D1346632

E·CHE·1·285·9

30130 086723516

Thomas Hooker's England

Thomas Hooker

"Father of American Democracy," founder of the State of Connecticut, originator of its "Fundamental Orders," first written instrument of American government, instigator of the Federation of American States, author of a Preparationist Theology which opened up New England to world immigration, and of "A Survey of the Summe of Church-Discipline," the foundation work on New England Congregationalism.

Thomas Hooker

1586 – 1647

Father of American Democracy

by
Deryck Collingwood

A pilgrim's guide to the England he knew, the great people, and the stirring events leading to his becoming a pre-eminent figure in the founding of Puritan New England.

Heart of the Lakes Publishing
Interlaken, New York
1995

Library of Congress Cataloging-in-Publication Data

Collingwood, Deryck, 1916–
    Thomas Hooker, 1586–1647, Father of American Democracy:
a pilgrim's guide to the England he knew, the great people, and
the stirring events leading to his becoming a pre-eminent figure
i nthe founding of Puritan New England / by Deryck Collingwood.
        p.   cm.
Includes bibliographical references and index.
ISBN: 1–55787–127–2
    1. Hooker, Thomas, 1586–1647—Homes and haunts—Eng-
land.   2. England—Description and travel.   I. Title.
BX7260.H596C65
285.8'092—dc20   94–45609
[B]   CIP

ISBN: 1–55787–127–2
LC: 94–45609
Manufactured in the United States of America

Published for
Family Society Tours
62 Weston Road
Weston, CT 06883
(203) 846–8486

Quality book production by
Heart of the Lakes Publishing
Interlaken, New York 14847

Dedication

With the lives of the women pioneers of New England foremost in my mind (although for the most part unwritten), the risks they took for the faith within them and their family circles, the hardships they suffered, the talents they displayed and secured for later generations, the Commonwealth they planted in what was, for them, invariably an hostile environment, in particular Susannah Hooker of Amersham, her daughter Joanna Shepard of Cambridge, Massachusetts, Dorothy (Hooker) Chester of Blaby, Hannah Eliot and Agnes Blake of Little Baddow, Margaret Winthrop of Great Maplestead, Lady Arbella Jonson and Anne Bradstreet of Sempringham, and Anne Hutchinson of Boston, I present this book in memory of Barbara Opie, first Secretary of the Little Baddow Historical Society, Margaret Martin, first Chairman, Judith Johnston, Secretary, Joan Barker, Olive Gibson, Patricia Herniman, Audrey Mossman researchers and committee members, Mary Clare Klaber, who resides at Cuckoos and has welcomed innumerable Hooker visitors, Hazel (Marven) Rowland, Treasurer of the Little Baddow United Reformed Church (URC), and Dilys my patient wife, without whose friendship and help this work could not have been undertaken or completed.

There are many others whom I should thank: Andy Coppell, Little Baddow URC Secretary, and his daughter Lynn, computer-programmer, who together, with a tolerance and affection beyond my desert produced a fair copy from my fuddled word-processor; Michael Herniman who with Patricia offered their help as personal researchers and advisors years ago; Ronald Bond, archivist with the Essex Record Office, the Essex Record Office and Cardiff Reference Library for unfailing guidance; and the hundreds of unexpected friendships which emerged from my tentative letters of enquiry, advancing information and hospitality willingly, often enthusiastically, on both sides of the Atlantic, including Alan McLean, Pastor of Hooker's Centre Church at Hartford, Connecticut, Herb Davis, Pastor of the Eliot Church of Newton, Massachusetts, Helen and Isabelle Conway, my first American visitors from the same Church in the early 1980s, Tony Jarvis, Headmaster of the Roxbury Latin School, Harold Worthley, Librarian of the Congregational Library, Beacon Hill, Boston, and Donald Bergquist of Family Society Tours, Connecticut—all of whom have sustained me, and have provided the pleasantest experiences of this private investigation. To all these and many more, my Thanks.

And not least to Thomas Hooker, John Eliot, the Cuckoos Company, the army of the faithful represented by the 738 names listed in the Index, with each of whom I hope to discuss those trembling Puritan days if, in heaven, I may meet them face to face.

Deryck Collingwood

Contents

Foreword by Donald C. Bergquist   11

Introduction   15

Chronology of Reigns   21

Abbreviations   23

Thomas Hooker, 1586–1647. A Brief Biography.   27

Chapter 1:

Marefield In Leicestershire. Security, Confidence in Conflict, Expectations of Expansion. 1586–c. 1596.
How to get there and where to stay.   41

Round Tour A.
Marefield, Birthplace of Thomas Hooker, and The Rise of The English Yeomanry.   42
Tilton-on-the-Hill, The Digbys, Puritan Patrons.   50
Melton Mowbray, Seat of Sir John Digby.   63
Belvoir Castle, Royalist Stronghold.   66

Round Tour B.
Blaston, Birthplace of Thomas Hooker Senior.   68
Stoke Dry, Seat of the Everard/Kenelm Digbys.   71
Rockingham Castle, Home of Lady Anne Digby.   73
Deene Park, Seat Of The Brudenells, a diversion.   74
Fotheringhay, Last Home of Mary, Queen of Scots.   74
Apethorpe, Seat of Sir Walter Mildmay.   76
Uppingham, Archdeacon Jonson's School.   77

Leicester, Early Evidence of Democracy And Unrest.
Leicester City, Cradle of Constitutional Democracy.   78
Blaby, Home of Dorothy (Hooker) Chester.   85
Stoke Golding, in the Shadow of Bosworth Field.   86
Towcester, Lectureship of Samuel Stone.   87

Chapter 2:

Market Bosworth. Isolation, Insecurity, Introspection, c. 1596–1604.

Kirby Muxloe, Perfidy of Kings.   93

Market Bosworth, Sir Wolstan Dixie, Puritan Patron.   96

Bosworth Battle Field And Visitors Park.   105

Birstall, First Educational Practice, 1602–1604?   110
Thurcaston, Such A Candle.   112

Chapter 3:
Cambridge. The Maturing of the Godly Preacher, 1604–1618.
    Various Routes To Cambridge.   115

Diversion Into Lincolnshire
    Stamford and Burghley House, Home of William Cecil.   115
    Bourne, Birthplace of Hereward and Burghley.   116
    Sempringham, A Bay Company Headquarters.   117
    Boston, John Cotton Vicar, 1612–1633.   123

Diversion Into East Anglia
    Choice of Three Routes to Cambridge.
        Direct Route.   126
        Diversion to Peterborough.   126
        Diversion to King's Lynn and Norwich.   126
    Ely, Cathedral Over Cambridge.   128

Cambridge, via the Great Fen of East Anglia, to Wicken Fen.
    Huntingdon, Birthplace of Oliver Cromwell.   131
    St Ives, Cromwell's Sometime Home.   133
    Grantchester.   133

Cambridge, University Town, and Selected Colleges.
    A Brief History of Cambridge.   135
    Walk From Queens' to St John's Colleges.   137
    Walk From Emmanuel to Jesus Colleges.   140
    Jesus College, Alma Mater of John Eliot.   152
    American War Memorial and Cemetery.   156

Chapter 4:
Esher, Surrey. Pastoral Practice and Counselling Perfected
    c. 1620–1625.

Esher St George's, Thomas Hooker's First Pastoral Charge.
    How to Get There.   159
    Sir Francis Drake, and the Drakes of Esher.   160
    Illustrious St George's, Thomas Hooker's First Church.   163
    Esher Place, Wolsey, Henry VIII, Howard of Effingham,
        and 'Mrs Drake Revived.'   167
    The Effect of Esher upon Thomas Hooker.   174
    Claremont House and Garden.   178
    Diversion to Hampton Court.   179

Amersham and Susannah Hooker.
    How to Get There.   180
    Old Amersham, Home of Mrs Joane Drake.   180
    The Drake Memorials at St Mary's Parish Church.   181
    Susannah Garbrand Marries Thomas Hooker.   183

Chapter 5:
Chelmsford and the County of Essex. Political Involvement for a
Godly Commonwealth. 1626–1631.

Chelmsford, The County Town.
    How to get there.   193
    A Brief History of Chelmsford.   193
    The Mildmays, a Chelmsford Dynasty.   198
    Essex, "The English Goshen."   204
    William Laud, Ecclesiastical Disciplinarian.   205
    Socio-political pressure moves towards Civil War.   206
    Excursion to St Peter-ad-Murum, First Essex Cathedral.   207
    The Cathedral Church of St Mary, and Hooker's Lectureship.   208

Little Baddow, Hooker's And Eliot's Hillside Hideout.
    How to get there.   220
    The Parish Church of St Mary.   220
    Sir Henry Mildmay of Great Graces Manor.   221
    Little Baddow Hall.   224
    The Lords Barrington, Puritan Patrons.   225
    The Meeting House and Manse-cum-Nonconformist-School.   232
    Cuckoos, home of the Hooker Family and John Eliot.   239
    The Cuckoos Company and the Making of Connecticut.   239
    Two More Manors: Tofts, home of the Barringtons and
        Bassets, home of the Blakes.   242

Excursions Into Thomas Hooker's Essex.
    Colchester and its Environs.
        Colchester, Ancient British Capitol.   244
        Copford, home of John Haynes.   248
        Messing, home of the Bush family.   252
        Constable Country: Dedham (John Rogers, Shermans)
            and Flatford Mill, East Bergholt.   255
    The Braintree Area.
        Braintree and Bocking, (Goodwin and "The Braintree
            Company": The Company of Twenty-four).   260
        Round Trip A: Leez Priory (Warwick), Felsted, and
            Great Waltham.   272
        Round Trip B: Stisted (Stone), Coggeshall (Stoughton),

Earls Colne (Shepard), Castle Hedingham,
Wethersfield, Finchingfield (Marshall).   278
Villages Around Chelmsford.
Group One: Writtle, Roxwell, Springfield (Pynchon),
Boreham (Benjamin Rush), Terling (Weld).   290
Group Two: Ingatestone, Stondon Massey (the Simple
Cobler of Agawam, and William Byrd).   306
Group Three: Danbury, Purleigh (George
Washington), Maldon, Port Of Exile.   318
John Eliot, Apostle To The Indians, 1604-1690.
A Brief Biography.   324
Widford, Herts, Birthplace Of John Eliot.   330
Ware, Essex, A Window On A Wider World.   331
Hertford, Birthplace Of Samuel Stone.   334
Nazeing, Essex, John Eliot's Boyhood Home.   339
Waltham Abbey, Essex.   344

Chapter 6:
The Dutch Disillusionment. 1631–1633.

The English Reformer Becomes The American Founder,
Influenced By Paget at Amsterdam, Ames at Franeker,
Disease and Disappointment.   347

At Rotterdam, With Hugh Peter.   350

At Delft With John Forbes.   351

Preparation For Exile, With Cotton, Whitefield, Davenport,
Stone.   352

The Final Phase. Flight From the Downs to contrive a
Commonwealth beyond mortal competence—The
Unending Pilgrimage.   353

Notes   357

Bibliography   447

Index   469

Illustrations

Thomas Hooker Statue, Hartford	Frontispiece
Marefield Farm	43
The Author Visits Marefield Farm	44
The Gardens, Marefield Manor Farm	45
St Peter's Church, Tilton-on-the-Hill	50
Baptizmal Font, St Peter's Church	51
The Stone House, Blaston	69
St Giles Church Ruins	69
Kirby Muxloe Castle	94
Sir Wolstan Dixie	97
Bosworth Hall Today	98
Dixie Grammer School in the Market Square	100
Headmaster Jarvis and Lady Dixie, Roxbury Latin School	101
Plan of Battle of Bosworth, 1485	109
Burghley House, Stamford	116
William Cecil, 1st Baron Burghley	117
St Andrew's, Sempringham	118
View from St Andrew's	122
Boston Stump, St Botolph's ChurchTower	123
Cotton's Pulpit, St Botolph's Church	125
Ely Cathedral	129
Cromwell Museum, Huntingdon	132
Map of Cambridge	135
Mathematical Bridge, Queens' College, Cambridge	137
President's Lodge, Queens' College	138
King's College Chapel, Cambridge	139
Emmanuel College Chapel	141
Sir Walter Mildmay, Founder of Emmanuel College	142
Emmanuel College, From the Air, c.1690	143
The Author Presents a Copy of the Hooker Genealogy	145

Esher Place Gate House   160
The Hooker Pulpit, St George's, Esher   164
Sir Richard Drake Memorial, Christ Church, Esher   167
Market Hall, Amersham   180
Amersham Parish Church of St Mary   185
Shardeloes, Home of Joanna Drake   186
Martyts' Memorial, Amersham   190
Map of Chelmsford, 1591   196
St Peter-ad-Murum, Chelmsford's First Cathedral   208
St Mary's, Chelmsford   210
Thomas Mildmay's Tomb, Chelmsford Cathedral   211
Chelmsford Cathedral   212
Little Baddow Hall   225
Little Baddow Manse, 1794   236
Hooker's Schoolroom, Cuckoos Farm   238
Colchester Castle   245
Copford Hall   249
Copford Church of St Mary the Virgin   251
Parish Church of St Mary, Dedham   256
The Sherman Glass   258
The John Rogers Monument   259
Deanery Church of St Mary the Virgin, Bocking   266
Dorewards Hall, Bocking   268
Lyons Hall, Bocking   269
High Street, Earls Colne   284
Tower of Earls Colne Church   285

Genealogical Tables

1. The Hookers of Leicestershire — 28
2. The Digbys of Tilton — 52-53
3. Relevant Reigning European Families — 56-57
4. Families Concerned in the Wars of the Roses — 106-107
5. The Garbrands of Oxford — 184
6. The Family of Thomas and Susannah Hooker — 197
7. The Mildmays of Chelmsford — 200-201
8. The Family of John and Hannah Eliot — 325
9. John Martyr and the Essex Rogers — 426-427

Foreword

This story has its genesis more than four centuries ago (1586) in the tiny Leicestershire hamlet of Marefield, birthplace of a boy named Thomas Hooker. If you go there today, go carefully for little has changed throughout these four centuries. Yes, the road is now paved, the homes enjoy electricity, and the year is 1995. But were Thomas Hooker to revisit Marefield today, he would surely recognize it. But would the people of Marefield recognize the name "Thomas Hooker"? Possibly not. Yet the world of the 1990s is remarkably different, in part, because of changes brought about by that Marefield lad, Thomas Hooker.

Half a century (1636) after his birth, Reverend Thomas Hooker found himself five-thousand miles from Marefield in the budding Massachusetts Bay Colony. He would soon depart "New Towne" (or Cambridge as we know it today) as leader of America's first westward migration, trekking 110 miles along the uncharted Bay Path with women, children, and barnyard animals to a place the Indians called Suckiaug (now Hartford) on the fertile banks of the Connecticut River. There, in 1638, Hooker preached a sermon to his congregation which articulated God's fundamental rights over human societies. That those who heard it or who later heard about it set forth to codify it into law in the Connecticut colony's infant legislature in the early days of 1639. The Hooker sermon and subsequent legislation are known as Connecticut's "Fundamental Orders." Many of the principles set forth in these Fundamental Orders were later incorporated by America's so-called "Founding Fathers" into the United States Constitution 150 years later. Indeed, in 1995 Connecticut automobiles bear license plates with the legend "Constitution State." Could it be that Thomas Hooker was really the "founding father" of American democracy?

I was born in Connecticut sixty miles from Hooker's Hartford about three hundred years after the 110-mile trek from New Towne. My maternal grandmother, Mary E. Keep, was a direct descendant of William Spencer, Hooker's trusted Town Clerk both at New Towne and at Hartford. She was a teacher and a firm believer in the beauty of our Connecticut system of democracy which Hooker established in the wilderness. She passed her knowledge along to her grandson so that when I first met Reverend Deryck Collingwood in the 1980s I "knew" Thomas Hooker, the Fundamental Orders, etc. But it didn't hurt to have been an undergraduate history major, nor to have studied Connecticut history one semester under Christopher Collier, now Connecticut's highly respected State Historian.

My personal knowledge of a Hartford man named Hooker was certainly not unique, however. He is depicted in the form of a statue in a niche on the exterior of Connecticut's State Capitol completed in 1879. A statuary depiction of what he might have looked like has stood for decades near Connecticut's Old State House, built 1796, in Hartford. There are no paintings or pictures of Hooker so what we see today is nothing more than an artist's conception of what he might have looked like. Nevertheless, it serves to provide us with an image around which we may build our own "Hooker."

But how did Hooker happen to be in Hartford? What were the formative influences which led to his becoming such an important and contributory figure in the embryo republic we know now as the United States of America? Very little of the story has ever been told . . . certainly very little has been told with the depth of understanding that has been provided by Deryck Collingwood via his incomparable manuscript which has been further embellished by some magnificent footnotes. Please don't overlook the footnotes which add immensely to these works.

The reader will correctly ask, "How did this book come about?" Researched and written in Great Britain, published and distributed in the United States, this book follows an unlikely trail. It begins, as the author explains, in England. A seed was planted when a young Deryck Collingwood, ordained as a Methodist clergyman, received his first pastorate in the North of England. The area included the village of Sturton-le-Steeple, once home to the Reverend John Robinson, leader of the Mayflower Pilgrims. The seed germinated for many years until it burst forth in the early 1980s as Deryck initially "retired" to Little Baddow in Essex to serve the United Reformed Church. For it was here near Chelmsford that Reverend Thomas Hooker fled in 1629 when he was driven out of Chelmsford by the Bishop of London, William Laud, the most powerful anti-Puritan of his time.

Perhaps it was the air he breathed, perhaps it was his fervent intellectual curiosity, but Deryck Collingwood had "the bug." In 1986, The Collingwoods met Mr. and Mrs. Thomas Hooker, a twentieth-century American couple with a direct line of descent back to Thomas Hooker of Marefield. Upon meeting the American lady, Dilys Collingwood, (Deryck's wife), exclaimed that she felt it was *she* who was married to Thomas Hooker. Deryck Collingwood's mind began to ask questions of himself about this chap, Hooker. He then learned about the Chelmsford lectureship, the flight to Little Baddow, Cuckoos Farm, the neighboring farmhouse . . . and so much more! The story began to take shape . . . a story that only Deryck knew, however, because there were no memorials, no local legends, no one initially seemed to care. And even worse, he had never visited New England where some Yankees might have told him about Hooker. However, the

Collingwoods had earlier visited Kansas and pictured America as a land where buffalo roam.

But all soon changed. Realizing that 1986 would mark the 400th anniversary of Hooker's birth, contact was made with Center Church in Hartford, Connecticut, leading to a pilgrimage that year by present-day members of that church. The link was now complete and in 1987 the Collingwoods paid a return visit when Deryck delivered the 14th Hooker Lecture, sans buffalo! The lecture, one of a long series to honor Hartford's founder, was entitled "Growing Toward Greatness," telling the Hooker story from an English viewpoint.

Meanwhile, I'd first met Deryck and Dilys Collingwood at Little Baddow prior to the 400th Hooker birthday commemoration. The month was June and you could literally smell the strawberries ripening behind Little Baddow Hall, near the Manse. Arriving at the Manse, I was served tea and the most delicious strawberries and cream this New England-born lad had ever eaten. As complete as this guide may be, Deryck fails to tell you that Little Baddow is only a short distance from Tiptree, Essex where Wilkin & Sons, Ltd. have been packing their wonderful fruit jams and marmalades for more than 100 years. Queen Elizabeth II regularly enjoys these delicious foods and Americans pay dearly for a small jar. No wonder the strawberries Dilys Collingwood served that June afternoon in the midst of the berry-harvesting season tasted so good.

I didn't realize it at the time but Deryck Collingwood was already becoming my "mentor." As I curiously asked about Springfield and Felsted, Marefield, and Tilton-on-the Hill and numerous other places in Hooker's England, I received patiently-worded answers more complete than I'd ever imagined possible. Soon the places became more than words on a map: they are real places where Englishmen live and worship in the twentieth century ... all very fascinating and all so terribly different from London, Stratford, Bath, and the normal tourist stops which American visitors usually know as England. I met Andy Coppell, Pat Herniman, Hazel Rowland, and a host of other wonderful people at Little Baddow. I once said to Dr. Mary Clare Klaber, the Collingwood's neighbors at Cuckoos Farm, that I was beginning to know their twin daughters well enough to feel "cheated" if I'm not in attendance at their weddings some future day.

When the Collingwood's "retired again" in 1988, out to Penarth in South Wales, Deryck now had sufficient time to record his knowledge for Englishmen and Americans alike to partake of in the form of this book or "guide" as he likes to call it. It isn't a guide in the sense of the traditional "AA" book but a very successful and unique endeavor to point venturesome souls toward the extant English venues where one may recapture Hooker's life. The places are real and while Sir Wolston Dixie is no longer there, his portrait remains at Emmanuel College. While the Mildmays aren't there, many memorials remain in the churches and Guy Harlings (the ancient Mildmay home at Chelmsford) is in daily use by the Church of England. See the communion table given to All Saints Church in Springfield by William Pynchon, Hooker's neighbor in Essex as well as in New England.

I've been very fortunate to have been blessed with the friendship of Deryck and Dilys Collingwood. I've spent many evenings in their home in South Wales where I've seen this tome progressing into what I believe is a remarkable contribution to knowing and understanding our Puritan forebears both here in New England and in our Mother Country across the pond. God was most generous in sharing Thomas Hooker's life with us. He has been equally generous in giving us Deryck Collingwood, a remarkable chronicler of the life and times of Reverend Thomas Hooker. I commend this story to all who share my intellectual curiosity about the seventeenth century. I guarantee that you will be well rewarded for your time invested.

Donald C. Bergquist
Weston, Connecticut
August, 1995

Introduction

Thomas Hooker, 1586–1647, is amongst the most remarkable and enduring of the Founders of New England, whose influence over the emergent culture of the United States of America went far beyond normal human expectation. His achievements may appear to be puny compared with the gigantic advances made by the United States' subsequent exploitation of the land and its resources, especially during the past century, brought about by modern technology, and America's global diplomacy. But the emergence of a new cultural world-model (enshrined in the Declaration of Independence of 1776, and the subsequent Constitution) was set in motion by a handful of Puritan pioneers in the 17th Century, amongst whom Thomas Hooker was pre-eminent.

This is the marvel we shall explore if, as tourists, we return to their place of origin, the hamlets and small towns, the country manors and parish churches, where Puritanism seized the imagination of a generation, and drove them to subdue a sub-continent, to plant a new Commonwealth.

However, whilst Thomas Hooker is known and respected in the land of his adoption, in the land of his birth he is one of the least known of the Founding Fathers. "You must mean Richard Hooker, ecclesiastical statesman of the Elizabethan Settlement," I am invariably told by people with a sense of history in England; not altogether surprisingly, for some Hooker descendants, notably in Commander Edward Hooker's large *Genealogy* (1909), have attempted to trace a connection with the celebrated West Country Hookers, although without any success.[1]

So total has been the neglect of Thomas Hooker in England that no tangible memorial can be found in his native county of Leicestershire. There is no visible reference to him, or his family, in their major place of residence, at Marefield (pronounced Marfield), in the Parish of Tilton-on-the-Hill.[2] And such authoritative publications as the English *Dictionary of National Biography*, or the Harvard Theological Studies XXVIII *Thomas Hooker Writings in England and Holland, 1626–1633*, confuse his birthplace with Markfield,[3] a village near Coalville situated towards the north-west of the county. The Harvard Press even includes a map of Hooker's travels[4] which, if taken seriously, would divert the unwary traveller into the opposite corner of Leicestershire, far from his true birth-place at Marefield in the east.

The definitive *Alumni Cantabrigienses* has "S. of Thomas, yeoman, of Birstall, Leics. B. there 1586,"[5] presumably because Birstall was given as his address when he entered Queens' College (see discussion in *A Brief Biogra-*

phy, following). Worse still, Venn has Hooker ejected from Chelmsford in 1626, the date of his arrival, and by "Archbishop Laud" when Laud was still the Bishop of London.

This guide is an attempt to redress the balance as well as to offer more accurate directions, and to accord Thomas Hooker the status he merits in the story of his native land. I am also aware that today's traveller is often looking beyond the traditional tourist centres, and wishes to enjoy a more personal adventure, or to take advantage of the growing number of Heritage Tour Companies which are offering programs like my Thomas Hooker Trail.

The Itineraries sketched here take the pilgrim deeper into the England of our ancestors. To Colchester (Camulodunum) capital of the ancient Britons, or Ely, stronghold of Hereward the Wake, and many other ancient towns and villages, some refreshingly unaffected by the passage of 300 years.

It is my hope that, by a heightened appreciation of the mould in which Thomas Hooker was cast, a wider familiarity with the places where he lived and worked for the first 47 years of his life, and a better acquaintance with the people he knew and loved (or else fearlessly opposed), a deeper understanding of the man and his achievements may be gained.

One word of caution is appropriate. Some of the places here described, gentle nurseries where many a founding family gained its distinctive culture, are remote, unspoiled, and by no means attracted to tourism. It will be well for the future if we can continue to treat such shrines as holy ground, and to tread softly as we come and go. Most people in Britain warmly welcome visitors from abroad, provided they respect the privacy of their homes, and exhibit the same determined care for the green countryside with which they (alas, by no means everywhere, but certainly in and around Marefield) have preserved its beauty over so long a period, and hopefully will for years to come.

My qualification for attempting this guide began in 1940, when I was sent, on completing theological training for the Methodist Ministry, to Retford in Nottinghamshire, with a bicycle and twelve mostly very small rural congregations to care for, spaced round the market town. One of them was at Sturton-le-Steeple, where John Robinson, pastor of the Pilgrim Fathers' congregation at Leiden, Holland, was born c.1576.[6]

The Robinson home was at "Crossways," which still stands at Cross Street, slightly to the north of the fine Parish Church of St Peter and St Paul, (known as "the Minster of the Clays"), and in between it and the Methodist Chapel, from the elevated rostrum of which I could almost have seen the Robinson home when officiating at Sturton, had my attention not been diverted to the attractive girls in the choir gallery behind the pulpit, for a pastor must always look to the future! But the Mayflower memory and heroic presence was there, in those desperate days of World War II, when, like John and Bridget Robinson, we scarcely dared to look into the fate which menaced ahead.

John's father was born at Sturton before him, and enjoyed a sufficient income to be able to send his son to Corpus Christi College, Cambridge. There John graduated MA, was elected a fellow, and ordained into the Church of England. He married a Sturton girl, Bridget White, on resigning his fellowship on 10 Feb 1604. Thomas Hooker was admitted to Queens' College on March 27 that same year. They surely met. Corpus Christi is on Trumpington Street opposite Silver Street, where Queens' hugs the river bank almost within touching distance, and John returned to Cambridge from time to time, not least because he had come under the influence of Laurence Chadderton, Master of Emmanuel, where Hooker was by then a student.

At first the young Robinsons ministered at Norwich, then a stronghold of Puritan sentiment. But King James' decree of July 1604, requiring all clergy to conform to a new Book of Canons, which curbed Puritan practices, forced their withdrawal. They returned to Sturton-le-Steeple, and were at once caught up in the ever increasing circle of Reformers who met under William Brewster at Scrooby, and others like John Smith of Sturton, then at Gainsborough. I had friends in both places, and frequently visited them, headily breathing the Nonconformity which still hung on the air.

Scrooby is not ten miles north-west across the fields from Sturton, and Gainsborough, where the John Robinson Memorial Church and a new Pilgrim Tourist Centre is to be found, not four miles directly north. The separatist Congregation clung together in growing danger, then fled into Holland.

John's sister-in-law, Catherine White of Sturton, married John Carver, who was Deacon of the first Pilgrim Church at Leiden, and first Governor of Plymouth Plantation in New England. John died (1625) before he could join the new Colony, partly held back by some of the Pilgrims' opposition to his more liberal views about church government and order, as happened to Hooker when he too was in Holland. I learnt all that matters about pastoral ministry as I slogged round my twelve churches, singing Charles Wesley's hymns to keep out the worst of the snow or driving rain, and knowing that I cycled where Saints had gone on foot, to give life itself for a distant dream of holiness.

Six years later I was dispatched to Leicester, with, wonder of wonders, Markfield one of the churches I served. I remember it vividly. After Sturton-le-Steeple, some of the prettiest girls ever were to be seen at Markfield Methodist. We talked of many things, but no one ever mentioned Thomas

Hooker! So I knew he was not from Markfield as soon as I came across his name. Thus history is made.

During my six years there I became Secretary of the Leicester and Northampton District Synod of the Methodist Church, and gained a wide and personal knowledge of Hooker's childhood localities. Every free Saturday I dragged my long-suffering wife and four children round the Shires in the wake of my enthusiasm for old churches, great castles like Rockingham, Belvoir, or Ashby-de-la-Zouch (with its exciting underground passageway), or boating on the Soar, or roaming the bluebell woods of Charnwood Forest, and the rolling Wolds.

During the week days of fifteen years in the Midlands (at Leicester and then at Birmingham) we enjoyed the hospitality of hundreds of Midlands farmers, landed yeomen, direct successors to the Hookers, as I attended District Visitations, or Commissions on the future of their rural churches, or preached at their numerous Church Festivals. These latter were the most popular with the children, for the huge farm-teas which followed the afternoon Preaching Service, replete with vast home-cured hams, hand-raised pork pies, basins full of fried chitterlings (heavenly Methodist pigs' intestines chopped small), cakes enough to stuff a Brigade of Guards, all the delights of that prosperous agricultural region.

Later on I became, for a decade, Chairman of the London North East District, with responsibility for 250 churches spread across the Capital, the whole of Essex, and much of Cambridge and Hertford shires (now amalgamated), all "Hooker Country," of which I must have trodden every other acre. This included the University towns of Colchester and Cambridge, where the Methodist Church has a college (Wesley House) next to Jesus College where John Eliot, "The Great Apostle to the Indians," attended, and a residential school (The Leys) for which I had responsibilities such as sharing in joint Confirmations with the Bishop of Ely (whose predecessor just may have ordained Thomas Hooker, and probably did Eliot).

English History has always been the second passion of my life, the first being to represent the way of Christ's love to people within themselves, their homes, and their total life situation, in order to discover how Christian caring can be applied to every situation, which I understand to be the office of a pastor.

It was natural, therefore, on retirement in 1981, that I should accept a call to become the resident pastor of the Little Baddow United Reformed Congregation, a Unity Church serving all Free Church people in and around the village, and there became immersed in Thomas Hooker's teaching and accomplishments.

The 1794 Manse at Little Baddow, built to include a residential school for Nonconformist children in the tradition of Hooker's and Eliot's school of the 1620s, stands next door to Cuckoos Farmhouse; between the place where he and his family lived, and the Parish Church of St Mary the Virgin, lower down the hill.

I eagerly sought to restore connections with Thomas Hooker's continuing congregation at Centre Church, Hartford, Conn., and with many of the churches and institutions in the U.S.A. which descend from the work he and his associate John Eliot, "Apostle to the Indians," began to explore in Little Baddow. This led to a number of visits to the river towns of Windsor, Wethersfield and Hartford, to Eliot's Roxbury Latin School, Harvard and Boston, particularly to read at the hospitable Congregational Library on Beacon Street, and other facilities.

Over the years this has taken me to William Pynchon's Springfield, Massachuetts, (the Little Baddow Manse bedroom windows overlook Springfield, England, a mile across the Chelmer River valley), and to many other New England towns. Groups of pilgrims have exchanged visits on both sides of the Atlantic, and a small History Centre has been established at the Little Baddow Manse, to research and collect Hooker material gleaned from British sources.

I have written of the little I know personally in much consciousness of the greater whole outside my range; but in the hope of making a small contribution to a better understanding of our indebtedness to the Anglo-American Puritan Movement, and its doughty exponents. They have been widely and at times ignorantly criticised, but remain the vital spring of the greatest experiment in the founding of a Nation known to history.

Route-Wise Warning!

At the time of writing, large scale road developments are taking place all over Britain, and in particular round Leicester (a new 'Distributor' highway) and Chelmsford-Colchester (new Ring Roads). These will affect some of the route-descriptions offered in the following pages. It will be important to get hold of some up-to-date Route Maps before exploring "Hooker's England."

Note on Dating

There is no end to the small confusion caused by the change in 1750 to new Calendar Dating, when the old year's beginning on March 25 was altered to a New Year on January 1st. As far as possible I have updated 16th/17th c. datings to match our current practice.

20

Chronology Of Reigns

Normans

Normans			
William I	1066	Henry I	1100
William II	1087	Stephen	1135

Plantagenets

Henry II	1154	Edward I	1272
Richard I	1189	Edward II	1307
John	1199	Edward III	1327
Henry III	1216	Richard II	1377

Lancastrians

Henry IV	1399	Henry VI	1422
Henry V	1413		

Yorkists

Edward IV	1461	Richard III	1483
Edward V	1483		

Tudors

Henry VII	1485	Mary I	1553
Henry VIII	1509	Elizabeth I	1558
Edward VI	1547		

Stuarts

James I	1603	Charles I	1625

Commonwealth 1649

Stuarts

Charles II	1660	William & Mary	1689
James II	1685	Anne	1702

22

23

Abbreviations and Sources

See also the Bibliography on page 447

Abp	Archbishop
Achdea	Archdeacon
C	Curate of Parish
R	Rector of Parish
V	Vicar of Parish
BCP	*Book of Common Prayer*
BOTT	Banner of Truth Trust, 3 Murryfield Rd, Edinburgh EH12 6EL
Bush	*Thomas Hooker, Spiritual Adventure in Two Worlds*, S. Bush Jr. , 1980
CambU	Cambridge University
CCH	*Cambridge Cultural History*, 9 vols, 1992
CUP	Cambridge University Press
ConnHS	Connecticut Historical Society
ConnSG	Connecticut Society of Genealogists
CPPG	Corporation for Promoting & Propagating the Gospel in New England, 1649
DAB	*Dictionary of American Biography*
DNB	*Dictionary of National Biography*
EAS	Essex Archaeological Society Library
EAT	*Essex Archaeological Society Transactions*
ER	*Essex Review*
ERO	Essex Record Office, Chelmsford
EncBrit and EncBrit(15)	*The Encyclopaedia Britannica*, 11th edition 1910/11. I have preferred this edition because of its outstanding articles on the people & events of 16th/17th century England. I have also extensively used the 15th edition of 1986, for its wider and latest coverage. But you should know that I still prefer the biographical articles in the 1911 edition!
Guide	This work: *Thomas Hooker, 1586–1647, Father of American Democracy*
Genealogy	*Descendants of Thomas Hooker, 1586–1908*, Commander Edward Hooker
HTS	*Thomas Hooker Writings in England and Holland, 1626–1633*, Harvard Theological Studies XXVIII, ed. G. H. Williams, N. Pettit, W. Herget, & S. Bush Jr, Harvard, 1975
LBHS	Little Baddow Historical Society

Magnalia	*Magnalia Christi Americana*, Cotton Mather, 1702
Martyrs	*Book of Martyrs*, John Foxe, revised edition. W. Bramley-Moore, Cassell
MassHS	Massachusetts Historical Society
NEHGS	*Hooker Genealogical Material compiled by the New England Historic Genealogical Society*, Boston, for the Little Baddow Historical Society's 400th Celebration of Hooker's birth, monograph, 1986
ODCC	*Oxford Dictionary of the Christian Church*, 1957
OUP	Oxford University Press
OxfordU	Oxford University
Oxons	*Alumni Oxoniensis 1500–1714*, James Foster, 4 vols, London, 1887–91
Saints	*Penguine Dictionary of Saints*, 1965
Pevsner	Pevsner, Nikolaus. *The Buildings of England*, 2nd ed, Penguin 1965–75
rep	reprinted
Rowley	History of an English Village, 3 vols., Sheila V. Rowley
Shuffleton	*Thomas Hooker, 1586–1647*, 1977
TEAS	*Transcripts of the Essex Archaeological Society*
Venn	*Alumni Cantabrigienses*, J.& J.A. Venn, Part I, 4 vols, Cambridge University Press, 1922–27
VicHist—	*The Victoria History of the Counties of England*—[various counties], Oxford University Press, London

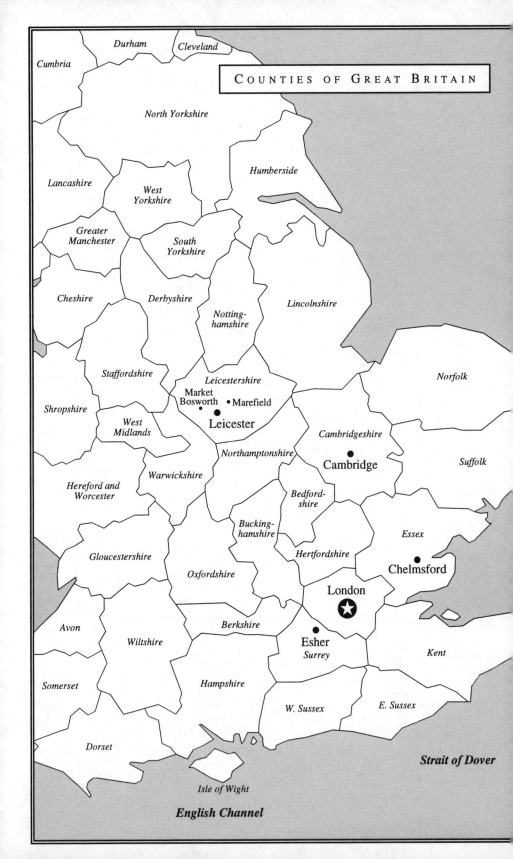

COUNTIES OF GREAT BRITAIN

Cumbria

Durham

Cleveland

North Yorkshire

Lancashire

West Yorkshire

Humberside

Greater Manchester

South Yorkshire

Cheshire

Derbyshire

Nottinghamshire

Lincolnshire

Norfolk

Staffordshire

Leicestershire

Shropshire

West Midlands

Market Bosworth • Marefield

Leicester

Cambridgeshire

Suffolk

Hereford and Worcester

Warwickshire

Northamptonshire

Cambridge

Bedfordshire

Buckinghamshire

Gloucestershire

Oxfordshire

Hertfordshire

Essex

Chelmsford

London

Avon

Wiltshire

Berkshire

Esher

Surrey

Kent

Somerset

Hampshire

W. Sussex

E. Sussex

Dorset

Isle of Wight

Strait of Dover

English Channel

Thomas Hooker, A Brief Biography

The story of Thomas Hooker in England is fully related in the following pages. I confine myself here to a resume of those English years, and to a short evaluation of his achievements in New England, which seem to me to progress naturally out of his English background.

He was born at Marefield in Leicestershire on 7 July 1586, as best one can tell, into the home of Thomas Hooker of Blaston. Blaston is a small village barely 10 miles away, where the family had lived for several generations past, as is shown by an examination of Leicester wills.[7]

Our Thomas' great-grandfather, "THOMAS HOKER of Blaston in the countie of Leycester, yoman," (will dated 2 September 1559), was predeceased by his grandfather "JOHN HOOKER of Blaston in the countie of Lecestre, yeoman," whose Will is dated 6 November 1558. In this latter will, John bequeathed the use of his house at Blaston to his father during his lifetime, and to his son Thomas (c.1553–1636) afterwards. This Thomas was our Thomas' father.

The family was rising in the world. Old Thomas had no house of his own, and little enough to distribute apart from it, when he died. "Cecely my wief all my household stuff in the halle, parlor, chambers and kitchen, excepte one fetherbed which I doe giue vnto Agnes Bellamy my daughter. The residue of my goods I will shall be diuded vnto Kenellyne Hoker my sonne."[8] The house was already entailed on his grandson, Thomas.

John Hooker had had livestock to distribute to his family, servants, and friends, as well as the house. And some ready cash. "To Frances Hocker my daughter £20 to be paid to her at the age of xix yeres. Thomas Hocker my sonne to have £10 of it in case my daughter die before attaining that age, and the other £10 to be bestowed upon hight wayes and poor people." The Inventory of the goods remaining was calculated at £82.0.4.[9]

When Thomas senior (our Thomas' father) eventually inherited John's estate, he quickly turned it into profit. By 1584 he had bought "one messuage, two tofts, one cottage, one barn, one dovehouse, four gardens, one hundred acres of land, eighty acres of meadow and forty acres of pasture in Marfield alias Sowth Marfeld."[10] This respectable property, part of his perquisites as an Estate Manager to the Digbys of Tilton-on-the-Hill, was supplemented in 1616 by a house and 154 acres, "and common pasture for all manner of cattle at Blabye and Countesthorpe" (south of Leicester, within easy distance of Marefield); and also by property of some sort at Birstall (due north of the city).

28

GENEALOGICAL TABLE, NO. 1: THE HOOKERS OF LEICESTERSHIRE.
(b=born: bp=baptised: bu=buried: d=deceased: da=will dated: do=domiciled:
m=married: n=nee: p=parish: pr=will proved: 1/2/1500 = day/month/year)

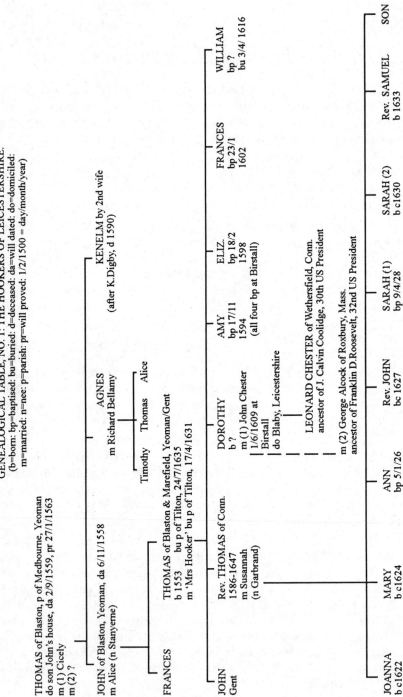

This family continues on Chart 6, page 197

That the family lived for some time at Birstall[11] is clear. Three of the children were baptised there, namely Amy, 17 November 1594; Elizabeth, 18 February 1598; Frances, 23 January 1602. Dorothy was married to John Chester there, 1 June 1609, and William was buried on 3 April 1616. But Thomas senior and his wife were buried at Tilton, so Marefield remained their principal home.

The fact that Thomas Hooker gave Birstall as his address on entering the Queens' College at Cambridge need not surprise us. It certainly does not follow that he was born there. His name is not on Birstall's baptismal records, nor is there any mention of Birstall until eight years after his birth. Not even Tarleton's Deposition is necessarily determinative.

In 1631 Hooker fled to Rotterdam, where he lodged with his friend Hugh Peter. His wife and children were sheltered by the Earl of Warwick at Great Waltham, near their former home at Little Baddow. The text is as follows: "John Tarleton, of the parish of St Olaves in the Borough of Southwark, brewer, aged 46, deposes 30 December, 1631, that in July last he, at the entreaty of Susan Hooker, wife of Thomas Hooker of Waltham in the county of Essex, preacher of God's word, now resident of Delph in Holland, did lade aborde the Jacob of London, Robert Jacob master, one small truncke of apparrell to be delivered to Mr Peters, a minister dwelling at Rotterdam, for the accompte of the said Thomas Hooker. Also he sayeth that the said Hooker was borne at Burstall in the county of Leicester, and went to Holland in or about the month of June last past."[12] That he was occasionally known as Thomas Hooker of Birstall would be natural. That he was born there is unsure.

He was sent, another sign of affluence, as a boarder to the Dixie Grammar School at Market Bosworth. From there, possibly after a spell as school-teacher at Birstall,[13] to Queens' and Emmanuel colleges, Cambridge, where he gained a reputation as an outstanding preacher and disputant. He added to it an unusual skill in pastoral counselling, which revealed itself during his first church appointment, as Rector of Esher in Surrey, after some fourteen years as scholar and fellow at Emmanuel.

From Esher he went to Chelmsford, county town of Essex, and at once exerted an immense pressure for reform on the county, nearby London, and the government both ecclesiastical and national. It led to his silencing by William Laud, and his flight to Holland.

On 10 July 1633, he set sail with his wife and four children,[14] for New England. In the *Griffin*, a 300 ton ship carrying some 200 passengers, there were other influential immigrants destined to make their mark in the new colonies. John Cotton of Boston; John Haynes, third governor of the Bay Colony and first of Connecticut; Samuel Stone, Hooker's associate from

Hertford, England, soon to negotiate the Indian Treaty which established a new Hartford on the banks of the Connecticut river.

The Hooker family went to Newtown (now Cambridge) four miles by boat from Boston across Back Bay and up the Charles River. This site was, at first, proposed as the capital of the colony, and Thomas Dudley (second governor) erected a large house there with an obvious eye to the governorship later on. The Hookers and the Haynes stayed with the Dudleys until their houses were completed. The settlement was now rapidly enlarged by members of "Mr Hooker's Company,"[15] who had sailed with William Goodwin of Braintree, Essex, (Hooker's ruling elder) in the *Lyon* the previous year. They ordained Thomas as pastor over the congregation on October 11, 1633, with Samuel Stone as teacher.

By 1636 Newtown felt itself constrained "for want of land,"[16] and, after some resistance, obtained permission from the General Council to re-establish itself as a second Newtown (afterwards Hartford) in the Connecticut river valley. They were part of a wide-scale development which initially included Windsor, Wethersfield, and Springfield. The Dutch already occupied a trading fort nearer the mouth of the river, Huysettoop (House of Hope).[17] Plymouth Plantation also had prior interests in the fertile river valley. But the residents of the four river towns were commonwealth-builders, come to stay, and they proved irremovable.

There is some suggestion that the epithet "Yankee"[18] was originally hurled derogatively at the new settlers by the outraged, and outmanoeuvred, Dutch, "Jankes" meaning "pirates," or, more acceptably, "intransigent interlopers!" Nothing moved the intruders. They had not come simply as traders, but as families, to settle. By design of Almighty God they had been granted this patch of earth, and they proceeded to build His Kingdom upon it.

The achievement was decisive. The Puritans had exploded out of Boston Bay and swept through the whole region. Convinced of divine approval, they set aside the claims of whoever else might be there and, by the strength of purpose within them, surmounted every obstacle.

The swift appearance of the new Connecticut settlements provided the visible proof that the colonisation of the North American seaboard had succeeded. With its seemingly limitless fields, its growing flocks and herds, its maritime trade, and vital industries such as armaments presently to be started, there would be no turning back. Even more significant developments were to follow. The next step was to Federalise the inceptive settlements.

As early as 1637 Thomas Hooker was discussing with Governor Winthrop the advisability of some form of Federation between the New England colonies, which might preserve their separate autonomy whilst ensuring their collective security.[19] It would be quite inaccurate to imply any advanced form of federalism at this stage. Indeed, Hooker was to write angrily to Winthrop in defence of Connecticut's rights, and his magistrates backed him.[20]

Reconciliation came only slowly. Rhode Island remained determinedly isolated. But by 1643 Plymouth, Massachusetts, Connecticut, and New Haven were calling themselves the United Colonies of New England. The seeds of a United States of America were thus cast over the very first settlements, and Hooker was a pioneer of their sowing.

Much the same may be said about his title to be "The Father of American Democracy." Taken literally, the claim is nonsense. S. E. Morison was surely correct when, in *The Founding of Harvard College*, he wrote "Certain phrases of his, taken out of their context by later writers, have been used to build up a false picture of him as a democrat: Hooker, on his political side, was essentially a medieval church autocrat."[21]

But this was no longer a medieval age. In New England Hooker preached to and wrote for a community of people who had left the last vestiges of feudalism behind. They had gained an entirely new type of freedom at great personal cost, and this gave a new direction to his words. In the long run their impact could be nothing other than democratic, and in this sense he is indeed a founding father, possibly the outstanding founding father, of American Democracy.

Let us consider, for instance, the Fundamental Orders of Connecticut 1639, said to be "the oldest truly political Constitution in America,"[22] and as such the precursor of the present-day Constitution of the United States. Every New England settlement had a Foundation Covenant, entered into by every citizen. The Covenant granted status of citizenship (church membership, property ownership, voting rights), and fortified all citizens together in loyalty to an agreed religious commitment, and to each other in binding relationships.

Each Colony had a Charter, which gave legal form under the English crown to their land titles, their legislature, and their commerce. These, however, were Trading Company charters, organs of corporation government under the King. The Fundamental Orders of Connecticut were organs of political government, independent of English authority, and therefore not to be confused with, for instance, Massachusetts' *Body of Liberties* of 1641.[23]

The Body of Liberties sought to control arbitrary government by Governor John Winthrop and his Deputies, who constituted an executive council operating outside the General Court in Massachusetts. The Fundamental Orders were to constitute an Independent Colony, and were therefore "a landmark in the development of the written constitution."[24]

It all came to a head with a sermon preached by Hooker before the General Court of Connecticut on 31 May 1638, formulated into law by Roger Ludlow of Windsor, Connecticut (one of the few members of the legal profession in the colonies at that time, and a lawyer of the highest attainments', cf. n.22), on which the Statute was approved by the Court, 14 January 1639. Hooker's text was Deuteronomy 1:13, "Choose men of wisdom, understanding and repute from each of your tribes, and I will set them in authority over you."[25] The sermon discussed what it means to authorise the people to choose their governors.

Hooker, even allowing for the different outlook and expectations of his hearers, laid down a basis for New England Law in unmistakably democratising terms:

1. That the choice of public magistrates belongs unto the people, by God's allowance.

2. The privilege of election, which belongs to the people, therefore must not be exercised according to their humours, but according to the blessed will and law of God.

3. They who have the power to appoint officers and magistrates, it is in their power, also, to set the bounds and limitations of the power and place unto which they call them.

Dynamite! It is not my purpose here to do other than note en passant the unique contribution Thomas Hooker made to democratic world history during his leadership at Connecticut, but the conclusion is as startling as it is inescapable.

Recognition must also be given to the democratic effect of his Preparationist Theology, if only that it found its natural outlet in the "Half-Way" Covenants which Hooker might have resisted, but which flooded the colonies shortly after his death. They eased the regulations governing church, and therefore state membership, in order to accommodate the diminishing dedication to a narrow theocracy evidenced by third-generation settlers. They were the natural outcome of Hooker's teaching, which was experimental not systematic, and gradually won approval. Preparationist theology saved New England from self-destruction.[26]

Reader, you thought you were getting hold of a Tourist Guide to Hooker's England. Take comfort, it awaits you in the coming pages! This is not a theological treatise in disguise. But consider a moment. Theology, i.e. what we believe about Ultimate Truth, cannot be excluded from the study of people. In Hooker's case, it furnishes the most relevant information available. You simply cannot see the England he grew up in unless you understand something of the way the spirit worked his mind.

The issue for New England was one of expansion towards nationhood or of narrowly declining into sectarian oblivion. The Calvinist settlement assumed that only discernible saints were fit for membership of the Church, and of the State. But how was a judgement to be made? On the one hand there were leaders like John Cotton. For him, election to sanctification was brought about solely by God's arbitrary choice. The recipient was entirely passive, could do nothing to gain it, and was instantly, wholly, demonstrably saved, or irretrievably damned.

Citizenship consequently tended to depend on the individual's ability to convince the Church Meeting (under the watchful eyes of the Ministers and Elders) that you were one of God's elect. The duplicity and hypocrisy engendered by such a system, especially when property rights depended on your manifest sanctity, needs no further elaboration. The outcome was, and always is, a narrow, exclusive Sectarianism.

On the other hand there was Thomas Hooker, and other likeminded ministers, some trained by him at Emmanuel and Little Baddow, who eventually generated a majority opinion amongst New England statesmen in favour of preparation for holiness, thus enlarging the breadth of the commonwealth.

At Cambridge Hooker had entered into a heritage of godly scholarship and personal practice, epitomised by the concept of Divine Mercy, which had become the aim of many Puritans. He followed men of immense influence like Dutch Erasmus,[27] New Testament translator, initiator of the Reformation, Lady Margaret professor of Greek at Cambridge, advocate of religious peace; Martin Bucer,[28] German Lutheran, Regius professor of divinity at Cambridge, "the dear politicus and fanaticus of union"; Theodore Beza,[29] Calvin's French biographer, stern contender for reconciliation; William Whitaker,[30] Master of St John's, hard-line Calvinist, champion of Church of England compromise; William Perkins,[31] prince of preachers at Great St Andrews, in death saluting God's "Mercy, Mercy", reminiscent of Hooker's last words, "I am going to receive Mercy"; Laurence Chaderton, first Master of Emmanuel, a giant of a moderate Puritan teacher and administrator whose Calvinism assumed that a Reformed English Church must succeed; and, closest of all, William Ames, irreconcilable opponent of petty ecclesiasticism, assured in his Calvinistic Anglicanism, sometimes termed non-separating Congregationalism.

From these, and others too numerous to enumerate, Hooker mastered the task of reconciling the absoluteness of the Sovereignty of God with the need for expansive ethical growth. It was made possible by distinguishing a double effect in Election. "There is a double repentance," he wrote. "The first is of preparation, wrought by the almighty and irresistible power of the

Spirit. Second, there is a repentance in sanctification—and it comes after faith."[32]

Being elected by God for salvation was entirely passive. Basic Calvinism was upheld. But now with election came saving grace for further development, an ingrafting into the parent-stem of God for growth. This comprehension helped Hooker and his followers to present Calvinism as a progression, confirming faith in a Divine Call, without which Puritan colonisation would have collapsed, but liberating it from the anomoly of seeming to inhibit expansion thus making feasible the forward progress of the New England experiment.

Hooker's theology had the immediate, if unrealised, effect of switching the emphasis from a demonstration of what had already been achieved by God (necessarily backward looking and restrictive) to a co-operation with God for growing in grace, for preparing a better relationship with Him, and therefore with the State. It is not too much to claim that Hooker's Preparationist Theology made possible the establishment of the open nationhood of the United States of America, to which all classes and creeds might come and find a welcome. It was Hooker, through his homesteading heirs, who first conquered the West.

The key issue was that of a contagious as against a cooperative Church/State. Cotton's was a "contagious" Church/State, bent on demonstrating its elected glory, and driving away those who could not claim it. Hooker's was, although I think he never fully realised it, an "open" Church/State, made up of Christ-willed co-operators, preparing for a glory still to come.

Through God-given contrition and humiliation, rather than through an instantaneous sanctification, "The Soule must be fitted for Christ before it can receive him,"[33] he taught. He called for "the judgement of charity."[34] The anonymous author of an Epistle to the Reader sometimes bound with Hooker's sermon on "The Danger of Desertion" wrote, "he loved such as he observed sincere—though hee differed from them."[35] He himself wrote "hee doth bring all the riches of His grace into the soule truly humbled."[36]

In tune with Preparationist Theology, the Fundamental Orders authorised government "by all that are admitted freemen,"[37] and defined citizenship as acceptance of the State Laws, not of Church Membership as in Massachusetts. Once cooperation became the Way, rather than the public demonstration of a sanctity already received, a door opened through which the world might walk into America, and did.

The above is an over-simplification of the most attenuated kind, but it does at least suggest the need for a reappraisal of Hooker's significance by English historians, and I make no apology for that.

Hooker's final work was *A Survey of the Summe of Church-Discipline*, printed posthumously by his executors Edward Hopkins and William Goodwin, at London in 1648.[38] It was written at the request of the Cambridge Synod of 1643, a 400 octavo manuscript, completed within two years, lost at sea on its voyage to the printer, and laboriously rewritten by the ailing author shortly before his death.

Although composed as a counterblast to Rutherford's *Peacable and Temperate Plea for Paul's Presbyteries in Scotland*, 1642, (by Samuel Rutherford, 1600–61, the ablest advocate of Presbyterianism in Britain), and his *The Due Right of Presbyteries*, 1644,[39] the book has a literary and logical flow of its own, presented with wit and conciliation, deserving to win Hooker a place in the realms of ecclesiastical literature on its own account.

The Preface offers a brief sketch of the history of Christendom, where Hooker sees Christ's unique role as Prophet, Priest, and King usurped by political ambition vested in the Papal office, and only restored to Christ at the Reformation. In England, however, Henry VIII only "cut off the head of Papacy." Not until the Commonwealth was "Parity in the Ministry" reintroduced, as Christ had intended (away with the Bishops!).

The remaining choice, as Hooker understood his current situation, was therefore between two forms of Reformed Church, Presbyterian and Congregational. The *Survey* proceeds to justify Congregationalism above all others.

The book falls into four parts. The first claims Scriptural authority for the vesting of power in the gathered congregation rather than in church officers or courts: the concluding three deal with the structure of individual congregations; their appropriate government in relation to membership tests, and excommunication—where caution and compassion are urged; and the use of synodical government without granting any over-riding authority away from the local congregation. Key-words were "con-sociation," "moderation," "unamity"—"that we do not spoil the ordinances of God by our management."

It was not the only such book. John Cotton wrote at least three, culminating in *The Way of the Congregational Churches Cleared* (1648). Richard Mather, John Davenport, Thomas Shepard, and others whom you will meet in the body of this book, added their contribution. But Hooker's was the model. The *Survey* provided a platform from which the Congregational churches dominated the New England scene for the next century, and beyond.

They still stand, those great white First Churches of Christ, central on any New England town common, symbols of the religio-political ideals of their first families. An expression of that progressive and hopeful spirit characteristic of the colonists, to whom Hooker's theology had contributed so much.

Thomas Hooker died, as he was born, on July 7th, following a bout of fever in the year 1647. The eulogies poured in. "Mr Hooker," wrote John Winthrop, "who for piety, prudence, wisdom, zeal, learning, and what else might make him serviceable—might be compared with men of the greatest note—and he shall need no other praise."[40] John Cotton's elegy "On my Reverend and dear Brother Mr Thomas Hooker late Pastor of the Church at Hartford, Coonectiquot" concurred.

> That well did learned Ames record bear,
> The like to Him He never wont to hear.[41]

Cotton Mather invited his readers in the *Magnalia Christi Americana* (1702—the first full account of the New England experiment) "to behold at once the 'wonders' of New England, and it is in one Thomas Hooker that he shall behold them: even in that Hooker, whom a worthy writer would needs call 'Saint Hooker'," and named him "The light of the western churches."[42] John Fuller (1631–1687) spoke of "that great Elijah, that renowned man of God."[43] Frank Shuffleton, writing in 1977, confirmed "one of the most famous Puritan divines of his day and one of the chief architects of the New England experiment."[44]

My own esteem will become apparent in the travelogue which follows. Here is a man to know, and knowing better, to walk the human way with a keener awareness, a surer grasp of the compassion and integrity which changes all by changing not.

One further consideration remains: the pressure of the pulpit.

Thomas Hooker was a preacher of transcendent quality. His output was also prodigious. His biographers therefore necessarily begin their personal assessment of the man with a careful study of his voluminous writings. Three major works have been published in the past fifteen years, the Harvard Theological Studies XXVIII, *Thomas Hooker Writings in England and Holland, 1626–1633,* (1975); Frank Shuffleton *Thomas Hooker 1586–1647* (1977); and Sargent Bush Jr. *The Writings of Thomas Hooker, Spiritual Adventure in Two Worlds* (1980). All rightly concentrate on his works, and my indebtedness to these three books and their several authors will become apparent as the story unfolds. I acknowledge that debt with gratitude.

In evaluating the contents of Hooker's writings, however, the text alone is not enough. The puritan sermon was more than an essay, an exposition of Biblical faith and morality, or the exposure of contemporary affairs to Christian comment. It was a feeling after absolute truth as exemplified in the idea of God. The preacher speaks under a sense of Divine constraint, in response to an inner spiritual imperative. He does not speak because he wishes to but because he perceives himself to be called of God, and in obedience responds.

This is altogether clear in Thomas Hooker. "Shall I tell you what God told me?" he asked in his farewell sermon at Chelmsford, when about to flee the country, and feared a collapse of stable government, in prophetic anticipation of the Civil War to come. "Nay, I must tell you on pain of my life. God has told me this night that he will destroy England."[45] You can feel the pressure under which he laboured. Since the days of St Paul the preacher has cried "Necessity is laid upon me; woe to me if I preach not the gospel!"[46]

Now the pressure of the pulpit is twofold. The Preacher sees himself as a messenger, representative of truths over and above himself. The message given conditions the words he speaks. He wrestles in an agony of self-doubt and of eager anticipation. He is in bondage to truths higher than his most inspired comprehension. He stands, says Hooker, on "the Pinnacle of the perfection of Happiness itself, and there seems to be something more, and one step higher than the glorious Grace of Heaven—Its the last resolution—and the top of the rock, whereon the soul rests. Its beyond all gunshot."[47]

At this level of intense obedience to a heavenly vision, we must look carefully into the Preacher's integrity. The temptations of pride and of dissembling, not least in the manipulation of human emotions, are ever-present pulpit pressures. This is never in question with Thomas Hooker. He displays no inclination or aptitude for hypocrisy. He never dresses his face with pretence. But in accepting his utter sincerity we need also to understand that it is not his message we receive, but that which he understands God to have demanded of him. We must look beyond the printed sermons if we are to see the man. We must visualise God as he saw Him, and share the beliefs of his generation.

The other pressure is the Evangel. Puritan preachers, almost in defiance of their claim that all saving initiatives come only from God, believed themselves nonetheless to have been enlisted by God to win others from error and self-destruction. This was especially true for Hooker. "You are bound prentice to the trade of holiness," he told his hearers. "I would have every Christian man—express such holy graces in his course and conversation that all the world should find no flaw."[48]

This laid heavy obligations on the speaker, and led Hooker to advocate a "plain style"[49] which directly conveyed the message to the hearer, which, as it were, enabled the merchant to sell his wares. Now this obedience to the conversion of others is always in danger of obscuring both the preacher and the truth. It is therefore the more important that we go behind the words to discover who the communicator is; and what the situation he seeks to address. This calls for a highly perceptive understanding of his congregation's socio-political orientation, their basic needs, and expectations, their prejudices and their life-experience.

If the essence of Puritan preaching lies in a redemptive disclosure-through-obedience, a willingness to put into the hands of other people the deep surges of insight and belief granted to the speaker for the conversion of his hearers, then it is vitally important to study the environment of the sermon, its historical setting in time and place and people, as well as the content of its message. This is what I shall now try to do in the rest of the guide.

Chapter 1

Marefield in Leicestershire

Security, Confidence in Conflict, Expectations of Expansion

1586 – ca. 1596

How to Get There.

Marefield is most easily reached from the A47 road, which runs due east-west from Wansford on the Great North Road (A1, London to Edinburgh) to Leicester. A minor road, B6047, turns off the A47 between Skeffington and Billesdon, signposted Tilton-on-the-Hill and Melton Mowbray. Follow the B6047 round Tilton, and down the hill outside. Where the road veers left, a single, gated track, signposted Marefield, meanders off to the right, winding its leisurely way through fields, carefully closing its gates on the world it has left behind.

Where to Stay.

Much depends on the anticipated duration, but Leicester is an excellent centre with ample accommodation of all types for visits to Marefield and Market Bosworth. There is also attractive accommodation at Melton Mowbray, Uppingham and Oakham, all within ten miles of Marefield. Good Hotels, Bed-and-Breakfasts, Guest or Farm Houses can be found in both the towns and the villages, advertised in tourist guide books and at the main Information Centres. If you stay at Leicester, you will need at least one day there, and two more for the two tours outlined below, plus one further day for Market Bosworth.

ROUND TOUR A

Tilton and Marefield, with a possible diversion to Melton Mowbray and Belvoir Castle. Distance from Leicester/Uppingham is about 60 miles.

MAREFIELD, birthplace of Thomas Hooker.

Take the B6047 as advised. This brings you first to Tilton-on-the-Hill, but I suggest you proceed direct to Marefield, and return to Tilton for luncheon.

In an Ecclesiastical Census held in 1563, the hamlet of Marefield returned six households.[1] It remains the same size today. A remote, rural settlement set in a green and peaceful valley. There is a single street of six houses, sheltered from the east winds by rising ground. To the south the sharp incline of Tilton Hill overtowers the pastures, and small fields roll away westward to the valley bed. Here the land rises again steeply upon the ridge, running back towards Tilton-on-the-Hill, two miles distant. Northward and to the east the lower-lying ground stretches out into pastoral Lincolnshire, and the emptiness of the Fenlands to The Wash.

When the 400th Anniversary of Thomas Hooker's birth was celebrated in 1986,[2] a double-decker coach took a party of British and American pilgrims along the gated track. The group consisted principally of people from Hooker's continuing congregations at Little Baddow, Essex, and from his First Church at Hartford, Connecticut.

The American group was led by their pastor, Rev. J. Alan McLean, who had already conducted an earlier trek from Hooker's first abode at Cambridge, Massachusetts, to Hartford where Hooker and his followers planted the State Capital of Connecticut. This trek marked the 350th Anniversary of the founding of Hooker's congregation in 1632, but the highlight event was a retracing of Hooker's epic journey in 1636, 100 miles of still distinguishable Indian trails, down which the pioneers drove their livestock, carrying a sick Mrs Hooker on a litter, and the church bell they had brought all the way from England, to hang in the new Meeting Houses first at Newtown, Massachusetts, then at Hartford, Connecticut.[3]

The giant coach precariously squeezed its bulk between the narrow gates, and over the protesting cattle-grids let into the lean lane to keep the loose grazing cattle and sheep in their simple pastures. This was the first known tourist expedition to Hooker's birthplace in recorded history, and hopefully will be the last! The handful of residents welcomed the invaders graciously, but there are no facilities for large groups of visitors, no parking or turning areas. Neither the hospitality nor the undisturbed tranquillity of the place, let alone the flimsy surface of the byway, could be expected to survive many more mass intrusions.

Now to quibble over the distinction between Markfield and Marefield (see Introduction) might seem the height of pettiness from across the Atlantic, but it is all important. Marefield was, and remains, inaccessible, out-of-the-way, unspoilt. Thomas Hooker was a countryman-born, with the uncorrupted single-mindedness and steadfast independence of his breed.

I do not suppose the ethos of Marefield has changed appreciably through-out the passing centuries, as you will find if you go there. Hooker would be as much at home there today as when he freely ran the fields, or climbed the hill to worship with his family in Tilton's parish church of St Peter.

Markfield, on the other hand, stands hard by the edge of the Leices-tershire coalfields. They lie in a tight-knit semi-circle from Coalville to Ashby-de-la-Zouch and Measham, to the west of the county. Theirs was a distinctive culture, partly formed of danger and the darkness. A different breed, a harsher world, deeply imbedded in a region where mining, long sprung from the early colliery village of Coleorton, next to Coalville, had scarred the land surface for at least two hundred years before Hooker was born.[4]

The Hooker home at Marefield's haven is not proven, but the choice lies between the two buildings you meet on entering the minute village. The first and most probable, is Marefield Manor Farm, immediately on your right. It is a lovely old three-storied house, with some mullioned windows and a steeply pitched roof, certainly not later than the 16th century. The golden-tinted iron-stone of its principal rooms faces south and glows in the sunshine. There are even roses round the door. Best of all, it remains a working farm-house, with all the accessories of stock and land-cultivation to dress it.

Marefield Farm,
probably the home of the Hookers in the 16th Century.

Thomas Hooker from Pennsylvania and the author visit with
M. Stuart Campbell, owner of Marefield Farm in the summer
of 1986.

It is thought that the Manor House was retained for one of the lordly
Digbys' farm bailiffs, the Manorial rights having long been exercised by the
Digbys up at Tilton's moated Manor House. If so, it would be natural for the
Hookers to live here. George Leon Walker, in his carefully researched
biography *Thomas Hooker, Preacher, Founder, Democrat,* claimed that Thomas
senior served "in some capacity as overseer of the large landed properties
of the Digby family,"[5] and that the Hookers had so served for some generations beforehand.

It is true that the Hookers very occasionally used Kenelm as a family
forename,[6] suggesting a close relationship with the Kenelm Digbys of Stoke
Dry, as has already been noted. Reference is made by Samuel Eliot Morison,
in *The Founding of Harvard College,* to a donation by Sir Kenelm (1603–1665)
the author-diplomat, to the earliest Harvard Library of "seventeen valuable
and curious works, including several Church Fathers, the *Bibliotheca de
Ratione Studiorum* (1607), of Antonio Possevino, S.J., the works of Jacobus
Alvarez, S.J., an *Epitome of the Annales Ecclesiastici of Cardinal Baronius* (Cologne 1630), *Harphius' Theologia Mystica* (1611), and the Rosselus edition
(Cologne 1630) of the *Poemander of Hermes Trismegistus,*" an interesting
sidelight on the catholic taste of the Puritan clergy, perhaps not always

appreciated. Morison comments that their literary interest was encyclo-paedic.[7]

"That noble and absolutely compleat Gentleman Sir Kenelm Digby Knight" appears later in our story. His donation to Harvard had been solicited by Thomas Weld, John Eliot's associate minister at Roxbury, Massachusetts some time after 1645, and confirms his family's connection with the Puritan Movement, and the Hooker family,[8] for Thomas Hooker was the first minister at Cambridge, Massachusetts, and it was his son-in-law, Thomas Shepard who succeeded him as pastor, and helped to nurse the infant Harvard College through its early traumas.

This family connection with the noble Digbys was a determinative factor in Thomas Hooker's development. In later life he showed no sign of subservience under any circumstances, be it to king or nobility. His pulpit style and public action display a man entirely at home with those in authority, one who from childhood familiarity feared no overlord but God.

Standing four-square to the narrow street, next-door to the Manor but at right-angles to it, you will find the second possible Hooker homestead, Marefield Farm. This too is a stone-built property of sufficient antiquity to have been the Hooker residence. It is plain and sturdy, like Thomas himself, a three-storied building until recently with an exterior stairway for access

Marefield Manor Farm, probably the home of the Hookers in the 16th Century. Inspecting the gardens is Dilys Collingwood, wife of the author.

to the space under the rafters, where the farm servants would have slept. And it was thatched with straw.

When the thatch was replaced with a new slate roof recently, a large quantity of walnut-shells, blackened with age, was uncovered. Squirrels' hoards for generations! But no walnut trees are now to be found in the vicinity, though once, presumably, they abounded.

Leafing through the Massachusetts Historical Society's Collections some years ago, I came across a letter of Governor Winthrop's in which he made reference to the fine oak, walnut and pine trees "more vigorous in former than in later years—the quality of the fruit greatly diminished."[9] I paid little attention to it at the time, but the "fruit" could only have been walnuts. One day I hope to return to Boston to check my notes and to enquire whether these trees could have been imported with the first settlers. If so, we may know where they came from, and where they disappeared to!

This in no way justifies a preference for the Farmhouse over the Manor Farm as the Hooker residence. But the present owners will welcome your discreet visit, and proudly show you their property if reasonable warning is given. The vista across the fields from the rear is virtually unchanged since the 16th century. No young boy could wish for a better prospect, with open fields inviting him to romp across them unfettered. The farmhouse is now a working Stables, with smells and sounds of stamping horses altogether appropriate to its situation. A deep sense of peace and joy sweeps over the pilgrim who pauses for reflection here.

There is nothing at Marefield out of step with the contemporary rise of the yeoman farmers of Tudor England, from obscure beginnings to comparative affluence, easily elevated to the ranks of the gentry, and beyond.[10] It was Tudor policy to exalt to positions of highest power those able, and above all loyal scions of the capitalist yeomanry, who lately had begun to own land in increasing volume. It was a time of low rents and rising prices, which enabled the more skilful farmers to buy out the impoverished of the old nobility, and replace them in high office. This to increase Tudor control.

The rise of the yeomen farmers, under the impetus of an upstart Tudor reign, always conscious of its insecurity, and needing to surround itself with influential supporters, is important to any understanding of the rise of the Puritans, and so of the founding fathers of New England.[11]

The mental as well as the material shackles (and protections) of Feudalism were being cast away. The reformation of religion and politics, which brought Puritanism into being, appeared in Europe at the same moment as new markets beckoned beyond. Newfound worlds of faith and prosperity invited merchants and the new nobility alike. But populations were increasing, there were fresh pressures on the Poor Laws, indigence advanced as quickly as land enclosures robbed the poor of common land, and the old protections of feudalism weakened away.

An air both of unrest and of excitement permeated from the Court of King Charles, intendedly the most brilliant in Europe,[12] down to the merchant adventurers and the depressed cloth traders, to the would-be founders of a reformed church at home, or of colonies overseas.

This was particularly true of the land-owning yeoman stock to which the Hookers belonged. The more enterprising among them could indeed buy or marry into land, increase their holdings until their sons might be educated at Oxford or Cambridge, read Law as a stepping stone to State office, and be raised to the peerage overnight. It was into a land of such rapid social change as this that Puritanism was born, with its emphasis on industry, morality, thrift reaching out from the reformed service of God.

The emergence of the Salisbury dynasty, from 15th century Herefordshire yeomen farmers, is the most remarkable instance of this social movement; and is by no means untypical. They, soon to be amongst the foremost families in the realm, were descended from Richard ap Seyseld of Allt yr Ynys, whose Will in 1508 bequeathed some land in the Welsh Marches to his younger son David ap Richard Seyseld.[13]

This David appears in the ranks of the Yeomen of the Guard at the funeral of Henry VII (1509). He rose to be thrice Mayor of Stamford, and its Member of Parliament, then Sheriff of Northamptonshire. He died in 1536, and his son Richard inherited the growing family fortune, and appears as a Yeoman of the King's Wardrobe under Henry VIII. He became Sheriff of Rutland, a Gentleman of the Privy Chamber, and secured a nice share in the distribution of Abbey lands at the Dissolution of the Monasteries. Being domiciled around Stamford, it is not surprising that St Michael's lucrative Priory there changed into Seyseld hands.

His son William Cecil, grandson of David ap Seyseld, was born in 1520. First he served Somerset,[14] the Lord Protector of Edward VI. He displayed such outstanding administrative ability that, when Somerset fell from favour, he became a Secretary of State to the Crown. On Elizabeth's accession he was made her principal advisor, and in 1571, sixty-three years after his grandfather had inherited a small property in Wales, was created Lord Burghley, and Lord High Treasurer of England.

It was his son, Robert Cecil (Secretary of State in succession to his father), who created the House of Salisbury. The family seat is at Hatfield House in Hertfordshire, one of the most splendid in Britain, straight down the A1(M) from its junction with the A47 at Wansford, easily gained from Exit 4, signposted to Hatfield.

Hatfield House naturally finds a place on the itinerary of the intelligent traveller, with its magnificent architecture and furnishings, its exquisite collections (including such fanciful objects as Queen Elizabeth's gloves and stockings, and the superb portraits of the Virgin Queen—the *Ermine* by Nicholas Hilliard, 1547–1619, and the *Rainbow* by Isaac Oliver, 1565–1617).[15] A wild diversion from the Hooker trail? Be sure no one will complain! Hatfield could also be conveniently en route to Chelmsford, Essex, where we shall catch up with the ubiquitous Cecils again.

What the Cecils achieved in two generations was parallelled all over England (again Chelmsford will bring us examples from the Mildmays, the Warwicks, the Petres, etc.) and helps to explain how the son of a village yeoman (albeit already gentleman Estate Manager) could become one of the leading Reformers in the land, simply for the spiritual gifts within him. In this respect it is significant that, when Hooker was bound by William Laud in 1631, in a forfeit of £50, to attend a meeting of the Court of High Commission in London, it was a yeoman who advanced the money, no inconsiderable sum in those days. His name was Nash, a tenant farmer on the Earl of Warwick's estate at Much [Great] Waltham, near Chelmsford.[16]

This is not to say that life was without physical hardship in Marefield. By present standards, conditions in the Manor house would be primitive and harsh. But in the economy of the day it was doubtless privileged and secure. A useful examination of the extended family living in a Puritan establishment can be found, for instance, in Edmund S. Morgan's book *The Puritan Family*.[17] This is based on the early New England families, where Puritans at last had free rein to bring up their children as they believed; much of it more attractive to present day taste than has sometimes been imagined.

Children were all important to Puritan parents, whose first charge under God was the creation of a Christian household as the microcosm of the Divine Commonwealth.[18] In the Hooker household there would be a full regimen of family prayers morning and evening, a conscious direction of the children's minds towards an understanding of the meaning of Creation, an acknowledgement of the Judgment of God and of His Mercy in Salvation, and thereby a proper sense of morality or of positive living, which clearly stood them in good stead throughout their lives for they were a godly and a prosperous family.

The material welfare of a well placed family within a powerful Estate such as the Hookers and Digbys enjoyed would be enviable. Industrial Leicester, such as it was, lay away to the west. Wool had been a principle source of income since Norman times, and Leicester wool was of the highest quality. There was a flourishing hosiery trade, carried on by hand-frames in a hundred villages.[19] This brought a prosperity to the county that must have been felt in the rural communities too.

Leicester and Rutland shires, with their rich grazing lands were predominantly Puritan and Parliamentarian. This in itself suggests a populace of independent status, an expectation of freedom to improve their lot. They were not beggars fighting for bread, but the better-off demanding their full liberty.

Whom have we here, growing up in the small manor house at Marefield? Perhaps a weakling child. Thomas complained throughout his life of indisposition. He wrote to his friend John Cotton from exile in Rotterdam, "my ague yet holds me," and again "in this long time of my sickness, and wherein I have drawn forth many wearyish hours under his Almighty hand (Blessed be his Name)."[20] In the same letter he speaks of "my weak eye," probably an oblique reference to his unwillingness to make a hasty judgement about the Dutch churches, but an interesting choice of words none-the-less. He was prone to illness all through his life, and died untimely of a fever when sixty-one.

There is evidence too, that he was a late-developer (see under Market Bosworth school). Yet in maturity a calm, almost god-like confidence came over him, as if welling up from the comfortable depths of a settled and happy childhood. He became an outstanding tutor as well as disputant at Cambridge. He was welcomed as a preacher all over the country. He blossomed into a pastoral counsellor without equal with his "new answering method."[21] He was sought out as a trouble-shooter in the colonies.

He wrote one of the definitive defences of New England Congregationalism (*A Survey of the Summe of Church-Discipline*)[22] at the particular insistence of those high-powered New England clergymen and educated laymen, some of the best minds ever to quit England, even though he had come very late to an acceptance of the Congregational way. He was founder, mentor, bedrock of faith and hope and charity to thousands of trembling souls in their search for God.

In everything that emerges after graduation at Cambridge, he appears as a well-balanced, comfortably settled, authoritative, hugely compassionate, highly sensitive man of letters and of action. In addition to his many and commanding writings,[23] his pioneering ministry at home and in America, his later management of a new church colony, he, the primate of Connecticut, would seek out the boy whom he had wrongly accused of stealing his apples, in order to make a personal apology. He would catch, briny-handed, the thief who was helping himself to the Hookers' precious pickled-pork, and over-generously absolve him in the name of their common necessity. He would charter a ship-load of corn for the relief of starving settlers on Long Island. This was known, and became part of the folk-law of the first New England settlements.[24]

Must it not be that the serenity and security of the Marefield home, with the assurance of his socially expanding yeoman class, and a Puritan upbringing in the practical liberties of that most spiritual reformation, made him the man he became?

TILTON-ON-THE-HILL, The Digbys, Puritan Patrons.

From Marefield, continue east and south to Halstead, another hamlet in the parish of Tilton. After its intersection with a lane coming in on your left from Owston,[25] the lane bends narrowly to the south (right) to its junction with the Braunston to Tilton road. At this junction turn right (west), to Halstead at the summit of the steep hill up and adjacent to Tilton. Halstead is the highest hamlet in Leicestershire, 700 feet above sea level. Tilton enjoys the same elevation, so that St Peter's spire dominates the approaches to the village. The distance from Marefield to Tilton via this route is 3½ miles.

The village centre is marked by a cross-roads, with St Peter's Parish Church on your left, and the Rose and Crown across the road also on your left. If you walk down the lane between the Church and the Inn, another steep hill, towards Loddington, you immediately pass Tilton Manor Farm on your right, site of the old Manor House now demolished, with the remains of its one-time moat.

St Peter's Church, Tilton-on-the-Hill.

There is a large car-park at the Rose and Crown. I suggest you stop there for luncheon whilst visiting the church. You will wish to visit the inn in any case. It is as old as the church, and its low-slung beams, good food, facilities, and welcoming atmosphere, make it an attractive place to visit.

The gold-tinted stonework of the medieval church stands as commandingly in its ancient churchyard as the 14th century tower, topped by a slender spire, reaches above the surrounding countryside. The roof, with its crenelated parapet, carries a profusion of pinnacles, and the finest set of gargoyles in the county. The work was carried out c. 1490, under the patronage of Sir Everard Digby (d. 1509, his tomb is inside the church), when the magnificent clerestory was also built above the nave arcades.

This was a pious by-product of the Digby's increasing wealth, following their support for Henry Tudor at the battle of Bosworth, fought five years earlier where Thomas Hooker was to attend school. Sir Everard's seven sons took part in the battle, "several of them 'graced and rewarded' by King Henry VII," as John Nichols reports in his *History and Antiquities of Leicestershire.*[26]

At the southern corner of the churchyard you will see the old School House, reminiscent of the little group of village boys with whom Thomas Hooker must have begun his education, probably tutored by the resident incumbent, Thomas Boyle, a noted Puritan.[27] The shaft of an open-air preaching cross also stands prominently before the South Porch. Somewhere here lie the unmarked graves of Thomas' mother and father. It was not the custom in rural England to set up marked gravestones until the next century. We do not even know his mother's name, only that her death is registered at St Peter's, "1631—Mrs Hooker, wife of Mr Thomas Hooker of Marfield, buried April 16." Her husband followed her, "1635—Thomas Hooker of Marfield buried 24 July."[28]

Enter the Church by the South Porch, rebuilt in 1600, as teenage Thomas would have vividly remembered. Inside, the building is impressively proportioned and ornamented. Faces peer down from the roof bosses, supporting some original oak beams. Angels' wings sweep round capitals in the north aisle, or a lion with a lamb that has given up without a struggle, a fox making off with a goose, a battered head. It all

Font where Thomas Hooker was probably baptized. St Peter's Church, Tilton.

GENEALOGICAL TABLE, NO. 2:   THE DIGBYS OF TILTON AND STOKE DRY

SAXON AELMAR held "lands in Tiletone", Leicestershire under Edward Confessor (1003-66). His descendants took their name from Dikeby, or Digby, Lincolnshire, where they lived

Sir JOHN DIGBY of Tilton, d 1269 (Tilton tomb) , m Lady Arabella (n Harcourt) (Tilton tomb)

ROBERT DIGBY of Tilton, d before 1413, inherited Drystoke Manor, m Catherine (n Pakeman)

SIMON of Tilton & Drystoke, d before 1422, m Joan (n Beler)

EVERARD DIGBY of Tilton & Stokedry; d Battle of Towton, 29/3/1461, m Agnes (n Clarke)

SIR EVERARD of Tilton & Stokedry, d 1509 (Tilton tomb), m Lady Jaquetta (n Ellys) bu Dry Stoke, 1496

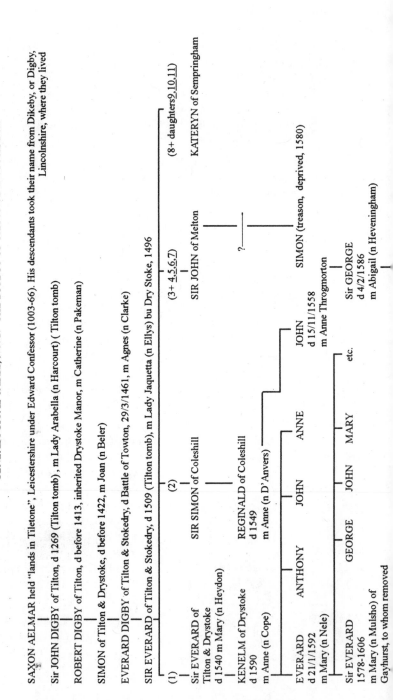

(1)

(2)

(3+ 4,5,6,7)

(8+ daughters9,10,11)

Sir EVERARD of
Tilton & Drystoke
d 1540 m Mary (n Heydon)

SIR SIMON of Coleshill

SIR JOHN of Melton

KATERYN of Sempringham

KENELM of Drystoke
d 1590
m Anne (n Cope)

REGINALD of Coleshill
d 1549
m Anne (n D'Anvers)

?

EVERARD
d 21/1/1592
m Mary (n Nele)

ANTHONY

JOHN

ANNE

JOHN
d 15/11/1558
m Anne Throgmorton

SIMON (treason, deprived, 1580)

Sir EVERARD
1578-1606
m Mary (n Mulsho) of
Gayhurst, to whom removed

GEORGE

JOHN

MARY

etc.

Sir GEORGE
d 4/2/1586
m Abigail (n Heveningham)

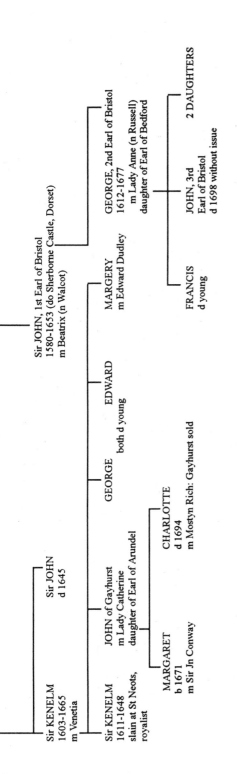

Sir JOHN, 1st Earl of Bristol
1580-1653 (do Sherborne Castle, Dorset)
m Beatrix (n Walcot)

Sir KENELM
1603-1665
m Venetia

Sir JOHN
d 1645

Sir KENELM
1611-1648
slain at St Neots,
royalist

JOHN of Gayhurst
m Lady Catherine
daughter of Earl of Arundel

GEORGE   EDWARD
both d young

MARGERY
m Edward Dudley

GEORGE, 2nd Earl of Bristol
1612-1677
m Lady Anne (n Russell)
daughter of Earl of Bedford

MARGARET
b 1671
m Sir Jn Conway

CHARLOTTE
d 1694
m Mostyn Rich: Gayhurst sold

FRANCIS
d young

JOHN, 3rd
Earl of Bristol
d 1698 without issue

2 DAUGHTERS

depends on your taste, but you will reach out a trembling hand for the lightest touch on the square-cut bowl of the font (the upper part is 11th century), where Thomas Hooker was baptised. It stands at ease inside the south entrance, unadorned by any inscription, almost as if it were not one of Britain's most precious possessions!

On the south side of the nave there are three priceless Digby tombs, with effigies of Sir John of Tilton, d. 1269; his wife; and Sir Everard, d. 1509.[29] Sir John's effigy is sculptured in stone, clad in chain-mail with a sleeveless surcoat. His shield bears the fleur-de-lys which recur in the Digby coat-of-arms, his feet rest on a recumbent lion.

The Digbys descended from Saxon Aelmer, who held land at "Tiletone" in the reign of Edward the Confessor.[30] It is claimed they "cummith by lineal descent owt of the towne of Dikeby, a village yn Lincolnshire, wher as yet the heir of the eldest house of the Dikebyes hath a xli land by the yere. As far as I can lerne, the eldest place that the Dikebyes of Lincolnshir had in Leircestershire was at Tilton," according to the Itinerary of John Leland (1506–1552) appointed 'King's Antiquary' by Henry VIII, the manuscript of whose tours in England and Wales were deposited in the Bodleian at Oxford, and have been variously published.[31] Dikeby is present-day Digby, 5 miles north of Sleaford in what used to be Lincolnshire fenland, where hidden hamlets rose (sometimes on stilts) beside (By) the Dykes, which slowly drained the marshlands.

The tomb of Lady Arabella, wife of Sir John, lies under the adjacent arch in the south aisle. Her elegant figure has a draped headdress, and a cloak embroidered with the fleur-de-lys. Her lapdog supports her feet. The third tomb is that of Sir Everard, in armour, the fleur-de-lys conspicuous on his shield, a lion again at his feet. To him more than any other of this ancient line, the family owed its always fluctuating, but steadily improving good fortunes.

His father, Everard, lord of Tilton and Stoke Dry, Member of Parliament for Rutland, and Sheriff, resisted Edward IV's seizure of the crown, and, with three of his brothers, fought against the new king at the decisive Battle of Towton (just south of Tadcaster, south-west of York). There, on March 29, 1461, he was slain.[32]

The victorious Edward stripped the Digbys of their lands and titles, but the Sir Everard commemorated in the Tilton tomb (d. 1509), eldest son and heir to his father's forfeited properties, must already have been possessed of the Digbys' intoxicating charm, which was to gain his descendants many another redress of ill chance. He got everything back, apparently before Sir Walter Devereux (to whom the properties were forfeited by King Edward) could enter into possession, and for the next 48 years presided over the family's growth in numbers, wealth, and influence. Salute the sculpted effigy with the deference due to its model as well as its artistry. He was a remarkable man.

He married Jaquetta Ellis (d. 1496), by whom he had seven warrior sons.[33] He astutely sent them to fight on the side of Henry Tudor at the Battle of Bosworth, and reaped the appropriate rewards. Jaquetta was laid to rest, not in the tomb later erected for her husband at Tilton, but at the new family home of Stoke Dry (Drystoke). For 100 years, and more, Digbys had been styled "of Tilton and Drystoke," since Robert Digby (d. before 1413) inherited the Drystoke Manor from a Richard Digby (d. 1379) of a collateral branch. In due course Stoke Dry became their principal seat. Besides Jaquetta, her eldest son Sir Everard (d. 1540), his wife Mary (Margaret), and their son Kenelm with his wife, down to the Everard (d. 1592), father of the Gunpowder Plotter, they lie in the Digby Chapel at Dry Stoke Parish Church.

Of the seven sons who fought at Bosworth, the eldest, Sir Everard (d. 1540), was confirmed in the family possession of Tilton and Dry Stoke so carefully kept for him by his father, who lonely lies in Tilton Church. One wonders why, when his wife was already interred at Stoke Dry, the family wished for this last ornate memorial in their ancestral church. At least it secures the Digby connection, long after the family had outgrown the local Manor House

The second son, Sir Simon, lord of Uppingham amongst other manors in Rutland, and many additional holdings from Suffolk to Surrey, "comptroller of petty customs in the port of London,"[34] and so on, had his seat at Coleshill, Warwicks. There he was buried. From him the Digby Earls of Bristol descended.

The third son, Sir John, at times Sheriff of Warwick,[35] Leicester, and Rutland, "knight-marshall of king Henry VII's household," Captain of Calais (Digby hands had wide open palms, and their feet were no slouches!), lived at Eye-Kettleby, Leicester, and was buried at neighbouring Melton Mowbray, where we shall catch up with him again.

Sir Everard and the Lady Jaquetta also had four daughters, of whom the third, Kateryn, was a Gilbertine "nunne at Sempringham." Her father's will granted her "xxs in money, and a pair of flexyn shete, and a white sparvar"[36] (bed-canopy). You will, I hope, go with Thomas Hooker to Sempringham, northern headquarters of the Massachusetts Bay Company, later on.

Tragedy struck again in the person of the Sir Everard (great-great-great-grandson of the Sir Everard slain at Towton, and a contemporary of Thomas Hooker) who was executed for his part in the Gunpowder Plot.

GENEALOGICAL TABLE, NO. 3

Table showing major relationships of reigning families in Europe which affected Sir Kenelm Digbys' career.

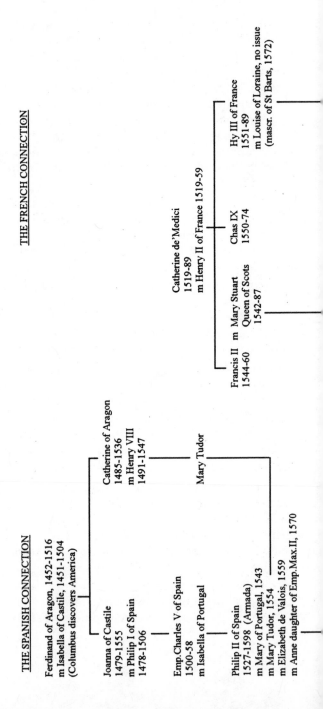

THE SPANISH CONNECTION

THE FRENCH CONNECTION

Ferdinand of Aragon, 1452-1516
m Isabella of Castile, 1451-1504
(Columbus discovers America)

Catherine of Aragon
1485-1536
m Henry VIII
1491-1547

Joanna of Castile
1479-1555
m Philip I of Spain
1478-1506

Mary Tudor

Emp. Charles V of Spain
1500-58
m Isabella of Portugal

Philip II of Spain
1527-1598 (Armada)
m Mary of Portugal, 1543
m Mary Tudor, 1554
m Elizabeth de Valois, 1559
m Anne daughter of Emp. Max. II, 1570

Catherine de'Medici
1519-89
m Henry II of France 1519-59

Francis II m Mary Stuart
1544-60   Queen of Scots
              1542-87

Chas IX
1550-74

Hy III of France
1551-89
m Louise of Loraine, no issue
(mascr. of St Barts, 1572)

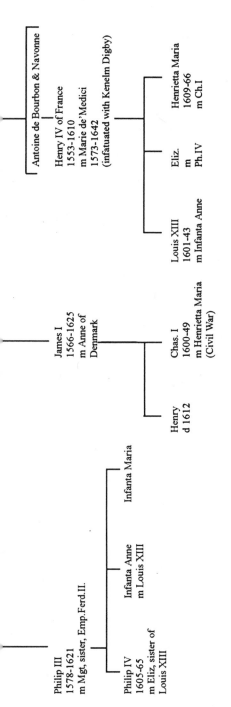

Antoine de Bourbon & Navonne

Henry IV of France
1553-1610
m Marie de'Medici
1573-1642
(infatuated with Kenelm Digby)

James I
1566-1625
m Anne of
Denmark

Philip III
1578-1621
m Mgt, sister, Emp.Ferd.II.

Philip IV
1605-65
m Eliz, sister of
Louis XIII

Infanta Anne
m Louis XIII

Infanta Maria

Henry
d 1612

Chas. I
1600-49
m Henrietta Maria
(Civil War)

Louis XIII
1601-43
m Infanta Anne

Eliz.
m
Ph.IV

Henrietta Maria
1609-66
m Ch.I

NB. John Digby 1st Earl Bristol failed 1611 to arrange a marriage with Prince Henry (d 1612) ditto in c. 1620 for Prince Charles (I) marriage with Infanta Maria, assisted by Sir Kenelm Digby (1603-65) both times. Whilst James (I) unsuccessfully sought an alliance with Catholic Spain, his daughter Elizabeth m the Protestant Elector Palatine, Fredrick V.

"Gunpowder" Digby was born at Dry Stoke in 1578.[37] He inherited from his father Everard, a scholarly Master of Arts and Fellow of St John's College, Cambridge (then a "Puritan" academy), when only 14 years of age, and considerably augmented his large estate by marriage, at 18 years, to a wealthy Catholic heiress named Mary Mulsho, of Gayhurst (Gothurst), Buckinghamshire. From this time onwards, Gayhurst became the family seat of the Tilton Digbys.

On his father's death, Everard was made a Ward of the Crown, and given a place in Elizabeth's household. He grew up at Court. But three years after his marriage he came under Jesuit influence, embraced Catholicism, and enthusiastically supported the accession of James I in the belief that this would bring a wider toleration of Catholics in England. He was even knighted by James at Belvoir Castle on April 23, 1603 (his wardship had, in fact, been purchased from the crown by Roger Manners, of the family of the Dukes of Rutland of Belvoir Castle, on behalf of his widowed mother).

When it became plain that no favours awaited the Catholics (or anyone apart from James' favourites) Sir Everard joined the Gunpowder Plot. He financed a rising in the Midlands, and, on pretence of organising a hunting party, on November 5 mobilised an armed troop at Danchurch near Rugby, Warwickshire.

With the failure of Guy Fawkes,[38] Everard too was arrested, imprisoned in the Tower of London, tried at Westminster Hall, and hanged on January 30 in St Paul's churchyard. According to Father Gerard, the Jesuit priest involved in Everard's conversion, he was the only conspirator to plead guilty for the sake of the faith within him. "A handsome man, of fine presence, with skill in riding of great horses as well as in music, he was as complete a man in all things that deserved estimation or might win affection as one should see in a kingdom."[39] "He was one of the most beautiful men of his time, and, by the accomplishment of his mind, reputed one of the finest gentlemen in England," was the unexpected verdict of John Nichols in his "Antiquities."[40]

The Digbys were legendary for a charming ability to retrieve their lost fortunes. Thus Sir Everard's elder son, Sir Kenelm (1604–1665) quickly regained the royal favours both easily won and lost by his father. His rapid advancement no doubt owed something to the infatuation he inspired in the ageing Marie de Medici, mother of King Charles' wife,[41] Henrietta Maria. Edward Hyde, Earl of Clarendon (1609–1674, who with Ben Jonson the dramatist was amongst Kenelm's closest friends) described him as "a man of very extraordinary person and presence which drew the eyes of all upon him, a wonderful graceful behaviour, a flowing courtesy and civility, and such a volubility of language as surprised and delighted."[42]

Sir Kenelm was highly gifted, and, as we have seen, remained a friend of the Puritan cause. He was a founder member of the Royal Society (in 1663), having been a celebrated author and dipomat long before that. At only fourteen years of age he had joined his cousin Sir John Digby (afterwards first earl of Bristol) at Madrid,[43] where Sir John, as English ambassador, was abortively negotiating a match between Prince Henry (James' elder son), and the Infanta Anne of Austria, daughter of King Philip III of Spain. But Anne married King Louis XIII of France instead.

Six years later Kenelm was again in Madrid, assisting his cousin to service the Duke of Buckingham's and (then) Prince Charles' bid (Henry having died in the meantime) to marry Anne's younger sister the Infanta Maria. This attempt to form a Spanish alliance also failed, with the consequence of damaging the already unpopular Buckingham's reputation even further.[44]

George Villiers, 1592–1628 was, you may recall, chief amongst the young men favoured by James I, who created him Duke of Buckingham, of Boreham Hall next to Little Baddow, as we shall see in Chapter Five. Villiers had married the Catholic Lady Katherine Manners (whose kinsman Roger was patron to Kenelm's father), but apparently never forgave the Digbys for the failure of the Madrid mission, and tried to impede their careers, until his own assassination five years later.[45]

Nonetheless, King James was captivated by the youthful charm of the twenty year old Kenelm. He knighted him on his return, exactly as he had done his traitorous father twenty years before. Kenelm became a gentleman of Prince Charles' privy chamber, and was much favoured at the court.

Two years later, in 1625, he married Venetia, daughter of Sir Edward Stanley of Tonge Castle, Shropshire (demolished in 1954, the ruins, and park landscaped by Capability Brown, are now part of the M54 motorway; but the village, where Dickens set the final scenes of *The Old Curiosity Shop*, and the church of St Mary and St Bartholomew, with its unique array of tombs, remain).

Venetia was "a lady of extraordinary beauty and intellectual attainments, but of doubtful virtue."[46] This brilliant match, extolled by Ben Johnson in his poem "Eupheme," was also a happy one. When Venetia died eight years later, Kenelm was inconsolable, and withdrew from society for the following two years.

The vivid story is too complex for more detailed telling here. Sir Kenelm (once more in consort with his cousin, the Earl of Bristol) turned privateer, and soundly whipped the French and Venetian fleets in the Venetian harbour of Scanderoon, on June 11, 1627. He was feted on his return, made Commissioner of the Navy, and then dismissed at the insistence of the Venetian government. He now turned Catholic, as his father had before him, and was banished to France. Returning to England, he was imprisoned in "The Three Tobacco Pipes nigh Charing Cross" (who wouldn't be, given half the chance!), and was said to have turned this Inn of Correction into "a place of delight" by his effervescent conversation.

When released, he returned to France, intrigued with Queen Anne of Austria in the Royalist cause; defended his close friend Archbishop William Laud against pro-Catholic charges, to the anger of Parliament, and had all his property confiscated. Queen Henrietta appointed him her Chancellor, and dispatched him to Pope Innocent X at Rome, to negotiate support for King Charles. Banished again, he resurrected his former Puritan relationships, opened negotiations with Oliver Cromwell (in 1654, after Charles' execution), and was employed by Cromwell as a Catholic-European adviser.

He was in Germany at the Restoration in 1660, and returned for his own reinstatement to royal favour only to forfeit it again for too avid a defence of his kinsman George, second Earl of Bristol,[47] who was in trouble with the House of Lords for charging Lord Clarendon with High Treason. The quarrel with Clarendon seriously disrupted the Digbys' influence. Clarendon had been a chief architect of the Restoration. He was Charles' Chancellor of the Exchequer, and speaker of the House of Lords. At that time he was the most influential man in England.[48]

Fortunately for Kenelm, his other interests were boundless. Scholarly papers and larger works flowed from his pen throughout his life-time, ranging over the known fields of science and philosophy, and rich in Catholic polemics. Yet he retained his acceptability amongst the Puritan founders of New England, and was, as already noted, an early patron of Harvard College. He died, this son of the squire of Stoke Dry near Tilton, on 11 July 1665, surely never to be forgotten by the neighbourhood families, at least one of whom had already taken his name for their own—Kenelm Hooker.

The first Earl of Bristol, now of Sherborne Castle in Dorset (great-great-great-grandson of Sir Everard, d. 1509, of Stoke Dry, as was Sir Kenelm), had died in 1653. He was succeeded by his son George, who also saw personal service with his sovereigns Charles I and Charles II. His long career of political intrigue made him one of the most conspicuous figures of his time. He too alternated between royal favours and impeachments, betrayed as well as advanced by the Digby charm.

The impact of this astonishing family on small, sober Tilton-on-the-Hill could not but have made a commensurate impact on the fertile mind of young Thomas Hooker. Indeed, many of the Digby traits rubbed off on him, whether coincidentally or no. He too had a charm matched only by his controversial interventions into politics. At the very least the Digbys brought the sphere of State, and World affairs close home to lowly Mare-field.

A brief consideration of the epithet "Puritan" will be helpful here, though the word is not easy to define.[49] It never had a precise use, and has been subject to considerable misunderstanding. Groups quite unacceptable to the Puritans, such as Brownists, Independants, Quakers,[50] have been lumped in with them, to the outraged annoyance of the New England Puritan leaders, who would have run any of these out of the State, had they dared to stray into Massachusetts Bay.

The 17th century Puritans were the more extreme party of English Protestants who had been disappointed by the Elizabethan Settlement,[51] as determined by the 1559 Act of Uniformity. This had restored the partial reforms made under Henry VIII and Edward VI, but no more. The Puritans saw themselves as the elect of God for the establishment of His Kingdom on earth, and wished to build a divine commonwealth dictated solely by His Word as revealed in the Bible.

Their theology was that of John Calvin, their model Calvin's city-state at Geneva.[52] To this end they campaigned relentlessly for a purification of public and private affairs, but remained members of the Church of England, and generally loyal to the monarchy even into the first settlements in America. They simply wished to improve everything.

Francis Higginson (Hooker's friend, whom we shall meet in greater depth when we reach Leicester) was typical of his generation. He sailed for Salem, Massachusetts, in 1629, and was reported by Cotton Mather, in the *Magnalia Christi Americana*, as calling the ship's company to the stern for a last look at his native country, and to have said "'farewel, dear England! farewel, the Church of God in England, and all the Christian friends there! We do not go to New-England as separatists from the Church of England; though we cannot but separate from the corruptions in it: but we go to practice the positive part of church reformation, and propagate the gospel in America.' And so he concluded with fervent prayer for the King, and church, and state, in England."[53]

The following year, in the same vein, Governor John Winthrop published from the *Arbella,* flagship of the Bay Company's fleet which colonised Massachusetts, a "Humble Request of His Majestie's loyall subjects the Governour and Company late gone for New England; To the rest of their Brethren in and of the Church of England. For the obtaining of their prayers and the removal of suspitions, and misconstructions of their Intentions," calling the Church of England their "dear Mother," for whom they "rejoice in her good and unfeignedly grieve for any sorrow that shall ever betide her."[54]

The pragmatic reason for the persecution of the Puritans came from their opposition to the bishops (to be exact, to prelacy). The Elizabethan Settlement had been a delicate political compromise, designed to secure the stability of the throne by striking a balance between the old English Catholics (who had temporarily returned to power under Queen Mary, and still enjoyed widespread support amongst the populace) and the up-and-coming Protestant reformers, of whom the Puritans demanded not only a church cleansed from unscriptural practices, but of the whole hierarchy, the very machinery of domestic government right down to each local parish and household, and of the bishops who were amongst the staunchest upholders of the crown.

The Puritans wanted a democratisation of the clergy, a simplification of religious ceremonies, no fussy vestments, no genuflexions, no sign of the cross, no organ to drown out the words of chanted psalms, nothing to intrude between the believer and his God. They wanted simplicity and sobriety in behaviour, integrity in public affairs, honesty in commerce, and to be left free to pursue the prosperity so many had begun to enjoy as a sign of their divine election.

The ordinances of their faith were perhaps means rather than ends. They tended to call Sunday "The Market Day of the Soul,"[55] and that neatly described their attitude to public worship. They could also be sacramentalists and mystics. Their personal diaries and letters, like their lives, could be full of tender, joyful love.[56] They are not to be dismissed as narrow-minded individualists questing for personal piety, nor simplistically as kill-joys bent on blighting normal human pleasures. But they could be tribal, censorious, vindictive when vagrancy or intemperance threatened their carefully tended economy, or irreligion the New England way they had suffered so much to set up in North America.[57]

They were invariably a minority group. A number of contemporary historians such as Wrightson and Devine (*Poverty and Piety in an Essex Village*),[58] or William Hunt (*The Puritan Moment*), have shown that for a community to be "Puritan" generally meant having Puritan patrons or clergy. Rarely did a community express a common theological or political view. The manor or the village, even the town which espoused Puritan reforms in England, and fought on the side of parliament in the Civil War, was likely to have a majority of inarticulate adherents to the old regime, superstitions, and customs. They went along with the new reforms because they lacked the power to resist, or out of personal loyalty to their squire, or their parson. As soon as the lordship of the manor changed, or a conforming vicar returned to the parish, the populace returned with shouts of relief to their unreformed state. They did not know what was good for them!

When the term Puritan is used of an English community in this Guide, it refers to people and situations under the control of leading Puritans locally resident or empowered. They mistakenly supposed that the kingdom of God could be intellectually ordered and governed by godly rulers. In this they were misguided, and disappointed, but the dream beckons men and women of integrity still.

A corrective postscript needs to be added here, reminding us of the waves of Popular support given to Puritanism at recurring times and places, which eventually flooded into civil war. It was the people at large in villages like John Eliot's Nazeing (see pp. 333-35) who opposed the petty tyranny of eg. imposed liturgical practices (the surplice, square cap, fixed altar, etc) as much as the clergy, however muddled their motives.

For all the Catholic persuasion of some of the Digbys, the Tilton and Drystoke branch remained sympathetic to Puritan reforms. They certainly approved a Puritan rector, Thomas Boyle. His painful preaching was Hooker's first introduction, outside his home, to the majesty of God and the depravity of a human race in dire need of God's gracious salvation, which was to dominate Thomas Hooker's manhood.

MELTON MOWBRAY, Seat of Sir John Digby.

From Tilton to Melton Mowbray, via the B6047, is less than 10 miles. You will thank me warmly afterwards, for recommending this marginal incursion into Hooker's boyhood countryside. Melton is a tourist centre in its own right, as you will instantly recognise on turning from the pleasantly rural B6047, onto the A607 into the town. You enter via widespread Egerton Park, where the Earl of Wilton entertained royalty at Egerton Lodge up to modern times, up for the hunt. If you have time for a walk in the park later on, you will see the ancient door, now standing at the side of the Lodge, facing the main road, in which a loaf shaped opening of generous proportions is cut, through which bread was once freely distributed to the hungry poor outside.

I suggest that you call first at the Tourist Information Centre, at the Carnegie Museum in Thorpe End, for up-to-date directions.[59] It is clearly signposted. If you are lucky, you may park for a short time outside. There are several long-stay car-parks nearby, again well sign-posted. The one off Wilton Road, behind the Bus Station between Egerton Lodge and the Library, as you enter, is perhaps the most convenient. Whilst at the Information Centre, you may wish to inspect the Stilton Cheese factory of Tuxford & Tebbutt, almost next door. Stilton Cheese, a delectable cylindrical concoction, once the proud produce of many surrounding villages, has been manufactured here since 1780. It is a delicacy to be experienced by the wise. I understand that Tuxford & Tebbutt have a video presentation of this unique cheese-making process, available only by prior arrangement.

The Saxon Lord of the Manor was none other than Leofric, shamed husband of Lady Godiva. The Mowbrays came later, granted the Melton estates by King William Rufus (1056–1100, third son of William I). They stayed for over 300 years. In the Civil War Melton was a Roundhead Garrison town, twice assaulted by Royalist forces, with considerable loss to the Parliamentary side.[60] Thomas Hooker would be well aware of these radical events in his native region. They sustained the tally of conflict he had experienced from boyhood.

Leicester is the Fox-Hunting Shire, with the Belvoir, Cottesmore and Quorn hunts historically associated with the town. There is still a Meet on New Years Day in the Market Place, and the Harboro' Hotel in Burton Street was the place where fox-hunting people used to stay. Indeed, there are Hotels and Guest Houses a'plenty in and around Melton.

Make your way to the Market Place. From there you will see another early coaching inn, the George Hotel, in High Street. And in Nottingham Street, the Olde Pork Pie Shoppe, for you are in the home of the mouthwatering Melton Mowbray pork pie, and the Melton Hunt Cake, both still baked on the shop premises by the long-time proprietors, Dickinson & Morris Ltd, and truly unsurpassed.

Anne of Cleves House is in Burton Street, just off the Market. This is a 1384 property, given to Anne on her divorce from Henry VIII[61] (a welcome change from the headman's axe), now surely one of the most historic restaurants in England. The graceful Bede House stands opposite, erected in 1640 as an almshouse, still a residential home for senior citizens. If you are interested in what was considered to be a suitable retirement condominium in Hooker's day look discreetly at this low-lying, two storied, stone-gabled masterpiece.

But first you will meet the magnificent Parish Church of St Mary.[62] It stamps its image on your mind almost wherever you are. Local residents will assure you that it is the most beautiful in the county, and you will not easily disprove the claim. The upper section of the mighty, 100–foot high tower, battlemented, with slender spire, and, in the nave "a glorious array of 48 clerestory windows—containing over 15,000 pieces of glass" (Gilbert M. King's description in his excellent *St Mary's Parish Church*), with the vestry north of the chancel, were erected by Sir John Digby amongst others, in a major reconstruction of 1532, as the date-stone, visible from the church walk along Burton Street shows. The church has changed little from that date.

Sir John of Eye Kettleby, you will recall, was the third of seven brothers, sons of Sir Everard Digby of Tilton, who fought to place Henry Tudor on the throne. He was knighted at Bosworth's battle field, and continued to serve his king in many distinguished, and very lucrative ways (which found expression, as at Tilton, in improving the architecture of his church). In Sir John's case, this included Henry VIII's campaign in France (1511–14), where he fought in the siege of Therouenne, and Tourney, and was appointed Warden of Calais.

He died in 1533, and his tomb used to stand in the south aisle, then called the Digby aisle,[63] close behind the Crusader knight's tomb, which you will find there, in a round arched niche. But the Digby monument was defaced as early as 1583, according to a Harleian manuscript (2017–84) in the British Museum, and then altogether dismantled. It is possible that Sir John's grandson, Simon, was responsible, attainted for high treason, and dispossessed of all his lands in 1580. The ups and downs of the Digbys were a permanent feature of their undoubted accomplishments.

However, his later kinsman Everard of Holwell, by Ab Kettleby (d. 1628) is still fondly memorialised in that church. If you have time to spare, you can easily drive there to see it, in its charming village setting. But first, do explore the interior of St Mary's. Its treasures, too numerous to detail, repay every minute spent there. It is normally open on weekdays 10:00–noon, and 14:00-17:00 in summer, as well as for Sunday Services.

AB KETTLEBY is a small village 3 miles north of Melton, on the A606 to Nottingham. Turn left on entering, and drive down narrow Church Lane, where you can park alongside the tiny triangle of grass under the tree where a narrow footpath runs on to the church of St James the Greater. The church will probably be locked, but the key may be had from 24 Chapel Lane, at the far end of a grassy track, which leads across the fields beyond. You tread a legendary way, for there is evidence here of a Bronze Age settlement before the Romans built their villa, and Domesday records 17 households. The square church tower holds three bells, one inscribed "God Save His Church 1653," another "Jesus Be Your Speede 1662."

Inside the church you will find the Digby epitaph:

> When his pure soule from Holiwell did hast
> Of light and life the eternall springe to tast
> Within this stonie caskett was enclosed
> The dust of Everard Digbie here deposed
> Whose name still fresh, like pretious ointment finds
> A sweeter cabynett in good men's mindes
> Whose goodness here in vaine ye readers seek
> Tis writ in teares on many a neighbring cheek
> And such sadd dropps doe more adorn an herse
> Than painted coats or brass or flattring verse.

HOLWELL is reached by returning to the A606, turning left, and then by taking the first right-hand lane outside the village, signposted Holwell.

This isolated hamlet again more than repays the effort of getting there, though the Digby residence is no longer known. Enquire at the Village Store, and you will obtain the huge church key from an adjacent house, with the Manor Farm at the corner beyond.

The Church of St Leonard perches on a steep bank opposite, its low-lying outline broken by a small bell-tower. The unadorned nave within is only some 53 by 16 feet of 13th century iron-stone, too unpretentious for a Digby epitaph, but with a simple, earthy relevance never to be dismissed. You do not know old England unless you have worshipped in such homely places, and have gossiped in the houses round about. They were complete communities up to recent times, with traditions, expectations, obligations all their own.

EYE KETTLEBY completes the trio of Digby possessions around Melton. To reach it you need to retrace your journey, through Melton, to the B6047. At the town end you reach a cross-roads, signposted to Kirby Bellars on the right (the road goes on to Great Dalby, with a gated road to Burton Lazars to the left—you could, of course, have diverted down this lane on your way into Melton Mowbray from Tilton, but I think you will wish to ensure the maximum time for exploring Melton first).

If you drive a short way along the lane, you will enter Eye Kettleby, clearly marked by a name-plate, and see the Hall, at the top of a private drive on your left. Beside the Hall there is Eye Kettleby Hall Farm, and perhaps three other houses.

The site of the original village lies across the fields to your right, skirting the A607 at the end of the lane, as it runs back into Melton, a mile from the town. The village, with the Digby residence, disappeared 300 years ago, marked by a series of mounds and depressions in the fields, and nothing more.[64] Nonetheless, you get the feel of the locality, and understand how effectively the high-handed Digbys covered a lot of the countryside, as you have done today!

BELVOIR CASTLE, Royalist Stronghold.

An unforgettable experience awaits you, if your itinerary permits this diversion to Belvoir Castle (pronounced Beever). Follow the A607 Thorpe Road from Melton Mowbray, signposted to Grantham and Waltham-on-the-Wolds. The total distance to Belvoir is little more than 10 miles.

As you drive into Waltham-on-the-Wolds you will be intrigued with the many old cottages with distinctive blue-black pantiles, glazed against the cold winds. The Wolds (open, undulating hills) rise above the surrounding countryside, so that Waltham is unprotected from the intemperate North Sea some forty miles away.

The 13th century church of St Mary Magdalen with its tall spire is visible from afar. A key used to be kept at the Village Post Office in High Street. O that you could have shared the jolly hospitality of the Methodist family who kept it, and entertained the preacher at the Methodist Church Anniversary Services of fifty years ago! My heart warms and my mouth waters still!

If you require refreshment there are two Inns. The Marquis of Granby,[65] commemorating John Manners, eldest son of the 3rd Duke of Rutland, a hero of the Seven Years War (1756–63) in which Britain supported Frederick the Great of Prussia against a coalition of Austria, France, Russia, etc, which laid the foundation of modern Germany, and ended French domination in Canada and India. And the Royal Horseshoes, reminding you of the two Racing Stables at Waltham, but you may have seen the racehorses at exercise as you drove in.

Belvoir is a further six miles from Waltham via the A607. You will see the Castle signpost as you approach the cross-roads, where High Street veers off to the right. Go "straight on." Follow the signs cross-country to Belvoir.

The view from the Castle down the Vale of Belvoir is as memorable as anything in Midlands Britain. The garden terraces are superb. The battlemented, turreted house, with its art treasures, oil paintings, furniture, ornamentation (wait 'til you see the Elizabethan Saloon) and military collection, demand as long a visit as you can contrive. You will especially wish to see Holbein's portrait of Henry VIII, so significant for the rise of the Puritans.

Belvoir Castle was built by Robert de Todeni, standard-bearer to William the Conqueror. It passed to Lord Hastings, whom we shall meet at Kirby Muxloe, and after his murder it finally came (because of the friendship of Henry VIII) to the Manners family, then earls of Rutland.[66] You will remember that Everard (Gunpowder Plot) Digby was knighted here by James I, enroute from Scotland to assume the English throne. He was one of 46 to be knighted at the royal stopover; they say, all before breakfast. But James was in a hurry to reach London. Maybe he was hungry too![67]

Thomas Hooker would be keenly aware of this prominent family, and their alignment with the Digbys, if only as background Catholic nobility in his boyhood world, adding their considerable weight to the clashing inner competition which was to drive him into exile, that is, between the sovereignty of Almighty God, and the authority of his family's overlords, each so far removed, yet each, both God and the nobles, near at hand.

The Manners remained royalist when other leading Leicestershire families turned parliamentarian. The Castle was extensively damaged in consequence, during the Civil War. It was rebuilt on its original foundations by successive owners, until it reached the splendour you will admire today. I only wish I could come with you. Thomas Hooker would have stayed at home!

ROUND TOUR B

Blaston, Stoke Dry, Rockingham Castle, Deene Park, Fotheringhay, Apethorpe and Uppingham.

Approximate Distance, seventy miles, or, if returning to Uppingham direct from Rockingham (omitting Deene Park, Fotheringhay and Apethorpe), about 45 miles.

BLASTON, Birthplace of Thomas Hooker senior.
From Tilton-on-the-Hill return to the A47, turn left (east) to Tugby, a distance of no more than three miles. At Tugby, turn right across the busy main road into Main Street, signposted to Hallaton. You pass the Church of St Thomas Becket on rising ground to your right. Its square tower has four stories, the lower two, with the little doorway and window, a rare Saxon construction; the upper two, Norman work.

Follow Main Street, now Hallaton Road, down the hill, bending left. It runs up and down the hillsides a further four miles, past small fields split by lush hedgerows, great trees springing here and there, lambs in Spring-time and daffodils at the wayside, a taste of old rural England long lost elsewhere.

You enter Hallaton at a duck pond on the rise of the last hill, with the Fox Inn at its bank, and, round the corner, a sharp left-hand turn for Blaston, as the signpost says. But, if you can, do first penetrate into Hallaton Village. You drive past the lane to Blaston, take the immediate right-hand turn into a winding High Street, and there you are, at a sculpted green-sward square of most amiable proportion, with a rare conical market cross alongside a modern war-memorial, scattered thatched cottages, the Berwicke Arms opposite, and the great church of St Michael, its 13th century spire amongst the finest in the county, on the western rim beyond.

Hallaton well repays a nearer acquaintance, including, if you were so lucky, its unique "bottle-kicking" on Easter Monday, a bruising team contest with the neighbouring village of Medbourne, to capture a small cask, a ritual said to have survived from the rites of the pagan goddess Eostre, which the Puritans evidently failed to curb![68]

From the Village Green you go back up the High Street, left past Torch House, and right into the same lane to Blaston just before the Fox Inn. This is a further 1½ miles, but watch for the sudden left-hand turn outside Hallaton. Wherever you look, the scenery is verdant, undulating, enclosed,

Blaston, ancestral home of the Hooker family. The Stonehouse stands opposite fields where the Village originally stood and the site of St Giles.

The ruins of St Giles Church, Blaston, probably the place of worship of the early Hookers.

safe; a place to breed a contented, independent, self-sufficient people, you will say.

Blaston (pronounced Blayston) is another cluster of attractive dwellings, once of thatch like the handsome 1647 Thatch House where you will stop the car on entering. Here you can obtain a key to the church of St Michael and All Angels, a diminutive building, free-standing in the fields, with semicircular apse, and bell-turret above. Did the insistence of Hooker's Company to ship its bell from England to Hartford, Connecticut via Cambridge, Massachusetts, and hang it in each of their Meetings Houses to this day, echo some childhood memory? No bell-turret, no proper place of worship?

The church has been newly rebuilt, but stands on a Saxon foundation. It is possible that the Hookers worshipped here. But there is a stronger claimant not five minutes walk away. St Michael's lies at the edge of the village, in the Parish of Hallaton. Go on into Blaston, and you will find a second small chapel, this time in Medbourne Parish (where the Hookers of Blaston were buried) named St Giles. Surely this was the family church.

You can walk the short distance between the two, or park your car in front of the gracious Stonehouse, a hundred yards further on, its paddock stretching down to the ruins of St Giles, no longer in use, lying lonely by a small lake at the field's end. There is the Manor, further down the road. And, it is said, a row of houses stood where the grassy paddock now is, decimated and left to decay by the medieval plagues. No one now knows where the earlier Hooker homes may have been, or at which church they worshipped. But you will be grateful for the place. Held within a circlet of low hills, the village enjoys an idyllic English Country setting.

It has another claim to fame. Richard Vines, 1600–1656, of Magdalene College Cambridge,[69] a contemporary of Thomas Hooker and Vicar of St Lawrence Jewry, London, during the Civil War, was born at Blaston. He was one of the Puritans who offered their services to Charles Stuart on his execution morning. Sir Thomas Herbert (1606–82), English traveller and author, described the incident in his *Threnodia Carolina, or, Memoirs of the last two years of the reign of that unparallelled prince of ever blessed memory King Charles I.*

"They presented their duty to the king with their humble desires to pray with him and perform other duties if his Majesty pleased to accept."[70] The king had already chosen his confessor, Bishop William Juxon, William Laud's successor both as President of St John's College, Oxford, and as Bishop of London when Laud went to Canterbury in 1633.[71] Juxon was to follow his friend Laud as Archbishop in 1660. He was also a close friend of the royal family, so that it was natural for him to stand by his sovereign at his death, secretly to bury him in St George's Chapel, Windsor, and to crown Charles II at the Restoration.

The story illustrates the complexity of the Puritan dilemma. They were often born into settled, loyalist countryside. They were Reformers, not Revolutionaries. They desired peace and prosperity under God in the land, not the armed strife which nevertheless came from their reforming zeal.

STOKE DRY, Seat of the Everard/Kenelm Digbys.

Continue through Blaston (going east) to the B664. At the intersection, turn left, towards Uppingham. At the bottom of the hill turn sharp right at the signpost for Stoke Dry. Then bear left, up another hill, into the village. It is approximately three miles from Blaston.

The small village of Stoke Dry tops the Eyebrook Reservoir, a long stretch of placid water, a small world on its own, the dozen houses with a church and manor house opposite caught up in the high wooded slope above the scimitar-shaped lake.[72] You are now in the southern tip of England's smallest County, Rutland, a rough triangle wedged between the shires of Leicester, Lincoln and Northampton, covering an area of about 150 square miles, still principally agricultural. It has been absorbed administratively into Leicestershire, but tell that to the residents! Note the many proud public references to "Rutland!"

The Digby connection was of long duration. *The Victorian History of the County of Rutland* makes mention of an Agnes Clarke of Stoke Dry, who married "Simon alias Everard Digby of Tilton; thus the Digbys came to Stoke Dry, which they made their chief seat."[73] This Everard, as we have seen, forfeited his estates at the Battle of Towton (1461), but his son, Everard (entombed at Tilton, 1509) restored the family fortunes. They remained in possession of Stoke Dry until Sir Kenelm (1604–1665) altogether removed to Gayhurst in Buckinghamshire, and the Great House was finally demolished, c. 1615–1620.

Nothing now remains of the Digby Mansion, though some of its material is said to be incorporated into the old rectory garden wall. But the Church of St Andrew remains, eminently placed above the narrow street, opposite the Manor, where you can scarcely squeeze your car, to park and see.

As you climb up to the north door into St Andrews, conflicting memories may crowd upon your mind. Behind the oriel window in the parvis, or priest's room above the doorway, some say the Gunpowder Plot was hatched. It had no such sinister usage so far as I know, but "Gunpowder" Everard was born here, and inherited the estate at fourteen, only removing to Gayhurst, his wife's property, after their marriage.

You can explore the room, up its staircase behind the north door, on entering but perhaps first you will say a prayer against intemperate ambitions, or beliefs which lead us into unjustifiable violence. If so, your eyes will focus on the East End, and you will be struck by the 14th century murals on the walls there, and elsewhere in the church. St Andrew is painted to the left of the altar, the Virgin and Child to the right. As you move towards the large monument also standing there, you will pass through the chancel arch, with its slender Norman pillars vividly carved in foliage, figures, even a cheerful bell-ringer, one of the earliest examples of campanology in England.

The large tomb beside the altar, arrogantly crowding it, commemorates "Kenelm Digby esquire" (d. 1590), and "Anne his wife." He it was who sponsored Kenelm Hooker, younger son of old Thomas Hooker of Blaston (d. 1563). He even acted as Supervisor to old Thomas' Will. They were the parents of an Everard who fathered "Gunpowder" Everard, but he was a gracious intellectual, who deserves to be remembered for his scholarship, rather than for the son he died too young to control. He, and his ten brothers and sisters, are carved into the base of the tomb.

Alongside is the Digby Chapel, with murals of St Christopher, and St Edmund, martyr king of East Anglia, being shot by two bowmen as he stands tied to a tree.[74] These are dated c. 1280–1284. The bowmen are thought to be modelled on North American Indians, described in Norman ballads from stories of the early Viking raids on the American coast, which is indeed food for thought.

A notice there displayed suggests that the Chapel was "built in the 13th century when Richard Digby, Lord of Tilton, resided, and was at last buried—with his wife—at Stoke Dry." But only the massive monument, the Digby fleur-de-lys prominently displayed, of a headless Sir Everard (d. 1540, eldest son of Everard of Tilton, and Jaquetta) remains.

Jaquetta lies in the south aisle, her portrait finely incised onto the lid of her alabaster box tomb. She bore her husband fourteen children, but the pull of Stoke Dry was stronger, for he lies companionless at Tilton, and she lies here, in her beloved Stoke Dry.

Drive away slowly, up the hill outside, and turn right onto the main road, the A6003 signposted to Caldecott, and Rockingham. You will then be on the edge of the Vale of the River Welland, which flows east to Stamford, and away to The Wash south of Boston, Lincolnshire. It parallels the Vales of Catmose and Belvoir to the north. This is a land of lolling hills and river valleys whose villages lie half-hidden in the solicitous Wolds, their presence often made known only by the peeping spires of their churches. They preserve a rural England now destroyed by the industrial Midlands Shires to the west.

They were the breeding ground of a progressive yeomanry interwoven with a reactionary feudalism of which vestiges can be found today. Both traits, the Radical and the Conservative, are endemic to Puritanism, and easily traceable in the villages of 17th century New England. Ill-suited bedfellows, they nonetheless vastly enriched the American heritage, which is expansionist, and was busily destructive of the indigenous culture, yet managed to preserve many of its own native English traditions.[75]

Oakham in the Vale of Catmose is the old county town of Rutland-shire.[76] Its 1180 Castle Hall is a remarkable example of Norman domestic architecture, the interior walls lined with over 200 huge horseshoes, the traditional fee required by the Lord of the Manor from any Peer of the Realm who passes through the town. Nearby lies Rutland Water, one of the largest man-made lakes in Europe, covering over 3000 acres, with leisure facilities, and a picnic site in its 350 acre Nature Reserve, if you are inclined for an alfresco luncheon.

I must tempt you no further for this is off our beaten track. But this is a countryside to know, and slowly, respectfully, grow to understand for the part it played in the rise of English Democracy, as we shall see when we reach Leicester.

ROCKINGHAM CASTLE, Home of Lady Anne Digby.

From Stoke Dry proceed as advised to Rockingham, four miles altogether. As you approach the small town you cross the river Welland, which marks the boundary between Leicester and Northampton shires. To the residents of Marefield it must have seemed a journey to the end of the world when Anne, daughter of Kenelm Digby of Tilton and Drystoke (d. 1590) married Sir Edward Watson of Rockingham Castle in April 1567.[77] The giant Rockingham Forest stretched over much of Northamptonshire, making it a land apart, where the early kings of England came to hunt for 400 years.

Edward's and Anne's son, Sir Lewis, became the First Lord Rockingham. He was a royalist, but he married the Earl of Rutland's sister, Eleanor, whose branch of the Manners family unexpectedly supported Parliament during the Civil War. Rockingham fell to an investing parliamentary force, and Lord Lewis was ironically imprisoned at his royalist in-laws' Belvoir Castle by Charles I for losing his castle, before Belvoir too fell to Cromwell. Lord Lewis was reinstated in 1644, but his mother had died long before then, in 1611.

Rockingham Castle[78] stands boldly above the town, and is open to the public, Easter to Sept. 30, Sundays and Thursdays (Tuesdays also in August), 1:30–5:30 pm, or by arrangement. A fort was built there by the Ancient Britons to guard the strategic river crossing. William the Conqueror replaced it with a Norman Keep, and used it as a royal residence. Such it remained until granted by Henry VIII to Edward Watson (d. 1584, second son of the 15 children born to his wealthy father, Edward, Surveyor General to the Bishops of Lincoln). It was his son, Edward, who married into the Digby family, and was knighted by James I, who visited Rockingham for the hunt. The Castle has remained in the family ever since.

The entrance gateway dates from Edward I (1239–1307), but the rest is largely Tudor, the whole feel of the place, from the dependent village clustered at the foot, to the formidable towers of the castle, regal, aristocratic, and all the better for that! I think you will sense the isolation of this Royalist forest site from the affluent, agrarian holdings of Puritan Leicestershire over the Welland water. It bred a very different population, and outlook.

Fortunately the Cavaliers kept an even better table than the Round-heads across the river, and the tradition has held. You will get an excellent lunch at the Sondes Arms Inn in the main street below the castle, and will need it before this long day's trip is completed. Afterwards, go up the hill, as if to the castle, onto the A6116 skirting Corby, to the A427 into Weldon, and so to the A43, direction Stamford. Almost immediately on gaining the A43 you come to Deenethorpe on your right, and, continuing towards Bulwick on the A43 catch a glimpse of Deene Park on your left.

There is a back lane from Rockingham, via Kirby Hall, which is nearer; or via Gretton. I got lost in the welter of a new Industrial Estate at the Deene end of the lane so do not recommend this shorter route.

If time presses, you can return north from Rockingham, back up the A6003 to Uppingham, and return to where you are staying; but this denies you historic Fotheringhay, and the Mildmay mausoleum and manor house at Apethorpe.

DEENE PARK, Seat of the Brudenells, a diversion.

Turn aside from the main road if you possibly can, to drink in the splendour of this country mansion. Since 1514 it has been the home of the Brudenells, widely known for James Thomas Brudenell (1797–1868) 7th Earl of Cardigan who led the charge of the Light Brigade with incredible courage at Balaclava (25 Oct 1854) in the Crimean War.[79] The house and grounds are open to the public, I believe, on Sundays during the summer.

Deene Park, a manor house when Thomas Hooker was born, was transformed into the elegant mansion you find today during the following centuries. Situated in wooded grounds behind its lake and gardens, it is a place to photograph for its beauty as well as its history.

FOTHERINGHAY, Last home of Mary, Queen of Scots.

From Deene Park turn left again (north) up the A43, and at once turn right for Bulwick, Southwick, and Fotheringhay, a further seven miles. Why

not park in the road outside the imposing giant of a church, St Mary and
All Saints, which dominates the meadows round the banks of the river,
before the Nene drifts down to the Soke of Peterborough, to empty the
fenland wet-marshes into The Wash in consort with the Welland, and many
another mighty drain above the Great Ouse? Everything flows from this
eastern extremity of Hooker's boyhood playground to the East Coast and
to the North Sea. It could not have failed to shape their minds, these children
of the easterly plains, who were to swarm as seafarers across the Atlantic.

A short step along the same road leads you to Castle Farm, and a
footpath to what remains of the castle mound, once a formidable penitentiary. The river provided one side of a deep moat which surrounded the
heavily battlemented walls and corner towers, the keep rising sturdily
above the hillock where you will find nothing erect except the wild flowers.
Poor captive Queen! Local residents assure you that the Scottish thistles you
find growing there descend from seeds the fated Queen sowed, and who
shall doubt it.[80]

Here was born King Richard III, in 1452,[81] himself to die at Bosworth
Field, like Mary largely from his own misjudgement. A sombre place for
sombre thoughts. But St Mary's Church is filled with colour and with light.
After visiting the castle mound you will wish to enter the church, and trace
its story from the original display-panels within, which speak of its history,
its Yorkist connections, and of Mary's tragic end; that is, if you can drag
yourself from admiring the superb exterior, crowned by its glorious tower.
But watch the time. Recent vandalism has caused the church to close early.

Mary's final trial was conducted in the great hall of the castle by
William Cecil, Lord Burghley, on October 14/15, 1586. Here she was executed on February 8, next year, when Thomas Hooker was seven months
old. She was buried in Peterborough Cathedral, but James I had his mother's
body transferred to the Chapel of Henry VIII, at Westminster Abbey, after
his coronation.

Surely the much publicised machinations of the reputedly wicked
Catholic Queen of Scots, held captive but a short distance from Marefield,
were fed eagerly to the infant Thomas as morally-improving bed-time
stories. His mind was to be clouded with anger against Catholics for the rest
of his growth towards manhood. He was to castigate Charles I for his
marriage to another Catholic princess brought up at the Catholic French
Court, on a celebrated occasion at Chelmsford. He shared this hatred with
all Protestants of the day. It had many other causes. But we may surmise at
the causal connection.

APETHORPE, Seat of Sir Walter Mildmay.

At Fotheringhay take the road opposite the church signposted Nassington and Yarwell. In Nassington turn left at the Apethorpe sign. It is the next village. The estate was purchased by Sir Walter Mildmay of Danbury Place, Chelmsford, in 1552, and became his principal residence. We shall come across his name frequently at Cambridge (where he founded Emmanuel College, alma mater of many a Puritan divine), and at his birthplace, Chelmsford.[82]

Sir Walter was a leading Tudor statesman, adviser and Chancellor of the Exchequer to Elizabeth, friend and colleague of her most trusted Secretary of State, Lord Burghley. The move to Apethorpe brought the two men into closer contact, with Burghley House at Stamford not seven miles away. It also extended Sir Walter's influence into the Midlands, where he was elected Member of Parliament for Peterborough, and then for Northamptonshire.

Burghley and Mildmay teamed up to represent their monarch's interests on a number of occasions. These included an abortive Treaty with Mary Queen of Scots at Chatsworth House in Derbyshire, October 1577. Had they been successful in binding her to a limitation of her sovereignty, she might have been restored to her Scottish throne, but Mary was an inveterate schemer, and negotiations broke down. More ominously, they visited her together at Fotheringhay for a final plea to renounce all claims on the English crown before Burghley's fateful trial there, which sealed her doom. You did not trifle with men of such high standing unless it was to the advantage of their Tudor Queen.

Sir Walter died at Apethorpe in 1589, and the estate passed to his eldest son, Sir Anthony. The route from Nassington bends left into a cul-de-sac at the standing cross in the middle of the road. Here you may park, the gates of the lordly manor before you, St Leonard's Church proudly at your side. I trust you will sit for a moment to consider Mildmay, and Burghley, the huge distances between their many seats of power, the range of their influence, the destinies they controlled. These men were monarchist, establishmentarian, autocratic, but so determined also to effect power-sharing for the expansion of trade and empire that, though they knew it not, they sculpted democracy from the air they breathed.

Inside St Leonard's you can visit the almighty tomb of Sir Anthony, with its suitable tribute to his greater sire. He became Ambassador to France, but never attained his father's stature. Who needs a reputation who lies beneath such a tomb? His lady Grace, heiress of Sir Henry Sharington of Lacock, Wilts, at his side. It was Sir William Sharington who, in the 1540s, had converted Lacock Abbey into a mansion, but the 13th century cloisters remain. It was the last religious house to be dissolved under Henry VIII, so that the Mildmays were in at the beginning (as you will discover) and at the very end.[83]

Lacock is unquestionably one of the most beautiful villages in Britain, but it has to belong to another story, unless you find yourself near Chippenham, and can explore for yourself. The property is owned by the National Trust. It is open from April to November daily, except Tuesdays.

On leaving St Leonard's, you follow the road in the same direction out of Apethorpe. It takes a northwest direction to King's Cliffe, and from there turns north to the A47, some four miles in all. Turn left (west) at the A47, towards Glaston and Uppingham, another ten miles.

UPPINGHAM, *Archdeacon Jonson's School.*

Uppingham is the second largest town in Rutland, top-heavy with its famous school, but the two go vivaciously together. You will enjoy the liveliness of this small, high-quality town.

The school was founded in 1584 by Archdeacon Robert Jonson (1540–1625), son of Alderman Robert Jonson of Stamford, whose forebear Morris ap Jonson and David ap Cecil (later Lord Burghley) came from the Welsh Marches and rose to eminence in the train of Welsh-connected Henry Tudor. The two sires at one time representing Stamford in Parliament together.[84]

Archdeacon of Leicester, son Robert was also Rector of North Luffenham, and near neighbour of Sir Walter Mildmay, whom he long outlived. His son Abraham married Elizabeth, daughter of Mildmay's first Master of Emmanuel College, the legendary Laurence Chaderton. Their son Isaac married the Lady Arbella, sister of the Earl of Lincoln, another leading Puritan. Arbella gave her name to the flagship of the Winthrop Fleet, and sailed with her husband for the founding of Massachusetts in 1630. She and Isaac Jonson died there that first bitter winter.

Robert Jonson founded two Grammar Schools, one at Uppingham,[85] the other at Oakham. They were Puritan foundations, and Uppingham has become one of the foremost schools in England. The original school can still be seen at the corner of the churchyard of St Peter and St Paul in the Market Place. The many other buildings stretch on both sides of the town.

You can park, with patience, in the small, irregular market square, from which the town radiates. The Church of St Peter and St Paul, a Saxon foundation, occupies most of one side, where Jeremy Taylor (1613–1667, author of *The Rule and Exercise of Holy Living*, and *of Holy Dying*, royalist friend of William Laud, and later bishop of Down and Connor, and of Dronmore, Ireland) once exercised his ministry.[86] So did Edmund Bonner (1500–1569) before him, London's last Catholic bishop, buried at Copford, Essex.[87] It is not easy to envisage any blood-letting religio-political controversy in Uppingham today, but the tokens of the uneasy coexistence of Catholics, High Anglicans, and Puritans are here, in this part of England where Thomas Hooker grew up.

It is surprising that he was sent to Market Bosworth, rather than to Archdeacon Jonson's school, so much nearer home. The Foundation Charter granted by Queen Elizabeth may provide the answer. It says "inasmuch as no free grammar school exists in our County of Rutland."[88] The Hookers entertained educational aspirations for their son, and Bosworth was already an ancient foundation. Uppingham had yet to make a name for itself. It was, nonetheless, part of the ambitious rural community in which Thomas began his growth towards greatness.

The Falcon Hotel stands opposite the church, with other hotels and guest-houses nearby, and quaint old-fashioned shops to attract the discerning visitor.

LEICESTER
Early Evidence of Democracy and Political Division.

LEICESTER CITY, Cradle of Constitutional Democracy.
What influence the County Town of Leicester may have exerted over the formative childhood of Thomas Hooker cannot now be ascertained. However he would know it well. It was the only large town available to his family, and his father's duties as a Digby estate manager must have brought them into frequent contact with this centre of civil government and commerce. Young Thomas had to pass through the town whenever he journeyed to and from his residential school at Market Bosworth, some 14 miles due west of Leicester, approximately 25 overall from Marefield.[89]

It will therefore be convenient to explore Hooker's many later experiences in Leicester now, as we too prepare to move on to Market Bosworth for the second major phase of his development.

The long sequence of visits to the city (then a town, under the ecclesiastical jurisdiction of the Bishop of Lincoln: the present Diocese of Leicester was only re-created in 1926)[90] continued right up to Hooker's embarkation for Massachusetts in 1633. The question we shall wish to keep closely under review is "What impressions were printed onto Hooker's most critical, most logical mind by his early proximity to, and frequent later visits at Leicester, aside from his growing up in secluded Marefield?"

The confused political impact is worth noting to begin with. Leicester had a unique history of emergent democracy, yet the mayor was still royalist when the Civil War broke out, and so too was an influential minority of the town council, as Hooker was to discover to his cost. Royalist troops were to occupy the castle, and practical aid was made available to the crown.[91]

When Charles I made his effective "progress" through the Midlands in 1634, accompanied by Queen Henrietta Maria, they stayed at Leicester. He attended St Martin's Church on the Sunday, but the Queen, being Catholic, refrained. Nonetheless, considerable acclaim surrounded them throughout the progress. "The Church was strewn with rushes and adorned with green boughs, and flowers decorated the King's cushion."[92]

However, when Charles came a second time, in 1641, a general hostility from the populace transformed his reception, despite official sanction. "Many who had once entertained him stood coldly aloof."

Tilton-on-the-Hill might be something of a haven of Puritan peace under the dominion of the Digbys, the Hookers and the parson. But, as was only to be expected in an industrial and administrative centre, ecclesiastical and political divisions seethed merrily. This must have been well known to its rustic neighbours, especially to educated people like the Hookers. Thomas would grow up knowing he had a fight on his hands, and that the forces ranged against Reform were formidable.

Leicester was, even then, an ancient Borough. Captured and fortified by the Roman occupying forces in A.D. 52, and renamed Ratae Coritanorum, it stood astride the Fosse Way, a Roman road of exceptional importance which ran from Lincoln in the east to Exeter in the south west, via Leicester and Bath.[93] It enjoyed, additionally, a river route of some importance; for the River Soar (formerly the Leire, hence Leicester, the Camp on the Leire) runs alongside the city, to join the river Trent at Nottingham, and so reaches the Humber, and gains access to the North Sea trade.

The excavated Roman Forum, ruins of a huge Basilica, with its Jewry Wall and Holy Bones street, together with other Roman remains imaginatively exhibited at the local museums, make it an entertaining and significant location for Romano-British studies.[94]

Today the city is one of the centres of the British footwear industry, and has for many years been a leading manufacturer of hosiery, clothes, and many other commodities. It is heavily congested with traffic and subject in recent years to large scale road, and inner-city redevelopment schemes. Up-to-date routes are a pre-requisite for any motorist travelling this whole area. Nonetheless it retains many attractions for its visitors amongst the excellent modern hotels, and ancient buildings, which are easily discovered in the old town centre, and perpetuate its unique contribution to the growth of English Democracy. If Thomas Hooker was destined to be the Father of American Democracy, truly he should have been born near here!

It is possible that he preached at St Mary de Castro,[95] as John Wycliffe the Bible translator and earlier reformer certainly did. Local residents will assure you that Chaucer was married here. A Saxon foundation, the church was rebuilt when Robert de Beaumont, first Earl of Leicester, constructed the Norman Castle on the same site, in 1107.[96]

If so, Hooker must have sat in one of the three fine sedilia reserved for officiating clergy, with round-arched canopies resting on double pillars rarely carved with foliage capitals, well worth viewing. No flower-decked cushion for the godly preacher, but other treasures await the perceptive visitor in this unusual building.

Little remains of the Castle, but the Great Hall was used as a Hall of Justice from 1274 up to modern times.[97] It was here, in 1201, that a first meeting of the English Barons began a protest which led to the signing of the Magna Carta by King John at Runnimede, in 1215; here Simon de Montfort (1200–1265), last of the Norman Earls of Leicester, but first among the founders of Parliamentary Democracy,[98] entertained Henry III and his son (later Edward I) at Leicester Castle in 1264, but then, finding them obdurate, fought and took them captive at the Battle of Lewis in Sussex on May 14, 1264. Once in his power, he forced the Crown to call the first regular and representative parliament in English history, an exercise in rough-and-tumble diplomacy never quite forgotten by succeeding generations.

One of these early parliaments actually met at Leicester Castle, in 1349.[99] How much the young Thomas Hooker was aware of this struggle towards a representative government rather than an absolute monarchy, which took place on his doorstep, cannot be determined. It is, however, difficult to suppose that the heroic conflict was not bred into the bone and sinew of all founding Puritan families. They, however, recognized it as the Divine Commonwealth.

Here, at this same castle, John of Gaunt, third son of Edward III, entertained John Wycliffe (1329–84) and Geoffrey Chaucer (1340–1400),[100] sparkling emblems of the religious and literary Renaissance that was to be the glory of Tudor England.

And to the old Blue Boar Inn came Richard III,[101] reputedly the murderer of his young nephews in the Tower of London, to rest and dream, then ride out a king to Bosworth's fateful field, to be dragged back a corpse, hastily buried in the Grey Friary church next St Martin's, leaving crown, field, and kingdom to Tudor Henry VII.

Here the English parliamentary system found its birth. Here Tudor England, with its very English-Protestant Church, and from it the Puritan Movement, and indeed the founding of a New England in North America, struggled into the fresh air of a new learning, a new political system, a new liberty, and many new achievements from literature to lands overseas. And was not Thomas Hooker to have his suspicion of the revolution flying in that wind of change?

That was the very theme of his farewell sermon in Chelmsford St Mary's, on the eve of his flight to Holland, "The Danger of Desertion" (March 1631).[102] In it he warned England of the impending, irresistible doom he knew must come. He had lived with the knowledge all his life. He was born here. His people were the inheritors of Simon de Montfort's parliamentary liberty and privilege. He was educated at Bosworth, crucible of violent change. He went to Cambridge, cradle of Puritan reform. What else would you expect!

The traveller will enjoy other aspects of this city. The medieval Guildhall is exemplary.[103] It is now a museum, and possesses, amongst other items of interest, a rare collection of early 16th century painted glass. The timber arches in the Great Hall contain three bays of original 14th century work. Shakespeare is thought to have acted in one of his plays in this room.

On the banks of the Soar you will find Abbey Park,[104] a public garden planted around the skeletal remains of the Abbey of St Mary de Pratis. It was founded by Robert de Bossu (Beaumont), first Earl of Leicester, and became one of the wealthiest in the land. To it came the dying Cardinal Wolsey, summoned, after his disgrace, from his Archbishop's palace at York to London, on a charge of treason. Wolsey died the following day, 30 November 1530, more than fifty years before Thomas Hooker's birth. But the memory of the king's vengeance did not die.

Two more churches invite exploration on Thomas Hooker's trail. First, there is the Cathedral, formerly St Martin's Parish Church, but thought to occupy the site of the first Saxon Cathedral. Nothing of this remains, and very little of the cruciform Norman construction which succeeded it, apart from some of the moulding, and of the walls in the majestic 19th century tower, crowned with a spire which soars to 200 feet.

The Church has been extensively altered in succeeding centuries. However, the aisles added in the 13th and 14th, the chancel renewed in the 15th, and more recent restorations into the 20th, have built it up into an impressive Cathedral. No family has contributed more to this than the Herricks.[105]

The Herrick family came into possession of the Grey Friary, built by Simon de Montfort on land adjacent to St Martin's, at the dissolution of the monasteries in the 16th century. They established themselves as major contributors to the Church, and enriched its fabric. But they are best known through the works of Robert Herrick (1591–1674), poet and priest, who was brought up by his uncle, and guardian, Sir William Herrick, a wealthy London goldsmith, banker to Queen Elizabeth. Sir William's body lies interred in St Martin's church. It was his son, Henry, who emigrated to America in 1627.

Robert Herrick was five years younger than Thomas Hooker, but they were at Cambridge together, Robert at St John's College, Hooker at Emmanuel. Thomas had gone up to University in 1604, and was made a fellow of his college four years later. Robert did not go up until 1614, by which time Hooker was established as a noted controversialist and preacher. Herrick could not but have known him well. Their colleges were close together and both colleges had shared Puritan sentiments. They both took Holy Orders, and left University in or about the same year, 1620.

Robert remained a royalist throughout his long career and, coincidentally, was presented by the King to the incumbency at Dean Prior in Devon (where he was to spend the greater part of the rest of his life) in September of the year 1629, when, two months later, Hooker was deprived of his living in Essex.

The poet who could write:

Cherry ripe, ripe, ripe, I cry,
Full and fair ones; come and buy.

and:

Gather ye rose buds while ye may,
Old time is still a-flying:
And this same flower that smiles today,
Tomorrow will be dying.

or:

I sing of brooks, of blossoms, birds and bowers;
Of April, May, June and July-flowers.

might have scandalised Hooker and his pious friends with:

I sing of May-poles, Hock-carts, wassails, wakes,
Of bride-grooms, brides, and of their bridal-cakes.

But for all Hooker's scant reference to the secular literature he must have read, the two young men might not have been so out of sorts in the celebrated, flower scented gardens of Emmanuel. Some echo of their mutual delight in Nature may even appear in Hooker's sermons. His use of natural and normal sights and sounds can be compelling. Take, for instance, his pleasure in the heliotrope (the popular English name is "cherry pie"), and who shall say that Herrick had no influence over him?

"The soul should be like the Herb Heliotropium, the Nature whereof is such, as the Philosopher observes, it turns the face of it towards the Sun, what way soever it turns. In the morning looks to the East, the Sun rising.

In the evening to the West, the Sun setting. So it should be with the believing sinner, the face and Eye of the Soul ever towards God in Christ."[106]

The pilgrim will wish to visit St Katharine's (sometimes called "The Heyricke") Chapel, on the north side of the Chancel. It is lined with Herrick memorial stones. The stained-glass window depicts Robert Herrick and his church at Dean Prior, together with St Katharine, and St Francis of Assissi.[107]

The chapel was rebuilt in 1865, and has since been restored at the charge of the American Herrick family. Stand here, and spare a thought for Sir William, Robert's guardian, and wonder if he, and son Henry who was to emigrate to New England within a few years, ever visited his nephew in Cambridge, or went with him to hear the famous Thomas Hooker preach.

Sir William could even have heard Hooker in St Martin's. Cotton Mather tells us that Hooker "had an invitation to preach in the great church of Leicester."[108] Since St Martin's had a Puritan Lectureship at that time, this is entirely possible.

The Lectureship[109] was a device for side-stepping those ecclesiastical laws which controlled who might preach, the hated surplice he must wear (badge of spiritual servitude), and what the content of the sermon might be. Local Puritan gentry would arrange to finance an acceptable godly preacher, and accommodating patrons, or clergy, would make room in their pulpits for him to preach (technically only to "lecture," but no one could tell the difference) outside normal times of "Prayer-Book" worship. This released the lecturer from every legal restraint, and by proliferation provided pulpits for reforming clergy throughout England, until suppressed by Archbishop Laud.

Wherever it was, Hooker was made uncomfortably aware of the tension his Puritan preaching brought to this divided town. One of the chief burgesses, according to Mather, sent fiddlers in the courtyard to distract Hooker, while preaching.[110] As you would expect, Hooker's charm and eloquence won over his detractor, and converted him instanter into the Reformed Genevan tradition of John Calvin. It may well have been so, his sermons have the power to convert the casual hearer today.

One wonders how frequently Hooker was accustomed to appear in Leicester pulpits, that so orchestrated an opposition should have been feasible.

There remains a third church within the old centre of Leicester which he must also have visited, namely St Nicholas at the Forum.[111] It stands on the brink of the excavation trench, like some great hanging stone overlooking the foundations of the ruined Roman Basilica. Fragments of Roman, Saxon, Norman and Medieval work went into its construction, rendering the building as stimulating as the situation. But its importance for New

England descendants is that Francis Higginson (1586–1630) was Lecturer here from 1617–26, the year when Hooker went to Chelmsford.

Francis Higginson[112] was the second of nine children born to Rev. John and Elizabeth Higginson of Claybrooke Magna, a dozen miles south of Leicester, seven miles from Blaby, well within Hooker's boyhood range. He entered Jesus College, Cambridge, completed his Master's degree in 1613, was ordained by the Archbishop of York next year, and joined his father as curate at Claybrooke until elected to the Puritan lectureship at St Nicholas.

His friendship with Thomas Hooker was even closer than their geographical ties, for Hooker (with Arthur Hildersham, see below) was credited with Francis' conversion to a consistent Puritanism. Higginson remained at Leicester, guest-preaching at his many friends' churches even after his eviction from St Nicholas. This lasted up to his embarkation for Massachusetts with his wife Anna, neé Herbert, and eight children, in the Talbot, on 25 April, 1629. His *New England's Plantation, or A Short and True Description of the Commodities and Discommodities of that Country*, published 1630, went through three editions in the first year, and was amongst the earliest of many similar publications which advertised the potential of emigration.

Years afterwards, following Francis' too-early death at Salem, his son John (born at Claybrooke, 6 August 1616, so only 13 when his father removed to New England) went to live in the Hooker's home at Hartford, so that he might complete his theological training under Thomas' guidance. He is known to have transcribed many of his master's sermons ready for publication. It is thought that some 200 manuscripts were lost at one time, by shipwreck, when the vessel to which John had committed them for transport to England, foundered at sea;[113] an irreparable loss.

Francis Higginson is thought to have been behind the direct reference to Leicester made by Hooker in his Preface to the posthumous *A Fresh Suit Against Human Ceremonies in God's Worship* of William Ames.[114] Ames had been Hooker's contemporary and friend at Emmanuel, Cambridge. He was forced to fly to Holland, and had been Professor of Divinity at Franeker University. He transferred, for health's sake, to become pastor of the English Church at Rotterdam shortly before re-issuing his *Suit*. He died before his book came fully off the press, in November 1633, not long after Hooker had sailed for Massachusetts. The preface would be written when Hooker was serving the English Church at Delft, and was published with the *Suit* in Amsterdam.

Hooker's 'Preface' is really a separate volume, complementary to Ames' work, but providing parallel arguments in support of his friend's attack on the mounting imposition of unscriptural ceremonies (so they thought) in Anglican practices. It dramatically examines the reactions of different people to the pressures which Puritans were then experiencing. It had become expedient for many of the clergy to recant from their Reformed opinions, or to pretend to a reasoned change of mind.

"This kind of declining was done at Leicester," wrote Hooker. "Pressures were growing heavy upon such that would not conform themselves. The Court censures of the Commissary, proceeding to the excommunication of such as refused conformity, and adding aggravations thereunto—to wit, forbidding to buy or sell with such that were so excommunicate—one amongst the rest was not able to undergo the burdens—and therefore he professeth his judgement was changed."

Hooker does not name the turncoat, nor his informant. This latter may have been Francis Higginson, even though he had sailed in the Talbot with Samuel Skelton (chaplain to the Puritan Earl of Lincoln who gave much help and protection to the New England founders), for the early settlement of Salem, Massachusetts.

A further possible informant was the influential and highly connected Arthur Hildersham (1563–1632).[115] He was another of Hooker's friends near Leicester, and a celebrated Puritan Divine. He had been appointed Lecturer at Ashby-de-la-Zouch by his mother's second cousin, the third Earl of Huntingdon.[116] He was suspended more than once for his outspoken views, but his relationship with the Earl probably accounts for his several releases.

Hildersham influenced many young men, among them Hooker's sizar at Emmanuel College, Simeon Ashe, to take Holy Orders. We shall hear more of Simeon later on. His name simply adds to the circle of friends in and around Leicester who drew Thomas Hooker back to his birthplace, and thus enlarged its influence over him.

Cotton Mather commented "It was Mr Hooker's manner once a year to visit his native county."[117] Presumably that included his parents at Marefield, and his married sister Dorothy Chester at Blaby. From all that we know, Mather's estimate of an annual visit appears to be conservative.

BLABY, Home of Dorothy (Hooker) Chester.
Blaby is quickly reached from Leicester, on the A426, travelling south. Thomas Hooker senior had substantial holdings there, and at adjacent Countesthorpe. It would therefore be well known to his daughter Dorothy, even before she married John Chester of Blaby. Their son, Leonard, emigrated with his widowed mother to New England, and became one of the founders of Wethersfield, Connecticut. From his marriage to Mary Wade there, Calvin Coolidge (1872–1933), 30th President of the U.S.A., descended.[118]

In Dorothy's day, Blaby was a small village three miles from Leicester, and 15 from Marefield. The spire of its 13th century church,[119] decorated with three rows of heads fantastically carved, reached high into the air for all to see, like many another in this county of spires. Today it is swallowed up in the urban sprawl of the city, but in the 17th century it would have provided another refuge of "middle-class security"[120] for Thomas to visit, away from the tumult of London and Chelmsford.

Whetstone is another village associated with his preaching tours.[121] It is now a part of Blaby, indistinguishable from it.

This is an area for us to note rather than to visit. The Chester home is not known. When her husband died, Dorothy followed her brother to Massachusetts. She married George Alcock M.D., of Roxbury, Deacon of the First Church where John Eliot, Apostle to the North American Indians, and formerly Hooker's assistant at Little Baddow, was one of the ministers. From her union with Alcock, Franklin D. Roosevelt, 32nd President of the U.S.A. descended.[122] It is a small world.

STOKE GOLDING.

In the shadow of Bosworth field, another local name crops up in the scanty records, suggesting a series of post-graduate preaching tours when Hooker visited his native county. For instance, there was the case of Constance Wallen.[123] When arraigned before the magistrates for non-attendance at Divine Worship, her excuse was that she followed Mr Hooker from place to place.

The name in question is Stoke Golding. As the lanes wind, it is approximately four miles south of Market Bosworth, and is best reached from that town. The church was probably built in the reign of Edward III, as his carved head appears with that of his queen, Philippa, on the panelled parapet below the spire.[124] This is a particularly lovely church, and touches on our story.

In the vestry you will find a marble monument to Sir Henry Firebrace, who assisted Charles I in his unsuccessful attempt to escape from Carisbrooke Castle on the Isle of Wight. Charles had given the slip to Cromwell's guard at Hampton Court on 11 November 1647, and gave himself up to Sir Robert Hammond, Governor of Carisbrooke, hoping for sympathy. But Hammond was a supporter of Cromwell, and Charles was made prisoner again. For all his intrigues, coded messages sent in and out of the castle in laundry baskets, and the active assistance of loyalists like Firebrace, he was moved from prison to prison until, in January 1649, he was put on trial in London.

In the fields outside Stoke Golding you will no longer find the thorn bush into which, legend has it, the crown of Richard III fell when he was killed at Bosworth Field, just along the old Roman road. Sir Reginald Bray,[125] whose family thereafter adopted a crown in a thorn bush on their escutcheon, as evidence of the story's veracity, accidentally found the crown after the battle ended. He dutifully handed it to Lord Stanley, who placed it on the victorious Henry Tudor's head. Maybe so, maybe not. But young Thomas Hooker, like every other boy in the vicinity, would have taken you straight to that bush for a half-penny!

For your passing interest, three miles due west across the fields from Stoke Golding lies Fenny Drayton (originally Drayton-in-the-Clay because of the marshes which hemmed it round), where George Fox, founder of the Society of Friends, or Quakers, was born.[126] It can be reached via the lane which elbows out westwards, or more easily from the A5 where it intersects with the A444.

George Fox was born in July 1624, and first imprisoned at Nottingham for his pacific but uncompromising nonconformity in 1649, two years after Hooker's death. His first visit to North America took place nearly thirty years later. The disturbing effect of the early Quakers on the New England Puritans does not, therefore, belong to the Hooker saga. But you may wish to know how close you are to Fox's birthplace, and to the fenland tradition of indomitable independance, when at Market Bosworth.

DIVERSION TO TOWCESTER, NORTHANTS., Samuel Stone's Lectureship.

How to Get There. Towcester is situated south-west of Northampton at the junction of the A5 (Roman Watling Street) with the A43 from Northampton. If journeying from Leicester, continue south along the A426 from Blaby to Lutterworth. There join the A5 south to Towcester, a journey of about 35 miles. This Diversion is marginally a part of the Hooker Trail, although the event related to it is most revealing. The location is so central to England, that you may well find it convenient to turn aside from any number of trips, to take in this small, and rewarding portion.

LUTTERWORTH.

John Wycliffe, 1329–1384, was born a Yorkshireman, near Richmond,[127] but spent the last ten years of his life as incumbent of the Parish Church at Lutterworth. You cannot miss it, even in the crush of modern traffic. From the river Swift the High Street climbs up towards its dominant tower, beneath which the courageous early church reformer sent out his message of human lordship (an inalienable right conferred by Christ's grace), and his Poor Preachers, or Lollards, for the purification of a corrupt organised Christianity, and the restoration of personal religion.

"The Morning Star of the Reformation," as he was, he is in England also the dawn's breaking of the Puritan movement. It could not be other than that Thomas Hooker looked down the Lutterworth road from Blaby, and remembered.

TOWCESTER.

The Romans set up a small Staging-Post, and named it Lactodorum (Towcester)[128] when they built their great highway from London past St Albans to Wroxeter (A5). They called the road Watling Street. It carried its dense quota of London's north-bound traffic until the first Motorway (M1) eased the burden in the late 1950s. This was frenziedly true of Towcester, where the main road from the north ran into the High Street, which opened out into Market Hill, and slap into an Italianate Town Hall (erected 1865 above an earlier building) placed athwart the end of the Market Place. Traffic in my boyhood squeezed slowly past the side of the Town Hall into the southern strip of the High Street, and so regained the A5 beyond.

The presence of a number of Coaching Inns bears witness to the congestion. Over the years there have been the Wheatsheaf, Saracen's Head (which features in Charles Dickens' *Pickwick Papers*), the Tabard, later Talbot (now Sponne House, entrance to a shopping precinct), the Brave Old Oak, the George later White Horse, with the Bell and Reindeer next door (all on High St/Market Hill inside the original Roman fortification), with the Peacock further south, and the Bull on the A43 approach from the west, and probably more.[129]

The Tabard had been given to the town by Archdeacon Sponne[130] in 1440 to help finance his charities, and was certainly known to Samuel Stone.[131] Stone liked his pipe of tobacco, so might even have been seen there. It is across the High Street from the 16th century Grammar School (now Chantry House), close by the Town Hall and Parish Church. Thomas Hooker knew, clandestinely, exactly where to find Samuel, when he returned from his Dutch exile, some time in 1633, to complete their joint plans for emigration.

Stone had been chosen as his American Associate, so Hooker made his way to Towcester incognito, where Samuel held the Puritan Lectureship (from 1630–33), having been evicted from Stisted, near Little Baddow. Mather tells us what happened.[132] Pursuivants acting for the Court of High Commission had kept Hooker under close surveillance. Now they turned up at Stone's door.

Samuel had been caught smoking tobacco by Hooker. His senior partner began to reprove him. The door-knocker hammered its doom-filled message. Hooker, the brave inquisitor, hastily hid himself. Pipe nicely drawing, all unabashed, Stone (named by Mather "Doctor Irrefragabilis"[133]—"whom none could confound") confronted the law-officers, blandly puffing out his innocence. He agreed he might have seen a Mr Hooker "that once lived at Chelmsford—about an hour ago, at such an house in the town; you had best hasten thither after him." So Hooker was saved, if not his integrity, or the veracity of his host's speech and personal habits.

Smoking the noxious weed! Half-truths justified by expediency! One wonders that either of these righteous clergymen should recount the story, or pious Mather print it. This ready accommodation of truth, let alone of sinful habits, to necessity, catches both gentlemen in a decidedly unexpected posture. The rigidity of their supposedly narrow puritanical principles, so often the butt of misplaced criticism by later generations, apparently belonged to the American rather than to the English phase of Hooker's self-development!

Where this meeting took place is not known. Mather makes only the laconic comment, "Mr Stone, then a lecturer at Torcester in Northamptonshire."[134] The *Memorials of the Independent Churches in Northamptonshire* (Thomas Coleman, 1853) says simply "In the early part of the 17th century Mr Samuel Stone, one of the Puritan divines, ministered in the Church at Towcester."[135] Two pursuits were linked with that of a lecturer, both could affect the place where he resided—to be Curate at the Church (possibly implied by "ministered in the Church"), or Usher at the Grammar School.[136] But no record remains of either, and as Towcester was a Royalist stronghold in the Civil War, it seems unlikely that Samuel was on the staff of the Parish Church of St Lawrence.[137]

The Church is visually dominant, and has much to interest visitors. It was probably first built c. 920 when the town was fortified against the Danish invaders by Edward, son of King Alfred.[138] It has grown in size and proportion over the years, welded into an architectural whole by a substantial reconstruction, in perpendicular style, c. 1480–85. Archdeacon William Sponne's table tomb stands in his chantry chapel, at the east end of the south aisle. He was a major benefactor of the town. His charity priests' house, purchased by his trustees at the Dissolution, in 1552, was turned into a Grammar School and Master's residence. Samuel Stone would have been familiar with it, and could even have lived there.

We also know that Samuel enjoyed the support of an influential Puritan nucleus in the town. The *Descendants of Thomas Lord* (Kenneth Lord, pub. New York 1946) shows that a Thomas (16 years), Ann (14), William (12), John (10), Robert (9), Aymie (6), and Dorothy (4), sailed with their parents to Newtown, Massachuetts, in the *Elizabeth and Ann*, Captain Roger Cooper, from London on 29 April 1635.[139]

Their eldest son Richard (baptised at St Lawrence, Towcester, Jan. 5., 1612) had gone ahead in 1632, in readiness for Stone's arrival the following year, and to provide for his parents when they too followed their pastor.

Thomas' own father, Richard Lord, "of Towcester—husbandman," as his Will of 30 May 1610 reveals, had bequeathed a considerable estate to his son. He and his wife Joan were buried in the churchyard. Thomas was born to them c. 1583. He was a solid and successful citizen in his early fifties when he removed to New England.

The Lord family quickly joined the great trek from Newtown to Hartford in 1636, as original proprietors, and took up residence on the north side of the highway on the bank of the Little River (Wells Street) close to Hooker, Governor Haynes, and Stone. Thomas' sons Richard and Thomas occupied the sites on either side of his lot. His name, with that of Richard, is inscribed on the Founders Stone, and he is buried in the old graveyard at the rear of the First Church, Hartford, with his wife, neé Dorothy Bird, also of Towcester.[140]

There can be no doubt that they were amongst the leading families who subscribed to the lectureship held by Samuel Stone at Towcester, and formed his support group. It is a familiar pattern, one we shall observe over and again.

* * * * *

We surely feel ourselves drawn closer to the living Hooker as we revive these various episodes at Leicester and its environs. So much of England's story was enacted here. Indeed, within a narrow Midlands triangle between Leicester and Northampton, three giant turning-points were fought out: Bosworth Field, 1485, terminus of the Wars of the Roses, and the beginning of the United Kingdom; Edgehill, 1642, thirty miles to the south, first battle in the Civil War for a parliamentary liberty initiated under Simon de Montfort Earl of Leicester; and Naseby, 1645, some twenty miles to the south east, the defeat which ended Charles' hope of an absolute monarchy, and set up a Commonwealth which proved to be the summit of Puritan achievement in England, matched, and outmatched, only by the astonishing achievements of small groups of Pilgrims in North America.

A man and his inheritance may not lightly be separated. The growth of Leicester towards a system of regulated democracy started with the Lex Romana, continued to Magna Carta under Simon de Montfort and the Barons, and found its most unpredictable issue in the Fundamental Orders of Connecticut. They were inspired by one of Hooker's sermons, the first written instrument of political government in the United States of America, the logical consequence of being born at Marefield, bred to Leicestershire.

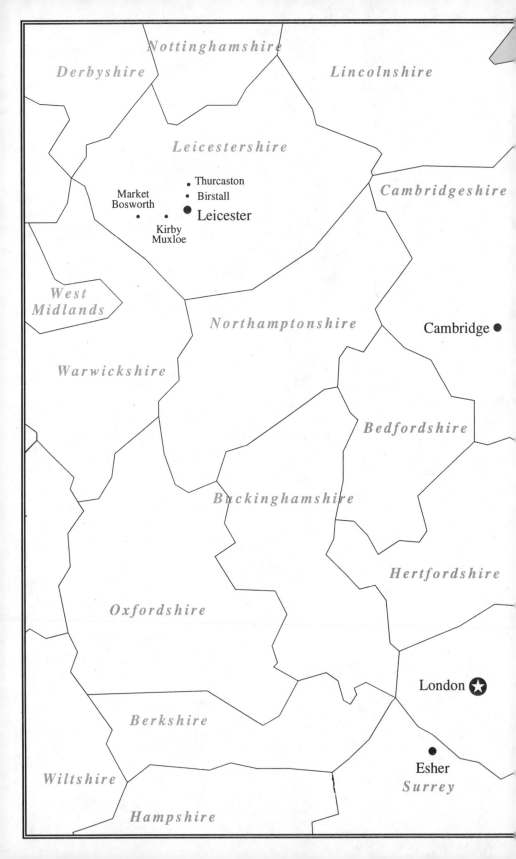

CHAPTER 2

MARKET BOSWORTH

Isolation, Insecurity, Introspection

c. 1596–1604

KIRBY MUXLOE, Perfidy of Kings

How to Get There.

The route from Tilton-on-the-Hill to Market Bosworth conveniently lies via Leicester, along the A47, through the city centre, to Hinckley Road on the west side of the City (still A47). Once past Western Park (on your right) you come to a large roundabout, meeting place of Braunstone Lane (on your left) and Ratby Lane (far right) with Hinckley Road. Take Ratby Lane, signposted to Kirby Muxloe, Glenfield and Ratby, flying over the M1, to the next roundabout. Turn left into Main Street, Kirby Muxloe. You will see the castle on your left.

At the time of writing, the proposed distributor road which will run clean round Leicester on the north, linking Kirby Muxloe directly with Melton Mowbray, is incomplete. Enquire later on if there is not an easier route from Tilton via this new road, which will avoid your fighting your way through the congested city centre, should you drive from Tilton and not wish to stop in Leicester en route.

The castle (more correctly, a prime example of a fortified manor house)[1] is in the care of English Heritage, which looks after over 350 historic buildings open to the public in Britain, amongst those nearby being Leicester's Jewry Wall, and Ashby-de-la-Zouch Castle (another Hastings house) with Kenilworth Castle further afield. It is approached by a car park at the edge of the four-square moat, restored to its original depth and dimension, a gem of a setting for the mellow red-brick castle built by Baron William Hastings (c. 1430–1483) when he was Grand Chamberlain to Edward IV.[2]

Begun in 1480, the work was never completed because of Lord Hasting's summary execution. Only the great gatehouse by which you enter, and the west tower remain, with the foundations of the fortress and earlier manor house outlined at ground level.

Kirby Muxloe Castle

Lord Hastings was a distant descendant of the Sir Henry Hastings who had supported Simon de Montfort, and sat in his Parliament of 1264.[3] Sir Henry remained loyal to de Montfort after the latter's defeat and death at Evesham in 1265. He commanded the remnant of the Baronial Party (which had wrenched the Magna Carta out of an unwilling King John at Runnimede in June 1215)[4] when they made a last stand against Henry III in the Isle of Ely, in July 1267. Thus history repeated itself, for even so the Saxon nobles' resistance under Hereward the Wake[5] against William the Conqueror, sank in the Isle of Ely marshes, as we shall discover when we visit Ely later on.

Sir Henry's son John became the first Baron Hastings. Sir William was the inheritor of a long line of masterful men who gave their loyalty to those whom they chose. He had been one of the most trusted advisors to Edward IV, and most lavishly rewarded. He was Lieutenant of Calais, Lord of Belvoir as well as of Kirby and Ashby, Steward of Fotheringhay, and of Leicester. At first, when Edward died, he lent his influence in support of Richard's Protectorate, but he did not choose to transfer his allegiance from the boy King Edward V (murdered in the Tower of London) when Richard III claimed the crown. He quickly paid the price.

If by this time you are wet, cold and hungry (more so if the sun dazzles) you will enjoy the hospitality of the new Castle Hotel and Restaurant which looks out over the moat and gatehouse, a superb situation. It has been developed out of the old Castle Farmhouse, its main structure composed of bricks and oak timbers taken from the castle.

Lord Hastings was less fortunate in his opportunities for pleasant self-indulgence. Shakespeare recalls the extraordinary scene in his *King Richard The Third*. It was on 13 June 1483, nine days before the date fixed for the young King Edward's coronation (22nd June), that members of the council for Richard Duke of Gloucester's Protectorate met to dine at the Tower of London. Suddenly, Richard accused the Queen and Jane Shore, abetted by Hastings, of withering his arm by witchcraft. Jane Shore had been the mistress of Edward IV, and probably also of Hastings, a bewitching lady by all accounts, but she was no more a witch than any of the others accused.[6]

Richard ordered Hastings' immediate execution. No Trial. No Justice.

Protector of this damned strumpet—Thou art a traitor:
Off with his head!—now, by Saint Paul I swear
I will not dine until I see the same.

Richard The Third, act 3, scene 4

It was an inexcusable outrage, and contributed to Richard's unpopularity, and subsequent overthrow.

You will appreciate that 16th century England had a small population thinly spread, and closely inter-related. No accurate population statistics exist before the 19th century, but approximately one-and-a-half million is a generally accepted figure up to the close of the 11th century; probably two-and-a-half million according to a rough Poll Tax consensus in 1377; and around five million by the year 1700.

It is inconceivable that the great events which occurred in so small a population, and the general gossip surrounding the passage of kings and local dignitaries were unknown to up-and-coming families like the Hookers. I cannot say that the fate of Lord Hastings of Kirby Muxloe meant as much to Thomas Hooker as it did to William Shakespeare. But the proximity of the castle to Market Bosworth, and its poignant reminder of the perfidy of kings, belonged to Thomas's upbringing. It therefore needs to be considered.

MARKET BOSWORTH,
seat of Sir Wolstan Dixie, Puritan Patron

How To Get There.

From Kirby Muxloe the B5380 joins the B582 at Desford, and the B585 at Newbold Vernon, with Market Bosworth further along the B585, a total journey from Leicester of not more than 12 miles.

Visitors from other parts of the country may take the M1, or the M69, to Leicester and exit at Junction 21. There follow the signs for Enderby and Desford, and proceed as above.

Market Bosworth is another small English country market town worth visiting for its own sake.[7] The Market Charter goes back to 1285. There is still a street market every Wednesday, a cattle market on Mondays, and the flavour in the air of a confident, meaningful community, happily combining antiquity with contemporary achievements.

It was the administrative headquarters of a Rural District Council until the 1972 Local Government reorganisation brought it into a larger Hinckley and Bosworth Borough Council, with a new Council House at Hinckley, a lively and helpful Information Centre there, and some unusual Tourist attractions.[8]

The tiny Bosworth Market Square draws the ancient streets together at the very point where Thomas Hooker was sent to board, at the celebrated Dixie Grammar School. Close by stands the 15th century church of St Peter, tree-sheltered on the borders of Bosworth Park and Arboretum, where Richard placed his command-post on a small hillock known as Richard's Clump, before the Battle of Bosworth began.

In St Peter's the young Thomas worshipped on Sundays, under the "painful" (serious) preaching of the Puritan rector, William Pelsant.[9] There is a tower dating from 1325, a font of similar lineage, and numerous memorials to the Wolstan Dixies. Indeed, the association of this remarkable family with St Peter's is amongst its chief claims to fame.

The first Sir Wolstan Dixie, 1525–1594,[10] was an exceedingly wealthy London merchant. He purchased Bosworth Hall from the Earl of Huntingdon. Baron William Hastings of Kirby Muxloe was grandfather to George Hastings, 1488–1545, who became the first Earl of Huntingdon in 1529, nicely keeping our story within one of the circles of acquaintance we have already made. The third Earl, you may remember, was related to Thomas Hooker's great friend, the Reverend Arthur Hildersham of Ashby-de-la-Zouch.[11] The circles amongst the early puritan families tended to be small, and closely concentric.

Sir Wolstan was born at Catworth, near Huntingdon, where his family had resided for several generations, and owned considerable estates. He,

Sir Wolstan Dixie

being the fourth son, was apprenticed to Sir Charles Draper of the Ironmonger's Company in the City of London. Sir Charles was a native of Melton Mowbray and the young Wolstan married his daughter Agnes.

He became a Freeman of the Skinners' Livery Company in the City, an Alderman of the Broad Street Ward, and a Sheriff of London. He was also a founder of the Muscovy Company, and a patron of the Merchant Adventurers' Livery Company, with a wide experience of promoting overseas trade, and the first tentative overseas colonies. From the vision and expertise of influential merchant adventurers such as he, sprang, eventually, the New England experiment. No more suitable patronic family could have been devised for the oversight of Thomas Hooker's education.

Thomas could scarcely have known his benefactor personally, as Sir Wolstan died in, or shortly after, the probable year of his admission to the school, and long before Hooker was to enjoy a Dixie Scholarship and a Dixie Fellowship, at Cambridge. But Sir Wolstan's interests and influence continued both in the school and in New England.

His family were to be amongst the first of the New England settlers. A William Dixie is said to have landed at Cape Ann in 1629, having sailed in the *Talbot* with Frances Higginson and Samuel Skelton, founders of Salem, Massachusetts. He became an early Freeman of Salem (14 May 1634), and his son, William, kept the "Horse-boat Ferry" to Beverly in 1643. His brother Thomas kept the ferry from Darby Fort to Marblehead, in 1644.[12]

Other members of the Dixie family adventured further south, and one of them, Alexander Dixie, commanded the frigate *Chesapeake* for the British in the War of American Independence. He fled afterwards to Canada, but left his name behind, for the Southern States had become "Dixieland."

Bosworth Hall, home of the Dixies, as it is today.

Bosworth Hall[13] still stands within the remains of the great park, near the Market Square. The present Paladian building dates from c. 1700, and only ceased to be the family residence in recent years. The fine entrance gates were those of the old Newgate Prison in London (of which Sir Wolstan was a benefactor), removed here when the prison was demolished to make way for the Old Bailey, near Saint Paul's Cathedral. But the Hall has a varied history of its own.

Sight of the ghost of the "Grey Lady," Anna Dixie, daughter of the Fourth Baronet, is still being claimed, albeit only at the witching hour. Around the year 1720 she loved one of her father's tenant farmers too well, and herself accidentally fell into the man-trap her father had caused to be set in the grounds, to catch her lover at their secret assignations. She dragged her mangled body to a room above the entrance hall, and there died in a pool of her own blood. The stain is visible on the ceiling of the hallway, despite repeated attempts to remove it during a period of 250 years. So I was assured when visiting the Hall (at that time, a Nursing Home, now a Hotel, you may like to know), by staid members of the Nursing Staff, two of whom stoutly affirmed their sightings of the Grey Lady, "at the dead of night", in the upper rooms. A stain of some sort certainly remains on the hall ceiling, painfully visible.

The rhyming Will (1815) of a later owner of the Hall, is equally illuminating:

> I, Willoughby Dixie of Bosworth Park
> Without the aid of scribe or clerk
> Or pettifogger of the law
> Ready to make or find a flaw
>
> To my sister Eleanor of Bourne
> Lest she her brother long should mourn
> The welcome news she must bear
> That I give her £800 a year.
>
> To sister Rosamund, whose bower
> Of happiness ne'er knew one hour
> I 12d give, far more than's due
> To such a sad, vexacious shrew.
>
> To Tom Drakeley my steward ever true
> Who did for me all that man could do
> I give in cash and notes, no little sounds,
> The sum of £20,000.

It goes on in the same strain, with minor bequests to all his household, in an original, whimsical style which suggests that the inventiveness of the first Sir Wolstan had not yet died out. This, again, has little bearing on the Thomas Hooker saga, except in so far as family traits and traditions have a tendency towards self-perpetuation.

At the very least no one can gainsay the excitement of living close to, and under the personal patronage of, the Dixie entourage, which has maintained its connection with the school to this day. Combine these years at Market Bosworth with his earlier childhood experiences under the protection of the Digbys of Tilton-on-the-Hill, and one can only conclude, with due gratitude to the great families concerned, that Thomas' nurture fitted him for any company, any vicissitude, any task; and he proved an apt pupil.

The Dixie Grammar School had its own contribution to make to his growth and development. It is possibly the oldest remaining Grammar

The Dixie Grammar School in the Market Square

School in England. The Prospectus claims "There is a document dated 1094 which refers to a school at Market Bosworth, and papers relating to a 'Grammatic' school in the 12th century."[14] Accurate records go back to 1320. It is an astonishing survival, made the more notable because the Governors are actively planning a renascent curriculum today.

The school was closed by the County Education Authority in 1969 and amalgamated with the nearby Desford Comprehensive School. As time went on the town increasingly mourned the passing of its historic Grammar School. At last an amendment to the National Education Act enabled local people to set up an organization for its restoration.

Penelope, Lady Dixie (still resident at Bosworth) became the patron, together with Professor D. S. Brewer, Master of Emmanuel College, Cambridge, and Sir Rex Hunt, former Governor of the Falkland Islands. The school re-opened in September 1987, one of the first such renewals of a grammar school foundation after their widescale closure for politico/educational theory (Comprehensive Education for all children) in England in the 1960s.

Whatever one's opinions about educational theory and practice, the valiant fight to re-open their most ancient school, and to restore it to its historic site at the centre of Market Bosworth, reflects most creditably on all concerned. Their pride in their school is only equalled by the new-found

Headmaster F. Washington Jarvis and Lady Dixie, in May 1992, with a print of the Dixie Grammar School at Roxbury Latin School, West Roxbury, Massachusetts.

pride of its staff and scholars, as any visitor will discover. This is as positively refreshing as it is all too rare, in British schools today. The spirit of New England, not to mention far-sighted Sir Wolstan Dixie and his patron, Queen Elizabeth I, has surely risen again!

The school building in Market Square dates from 1828, a rectangular grey-stone construction, with stone-framed windows, of austere but pleasing appearance. Above the entrance a distinctive cast-iron plaque, in Latin and Greek, is affixed, which may be translated "The buildings of this school (founded by Wolstan Dixie, Knight, in A.D. 1601), having collapsed with age, the governors of the same had restored in A.D. 1828. Education is a possession which cannot be taken away from mortal man."

The assumption that Thomas Hooker attended here is based on his enjoyment of a Dixie Scholarship, and Fellowship, at Emmanuel College, Cambridge. Sir Wolstan had founded both, and they were reserved for graduates from the Bosworth School, or for family connections. The distance from Marefield made it imperative for Thomas to have been a boarder during term-time.

We do not know precisely when he arrived. Possibly at a later rather than an early age. He did not enter Cambridge until 1604, when he was eighteen. This was somewhat late for an era when University normally followed the completion of a grammar school curriculum, irrespective of age. Quite often, as in the case of John Cotton, and John Eliot (who went up to Jesus College, Cambridge when only fourteen), an intelligent scholar had completed the limited courses available at his local grammar school well before the normal entrance age today.

One reason for Hooker's late arrival at University, and therefore, perhaps, at grammar school, could have been his indifferent health, already noted. He may also have been a late-developer. His great friend, and near contemporary John Cotton of Boston Lincolnshire, as well as of Boston, Massachusetts, was only one year older. He was already a Fellow of Emmanuel at nineteen years of age (by no means unusual at that time), when Hooker reached the College.

Hooker does not appear to have attained that maturity and authority which was to characterise his later life, until he reached the mid-twenties. He was forty when he commenced his political career at Chelmsford. He was forty-seven when he landed at Massachusetts, and fifty when he planted his great work at Hartford on the banks of the River Connecticut.

His intelligence is not in question. No one can read the large literature he has left behind him (cf. *Establishing the Hooker Canon*, Sargent Bush Jr. Essay 4, *Thomas Hooker, Writings in England and Holland*, Harvard, 1975: but a fraction only of his output; cf, the 200 volumes transcribed for publication in London by John Higginson, thought to have been lost at sea), without respecting his intellect.[15]

His sermons make a powerful impact on the hearer today. Their logic is exacting, as Hooker examines every conceivable aspect of the subject under discussion. Their application ("Uses", he called them)[16] can still feel threatening, as he explores all the avenues of action which spread out from the basic tenets he has laid down. His was a monumental mind, awesome yet attractive, often irresistible in its pressure; and as for his sensitivity and sensibility, he was an automatic choice by the New England colonists whenever they needed exceptional help or advice.[17]

It all suggests that he may well have been a late developer, and therefore would leave his insignificant little village school at Tilton-on-the-Hill for the more prestigious Market Bosworth Grammar School at, say 10–12 rather than 7–9 years of age. That was around the period of the School's largest reconstruction, and its greatest confusion, under the first Sir Wolstan Dixie's new foundation, between the years 1593–1601. Thomas was then between seven and fifteen.

The situation confronting the Headmaster and the Governors at that period would have been formidable.[18] There had been an honoured foundation in the town for 500 years, since 1094. Sir Wolstan, fresh from London, does not seem to have taken that venerable first school much into account. Moreover he was a man in a hurry, with little time left to him. His mercantile accomplishments suggest that he would, in any case, look for a reasonable return on his capital, and that speedily.

He was also an energetic, and doubtless dedicated, educational re-former. In 1584 he had joined with Sir Walter Mildmay of Chelmsford, and other leading Puritans, in opening the "Puritan College" of Emmanuel,[19] at Cambridge. He endowed it with two Scholarships and two Fellowships, which now provide income for the Dixie Professor's Chair of Ecclesiastical History at the University. It still carries with it a Fellowship at Emmanuel.

He also contributed largely to Cambridge's oldest college, Peter-house.[20] He financed public works in London such as his "Pest Houses" (Isolation Hospitals), and at St Thomas's and St Bartholomew's hospitals, and for the poor in Bridewell (house of correction),[21] the prisoners at Newgate, a Skinners' Company fund for struggling young merchants, and other benevolent causes.

It was tragically ironic that Sir Wolstan should die, in 1594, from one of London's many plagues, in the year when his new school at Market Bosworth superseded the earlier one.

One can imagine the anxieties which would be expressed in the small town at the displacement of its former grammar school after 500 years, by a fairly new resident at the Hall, who thereupon died. What then of the pressures on Roger Amson, headmaster from 1586, and on the governors, one of them William Pelsant the rector, all of them appointed by Sir Wol-stan? What of the effect on the sole resident scholar?

The new school had to be rapidly organised, the long drawn-out negotiations for its Constitution successfully concluded. But although granted to its founder by Queen Elizabeth before his death the Constitution was not incorporated until 1601. There were evidently major obstacles to be overcome, and to frustrate the continuing management. It was a time of maximum confusion and insecurity.

There were only eight pupils at the time of this major reorganization, of whom Thomas Hooker was the only known boarder. He would have been housed with the family of his headmaster, or some other approved household in the town; but the time must have hung heavily on the slender shoulders of a delicate young boy from a remote rural hamlet, used to the security of his small home circle.

He would be busy enough. School classes were held six days a week, from 6:00 a.m. in summer (7:00 a.m. in winter) until 5:00 p.m., with breaks for breakfast and lunch.[22] Latin, Greek and maybe some Hebrew would be standard subjects, with an introduction to Logic and Mathematics. Under the surveillance of committed Puritans such as the Dixie family, and the Rector, there would be prayers morning and evening as well as Sunday Worship, with much study of the Scriptures. But what of the long nights so far from home?

Frank Shuffleton in his *Thomas Hooker, 1586–1647* (Princeton, 1977) notes that "Learning was a dialectic process between reader and writer, teacher and student, knowledge and ignorance, and the young scholar was implicitly encouraged to conceive of his studies as a training in the art of communicating truth to men."[23] There can be no doubt that Thomas would thrive on such a diet. The disorganisation and insecurity would be there too.

Nearly contemporary with Hooker at the school, was William Bradshaw (1571–1618), who became one of the outstanding thinkers and writers of the Puritan Movement in England.[24] That they were acquainted with each other is evident. Hooker defended Bradshaw's views in his Preface to *A Fresh Suit Against Human Ceremonies in God's Worship* already discussed.

Bradshaw was born at Market Bosworth, and began his education at the old grammar school. He entered Emmanuel College, Cambridge, in 1589, five years after the college opened. On the recommendation of Emmanuel's first Master, the redoubtable Chaderton, he was appointed tutor to the family of Sir Thomas Leighton, Governor of the Channel Island of Jersey, and there framed the Ecclesiastical Discipline of the Channel Islands on Calvinistic principles, much as Calvin had done at Geneva, and as Hooker (can it have been only co-incidental?) was to do in Connecticut's Fundamental Orders.

Bradshaw returned to Cambridge as a Fellow of Sidney Sussex College (the earls of Sussex of Boreham, near Little Baddow), and became a prolific author of Reformist policy, publishing *English Puritanism* in 1605, the year after Hooker's entrance at Emmanuel.

Two such outstanding students within a decade reflects favourably on the abilities of the headmaster, Roger Amson, who presided over the transition from the old grammar school to the Dixie school. We can be sure that Hooker relished the intellectual challenge, and the opportunities afforded by such a school. He was always an avid reader, his library amongst the largest shipped out to New England.

Hooker was also a "workaholic," remorselessly writing down in longhand his multitudinous articles, and full-length manuscripts. But I repeat, how lonely the single-boarder must sometimes have been.

That he went through a period of intense spiritual insecurity, and of introverted doubts, when first at Emmanuel College, is made clear by Cotton Mather amongst others. Mather's description is worth quoting. "It pleased the spirit of God very powerfully to break into the soul of this person with such a sense of his being exposed unto the just wrath of Heaven, as filled him with most unusual degrees of horror and anguish, which broke not only his rest, but his heart also, and caused him to cry out, 'While I suffer thy terrors, O Lord, I am distracted!' "[25]

This may not have been an unfamiliar experience amongst the more earnest Puritans. Their personal diaries are full of soul-searching after the assurance of salvation. They needed to be certain of their election to the people of God. It could lead them into excesses of anxiety and doubt, such as reverberate from Hooker's cri de coeur.

Hooker found his peace with God whilst at university, and never looked back. Nor did he ever lose his sensitivity for *The Poor Doubting Christian Drawne Unto Christ*, his earliest published sermon (London 1629).[26] His was a finely responsive nature, graciously sensitive to people's needs as well as to the absolute demands of God. This is what made him so fearsome a protagonist, so endearing a censor. He could both penetrate to the unacceptable heart of the truth, and present it in homely similies any peasant could grasp, and accept. So much belonged to his character.

One wonders, nevertheless, to what extent his isolation as a lone boarder in the influential Dixie Grammar School, when it was undergoing a period of radical change, under a Master whose interests must have been forcibly diverted away from the child's personal needs, contributed to his subsequent insecurity and introspection. Order was only finally restored to the School in 1601, when Hooker would be fifteen years old, and ready to leave. He may never have known the school other than in a state of flux.

BOSWORTH BATTLEFIELD
Visitor Centre And Country Park

Two miles from Market Bosworth, between the villages of Sutton Cheney, Shenton, and Dadlington, close beside the Ashby-de-la-Zouch canal, you will find the carefully signposted site of Bosworth Field. This lies a mile to the north of Stoke Golding, to which reference has already been made.

Here, at Ambion Hill Farm, a well appointed Visitor Centre was created to mark the 500th Anniversary of the Battle, in 1985. It is open to the public from Easter to the end of October. There are exhibition halls, which display every aspect of the conflict and its history, a small theatre, a cafeteria, and guides to assist the newcomer.

Outside, you can stand on Ambion Hill, as Richard did to survey the field, or walk the trails which trace the course of the battle, and mark the spot where Richard died. In the summer enactments of the battle, and jousting tournaments are organised. Do plan the time to visit here, where modern England essentially began.

When Richard drew up his 10–12,000 strong army on Ambion Hill, that morning of 22 August 1485, he had every expectation of a Plantagenet victory.[27] Henry Tudor had landed from Harfleur, France at Milford Haven

GENEALOGICAL TABLE, NO.4: JOHN OF GAUNT AND THE WAR OF THE ROSES

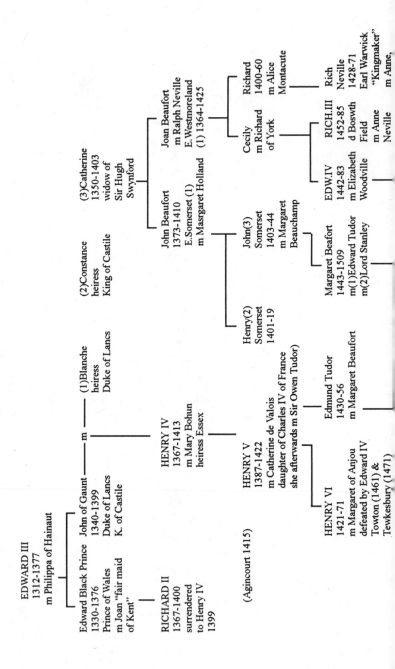

EDWARD III
1312-1377
m Philippa of Hainaut

Edward Black Prince
1330-1376
Prince of Wales
m Joan "fair maid
of Kent"

John of Gaunt
1340-1399
Duke of Lancs
K. of Castile

——— m ———

(1)Blanche
heiress
Duke of Lancs

(2)Constance
heiress
King of Castile

(3)Catherine
1350-1403
widow of
Sir Hugh
Swynford

RICHARD II
1367-1400
surrendered
to Henry IV
1399

HENRY IV
1367-1413
m Mary Bohun
heiress Essex

John Beaufort
1373-1410
E.Somerset (1)
m Masrgaret Holland

Joan Beaufort
m Ralph Neville
E.Westmoreland
(1) 1364-1425

(Agincourt 1415)

HENRY V
1387-1422
m Catherine de Valois
daughter of Charles IV of France
she afterwards m Sir Owen Tudor)

Henry(2)
Somerset
1401-19

John(3)
Somerset
1403-44
m Margaret
Beauchamp

Cecily
m Richard
of York

Richard
1400-60
m Alice
Montacute

HENRY VI
1421-71
m Margaret of Anjou
defeated by Edward IV
Towton (1461) &
Tewkesbury (1471)

Edmund Tudor
1430-56
m Margaret Beaufort

Margaret Beafort
1443-1509
m(1)Edward Tudor
m(2)Lord Stanley

EDW.IV
1442-83
m Elizabeth
Woodville

RICH.III
1452-85
d Boswth
Field
m Anne
Neville

Rich
Neville
1428-71
Earl Warwick
"Kingmaker"
m Anne,

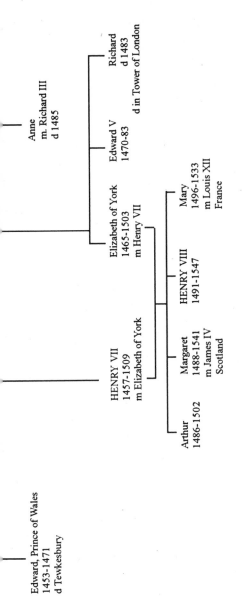

in West Wales on August 7/8.[28] But he had scarce 2,000 troops, and they were reputedly mostly French convicts enlisted with the promise of a free pardon. Welsh levies and disaffected English hurried to his banner, but his army was still considerably smaller; his claim to the throne as tenuous.

From his mother Henry narrowly managed to scramble a descent from John of Gaunt, the great Duke of Lancaster, fourth son of Edward III and father of Henry IV. Gaunt established the royal House of Lancaster, and in the Wars of the Roses his red-rose descendants produced a series of warring kings, Henry V, Henry VI, and finally Henry VII of the new House of Tudor.

The embarrassing factor was that Henry Tudor's mother was descended from only the third of John of Gaunt's wives, whereas the descent up to that time had rightly followed the line of his first wife's issue. Come too lately, the Tudor branch nevertheless sprouted onto the family tree somewhat too early! In fact, before his great-great-grandmother, then Catherine Swynford, had found it convenient to marry John of Gaunt.

Their children were legitimised in due course, and Henry Tudor traced his descent from the eldest Swynford male, the powerful John Beaufort Earl of Somerset. Somerset's second son was also named John Beaufort, and inherited the title. Now he had a daughter named Margaret, and she married an Edmund Tudor. Their son was Henry Tudor, victor at Bosworth, later Henry VII.

As if this were not confusion enough, Henry's father, Edmund Tudor, was the son of a Sir Owen Tudor who had married Catherine, widow of King Henry V. By her first union she was the mother of Lancastrian Henry VI. But Edward Duke of York seized the crown from the ailing Henry VI, and had himself proclaimed King Edward IV. He was succeeded by his young son, Edward Prince of Wales, but Edward was "murdered" in the Tower, presumably by his Yorkist uncle Richard of Gloucester, who then became King Richard III, and was vanquished at Bosworth Field.

Thanks to his grandmother's second marriage to Owen Tudor, Henry VII just managed as it were to slip both feet under the Lancastrian table. His toehold on Yorkist support was secured by his marriage to Elizabeth, eldest daughter and heiress of King Edward IV, and so the Wars of the Roses came to an end. Credit is due to Henry VII for this, but the fragile nature of his claim kept the Tudors uncomfortably on their thrones long afterwards. This partly explains why they felt a need to create a new nobility from amongst their supporters. The old families had long memories!

Victory was denied to Richard III that fateful day at Bosworth, partly because of his assumed treachery. There was the death of the Princes in the Tower. The young Edward (V[th]) was only 12, his brother Richard a mere 10. There were other charges against Richard III, such as the case of Lord

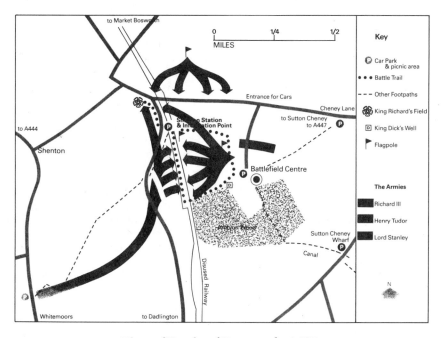

Plan of Battle of Bosworth, 1485.

Hastings of Kirby Muxloe. And it was Richard's own army which brought about his defeat.

His steward was Lord Stanley, who, with his brother Sir William Stanley commanded Richard's flank, with 5,000 men. At the crucial moment of the battle, as Richard led a charge across the face of Stanley's troops, to challenge Henry's centre, the Stanleys turned traitor and attacked Richard's flank instead of defending it. Richard died shouting "Treason! Treason! Treason!" as well he might.[29]

The battle was over from that moment. But Stanley's eldest son, Lord Strange, was being held hostage by Richard, as a surety for his father's loyalty. A most odd arrangement! At one stage in the battle Richard had even threatened to kill the young man, in order to encourage the Stanleys to take action on his behalf! The outraged steward may well have felt as betrayed as his master.

It was an age of the roughest justice. Could Thomas Hooker, and his companion Puritan leaders, really have supposed that they would totally cleanse the Tudor/Stuart Court, or its Parliaments, or its Church? The corruptions of the past were too interwoven with the fabric of the State. Yet, for a few ideological years round the turn of the 16th century, it seemed as if they might.

They had influence throughout the courts of government, and high hopes when Elizabeth ascended to the throne that a purer Reformation than Henry VIII had effected, might ensue. Her gift of engendering the loyalty of her people kept her throne safe. But James' ascent in 1603 disabused the reformers. His first conference at Hampton Court, in 1604, led to his outburst "awaie with your snyvelings. If this is all your party has to say I will make them conform, or I will harry them out of the land."[30] The Godly Commonwealth disappeared from sight, nor reappeared for forty years.

Hooker wrestled long with his conscience before crossing his Rubicon. Was he to remain in England, working to reform the Church and State, and risk imprisonment or worse? Was he not to join the Exodus of Belief, cast off the old, and build a New England in another place? Surely no intelligent boy could grow up near Bosworth and not know, in his bones, that political success is inseparable from rational compromise? That there never was a serious hope of Pure Reformation in Tudor/Stuart England?

There was no realistic hope of a Puritan compromise either. In his providence, God brought a new form of United States into being. And as Henry Tudor had come from overseas to initiate a new dynasty, so eventually Hooker came to terms with Bosworth Field, and claimed his Commonwealth of Connecticut by invasion.

BIRSTALL, Hooker's First Educational Practice, 1602–1604?

How To Get There.

If a visit to Birstall is intended, it will perhaps be better to go from Leicester city, rather than attempt a cross-country route from Market Bosworth via Desford, Ratby or Glenfield, and Anstey, for Birstall lies on the A6 going north from Leicester to Loughborough and the attractive countryside of Charnwood Forest.

At nearby Cropston you are on the edge of Bradgate Park, former home of the tragic Lady Jane Grey (1537–1554).[31] The sad story of the youthful nine days Queen comes flooding back as you wander through the 850 acres of open parkland to the ruined Bradgate House. The remains of the once great mansion stand there skeletal and headless, as if in sympathy with her beheading. If this is indeed Hooker country, it lends a further dimension of pathos to the struggles for power which erupted every other step of his earthly journey.

Thomas was about eight years of age when his parents temporarily removed to Birstall (if such they did), and 18 when he finally left home for Cambridge.[32] He could not have avoided an encounter with the story of the scholarly girl who wished only for a life of learning and devotion to religion, as he did, but who was forced by circumstances over which she had no control to engage disastrously in politics, as he was to do.

Birstall stands close by the river Soar, within two miles of Leicester, downstream from Abbey Park and twelve miles from Marefield. It is now part of the Leicester conurbation, but was then a small, impoverished hamlet without a manor. Its open-field system was controlled by the church-wardens within the very large Leicester Parish of Belgrave, of which the local church was an appendage, with no resident curate. The church is 13th century, the more interesting for a Saxon window in the chancel. But Thomas Hooker would not have known. It was only rediscovered last century. A school might have been held at the church, but if so no record remains.[33]

Thomas Hooker senior is known to have owned property at Birstall. We have already noted that the three younger children were baptised there, Amy in 1594, Elizabeth in February 1598, and Frances in 1602; that Dorothy was married to John Chester at Birstall in 1609; and that a "William Hooker, sonne of Thomas Hocker" was buried there on April 3, 1616. This suggests a minimum residence of 7 years, and a maximum of over 22 years, before the Hooker parents returned to Marefield where they died, unless they used both properties, only some 12 miles distant, concurrently.

This explains why Venns' *Alumni Cantabrigienses* gives Birstall as Thomas Hooker's address, and why Tarleton's deposition (both already referred to), as late as 1631 assumes that he was born there. However, Professor Frank Shuffleton in his *Thomas Hooker 1586–1647* (1977) thinks that Hooker may have left Market Bosworth Grammar School in 1602, or there-abouts, and that he accepted a teaching post at Birstall. I know of no other evidence for this.[34]

Thomas may well have wished to build up a small fund towards his university fees. He was not awarded a Dixie scholarship until after he had gone to Queens,' and the fact that he entered Queens' as a sizar (working his way through college) suggests that he could have been financially embarrassed until the scholarship was confirmed.

This would provide a reason for his late entrance at university. It would also have contributed to the sense of insecurity he may have gained from boarding-school experience. The nearer to 1601 that he finished at Market Bosworth, the more certain it becomes that his time there coincided with the school's period of greatest reorganisation. Was his well-ordered mind in part a reaction against the uncertainties of this prolonged period of transition, as well as the product of his Master's excellent teaching?

There is no connection between Hooker's experiences and the unhap-piness of a further celebrity who was also at the Dixie school. Dr Samuel Johnson (1709–1784) the Great Lexicographer, joined the staff at Market

Bosworth as a young usher in 1731. His appointment carried a personal tutorship to the Dixie household, where he catalogued the library, and where his interest in the famous Dictionary probably began.[35]

He was poor, ill-suited to teaching, and stayed but a short time. He complained that his life was as unvaried as the cuckoo's note, and he wondered whether it was more disagreeable for him to teach the boys or for the boys to learn from him. However misplaced his choice of the school, his attraction to it in the first place points again to its high standing.

The variegated enigma of life in late 16th century Market Bosworth, and beyond, remains to tantalise and enliven the pilgrim's enquiries. You will drive away from this area regretting that you can stay no longer, possibly musing to yourself, "could the founder of Connecticut have become the man he was, had he not boarded at Sir Wolstan Dixie's grammar school?"—let alone grown up at the Digby's Marefield, possibly having learnt his teaching practice close by Jane Grey's studious home near Leicester, cradle of English democracy!

THURCASTON, Such A Candle

You will scarcely have time to touch the font in All Saints Church,[36] Thurcaston, where Hugh Latimer was baptized, even though it lies adjacent to Birstall at the north-westerly exit to Bradgate Park, but you need to know.

Hugh Latimer, 1485–1555,[37] Bishop of Worcester and martyr, was born here, as doubtless the wide-awake Hooker family well understood. Even today obliging natives will take you to a site on the Rothley Road where the Latimer yeoman farmhouse traditionally stood. What did that say to the young yeoman T. Hooker, himself en route to becoming a reforming churchman!

Latimer probably entered Peterhouse, Cambridge, as an undergraduate (Venn 3:49). He was a Fellow of Clare, University Chaplain, and University Preacher (1523) before leaving Cambridge to be Chaplain to Anne Boleyn. His Protestantism was slow to develop, and the more effective as, with homely wit and disarming directness he began to advocate Reform. When elevated to Canterbury, Cranmer[38] advanced him. Once the break from Rome was made, Henry VIII turned to him for advice. He was made Bishop of Worcester, but continued to preach against social injustice. His integrity was never in doubt.[39] He resigned his See when Henry introduced *The Six Articles* in 1539 (a reactionary reimposition of clerical celibacy, transubstantiation, auricular confession, etc; cf. ODCC, p. 1262), when it seemed to Henry that reformation had gone too far for Tudor comfort, and served a short term in the Tower. He was reinstated under Edward VI, but at Mary's accession was committed to the Tower again, condemned for heresy, and burnt with Ridley at Oxford, brave, persuasive to the last.[40]

"Be of good comfort, Master Ridley;" he said. "We shall this day light such a candle in England as I trust shall never be put out." Who can doubt Hooker heard him clearly, and with neighbourly premeditation chose the same route.

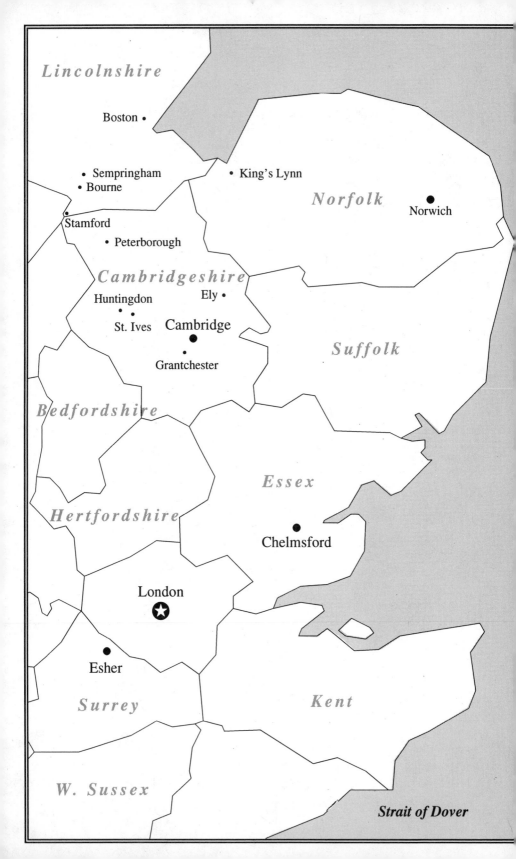

CHAPTER 3

CAMBRIDGE

The Maturing Of The Godly Preacher

1604–c. 1618

Various Routes To Cambridge.
If it proves feasible to plan a chronological tour, and thereby to enjoy
an experience of the unfolding life of Thomas Hooker from his birthplace
to his flight to Holland, then the starting point for Cambridge will be from
Market Bosworth, or Leicester. Some alternative routes are also described
in the following pages.

The direct route from Market Bosworth runs eastwards along the A47
to Wansford, where it links with the Great North Road (A1) some seven
miles short of Peterborough. Turn right (south) onto the A1. Continue some
20 miles to the Huntingdon exit (A14), also signposted to Cambridge and
the M11 via the A604.

Diversion to Sempringham and Boston, Lincolnshire.

If time can be found for a major diversion it will certainly prove to be
entertaining, and is instructive for the Thomas Hooker story. If so, turn
northeast beyond Glaston on the A47 (next village beyond Uppingham),
some ten miles before Wansford, and take the A6121 to Stamford and
Bourne in Lincolnshire.

Stamford.
It stands on the banks of the river Welland,[1] the eastern extremity of
Hooker's world of Marefield and the Leicestershire countryside, where the
Roman Ermine Street (A1) ran from London to York, that mighty highway
between two major military outposts.

At Stamford the Great North Road (as Ermine Street became) used to
spin in and out of the six historic churches, before a modern by-pass took
the traffic off to the west of the town. The George Hotel still has a London
room, originally for travellers by stage-coach. It will prove a pleasant rest-
ing-place, not least because Stamford provides you with an opportunity of

Burghley House, Stamford

visiting one of England's Great Houses, Burghley,[2] built by Sir William Cecil, Lord Burghley before his family came into possession of Hatfield House. Anyone will direct you to it once you reach Stamford.

It is surrounded by a spacious deer-park. Tall chimneys and domed towers top its grand facade. Inside you will find a wealth of fitments, furnishings, and works of art to enrich your visit. Burghley House offers an introduction to high society in the 16th and 17th centuries, familiar to Thomas and Susannah Hooker, and setting the standards at which some New England aristocrats aimed.

Bourne.

From Stamford continue along the A6121 to Bourne in Lincolnshire. You are now approaching the fertile, low-lying Fenlands where Hereward the Wake, last of the Saxon freedom-fighters, held out against the Norman invaders. Though outlawed and frustrated, his family nevertheless enjoyed a long association with this independent region, a Hugh Wake being Lord of Bourne as late as 1166. Hereward was probably born here, in the Castle.[3] So was Sir William Cecil, at a house now enclosed within the Burghley Arms.

You will enter the town centre down West Street. The Burghley Arms is in front of you at the central crossroads. There is a car-park, at the rear, entered by turning left into North Street, and sharp right at the first exit. There is no longer any overnight accommodation, but as a Pub the Burghley Arms offers a good meal, and an ideal stopping place. The rafters of the old Cecil dwelling, dating from c. 1420, can be seen from the upstairs rooms. There are several other early Inns in the small town, a variety of interesting buildings, including the Church of St Peter and St Paul, originally an Augustinian monastic foundation dating from 1138, in Abbey Road, and an engaging park off South Street, all within a very short distance from the central crossroads.

The Castle Park occupies the original castle site. Ducks cluster where the Bourne Eau stream was diverted to make a moat around the castle, of which only the mound is now visible. You enter from South Street (the A15 to Peterborough) past the car park (which you could also use on entering the town), and walk over the greensward, past the Well House (built of stone filched from the castle). With young Hereward's footprints in the

William Cecil,
First Baron Burghley
1520–1598

damp grass stretching away to left and right, you simply have to create your own imaginative masterpiece, a photo of your companion(s), *Freeborn Man on Hereward's Monticule*, or *Liberated Lady Beside the Waters of Bourne Eau.* I promise your friends will not have a replica and you will have a memento of the threshold to this Free Fen World you are about to enter.

As you drove up to Bourne on the A6121, and joined the A151 to enter the town, you were three miles from Grimsthorpe, once home of the formidable Puritan Catherine Duchess of Suffolk, its castle on the hill before your eyes as you draw near, a noble skyline. The great hall was reconstructed in 1722–24 by the dramatist Sir John Vanbrugh, architect extraordinaire of Blenheim Palace, Castle Howard near York, Esher's Claremont and much else besides. Grimsthorpe was his final major work, a majestic pile on its southerly hill-top; the grounds laid out by Capability Brown. It is only open in August/early September afternoons, so far as I know, but the recompense is unmatched if you can arrange a visit.[4]

Similarly, Spalding, away east on the other side of Bourne, along the A151, is the centre of the tulip and other bulb-growing acres of England, each May celebrated with a parade of flower-decorated floats. I must not tempt you to stay overlong, for you are enroute to many other places; but you will not regret succumbing to the magnetism of this wide flat country, with its mixture of architectural styles, endless patterned fields, vast skies, once autonomous marsh culture, if you do fall for its spell, and decide to linger.

Sempringham.

At Bourne you have joined the A15 going north, so take North Street out of town, go past Morton and (not more than three miles altogether) switch right onto the B1177 signposted Billingborough. Just past Pointon you will see the sign "Sempringham,"[5] eight miles from Bourne. There is

St Andrew's, Sempringham, with the original porch
above which St Gilbert's cell was built.

little else, apart from the far horizons across cultivated country, once impenetrable marshland.

Immediately after, a Notice Board on the left side of the road an-
nounces: "Parish Church of St Andrew—Birthplace of St Gilbert Founder of
the Gilbertine Order AD 1102—Holy Communion 2nd Sun. 11:15 am Evensong 1st & 3rd Sun. 3:00—All other Services at Christ Church Pointon—Key
Opposite." If you can find anyone at the lone house opposite the narrow
driveway to St Andrew's you can gain admission. If not, the site alone is
magic.

In July 1629 Thomas Hooker rode from Little Baddow in company with
Roger Williams to confer with John Cotton at Boston, Lincolnshire.[6] I
imagine they went via Cambridge and Ely as they were familiar with those

roads from their student days. But with whatever short-cuts they might take, it was a journey of over 100 miles.

John Cotton (1584–1652)[7] had graduated MA from Trinity College, Cambridge, at only 21 years of age. He received a Fellowship at Emmanuel, and began there an abiding friendship with one of his students, Thomas Hooker. His distinguished career as Senior Lecturer and Dean ended with his appointment to St Botolph's Parish Church at Boston, in 1612. Before this, Hooker had gained his Emmanuel Fellowship. They remained close colleagues for life, despite strongly held theological differences, and the inevitable conflicts which attended their dangerous pioneer ministries in New England.

Roger Williams (1604–1683)[8] was then resident chaplain to Sir William Masham at Otes,[9] Masham's estate at High Laver, Essex. Sir William was a noted Puritan Member of Parliament. He had recently suffered imprisonment for opposing the forced loans which Charles I had attempted to levy without Parliament's approval. This must have been particularly unsettling for his many friends amongst the reforming clergy in Essex, round whose heads the storm-clouds of Bishop Laud's lawsuits had already gathered.

Hooker and Williams undertook the arduous horse-back journey to discuss their own future prospects with their friend John Cotton. In point of fact, according to Williams' later admission in *The Bloody Tenement, Yet More Bloody*, volatile Roger was more interested in attacking his two companions for refusing to separate altogether from the Church of England;[10] but that was Roger all over, virtuoso fiddling whilst the world was burning, and such music as only angels dare to make!

Williams emigrated two years afterwards, and was invited to join John Wilson, pastor of the First Church of Boston, Massachusetts as his assistant. He refused because he "darst not officiate to an unseparated people."[11] He removed to Salem, to the general relief of many Boston citizens, for angels make uncomfortable roommates, was banished for litigious conduct when Hooker's friend John Haynes was Governor, and founded Rhode Island State. There his impassioned belief in religious liberty found a wider acceptance. His successor at High Laver was John Norton,[12] who also married whilst there and migrated to New England. Thus the Puritan springs grew to be floods.

Once in Cotton's company the friends set out to ride the 18 miles from Boston to Sempringham, one of the manor houses belonging to Theophilus Fiennes Clinton, fourth Earl of Lincoln.[13] He was one of the foremost proponents of the Massachusetts Bay Company, Sempringham its northerly headquarters.

It will be remembered that the Lady Arbella, sister of the earl, accompanied the Winthrop fleet in 1630 with her husband, Rev. Isaac Johnson, and lent her name to the flagship *Arbella* (formerly the *Eagle*). Both were present on this occasion, as were her sister and brother-in-law (the Lady Susannah and John Humfry, first treasurer of the Bay Company) together with John Winthrop,[14] Emmanuel Downing of the Inner Temple his brother-in-law, and Thomas Dudley, capable administrator of the vast Lincoln estates, later occasionally to share the governorship of Massachusetts with John Winthrop.

The Earl of Lincoln's other sister, Lady Frances, was equally at home with the planners of New England, though not present at this meeting. She had married John Gorges, elder son of the Sir Ferdinando Gorges (1566–1647), who was amongst the earliest and largest land prospectors under the Council for New England.

Sempringham had an even wider importance for the Bay Company. There was Samuel Skelton,[15] chaplain to the Earl of Lincoln and vicar of Sempringham, who sailed with Francis Higginson to establish a preliminary settlement at Salem in 1629. There was Simon Bradstreet, brought up in the Lincoln household and married to Dudley's daughter Anne, he to become Governor of Massachusetts, she one of the colony's first poets.[16]

But more than this, St Gilbert's Priory at Sempringham had come into the possession of Lord Edward Clinton, first Earl of Lincoln, at the Dissolution. The immense monastic buildings were stripped of valuables. A mansion, "that passing fair house,"[17] rose from the rubble of the old, to be the new seat of the earls of Lincoln. But at the death of the first earl it was apparently allowed to fall into decay, never inhabited, and an older manor house on the same monastic site was made available to the planners of New England.

Whether they realised it or not, by an extraordinary coincidence they were meeting on the original Gilbertine site to plan an effectual restoration of St Gilbert's work, which was the training of a new society, through carefully regulated sexual and communal relationships, within an ordered and unified religious community—and that almost describes Puritanism.

St Gilbert of Sempringham (1083–1189)[18] founded the only recognised English Religious Order, the Gilbertines, when presented to the living of Sempringham by his father Jocelin, a wealthy Norman knight, because he had proved useless as a warrior. Ridiculed even by his father's retainers, Gilbert had fled back to France in the hope of finding a more tolerable life; but his mother's affection seems to have produced in him an answering tenderness, and an exceptional consideration for women and for disadvantaged children.

When he returned to Sempringham as Rector he was not ordained. He employed a priest, Geoffrey, with whom he shared a tiny room over the south porch of the present church, their sole lodging. He had considerable experience as a scholar and teacher in France, and at once offered to educate the local peasant boys and girls, something almost unheard of.

The Bishop of Lincoln demanded his services as a clerk, and he humbly pursued his duties at Lincoln for ten years, giving most of his money to the poor whilst expanding his dream of a fuller life for his flock of serfs at Sempringham. He was now ordained, and rich, having inherited his father's lands. In 1131, at the age of 48, he returned home to start a small community for seven of the women he had taught as girls, out of which grew the new Order, "culled from the statutes and customs of diverse churches and monasteries," but uniquely one Order in two-kinds, with both nuns and lay canons (male).

They lived together in strict segregation, physically separated from each other at worship, as the Puritans liked to do, and also in their residences. But they coexisted as a single society, partners in double-monasteries, a single complex with a wall down the middle of their chapels dividing the sexes. The Puritans would have nodded their heads in grave approval, had they been alive to inspect Gilbert's houses.

Papal approval was secured in 1148, and by the time of his death Gilbert presided over an Order of some 1500 women and 700 men. At the time of the Dissolution, 26 houses were spread over England. Their effect was to weld together mixed communities in shared labour and learning, under a consistent rule which might well, however unconsciously, have provided a model for the enclosed towns of New England.

The analogy applies even to their temporary breakdown, for Gilbert's enfeebling longevity (he lived to be over 100) led to a partial collapse of his disciplines at the end of his life, especially under the misdemeanours of two unscrupulous members, Gerard and Ogger Carpenter. The Old Adam could not be entirely rooted out of either experiment, Gilbertine or Puritan, by education and regulation, as John Winthrop would sorrowfully have agreed.

The Sempringham group joined by Hooker, Cotton, and Williams met on 25 July 1629, at a time when others were meeting in the London home of Thomas Goffe, deputy governor of the Bay Company,[19] in the presence of governor Matthew Cradock.[20] At this fateful London meeting it was decided to transport the whole apparatus of the government of the Settlement to its future place of residence, thus setting up a colony, not merely the trading station of a merchant company. New England was born. It was a turning point for Hooker and Cotton, for though they were to wait a further four years before themselves emigrating, they had ridden in at the beginning, and were never afterwards far from the eye of the storm.

Drive slowly along the single track to the secluded church of St Andrew, or take off your shoes and walk, as the first postulants would have done, preferably the rain sheeting down, the wet soil between your toes (the road today is metalled, but you have only to trudge in the verge!), not a soul in sight, nothing but low-lying plain as far as sight can reach, almost as remote as you can get in over-populated Britain.

Here, to your right, stands the Parish Church of St Andrew, solitary but for its memories. A Norman House of Prayer first sprang up here in 1100 AD, above the foundations of a yet more ancient Saxon predecessor. When the cathedral-size Gilbertine Priory Chapel grew within the acres of monastic buildings, spread over the fields to the south and west (c. 1160), alterations were made to the simple Norman Church as well. But Gilbert's South Porch remains, without the little room above, where he once lived.

The Norman Nave inside gives a surprised delight to the first-time visitor, its austerity enlivened by more colourful furnishings, and beautifully kept. The Victorian Apse provides a pleasing addition, as it peeps out underneath the weighty 14th century tower, crowned with reaching pinnacles outside. It was in this small space that the Gilbertine Order first gathered, the nuns' quarters splayed outside the north wall.

Nothing remains above ground of the Priory, or its Church, or the Lincoln Mansion. But here, to your left, is the Holy Well, neatly tiled with stones, from which the Community drew its water. Here Gilbert dreamt of an ordered holiness which, parasitically, leaped aboard the Pilgrim ships from the ruined priory, and relived his Vision in North America. Here he was buried.

My wife and I stood sheltered from dark storms under the sparse trees that shield this sacred spot. Suddenly the clouds lifted, and a rainbow spanned the limitless fens, lit by a dying sun from the west, as if from pilgrims coming home.

Boston.

From Sempringham continue northwards up the B1177 to the A52 beyond Billingborough. Turn right (east) on the A52 into Boston, a journey of some 18 miles.

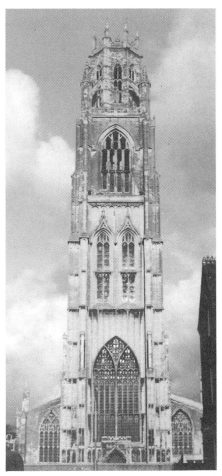

In the 12th century Boston was a major port, second only to London in the harbour levies it paid to the Crown,[21] despite the four miles which now separate the town from the River Witham mouth. The river temporarily silted up, and the pattern of trade shifted elsewhere, notably to Bristol in the west, along with the growing predominance of London and the Essex ports in the east. The importance of Boston slumped, but it was still a highly influential appointment for the young John Cotton, vicar from 1612–1633.

Today Boston may feel remote (the more attractive for that!), but it is still a busy port and commercial axis for the large agricultural area over which it presides. The town is dominated by Boston Stump, the magnificent tower of St Botolph's church in the old central Market Place. Drive right up to it. There is a small car park in the open air mar-

Boston Stump
St Botolph's Church Tower

ket, and you may be lucky enough to find a space in it, close by the Information Centre, the 15th century Guildhall, and St Botolph's. But beware. Two annual fairs and two weekly markets were granted in 1546 by Henry VIII, in a Charter which declared Boston a Free Borough. They are held to this day, in Market Place and Bargate Green, on Wednesdays and Saturdays, and congest access through the narrow streets all too effectively.

The Guildhall, a fine 1450 brick structure, was once the hall of a medieval religious guild, then later the meeting place of the Boston Corporation. Its most celebrated "guests" were William Brewster,[22] William Bradford,[23] and others of the original Pilgrim Fathers. Thirteen of them had set

Cotton's Pulpit
St Botolph's Church

out from Scrooby in Nottinghamshire in 1607, to flee to Holland. But
their ship's captain (not the *Mayflower* of 1620) betrayed them, and
they were held for trial in the Guildhall cells, as you can see, later to
escape to Leiden.

The period Queen Anne (c.
1700) Fydell House, alongside the
Guildhall, is well worth visiting. It
was opened in 1938 by Ambassador
Joseph P. Kennedy, with an American room set aside for visitors from
Boston, Massachusetts. How will
you tear yourself away! But you will
wish to hurry into St Botolph's
Church, one of the grandest deco-
rated parish churches in the kingdom, so near at hand.

St Botolph was, according to the Anglo-Saxon Chronicle, the founder
of a monastery at Icanhoe later St Botolph's Town, or Boston, in the mid-
seventh century.[24] He was a popular saint, especially in East Anglia. A
number of churches were dedicated to him, but none the equal of Boston.

The "stump" rises 272 feet above the flat fens, crowned with a graceful
octagonal lantern, visible for miles inland, and a prominent landfall for
seamen from its erection in the 14th century. Inside the church you will
immediately discover Cotton's pulpit, richly carved, elevated for the
preacher's art. The modern stained glass window in the north aisle depicts
Cotton's farewell to the Boston group who emigrated in 1630. He followed
them three years afterwards. But first you will glory in the splendidly
proportioned and ornamented interior, and perhaps say a quiet prayer for
the present-day worshippers in this congregation once enthralled by one of
the most persuasive preachers of his day.

Inside the south door, on your left, you will also find the Cotton
Memorial Chapel, restored in 1857 by citizens of Boston, Massachusetts, in
memory of their long association through John Cotton and the New England settlers. The story behind the Chapel is almost too good to be true. It
had direct access to the Market Place outside, and had been inexcusably but
conveniently deconsecrated for use as a fire-engine shed. A hand-ported
manually operated pump, more impressive for whooping behind as it was

The Cotton Chapel
St Botolph's Church

carried through the town than for any value it had for quenching fires, but portentously symbolic for all that.

John Cotton, fiery preacher, striking heat from the hearts of his hearers, and equally effectively quenching the evil within them! You can sit here in blissful silence, and think, if you will, of the flames of persecution which charred the very bones of the early English Free Church men and women, and reflect how strangely history unwinds towards the creation of marvel out of misadventure, the fires quenched before they fully destroy. Another name for it is Divine Providence.

The human factor merits careful examination too. Hooker's career was in many ways modulated by Cotton, whose brilliance probably brought out the best in his more introversive friend. The friendship began at Emmanuel, Cambridge, with the warmth a freshman can conceive for a popular senior, for Cotton was made a Fellow of Emmanuel within two years of Hooker's entry, though he was but a year older.

I think Hooker felt disadvantaged in comparison with Cotton. I doubt the division often claimed between them, and sometimes advanced as the reason for Hooker's leaving Massachusetts for Connecticut.[25] Cotton's fulsome Eulogy on Hooker, when his friend predeceased him, disposes of any prolonged antagonism between them.[26] But Cotton's was a less sensitive mind than Hooker's. He tended to act impulsively, without first analysing the logical outcome of his generous responses, as in the case of Anne Hutchinson, the plausible antinomian.[27] Cotton at first championed her attacks on the Massachusetts clergy, then recanted. There was nothing impetuous about Thomas Hooker.

We see them riding side-by-side through the waste Lincolnshire fens, cheek-by-jowl again in cramped quarters on board the same ship bound for America, or locked together in the initial conflicts of the New England commonwealth, their considerable talents complementing each other. Each was cast in the role of a prince in his own pulpit, exercising his strength over a distinct region, and advancing their godly cause the more for each separate development. Who shall say that was not Providential too?

Diversion Into East Anglia

Choice of three routes to Cambridge.
   From Boston, Lincolnshire, three routes to Cambridge await your selection.

Direct Route.
   You can drive south-south-west down the A16 back to Stamford, and resume your journey from there. This makes possible a brief stop at Spalding. It is approximately sixty miles to Cambridge by this way.

Diversion into Peterborough.
   You may prefer to leave the A16 at Market Deeping, after Spalding, to take the A15 south into Peterborough, and break your journey there. Thomas Shepard, Thomas Weld, John Rogers of Dedham and his son Nathaniel were ordained in Peterborough Cathedral, along with other puritan clergy.[28]

   The Cathedral[29] is amongst the finest of Norman Romanesque buildings in Britain. It began as a Benedictine Abbey church in 655, conservative monks carrying on their traditional designs long after Gothic architecture had superseded Romanesque. They had access to the Barnack stone quarries, creamy-white stone which provides a delicate contrast to the golden wooden ceiling inside, a dense medley of diamond-patterned paintings completed by 1220.

   The AD 1118 west front will greet you before you enter the building, and is incongruously but superbly Gothic, like some richly chased sword-hilt added to an earlier blade. The three huge arches are deeply recessed, the narrowness of the central archway compelling the eye to penetrate within. A late Gothic porch ties the ends together in dramatic unity.

Diversion To King's Lynn And Norwich.
   If in an adventurous mood, you may decide to quit the A16 almost straightaway after leaving Boston, and, at Sutterton, switch east onto the A17 to King's Lynn. A full description of this journey unfortunately lies outside the scope of this guide. Its value derives from the fuller exploration of East Anglia it offers, if need be all the way down to Ipswich and Chelmsford, cutting out a return to Cambridge. But only if you've been to Cambridge before!

King's Lynn.

Once a major European port near the mouth of the Great Ouse, a member of the lucrative Hanseatic League of north European trading partners which sprang up in the 13th century, King's Lynn[30] is still a busy maritime and market town with many intriguing old streets and buildings. Near to St Margaret's Church with its twin 13th century towers you will find the Holy Trinity Guildhall, on Saturday Market Place—and the Guildhall of St George behind the Tuesday Market Place—with Hampton Court from the 14th century, and the waterfront Customs House from 1683, and more of interest besides.

From King's Lynn the world of East Anglia lies open before you. This was the heartland of Oliver Cromwell's Eastern Association, where he raised and trained his victorious armies from the people of Norfolk, Suffolk, Essex, Cambridge, reaching right across to the Midland counties, Marefield just over the horizon. Without this hinterland, this reservoir of freeborn Fenmen, resistance to King Charles I would have proved vain. Unfettered land! Open skies! Liberty!

King's Lynn is approximately thirty miles from Boston, Norwich a further 45 miles.

Norwich.

Norwich[31] stands some 45 miles to the east, along the A47 via Swaffham and East Dereham. With its great castle (now a Museum of local history and the surrounding countryside) and cathedral (are there cloister carvings to equal those at Norwich, or a cathedral setting to outrival the approaches from the Wensum River at Pull's Ferry watergate, or from Tombland through the 14th century Ethelbert Gate?) and with its delectable central Market, its many churches, narrow alleyways, and heterogeneous period buildings—it had many claims to be one of Britain's most outstanding cities.

Three times in 300 years the citizens rose in popular revolt for personal freedom. Against a tyrannical Church in 1272, in sympathy with Wat Tyler's peasant revolt of 1381,[32] and to support Robert Kett's doomed rising in 1549,[33] against the enclosure of common lands whereby the landlords turned sturdy peasants into landless beggars overnight. Norwich was as nonconformist as the fens from the beginning of modern times.

The Burnhams await you to the north. Burnham Deepdale, Burnham Norton, Burnham Market, Burnham Overy, and Burnham Thorpe the vicarage birthplace of Horatio Admiral Lord Nelson.[34] Lonely little villages open to The Wash, the salt marshes, and every bitter northeast wind that howls across bleak winter waters, a stern training-ground for the scorning of pain and an heroic self-reliance fit for founding a purer faith or a larger England anywhere. Then there is Palladian Holkham Hall,[35] and Jacobean

Blicking[36] once home of Sir John Falstaff, and of the Boleyns, and magical Walsingham with its ancient Shrine still drawing crowds to its pilgrimages, too much to detail, a region open to God and Destiny.

You understand here, traversing the fenlands as they stretch endlessly from The Wash to Cambridge, that this is a country belonging to no one but itself. Hereward was its hero figure, impenetrable marshes were its sanctuary. From long-born instinct the men would enlist in Cromwell's New Model Army. They were the Ironsides. They played their part in the remaking of England under the Commonwealth, then lapsed into their lowland anonymity again. They were equally at home in the creeks and river-swamps of Massachusetts. Inured to isolation, fever, deprivation, they helped make New England too.

According to the Domesday Book, Hereward the Wake had large landholdings under Peterborough and Crowland Saxon Abbeys. When William the Conqueror handed them to his new French Abbot, Turold, Hereward defended his lands and swept aside the Norman invaders. In 1070 he sacked their new Norman Abbey at Peterborough, and took its treasure to finance his resistance. He established a base camp on the Isle of Ely, then an "island" of high ground rising out of the marshes. He gathered Saxon and Danish malcontents from the breadth of the land and, for more than a year, held out against the enclosing Norman forces. The odds against him were too heavy. He was finally outmanoeuvred, his outlaws dispersed. He disappeared into the murky fens by hidden tracks and vanished undefeated into history, reputedly buried at Crowland Abbey north of Peterborough.[37]

A cycle of legends grew round the name of Hereward. He was "in popular eyes the champion of the English national cause."[38] Like Queen Boadicea of a former era,[39] and Robin Hood[40] after him, his cause was hopeless. That was the point. His inheritors of the fens grew up treasuring a myth of Hopeless Freedom. They never gave up. Under threat, they simply vanished into the mists. As we drive from Boston to Cambridge, we traverse a region of irrepressible liberty ever close to the folk law of Cottons, and Winthrops, and Hookers.

Ely, Cathedral Over Cambridge.

How To Get There.

From Norwich take the A11 through Thetford (once a hidden place, but now overlaid with new building developments) to Mildenhall, and the B1102 west to Fordham where you turn north on the A142 to Ely, a journey of about 55 miles.

Newmarket.

You may prefer to go on to Newmarket on the A11, and to take the A142 from that English metropolis of horseracing. At Newmarket you can visit the National Horseracing Museum at 99 High Street, and take one of their tours of the town and National Stud (prior booking advised). This is flat country bordering Breckland, often slow and tedious to drive, though plentiful of interest for the discerning travellers, as any tourist agency will inform you if you have a mind to explore round Dereham, Swaffham, Watton, Attleborough, and Thetford, its sandy heaths and pine-forests.

Undoubtedly the quicker route is direct from King's Lynn, south down the A10. But you should not miss Norwich (or Newmarket) if you can help it.

Ely.

The Ely[41] Information Centre deserves special mention because it is at Oliver Cromwell's House, off St Mary's Street, the road by which you will enter the town centre from the A10. Here Cromwell resided from 1633–1647. As you drive past St Mary's Church on your right (before reaching the town centre) you will see a small parking area (three hours free) at the entrance to the one-way Church Lane. Cromwell House is alongside. As always, full information is available for overnight accommodation, places to visit, etc.

From here you can enjoyably walk across Palace Green to the West Entrance of the Cathedral, and the old town attractions. These are perched

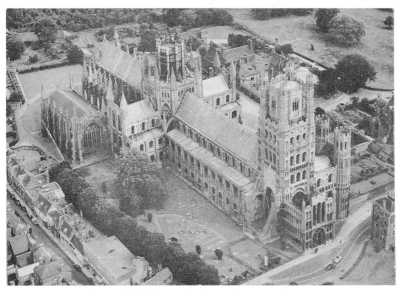

Ely Cathedral from the north-west.
The High Street of the little city is on the left.

upon the summit of steeply rising ground, on the west bank of the great Ouse, an insular refuge before the large scale drainage of the fens in the 17th century, of importance to our quest because of Ely's close association with Cambridge and the University.

When Henry III issued a Writ for the governance of Cambridge as a centre of learning, he conferred certain disciplinary powers on the bishop of Ely. For this reason it was Bishop Hugh de Balsham[42] who founded Cambridge's first college, Peterhouse (1281–84). Trinity Hall was founded by the Prior of Ely, John de Crander (1320); Gonville and Caius by Edward Gonville, vicar-general of the Diocese (1348); Magdalene by the monks of Ely, Crowland, and Ramsey abbeys, nearby (1428); and Jesus College by Bishop John Alcock (1496).

Cambridge remains in the diocese of Ely. John Eliot, Apostle to the Indians of New England, is said to have been ordained here (along with many others), as is claimed by a memorial plaque at the Roxbury Latin School, Roxbury, Massachusetts, founded by him from Little Baddow in 1645. More of that later. The bishops as it were brought the Fen Country into the University Town, with a touch of savagery and an aroma of peat, good earthing for the morale of young Puritan ordinands, menaced by conflict, exile, civil war.

It was to this haven that St Etheldreda,[43] daughter of the early Christian King Anna of East Anglia, fled in AD 673 Her husband Tonbert, a prince of the Girvii (fen people) had given her the Isle of Ely for dowry. But he died, and from an enforced second marriage she sought sanctuary with Wilfrid, Bishop of York,[44] and, with his support, established herself as Abbess at Ely.

The Abbey was raided, and destroyed by marauding bands of Danes, and outlaws, but when Simeon, Norman Prior of Winchester, was appointed Abbot in 1081, he immediately began to construct the present building, and in 1109 it was detached from the Diocese of Lincoln, and became the cathedral of an Ely Diocese which stretched over the shires of Cambridge, Huntingdon and Bedford with segments of Essex, Suffolk, Norfolk, Northampton, Hereford, and Buckingham in tow. The bishops wielded a regal power over this vast area.

The Cathedral is breathtaking in its beauty. Walk into the austere nave alone, on Sunday, for early communion, and hear the ghosts still whispering before the mists have time to lift from the marshland spread blackly below. The great church seems to float in the air above, perched on its eminence, signalling light. Or attend Evensong (5:30 pm, but better to check) allowing ample time to revel in the multiplicity of chantries, canopied tombs, mazes of stone and wood carvings, the many patterned ceilings, the majesty of the

Lady Chapel, bewildering in diversity, yet one harmonious paean of praise to Almighty God.

The most unique feature is the exquisite Octagon, with a 400 ton, timber-framed lantern on top. It replaced the original central tower, which collapsed in 1322. Architecturally it is unsurpassed in England, and aesthetically it richly enhances the central crossing within, the arches of the nave and choir aisles being set obliquely to accommodate the octagonal form, and diffuse its ethereal light.

As time passed St Etheldreda was shortened to St Audry. At her annual fair the trinkets sold to pilgrims came to be called St Awdrys, or tawdry! But it is an entrancing town, with the handsome Cathedral Close terminating in the 1398 Porta, and the 15th century Monks Granary where the one-thousand-year old Kings School occupies other monastic sites. There is a Thursday Market, interesting shops and other buildings, a Museum in Sacrist's Gate at 28 High Street with a "Hereward in Fact and Fiction Exhibition," pleasant riverside walks, and Cambridge only 16 miles down the A10.

Cambridge via The Fens of East Anglia To Wicken Fen, Wetland Nature Reserve.

If, however, we may now return to the Direct Route to Cambridge, and pick it up at Stamford, or Peterborough, we shall proceed down the A1, as first advised. This route visibly skirts the Great Fens of East Anglia, at their western and southern extremities. They once covered 2,500 square miles. The Roman roads A15 and A1 are linked via the A14 with the A604 causeway, and acted almost as a rampart against any penetration of those closed-in wetland fastnesses. Trace them on a map. Deeping Fen, North Fen and Morris Fen, Flag Fen and White Fen, Holme Fen (listed in the Guiness Book of Records as the lowest stretch of land in Britain), Pidley Fen, Chatteris Fen, and Smithy Fen, the roads follow them round.

Wicken Fen comes last on this journey, 17 miles north-east of Cambridge via the A10/A1123. Some 600 undrained acres of fenland remain. It is, scientifically, one of the most important wetland nature reserves in Western Europe, managed by the National Trust since 1899. The Trust has mounted a display of the history and development of the fens in their William Thorpe building. The only complete windmill for pumping in the fens is also preserved here. Wicken is open daily all year, except on Christmas Day.

Huntingdon.

Shortly after leaving the A1 (A14 exit), a newly elevated stretch of road by-passes Huntingdon. You may wish to turn aside. Oliver Cromwell (1599–1658)[45] was born at Huntingdon, in a house long since demolished.

Cromwell Museum, Huntingdon

The site, now a small office building, can still be seen in the narrow town centre, along which the Great North Road traffic flowed in slow congestion not many years ago. You can also visit the Grammar School in High Street where Cromwell attended, as did Samuel Pepys the diarist (1633–1703), in what is now the Cromwell Museum. The headmaster in Cromwell's day was the celebrated Dr Thomas Beard, a controversial Puritan. The Information Centre is at the Library, Princes Street.

Memorials of the Cromwell family abound. As you approach the town from the western section of the A604, you pass Hinchingbrooke House, now a school, the mansion where Oliver's great-grandfather, Sir Henry Cromwell, lived. His grandfather owned what is now the George Hotel in George Street, Huntingdon. His father lies buried in All Saints Church.

Across the Great Ouse, which skirts Huntingdon on its southern and eastern sides, lies Godmanchester (where Stephen Marshall was born, see pp. 289–90), a collection of 17th and 18th century properties, for instance Island Hall, a 1740 riverside mansion. It is joined to Huntingdon by an early pack-horse bridge, dated 1332, most narrow, with passing places for pack-animals spaced here and there; a mulish nightmare for the single-line traffic not long since bearing down on London.

The Ouse has flowed here from John Bunyan's Bedford[46] to the west. It does not stop until it reaches The Wash opposite John Cotton's Boston. These water-ways draining the fens, the Welland, the Nene, the Delph, the Great Ouse, carried the Midlands trade to the east coast ports, and formed a culture contact from northern Europe into the heart of England.

Traces of the Hereward saga perhaps surface in the popular association of another freedom fighter, Robin Hood,[47] with the earldom of Huntingdon. He is another English folk hero in the long struggle against serfdom, genesis of Thomas Hooker and the Puritans. Alas, little if any truth resides in Robin's claim to Huntingdon. The connection probably derives from Robin the Hunter of Sherwood Forest.

William Langland (c. 1330–1400),[48] in his early poem-cum-social statement *The Vision of William concerning Piers The Ploughman* (1377) makes reference to Robin, but not to Huntingdon. Says Sloth: "I can noughte perfitly my pater-noster, as the prest (priest) it syngeth: But I can rymes of Robyn Hood and Randolf Erle of Chestre."

Robin takes his place in English folk-law with special distinction in that, whereas the old heroes were invariably of noble birth, Robin was a man of the people, "the ideal yeoman."[49] Anyone who has read so far knows what that signifies, in tracing the rise of Puritanism. So welcome Robin to Huntingdon whether he had title there or not. His myth belongs to any understanding of the Puritans.

St Ives.

The road next passes the small town of St Ives, named after an obscure Persian saint who lived on the banks of the Ouse, c. 600.[50] Cromwell also lived here for a time. The town is again reached across a 15th century bridge of equally graceful proportions to the one at Godmanchester, with a rare two-tier bridge chapel suspended over one side. A statue of Cromwell stands on Market Hill. From St Ives the A604 bypasses the village of Fen Stanton, where Capability Brown (1715–83), the great landscape gardener, is buried. His tomb inscription is worth quoting. "Ye sons of Elegance, Come from the sylvan scenes his genius grac'd, and offer here your tributary sighs."[51]

Fen Stanton is followed by Fen Drayton, and Dry Drayton is not far along the road. These are evidence of Fenland culture, being the hamlets, or stray settlements, that gathered beside the hard ground where a boat might be dragged (dray), or safely housed (stand), in transit across the wastes of marsh waters.

So at last you come to Cambridge.[52]

Grantchester.

If you overshoot Exit 14, and find yourself on the M11, do not despair. Any of exits 13, 12, 11 will bring you as comfortably into the centre of the town. Indeed, if you enjoy the poetry of Rupert Brooke (1887–1915), your chosen exit will be no 11. Turn north onto the Trumpington Road (A10), and take the left-hand turn signposted Grantchester a mile along.

Grantchester is a very pretty village, on the banks of the river Granta (the original name for the Cam) made famous by Rupert Brooke's poem *The Old Vicarage, Grantchester.*

> For England's the one land, I know,
> Where men with splendid hearts may go;
> And Cambridgeshire, of all England,
> The shire for men who understand;
> And of that district I prefer

The lovely hamlet Grantchester . . .
Stands the Church clock at ten to three?
And is there honey still for tea.[53]

The hands of the clock pointed correctly, if unpoetically, to 1:30 pm when last I was there, and the honey-serving Orchard Tea Rooms was closed; but there are other poems of Brooke to enjoy. *The Great Lover, Heaven, The Dead,* and *The Soldier;* and Grantchester furnishes a most agreeable entry into the University town. Return to the A10 the way you came in, and continue along Trumpington Road into Cambridge.

The direct route (exit from the A604 before the M11, using the Huntingdon Road) had the advantage of bringing you into the town centre past the celebrated first women's college, Girton; past the castle mound, also on your left; and over Magdalene Bridge into Bridge Street, where there is a multi-storey car park on your left, in Round Church Street.

Holy Sepulcre, The Round Church, is one of only four examples of a circular Norman church in Britain. The eight massive Norman pillars with individually carved heads, the fine triforium above with double arches, as · wide as high, are quite awe-inspiring in so miniature a building. It dates back to the Knights Templar, 1130, and is well worth a visit.

However, the advantage of using Exit 11 from the motorway is that it brings you straight into the heart of Cambridge, down Trumpington Road, alongside Hobson's Conduit. The conduit is a supply of fresh water, conveyed by an open channel devised by a well-known 17th century carrier, Tobias Hobson.[54] He also hired out horses, but insisted you take the one nearest the stable door, or do without—hence "Hobson's Choice." Then past the Fitzwilliam Museum, which you will wish to visit, and Cambridge's oldest college, Peterhouse, endowed by Sir Wolstan Dixie, to another multi-storey car park off Pembroke Street, on your right, well signposted.

This most central car park opens onto Lion Yard shopping precinct, with the Information Bureau in Wheeler Street adjacent, and takes you into the open air market, with Great St Mary's, the University Church. Here veer left, cross over King's Parade (an extension of Trumpington Street), and straight into King's College Chapel, hopefully in time for Evensong, 3:30 pm weekdays, 5:30 pm Sundays.

King's is the most perfect perpendicular chapel, begun in the reign of Henry VI (1446), comparable only with the Chapels of St George at Windsor Castle, and of Henry VII at Westminster Abbey. Hear the music of the choir reach up to the fan-vaulted ceiling like sun-lit spray from some ornate fountain, vibrating, convoluting on the still evening air, and experience a harmony of the human spirit which untainted artistry can create, if only momentarily.

CAMBRIDGE, University Town.

A Brief And Inadequate History Of Cambridge.

In early days, water-borne traffic from the North Sea could reach up to the Cam crossing, where Magdalene Bridge spans the river today. The Romans built a settlement there, covering some 25 acres. The Normans fortified it with a castle, in 1068. Beside the small wharves of those simpler times ran an east-west highway, roughly the line of the Roman causeway (A604) from Colchester, through Cambridge, to Kettering near Leicester. It edged round the southern Fenlands into the Midland Shires, traversing (and so giving access to) the great north-south highway, Ermine Street, as we have seen.

At this prominent meeting place of river and road routes the largest of the medieval fairs sprang up, at Stourbridge (Sturbridge), two miles from the bridge head, near Barnwell and Chesterton. Founded in 1211, it ran from mid-September to the beginning of October and only finally ended by Royal Decree in 1933.[55]

In its heyday it covered an area two miles in circumference, a tented town divided into squares for the widest variety of goods: wool in bags up to a ton, grain, cheeses, coal, Staffordshire ware, Spanish iron-ware, silks from Venice and Genoa, wines from France and Greece, Norwegian pitch. Later a pulpit for preaching in the Duddery Square, taverns, coffee-houses, and a hackney-coach service daily from London, to supplement the river

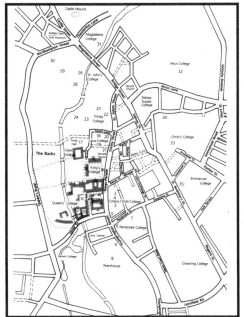

barges and earlier pack-horse trains, which brought people and goods from all over the country and Europe.

Daniel Defoe, in his 1724 *Tour of Britain* declared he had never seen such large crowds so well behaved. They had their own "Peid-Poudre," or Court of Dusty Feet, which controlled the fair under the local mayor. Bron Surrey, in *Stourbridge Fair*, writes of it as "one of the greatest and best-known of the medieval European markets, which made Cambridge a famous centre of commerce long before the first stone of its University had been laid." The town has remained an important manufacturing, commercial and administrative centre ever since.

Inevitably the main Religious Houses quickly established themselves in so strategic a settlement.[56] The Augustinians came first, their monastery of St Giles founded in 1092 by Hugoline, wife of Roger Picot the Norman sheriff. The Franciscans followed in 1224, the Dominicans, Gilbertines, and Carmalites within the same century. Students flocked to the town to be taught by the monks so that, when Henry III issued a writ in 1231 for the government of the growing community, Cambridge could already be referred to as a centre of learning and the Bishop of Ely was confirmed in his disciplinary powers over the embryo colleges.

A need to broaden the curriculum of the monastic houses was first recognised at Oxford, where Walter de Merton drew up a set of statutes for his "House of Scholars," founded in 1264. These 1270 statutes constituted Merton as a University College rather than a Religious House, with the scholastic authority vested in an independent Warden and a group of Fellows. Hugh de Balsham, Bishop of Ely, took the Merton statutes as his model for Peterhouse, the first Cambridge College, in 1281–84.

Tensions between town and gown, arising from their separate and often competing sources of authority, peaked during Wat Tyler's Peasants' Revolt, in 1381.[57] Discontent amongst rural labourers in Kent and East Anglia brought on by the economic distress which followed the Black Death, boiled over at the introduction of a Poll Tax, first at Brentwood, near Chelmsford in Essex, then in Kent where Tyler was chosen as rebel leader. Canterbury was seized, the Archbishop's palace ransacked, and the mob moved to London.

King Richard II, a mere boy of fourteen, courageously faced the rioters at Mile End, and agreed to their demands. However, after days of rioting in the city, Tyler was struck down by the mayor at a further conference at Smithfield and Richard resumed command crying "Will you shoot your king? I will be your chief and captain, you shall have from me all that you seek." The too-trusting peasants were dispersed, many were executed, and little benefit accrued to them until they rose again in civil war, in Thomas Hooker's day.

A small side-line of the same revolt led to the sacking of some of the Cambridge Colleges. East Anglia even then was ripe for an affray. The monarchy never held sway in Cambridge as it did in Oxford. When, for instance, Henry III (1207–72) had tried to exert his authority over the town by having two great gates placed at either end the local barons burnt them down. Cambridge never became the royalist stronghold that marked Oxford. How could it be otherwise? The independent yeomen of East Anglia lived everywhere around.

The contribution of the growing University was even more determinative for the history of Cambridge than its environment. We turn now in eager expectation to look into some of the great self-governing Colleges.

Walk From Queens' To St John's Colleges.

Our interest bends towards the University because Thomas Hooker's connection with Cambridge derives from his university entrance. He first entered Queens' College. This provides a useful starting point for a walking tour of the colleges—the only way for a tourist to enjoy them to the full. Visitors are generally welcome to stroll through the main grounds and passageways of most colleges, outside examination times, and into some of their chapels. You can always check at the Porter's office.

From King's Parade, where our journey stopped the previous day, turn south past St Catharine's College on Trumpington Street, to Silver Street. There turn right (west), and Queens' is the next college, backing onto the river.

St Catharine's College.

St Catharine's was founded in 1473, but the present buildings date from 1675–1775. You may wish to look in as you pass, they form an attractive architectural whole. A former student in whom we have an interest was John Ray (1628–1705) of Black Notley, Braintree, Essex. He was the first great English Botanist and Zoologist. You may see some of his work at the Braintree Heritage Museum.[58]

The Mathematical Bridge, Queens' College, Cambridge

President's Lodge,
Queens' College

Queens' College, 1604.
The Master of
Queens' when Hooker
entered in 1604 was Hum-
phrey Tyndall,[59] known
for his Puritan persua-
sion. He had been chap-
lain to the Earl of Leicester, and this may have provided a further reason for
Hooker's entrance as a sizar there. Hooker matriculated on 27 March 1604,
and moved to Emmanuel.

Opposite St Catharine's you might have noticed another St Botolph's
Church (as at Boston). Its erstwhile rector, Andrew Docket, was also warden
of a student's Hostel of St Bernard. He obtained the patronage of Margaret
of Anjou, wife of King Henry VI, for the founding of a new college, in 1448.
He became the first Master. Elizabeth Woodville, wife of Edward IV, was
the second benefactress, in 1465. Queens' indeed![60]

The quadrangle within the towered gateway, with its fantastic 17th
century sundial, dates from the foundation, and so does the cloister court
beyond, in which is found the sublime half-timbered President's Lodge. An
unusual wooden bridge, the "Mathematical Bridge" leads over the Cam,
said to have been designed by Isaac Newton (1642–1727). Since it is dated
1749 this appears to be somewhat doubtful. It is mathematically ingenious,
constructed without nails or bolts, maybe posthumously erected.

Erasmus (1466–1536)[61] had rooms in the tower at Queens,' after he
came to England in 1509. The former Master, St John Fisher (1469–1535),[62]
later the martyred Bishop of Rochester, gave him the newly created Lady
Margaret Professorship of Greek and Theology and he stayed until moving
to Brussels in 1516, after completing his translation of the New Testament,
a further reason for Hooker's attendance.

King's, Clare, and Trinity Colleges.
You may now wish to retrace your steps to King's College by crossing
over Silver Street bridge into Queens' Road, so as to enjoy the views across
the river, especially of King's College Chapel. Walk back to the next bridge
leading into King's or go on, through Clare, founded 1326, via its parallel
bridge over the river. Hugh Latimer (1485–1555), Bishop of Worcester,
another Leicestershire yeoman's son, was a Fellow of Clare. He was martyred, with Bishop Ridley, at Oxford, on 16 October 1555, when they lit
"such a candle."[63]

King's College Chapel, Cambridge.

Next comes Trinity Hall, founded on the site of a house of monastic students from Ely (1350). Then, via Trinity Lane, you come to Trinity, the largest of the colleges since Henry VIII brought together several earlier foundations in 1546. Its great court, surrounding Thomas Neville's fountain (he was Master from 1593–1615) has no equal in Cambridge. The chapel was founded by Queen Mary. A statue of Isaac Newton stands in the anti-chapel. He is but one of a plethora of distinguished alumni who include Byron, Dryden, Rutherford, and many others too numerous to mention here.

King's Parade, where you first entered King's College, becomes, without altering its line, Trinity Street outside the main entrance to Trinity College. It immediately renames itself St John's Street as you leave Trinity and turn left into St John's College, going towards Bridge Street at the Round Church, with Magdalene Bridge and College round the corner.

St John's.

St John's was founded in 1511 by Lady Margaret Beaufort,[64] mother of Henry VII, as you might deduce from the Beaufort Arms splendidly carved above the entrance gateway. Thanks to her generosity St John's grew into one of the largest colleges, extending across the Cam by the "Bridge of Sighs," with gardens planted all the way to Queens Road. There, free car parking awaits those who arrive early enough, and the best views back over the Cam (or Granta), past King's College Chapel to Queens.'

St John's was a Puritan college until the staff was purged in the first King James' reign. Thomas Cartwright,[65] father of English Puritanism, was there, and others of different ilk, like Roger Ascham,[66] Lord Burghley,[67] Wilberforce,[68] the poet Wordsworth as well as Robert Herrick.[69]

You can return to the central Market along Trinity Street, with places of interest before you at every alleyway; so do arm yourself with the Official Cambridge Guidebook. There is so much more to discover.

Walk From Emmanuel To Jesus Colleges.

Emmanuel College, 1604–c. 1618.

From Queens' College, Emmanuel[70] is a short stroll up Botolph Walk, alongside St Botolph's church (or Pembroke Street parallel with it) into Downing Street. The entrance to Emmanuel is immediately opposite the end of Downing Street, where it connects with St Andrew's Street.

From Market Hill, should you wish to continue your walk from there, cross the market in front of the Guildhall into Petty Cury, turn right at St Andrew's Street, and Emmanuel is on the left, at the junction with Emmanuel Street. Or, if time permits, you could follow Peas Hill, the south exit from the market, along the west end of the Guildhall. This takes you to the Arts Theatre, or into St Edward's Passage, and the church of St Edward, King and Martyr.

Peas Hill leads into Bene't Street. Turn right for the Church of St Benedict, in part the oldest building in Cambridge. The tower is almost pure Saxon though the nave was rebuilt in the 13th century. On leaving the church, turn back to Peas Hill and Wheeler Street, which takes you to the multi-story car park and the large new Lion Yard shopping precinct. Continue in the same direction through the precinct and you will emerge onto St Andrew's Street.

These directions are necessarily sketchy and selective, as our main purpose is to visit colleges with a Puritan association. But do linger, and look.

Emmanuel College Chapel,
designed by Sir Christopher Wren.

Emmanuel College was founded in 1584 by Sir Walter Mildmay of Chelmsford.[71] His portrait hangs in the Great Hall. He was typical of many Puritans of his generation. Born into an enterprising family of market stall-holders, he rose to be Elizabeth's Chancellor of the Exchequer and a very wealthy man. His benefactions in his native Essex, and in London, were correspondingly large. He was a patron of Christ's College, Cambridge, where he had himself been a scholar, before he invested in Emmanuel.

There had been a Dominican priory on the site, part of which was absorbed into the new college. John Hammond's plan of Cambridge in 1592 shows the first buildings, with the entrance on Emmanuel (not, as now, on

Sir Walter Mildmay, c. 1588
Founder of Emmanuel College.

St Andrew's) Street. The Dominican chapel was turned into the Great Hall, with the kitchens at right-angles to it, to the west, and the Chapel (now the Old Library) to the east, forming a three-sided court. This brought about an incorrect orientation of the Old Chapel, on a north-south axis instead of the conventional east-west, which no doubt pleased later Puritan scholars.

Some see in this a deliberate Puritan act of defiance against the supposed foibles of the established church. A number of Independents did, indeed, make this statement, by building their Meeting Houses on a north-south axis. "God's Elect may worship Him facing in any direction, in any posture." But I think Sir Walter was too genuinely an establishment man to have deliberately schemed this. Rather, as a very wise reformer, he planned his college as thriftily as possible, making full use of buildings already on the site. That would be the "Puritan" way.

The first Master was Laurence Chaderton (1536–1640),[72] a legend in his own time. He was born into a wealthy Catholic family at Lees Hall, Oldham, Lancashire, but entered Christ's College, Cambridge where he became a Fellow and adopted reformed doctrines. For this his family renounced him. Chief amongst his new Protestant confidants was Thomas Cartwright of St John's.[73]

Cartwright was driven from his fellowship at St John's under Queen Mary, but returned on the Queen's death, to take up a fellowship at Trinity and to become Lady Margaret professor. He wrote the Millenary Petition presented to James I on his accession in 1603, but died before he could lead the Puritan deputation, which included Chaderton, at the decisive Hampton Court Conference next year. These two were giants of the English Reformation.

Another of Chaderton's close friends was William Perkins (1558–1602), also a Christ's graduate, lecturer at St Andrew's the Great (where St Andrew's Street meets Petty Cury), and the golden preacher of them all. He drew thousands to Calvin's way by his preaching and writing. He deplored the manner in which Protestant writers were neglected for the Church Fathers and Schoolmen. He stood for "The truth, that is—the Calvinist doctrine."[74] If Thomas Hooker had a model, it was surely the image left behind by Perkins' glowing character.

Chaderton also held a popular lectureship, at St Clement's. Then, at 48 years, Mildmay appointed him to Emmanuel. Here he remained until, at 86, reluctantly, he stood down for the brilliant Puritan Court Preacher, John Preston,[75] friend of Prince Charles and Buckingham. Chaderton lived for 103 years of muscular Christianity, with an influence over tutors and students beyond description.

Not only university personnel either. Richard Bancroft[76] was his contemporary, adversary, and friend. He too had been at Christ's, but removed to high church Jesus College, eventually to become the Elizabethan scourge of Puritans when Bishop of London (1597), and Archbishop of Canterbury (1603). There is no doubt that Emmanuel escaped the worst strictures of repression under James I because of the estimation in which Chaderton was held in Church and State.

Plume's Library at Maldon, Essex (Thomas Plume, 1630–1704, Archdeacon of Rochester, bequeathed his library to his native Maldon)[77] has Dr Plume's notebook. It records a meeting between the two men in 1611, when Bancroft was Archbishop, and Chaderton an even older Don. "Come," says Canterbury, "we must have a fall the first thing we do, put off yr cloak, now do yr best." But the septuagenarian scholar had the best of the impromptu wrestling match! "I see the cares of the council table are greater than the lectures of the Round Church or Trinity Church in Cambridge," groaned

Emmanuel College, seen from the air, painted about 1690.

the fallen archbishop as he picked himself up, despised vestments in disarray. "If we should report it as an omen, I see bishops may fall and puritans rise."

Well, Chaderton had rescued his friend in undergraduate days from the anti-faculty mobs in Cambridge, but it was not for that alone the Archbishop felt beholden to this redoubtable Master of Emmanuel. King James shared his respect, and included Chaderton amongst the authorised Bible translators. So it was that, when James paid his first royal visit to the university in 1615 decorative and diplomatic celebrations were planned by cautious heads of colleges, but not by honest Chaderton.

> But the pure House of Emmanuel
> Would not be like proud Jesabel,
> Nor show herself before the King
> An hypocrite or painted thing
> But that the ways might all prove fair
> Conceived a tedious mile of prayer.[78]

The students did not find Emmanuel's devotions tedious. They crowded in to sit round a central table (possibly the one now in St Edward's church) when celebrating the Eucharist, in plain attire, with an informality present-day undergraduates would warmly applaud.[79] That Chaderton and his colleagues survived intact speaks volumes for his scholastic eminence, and that of his college. Its enrollment was amongst the highest of that day.

If it is convenient to write to the librarian before your visit, it might be possible for you to be shown some of the college treasures, such as the 1584 Charter obtained by Mildmay from Queen Elizabeth; the authorisation of Hooker to a Fellowship (1609); and John Harvard's enrollment, at a ten shilling fee. You will also wish to visit the New Chapel, built by Christopher Wren in 1677, with its windows depicting Chaderton and Harvard.[80] Then there is the Hall, the Old Library, and, not least, the gardens outside, distinguished for their beauty throughout the centuries.[81]

Queen Elizabeth, with Tudor acumen for the safety of her crown, chided Sir Walter Mildmay. "I hear, Sir Walter, that you have been erecting a Puritan foundation." He is said to have replied "Madam, far be it from me to countenance anything contrary to your established laws, but I have set an acorn, which when it becomes an oak, God knows what will be the fruit thereof."[82]

That was not to say that Sir Walter was ignorant of the genus he had planted, nor its probable shape on reaching full stature. But he was most certainly nurturing an English (*Quercus Robur*) not a Spanish (*Quercus Ilex*), or any other Continental oak. The fruit of at least one Spanish oak (*Quercus*

Deryck C. Collingwood presenting a copy of the *Hooker Genealogy*, by Commander Edward Hooker, to Dr. Frank Stubbings as they stand in front of Queen Elizabeth's Charter to Emmanual College, Cambridge, granted to Sir Walter Mildmay in 1584.

Ilex Gramuntia) was regularly eaten, as the Armada was eaten up four years later, assisted by some very English Protestant hearts of oak, Sir Francis Drake foremost amongst them!

The foundation charter of 1584,[83] preserved at Emmanuel College, makes his intention crystal clear. It begins with a ravishing portrait of Queen Elizabeth, illuminated around the initial letter E, painted by Nicholas Hilliard, the master miniaturist. This reveals Sir Walter's stance from the outset. It was not so much a Puritan college as, first, a Tudor establishment.

Its purpose as its statutes declared was "for the sending forth of as large a number as possible of those who shall direct the people in the Christian faith." It was to be "a school of prophets." For this it must be academically amongst the best in the University. More than that, learning was to lead to teaching. "We would not have any Fellow suppose that we have given him in this college a perpetual abode" continued the statutes. Out they must go, tutors and scholars alike, to modernise and reform the land.

The Christian Faith handed down by the new national church of Henry VIII and Edward VI, had a distinctly Calvinistic flavour. That was the mould in which the English Reformation had roughly been cast, and the taste clung to the plaster, despite Mary's and Elizabeth's very different determination to soften the Calvinist savour. So Emmanuel started out as an English

Calvinist institution. But there was no license for a Continental or a Genevan copy, any more than a Catholic one, on the part of Sir Walter. Emmanuel was to be contemporary, and to fit England for an empire. Given the time, and the men involved, only Puritanism could eventually fill this bill.

"The Fruit Thereof," Thomas Hooker's Conversion.

There are three things we know about Thomas Hooker which are beyond question. He was overwhelmed by doubts about his relationship with God when he entered University, a state which continued at least until he was 27 (another sign that he was a late developer). At Emmanuel he underwent a deep, and abiding conversion experience. He emerged from this religious experience a mature, confident leader who never looked back.[84]

Whilst entering Queens' College as a sizar,[85] that is to say, a student without adequate private financial means, who worked his way through college, he moved over to Emmanuel as a scholar, with a Dixie scholarship. The difference in status was considerable. As a sizar he would be appointed a variety of menial tasks, and probably be attached to a scholar, or fellow, as a servant. Now that he was a scholar, especially after receiving his fellowship, he would enjoy his own rooms, with a bed, a notable possession, and a sizar who might, in certain circumstances, sleep on a mattress in his master's room, or on a truckle-bed (a low-slung contraption on wheels) which could be pushed under the master-bed.

In 1613, when Hooker was 27 years old, and had been a Fellow for five years, Simeon Ashe entered college and became his sizar.[86] They may have had an earlier connection through their mutual friendship with Arthur Hildersham, who helped Simeon prepare for the Ministry. This suggests that they were both natives of Leicestershire. At any rate they swiftly forged a close and confidential relationship. This helped to remove Hooker's inner uncertainty. Cotton Mather says "While he [Hooker] long had a soul harassed with such distresses" (ie. "While I suffer thy terrors, O Lord, I am distracted") "he had a singular help in the prudent and piteous carriage of Mr Ash, who was the Sizar that then waited upon him; and attended him with such discreet and proper compassions, . . . at length he received the "spirit of adoption," with well-grounded perswasions of his interest in the new covenant."[87]

Ashe's exact age (d. 1662) is not known, but he was a remarkably perceptive teenager, and revealed an unusual maturity as he gently led his master into a state of peace with the majestic and judgmental God of the Puritans. We can imagine them, Hooker tossing and turning on the bed above, agonising over his election, Simeon on his matress, hardly an accepted counselling posture, easing comfort upwards.

Simeon Ashe went on to ordination himself. He held livings under various Puritan patrons, Sir John Burgoyne, Lord Brooke of Saybrook Plantation, Connecticut, and the Earl of Manchester.[88] It will be remembered that Manchester was the moderate commander of the Parliamentary forces at the beginning of the Civil War, continually at odds with his junior commander, Oliver Cromwell. Cromwell saw the revolution as a religious crusade, to be pursued to the bitter end if need be. Manchester belonged to the party of compromise. Evidently Ashe was of the same view. He defended his general in two works, *A Particular Revelation of the most Remarkable Occurence from the United Forces in the North,* and *A True Relation of the most Chiefe Occurences at and since the late Battell at Newberry.*

For his last seven years he was Rector of St Austin's in London. He preached before both Houses of Parliament, and was attached to the Commission which negotiated the Treaty of Breda in April 1660. In it, Charles II promised "liberty to tender consciences,"[89] were he to become king. This paved the way for the Restoration. For such a delicate task the Commissioners had to be acceptable to both Commonwealth and Royalist parties. Simeon Ashe was a reconciler to the end, as was Thomas Hooker. He died in office on 24 August 1662, the very day by which ministers were required to subscribe to the Act of Uniformity which would have brought about his own exclusion.

If we now ask "What influence did Cambridge exert over the development of the character, beliefs, and actions of the future Founder of Connecticut?" numerous answers leap to the mind from what has so far been discovered.

He came to the University versed in Puritanism. The syllabus he followed, as well as his conversion experience, would have confirmed and expanded that training. The scholasticism of an earlier generation provided a platform of basic assumptions which still pointed to theology as the Queen of sciences. The emphasis on rhetoric, in the new Ramus mode, aimed at a flexible and elegant latin style, culled from a wide knowledge of the classics, intent on impressing the truth on the hearer, which Hooker was to perfect. This enabled succeeding Calvinist teachers to take an absolute stand on the Biblical revelation, but to deduce moral codes and political practices from it without seeming to disregard the contradiction between their determinist belief, and a determined humanist behaviour pattern.

At Cambridge Petrus Ramus, alias Pierre de la Ramee (1515–1572)[90] opened the way for Puritan scholars, following his conversion to Calvinism in 1562. He was professor of rhetoric and philosophy at the Collège Royal in Paris, gaining his reputation by attacking Aristotle's *Ethics* as untrue to the innate logic of the human mind. He initiated a long-running debate on the distinction between "inventio" (idea) and "iudicium" (judgment), de-

claring deduction to be the summit of scientific method. As he was murdered in the Massacre of St Bartholomew in Paris, 1572, his reformed status
was almost above question.

Ramus was in no sense a Platonist,[91] but with hindsight one can
recognise a direct connection between his insistence on the primacy of
deductive logic in Calvinism, so eagerly seized on by thinkers like Thomas
Hooker, and the emergence of the Cambridge Platonists immediately after
the exodus of so many leading English Calvinist theologians to New England.

If you are looking forward to a pleasant prowl round antique Cambridge, and couldn't care less about Ramus' rhetoric or the Platonists,
forgive the last five and jump the next seven paragraphs! But when I claim
that Hooker's brand of preparationist Congregationalism contributed
(against many outward appearances to the contrary) to the opening of the
American mind (not its narrowing, as is too often the popular complaint
against the Puritans), and consequently to the opening of its physical
boundaries (not their closing against undesirables, as was the Puritan New
England practice at that time), so that America became the melting-pot of
many nations; you will find some of the evidence in the Cambridge Platonists. That is why I introduce them.

They were a distinguished group of Christian philosophers who
stepped straight out of Hooker's Emmanuel around 1633, and made a
considerable impact on English University thought during the following 55
years. Their founder was Benjamin Whichcote, D.D. (1609–1683),[92] a student and fellow at Emmanuel, later Provost of King's College and Vicar of
St Lawrence Jewry, London where he is buried. His works were mainly
published posthumously but in his lifetime he held up humanity as the child
of reason, pleaded for freedom of thought, and even advised Cromwell on
toleration for the Jews.

Ralph Cudworth (1617–88)[93] is the best known of the group, which
included Nathanael Culverwel;[94] the dramatist Richard Cumberland;[95]
Joseph Glanvill[96] the Oxford prebendary of Worcester Cathedral, and chaplain to Charles II (cf. his *The Vanity of Dogmatizing*, 1661); John Norris,[97]
lengthy correspondent with Cudworth (cf. his platonic essay *The Theory and
Regulation of Love*, 1688); and others, generally referred to as *Latitudinarians*.

Cudworth too was a Fellow of Emmanuel, later Master of Clare and
then of Christ's. His works include *The True Intellectual System of the Universe*
(1678), and the posthumous *Treatise concerning Eternal and Immutable Morality* (1731). With the rest of this small "School," he opposed religious dogmatism equally with atheism, and for the same platonic reason that what is
known to finite mind is but a reflection of the Truth itself.

Henry More (1614–87) of Christ's College followed a similar pattern in his *Antidote to Atheism* (1653), and *Manuel of Ethics* (1666), both aimed at the materialism of the English philosopher, Thomas Hobbes (1588–1697),[98] author of the *Leviathon*, which left no room for any genuine distinction between good and evil. Hobbes had to face the threat of a parliamentary enquiry into his alleged atheism in 1666, when superstitious fears ran high in London following the Great Plague and the Great Fire. Hobbes' threat to their faith provided a prime target for the Cambridge Platonists, as well as their distaste for the dogmatic separatism of the English Commonwealth Sectaries.

Plato (427–347 BC)[99] may not be summarised in a few sentences. Even the hurry of a holiday could not excuse such cavalier treatment! In any case, I owe too much to Plato's mysticism and literary style, and responded too deeply to his passion for human improvement, and his persistent faith in the supremacy of the mind, his identification of truth with goodness, and his vision of sense-experience as but a reflection of the true and higher world of Ideas ("Forms") when, as a young student, I first read him in the original greek editions of his dialogues, to dishonour him with my paltry summaries now (although I've done it to others in this guide with equanimity!).

The point for our understanding of the early New England Founders, is that, whilst far from acknowledging this later group of Cambridge Platonists themselves, they actually fathered them. Their determination to reach logical conclusions about Biblical law, and to translate it into practical uses, incubated Cudworth and company into fledglings who flew the narrow nest of official Calvinism, and grew into great birds of prey to gobble up its more extreme exclusive sectarian aspects for ever; as, in fact, teachers like Hooker did also.

Thanks to this whole movement of thought it became easier for Calvinists in the English tradition to accept that Faith and Reason must live legitimately together. This did not happen to the same extent on the Continent of Europe, where Dogmatics flourished into the 20th century. But the Platonists were post-Hookerites, his natural successors. And the word was toleration, freedom of thought. If New England at first voted "perish the thought," it nonetheless eventually opened the highway for all sorts and conditions to come in.

In Hooker's Cambridge, an extended study of logic sharpened the student's perception, and elucidation, of demonstrable truth. The curriculum also included academic psychology, the science of the nature and function of the mind through the faculties of understanding, memory, and will; and metaphysics, the study of being and knowing; and moved towards the final goal of Biblical theology. The scene was set for the production of a godly, preaching, and intellectually critical clergy. Hooker, as already observed, was an apt pupil.

It is important to note that this was not necessarily a moralistic process. Many of the great preachers of the 17th and 18th centuries were anything but "moral." Pepys preferred them witty, scholarly, and inventive. The thrust of those colleges which had come under Calvinist influence, however, was that they bent these skills in rhetoric, logic, and metaphysics to an understanding of Scripture as the sole means of attaining a society acceptable to God.

The morality which flowed from, and all over, the Puritans was scriptural, not ethical, deriving from an intense longing to practice what they deduced the Scriptures required in the name of a moral God.

There was no remarkable outward change in Thomas Hooker, following his entry into a personal faith in his election to salvation. Just an assurance of mercy, and a confidence in the divine love which had stooped to save him. It was enough. Everything came together. Family training, neighbours and patrons of similar outlook, influential puritan clergy, the enviable status enjoyed by preachers, the market forces which invited young men of little fortune into the pulpit, and offered them a socio-political platform there. Add to these a personal inclination to counselling and the pastoral office, the vital equipment of education, and finally his own personal conviction of a sufficient mercy, and a divine calling. These comprise the historic ingredients of an effective call to ordained priesthood, and compelled Hooker into Holy Orders.

Cambridge contributed to the reconciliation of a further inner contradiction which Hooker shared with other Puritans. They acted all along as if the City of God were round the next corner, assuming its practicability, yet must have known how fragile were the promises. This was particularly so for Hooker. He spent his life within influential Puritan circles where the dream of the Kingdom of God on earth seemed in the process of becoming a reality. Yet they must have known the strength of the civil power ranged against pure reformation, the improbability of a Puritan coup.

And these same young Puritan parents must early have suspected that their children were not destined to become the saints they themselves sought to be. Many were disappointed, as the Hookers were to be in their eldest son John,[100] who quickly forsook the New England dream. Yet they never relinquished the expectation of rapid success. Such hope in hopelessness could come only from the extraordinary spirit within their group. It seems to have been established, at least in large part, by their experience at University.

It was Cambridge which welded together Hooker and many of his associates into a company of kindred spirits, several Jasons commanding some hundreds of Argonauts! And secured the comfort they needed for the conquest of a new world. Some followed the vision at home, like Robert Rich (1587–1658) second earl of Warwick,[101] Parliamentary High Admiral of the fleet, or Stephen Marshall (1594–1655)[102] born at Godmanchester, educated at Emmanuel,[103] lecturer at Wethersfield (name of one of the three original river towns of Connecticut), then at St Margaret's, Westminster, preacher to Parliament, another of the men who remade England by civil war. Others emigrated, many of them Emmanuel men. One third of the first 100 university graduates who planted New England were from Emmanuel, all Hooker's friends. And there was John Eliot, the Apostle.[104] He was at Jesus College from 1618–c. 1625, met Hooker whilst there, and followed him to Little Baddow as will presently appear. It will be convenient to visit Jesus now, rather than delay until the Chelmsford Section is reached.

Turn right when you leave Emmanuel, and return towards the town centre. Almost at once you will reach, on the right, the gateway of Christ's College.

Christ's College, In St Andrew's Street.
This is another Lady Margaret Beaufort foundation.[105] The gateway bears her coat of arms. Several noted Puritans were students or fellows here. You may wish to look in en passant. If you did not have time previously, carry on down Sidney Street from Christ's, and at the bottom of the road, where it joins Jesus Lane, call in at Sydney Sussex.

Sidney Sussex College.
Lady Frances (neé Sidney) widow of the Third Earl of Sussex of New Hall, Boreham (next Little Baddow) bequeathed the money to build "a goodly and godly monument for the maintenance of learning," in 1588.[106] It was completed in 1598, but largely restored in the 19th century. Oliver Cromwell was briefly here. He matriculated on 23 April 1616 before reading Law in London. The College had decidedly Puritan views. As Hooker was currently at the peak of his university career, Cromwell at least must have been well aware of him. Much of Cromwell's early life was focused on Cambridgeshire, much of his early energy absorbed in defending the rights of fellow commoners against evictions from the land enclosures which followed the draining of the marshlands especially round St Ives and Ely where he inherited land.

His wife was Elizabeth Bouchier, from Felsted in Essex, his aunt was Lady Barrington of Hatfield Broad Oak, whom we shall hear of at Little Baddow. It was only to be expected that he should lend his name to the petition addressed to Hooker in Connecticut, urging his return to England to advise the Westminster Assembly of 1643.[108]

Originally the Assembly was to revise the 39 Anglican Articles of 1563. Under pressure from the Scottish Presbyterians, and at the insistence of the Solemn League and Covenant (the agreement between the English and the Scots which ensured the overthrow of King Charles I) it produced instead the Westminster Confession of 1648, a Presbyterian not Puritan document. Hooker, forewarned, wisely refused so unpromising a voyage.

Now turn into Jesus Lane, bearing right, and Jesus College is on your left. Or from Christ's take Hobson Street at the three-way junction of St Andrew's and Sidney streets. This brings you into Jesus Lane via a right and left turn into Malcolm Street. Jesus College is across the road, on your right.

Jesus College, alma mater of John Eliot, Apostle to the Indians.
Our personal reason for visiting Jesus College is that John Eliot entered as a scholar in 1618, before joining Thomas Hooker at a grammar school they opened together at Cuckoos Farmhouse, Little Baddow, some time after 1625. The two men, their families, and their careers are closely linked from Cambridge onwards. Thus Jesus College becomes a vital part of the Thomas Hooker story.

A brief life of John Eliot will be found in Chapter 5, Chelmsford, of this volume.[109] His was an equally exceptional career, pregnant with Hooker's influence, but with his own natural genius contributing to one of the outstanding achievements of the New England plantation. His fame in his generation, and through the subsequent history of the United States of America, has received an even wider recognition than Hooker's. When we reach Little Baddow, we shall enter the world of John Eliot more closely, but we begin conveniently here, for it was at Jesus college that the paths of the two men first crossed.

Enter through the main gateway, an imposing seasoned brick structure of late 15th century date, superbly ornamented. Alcock's rebus, the cock predominant, is boldly displayed. You instantly breathe in another, more gracious age. The quadrangle lies before you, old buildings spilling into flower beds and miniature parkland, architecturally close to its original appearance when John Alcock, Bishop of Ely, established it in 1496.[110]

There had been a Benedictine Nunnery on the site since the year 1133, dedicated to St Radegund, 518–87.[111] She was a princess of Thuringia, but as a child was captured by invading Franks, and forced into marriage with King Clothaire I, a man reputed to be of debased character. His murder of her brother forced her to flee. She was ordained a deaconess, and founded her own monastery of nuns outside Poitiers. For thirty years she conducted it with outstanding piety, in recognition of which she was given "a large fragment of the true cross." This is said to have inspired her friend and chaplain, Venantius Fortunatus (535–600, Italian poet, author of a dozen volumes of occasional poems, and many hymns, bishop of Poitiers after her death) to write his well known *Vexilla regis*, "The royal banners forward go; The cross shines forth in mystic glow."

On a visitation in 1496, good bishop Alcock discovered only two nuns in residence besides the prioress. Some impropriety was suspected, and the Nunnery was hastily closed. At first he replaced it with a boys school, but it quickly blossomed into a full, if small, University College, with a Master, six Fellows, and a High Church tradition.

Many influential students came to Jesus College. Thomas Cranmer, 1489–1556,[112] Archbishop of Canterbury, and author of the Book of Common Prayer, both 1549 and 1552 editions, was here. An Erastian theologian, and a progressive Protestant, certainly from the time of his secret marriage to Margaret, niece of Andreas Osiander the celebrated Lutheran reformer, he was responsible for the abolition of many church ceremonies, and of the veneration of images and relics, which gave great hope to the more radical religious reformers. He also genuinely believed in the supremacy of the State over the Church, and served Henry VIII, apparently without qualms, in annulling his marriages to Catherine of Aragon, Anne Boleyn, and Anne of Cleves. He died a martyr's death under Queen Mary, burnt at the stake in Oxford, on 21 March 1556, and lives for ever in the incomparable english of the Prayer Book. His skills bear testimony to a tradition in linguistics at Jesus from which John Eliot was to benefit.

In 1554, two years before Cranmer's death, Thomas Thirlby, 1506–70,[113] was made bishop of Ely by Queen Mary. Years before, he had received the personal support of Cranmer, then a Fellow of Jesus College, and shared his wish to establish the new Church of England as a National Institution, not merely a repetition of the Continental Reformed churches. But his was the Roman Catholic wing of the English church, and he had opposed Cranmer's Prayer Book, much to Catholic Queen Mary's approval.

He had resisted the Puritan tendencies then sweeping Cambridge, and fully approved Thomas Cartwright's exclusion from St John's. He had the Prioress' Oratory restored at Jesus, and "the old ritual and ornaments." Surprisingly, "the Genevan psalms in metre" were introduced into the College liturgy a few years later, but by a Thomas Ithell[114] who was said to be "a safe man," presumably a royalist, so that legitimised the doggerel verse!

The emphasis from now on became Royalist and Conformist. Richard Bancroft, we have seen, moved to Jesus College from Puritan Christ's in the 1560s, and became an anti-Puritan Archbishop of Canterbury. The process was accelerated when Lancelot Andrewes (1555–1626;[115] Bishop of Ely in 1609) appointed his brother Roger to be the Master in 1618, the year of Eliot's admission.

Lancelot Andrewes was a most saintly man, dedicated to the ideal of the English Church. His aversion to Puritanism was only equalled by his love of Anglicanism, for him a reasonable, catholic faith, wide enough to include all true Englishmen. But his brother Roger's appointment was not a success.

One of Bishop Andrewes' friends was Richard Hooker, 1554–1600,[116] the famed Anglican ecclesiastical theologian, apologist for the Elizabethan Settlement of 1559, architect of an organic, not static churchmanship, reformed, but not too much. They cherished their continuity with the Medieval Church, and saw themselves firmly a part of the body politic, their churchmanship inseparable from it. Attempts have been made to trace a connection between Thomas and Richard Hooker, without success. Richard's family (alias Vowell) came from Exeter in Devon, and have no known relationship with the Hookers of Leicestershire.

When civil war broke out, Jesus upheld King Charles' cause. The college plate was melted down for payment of the royalist troops, in weight some 1,201 ounces of silver. The mild-mannered Earl of Manchester, parliamentary general, evicted all but two of the college staff in retaliation.[117]

From the above it could be assumed that John Eliot's family were good Anglicans, and that until he came under the aura of Thomas Hooker, his sentiments were conformist. There is no indication to the contrary during his college career. It cannot, however, be emphasised too often that many Puritans were outwardly, and patriotically conformist. Inwardly they longed to advance the reformation of the Church of England. They became angry, and afraid, when the opposite happened, especially under Archbishop Laud.

John was only fourteen when he entered college during the Lent Term of 1618.[118] He matriculated the following year, and graduated B.A. in 1622. By then his father, Bennett Eliot, had died. But he left a bequest for the deployment of certain land rents, to the tune of £8 per annum, to be made available to John until the completion of his college course. John is said to have excelled in languages, but that may be from the hindsight of his translation exploits in North America.

It is logical to deduce that he remained for his Master's degree because the reading of theology, and the natural progress towards ordination, habitually went with a Master's course; and Eliot is said to have been ordained by the orthodox Bishop of Ely before he joined Hooker at Little Baddow.

Cotton Mather makes this same assumption. "His liberal education having now the addition of religion to direct and improve it," he comments, "his first appearance in the world, after his education in the university, was in the too difficult and unthankful, but very necessary employment of a school-master—no more disgrace unto him than it was unto the famous Hieron."[119] In other words, Mather regarded it as degrading for Eliot to teach in a school when he could have practised as a clergyman.

Such a deduction is reinforced by Mather's inclusion of Eliot, in the *Magnalia*, as No. 18 in "the First Classis," a list of 77 Anglican clergymen "who were in the actual exercise of their ministry when they left England."[120] W. C. P. Tyack's doctoral thesis (found in the Essex Record Office) *Migration from East Anglia to New England Before 1660*, points to the same conclusion. Tyack shows Eliot's name on the ship's register of the Lyon as "cleric." Governor Winthrop met the vessel on her arrival at Boston. His wife and members of his family were on board. He describes their reunion in his Journal, but mentions no other passengers except "Mr Eliot, a minister."[121]

This by no means proves his ordination in the absence of any official evidence, but the fact that John Eliot was immediately called to become caretaker pastor at the First Church of Boston is another strong indication in its favour. The elders of New England churches did not countenance other than ordained clergymen of the Church of England as their ministers at that early stage, not with Archbishop William Laud fulminating in England against any irregular practices amongst the settlers, and sticklers for propriety in the congregation like John Winthrop at Boston, and Thomas Dudley at Newtown.

The case is further strengthened by the refusal of Roger Williams, himself an ordained clergyman to fill the place of Boston's minister, John Wilson.[122] Wilson was the son of Dr William Wilson, Prebendary of St Paul's, Rochester, and Windsor, and of his wife, a niece of Dr Edmund Grindal former Archbishop of Canterbury—impeccable credentials. Wilson had returned to England for family reasons, and Roger Williams, as already noted, refused to stand in for him because, he objected, the Boston church was "unseparated" from the Church of England; and that was as unacceptable to iconoclastic Roger as he was to the people of Massachusetts who summarily exiled him for contumacy later on.

That John Eliot was able, without warning, to undertake the pastorate at Boston, and to occupy its pulpit for the ensuing year so acceptably that the deacons urged him to remain as assistant to John Wilson when the latter returned, argues strongly for Eliot's practice of ordained ministry in England over a lengthy period. Else where did the knowledge of how to organise a large parish come from? Or the weekly sermons preached before one of the most critical, theologically advanced congregations in the whole world? They hadn't braved the Atlantic to be fobbed off onto an inexperienced boy fresh out of college!

The "Great Plague of London" in 1625, with 35,417 recorded deaths, may have been responsible for the lack of hard evidence. It was widely

.diffused throughout England. Life at Cambridge was paralysed, most of the undergraduates departed, no lectures were given for a period of six months, and graduation procedures were disrupted.[123] It is therefore possible that John Eliot continued his studies at Jesus College after 1622, that he completed his Master's degree and was ordained some time around 1625/6, and that he joined the ranks of ordained schoolmasters at Cuckoos at that same period, for the want of other preferment due to his nonconformity, or out of personal commitment to Thomas Hooker.

Bishop Alcock carefully preserved much of the original building at Jesus college, including the Nun's Chapel, the Hall, and the Old Library on the top floor. In the long fragrant Old Library a copy of Eliot's 1663 Indian Bible is stored, inscribed

> Pro Collegio Jesu,
> Accipias mater quod alumnus humillimus offert
> Filius, oro preces semper, habere tuas.
> > Johannes Eliot.[124]

which may be translated "To Jesus College. Accept, mother, I pray, what a most humble alumnus offers, a son ever having thy prayers."

To touch it is to tremble for the pain it communicates. "Prayer and pains through Faith in Jesus Christ will do anything,"[125] John wrote from the perils of serving the Indians in the wilderness. His Algonquian Bible is a living testimony to it, its inscription an indication of his indebtedness to his Cambridge experience. In this he was joined by many of New England's pioneers.

American Military Cemetery And Memorial, Coton, Cambridgeshire.

Before leaving Cambridge there is one further place to visit. The American World War II Cemetery maintained by the Battle Monuments Commission. It was begun on 7 December 1943, the second anniversary of Pearl Harbour. The thirty acre site, donated by the University, was selected for its scenic grandeur, and because a high proportion of American casualties occurred from their East Anglian bases.

Entrance is from the A45 going west towards St Neots on the Madingley Road three miles from Cambridge, past the new Churchill College (memorial to Sir Winston Churchill) on the right-hand side.

There is a well appointed Visitors Centre at one end, a Memorial Chapel at the other. These are separated by the long high Wall of the Missing, with the 5,125 names of those whose remains were never recovered or identified, standing in awesome, tragic tribute over the graves of 3,811 others who also died in the Atlantic and Northwest European battles.

The Chapel is adorned with magnificent bronze doors, symbolic stained glass, a mosaic ceiling, and a large wall-map depicting American participation in the European sphere of operations.

In front of the Visitors Centre a 72– foot flagpole has these words on its base: "To you from falling hands we throw the torch—Be yours to hold it high."

There is no fitter testimony to the Founding Fathers of this momentous Nation, as well as to its contemporary defenders, where pain is justly touched with pride, and death transformed to life.

CHAPTER 4

ESHER, SURREY

Pastoral Practice and Counselling Perfected

c. 1620–1625

ESHER ST GEORGE'S,
Thomas Hooker's First Pastoral Charge

How to get there.

Esher in the County of Surrey[1] is some 14 miles south-west of Central London, roughly between Walton-on-Thames to the west, Kingston-on-Thames to the east, and scarcely three miles due south of Hampton Court Palace. The most natural way for a visitor to Britain to investigate Esher would be whilst staying in London. It is a 25–minute train journey from Waterloo Railway Station, or accessible by car or coach from the London to Portsmouth Road (A3), or from the South Orbital Road (M25, exit 10), and is well sign-posted from both directions.

St George's Church is situated immediately behind the Bear Hotel, a well-known local landmark in the town centre where, after your tour, you may comfortably refresh yourself. If you travel by rail, leave Esher Station by Station Road, turn right at Portsmouth Road, and the town centre is about ten minutes walk away. If by road, the church stands, fronting tree-shaded grounds, at the multiple central cross-roads where Portsmouth Road (renamed High Street on its west-side) crosses Claremont Lane and Church Street, with Esher Park Avenue, Park Road, and Lammas Lane in close attendance, an islet in a motorised vortex which somehow retains an aura of undiminished peace not easily forgotten.

At the time of writing, there is limited car parking space in front of St George's, and at the rear of the Bear Hotel. Other central parking sites are also available, or in course of construction.

St George's is no longer in regular use, and is now in the care of The Redundant Churches Fund.[2] It is, however, open for visiting every Saturday from the beginning of April to the end of September, 10:30 am - 12:30 pm.

Esher Place Gatehouse,
all that remains of the
mansion where Hooker
lived, 1620–1625.

Access can be arranged at other
times, by prior appointment,
through The Parish Office at
Christ Church, just across the
road at The Green, Esher (Tuesday to Friday, 10:30am - 1:00pm).
You need to call at Christ Church
in any case, if only for the fine
Elizabethan monument in the
south aisle to Sir Richard Drake,
removed from St George's when
Christ Church was opened. Sir
Richard purchased Esher Place
in 1583, and bequeathed it to his
son, Mr Francis Drake, who invited Thomas Hooker into residence there, when Hooker came as Rector in 1620.[3]

Christ Church[4] was constructed in 1853 to accommodate the increasing populations of the last century, when Esher ceased to be the small rural village Hooker and his young wife knew so well, and was swallowed up in the growth of Greater London. It is a church of considerable Victorian distinction, its spire a pivot of spiritual direction wherever you look in central Esher, its interior appropriately lofty for Queen Victoria's frequent attendances,[5] its monuments to her uncle Leopold, King of the Belgians,[6] and her youngest son, the Duke of Albany,[7] adding to its attractions.

Sir Francis Drake And The Drakes Of Esher.

Our major interest, however, is fixed on St George's where Thomas Hooker had his first experience of pastoral ministry, and on the Drakes of Esher who worshipped there.

The connection of the renowned seafaring Drakes of Devon with Esher in Surrey was by no means fortuitous. Every family wishing for influence at court required a London residence, and Esher Place was suitably situated for that purpose, its attractive parklands close to Hampton Court, and accessible to Westminster by road or by the River Thames. It had been one of the residences of Lord Howard of Effingham,[8] High Admiral of the fleet as his father had been before him.

Now the seafaring fraternity of England was relatively small and Lord Howard well knew the men who ventured their lives at sea. Indeed, Sir Francis Drake, kinsman to Sir Richard of Esher, was Howard's second-in-command at the Armada, and is thought personally to have intervened in Sir Richard's advancement. No one would have been surprised when Sir Richard succeeded the High Admiral at Esher Place.

Lady Eliott-Drake, in her carefully researched *Family and Heirs of Sir Francis Drake*, thinks that Sir Francis was responsible for Sir Richard's appointment as an equerry to Queen Elizabeth, and for his consequent knighthood. Francis also purchased the moiety of Yarcombe, an estate near Honiton in Devon which belonged to Richard, in order that the latter might use the money to buy Esher Place, and set himself up at Court.[9]

Sir Richard Drake (1534–1603) and Tudor England's greatest seaman Sir Francis Drake (1542–1596) evidently had a strong attachment to each other, Richard being known as "one that Sir Francis Drake did specially account and regard as his trusty friend."[10] They called each other "cousin" although the relationship is not altogether clear. However, their fathers were Devonians, and are presumed to have descended from collateral branches of the same family.

The one was John of Ashe, grandson of old John Drake of Otterton who purchased a large property at Ashe (both in Devon) and started the family's fortunes. His eldest son was Sir Bernard Drake of Ashe, eldest brother of Sir Richard of Esher. The other was Edmund, father of Sir Francis Drake, the impoverished younger son of John and Margery Drake of Tavistock in Devon.[11]

The Drakes of Tavistock were yeomen farmers at Crownedale, a farm of only some 180 acres leased first from Tavistock Abbey and then, following the Dissolution, from Francis Russell second Earl of Bedford, into whose possession the abbey lands came, and whose patronage Sir Francis Drake was to enjoy at a later date.[12]

These two branches of the Drake family parted company when Edmund fled from Tavistock into Kent. He was implicated with a John Hawkins (probably of the famous seafaring family to whom the Drakes were related) in charges of theft and assault on the King's highway in 1548, and in the 1549 Cornish uprising against Edward VI's imposition of the new Prayer Book, and the related Act of Uniformity.[13]

Edmund earned a meagre income as a protestant lay preacher amongst the predominantly maritime population around the Medway Ports in Kent, where much of the royal fleet was concentrated, and where young Francis served his apprenticeship in seamanship. He was ordained Vicar of Upchurch, Kent, in 1561, but that was long afterwards, and his twelve sons, of whom Francis was the eldest, had a hard struggle to establish themselves, as they did with remarkable brilliance. However, Edmund bequeathed to them a strong protestant faith which linked his descendants with religious and political reform, if not with outright Puritanism.

So it was that, although intensely loyal to their sovereign, the Drakes were allied to the reformist parties in Parliament throughout the Tudor period. Under the Stuarts, Sir Francis' successors sided with parliament, and his great-nephew the second baronet, also named Sir Francis (who married Dorothea Pym, daughter of John Pym, 1584–1643, the great statesman of parliamentary liberty, and a long-standing friend of the Drakes) fought against King Charles as a colonel in Cromwell's cavalry during the Civil War.[14]

The solid wealth and social position at first lay with the senior branch represented by Sir Bernard Drake of Ashe, elder brother of Sir Richard of Esher. This Bernard was a privateer out of the same rip-roaring mould. Commissioned in June 1585 by Elizabeth to harry the Spanish ships operating against the English fishing fleets bound for Newfoundland, he executed his charge with such dispatch that she dubbed him knight at Greenwich on his return, as she had done his cousin Francis when the *Golden Hind* docked at Deptford four years earlier. We may have heard more of Sir Bernard at the Armada had he not tragically died of goal fever, contracted from the crew of the *Lion*, a Portuguese ship captured on his way home from Greenwich in 1586.

But when, on 26 September 1580, the *Golden Hind* had returned to Plymouth after circumnavigating the world, Sir Francis Drake had instantly become a national hero, and amassed such treasure and estates as enabled him to benefit many of his relations, as he did out of his generous heart. He loaned Sir Bernard £600, assisted Sir Richard's career as we have seen, and later permitted him to retain some £1,500 of the ransom paid for his Armada captive Don Pedro de Valdes. He also arranged in his will for the Yarcombe estate to be restored to Richard's son Francis (his godson, and Thomas Hooker's patron) at a considerably reduced cost. It appears that the Drakes of Esher lived beyond their means and were frequently in want of money.[15]

This gives the lie to a story once circulated that Sir Bernard was hostile to Sir Francis and boxed his ears for appropriating the Ashe crest (a red demi-wyvern) when awarded a coat-of-arms. Queen Elizabeth was said to have had a replica of the red dragon hung by the heels from the *Golden Hind's* masthead in support of her champion.[16] But the preposterous yarn was short lived. The fact is that the Drake boys adventured together. Bernard's eldest son John sailed with his uncle, as did Francis' brothers John, Joseph, and Thomas, and their nephew Jonas Bodenham, and Sir Richard is known to have adventured money in Francis' exploits, notably the San Domingo and Carthagena voyage of 1585–86, which accounts for John

Aubrey's[17] claim that the church bell from San Domingo was re-hung in St George's bell tower at Esher. Alas, it is no longer there. The present bell dates from 1799, its companions melted down to make a ring of six bells for the new Christ Church.

The captivity of Don Pedro de Valdes at Esher Place must have lingered on in local memories when Thomas Hooker took up residence there.[18] Its entanglements contributed to his pastoral responsibilities. Briefly, Don Pedro was Admiral of the Andalusian squadron of the Armada, and commander of the *Nuestra Senora del Rosario*, a 1150 ton, 52 gunned ship, one of the largest in the Spanish fleet. Sir Francis Drake forced her surrender. She proved a sumptuous prize for she carried one third of the Armada's cash, as well as jewels and private treasure. There was considerable jealousy of Sir Francis when his habitual luck placed his ship, the *Revenge*, in the Rosario's path at crack of dawn on 22 July 1588, early in the running sea-battle.

Don Pedro yielded himself prisoner, and spent the rest of his captivity at Esher Place under Sir Richard Drake's surveillance, with his two captains Don Alonso de Cayas of Laja, and Don Vascoe de Medoca y de Silva of Xeres de los Cavalleros (their ransom alone amounted to £900). Crowds of onlookers came to Esher in hope of catching a glimpse of these celebrated captives.

Sir Francis granted his cousin £4 per week for maintenance, liberally supplied the Place with fine wines, and allowed Sir Richard to receive the ransom of some £3,550, of which it was later admitted that he kept £1,500 to cover the expenses of his son, Francis' marriage to the heiress Joane Tothill.

John Sugden in his recent biography *Sir Francis Drake* (1990) amply shows that religion was the driving force of the Drake legend.[19] Sir Francis saw himself as God's avenger against the iniquities of Catholic Spain and the Inquisition. His part in the development of an aggressive Puritanism can hardly be denied. His contribution to life at Esher was theatrically large. And Thomas Hooker expressed the same urgent, uncompromising holy warfare. If he did not actually imbibe the Drake legend at Esher, he exemplified it. He would fight for his faith, as when the Pequot Indians threatened the survival of the founding settlements in New England. He was a hammer of the Lord against sinners, even though at Esher he was to produce a very different, reconciling result. Let us turn from the Drake legend to the Drake church.

Illustrious St George's, Thomas Hooker's First Church.

St George's occupies a site thought to have contained a church from Saxon times. The present building, however, dates from c. 1540. By then Henry VIII had taken possession of Esher Place, and proceeded to depopulate the area in order to absorb it into his Hampton Court hunting range.

The Hooker Pulpit, St George's, Esher

The church fell into decay, maybe disuse. It was extensively restored in 1548, when Edward VI was persuaded to exclude Esher from the chase, and the population was able to return, and resume normal Parish life.[20]

The diminutive chancel and nave (20 by 18 feet and 35 by 22 feet respectively) are typically Tudor, and, to my taste, of engaging pleasantness both in external appearance, and inner interest. The large extensions, of the Newcastle Pew in 1725, and the distinctive North Aisle of 1812, with its incongruously battlemented roof, harmonise happily with the original building.

The church is full of fascinating furnishings, intimations of English social history from Tudor to Victorian times. There were, for instance, three galleries to accommodate the compulsory attendance of earlier parishioners of which the lower, west end gallery was there in Hooker's day. It also enshrines stories of high drama, and some melancholy, such as Mrs Francis Drake's dementia (to be discussed later), and the Princess Charlotte.

The North Aisle opens out behind curtains on your left and holds a Monument to Princess Charlotte, only child and heiress presumptive of King George IV. She tragically died in childbirth the year following her marriage to Leopold Saxe-Coburg, later King of the Belgians.[21] It is grandly executed by one of Queen Victoria's favourite sculptors, F. J. Williamson of Esher,[22] who also designed the bust of the Duke of Albany in Christ Church.

Charlotte was born on January 7, 1796 at Carlton House, the London residence of her father, George Augustus, son of George III, when he was the dissolute if brilliant Prince of Wales. The columns from the great portico on Pall Mall were removed to front the National Gallery in Trafalgar Square when Carlton House was demolished in 1826.

The marriage of Charlotte's parents was a disaster from the start. Her mother, Princess Caroline of Brunswick,[23] was formally separated from her husband shortly after her daughter's birth, access to the child was severely restricted, and George neglected his daughter altogether, so that she was brought up in virtual isolation. But she was described as "bright, intelligent and very merry," and was popular with the populace.

When Leopold proposed to her in the Spring of 1816, the love-match received wide acclaim. They were married at Carlton House on May 2nd that same year, and went to live at Claremont House, Esher. Charlotte died a few hours after being delivered of a still-born son, on 6 November 1817. She was buried in St George's Chapel, Windsor amidst widespread sadness that so swift an end should blight so unfulfilled a life, expressed in a contemporary ditty:

Never was sorrow more sincere
Than that which flowed round Charlotte's bier.

Charlotte and Leopold worshipped at St George's during the early days of their marriage, but had to desist because of the bad behaviour of "The Quality," who came to flaunt their finery before them. They used the Newcastle Pew before being forced to withdraw to private worship in their home. You will have noticed it, for it dominates the south aisle.

Sir John Vanbrugh, creator of the Churchill home at Blenheim Palace, designed the Chamber Pew for the Duke of Newcastle.[24] It consists of a brick building clasped to the south wall, nearly as large as the chancel itself, which provided a private side-entrance, and private elevated accommodation, for the residents of Claremont and Esher Place. At the time they were the families of two brothers, Thomas Duke of Newcastle, and his brother Henry Pelham, each in his turn Parliamentary Prime Minister. But the families required an even greater privacy, for they erected a high partition wall down the centre of the pew, and a fireplace in each section, the eastern part reserved for Esher Place, the western for Claremont.

Princess Victoria spent many holidays at Claremont with her favourite uncle Leopold and is the source of a delightful story. A wasp with social pretentions beyond its proper station invaded the Newcastle pew one Sunday service, to the distraction of the occupants except for the young princess. She was required by her governess to report on the sermon each week, and with perfect aplomb proceeded to recite its contents afterwards, when nothing but the wasp filled the recollection of the others. *Verbum sapienti!*

Ask permission to enter the Chamber Pew, and you will look out onto the fine 18th century three-decker pulpit, the preacher in the top deck at exactly the right height for the convenience of the pew's occupants. The altar in the Chancel retains its Laudian fence, in obedience to William Laud's edict of 1640. You can still see the marks on the south side where a further rail prevented commoners from touching the communicants come down from the Newcastle Pew.

On the north wall of the Chancel you will see a monument to Lady Vere Lynch, a painting on wood which shows her kneeling at a prie-dieu. Her husband, Sir Thomas Lynch, was Governor of Jamaica in the 1670s, when sugar was first imported into Britain, a reminder of the maritime connections of this remarkable church.[25] Lynch was periodically in trouble because of his association with the infamous Captain (later Sir) Henry Morgan, the Welsh pirate of the Caribbean. Morgan was known for his ruthless slaughter of friend and foe alike, but he was useful to English interests in the face of the powerful Spanish presence, and the English had blind eyes a'plenty where profitable privateering was concerned.

Sir Richard Drake memorial in Christ Church, Esher, originally at St. George's, Esher

To the south of the Chancel, where Sir Richard Drake's monument was once suspended, there are two by John Flaxman (1755–1826),[26] the gifted modeller of Wedgewood pottery, and more celebrated monumental-sculptor. These commemorate members of the family of Charles Ellis, Tory leader, friend of William Pitt, who sold Claremont to the Crown in readiness for Charlotte's occupation. His second wife was the widow of Admiral Hardy,[27] Nelson's trusty friend, a further sea-faring relic, as could be the columns, reputed to be ships masts, used in the construction of the north aisle, and the cannonball weights (probably taken from one of Sir Francis Drake's ships) used in the antique clock, which were originally raised by a small capston, said to be the "first (such) form of turret clock winding." An account from 1682 for repairs is extant, which suggests that the clock dates from the reconstruction of St George's in the 1540s.

More remains to gratify the visitor, but we should hurry a little in order to include Esher Place and Claremont in this very full day's itinerary.

Esher Place, Wolsey, Henry VIII, Howard Of Effingham, And "Mrs Drake Revived."

A 13th century manor house was built by the Bishops of Winchester at Esher, a part-time lodge to shelter them when they toured their large Diocese. Bishop Wayneflete (1395–1486)[28] enlarged it into a palace, and there Cardinal Wolsey, as Bishop of Winchester, one of his many titles, came for refuge when he fell from power in 1529. He waited for the recall that never came, conveniently out of sight, yet near to court. But Henry VIII was by that time determined to take up the reins of government himself, and the broken Wolsey withdrew to his Archbishop's Palace at York, to die at Leicester Abbey, as we have seen, when finally summonsed back for trial in London.

Thus Henry entered into doubtful possession of Esher Place and enclosed the parklands for his better hunting when at Hampton Court. From the Crown, Esher passed to Baron Charles Howard of Effingham (1536–1624) of Armada fame. The place could scarcely have enjoyed a nobler connection, for Lord Charles, later first Earl of Nottingham amongst other honours, "a striking, almost heroic figure,"[29] was not only connected to the great family of Howards, Dukes of Norfolk, but exercised a determinative influence over Queen Elizabeth, for instance persuading her to execute Mary Queen of Scots against her better judgement. He was also Lord Lieutenant of Surrey, High Steward of Kingston-on-Thames, and needed a residence equally within the County but close to London. The village of Effingham is scarcely ten miles from Esher, but he soon moved into great Haling House, near Croydon in the same county. There he died, having held office as Lord High Admiral until retirement at 86 years, in 1618.

The inhabitants of Esher must have felt honoured at his residence, despite his royal predecessors; a comment too on the status of Sir Richard Drake, who followed Lord Howard, and enhanced St George's with trophies of his own.

Nothing remains of Wayneflete's Palace except "Wayneflete's (sometimes called Wolsey's) Tower." This was the gatehouse built by Bishop Wayneflete, c. 1478. It can be viewed via the private road which runs between Lammas and More lanes over the green from Christ Church.

You go through the two lodges at the entrance to Esher Place Estate, an unusually lovely building development of costly dwellings, flanked by well tended gardens and stately trees, down Wayneflete Tower Avenue. This is very private property, but a discreet peep at the bulky old red-brick tower from Pelham Walk will bring no instant arrest to the courteous, unobtrusive tourist. You might even sneak a photograph through the surrounding hedge.

The Emmanuel College accounts record a final payment to Hooker, dated 26 October 1618, which intimates that his Fellowship terminated at some time towards the close of that year. We do not know what interests he may have pursued in the interim, before taking up the Esher appointment, if any.[30] What is known is that it was worth no more than £40 per annum, insufficient for a rector's proper maintenance, and that he consequently lived at Esher Place with his patrons, Mr and Mrs Francis Drake.

It was a strenuous household for a sensitive pastoral counsellor, the crucial problem being Mrs Joane Drake. She was the eldest of three daughters born to wealthy parents (Sir William and Lady Catherine Tothill of

Shardeloes Manor, Amersham in Buckinghamshire) "whose too great indulgence towards her in her youth (by her own confession) occasioned so
much sorrow unto her riper years."[31]

As their principal heir she was a very wealthy woman in her own right,
but with that disastrous interplay of spoiling and tyrannising which comes
too easily to some over-indulgent parents, they insisted on a socially attractive match with Francis Drake which abhorred her. She was married against
her will, "wherein though she were obedient and dutiful unto her Parents,
yet it stuck close unto her."[32]

We are fortunate to have an eye-witness account of the disturbances
in the Drake household from a friend of the family, Jasper Hartwell, in his
Trodden Down Strength by the God of Strength. Or, Mrs Drake Revived, published
1647. He was a barrister, who frequently visited at Esher Place from his
chambers in Whitefriars, London, by the Fleet Ditch, where an Abbey of
Carmelite white friars once occupied the long strip of land which runs from
present day Fleet Street down to the Thames.

It is marked today by Whitefriars Street at the junction of Fleet Street,
and becomes Carmelite Street at its lower end, where it joins the Victoria
Embankment close by Blackfriars bridge. The two halves of the single street
are transversed by Tudor Street, half-way down—a precise historical description in street names of what has happened on this site for anyone in
the know, like you!

Hartwell's *Trodden Down Strength* was republished seven years afterwards as *The Firebrand Taken Out Of The Fire. Or, the Wonderful History, Care,
and Cure of Mrs Drake* (London 1654). The incident has been imaginatively
researched in recent years by George Hunston Williams in his *Called By Thy
Name, Leave Us Not: The Case of Mrs Joan Drake, A Formative Episode in the
Pastoral Career of Thomas Hooker in England* (Harvard, 1968), which presents
the events surrounding Joane Drake at Esher Place as a cause celebre, that
contributed to the experience and reputation of Hooker in no small measure.

The situation was further exacerbated by some unpleasant defects in
the character of her husband, Mr Francis Drake. Lady Eliott-Drake's conclusion is quite devastating. "For Francis Drake of Esher," she writes, "nothing
favourable can be said. A man who is willing for the sake of gain to blacken
his father's character would calumniate anyone else for a trifle."[33] Lady
Drake writes from the viewpoint of her branch of the family, who were
legally assaulted by a lawsuit concocted by Jonas Bodenham and Francis
Drake, and may be considered prejudiced, but the case was undoubtedly
scandalous.

It is too complicated for more than a terse review here, which cannot
do justice to all the factors involved. After the death of Sir Francis Drake, his

nephew Jonas Bodenham (his "secretary and receiver" for many years) and his godson Francis Drake appear to have connived together to incriminate the late Sir Francis for their own gain. Anxious for their inheritance, and suspicious of Thomas Drake (Sir Francis' youngest brother and sole executor) they charged Sir Francis with having embezzled moneys due to the Crown from the San Domingo adventure of 1586, and the capture of the Rosario in 1588, in the sum of £3,151 18s 5p, plus an unspecified number of gold pistolettes. And they claimed this amount for themselves, by way of reward. Francis implicated his own father in this knowingly false charge.

Francis of Esher's motives were complex. He feared that the dying Queen Elizabeth could not be prevailed upon to provide his near-to-death father (her equerry, Sir Richard) with a hard-earned and urgently needed pension. Lady Eliott-Drake calls Sir Richard "extravagant, and in mature age grasping and not too nicely scrupulous where the advantage of his son was concerned." The Esher Drakes, as we know, were habitually short of money. They had expected the return of the lucrative Yarcombe estate from the will of Sir Francis Drake (sold to Sir Francis years before in order to buy Esher Place, and half promised by Sir Francis to his godson), and were angry that the will required an advance of £2,000 in exchange. They could not afford the price, even though the estate was worth four times as much. But they would have had the money if Queen Elizabeth had provided the pension for Sir Richard they considered his due. Thomas Drake, as executor, demanded the full amount. So they lost Yarcombe, and never forgave him.

Queen Elizabeth died in the same year as Sir Richard without settling any pension on her old servant. Francis of Esher immediately pressed the claim on King James I, to whom he was appointed an equerry as his father had been, and the king supported the outrageous proposal. The case dragged on until summarily concluded by the death of Thomas Drake in 1606, bringing satisfaction to none of the participants, except for the complete exoneration of Sir Francis Drake.

It appears to have been a disgraceful affair so far as Francis Drake of Esher was concerned, and suggests that his need for a lucrative marriage in order to recoup his own fortune may well have outweighed any consideration of suitability. In his own eyes Francis may have been justified, for he regarded both Yarcombe and the pension as properly belonging to him. But his exposure in the courts, the legal costs he sustained, and, one hopes, the pangs of conscience his devout Puritan spirit should have suffered, must have contributed to the failure of his marriage, and to the tension within his household. That Thomas Hooker emerged without criticism or stain from the Esher-syndrome, reflects his own integrity and sensitivities.

After ten years of misery, despite the propitious birth of two sons, the delivery of a baby daughter brought on a complete collapse for Mrs Drake.

The midwife was blamed for bungling the birth. "She was ever after troubled with fumes and scurvie vapours—which no physic could remove."[34] Her mother came to nurse her, probably the worst possible solution for Joane's paedo-psychotic needs, and blame was transferred to her. The tantrums increased. "She was undone, she was damned, and a castaway, and so of necessity must needs goe to Hell, and therewith shook, dropt down with sweat, and wept exceedingly." She was convinced she had committed the unforgivable sin against the Holy Ghost and, being beyond divine help, seems to have determined to make her household share in paying for her miseries.

It was an extraordinary, and pathetically painful case, which arouses our sympathy for the pampered, spoilt girl who was forced into an incompatible union with all the binding prohibitions of a condemnatory religious upbringing. Sick of life, terrified of death, ridden with guilt, desperate for a way out. Poor Joane! In this more liberal age we feel only understanding and shame for the narrow cultural demands which brought about her condition. But one cannot resist the feeling that the lady was also enjoying herself!

She had a dozen clerical counsellors flocking round her, amongst them the venerable John Dod[35] who introduced Hooker to her husband as a suitable spiritual physician for his wife. Born at Shotlidge, in Cheshire, the youngest of seventeen children, Dod entered Jesus College, Cambridge when fourteen years old, in 1563. As a scholar and a fellow he earned a high reputation. He was "witty and cheerful," though, as a good Puritan, a severe critic of drunken roisterers.

On one occasion he was waylaid by students indignant at his pulpit polemics against alcohol. They thrust him inside a hollow tree, threatening to keep him there until he had preached to their greater satisfaction on a subject more congenial to them. It was the pregnant if intoxicating word "malt." His unpremeditated response explains his popularity as a preacher. "Beloved I am a little man, come at a short warning to deliver a brief discourse upon a small subject, to a thin congregation, and from an unworthy pulpit." He then proceeded to expand upon every letter of his text, and his ad hoc congregation let him go.

His ministry alternated between long and acceptable pastorates interrupted by his silencing for nonconformity, but his faith had been born out of an illness which came in the wake of false accusations of embezzlement when at college, and was not easily overborne. His natural humanity together with his scholarly gifts led people to welcome him. His *A Plaine and Familiar Exposition of the Ten Commandments* proved widely popular, and earned him the name of "Decalogue Dod." His admirers even pasted it on the walls of their houses.

I mention this because one would suppose him, at nearly seventy years of age, with his wide experience of people under stress, his common touch and lively mind, to have been ideally suited for the easing of Mrs Drake's condition. On the contrary, a further incredible story was laid at his door, or on his unprotected pate. Whilst he was praying with the sufferer, Joane Drake took down one of the bed-rails and belaboured him with it!

Picture the scene. Ancient Dod on his knees beside the four-poster bed, beset with costly hangings as fitted a lady of wealth. His fine voice takes on a richer resonance from the solid wood, polished oak or beech for a great bed from her native Amersham. The lady is perhaps moved with gratitude, if not with comfort; but the little incubus within guides her eye to one of the railings which uphold the canopy overhead. Up goes the tiny hand, down plunges the mighty beam, and out flies the diminutive Dod!

Now Thomas Hooker "being newly come from the University had a new answering method—wherewith shee was marvellously delighted,"[36] and the cure began. It sounds like an early form of psychoanalysis, but it was more than that. The young chaplain needed to meet his hostess at every point of scripture and doctrine with a clarification even her argumentativeness could not distort into some twisted, self-gratifying condemnation. Then he must advance irrefutable yet attractive reasons to the contrary, never missing a trick, nor declaring his hand until she was ready to be convinced and converted. Miracles of patience as he kept the initiative in his own hands, with adequate wisdom and understanding. This was to become a commonplace experience for those who sought his guidance, or received his correction, as his ministry advanced upon the founding of new cities in an empty land, but it blossoms here, in fragile Esher Place.

The birth of a third son, John, at about the time of Hooker's arrival in Esher, had finally brought the matter to a head.[37] The infant lived only 3 years, and was taken back by his mother, after his death on 2 April 1623, to Amersham for burial in what is now the Drake Chapel. One wonders if this tragic episode jolted her mind from the self-centred obsessiveness which may even have contributed to the child's death. There she followed him two years later. It is of passing interest to observe that after twenty years of marriage, Joane Drake's spirit remained in her childhood home at Shardeloes Manor, Amersham. She would never come to terms with Esher.

Others were involved. Stories circulated of her barricading herself inside her Esher bedroom, "whereupon her husband took the great iron fork, and run up after her, threatening to beat down the door if she would not open it."[38] Even the saintly John Preston, who succeeded Chaderton as Master of Emmanuel tried his skills; and the formidable "Roaring" Rogers, friend of Hooker, long-time lecturer at Dedham, Essex, was talked into offering her the sanctuary of his home, though mercifully for his family, the scheme came to nothing.

John Forbes,[39] Scottish Minister at Amsterdam, who sheltered Hooker in his Dutch exile, called to see her. James Usher,[40] archbishop of Armagh, Calvinist scholar and eminent divine, added his counselling aid. But to Thomas Hooker's patient strength, indomitable intellect, and boundless charity, Hartwell most accredits "Mrs Drake Revived." She died in 1625, not long before the Hookers removed to Chelmsford, upheld (it is said) by an adoring family, replete with sanctity, a woman restored to God and to herself.

The contribution made by Thomas and Susannah Hooker to unravelling the tangled lives of the Esher Place residents did not go unrecognised. Francis Drake left a bequest in his will, dated 13 March 1634, to the Hooker's first-born child, named after his wife, "Johana Hooker who is now in New England £30 to be paid her on the day of her marriage."[41] When the time arrived, Joane was with her parents in Connecticut, and returned to her father's former church at Newtown (Cambridge), Massachusetts, married to his successor and friend, Thomas Shepard. It would be nice to know what the £30 was spent on.

An outcome of the Esher days, it is generally agreed, was the first sermon by Hooker to be published (anonymously for fear of reprisal), *The Poor Doubting Christian Drawne Unto Christ*, printed in London, 1629. It proved to be his most popular work, reprinted and revised in a variety of editions throughout the next 200 years. It was undoubtedly the fruit of his protracted counselling sessions with Mrs Drake.

The opening sentence is revealing in itself. "There are divers lets and impediments which hinder poor Christians from coming unto Christ, all which I desire to reduce to these following heads;"[42] he then classifies the general categories ("hindrances as really keep men from coming to take hold of Christ at all; those kinds which make the way more tedious" etc.) and enumerates particular issues, some reminiscent of his struggle with Mrs Drake, as "see my sins I do, but this is my misery, I cannot be burdened with them, I have a heart that cannot mourn;" or "How ill I am, when all the means in the world do me no good—I feel my heart more hard and stubborn under God's ordinances, and therefore my condition is hopeless," but always with the cry "should I think that there is any mercy for me?" set against his text "Every man therefore that hath heard, and learned of the Father, cometh unto me." (John 6, v. 45)

Hooker is very positive in this sermon, as if he had been this way many times before and knew its healing termination from long experience. In it he lays the foundation of what has been termed "preparationist theology," a faith to lead people out of doubt into a position where belief becomes possible, rather than to condemn them, "or consider them so as to be hindered from coming to God for mercy, which God offers us and we want."

It is the counselling-practitioner's approach. "Now I will shew you some means whereby a man may so improve his time that at last he may obtain the blessed grace." Yet he remains true to his Calvinist theology, that all is of God alone. "You must wait upon God in the use of the means, for it is not the means that will do it, that will work faith, but the spirit of God."

The dilemma for the Puritans lay in the apparent contradiction of high moral demands with an absolute dependence on the grace of God. Why bother with ethical behaviour if ultimately nothing counts apart from God's own action? Hooker's contribution was crucial. He accepted people as they were, and bent his energies towards preparing them to receive something better.

This permitted a much more open approach to vexed problems like church membership, and rights of citizenship for those who did not evince the marks of a fully sanctified life. Who did! How prone to hypocrisy and dissembling must have been the policy of "No visible sanctity, no church membership, no property ownership, and no vote," such as prevailed at first in Massachusetts but never in Hooker's Connecticut.

With Mrs Drake's cure Hooker's long apprenticeship was almost complete. With her death, the time had come to move to a more settled family life, away from the apartment in Esher Place. John Rogers made an approach to Colchester which came to nothing. Mather suggests that Hooker "did more publickly and frequently preach about London and in a little time he grew famous for his ministerial abilities, but especially for his notable faculty at the wise and fit management of wounded spirits."[43] Then the call came from Chelmsford to join the staff at St Mary's Parish Church and take up the post of town lecturer. The final phase was about to begin in the political arena of nonconformist Essex.

It was a more mature, more confident, more settled man who left Esher than the inexperienced young Don who had made his first essay into the pastoral office only five years earlier. At the least, from then on he was to be amongst the most sought after spiritual directors of his generation.

The Effect Of Esher Upon Thomas Hooker.

St George's church records claim that Hooker began his work as rector in the year 1620.[44] He was 34 years old. To assess the effect of his removal from nearly sixteen years of bachelor existence, ten of them as a university fellow, with a privileged lifestyle and selective companionship, into a high profile pastorate in a notably original parish, actually living in the home of his distraught patrons, plainly requires more data than is now available. However the following factors deserve our careful consideration:

First, Hooker had looked forward to the event with customary and careful preparation. Not only was it his nature to do so, but his career demonstrates a predisposition towards the small, intimate pastoral office. "He was not ambitious to exercise his ministry among the great ones of the world, from whom the most preferment might be expected—he chose to be where great numbers of the poor might receive the gospel from him,"[45] commented Mather. He would search, at times desperately, for a local pastoral appointment, as in Holland. He would choose Newtown in preference to Boston. He quit the comparative security of Massachusetts in order to nourish an infant retreat in Connecticut. This was his consistent pattern, throughout his country born life.

Sargent Bush, in his excellent *The Writings of Thomas Hooker, Spiritual Adventure in Two Worlds* notes, "as chaplain to the family, pastor to a small congregation—Hooker's years at Esher must have been rather quiet and uneventful, particularly for a man who while at Cambridge had gained a reputation for scholarship and disputation as well as for preaching."[46] But Hooker was there because that was the ministry he believed in; and it was anything but uneventful!

Second, he had anticipated leaving his chambers in Cambridge for some years, and was therefore unlikely to have taken the first appointment presented to him. Sir Walter Mildmay had declared his intention, in the Charter. Emmanuel was you may remember, "for the sending forth of as large a number as possible of those who shall direct the people in the Christian faith."[47] The need was urgent, and fully understood by Emmanuel men. One example will suffice. The Essex churches at that time had some 162 unpreaching ministers, either incapable of meeting the current thirst for Biblical teaching, or unwilling, with 58 clergy holding multiple charges.[48] The least admissible case was that of the Freakes of Purleigh, a village close by Little Baddow now famed for the later ministry of Lawrence Washington, ancestor of George Washington.[49]

Edmund Freake was Rector of Purleigh from 1567–1575. During that period he was also Dean of both Rochester and Salisbury cathedrals, far separated with no possible connection between them apart from his cupidity. At the same time he was Archdeacon of Canterbury and Bishop of Rochester. But he still continued to enjoy the living at Purleigh. One wonders if his congregation ever saw him. That he enjoyed the emoluments there can be no doubt.

Eventually he yielded Purleigh to his elder son John Freake, but only after he had secured an additional, and lucrative, post for himself, as the Queen's Great Almoner. John inherited his father's practice as well as name. He became Dean of Rochester in succession to his father and Archdeacon of Norwich together with Purleigh, 130 miles away as the crow flies, but he travelled by slow coach, or on horseback if at all.

What other reasons might there have been for Hooker's choice of Esher, apart from his predilection for small time pastoral work, and that it was a part of his contract to quit Emmanuel whenever his Church had need of him elsewhere? We need to understand that he habitually made debatable choices on grounds of personal conviction. Why, then, did this most conceptual of men accept so undeniably eccentric an appointment, and what did he learn in it?

Third, he could not have been altogether unaware of, or unreceptive to Esher's unique history. There was no haughty chamber pew in his time, but the imperious legacy of Henry VIII hung about the place, echoes of imperialism reverberated whenever the San Domingo bell summoned believers to worship. Did he not think of it, as he stood to preach? Surely the memory of England's miraculous deliverance from the Spanish Armada, due in no small measure to the former owner of Esher Place, Lord Howard of Effingham, lingered on in conversation at table, or when Hooker visited his parishioners around the estate? Lord Howard only resigned as High Admiral in the year that Hooker's Cambridge Fellowship terminated, and died in 1624, the year before Hooker moved from Esher. A similar liberation was certainly in his mind when he preached 'The Church's Deliverance', a thanksgiving for the failure of the Gunpowder Plot. Indeed, in it he made a direct reference to the Armada.[50]

He took his text from Judges 10, v. 13. "Wherefore I will deliver you no more." He warned, "whence is it, that the Lord hath had an eye unto me above all the rest, when the fire of God's fury hath flamed and consumed all the country round about us; Bohemia, and the Palatinate, and Denmark; when the fire hath thus burnt up all; yet this little cottage, this little England, this span of ground, that this should not be searched?—There is no other reason to be given of this but God's love will have it so.—And shall the Lord do this, and shall not we acknowledge it, shall we not observe it and remember it for ever, shall we not score up the kindness of the Lord, and set up pillars of his preservation and records of his mercy to our souls for ever? And above all other deliverances that in '88 was a great deliverance, but we specially record that upon the fifth of November. This we record unto all posterity." You clutch the edge of your pew, and bend to the amendment of England's sins that God may be appeased, and his mercies endure for ever!

Regrettably none of Hooker's sermons from Esher remain, unless embedded in subsequent manuscripts. But the Gunpowder Plot belonged to his Marefield folk-law.[51] It is, to say the least, improbable that the sermon preached on 5 November 1626, at Chelmsford, less than a year after his departure from St George's, did not have its first outing during the years he spent there.

Wolsey's demise was further away, but could it have been a non sequitur?[52] The two men represented the diametric opposites of christian ministry, Wolsey the prelatical prince, manipulating the church for secular power, excusing every corruption in the name of expediency. Hooker saw the church as a poor means to a much greater end, and ministry in terms of service, the preparation of souls for union with God. Every secular claim must give way before the spiritual objective, no excuse for corrupt thoughts and deeds might remain. Did he not go to Esher attracted by its place in history, and become the better equipped thereby for the political struggle about to erupt at Chelmsford?

Fourth, there was undoubtedly a personal factor which we must take into consideration whenever we think about the growth of Thomas Hooker's personality and performance. Francis Drake's predicament was tortured, his wife's was tantalising as well. Their needs would be paramount in Hooker's acceptance of a call to Esher. He was that sort of man. In responding to their personal dismay he grew in stature as a crisis-counsellor.

The power to assign the living was important, too.[53] Hooker was a celebrated Puritan divine. The Drakes were avowed Puritans, Francis' mother's family having been refugees in Calvin's Geneva. And the living was a donative, in the gift of the Lord of the Manor. Only so could known Puritans hope for security, for the die was cast against them wherever the bishops had control ever since the Elizabethan Settlement of 1558.

Hooker went to Esher because he was ripe for the security of his own group, a recurrent need and a facet of his strength. He could not live without God's approval, neither would he without the approving companionship of his fellows. Crowds of students flocking round him at Cambridge, a cluster of ardent disciples under his instruction at Little Baddow, a devoted company of followers awaiting him in New England, newly embarked from the ship they had chartered so as to anticipate his arrival, one hundred crusaders ready to march across Massachusetts to claim the Connecticut Valley under Hooker for God, that was the Hooker style.

He found the security he needed in the weakness of his patrons, in the strength of the fiancée who became his wife, and, how much more I wonder, in the fellowship of the people at St George's. J. Floyer (Rector of Esher, 1908–1934) in his *Guide Book*,[54] hints at a discontented contingent in 1636, and names royalists who rejected the Puritan tradition at St George's when Michael Hudson, a chaplain to King Charles I, was intruded by royal grant into the place of Hooker's Puritan successor George Speed. But this was all too common in those troubled times, and Hooker's total ministry speaks his need for ordinary, underprivileged folk.

Finally, most telling of all, Thomas Hooker emerged from Esher as a pastoral counsellor *sans pareil.*

Claremont House And Garden.

Claremont was built by Sir John Vanbrugh for his own use in 1708.[55] That was shortly after he had completed Blenheim Palace at Woodstock, Oxfordshire, for John Churchill first Duke of Marlborough, as a token of the nation's gratitude for Churchill's victories during the War of the Spanish Succession. The cost of the buildings alone was estimated at £240,000. Neither Queen Anne nor Parliament had paid for Blenheim, when Vanbrugh constructed Claremont.[56]

In urgent need of money, Vanbrugh sold his Esher property to Thomas Pelham-Holles, first Duke of Newcastle, in 1711. The Newcastles enlarged it into a great mansion with ornate pleasure grounds. In 1768 Baron Robert Clive,[57] founder of the Empire of British India, purchased Claremont as his English country seat. He demolished Vanbrugh's house and erected a Palladian mansion designed by Laurence "Capability" Brown, which still stands, though now adapted for use as a school. It is visible from the Portsmouth Road (A3), an extension of Esher High Street where it runs southwest from Esher. It stands on a hill top on the left hand side, across some fields.

The House is open to the public on the first Saturday and Sunday of each month (February–November, 2:00–5:00pm), access from the Portsmouth Road, or turn left by the Bear Hotel, down Claremont Lane, A244, and right, along Claremont Drive, to the House.

From Clive's family Claremont eventually passed to Princess Charlotte and her husband, Prince Leopold. He continued to use the house as a personal retreat after his wife's death, and there entertained his niece Princess Victoria. Her mother (Victoria Louise Saxe-Coburg-Gotha before her marriage to Edward Duke of Kent, fourth son of King George III) was Leopold's sister.[58] Princess Victoria was considerably influenced by Leopold, up to her accession in 1837. She spent many holidays with him at Claremont, the greater part of whose splendid grounds now belong to the National Trust.

Known as Claremont Landscape Garden, it is the earliest surviving example of "le jardin anglais," for Vanbrugh and Bridgeman had planned its layout from 1715. Charles Bridgeman, the "first professional English gardener to escape from the rigid formality of Versaille-inspired French garden design," was succeeded by William Kent, "painter, architect, and father of modern gardening." He extended and further naturalised the grounds, with later improvements from Capability Brown.[59]

You can stroll along the serpentine paths, past Bridgeman's large turf amphitheatre, and round the lake with its island pavilion, gaze up at Vanbrugh's belvedere, or into the romantic grotto, and be delighted with all you find in a park once described as "the noblest of any in Europe."

Access is from the Portsmouth Road, travelling the short journey southwest from Esher High Street, a little past the school. There are good car parks, and refreshment/tourist facilities. The extensive parkland is open to the public. I hope you can make a visit here, and envisage 17th century Esher from this unique vantage point. Nothing that you see was here in Hooker's day, apart from its potential. But this is as much the place which grew out of the rare advantages of this neighbourhood, as was Hooker himself. He became, to however small an extent, the man who once had lived at Esher.

Diversion To Hampton Court Palace.

Hampton Court[60] was built by Cardinal Wolsey in 1515, but by 1528 Henry VIII was casting envious eyes over this magnificent residence, and the Cardinal, whose position was already becoming insecure, felt it prudent to make a gift of the Court to the King. Five of Henry's wives lived here as reigning queens. It remained a royal residence up to the death of George II, in 1760. There are few greater attractions in London, and it is a part of the Esher story.

Enter its fantastic wrought iron gates, made by the French master Jean Tijou (who came to England with William III in 1688); go through the Great Hall with its superb hammer-beam roof, created for Henry VIII; see the wealth of work commissioned by William III from Christopher Wren, Grinling Gibbons and the like, apt setting for the Raphael tapestry and the collection of rare paintings; look into the Orangery with its 15th century Mantegna cartoons, *The Triumph of Caesar* (both somewhat surprisingly saved for the nation by Oliver Cromwell for those who do not understand the Puritan appreciation of excellence); go out into the grounds with their masses of flowers set against the Thames waters, but try not to miss the great vine planted in 1768, or the famous maze with six feet high and two feet thick clipped hedges.

It was as a master of this palace that Henry VIII next looked enviously at Esher Place, literally on his doorstep. It offered a desirable extension to his grounds. So Hampton Court went down in all its Tudor pomp to hunt, and Esher's royal connection, of which Thomas Hooker became a remoter feature, began. Hence entered the lordly founder of Connecticut into his domain, his church bell ringing, if no trumpets braying, for the self-effacing ruler! The weight of history in the shaping of a career may not be under-rated.

Amersham and Susannah Hooker.

How To Get There.
Amersham is eleven miles west of Watford, easily reached by car from the northbound M25, exit 18. Here take the A404 into the old town centre, not five miles west of the motorway. Or, if staying in London, take the underground system, Metropolitan line, from Baker Street or British Rail from Marylebone Station.

Francis Drake had married Joane Tothill at Amersham in the year 1603. It is an ancient market town, set in the Chilterns, a semicircle of chalk hills which form a protective ring around London from northwest to northeast. They stretch from the Thames at Goring (just north of Reading) to the head waters of the river Lea between Dunstable and Hitchin, in places reaching heights of 850 feet. Once covered with forests of beech, those noble trees still abound to beautify the undulating hills.

Old Amersham, Home Of Joane Drake.
The old town nestles in the valley of the river Misbourne,[61] green fields and wooded hills encircled; mercifully as yet not buried under the new town of Amersham-on-the-Hill, sprung up round the railway station. It stands athwart the early coaching-road from London to Aylesbury, and still displays a remarkable selection of old inns, notably The Crown, its Georgian facade concealing an Elizabethan interior; the attractive half-timbered, black-and-white King's Arms, now a quality restaurant; and some seven others, each adding to the architectural interest of Old Amersham, where many buildings date back to the 16th and 17th centuries.

King John granted a charter in 1200 for the market, a small residue of which still gathers in the open space under the gracious 17th century Market Hall gift from the Drake family.[62] There is a small museum alongside the post office, many charming old shops, and the parish church of St Mary the Virgin,[63] all conveniently bounded by the tiny Market Place and spacious High Street. You will never forget, or regret, visiting this archaic town centre, so little changed

Market Hall, Amersham, built in 1682 by Sir William Drake. The Drake family crest adorns the front of the building.

through the centuries, apart from its discordant swarm of motor traffic.

Amersham was a stronghold of nonconformity.[64] You can visit on foot, up a narrow lane off Station Road (running up to Amersham-on-the-Hill) a monument to the eleven protestant martyrs, who forfeited their lives to the Reformed Faith in the 16th century. William Tylsworth, a follower of John Wycliffe, the early Bible translator (1329–84), was burnt here in 1506. His daughter was forced to light the first faggot. So too the children of John Scrivener were hideously made to light the fire which killed their father, in 1521.

In step with this dire local tradition, Joane Tothill's parents too were devout Puritans. Her father, the wealthy Sir William Tothill,[65] was one of the six Clerks of Chancery, the Court of the Lord Chancellor with special responsibilities to the reigning monarch, and by tradition a court of equity for cases with no remedy in common-law courts.

Sir William (d 1626) purchased Shardeloes Manor in 1596. Here he lived in state, with Queen Elizabeth amongst his guests towards the close of her long reign. He married Catherine, daughter of Sir John Denham, and became the father of three daughters, of whom Joane was the eldest. She married Francis Drake of Esher, as we have seen, and predeceased her father.

At Sir William's death Shardeloes passed to Catherine,[66] his sole surviving daughter, who released the estates to Joane's eldest son, William Drake, the conveyance being completed in 1638. From that time the Drakes became Amersham's premier family, remaining in residence until Shardeloes was utilized as a nursing home during World War II. The property has recently been converted into most desirable apartments and can be viewed en passant at the far west end of Amersham High Street. Although the Drakes no longer reside in the county, their land ownership and influence remains very much alive.

The Drake Memorials at St Mary's Parish Church.

Many of the Drake Memorials[67] are to be seen within the solid grandeur of the parish church of St Mary, situated behind the Market Hall, where the High Street links up with Church Street. The well-tended churchyard and adjacent public park fill this threshold to the old town with colourful serenity, but you need a knee-jerk agility to dodge through the traffic whirlpool.

The church has a particular interest for Essex folk, because Geoffrey de Mandeville (d 1144), first Earl of Essex, conferred its income on Walden Abbey in 1140. Although considerably restored in 1870, much of the nave remains from the 12th, and the aisles are 14th century, well proportioned, and preserving some fine medieval brasses, and an east window containing 17th century Flemish glass, a gift of the William Drake of Shardeloes in 1760.

Our main interest, however, has to be with the Drake Chapel. It stands over the family vaults, to the north of the chancel, and is kept locked most of the time. I have no doubt that a courteous note to the rector beforehand would ensure that you gained access.

The Drake family traces its descent from the Drakes of Ashe in Devon, as we have noted,[68] but the Amersham branch adopted the distinctive name of Tyrwhitt Drake, as you will see from the host of Memorials scattered throughout the Church. On the west wall of the Drake Chapel you will find a large tablet which runs, astoundingly to those who know the full story, as follows:

> To the Glorie of God
>
> To Y blessed Memorie of Mrs Joane Drake
> Wife to Francis Drake of Eshere, in ye County of Surry
> One of Y Gentlemen of His Maties most Hon Privie Cham
> ber in Ordinary, Esq Daughter to William Tothill
> of Sharlees, one of Y 6 Clarkes of ye High Courte
> of Chancerie, Esq, who whilst shee lived, was a pattern of all
> Virtues of a Gratious Woman and Wife, as highly
> esteemed of all good yt knew her; as lowly in
> her owne eyes
> A living Monument
> of God's mercie above Sathan's malice,
> of his wonders in casting downe his children, yt hee may raise them up,
> of the Truth of his praises in refreshing the weary sowle,
> of the force of faythfull prayer,
> of the power of God's saving truth,
> of the gaine of godliness even in this life.
>
> For having fought the good fight of faith and wayted for
> the salvation of God, shee obteyned ye glorious vic
> torie; and beginning the life of Heaven upon earth, was
> translated from earth triumphantly to Heaven.
>
> 18 Aprill, Anno Domino 1625;
> having sent before her, her deare Childe, John D whome
> shee had nursed herselfe, & by whome she lieth
> buried, and leaving behind her 2 sonnes & one daughter
> viz, William, Francis, and Joane Drake.
>
> Her Husband lamenting his owne loss
> yet rejoycing in her gaine, dedicateth this Monument.

The effect of her dementia[69] can be read between these lines, and indeed her disinclination ever to quit Shardeloes for Esher Place, for here she brought her beloved baby John, and here she lies beside him, safe home at last. The briefer memorial to John nearby is no less poignant.

IOHN DRAKE SONN OF FRANCIS DRAKE
OF ESSHERE IN THE COVNTY OF SVRRY ESQ
BY IOHA HIS WIFE DAVGHTER OF WILLIAM
TOTHILL OF SHARLONS ESQ. BY KATHERIN
HIS WIFE DYEING YE. 2. OF APRILL IN THE 4
YERE OF HIS AGE 1623. LIES HERE BVRIED

Had hee lui'd to bee a man
This inch had grown but to a Span
Nowe is hee past all feare of paine
'Twere Sinn to wish him heere againe
Vewe but the way by wch wee come
Thowt say hees best thats first at home.

The evidence of the Chapel memorials corroborates the dramatic change which came over Joan Drake as a consequence of Thomas Hooker's remedial influence at Esher. If ever a story had a happy ending, it was hers. In the short five year period of their close acquaintance she progressed from hypochondriac to benign sanctity and founded a dynasty which would endure for over 300 years when her son was restored to the home she had left so reluctantly.

Susannah Garbrand marries Thomas Hooker.

Another dynasty sprang from her share in our story. She drew her "waiting-gentlewoman," Susannah Garbrand, from Amersham to share her life at Esher Place. There Susannah met Thomas Hooker. Their love quickly ripened. They were married on 3 April 1621, at Amersham St Mary's, and lived happily ever after. The ceremony was conducted (a month before he died on 1 May 1621) by the bride's uncle, Dr Robert Challoner, a Canon of Windsor, and Rector of Amersham from 1576/78 until his death.[70] He was married to Susannah's aunt Christian (neé Garbrand), to whose home at Amersham Rectory Susannah had removed when her mother died, in 1609. From the union of Susannah and Thomas, and their subsequent history, three United States Presidents traced their descent. William Howard Taft (1857–1920) 27th President, from the marriage of their daughter Sarah to John Wilson; John Calvin Coolidge (1872–1933) 30th President, and Franklin Delano Roosevelt (1882–1945) 32nd President, both descended from Thomas Hooker's sister Dorothy (who followed him to New England), by her two husbands John Chester and George Alcock respectively.[71]

GENEALOGICAL TABLE, NO. 5: THE GARBRANDS OF OXFORD

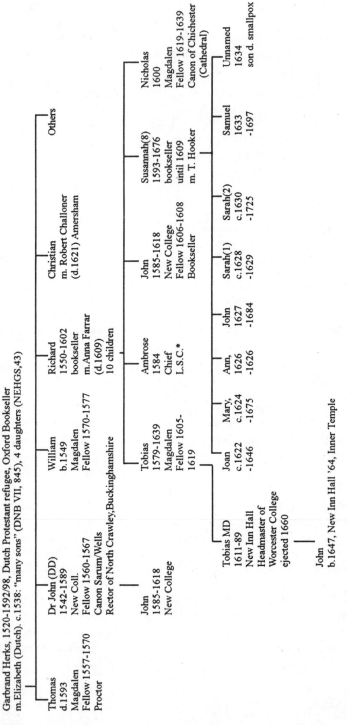

Garbrand Herks, 1520-1592/98, Dutch Protestant refugee, Oxford Bookseller
m.Elizabeth (Dutch). c.1538: "many sons" (DNB VII, 845), 4 daughters (NEHGS,43)

Thomas d.1593 Magdalen Fellow 1557-1570 Proctor

Dr John (DD) 1542-1589 New Coll. Fellow 1560-1567 Canon Sarum/Wells Rector of North Crawley,Buckinghamshire

William b.1549 Magdalen Fellow 1570-1577

Richard 1550-1602 bookseller m.Anna Farrar (d.1609) 10 children

Christian m. Robert Challoner (d.1621) Amersham

Others

John 1585-1618 New College

Tobias 1579-1639 Magdalen Fellow 1605-1619

Ambrose 1584 Chief L.S.C.*

John 1585-1618 New College Fellow 1606-1608 Bookseller

Susannah(8) 1593-1676 bookseller until 1609 m. T. Hooker

Nicholas 1600 Magdalen Fellow 1619-1639 Canon of Chichester (Cathedral)

Tobias MD 1611-89 New Inn Hall Headmaster of Worcester College ejected 1660

John b.1647, New Inn Hall '64, Inner Temple

Joan c.1622 -1646

Mary, c.1624 -1675

Ann, 1626 -1626

John 1627 -1684

Sarah(1) c.1628 -1629

Sarah(2) c.1630 -1725

Samuel 1633 -1697

Unnamed 1634 son d. smallpox

NB.   * = Chief Officer, London Stationers' Company.

The above Garbrand males regularly used the surname Herk(e)s, Herks-Garbrand or Garbrand-alias-Herks as well as Garbrand. NEHGS claims that Susannah's father, Richard, was "the only son who left issue". According to Oxoniensis, so did at least Dr John. But from this it may be assumed that 5 of the 6 third-generation children listed descend from Richard (ie. Susannah and 4 of her brothers).

Sources: NEHGS, Little Baddow 400th Anniv. mongraph, pp.42-44; DNB VII, pp.845-6; Alumni Oxoniensis, 1500-1714, vol.II, p.546

Amersham Parish Church of St. Mary

Susannah must have been an exceptional young woman. She endured, and survived her mistress' tantrums with sufficient equanimity to name her first child Joan (Joanna, later married to Reverend Thomas Shepard as previously noted), in honour of Mrs Drake, who became her godmother. Of the other children who survived, all born in England with the possible exception of the youngest—Mary married Reverend Roger Newton, first pastor of Farmington, Connecticut; John returned to Britain, and became a clergyman of the Church of England; Sarah married Reverend John Wilson; and Reverend Samuel succeeded his brother-in-law at Farmington, where he remained as pastor until death. Samuel married a Mary Willet of Plymouth Plantation. They had eleven children, of whom nine were sons. From them the name of Thomas Hooker has been perpetuated to this day.[72]

Susannah Garbrand was herself descended from a celebrated noncon-forming family.[73] Her uncle, Dr John Garbrand (1542–89) was a Prebendary of Salisbury Cathedral, and the protege of the esteemed John Jewell (1522–71),[74] bishop of Salisbury, whose works he published. Print was in his blood.

His brother Richard (1550–1602), Susannah's father, was the fifth son of Garbrand Herks, official stationer to the University of Oxford, and succeeded to the family printing and book-selling business. Susannah, 1593–1676, was the eighth out of ten children born to Richard and his wife Anna (who died 13 October 1609).

Susannah's grandfather Garbrand Herks (or Harkes, c. 1510–98) was a Dutch protestant refugee who found asylum at Oxford in about 1538. He opened a stationer's business, purchased Bulkeley Hall, and supported a conventicle which met secretly in the cellar during the Marian persecution. It became a focus for the ultra-protestants of Oxford, and further afield.

Herks (his family adopted the name Garbrand) bought up whole libraries from the monasteries at their dissolution. He made a fortune by supplying books to the Bodleian Library as well as the colleges. At least three of his sons graduated from Magdalen and New College. From immigrants this remarkable family not only assimilated successfully into English society, they were highly esteemed, especially amongst the more thorough-going English reformers. Susannah's credentials were impeccable.[75]

What may be deduced about Susannah from the above? We know so little. The nearest that Cotton Mather came to any awareness of her existence was when he informs us that during Thomas Hooker's exile in Holland, there was "a courteous and private recess provided for his family at a place called Old Park"[76] (near Great Waltham, Essex) by the Earl of Warwick. He also quotes from a lost manuscript in which John Eliot described his conversion experience at Cuckoos Farm, Little Baddow. "When I came to this blessed family I then saw, as never before, the power of godliness."[77] But Mather never mentions Susannah, apart from these two oblique references, and shows no appreciation of the implied contribution she and the children made to the ambience of Cuckoos, which so affected John Eliot.

Shardeloes, Amersham, home of Joanna Drake

First we should note that she was an orphan, when she went to live with her aunt at Amersham rectory. She was sixteen years old, of marriageable age, and from a wealthy family. But she did not marry for a further twelve years, and then it was to serious minded, academic, highly-complex Thomas Hooker, at 34 years of age perhaps shyly emerging from the male seclusion of his university chambers. Had not her background everything to do with that?

Her behavioural legacy from the Garbrands was unusually interesting. Dutch, Calvinistic, and persecuted. Maybe stolid, certainly independent, not easily deflected from basic beliefs and ideals. Highly intellectual, her uncles were all Oxford graduates, and Fellows of their Colleges. Her four aunts each married an Oxford graduate. Only her father, because he took over the printing and book selling business, missed out on an Oxford degree.

To her father Richard's commercial expertise, and extensive knowledge of literature, must be added the industry of his wife, for Susannah's mother carried on the business after her husband's death, for a further seven years. Susannah no doubt largely assisted her.[78] They inherited a tradition of good business management from old John Herks. And they were rich.

Courage was there in equal abundance. Her grandfather risked his life as a recent exile at Oxford, by permitting an illegal conventicle in his cellar during Mary's persecutions. And there was a gift for adaptation. The family successfully assimilated into English society, possessing personal attributes enough to win them high office within one generation. Perhaps Susannah was exceptionally unattractive, to remain unmarried for so long. But our scanty evidence does not bear this out. All the indications seem to suggest that her mind was too superior to stoop to the usual marriage of convenience where even small fortunes were concerned, too schooled in academics. She was content to wait for a man of Hooker's calibre. Nothing less than a marriage of minds would have satisfied either if them.

The girl who joined the Challoner household may have brought her own strong characteristics with her. She would receive much from residence with her uncle and aunt. Instead of a book shop she served a rectory, and received a training for her own unsuspected career as a rector's wife. It could have been pleasant enough, but her brother John's will, dated 1618 (nine years after her mother's death), notes that Susannah had not received her portion of their parent's estate.[79] Did her aunt take her out of charity? If so she may have been deprived of the many privileges a private income would have assured her, and experienced a drudgery which would prepare her only too well for the harsh conditions of a frontier parsonage in Connecticut.

The ornate alabaster and black marble memorial to Henry Curwen on the south wall of the chancel in Amersham St Mary's, may shed some light on her Amersham days. He died at the rectory in 1636, aged only fourteen, being a pupil of the rector at that time. It was normal practice to domicile the sons of wealthy families with some accredited divine for schooling, but Henry Curwen was sent the prohibitive distance from Workington in Cumberland. This suggests a close family connection with the then rector, or considerable fame for his Amersham school.[80] Now Dr Robert Challoner left provision in his will of June 1620, for the grammar school which bears his name to this day. His successor Charles Croke, a chaplain to King Charles I, actively supported the project. Interestingly, a William Tothill, "my well-beloved friend" was one of the founding trustees.

The Master of Dr Challoner's School was usually the Curate of the Parish, and, in 1649, one by name of Mr Angel successfully sent the son of Sir John Henden of Biddenden, Kent (another "prohibitive distance") to St John's College Cambridge,[81] as a fellow commoner. So there was a tradition of tuition of some note at the Rectory; and Susannah was to entertain young men in her frontier home, who came to live and study under her famous husband. Did Amersham begin her training for this duty too?

Her stay at Amersham was not lengthy. Joane Tothill married Francis Drake in 1603. We do not know when she took Susannah into her household at Esher Place. Her third child, Joane, the immediate cause of her final nervous breakdown, was born about 1612. This would seem a probable time for seeking additional help, and by then Susannah had established her reputation at Amersham, where Joane Drake always returned for support and comfort. She was then nineteen, with eight long years to go before Thomas Hooker came to rescue her.

For the purpose of this Guide to Thomas Hooker, Susannah's background is of some importance. There is no question of the suitability of the match. One would say they were made for each other. Nor could Thomas have survived as long as he did, with the intensity of his mind, his high-pressure destiny, and his ill-health, without the understanding as well as the affection of his wife.

I wonder too, at the influence of her most celebrated uncle Dr John, protege of Bishop Jewel. The bishop had been an outspoken Calvinist, who changed his stance when the nation was delivered from Catholic Mary. For him, as for others, the Elizabethan Settlement promised peace and prosperity for warring Catholic and Protestant alike, if a middle way compromise could be upheld. The need for reconciliation took precedence over his dogmatism. Former Puritan friends despised Jewel for his change of heart, but Calvinistic John Garbrand worked with him, posthumously publishing many of his works, the most famous of which was the *Apologia ecclesiae Anglicanae*, "first methodical statement of the position of the Church of England." And did not the family debate this issue whenever they met?

Thomas Hooker took, and suffered for, the opposite view of uncompromising belief, but his ministry was invariably touched by an accommodating charity. One wonders if his wife's spiritual inheritance from the moderate Dr John did not contribute to this contradictory trait in her husband's character, as surely as her material inheritance contributed to his wealth (when she finally received her portion of her parents' estate), for he died one of the richest men in Connecticut, a fact which has puzzled many commentators.

This at least is assured, that Thomas Hooker obtained a wife whose interests and upbringing matched his own. Her strong yet balanced Puritan faith outlasted the pangs of oppression, emigration, and every privation of the New England settlement. Her marriage appears to have been perfect by human standards, the harmonising of each one to the other so substantial, that echoes of wedded bliss surface throughout her husband's writings.

To listen to Hooker in his pulpit speaking of marriage, can be most tenderly revealing. In *A Comment Upon Christ's last Prayer/In the Seventeenth of JOHN/Wherein is opened/The Union Beleevers have with God and/Christ, and the glorious Priviledges thereof*, he wrote, "the Husband tenders his Spouse with an indeared affection above al mortal creatures. This appears by the expressions of his respect, that all he hath, is at her command, al he can do, is wholly improved by her content and comfort, she lies in his Bosom, and his heart trusts in her."[82]

Susannah's, and his own condition when exiled from his family in Holland surely underlies the following: "As a wife with the letters of her husband that is in a farre Country; she finds many sweet inklings of his love, and shee will read these letters often, and daily: she would talk with her husband a farre off, and see him in the letters—so these ordinances are but the Lord's love-letters."[83]

Again, "The man whose heart is indeared to the woman he loves, he dreams of her in the night, hath her in his eye and apprehension when he awakes, museth on her as he sits at table, walks with her when he travels and parlies with her in each place where he comes."[84]

Amersham has much to answer for, and may do so with pride.

Martyrs' Memorial, Amersham.

CHAPTER 5

CHELMSFORD AND THE COUNTY OF ESSEX

Political Involvement for a Godly Commonwealth

1626–1631

CHELMSFORD, THE COUNTY TOWN.

How to get there.

By rail: a simple matter. Go from Liverpool Street Railway Terminus in London. Take any of the frequent passenger trains to Chelmsford. It is worth an enquiry beforehand, as slow stopping trains along this congested commuter route alternate with express trains. It is not a scenic journey. The slow train trundles through the worst of London's East End and Docks area, now run down and rapidly changing to other uses so that the interest of massed ships' masts and maritime trade has long vanished. You will see all you need, for any joy it may bring, from the flashing vistas of the express.

By road: whether from London or elsewhere, look for the A12 via Romford, Essex. The lengthier but simplest route (depending on where you are staying) may be to get onto the M25, and to follow it eastwards to Junction 20. Here you join the A12 to Chelmsford/Colchester, exiting at Margaretting onto the A1016 into Chelmsford city centre.

The distance from central London is approximately thirty miles. There are good car parks, and the railway and coach stations are close to the town centre. The Tourist Information Centre is at County Hall, Market Road, and has lists of suitable accommodation. The Essex Record Office is close by, in Victoria Road South. Both offer a high class of general and detailed information.

A Brief History of Chelmsford, particularly as it relates to Hooker.

Three rivers merge at Chelmsford,[1] the Chelmer, the Can and the Wid. The old road from London to Colchester crossed two of these rivers (the Chelmer and the Can) and was first bridged by the Romans. They established a halfway staging post on the west bank of the Can (later Moulsham

Manor), a place of some importance since they named it Caesar Romagus, a hybrid Latin-Celtic word possibly meaning "Caesar's Plain." This is the only known instance of an imperial prefix to the name of a British town, and suggests that it was an imperial foundation. The explanation may well be that Claudius, on his way to investing Colchester in A.D. 43, won a decisive victory near here, which confirmed the subjugation of southeastern Britain.

After the withdrawal of the Romans early in the 5th century, the bridges decayed, the fords were impassable in rainy seasons, and the main road was re-routed through Writtle to the west of Chelmsford. The Roman settlement receded into anonymity. By Domesday, the main manors were Royal Writtle, and Moulsham (held by Westminster Abbey), with the manor of Bishop's Hall, on the north bank of the Can (held by the London Diocese) trailing behind.

It was Maurice, Bishop of London, who, c. 1100, bridged the rivers Chelmer and Can once again, and brought the main road back to what is now Chelmsford, but he centred it on Bishop's Hall on the north bank of the Can, not Moulsham as before. The bridge gave him a stranglehold over the London trade route and its growing commerce with the east coast ports. A Market Charter followed in 1199 and the right to an annual fair, an undoubted bargain for the rent was but two palfreys per annum.[2] Bishop's Hall (Chelmsford) flourished. Moulsham and Writtle declined.

Chelmsford quickly became the seat of regional government. Proximity to London increased its power and prosperity. You will find evidences of this steady evolution all round you, as you survey the town.

Why not take up your stand in Tindal Square? It is a short step from the central multi-storey car park, through the shopping precinct; and from the Railway and Bus Stations, down Duke Street. To the west you will see the splendid new County Hall with the Tourist Information Centre. You will wish to call there, and, at the rear, fronting onto Duke Street, at the Old County Hall, with its murals in the main hallway depicting scenes from Essex history as you ascend to the fine council chamber above. You will be welcome to look in.

Duke Street runs off to the northwest. As you look up it, you will see the cathedral spire rising above the buildings on the north side of Tindal Square. There is a narrow alleyway which leads into the Cathedral Close. A Hooker Memorial Civic Plaque is fixed high on the wall. It proclaims "Thomas Hooker, 1586–1647, Curate at St Mary's Church and Chelmsford Town Lecturer 1626–29, Founder of the State of Connecticut, Father of American Democracy." I should know. I wrote it myself. But plans are now afoot for an even worthier Memorial Foundation connected with the ongoing work of the cathedral and the community.

Alongside the alleyway you will note the Shire Hall. It boasts a ballroom upstairs, virtually unaltered since its erection in 1791, again well worth exploring. The High Street runs south from the Shire Hall, past the Saracen's Head (where Anthony Trollope wrote some of his novels), down to the old stone bridge of 1787, where the London Road used to enter the town. The market extended from the river bank to where the Shire Hall now stands. You can see the row of narrow shops on the right, backing onto a narrower Tindal Street at the rear, which marked one line of the medieval market stalls earlier known as Shoprow.[3]

Originally open barrows, the stall-holders cunningly protected them with shelters, which mysteriously grew a little, year by year, into a line of permanent buildings. From market barrow to town house! Several local families founded their fortunes on this soft-shuffle up the market place, most notably the very wealthy Mildmays.

In modern times large industrial concerns such as Ranson's agricultural machinery, Hoffman's Ball Bearings, English Electric Valves, and the pioneer electronics Company of Marconi have been sited at Chelmsford. The County Law Courts, now in New Street behind the Shire Hall, early brought the Assizes to the town. It provided Thomas Hooker with what he most needed—a central pulpit in an important Puritan town, within influential range of the City of London and the Court at Westminster.

Exactly when Thomas and Susannah removed to Chelmsford, or where at first they lived, remains uncertain. The earliest reference comes from the will of one John Marshall, a woolendraper of Chelmsford, dated 3 October 1625. This suggests that they were in residence before that date, but is not in itself determinative.[4]

By then they had at least one daughter, Joanna.[5] She was born at some time during or after 1622, and named after Mrs Drake of Esher. She was to marry Thomas Shepard at Newtown, Massachusetts in 1640, when no more than 18 years of age. She died there in 1646. A second daughter, Mary, who in 1644 was to marry Roger Newton (first minister at Farmington, Connecticut) may well have been born before her parents came to Chelmsford. There the family was enlarged by the birth of a son, John,[6] not 21 when Thomas Hooker's will was attested in July 1647, so requiring a birthdate after 1626. John returned to England later on, and was ordained into the Anglican Church. He married, had two children, and died in England in 1684. A third daughter Sarah was born (1630) during the Chelmsford period. She was to marry John Wilson Jr, Richard Mather's co-pastor at Dorchester, Massachusetts, and is said to have lived until 1725. A second son, Samuel (1633–1697), also minister at Farmington, was by tradition born at Newtown, Massachusetts where a third infant son's death was reported by Governor Winthrop in 1634.

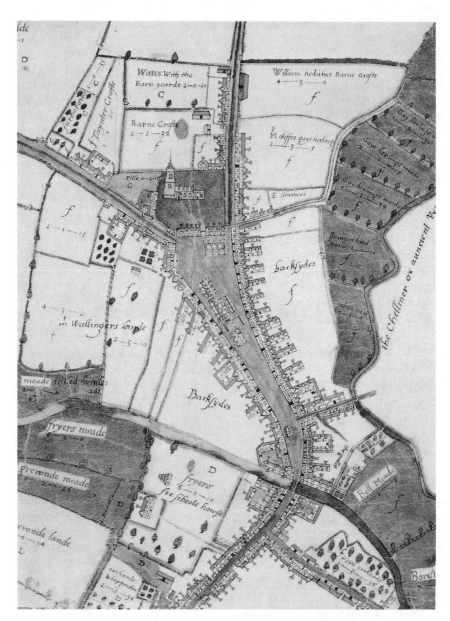

Map of Chelmsford, Jn. Walker, 1591.

GENEALOGICAL TABLE, NO. 6: THOMAS AND SUSANNAH HOOKER AND CHILDREN

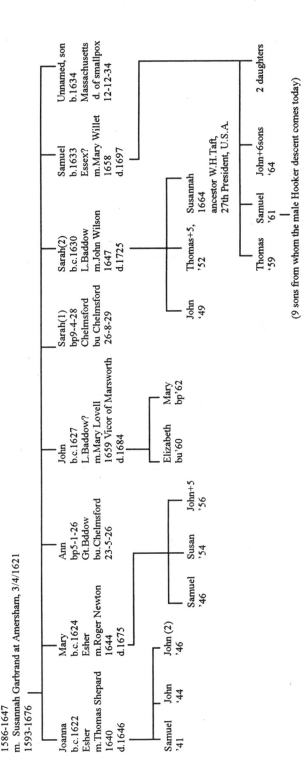

The above is little more than an illustration of the probable relationships between the Hooker children. The greatest anomoly is that the birth of John, traditionally placed between Ann and Sarah(1), is not registered either at Great Baddow St Mary's, or at Chelmsford St Mary's, as theirs was. This strengthens my feeling that Thomas and Susannah Hooker removed to Little Baddow before John and Sarah(1) were born, so that both would be born at Cuckoos, but variously registered, or not registered, due to the dangers to which the Hookers were subjected throughout their time at "Chelmsford." John was not 21 years of age when Thomas Hooker's will was published, 1647, so must have been born after 1626. Samuel, born the year of his father's return from Holland and flight to Massachusetts, could have been born at Old Park, Great Waltham, Susannah's temporary refuge.

Two other children were born at Chelmsford who died in infancy: Ann, whose baptism is recorded on 5 January 1626, in the Parish Register of St Mary's, Great Baddow (a village next to Moulsham manor, Chelmsford), and whose burial is recorded on 23 May that same year in the register of St Mary's, Chelmsford ("Ann the daughter of Mr Thomas Hoocker of Baddow Minister and Susan his wife")—and Sarah (1), baptised in Chelmsford on 9 April 1628, and buried there on 26 August the following year.

It is evident that when the Hookers arrived at Chelmsford they were immediately resident, presumably as close to his work at St Mary's Chelmsford as could be managed, in the Parish of Great Baddow, and that Ann was born there.[7] They must then have crossed the River Can to live somewhere within the Parish of Chelmsford soon afterwards, for her burial. It is, however, altogether conceivable, as the New England Historic Genealogical Society's monograph (presented in 1986 to the Little Baddow Historical Society on the occasion of its celebration of the 400th anniversary of Thomas Hooker's birth) claims that Sarah was born and died at Little Baddow, but was baptised and buried at St Mary's Chelmsford. This would imply that John and Sarah (2) were also born at Little Baddow.

Thomas Hooker was licensed to minister at Chelmsford alone, but was forced to withdraw secretly to Little Baddow at least by the year of Sarah's death, when the political controversies raging round him reached their height. He might even have gone quietly there before Ann died. At any rate, Cuckoos Farmhouse, Little Baddow, is the sole address we have for these Essex years.

Chelmsford had about 1,000 residents at that time, and a disproportionate number of ale houses with their attendant social disorder.[8] From earliest days it had been a wayfarers' town, busy with merchants, market-traders, hucksters, and vagrants pursuing their honest or dishonest affairs. It also had its share of ruling families who largely controlled the town. Like the majority of families they could produce peaceable and riotous citizens, and their quota who defended the old ways, or agitated for the new, all meat for Thomas Hooker's dressing, and in general clamorous for reform. None of them more so than the Mildmays.

The Mildmays, A Chelmsford Dynasty.

This family deserves a brief section to itself if only for its place in the story of Thomas Hooker. It also provides another instance of the confusion of the times, the hostile policies which divided families (not many Mildmays would have named themselves Puritans, some took the King's side in the Civil War, yet few directly and indirectly contributed more to the founding of New England), and the rapid rise to power and fame of those who had enterprise and ability. The Mildmay fortunes began on a market barrow. They spread over the Midlands and the Southeast of England.

The Mildmays[9] literally took off in 1506 when Thomas, a mercer from nearby Great Waltham (d. 1557), acquired the lucrative market stall rights in Chelmsford's Shoprow which had belonged to his kinsman John Cornish (also a mercer) when John's second wife, now widow Anne, made them over to him. This John Cornish's first wife had been a daughter of the well-to-do brewer Guy Harling, owner of "one of the most prestigious properties in the town," known as Guy Harlings, which Thomas himself was later to purchase (1530).

Thomas Mildmay prospered, expanded his Chelmsford holdings, and became one of its wealthiest residents. He was content to remain a "merchant and yeoman," and bequeathed his market stalls to his sons William and John,[10] of whom he and his wife Agnes Read had five, with three daughters, namely Thomas, William, John, Edward, Walter, Joan, Margaret and Thomasin. This numerous family opulently spread over Essex. Three of them interest us most, Sir Thomas, William (a branch of whose family came to live at Great Graces, Little Baddow), and Sir Walter.

The middle three sons followed their father's trade as dealers in textile fabrics, but the eldest, Sir Thomas the Auditor (d. 1566), served the Crown most notably as a commissioner of the Court of Augmentations for the Dissolution of the Monasteries, set up in 1537, of which Richard Rich, Baron Rochford of Essex, was Henry VIII's first Chancellor. Sir Thomas' title was Auditor, his fortune was made.

He and his brothers added to their father's holdings on both sides of the Chelmsford rivers, Moulsham's Dominican Friary and Manor, the Leper Hospital, bequests to religious guilds and chantries, lands and town houses, eventually Bishops Hall with the manor of Chelmsford. A survey of Mildmay properties drawn up in 1591 claimed "This towne is called the Shire towne-soe reputed and taken longe time before, by the keeping of all assizes and sessions of the peace, and many other certificacons and Inquisitions there. It is alsoe a greate thorowefare, and markett towne weekely uppon the Fryday,"[11] most of it by then Mildmay owned. They paid for their possessions as all honest Tudor land grabbers did, but the bargains hurt their purses passing well.

Sir Thomas was the prime mover. He had married Avice Gunson, daughter of the paymaster of the king's ships. He rebuilt Moulsham Manor into a grand hall. His descendants married into the family of the Barons Fitz Walter (Sussex earls of New Hall, Boreham), which title they incorporated in 1670. But the youngest of Thomas the mercer's five sons was the greatest of them all.

Sir Walter Mildmay (1520–89)[12] was educated at Christ's College, Cambridge, read law at Gray's Inn, and found gainful employment with his brother, the Master Auditor, on the Court of Augmentations. Henry VIII

GENEALOGICAL TABLE, NO. 7: THE MILDMAYS OF CHELMSFORD

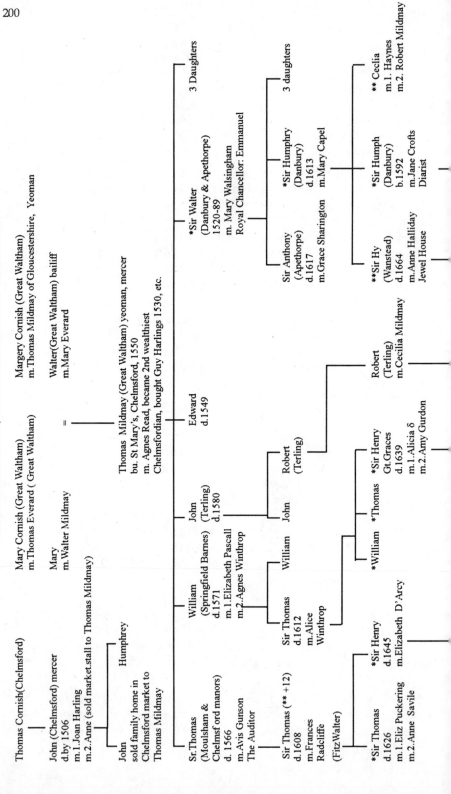

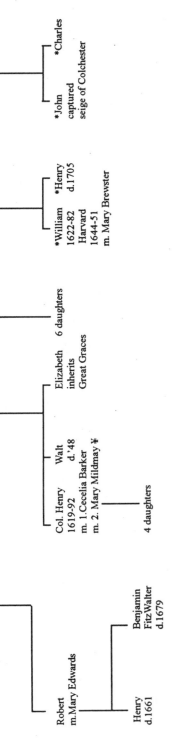

The above names are principally selected to simplify some of the complicated Mildmay family relationships, & because they contribute to the Hooker story,- ie. Sir Thomas the Master Auditor & the Chelmsford Lectureship: William of Springfield Barnes & Great Graces: John of Terling & Thomas Weld: Sir Walter & Emmanuel College, etc. It is not a complete Mildmay Genealogy.

* = some of the many Mildmays registered in "Alumni Cantabrigienses", eg. Sir Thomas d.1608, "(* +12)" = his two brothers Sir Walter & Henry not otherwise listed. Only 5 of the 15 children outlived their father, Sir Thomas the Auditor (d.1566).

Similarly "* *Sir Henry *Sir Humphrey * * Cecilia" = Sir Humphrey of Danbury's 5 sons, all at Camb, including Walter, John (royalist killed battle of Newbury), & Anthony (carver to Charles I) not otherwise listed.

δ = Joan, Management & Thomasin, daughters of Thomas the mercer (D.1550): δ again = Winifred, Christian & Martha (m.Sir William Fitzwilliam), dghts. of Sir Walter (d.1589): δ again = Alice (m. Richard Harlakenden, Earls Colne), Mary & Frances, dghts of Lady Alicia (Harris) of Great Graces.

+ Col.Henry Mildmay & Richard Harlakenden (above) together with Lt.Col. Carew Mildmay (2nd son of William of Spr.ingfield Barnes & Marks, Romford) fought with the Parliamentary forces investing Colchester v. their Royalist kinsman John inside the besieged town, see Cecile Rogers, LBHS Newsletter, Ap.1990,p.8.

¥ Mary "daughter of Robert Mildmay of Overton, Northamptonshire" (St.J.ohn Mildmay op.cit.p.34) descended from Sir Thomas the Auditor.

The chart shows the following names:

*Charles

*John captured seige of Colchester

*Henry d.1705

*William 1622-82 Harvard 1644-51 m. Mary Brewster

6 daughters

Elizabeth inherits Great Graces

Col. Henry 1619-92 m. 1.Cecelia Barker m. 2. Mary Mildmay ¥

Walt d.'48

4 daughters

Robert m.Mary Edwards

Henry d.1661

Benjamin FitzWalter d.1679

may have used the dissolution of the monasteries as one way of replenishing the Tudor purse. It came in mighty handy for these Essex entrepreneurs, already recognisable as embryonic "Connecticut Yankees," a term of highest praise.

Sir Walter received larger and larger responsibilities for the management of the royal finances. He was made Surveyor General for the sale of monastic lands, then Superintendent of the Royal Mint at York, Commissioner of Crown Lands, and, under Elizabeth, Chancellor of the Exchequer. A devout, and known Calvinist, his expertise guaranteed his survival under Mary. He became member of Parliament for Maldon, Essex in the year of her accession, and remained in Parliament for the rest of his active life, for Peterborough and Northamptonshire on taking up residence in that county.

His interest in education derived in part from a legal requirement, when disposing of monastic incomes, to transfer chantry endowments to "cy pres" objectives. For instance, Chelmsford Grammar School was made, thanks to Sir Walter, a beneficiary of the Mownteneye Chantry.[13] But his concern far surpassed any legal obligation. He made grants and personal bequests to Chelmsford Grammar School; Christ's College, Cambridge; Christ's Hospital on Newgate Street, London (the celebrated Blue-Coat School), founded by Edward VI after hearing a sermon on charity by Bishop Ridley, which Sir Walter may well have heard at the same time. He left it a legacy of £52 per annum.

On 24 November 1583, Sir Walter purchased a Dominican monastery in Preacher's (now St Andrew's) Street, Cambridge, for £550, and there built Emmanuel College, the chief cause of his enduring fame. The monastery had not long been dissolved. He may have used inside knowledge to get a bargain. But it was a noble benefaction. He designed it as a progressive rather than a Puritan college, in which the scholars were to look forward to spreading outside the knowledge they acquired within its walls. He was a loyal servant of the crown, never a revolutionary such as succeeding generations of his students became. But his contribution to the creating of New England in North America is second to none, in the volume of Emmanuel men who gave it leadership.

Sir Walter was brought up at Guy Harlings, and built his mansion at Danbury Place, between Great and Little Baddow. He also received royal grants of land in Oxfordshire, as far away as Cornwall, and in Northamptonshire where he purchased the Apethorpe Estate. There he died, although his magnificent tomb is to be seen in St Bartholomew-the-Great, Smithfields, London, for he was a Freeman of that city.

He was succeeded by his sons, Sir Anthony, who inherited Apethorpe, and was English ambassador at Paris; and Sir Humphrey who resided at

Danbury Place, and sired the infamous Sir Henry.[14] The latter lived in splendour at Wanstead House, a regal mansion in Essex more fit for the Master of the Royal Jewel House. Sir Henry had purchased Wanstead House from George Villiers, Duke of Buckingham, the favourite of James I, and virtual ruler of England prior to his assassination on 23 August 1628. James had been a frequent visitor to Wanstead in Buckingham's time. Henry Mildmay continued to entertain his royal visitor.

Edward Hyde, first Earl of Clarendon, and one of the principal architects of the Restoration of Charles II to the throne in 1660, wrote of Sir Henry that he was "a great flatterer of all persons in authority, and spy in all places for them."[15] Henry had been brought up at court, far from the common sense commercial circles of his native Chelmsford. He appears to have lost all sense of probity. A sycophantic courtier now by breeding, he easily switched loyalty from King Charles I to Parliament at the outbreak of the Civil War, and even acted as one of the judges at Charles' trial. At least he did not vote for his former master's execution.

He was finally called to account for the disappearance of various crown jewels, court robes, and other royal valuables at the Restoration. He was imprisoned in the Tower, degraded, and banished to Tangiers, but died en route. Yet the Puritan within him persisted. He sent his eldest son, William (1622–1682) to New England, to study at Harvard in 1644, accompanied by a personal tutor, Richard Lyon.[16]

This Richard Lyon is known to posterity for his collaboration with the then Principal of Harvard, Henry Dunster, in the revision of the *Bay Psalter*. This book had been the first to be published in New England, edited by John Eliot amongst others in 1640. *The Psalms, Hymns, And Spiritual Songs Of the Old and New Testaments, faithfully translated into English metre, For the use, edification, and comfort of the Saints, in publick and private, especially in New England* of Dunster and Lyon was printed at Cambridge, Massachusetts, by Samuel Green in 1651, and remained the standard Psalter until replaced by Thomas Prince's new translation in 1758. Thus the Mildmay hand spread wide over the new colony, devious though some of its motions may have been.

It should be noted that young William graduated both Bachelor and Master of Arts at Harvard, a small redeeming factor for his family; and that his disreputable father, Sir Henry, is not to be confused with his kinsman, the Sir Henry Mildmay who lies buried in Little Baddow parish church. He was descended, as we have noted, from Sir Walter of Danbury Place. The Henry of Great Graces, Little Baddow, descended from Sir Walter's brother, William of Springfield Barnes, another Mildmay manor in the same Chelmsford locality.

Sober old Thomas and his son the pious Sir Walter, not to mention his many other reformist offspring, could not breed the adventurous strain out of their stock, so strong in themselves. To know these people is to understand more clearly that age of godly buccaneers to which many good Puritan families belonged. Without much evident compunction, they would strip the assets from the virgin markets of a new world, or wipe out an Indian tribe that stood between them and their religious ambitions, if prayer and fasting could make it compatible with what they knew of the Divine Will. Their God was a Tudor deity, rough-hewn from a rumbustuous Old England, tinctured with the warrior God of the Old Testament.

Essex, the "English Goshen."

Essex is amongst the most varied of English Counties, a prime springboard for an ambitious career, and Thomas Hooker was ambitious for the Kingdom of God if never for himself. Large tracts have been absorbed into the five northeastern London Boroughs of Havering, Barking, Newham, Redbridge, and Waltham Forest. Indeed, from the day when Edward the Confessor erected his Bower House at Havering-atte-Bower,[17] Westminster and the City had encroached upon Essex for their summer palaces, hunting lodges, and ever larger supplies of food. With all the home counties, Essex was London's open space, offering a healthier life to its more prosperous citizens.

Havering-atte-Bower is now a hamlet on the hillside a mile north of the A12 Eastern Avenue, at Romford. The old palace was bought by Richard Deane,[18] one of the judges who signed Charles I's death warrant. He collaborated with Oliver Cromwell in organizing the New Model Army, rose to the rank of Major General then became one of the three Navy Commissioners who replaced the former Lord High Admiral (Hooker's protector, the second Earl of Warwick) and was killed in a naval battle off the North Foreland on 1 June 1653. Sadly he demolished the Bower House where for 500 years kings and queens, as late as its last owner King Charles, had enjoyed a country palace away from the polluted air of London. He cut down all the great trees in the park, an act of symbolic destruction which foretold the fate of his fellow regicides. His remains, buried in Henry VII's Chapel at Westminster, were disinterred and desecrated at the Restoration. The palace is commemorated by the Bower House, near the summit of Orange Tree Hill, off Havering Road, Romford, still witnessing to Essex' attraction for London.

"This Shire," wrote John Norden in his *Speculum Britanniae* (1594),[19] "is most fat, fruitful, and full of profitable things, exceeding (as far as I can find) any other shire." He called Essex "the English Goshen, the fattest in the land." We are especially indebted to Norden because he designed the first complete series of county histories, an enterprise followed by others, even though he did not finish his work.

After the Norman Conquest of Britain in 1066, William I set up his seat of government at Barking Abbey, built A.D. 666.[20] The largest fishing fleet in Britain once plied from Barking quays, situated on the bank of the river Roding below the Abbey, where it enters the Thames as Barking Creek. This was London's most regular supply of fresh fish, an Essex bounty which the Romans had enjoyed with the oyster beds in the Colne estuary, in addition to the wide acres of wheat and barley, the grazing lands for cattle and famed Essex saddleback hogs, and broad sheep-runs for the weavers' towns of Colchester, Braintree, Bocking, Dedham and Coggeshall, all contributors to the importance of Essex.

The Thames was a major source of wealth. To a lesser degree, so were the sheltered ports of the Crouch, Blackwater, Colne, and Stour estuaries. They sent their little ships across to the North European ports in constant trade, and, like as not, received them back with holds topped up with the forbidden literature of Protestantism, the latest reforms of John Calvin at Geneva, or his successors. It was not only the consequence of taking up residence in Essex, or in St Mary's pulpit at Chelmsford, it was the times themselves turned Thomas Hooker into a political agitator.

For instance, there was King Charles' proclamation on 24 January 1626, shortly after Thomas arrived at Chelmsford, which drove coffin nails into King James' earlier "harrying out of the land" of the Millenarian petitioners. "The King will admit no innovation in the doctrine, discipline, or government of the church—his majesty will proceed against all offenders against this order, with all the severity their contempt shall deserve."[21]

Hope did not altogether die in England for another fifteen years, when civil war at last broke out; but the sound of the hammering of patriot Puritans' coffins could be heard throughout the land, not least at Chelmsford, 33 miles from the Westminster Court.

William Laud, Ecclesiastical Disciplinarian.

A further contributory factor was the elevation of William Laud (1573–1645)[22] to the bishopric of London in 1628, two years after Hooker's appointment to Chelmsford. Now there was a hammering of reactionary high church practices in the ears of every ultra-Protestant, to add to the threat against their aspirations for further political reform. Hope plummeted to despair.

Laud was the son of a master-tailor at Reading in Berkshire, but proved himself to be more adept with shears than with scissors. He went up to St John's College, Oxford, became a fellow in 1593, and president of his college in 1611. From the beginning he was in conflict with the university authorities for his opposition to the Calvinist doctrine still enshrined in the 39 Articles of the Church of England, and for his determination to restore certain pre-Reformation practices. His first major church appointment came later (at 43 years of age), and in a similar fashion he clashed violently with his bishop when, as Dean of Gloucester, he removed the communion table from the centre of the choir, and replaced it at the east end of the cathedral.

But he pleased King James I, for he plainly venerated the old ways, and with them the divine sanctions of the crown. When Charles succeeded his father in 1625, Laud, by then bishop of St Davids, was made Bishop of Bath and Wells, and, two years later was translated to London with direct responsibility for all clergy in Essex, then a part of the London Diocese.

One of his first acts was to provide the King and the Court of High Commission (an ecclesiastical commission under the Crown from 1549, with authority to check heresy, and enforce forms of worship) with his *Considerations*, a list of all clergy in the London Diocese, each name marked with an "O" for Orthodox or a "P" for Puritan. He was again translated, this time to Canterbury in 1633, the year Hooker stepped ashore in Massachusetts.

An assiduous man, better fitted to be an inspector of taxes than a shepherd of souls, he worked through his list, threatening, banning, imprisoning those who demanded toleration or liberty, until himself imprisoned in the Tower by his outraged fellow churchmen. He was executed, 10 January 1645, on Tower Hill, without justification, even though the provocation had been severe.

Much of his work remains. He preserved the "Englishness" of the Church for the nation. He restored many of its good liturgical traditions, which needed only to have been reintroduced with greater tact and consideration to have been more widely tolerated. His reforms at Oxford University when Chancellor, "codifying the statutes, enforcing discipline, instituting professorships," and his personal donations to the Bodleian Library, were of permanent worth.[23] He chiefly lacked humanity. He saw himself as always in the right, inflexibly imposed his conviction, and that was something other reformers simply could not stomach.

Socio-political pressure moves toward Civil War.

There was a recession in the cloth trade.[24] It had been the bedrock of England's commercial prosperity ever since the Romans set up the first wool factory at Winchester, for clothing their armies of occupation. English cloth quickly established a reputation for fine quality, and was exported widely. The influx of Flemish weavers to East Anglia improved the quiddity of Essex cloth. It became the staple economy, and Essex was amongst the first to feel the effects of a recession.

The interminable hostilities with France and Spain led to an inevitable disruption of overseas trade. Recurrent and widespread poverty, vagrancy and unrest followed. The grievances of the godfearing, thrifty, up-and-coming Puritans were the hardest of all to bear. They believed that God had predetermined to prosper His Elect, whereas their burdens from a showy court, declining trade, and increasing numbers of vagabonds with their illegitimate children (all chargeable to local poor law relief), only increased. With a sovereign opposed to further religio-political reform, with bishops actually looking to reverse some of the liberties gained from the Tudors' limited Protestant reforms, and with new worlds beckoning them towards an Eldorado almost within their grasp, yet always seemingly unobtainable, it was at a time nearly meet for a popular uprising that Thomas Hooker rode into Essex.

St Mary's Parish Church, to which he went as Curate and Town Lecturer, stands at the top of Chelmsford High Street, the extremity of the lucrative market with its merchants' houses, and inns, near to where Bishop's Hall, the original manor house, used to stand. Today St Mary's is the Cathedral Church of St Mary the Virgin, St Peter and St Cedd.

The present-day Chelmsford Diocese dates from only 1914. It covers the County including the five London boroughs known colloquially as "Essex over the border." Before that, Essex had been included in the See of London from its inception in the 7th century, then transferred to Rochester (1836), and St Albans (1875). Its origins go beyond this.

Excursion to St Peter-Ad-Murum, first Essex Cathedral.

In A.D. 653 St Cedd, bishop of the East Saxons (d. 664) landed at the decayed Roman coastal fort round which had grown the flourishing settlement of Othona, or Ithancester, near Bradwell-on-Sea, Essex.[25] He and his brother St Chad were trained for episcopacy by St Aidan at Lindisfarne, the Holy Isle off the coast of Northumbria, between Bamburgh and Berwick-upon-Tweed (off the A1) which can still be visited at low tide. Monastic ruins and a rock castle at the extremity of a sandy causeway, cut off at high tide, wild, serene, reaching out to the same seas that bore its astonishing cargo of creative evangelists throughout 7th century Britain.

St Oswald (605–642), first Christian King of Northumbria, had sent to Iona, the Hebridean island off the west coast of Scotland, where St Columba had landed in 563 from Ireland, and founded a monastery which became the centre of Celtic Christian mission. Aidan was a monk of Iona. He crossed over to Lindisfarne, trained and dispatched a stream of gifted young disciples, St Egbert, St Wilfrid, St Cuthbert, with St Chad and St Cedd amongst them, whose labours planted Christianity from the Firth of Forth to the Thames estuary and beyond.

St Peter-ad-Murum, Chelmsford's first Cathedral.

St Cedd constructed Essex's first cathedral out of the ruins of the deserted Roman fortress, in 654. You can worship there on occasion still. A contemporary religious order, known as the Othona Community, resides nearby, and uses St Peter-on-the-Wall for its devotions. Parish Evensong is also held there on Sunday evenings throughout the months of July and August, together with an annual pilgrimage. It is one of the oldest places of Christian worship in Britain.

The primitive Celtic stonework arches overhead out of the Roman remains, creating a small, rectangular chapel. This is all that has survived, the apsed chancel and porticus, or side chamber, having collapsed years ago, as has the fort itself. But an atmosphere of awe remains. From here St Cedd founded a second church at Tilbury, on the banks of the river Thames, and slowly gathered pagan Essex into a more charitable faith.

You must drive to the Parish Church of St Thomas in the centre of Bradwell.[26] It is distinguished by its fine brick tower, built in 1706, and its 14th century porch, borrowed from another Essex village, Shopland near

Southend-on-Sea, when the latter was demolished. Amongst its monuments you will find one to Dr John Sherman (1616–1666), rector of Bradwell from 1644–1666. He was a Cambridge graduate like his kinsman Edmund Sherman of Dedham, Essex (whose son John emigrated to Wethersfield, Massachusetts, eventually to become its pastor). The celebrated general of the American Civil war, W. T. Sherman was descended from another Sherman of Dedham, Edmund's first cousin Samuel, who emigrated to Contentment, Connecticut in 1634.

You can drive a short distance down the lane which runs alongside the churchyard, and park at its termination. From there you must walk across the open salt marshes to the tiny building, cattle grazing at the gate, seabirds wheeling overhead, in the loneliness of the flat and empty beaches, great skies above you, wide spaces ever moving away from you, your littleness pressed upon you by one of the most distant, enchanted shrines in Britain.

St Cedd is remembered in the title of Chelmsford's present cathedral, and his seaborne mission by a lively carving of Peter the fisherman, in great big wading boots, as if just landed at Othona, which you will find squatting at the southeastern corner of the cathedral's outer wall.

To get to St Peter-on-the-Wall, why not drive into Maldon for lunch? Take the A414 from Chelmsford into Maldon, then the B1018 south to Latchington (where it becomes the B1010—you are now in the Dengie Peninsular,[27] an elfinland where time and the people stand still, but the lanes skip off in whatever direction they choose), and the B1020 to Southminster, and the B1021 to Bradwell-on-Sea. There you can take the lane on the south side of St Thomas' (see above) past the "jossing" or mounting block for horse-riders, to the rough car park. Be sure the weather forecast is set fair. It is a half-mile long walk, with no shelter until St Peter's is reached.

If time permits, Burnham-on-Crouch is well worth a visit, either going or returning. Burnham is on the B1021 back to Southminster, and south to the river Crouch, one of Essex's most picturesque yachting centres. Boatyards line the quay water front, mingling with restaurants and the White Hart hotel. There's boating everywhere if you're lucky, at the season-able week-ends.

If you wish to get the feel of Little Baddow as it was in Hooker's day, a trip round the Dengie Peninsular between the Blackwater and the Crouch will tell you as much as now remains to be experienced. Several of the villages have white weather-boarded little houses, an Essex tradition transferred by the settlers to New England. There was no building stone in Essex, but there was plenty of wood to protect the lathe and plaster walls.

You may also come across wayside chapels, their notice boards still proudly denominated "Peculiar People," direct inheritors of Essex independency. When a new international airport was mooted near Maplin

Sands, south of the River Crouch, in the early 1970s, a consultation on the challenge to the churches of that region discovered that approaching 100 such independent Christian groups persisted in the area. They had never bowed the knee to Baal, the Church of England, or even the Free Church Federal Council. A special envoy had to be appointed by the Essex Churches' Consultative Council to protect their interests, in case the project had proceeded. God sent a man whose childhood had fortunately been spent in going from one non-conformist church to another, who had providentially married into others, and was currently worshipping with the Baptists. In his person he represented so many of the Separatist traditions that he miraculously was acceptable to the majority. The world will be the poorer if Essex independency ever disappears!

The Cathedral Church of St Mary The Virgin, St Peter, and St Cedd, and Thomas Hooker's Lectureship, 1626–1629.

This is not one of the great cathedrals. In fact, much of its attraction comes from its atmosphere of a genuine parish church, with a close relationship to local people and affairs. It is a graceful, burnished structure, its 15th century West tower a charming feature, the interior excitingly refurbished recently, full of light and colour, set in well tended grounds.[28]

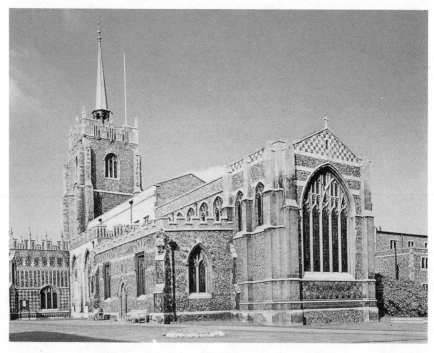

St Mary's, now Chelmsford Cathedral.

Thomas Mildmay's Tomb,
Chelmsford Cathedral

You enter by the spectacular
South Porch, dating from 1460 but
restored last century, and enriched
by "Essex friends of the American
people" in 1953, to commemorate
the U.S. Airforce personnel in Essex
during World War II. A memorial
window bears the arms of George
Washington, and the monogram of
the English-Speaking Union, and
the Essex Anglo-American Goodwill Association.

There is a library above the Porch, housing the collection of Dr
Knightsbridge, former Chelmsford resident, donated in 1679, which you
can visit on request. Much of the rest of the cathedral was rebuilt in 1800,
when the nave collapsed. On January 17 two workmen, engaged in opening
up a vault, excavated too close to the nave piers. They went home that night,
and at about ten o'clock the south arcade, clerestory, south aisle and roof
fell in, bringing down much of the north side at the same time. We can be
glad that a special Act of Parliament levied a sufficient tax on local residents
to supplement private donations, and enable the complete rebuilding of the
nave, including the finely carved and painted ceiling you will admire today.

Our main interest is with Thomas Hooker's dramatic ministry as St
Mary's, but you will wish to linger around the lovely interior, the modern
chapels of St Peter and St Cedd on your left as you enter; the startlingly
beautiful contemporary needlework hanging on the east wall, vibrant with
brilliant colour (depicting "Glory"); the free-standing altar, placed exactly
where Thomas Hooker wanted it (so that the communicants might gather
round the table as the first disciples did), but William Laud disallowed! It is
a massive single Westmoreland slate, which blends with the honey-toned
limestone floor; the lectern of steel and bronze, matching a pulpit which
stands where Hooker's thunderous vehicle made Westminster to tremble,
and more besides.

The area to the north of the Sanctuary was formerly known as The
Mildmay Chapel. Here a brass tablet high on the wall engraves the names
of this voluminous family. Two principal monuments commemorate Sir
Thomas (d. 1566) and his lady Avice, their eight sons and seven daughters

Chelmsford Cathedral
The free-set Communion Table is exactly as
Hooker wished but Laud prohibited.

in line on either side; the other, Lord Benjamin Mildmay, Earl Fitzwalter (d. 1756).

Hooker would preach at least once a week before work began on the main market day. He would catechize the children on Sundays, besides assisting his rector at whatever services his Puritan conscience permitted. It was said he "drew the people from the ale houses"[29] with his persuasive oratory. They came from miles around, from the Earl of Warwick and the other great families of Essex, from the clergy who formed the Cuckoos' seminars, from the many families who later founded two nonconformist congregations which still exist, one at Chelmsford, one at Little Baddow. From them "Mr Hooker's Party" was formed (as John Winthrop, first Governor of Massachusetts, called it), which established Newtown (Cambridge), Massachusetts, and Hartford, Connecticut besides many other New England settlements.

The Chelmsford Congregation, direct successor to Hooker's St Mary's following, is today housed in an exciting modern complex of church and community enterprises at the large Christ Church United Reformed Church in the New London Road. Further up the road you come to the Chelmsford and Essex Museum at Oaklands Park, with well-displayed collections of town and county history open daily from 10:00–17:00 (Sundays 14:00–17:00), free, with excellent car-parking space. You will enjoy visiting both.

John Michaelson had newly come to St Mary's as rector.[30] He had strong reformist sympathies, so uncomfortable with the compulsory use of the Prayer Book that he used to arrive late for Services, so as to walk in when most of it had been read. He warmly supported the Hooker family. It was a gross injustice that hotter and emptier heads than the founding Puritans rioted in Chelmsford at the outbreak of civil war. They smashed the East Window, assaulted Dr Michaelson, and drove him from the parish. Hooker has been unjustly blamed for the outrage, despite the 12 year interval since he had himself been harried out.[31]

The assault on the East Window "in a riotous manner and with long poles and stones," took place on 5 November 1641, and would be partially caused by the heightened emotions of a Gunpowder Plot celebration. We have already seen that Hooker would use the occasion for warning his congregation against any threat to their liberty. To be fair to the churchwardens, they had taken out the "scandalous pictures" of the Virgin, and of the crucifixion, the previous August, replacing them with plain glass. But the escutcheons of the Royalist nobility which decorated the edges of the window had been left intact. It was these the crowd attacked. You will be glad to know that although John Michaelson was forced to withdraw into semi-hiding in Writtle he was reinstated later on, Hooker's supporter to the end, so far as I know.

They were turbulent days. George Montaigne, Bishop of London before Laud, came to hear Hooker preach, and liked what he heard but "told him, for his sake, not to meddle with the discipline of the Church, the field was large enough besides. And he did promise him to do so."[32] If so, the consent was not very evident. Some time after Charles' marriage (16 May 1625) to Catholic Henrietta Maria, daughter of the ambitious Marie de'Medici, when memories of the Armada were still far from dead, Thomas was required to preach before the Judges of the Assizes then meeting.

Cotton Mather suggests that he called them to prayer, and invited their meditation on the theme of Malachi 2:11f, "An abomination is committed, Judah hath married the daughter of a strange God; The Lord will cut off the man that doeth this!"[33] A very brief period of silent prayer would be needed for every judge, and all their following, to grasp the point! Others of Hooker's sermons of that period also invited anxiety from his political opponents, if nothing more.

"Spiritual Munitions," 22 June 1626; "The Church's Deliverances," 5 November 1626; "The Carnal Hypocrite," also 1626; "The Faithful Covenanter," 1629; and "The Danger of Desertion," 17 April 1631.[34] This last, his farewell sermon before fleeing to Holland, challenges "Even so, England: Thou hast the temple and the priests, and yet may not God that destroyed Shiloh, destroy thee?—Will you have England destroyed? Will you put the aged to trouble, and your young men to the sword? Will you have your young women widows and your virgins defiled? Will you have your dear and tender little ones tossed upon the pikes and dashed against the stones? Or will you have them brought up in Popery, in idolatry, under a necessity of perishing their souls for ever, which is worst of all?"[35]

It is strong stuff. "Come, let us go hear what that bawling Hooker will say to us," Mather recounts of the Chelmsford mob.[36] "The man had not long been in the church, before the quick and powerful word of God, in the mouth of his faithful Hooker, pierced the soul of him; he came out with an awakened and a distressed soul, and by the further blessing of God upon Mr Hooker's ministry, he arrived unto a true conversion."

So it went on, week after week, as the crowds grew and the impact spread. This is surely the full import of Thomas Hooker's Chelmsford ministry. Up to this time he had been increasing in stature as a scholar, a counsellor, a preacher. There is evidence of preaching tours in the Midlands, and around London.[37] His skill in leading people to Christ drew larger and larger numbers to hear him, pledged to follow the way of God in the steps of Mr Hooker—"his Company." But before Chelmsford there is no semblance of a political edge to his work. Now it appears, and how!

It can be put down to his maturation. It was exacerbated by the importance of Chelmsford, and its proximity to the seat of government. It was enlarged by his followers, now amongst the most influential in the county. But it has also to do with his growing understanding of how The Truth (The Gospel) is implemented. "Heart religion" continued to be his beginning and his end. But in between, alive and kicking, the "uses"[38] of his faith grew to be more and more demanding, and inescapably political. No longer an academic exercise, no more a pastoral counsel, it seems that at last he had relinquished all expectation of a national evolution towards the godly commonwealth of Puritan dreams, and was openly courting a spiritual conflict which could climax only in civil war.

At Esher that would have been irrelevant. In Cambridge another matter altogether. Here in Chelmsford, it took on political significance for the first time, and he went with it. Nonseparating Congregationalism, towards which he was rapidly moving, became the battle cry of revolution.

Sit in the empty cathedral a moment, and listen. His spirit speaks there still. If you hear his seductive voice echoing down the years, calling you to face the consequences of our pitifully weak human choices, and to turn to God for a more meaningful existence, will you too not rise up and follow him? They did, or else they drove him away. There could be no middle path.

As you come out of the cathedral, you will see to your left, across New Street which girds the Cathedral Close, an ancient house, Guy Harlings. Today it is the Diocesan Centre, with offices, lecture rooms, archives, and secluded grounds for study courses where once the Mildmays strolled past beds of aromatic herbs.

The elder Thomas Mildmay, you recall, bought Guy Harlings in 1530, when he rose from marketeer to merchant. Thomas Hooker may have dined here often. There was a gracious side to the Chelmsford story and we should not ignore it.

The situation at Chelmsford could not be contained indefinitely. Laud had been appointed to the see of London in July 1628. He immediately started to weed out unacceptable (ie. Puritan) clergy. He conducted the investigations personally in many cases, either through the Court of High Commission in London, or himself visiting such courts locally. Thomas Shepard recalled the unnerving experience in his diary. "He looked as though blood would have gushed out of his face, and did shake as if he had been haunted of an ague fit, to my apprehension, by reason of the extreme malice and secret venom. I desired him to excuse me. He fell to threaten me, and withal to bitter railing, call me all to naught, saying "You prating coxcomb, do you think all learning is in your brain?""[39] Hooker was amongst the first to fall under suspicion.

So we find Samuel Collins, Vicar of Braintree, in correspondence with Laud's ecclesiastical chancellor, Dr Arthur Duck, with a view to the unobtrusive removal of Hooker from public office. "All men's eares are now filled with the obstreperous clamour of his followers against my Lord ... All would be here very calme and quiet if he might quietly departe."[40] The letter from Collins is dated 20 May 1629, less than a year after Laud had come to London.

It is a pitiful letter. We shall learn later of Hooker's association with Braintree, where he is said to have been involved with a conventicle which could not have met without their vicar's connivance. It appears that Collins attempted allegiance with both sides in the dispute, ingratiating himself with the strong reform element in his home town, and with his bishop in London at one and the same time. Small wonder he concluded his letter, "And now I humbly crave your silence, and that when your worship hath read my letter none may see it, for if that some in the world should have the least inkling thereof, my credit and fortune were utterly ruined;"—a back-handed compliment to Hooker's prominence and popularity.[41]

Sir Arthur Duck, M.A.,LL.D., 1580–1648,[42] was a formidable figure. He was a West Country man, born at Heavitree, near Exeter, in Devon, the birthplace of Richard Hooker, 1553–1600, the celebrated author of *Laws of Ecclesiastical Polity* who is sometimes confused with Thomas Hooker, but of no known connection. One can safely assume that the young Arthur was influenced by his famous older neighbour in the small Devon village.

Duck was MP for Minehead in Somerset from 1624. He had been admitted an advocate at Doctor's Commons (the London Society of ecclesiastical lawyers, with its own courts and chambers near St Paul's), as early as 1614. He became legal advisor to Laud at Oxford, Chancellor of the Diocese of Bath and Wells and then of the Diocese of London. He continued to work for Laud when Laud was translated to the Archbishopric of Canterbury, and was also close to King Charles, who sent for his support when a prisoner in the Isle of Wight. He died on 16 December 1648, and was buried at his Chiswick Manor, on the banks of the Thames not far from Westminster. Wealthy, influential, intimate with the Royalist Party, Samuel Collins must have known how much he endangered Thomas Hooker in opening a provocative correspondence with Dr Duck.

Hooker was summoned to appear before the Court of High Commission, and on June 3 a further letter was sent by Samuel Collins, promising his continued help in silencing Hooker, but that Hooker was inaccessible, being already in Leicestershire, and "All men's heads, tongues, eyes, and ears are in London and all the counties about London, taken up with plotting, talking, and expecting what will be the conclusion of Mr Hooker's business."[43] Mr Collins really was a persistent trouble maker!

On his return from Leicester, Thomas Hooker appeared before the Court of High Commission in London and was dismissed from his Lecture-ship at Chelmsford. A Mr Nash, tenant-farmer of the Earl of Warwick at

Great Waltham, next to Chelmsford, put up a surety of £50 for his later appearance before the court and Hooker withdrew into Little Baddow.[44] Had he been allowed to live unmolested at his school there, the later accommodation of New England's ruling Puritans to the emerging, ever more democratic, constitution of a United States of America had been the more painful, for he might have stayed at home.

He remained active at St Mary's, Chelmsford long enough to preach his Gunpowder Plot sermon there, that 5 November 1629. John Michaelson must have encouraged him still to preach, despite Laud's ban. But his detractors immediately pursued him again.

On 3 November 1629, not even waiting for the explosive gunpowder sermon, John Browning, Rector of Rawreth, informed against "one Mr Hooker, lately in question before your honour," directly to William Laud.[45] Rawreth is ten miles south of Chelmsford, on the A130 towards Wickford (birthplace of Elizabeth Reid, baptised 27 November 1614, who married John Winthrop Junior, later Governor of Connecticut: she renamed New Town, Rhode Island, Wickford, after her birthplace), and Rayleigh (where the Mount marks the place of the first Norman castle in Essex, the only one mentioned in the *Domesday Book*, 1086).

Here we are in the exposed southern valley of the River Crouch. Ashingdon stands to the east where a thousand years ago, King Canute defeated the forces of the Saxon king Edmund Ironside, and the Danes "thus for a time became masters of England." There is little to draw you into this rather remote part of the county, but it illustrates the openness of Essex to the invasion of North European peoples and ideas, and the extent of the hostility as well as of the devotion, which Hooker drew upon himself.

Rawreth's fine church spire points to the open marshlands which skirt the North Sea, and the wide open empty skies above, but its Rector's finger pointed accusingly at Hooker, and brought about his final exclusion.

Immediately upon hearing of Browning's attack, forty-nine of Thomas Hooker's supporters, "ministers in the partes adjoining, all beneficed men, and obedient to His Majesty's Ecclesiastical laws" spontaneously got together and petitioned Laud on Hooker's behalf, pleading, "we all esteeme and knowe the said Mr Thomas Hooker to be, for doctryne, orthodox, and life and conversation honest, and for his disposition peaceable, no wayes turbulent or factious."[46] To no avail.

That was on 10 November 1629. Seven days later a further petition was addressed to Laud, signed by forty-one of the clergy in the Chelmsford area. They did not mention Hooker by name, but the inferences were clear. They were, they said, being coerced by the popular opinions being advanced by the Puritan lecturers, "with nonconformists to runne the same waye," and they pleaded for Laud's protection.

Laud was ill at the time, but punitive action followed inexorably, and Hooker was again cited by an ecclesiastical court, sitting at Chelmsford on 26 July 1630, to appear before the Court of High Commission in London. He chose to break bail, and fled to Holland in the late Spring of the following year.

When we recollect the absence of good roads, and the shocking state of those that were available, so deeply and dangerously rutted that the use of more than two-wheeled vehicles was periodically banned in Essex,[47] these comings and goings of the eighty-seven ministers (three signed both petitions), over so large an area of the county, within the space of a few days, is highly significant.

In his June 3 letter, Samuel Collins had compounded the controversy with his fear that "It drownes the noise of the great question of Tonnage and Poundage."[48] This requires further elucidation.

King Charles I was at odds with Parliament from the moment he succeeded his father on 27 March 1625. His marriage to French-Catholic Henrietta Maria followed five weeks later. He straightway loaned English warships to his unpopular new relation, King Louis XIII of France, to help attack beleaguered French Protestants at La Rochelle in Brittany. This apparent attempt to curry favour with England's old enemy Catholic France, at the expense of their Protestant allies in La Rochelle, coming on top of the marriage with a Catholic princess, was hailed with dismay by most English Protestants. Even the mildly Puritan Rector of Earls Colne, Ralph Josselin (1616–1683), in his celebrated Diary, comments with consternation at "The strange carriage of King Charles—towards Rochelle in betraying same."[49]

England was still at war with Spain. Parliament, with a show of pique, resisted Charles' war levies. He summarily dissolved it on 12 August 1625. However, he soon found himself at war with France as well as Spain, and to raise the necessary taxes was forced to recall Parliament on 6 February 1626. But a Reformist Parliament was determined to win concessions for freedom of religion and trade, and it lasted only four months. The king again dissolved Parliament, on 15 June 1626.

Charles was hard pressed for money. His ambitions in Europe now forced him to support the Protestant cause. He promised £30,000 a month to the protestant armies of King Christian IV of Denmark, campaigning in Germany, on top of his Spanish and French campaigns. He tried to sell the crown jewels to the Dutch, but even failed in that. Almost as a last resort, he revived the highly profitable Tonnage and Poundage taxes.

These dated back to the reign of Henry VI (1421–71). They consisted of customs duties payable on wines (tonnage) and on merchandise (poundage) imported or exported. They could bring in as much as 12 pence in the pound. At first they were levied only in times of national crisis such as war, but later they were voted by Parliament to the incoming monarch for life. Charles was the sole exception in the long history of Tonnage and Poundage, from the 15th century until these taxes were abolished in 1787. He was, unfortunately, incapable of taking the hint, and attempted to impose them without Parliament's consent.

When Parliament was recalled for a third time, on 17 March 1628, far from learning humility from their two year banishment, the House of Commons formulated a Petition of Rights, which Charles was forced to sign four days later. This forbade him to imprison his subjects arbitrarily, or to levy taxes until the Commons had approved.

The king acted as if he had not signed the petition. He insisted that the tonnage and poundage taxes be enforced. Matters came to a head early in 1629. On March 2, he demanded the adjournment of the recalcitrant parliamentarians. Whereupon they, you may remember, forcibly held down Sir John Finch, Speaker of the House of Commons, locked the doors, and passed resolutions to the effect that religious innovations (ie. anti-Calvinistic practices—Laud was by now busily at work in London) should cease, and "those who levied or paid tonnage and poundage" were enemies to their country.

Charles immediately dissolved Parliament for the third time, and ruled without a Parliament for the next eleven years. He may have died like a martyr. At times he behaved like a fool.

Now in the midst of these explosive scenes, when the fate of a nation was tipping from comparative Elizabethan stability into Stuart genocide, Samuel Collins appears from nowhere, crying to the Bishop of London (Charles' most avid supporter) that the noise of Thomas Hooker's silencing in Chelmsford out volumes that of the critical tonnage and poundage controversy! We must not take turncoat Samuel too seriously, There can be little truth in the assertion that the tonnage and poundage issue, which contributed so dramatically to the subsequent outbreak of a civil war, was of less importance than the dismissal of a provincial lecturer.

Nevertheless the statement was genuinely made by an educated gossip, who did not dare to express his own ideas openly, but picked them up from the general conversation he overheard around him. It must indeed have seemed to many grave Puritan politicians that the furore caused by Laud's insensitive attacks on Hooker and the other Puritan clergy took precedence for them over most other current disputes, including crucial affairs of State. No Hooker, no hope! Additional credence has therefore to be allowed to Thomas Hooker's extraordinary influence in Chelmsford, and the political implications which flowed from his ministry there.

During these turbulent closing years in Essex, Thomas and Susannah remained at Cuckoos Farmhouse, Little Baddow. It is time to visit their place of residence.

Little Baddow, Hooker's And Eliot's Hillside Hide-out, c. 1626/9–1631

How to get there.

The six mile journey to Little Baddow from Chelmsford is somewhat demanding. Catch an infrequent bus from the main Bus Station in Duke Street. This takes 35 minutes as it meanders round Great Baddow and Danbury. The nearest bus stop to Cuckoos is at Holybread Lane off North Hill, with a walk of nearly a mile, compensated by views across the Chelmer Valley to Springfield and Chelmsford. Cuckoos, a 16th century half-timbered house, fronts Church Road at its junction with Holybread and Colam Lanes.

Or, drive south from Chelmsford along the A130 signposted Southend-on-Sea. Take the first exit onto the A414 marked Danbury/Maldon. At the first round-about cross over the dual-carriageway (A12 by-pass), and, at the second round-about, take the immediate left turn into Hammonds Road, parallel with the A12 going north. You first pass Graces Walk on your right, an avenue of trees climbing up to Great Graces (home of Sir Henry Mildmay in Hooker's day). Take the next major right-hand turn, signposted Little Baddow, which is Church Road. You come at once to St Mary's Parish Church on the left, the Hall opposite, and the Reformed Church further up the road, with Cuckoos on your right, beyond.

The Parish Church Of St Mary The Virgin.

The Hooker family undoubtedly worshipped here[50] during their sojourn at Cuckoos. The Vicar, John Newton, was "a very uneasy conformist," and welcomed the new residents. He was one of the 49 signatories who petitioned Laud on Hooker's behalf. When Laud made a visitation of the London Diocese in 1637, it was reported that Newton so objected to bowing at the name of Jesus, that he skipped around it to prevent any noxious nodding, when reading from the New Testament.

His congregation contained even more scrupulous members. Susan Cook hung up her washing to dry in the church. She said it was in protest at Newton's wearing a surplice, "her rags had as much right to be there."[51] Her daughter, a doughty replica of the mother of recognisable East Anglian independence, said it "were a good turn if he were hanged up there" with the washing. The memorials to the dead are less controversial. These include two rare wooden effigies in the south aisle most intricately carved, and the splendid Mildmay tomb near the altar. Any strident echoes from the past are now silenced by the serene yet homely beauty of the place. It radiates an atmosphere of vibrant parish life, along with an awareness of its historic treasures.

There is the priceless medieval mural of St Christopher (c. 1370) on the north wall, reminding you of the confluence of Sandon Brook with the river Chelmer close below the church, once a crossing of swirling danger in the perennial floods which isolated the village from its market at Chelmsford up to the last decade—and there is evidence of Roman and Saxon material in the tower.[52]

Stroll outside, through the quiet graveyard. If you shut your ears to the snarl of traffic on the new A12 by-pass, which cuts a desecrating swathe through the Chelmer valley below, the prospect is scarcely changed from Hooker's day. As he walked down the lane to worship, or take meals at the Hall, did he not enjoy the remoteness of this hillside hideout, as you will for very different reasons? Once across Sandon Brook, you enter a screened-off world with a secret life of its own, secure, select, a safe haven still from any corruption outside.

The Chelmer with its floodplain bounds the northern approach, the exposed Heather Hills and the Ridge make a barrier against the jagged indentations of the Blackwater North Sea Estuary to the east. The ancient heath formed by Lingwood and Danbury Commons guards the south, and Sandon Brook, a formidable obstacle under flood, completes the natural defences of an area of scattered dwellings, undeveloped up to the past half-century. A small nucleation settled round the church and hall, and at the far end of Holybread Lane, a mile away at Wickhay Green, and again at Coldham End where the two shops are found today. Otherwise, "Isolated farms and cottages were the rule rather than the exception,"[53] with never a village green or centre for easy expansion. I do not say this is necessarily a good thing. I simply rejoice that the sanctuary Thomas and Susannah found here, awaits you.

Sir Henry Mildmay of Great Graces Manor.

Sir Henry Mildmay (d. 1639),[54] Member of Parliament, Sheriff and Deputy Lord-Lieutenant of Essex, lived along Chapel Lane, at Great Graces. He supported the Puritan party as his forbears had done. You will wish to inspect his ornate tomb in the sanctuary at St Mary's, a "standing wall-monument with reclining figure, propped on elbow between black columns," as Pevsner describes it,[55] with both Sir Henry's wives kneeling at his either side. Alicia Harris to the left, who bore him three daughters, and Amy Gurdon to the right, the mother of another daughter, and two sons.

Lady Amy was an endearing person. Her younger son, Walter, died early, and left his large estate to "his deare and loving mother Dame Amy

Mildmay as a small testimony of my great thankfulness to hir for all hir love and extraordinary tender care."[56] She too came of a well-known Puritan family, being sister to the Brampton Gurdon of Assington (d. 1649) who sailed in the *Arbella*, his kinsman John Winthrop's flagship, to help found the Massachusetts Bay Colony in 1630.

The Gurdons had an allegorical nonconformist ancestry. They claimed descent from the robber baron, Sir Adam Gurdon, who died in 1305. He had supported the parliamentary reforms of Simon de Montfort, and forfeited his lands when the great Earl of Leicester met his end at the battle of Evesham (4 August 1265) in which Sir Adam also fought. The battle placed Edward I effectively in control of England, even though his father Henry III continued king in name for a further seven years.

Sir Adam armed a band of outlaws, rampaged up and down the country in the name of parliamentary democracy, and was trapped by Edward's army at Halton in Buckinghamshire, between Aylesbury and Wendover, not far from Amersham. The swashbuckling baron challenged Edward to single-combat (reminiscent of Robin Hood's famed cudgel fight with Richard Coeur-de-Lion), was worsted by the warrior king, and put up such a good fight that Edward granted him a full pardon and restored his estates.

The second son of Sir Adam inherited the Assington estate in Suffolk (between Colchester and Sudbury), where Brampton was living at the time of his emigration to New England. With nearly 400 years of such a family history behind them, it was small wonder the Gurdons supported religious and parliamentary reform.

Brampton was succeeded at Assington Hall by John Gurdon (1595–1679), MP for Ipswich, and a judge at the trial of Charles I, although in the event he refused to attend. Thomas Hooker was close to the family. His first published work (a preface to John Rogers' *The Doctrine of Faith*, 1627) was dedicated to Lady Amy Mildmay, and also to Brampton's second wife, Mistress Gurdon, and to Mistress Helen Bacon, relative of the celebrated Sir Francis Bacon—an interesting side-light on his circle of friends.[57]

Sir Henry Mildmay was a powerful Puritan. He was the third son of Sir Thomas Mildmay of Springfield Barnes, one of the Springfield Manors, and therefore neighbour to William Pynchon, later of Springfield Massachusetts. The Springfield Barnes Manor House stood near to the bank of the river Chelmer, opposite Little Baddow.

This Sir Thomas was the son of Sir William of Springfield Barnes (d. 1571), and a nephew of Sir Thomas of Moulsham (d. 1566, Master Auditor), and of Sir Walter (d. 1589, founder of Emmanuel), all three of them sons of the founder of Mildmay affluence, old Thomas the mercer of Guy Harlings (d. 1550).

To complicate matters, Sir William Mildmay had married Agnes, widow of Adam Winthrop senior (grandparents of John Winthrop, Governor of Massachusetts). And their son, Sir Thomas Mildmay, father of Sir Henry of Great Graces, married Alice, a daughter of the same Adam Winthrop, though by his first wife Alice Hunne. This looks like a brother-sister relationship, a by no means unprecedented instance of inbreeding in those days of high mortality in childbirth, when a wealthy man might lose several partners and the choice of suitably endowed women was limited. It also explains the very close relationships enjoyed by Puritan families spread geographically across the whole of England.

Being a younger son of Sir Thomas of Springfield Barnes, Sir Henry did not inherit the major estate, but was settled at Great Graces instead. You might well suppose him to have had the best of the bargain. Great Graces, a mile along Chapel Lane (which runs at the side of the present Little Baddow Reformed Church), looks out over the Chelmer vale from a wooded hillside, with elevated panoramas across the lowlands, whilst Springfield Barnes wallows in the floodland below.

Lady Alicia Mildmay, first wife of Sir Henry, "drowned herself in a pond by reason of her husband's unkindness,"[58] perhaps where the reservoir lies on the right-hand side of Chapel Lane as you approach Great Graces from the Reformed Church, in a deep dip which jumps up to the great house beyond. No one would have seen her. The old brick walls, Elizabethan windows now blocked up, and, I believe, some interior panelling, is all that has survived from the 16th century house. The mansion which replaced it is reduced in size: yet still great with grace.[59]

It was Sir Henry's elder son, also Henry (d. 1692), who fought for Parliament as Colonel of the 50th horse, and quarrelled with Sir John Bramston of Skreens, Roxwell. He was not much loved by anyone. MP for Essex, as so many of his family had been, he got his nose publicly tweaked by a Sir Edward Turner at an election. "For which he said he would complain to Parliament, and further said that since he was hated by all gentlemen in the country, he would make them fear him."[60]

However, his influence was a protection to the Puritan Congregation during the trauma of the 1662 Act of Uniformity, and for a time he was landlord to the first licensed Nonconformist Minister, John Oakes, at "Hillhouse otherwise Watts," now known as Walters Cottage, which still stands next the corner of North Hill and Tofts Chase (it was not alienated to Sir Gobert Barrington, the mainstay of local Puritanism, until 1670).[61] Walters Cottage was occupied by the Independent Pastor, Evan Jones, as late as 1764–80.

The youngest of the second Adam Winthrop's four daughters, Lucy (John Winthrop's sister), married Emmanuel Downing whose father had signed the Statutes of Emmanuel College with Sir Walter Mildmay in 1585. Lucy and Emmanuel stayed many times with the Mildmays at Great Graces. Their son, Sir George Downing (1623–84), when about fifteen, accompanied his parents to Massachusetts, and finished his education at Harvard. He was the second graduate in the first Class of 1642. Downing Street, Westminster, where the British Prime Minister has official residence at No 10, was named after him.

Unloved by the early settlers for his too eager transference of allegiance to Charles II at the Restoration, after being a member of the Commonwealth Parliaments, and his over zealous hunting down of the regicides Barkstead, Corbet, and Okey when they were in hiding in Holland, his reputation has been "stained by servility, treachery, and avarice."[63] Pepys wrote "All the world takes note of him for a most ungrateful villain." The informed tourist will therefore glance warily into Downing Street, when in London.

Postscript. Sir Henry Mildmay's daughter Alice married Richard Harlakenden of Earl's Colne.[64] He was a close friend and Emmanuel College contemporary of Hooker's son-in-law, Thomas Shepard. His brother Roger Harlakenden sailed with Shepard in the *Defense*, and bought Governor Thomas Dudley's large house (next door to John Haynes) when Hooker's trek to found Hartford, Connecticut, took place. Enter through the door of one of these founding families, and you're on a sliding staircase into one hundred more!

Little Baddow Hall.

Across from St Mary's Church, Little Baddow Hall overhangs. You can see the broken fireplaces in the ragged endwalls where once the Manor extended over the road into the churchyard. The road then ran round the other (north and west) sides of the church. The west wing of the hall was never rebuilt, and the shortcut has become the main road. It is still a graceful house, the 14th/15th century exterior and the interior great hall now divided into two rooms, full of character and charm.

There were two original Manors in the Parish of "Badwen," (probably derived from the Saxon name of the river Chelmer, Beadewan, meaning "birch-stream").[65] Badwen, consisting largely of the manor (built where Little Baddow Hall now stands), with Great Graces—and Mildemet, or Middlemead, which consisted principally of Tofts and Bassetts. They were in two different "Hundreds" (ie. a grouping of villages which together could make up one hundred pence in rents, or £1 per annum, according to the Domesday Survey),[66] Badwen in the Chelmsford Hundred, Mildemet in the Dengie Hundred (going towards Maldon).

The population at Domesday (1086) was little more than 100, rising to perhaps 250 by 1600. The two ruling manors then came together, effectively

Little Baddow Hall

under the lordship of Sir John Smythe (d. 1607),[67] a contentious figure, with a long record of overseas military service, but an undisciplined tongue which got him into the Tower of London in 1596 on a charge of treason, despite his having raised his own troop for the defence of the realm at the time of the Armada. He had marched his men to Tilbury in time to hear Queen Elizabeth's celebrated speech to her army there, when invasion threatened. He was released from the Tower under house arrest at Tofts.

Sir John had inherited Tofts from his father Clement Smythe, who married Dorothy, sister of Jane Seymour, Henry VIII's third wife, and from that time Tofts was the controlling manor. Little Baddow Hall was leased to various occupants, but Great Graces was sold by Sir John Smythe in 1591 for £1800 to an Arthur Herrys to clear his debts, and Sir Henry Mildmay had purchased it and was resident by 1612.[68]

Thomas Hooker and John Eliot must have been entertained at The Hall by the Jacob Maldons, tenants from 1607, and by the Mildmays at Graces, on numerous occasions. I wish you too could be included. Relax in either garden, after a meal, on some auspiciously chosen, warm May evening, amity in the air, flowers under your feet, birds at evensong in a thousand fruit trees planted in every direction, and you infiltrate England at her very best.

The Lords Barrington of Hatfield Broad Oak, Essex, Puritan Patrons.

The Barringtons were one of the few Saxon families to survive the Norman conquest and retain their lands. They had been woodwards of

Hatfield Forest for Ethelred the Unready (father of Edward the Confessor, d. 1066). Once part of the Royal Forest of Essex, Hatfield Forest today is reduced to a pleasant stretch of ancient woodland, administered by the National Trust, open to the public for walking, riding, and fishing all year.[69]

It is near to Bishop's Stortford in Hertfordshire, off the A120 (Roman Stane Street), and the A1060, which converge on Chelmsford a dozen miles away to the east. Hatfield Broad Oak lies between the two roads, on the B183 from Hatfield Heath to Takeley, a pretty village in a sylvan location.[70]

If you enter from the south, ie. Hatfield Heath, you come upon a wide main street, reminder of the markets once held there, and bend around the pubs, the remaining 16th and 17th century houses pleasingly distributed, and finally into the great sweep of road round the church of St Mary the Virgin, where the great priory stood, and back on its tracks to Barrington Hall, which stands across the fields to the rear.

The Benedictine Priory of Hatfield Regis was founded by Alberic de Vere, first Earl of Oxford, in 1135. An effigy of Robert de Vere, third Earl of Oxford will be found in the Sanctuary, as this was part of the vast Oxford domain, and Earl Robert was buried here (1221). The present imposing church structure, built upon the site of an earlier timber Saxon church, is only a small part of the nave of the great Priory church and ancillary buildings. There are Barrington memorials on every side. The family traces its ancestry to an Adam de Barrington, baptised by "him the sayd Augustine,"[71] first Archbishop of Canterbury, c. 597 AD. They had secured the estates around Barrington Hall from the 12th century, and purchased the domestic quarters of the priory from Lord Rich (purchased from the Crown at the Dissolution) in 1564, and lived there until the present hall was constructed, in 1740.

If you continue along the B183 northwards, from the narrow alleyway which took you into the Church, you quickly see Barrington Hall, above its lake, set grandly in landscaped gardens on your left. The Hall is currently used as an administrative headquarters, and creative perfume centre, of Contemporary Perfumes, Ltd., so it may be possible for you to arrange a visit. It is most tastefully designed and cared for. If you come away with a sense of opulence it will owe much to the grandeur of the place, and that was nothing foreign to the lordly Barringtons, Puritans, and patrons of people like Thomas Hooker.

Sir Francis Barrington[72] was a highly respected Puritan. He married Joan Cromwell, daughter of Sir Henry Cromwell of Hinchingbrook, Huntingdon (grandfather of Oliver Cromwell to whom Lady Joan was aunt). The Barringtons were a dauntless couple. She voluntarily shared her husbands imprisonment when, for conscience sake, he was committed to the Marshalsea, a prison formerly at Southwark, London, kept by the Lord

Marshal for "persons charged with contempt of His Majesty's courts," but abolished in 1849.[73]

Sir Francis was MP for Essex from 1603–28, an ally of the Earl of Warwick and the Reform Party in Parliament, opposed to the general drift of Stuart policies. When King Charles I attempted to exact forced loans without the consent of Parliament, Sir Francis and his son-in-law Sir William Masham of High Laver, Essex, refused to pay. They were imprisoned (1626), and Sir Francis, now 76 and in ill-health, died. He was widely regarded as a martyr, a memory long sustained in Essex.[74]

This was not without effect on Thomas Hooker, who had joined the ranks of leading Essex Puritans by the time Sir Francis died; nor, indirectly, on the whole Massachusetts Bay Colony, for the ubiquitous Roger Williams, long time friend of Hooker, was Sir William Masham's chaplain at Otes Manor, High Laver. He too left his lively, if idiosyncratic, mark on the new Colonies, as Hooker was to do in more orthodox manner. Williams got himself banished by John Haynes when Haynes was Governor, and founded Rhode Island. Hooker got permission to leave the Bay Colony and founded Connecticut.

Roger Williams, farsighted freedom-lover as he undoubtedly was, could leave mischievous fingerprints around when his obstinacy was roused, and did so all over High Laver. He decided to offer his hand in marriage to Lady Barrington's niece Jane Whalley,[75] whose mother was Frances (neé Cromwell), Lady Barrington's sister. Jane was staying with her cousin Lady Masham, who was also the daughter of Lady Barrington.

Jane's brother, it may be recalled, was the Edward Whalley[76] who rose to be one of the administrative major-generals of his kinsman Oliver Cromwell's Commonwealth. He was Warder of the captured Charles I at Hampton Court, "with due courtesy," for which he received a royal letter of thanks when the king escaped; and one of the signatories of his death-warrant (never was thanks so harshly rewarded), when Charles was captured again. He escaped in 1660 to Boston, Massachusetts, with his son-in-law William Goffe, and ended his days in hiding near Hadley, in the same New England State, c. 1675.

Roger Williams, employing diplomatic language he would have done well to imitate in his later New England controversies, approached the formidable Lady Barrington before putting the question to Jane, or to their mutual hostess Lady Masham. He reminded Lady Barrington, "who as an Angel of God discerneth wisely," that "Many and often speeches have long fluttered or flown abroad concerning your Ladyship's near kinswoman and my unworthy self—Like a rolling snowball or some flowing stream the report extends and gathers stronger and stronger—Good Madam, may it please you then to take notice: I acknowledge myself altogether unworthy and unmeet for such a proposition (but) to wrong your precious niece and answer her kind love with want, would be like gall to all the song of my life and mar my marriage joys."

Many blandishments follow: "The Lord that hath carried you from the womb to grey hairs crown those grey hairs by making your last days, like the close of some sweet harmony, your best—outshining all those stars that shine about you, going down in grace, rising in glory in the arms of your dearest Saviour, to which everlasting arms he often commits your soul . . .," in a word grant permission for the marriage and be rewarded with bliss hereafter!

Lady Barrington, not altogether to Roger's surprise I think, for he was aiming well above his station, dismissed the proposed match with outrage. Williams replied in kind. "Good Madam, it is not for nothing that the God of Heaven hath sent such thunderclaps of late and made such great offers at the door of your ladyship's heart—weaknesses in the outward and trouble in the inward man, what are they but loud alarums to awaken you? Remember, I beseech you, your candle is twinkling and glass near run. The Lord only knows how few minutes are left behind." But the threat of her mortality did him no good, so he quickly married Mary Barnard,[77] lady-in-waiting to Lady Masham. Everybody thought that about right. In fact, Lady Masham relented sufficiently to arrange the wedding at Otes—or was it that her mother told her to hurry up the nuptials for fear of another onslaught!

Sir Thomas Barrington, eldest son of Sir Francis and Lady Joan, was more circumspect. He quietly married his heiress, Frances Gobert.[78] The Little Baddow branch of the family perpetuated her name, for in 1650 Sir Gobert Barrington purchased the large manor of Tofts, in which the Hall, Cuckoos, and many other properties were held, and came to reside there.

The Gobert Barringtons were devout Puritans, and keen supporters of the congregation left behind by Thomas Hooker. This continued to worship within the Parish Church until evicted by the Act of Uniformity in 1662.[79] The Rector at that time was Thomas Gilson. He was sheltered by the Barringtons when dismissed his living for refusing to obey the Act (which enforced the *Book of Common Prayer*, and repudiated the National Covenant of 1638, which had licensed Presbyterian ministers). He stayed on in the village for a time, under Barrington protection vainly seeking a presbyterian license.

John Oakes,[80] ejected from neighbouring Boreham, was more fortunate. The Barringtons took him into Tofts Hall. He and his family then moved into Colonel Henry Mildmay's property at Walters Cottage, as already noted. He was granted a license for worship, and remained as pastor of the new Independent Congregation until 1678. However, this was not until 1672, when Charles II issued a "Declaration of Indulgence for Tender

Consciences."[81] In the meantime Cuckoos became again the main meeting place. Worship was held in a barn, the site of which has been preserved. There was no lack of preachers. A third clergyman, the celebrated Elias Pledger, ejected from St Antholin's church in London, had also found refuge in Little Baddow.[82]

The Pledger family put down roots, and in time provided members for both St Mary's and the Reformed Church. They were active in village affairs well into the present century, the last Miss Pledger to be a member of the Independent congregation in the early 1900s being also its organist. The family established Bequests, partly devoted to the work of the Independent congregation. This was in addition to trust funds in favour of the new Meeting House set up by the Barringtons; by Edmund Butler, nonconformist resident at the Hall, whose will in 1717 provided for a Butler Charity School, with a free distribution of clothes to children from Little Baddow and Boreham; and, later, but in the same tradition, by a William Ling for the distribution of coal and warm clothing to the adult members.[83]

In such ways an on-going concern for social as well as spiritual reform was indicated. It sprang directly from the example and teaching of Thomas Hooker and John Eliot. This helps to explain the astonishing growth of the early congregation. By the next century attendances exceeded 300, out of a local population of not more than 250! A complex of stables had to be erected to accommodate the travelling crowds.

After the death of Sir Gobert, his widow realised that such growth could only be accommodated in a new Meeting House. She made provision in her will and her son Francis, who married Elizabeth Shute, made further donations, including Bridge Croft, a plot of land carved out from the Little Baddow Hall home-farm on which the Chapel and Manse stand today. Thus in 1707 the Independent Meeting House, now the United Reformed Church, was erected.

The emergence of these small but trenchant Nonconforming congregations in 17th century rural Essex is little short of miraculous. Following the Act of Uniformity in 1662 came the 1664 Conventicle Act. It made illegal all meetings of more than five persons whether in a private house or elsewhere, enacting "that if any person, above the age of sixteen, shall be present at any meeting under colour or pretence of any exercise of religion, in other manner than is allowed by the liturgy or practice of the Church of England—he should be liable to fines, imprisonment, and transportation."[84]

A Five Mile Act in the next year prohibited any minister of religion from coming within five miles of any corporate town for the exercise of his ministry, except where authorised by a non-resistance oath. Not until the Toleration Act of 1689 under the newly crowned sovereigns William and

Mary was it possible for Nonconformists to practice their forms of worship with impunity. Yet in this period, thanks to the protection of its leading families, and owing everything to the remembered stature of Thomas Hooker, the Little Baddow congregation progressed from strength to strength.

Before leaving the Barringtons, we should note that their family's influence was perpetuated by a remarkable young man named John Shute, later Barrington (1678–1734),[85] who inherited Tofts Manor in 1710. He was the son of a wealthy Puritan London merchant, attending the Dissenting Academy of Mr Thomas Rowe, where Issac Watts, the great Hymn writer, had earlier attended, and finished his education at the Protestant University of Utrecht, and London's Inner Temple. He was an able theologian and lawyer, and rapidly rose to recognition as the leading Nonconformist of his generation. This did not prevent his becoming a favourite with king George I, nor of the ageing agnostic philosopher, John Locke. His was a most winning personality.

A ditty by Watts drew attention to Locke's influence over his young disciple—

> Shute is the darling of his years,
> Young Shute his better likeness bears,
> All but his wrinkles and his hairs
> Are copied in his son![86]

He published a number of well-received works, *An Essay upon the Interest of England in respect of Protestants dissenting from the Established Church, The rights of Protestant Dissenters*, and *A Dissuasive from Jacobitism* (supporters of the deposed James II, and the exiled House of Stuart, after the Glorious Revolution of 1688). All these books went into several editions, the last into four in its first year (1713). This established Shute as the Leader of Dissent, and greatly pleased many who were otherwise disinclined, because of his anti-Jacobite stance.

George I was delighted to have such a publication on the eve of his succession. He invited John Shute to a private audience on his second day in London, and used his influence to return him to Parliament as member for Berwick-upon-Tweed in the first Georgian Parliament of 1715. By this time Shute had inherited the Barrington estates through the marriage of his cousin Elizabeth to Francis Barrington of Little Baddow. He also inherited a second fortune from a John Wildman of Becket, in Hampshire. Wildman had no other connection with John Shute than admiration. He left his estate to "the worthiest person whom he knew." Dean Jonathan Swift (author of *Gulliver's Travels*, etc.) described Shute as "a young man, but reckoned the shrewdest head in England, and the person in whom the Presbyterians chiefly confide," adding "but he is truly a moderate man, frequenting the church and the meeting indifferently."

His general acceptability was employed by the Whig government to advance union between Scotland and England, officially ratified in 1707. John Shute was sent as a goodwill ambassador into Scotland to negotiate with the Scottish Presbyterians, and with complete success. This was reflected in his elevation to the Irish Peerage in 1720, as the first Viscount Barrington, Baron Ardglass of County Down.

Lord Barrington continued to occupy Tofts, and was one of the five foundation Trustees of the Little Baddow Meeting House.[87] His generosity enlarged the investments and the freeholdings of the congregation, and his presence lent a lustre to its work. So large were the numbers attending, eventually peaking around the 350 mark, that galleries were required round three sides of the small building, and the stables were extended round two sides of what is now the car park, to shelter the horses and carts which on Sundays brought people to worship from many miles away. Thomas Hooker had chosen wisely when he retreated to this attractive and strategic site.

Lord Barrington, however, made Becket in Hampshire his principal seat, and died there on 14 December 1734. He was succeeded by his eldest son, William Wildman, second Viscount Barrington, but here the story ends. In 1758 Lord William Barrington and his family decided to conform to the Church of England. He must have been living at Tofts at the time, because he persuaded John Steffe, then the Nonconformist Minister at Little Baddow, to go with him. The poor preacher possibly had no viable alternative.

The story is that Steffe preached one June Sunday, 1758, at the Meeting House; was received into the Anglican church by the Bishop of London that same week with his patron; was instantly ordained; and read the service at St Mary's Little Baddow, as their vicar, the next Sunday. It was a multiple blow to the Reformed congregation, the hurt reflected in the recorded comment that "his character was not such as to produce any regret among his former friends that he had taken the step which he did."[88]

John Steffe remained in the village as vicar until 1789, a source of embarrassment between the two congregations which persisted in strained interchurch relationships for a further one hundred and sixty years. Lord Barrington, however, sold his Essex properties, and more tactfully withdrew.

So ended a highly individualised first phase in the life of the Little Baddow Congregation. Like its founder Thomas Hooker, the congregation's identity stemmed from a burning quest for national reform. They too were opposed to Independency and Presbyterianism alike, wanting only the reformation of the established church, but social pressures dictated otherwise.

In New England the movement turned swiftly into Congregationalism as the tiny churches in the small pioneer settlements found themselves separated into independent units, with no useful recourse to larger alignments such as a resuscitated Anglican system would have brought to North America. In England on the other hand, movement was rather towards Presbyterianism, as affording the only practical defence against an established State Church. This tended, as persecution hardened after the Restoration of 1660, and Presbyterian hopes for a dominant role in ecclesiastical government faded away, to drift into Independency. This is what happened at Little Baddow. Hooker's dream of a reformed Anglican Church merged into an enforced Independency, quite contrary to his original intention. Not until 1965 did the Little Baddow congregation officially join the Congregational Union of England and Wales, although today it is contentedly within the British United Reformed Church.

The Meeting House and Manse-cum-nonconformist-school.

The Chapel Building.

The Meeting House, Independent or Congregational Chapel, now United Reformed Church, as it has variously been called, sits on a 1.6 acre site on the southern slope of the beautiful Chelmer Valley. Look first into the churchyard, its gravestones rising out of carefully managed grasses filled with wild flowers.

With so much of our ancient meadowland disappearing under roads or houses, and reduced as a result of modern agricultural practices, it has become essential to preserve the wildlife contained within the safehavens of churchyards. One additional bonus here is the increasingly rare Meadow Saxifrage which, with a sympathetic mowing regime in recent years, has increased from a dozen flowers to over a thousand. The grounds as a whole are an oasis for wildlife, 65 species of wild flowers being discoverable in the graveyard alone.

Together with the graveyard and the manse, there are the remains of an old orchard and nut walk beyond the 18th century cartshed. The chapel itself is rectangular in plan, and is built of warm red brick with blue headers. There are four excellent mullion and transom windows with semi-circular heads. Besides these there are two ovoid ("bulls eye") and two circular windows, providing upper light.

With financial help from the Barrington family the chapel was opened in 1707. Few buildings which boast the architectural claim of "Queen Anne" are genuine, for her reign lasted only 12 years, but this is one. Devoid of ostentation, it is disarmingly simple and dignified in design, upholding the best traditions of nonconformity at that time. Thankfully little has changed since, with the exception of a later entrance porch in the east wall (the old north doorway having been blocked up, as can be clearly seen), and a schoolroom or large vestry, added at the south end.

Inside, the building has a lustre of its own, the old oil lamps, so long in use, converted to electric light but retaining the charm of antiquity. A large renovation scheme at the turn of the century stripped the galleries from three of the walls, took the rostrum-pulpit from its commanding position on the west wall, between the two ovoid windows, enfolded by the people above and below, and placed a small pulpit behind a communion table at an elongated south end, turning the pews to face it. This has disturbed the true orientation of the building, and has taken away the visible gathering of the congregation around the open Bible in a central pulpit.

Fortunately, the sense of a gathering of the saints still persists, aided by the original intention of the proportions of the interior. Aesthetically worship here can still be nothing other than a meeting of people round about the Word of God. The truth of Independency, so long sustained here, that religion if of the heart and will, of personal vision and response, persists.

On the west wall, above where the rostrum used to be, are memorial tablets to the Morells, descendants of Huguenot refugees, father and son consecutively Ministers of the congregation from 1799–1877;[89] and one to a former church secretary for 34 years, David Marven, whose forbears Matthew and Rainold followed Thomas Hooker to New England and were founder members at Hartford, Connecticut. Their names are inscribed on the founders stone in the grounds of Centre Church, Hartford. Some of their descendants are still members of Little Baddow URC.

Beside the porch outside you will see another memorial tablet, to the family of William Parry, Minister from 1780-1799. It relates the death of his wife and two children, all within the space of three months.

Insatiate Archer, could not one suffice?
Thy shaft flew thrice and thrice my peace was slain;
And thrice, ere thrice yon moon had filled her horn.[90]

Bereft of family, William Parry proposed that a large manse be built alongside the church, half to be the Pastor's residence, half a residential school. Sick at heart, he filled his home with small boys. The project was completed in 1794; and for many years continued the Hooker tradition of providing urgently needed education for the children of Dissenting parents, who were often victimised by an otherwise predominantly Anglican school system, or none at all for poorer families.

The educational contribution of the Nonconformists at Little Baddow, a very small village up to modern times, is nothing short of phenomenal.

First the school at Cuckoos; then the Butler Charity school, which developed into a "British" school, part of a nationwide organization from 1830–1899 which provided non-sectarian education in distinction from the "National" schools, which were altogether Anglican.

Happily the two systems merged in 1899, at which point the assets were wisely devoted to the public good. The Butler School House became the Little Baddow Village Hall, occupying the site of the old Charity School, at the centre of the present village on North Hill. Finally, there was the Parry residential school at the manse.

Such was William Parry's benevolence that, aware of the financial penury suffered by the widow of his predecessor, still resident in the village, he pioneered a relief fund for the widows and orphans of ministers in the Essex and Hertfordshire region, which is still operative. He then involved himself in founding what became the London Missionary Society, the overseas wing of the Congregational churches, instrument of their evangelical and social work throughout the world.

The Manse.

To provide accommodation for future ministers and their families, the manse was built in 1794. Additional rooms for the accommodation of a small school and dormitory were added on the east and west shortly afterwards. The manse is a good example of a late 18th century dwelling, with well proportioned sliding sash windows and a double pitched slate roof with central valley gutter. The simple doorcase is also well-proportioned with pilasters and lintel. The walls of the original building are of lath and plaster, but some brickwork was used in the extensions and alterations which have been made from time to time, as required by each generation.

The manse ceased to be used as a school last century, but part of it is still in use as a Sunday school and small conference centre, favoured for day retreats in the three acres of grounds surrounding the house. It contains a small history centre set up in 1982 for Essex Puritan studies, and in these ways preserves the congregation's understanding of itself as the spiritual resource it has been, since its beginning.

The former classrooms, and the dormitory in what is now called "the Apple Room" (from a lapsed period when apples instead of boys were stored there), where the embryo historical collection is housed, can be viewed by appointment.

Notice the one remaining eighteenth century open-sided cart shed as you leave. It is listed by Essex County Council as being of historical interest, a reminder of the halcyon days when crowds travelled to worship here. An apocryphal story claims that the sheds backed onto the western, Chelmsford side of the grounds so that, when the Duty Elder stationed by one of the two elliptical windows over the old pulpit spotted an arm of the law legging it across the fields from Chelmsford, to apprehend some unauthorised conventicle (the Seditions Meetings acts long imposed limits on the number of permitted meetings), the Elder's warning cry would allow everyone to leap into the pony-traps or carriages, and vanish from sight, concealed by the intervening solid stable walls; but that I do not altogether believe!

Cuckoos Farmhouse and School, Home of the Hooker Family and John Eliot.
What is indisputable is the survival of Thomas and Susannah Hooker's place of residence. Across Chapel Lane and the home paddock, there it stands for all to see, Cuckoos Farmhouse. It is not from the hedgerows of this lane, with their hawthorn and blackthorn, sloe and elderberry, blackberry and spindleberry, honeysuckle and wild roses, that the ghost of Thomas Hooker materialises, but from darker, sunken Colam Lane the other side of Cuckoos. There, when nights are black and the wild winds shriek across the wide Blackwater Estuary beyond Maldon over Little Baddow Ridge, a desolate desperate tract 350 years ago, a stern Puritan figure, wrapped in a long cloak, stovepipe hat on head, emerges with unhurried dignity from the hedgerow, crosses the lane towards Cuckoos, and disappears. There is no recorded feeling of fear, only awe, as he strides purposefully past the pond into his house. The last known sighting was some thirty years ago.

This story is documented, and well vouched for amongst the papers in the History Centre, as is the appearance within Cuckoos of none other than, supposedly, the great John Eliot. He is a cheerful, bouncy little ghost seen by the children of the previous occupant. He sits on the end of your bed, smiles merrily, and, when last seen, insistently pointed to a section of the bedroom wall where, on investigation, an unsuspected stairway was disclosed which led into the kitchen below.

John Eliot was a young man when he lodged at Cuckoos, doubtless with the hearty appetite of a clerk in holy orders. He may have been concerned for the childrens' easier access to food. At any rate, the stairway was uncovered, and the children said to be filled with happiness from his apparition. He was always a favourite with children. Mather says he carried sweetmeats in his pocket, especially for the impoverished Indian children.[91] Sadly the ghostly Eliot stairs are in use no longer.

Cuckoos Farmhouse[92] is a handsome timber-framed building, typical of many other Essex buildings, with overhanging upper storey and moulded bressumer beams on carved brackets, its great brick chimney reaching up from the tiled roof, probably one of three originals in the larger structure of Hooker's day. No mansion such as a rich landowner would require, but a fine house nonetheless, fit for an eminent clergyman, spacious

Little Baddow Manse, 1794. The minister's dwelling is at right, school at left, Chapel left rear. From a 19th century painting.

enough for one of the largest libraries to be transported to early New England, with space for a growing family and a small residential school.

The present building dates from the early 16th century, but references to Cuckoos, or Cukkoks, as a freehold tenement, date back to 1369 when a Walter Cukkok of Rivenhall (some seven miles east of Little Baddow) sold the property. John Porter, whose family later emigrated to New England, held it in 1620 at a rent of two shillings and seven pence. He is said to have made it available to the Hooker family. This is the more probable because it was later sold to Sir Henry Mildmay of Great Graces and his Puritan and local interests are well known.

The date of the Hooker's arrival is not known, nor is that of John Eliot. But if Eliot was indeed ordained on, or before, leaving College, then any date after 1625 could have seen the Hooker entourage in residence. My inclination is towards an earlier date than 1629, when Thomas was finally excluded from Chelmsford.

The significant facts, however, are (1) that at Cuckoos Thomas Hooker consolidated a vision and a clergy-group which helped to democratise the religious and political life of both Old and New England; (2) that here the unique contribution of John Eliot to New England's educational practice was hammered out, under Hooker's tuition; (3) that the modern movement for the translation of the Bible began here, through John Eliot's conversion to a more positively evangelical Puritanism.

Cotton Mather quotes from a lost manuscript, "written by the hands of our blessed Eliot," which gave an account of the Cuckoos episode. "To this place was I called, through the infinite riches of God's mercy in Christ Jesus to my poor soul," wrote the apostle, "for here the Lord said unto my dead soul, live, and through the grace of Christ, I do live, and I shall live forever! When I came to this blessed family I then saw, and never before, the power of godliness in its lively vigour and efficacy."[93]

This scarcely reads as a conversion to Puritanism, but it plainly betokens a fresh revelation of new life in the Holy Spirit, which encapsulates Eliot's career following his tutelage at Cuckoos. The setting could not have been more idyllic.

The plain of Chelmer sinks gently to the river, and across to Springfield in front. The Danbury hills rise quite steeply behind. The house is girdled with flowering shrubs, and beds of old English garden flowers. Massed roses and honeysuckle scent the Summer air. Nothing obtrudes to spoil the memory of this cradle of America, with its dreams part-born of tranquil hearts grateful for the temporary sanctuary they found on this spot, after the bitter persecutions of Chelmsford. Certainly not the flock of rare, ring-straked Jacobs sheep which browse the home pastures as their predecessors did for the clothing of Susannah's children.

In the farmyard is the foundation of the barn where the first congregations met, and where, on a Sunday evening near to Hooker's birth (and death) on July 7, each year an open air commemoration service is celebrated. An illuminated vellum scroll hangs encased on the wall of a later barn, overlooking the original site, with the legend of the Hooker Saga inscribed by a local artist, the glass fronted case made by a local antique furniture restorer, for Little Baddow is still a highly self-sufficient community, and has had to be.

There is a second civic plaque outside the West Room, facing the front drive-way, commemorating the residence of Hooker and Eliot, and the school they kept here between 1626–31. It was unveiled during the first Open Air service on Sunday 6 July 1986, as part of the 400th Anniversary Celebrations of Hooker's birth, arranged by the Little Baddow Historical Society.

If you wish to see inside, it is essential to make prior arrangements via the Society. The reception hall has an early 18th century stippled pattern on the far wall, reminiscent of the decoration the Hookers would have expected prior to any general use of wallpaper. The low-ceilinged room opens onto the West Room, to the right, thought to have been the schoolroom where Hooker and Eliot taught. It is a charming room, backed by the later addition

The west room at Cuckoos Farm, Little Baddow
said to be Hooker's schoolroon.

of a long low lounge visible through what were the exterior slatted window-frames, both rooms opening onto an informal country garden.

Hooker had opened "the little academy, at the request of several eminent persons, in his own hired house," according to Mather, who added a characteristically imprecise but provocative comment, "having one Mr John Eliot for his usher, at Little Baddow, not far from Chelmsford; where he managed his charge with such discretion, with such authority, and such efficacy, that, able to do more with a word or a look than most other men could have done by a severer discipline, he did very great service to the church of God, in the education of such as afterwards proved themselves not a little serviceable."[94]

Who these eminent persons and their serviceable sons might be is not stated, but the inference, since the population of Little Baddow was scarcely more than 200, is that they included some of the wealthy Puritan families from the surrounding neighbourhood as boarders.

The West Room would also have been used for the monthly meetings of Puritan clergy, so frowned upon by William Laud and his officers, near-seditious groups in which, the Bible open before them, Hooker and the Cuckoos company wrestled with the principles of reformation, and planned a New Commonwealth when the hope of amending the Old had died.

There had been monthly clergy meetings in the Chelmsford area before Hooker arrived. He seems to have taken hold of these, and hardened them into a fellowship of theocratic criticism and development. They met for fasting and prayer. They went away to plan their voyages across the Atlantic, and the sort of Biblical society they would construct when they got there.

We do not know when his congregational convictions matured into their final form of a New Society based on a Covenant freely entered into by a local Congregation-State, strengthened by federal ties with agreed neighbours, as emerged on the banks of the Connecticut River, and defended in Hooker's definitive work, *A Survey of the Summe of Church Discipline. Wherein, The Way of the Churches in New England is arranged out of the Word, etc.* (1647). However, as early as 1624, Edward Winslow had returned from Plymouth Plantation to London to negotiate problems with their pastor, John Lyford, which largely arose out of his attachment to Anglican *Prayer Book* observances, and his lack of sympathy with New Plymouth's outright Independency. It was agreed "to choose two eminent men for moderators in the business: Lyford's faction chose Mr White a counsellor at law; the other part chose Reverend Mr Hooker, the minister."[95] He was then at Esher, already, you note, acceptable as an advocate for the Plymouth separatists.

However, for the time being, let us relax in this serene corner of a bygone age, and reflect on the mental and spiritual refreshment Hooker and his family found here. There were now four children living in the home, with two deceased in infancy during the past three years. Sarah's death in 1629 intervened between the fateful letters of Samuel Collins and John Browning that same year, which brought about Hooker's eviction from Chelmsford. Personal tragedy was never far from Thomas and Susannah Hooker's door and bore on the deepening of their outstanding sensitivities to the needs of others. Let us gratefully savour the charms of Cuckoos in remembrance of the brief interval of peace it brought the Hooker family.

The Cuckoos Company and The Making of Connecticut.

"Hooker became the spiritual leader of a large company of Essex Ministers of nonconforming sympathies." (Mather).[96]

The highways of East London and Essex moved upon Chelmsford from every point of the compass. When Thomas Hooker took up position in St Mary's central pulpit, huge crowds were drawn to him almost as a matter of course. But Little Baddow was a different case. By comparison it was a voyage into a backwater. Yet the flow of people concerned to listen, to consult, to plan new worlds with him continued unabated. Many were to follow him overseas. If the question is asked "What effect had residence at Cuckoos on Thomas Hooker?" some account needs to be taken of the drawing power of the place.

Little Baddow has a lode-stone quality, a property which invites exploration. This has something to do with its location on the northerly slopes of hills screening it from direct sunshine, so that the light has to force its way into the village, beckoning the traveller as to a secret haven. Part of the explanation lies in its history, the early waterway with its mills along the river inviting prosperity, the hill-fort on the Heather Hills inviting safety, the scattered farmsteads inviting investigation, the easy access to prime markets from the security of its seclusion combining commercial opportunity with freedom from stressful congestion to this very day.

Hooker himself was no stranger to personal magnetism, and provided the strongest drawing power. He attracted disciples wherever he went. But at Cuckoos it was the drawing together of a company of scholars, reformers, and empire builders for the clarification of their aims and their destiny. "It is the resolution of his friends and himself to settle his abode in Essex, and maintenance is promised him for the fruition of his private conference, which hath already more impeached the peace of our church than his public ministry," wrote Samuel Collins[97] to Dr Duck (28 May 1629) in a clear reference to the Cuckoos seminars.

"There be divers young ministers about us that seldom study, but spend their time in private meetings and conference with him or such other as are of his society, and return home in the end of the week and broach on Sundays what he hath brewed, and trade with his stock. He is their oracle in cases of conscience and points of divinity, and their principal library. Our people's palates grow so out of taste that no food contents them but that of Mr Hooker's dressing." Doubts predominated. His mind was not made up before a further testing of solitude and frustration in Holland. But the Cuckoos company launched Connecticut.

Who were its members? There is no record of attendance but the 49 clergymen who petitioned for Hooker's release from Laud's constraints in 1629 come within the ambit of the Cuckoos company. All were in sufficient unanimity with his views and with each other to compile and sign the petition at very short notice. Some of them lived close by Cuckoos, as a glance at the list of names, and a map of Essex, quickly shows.

John Michaelson at Chelmsford, Thomas Burr at next door Broomfield, John Newton at Little Baddow, Gilbert Dillingham at Sandon on the doorstep, Nicolas Bownd and Isaac Joiner at Springfield, Giles Alleyn at Great Waltham (where Susannah and the children were to hide), Thomas Weld (later Eliot's Associate at Roxbury, Massachusetts) at Terling, all adjacent. Nathaniel Ward (later Pastor at Ipswich, Massachusetts) at Stondon Massey, Robert Brooke at Woodham Walter, Robert Paley at Heybridge, Samuel

Collins (the Judas of the company) at Braintree, each only a few miles further off, with the renowned Stephen Marshall at Finchingfield, William Horsfield at Wethersfield, others a few miles more distant but mostly within a radius of ten miles from Chelmsford.

Some members were not available to sign the petition, as John Eliot, John Rogers of Dedham and his son Nathaniel (curate at Bocking later to succeed Ward at Ipswich, Massachusetts), Thomas Shepard (Hooker's successor at Newtown, Massachusetts) at Earls Colne, Samuel Stone (Hooker's Associate at Hartford, Connecticut) at Stisted, Roger Williams (later to found Rhode Island), and John Norton (of Ipswich and Boston, Massachusetts) both at High Laver, Hugh Peter (later to be Hooker's host at Rotterdam, and one of the first Overseers of Harvard) curate at Rayleigh. To this large group must be added "Mr Hooker's Party" from Braintree and Chelmsford districts, under William Goodwin of Bocking, who preceded him to New England, and a host of neighbour families, including the William Blakes of Bassett's Manor, Little Baddow, and the John Porters who earlier resided at Cuckoos. John had married a Sible Vessey of Little Baddow at St Mary's (12 September 1587), and settled into the family's prosperous tanners and glovers industry at Spring Elms Lane in the village, before making way for Thomas and Susannah Hooker. They removed to Felsted, whence his son John, by then married into the Loomis family of Braintree, emigrated with the Ephraim Huitt Party, to which Joseph Loomis' family was also attached, to Windsor, Connecticut, 1638. There the Porters and Loomis' were granted adjacent plots, and became influential citizens, thus supplementing the close ties between Hooker and the Connecticut River Towns.[98]

The Pynchons of Springfield (founders of Springfield, Massachusetts) belong to this group, as do the Marvens of Great Bentley (founders of Hartford, Connecticut), and the great families who supported Hooker but stayed in England, the Warwicks, Mildmays, Barringtons, Bacons, Gurdons, and not least John Haynes, who followed him into New England.

It is inappropriate to describe all these families here. Some have been introduced already, others will be covered in the following account of the towns and villages which are associated with Hooker's work. It is the breadth of his influence, and the volume of his effective leadership from exile at Cuckoos, that we need to comprehend. However, one predominating and mutually enriching relationship demands more detailed consideration, namely the presence of John Eliot at Cuckoos during the period c. 1626–1631. I shall deal with this in the final part of this Chapter.

Two More Manors.

Tofts Manor, Home of the Gobert Barringtons.

Eastwards, Church Road merges into Holybread Lane, and makes a T junction with North Hill at its end. Opposite, on North Hill, and a little to the right, you will see Walters Cottage, sometime home of the Reformed pastors. To the left is Tofts Chase, a back route to Maldon via Woodham Walter. The entrance to Tofts Manor lies on your right as you drive along this lane.

Tofts[99] is a shadow of its former grandeur, but still an impressive building, a very desirable reminder of its past splendour when, from the 14th century onwards, all this side of Little Baddow paid tribute to Tofts, formerly Mildemet Manor.

William Toft died in 1470; there is a brass plaque to his memory at St Mary's. His daughter Isabella married Thomas Smythe. Their son, Sir Clement married Dorothy, sister of Jayne Seymour, Henry VIII's third wife. The son of this union was the Sir John Smythe whose unbridled tongue landed him in the Tower of London. These all lived at, and enlarged, the manor house.

For a period Sir John held Little Baddow Hall, Great Graces and Riffhams manors, in effect the whole of Little Baddow except Bassetts. He was followed by Anthony, and then Henry Penninge, and by the Barringtons from 1652. Sir Gobert paid the large sum of £6,648 for the properties, in addition to the debts of its last owner the shiftless Henry Penninge (£500 owed to a London tailor, £600 to a London clothworker, £400 to a London grocer, etc., an interesting insight into the extravagance of some 17th century gentlefolk when others of their neighbours were selling up everything in order to establish a divine commonwealth in North America).

The Blakes of Bassetts Manor, Co-founders of Springfield, Massachusetts.

Continuing east from Tofts you will see Old Bassetts down a lane on your left, a barn-like timber construction which reverted to a farmhouse when new Bassetts was built some time after 1588. Proceed further and round a bend in the lane you run into Bassetts, facing towards you in all the beauty of its elaborate gleaming white pargetted facade. I consider it one of the most appealing, most livable of smaller buildings in Essex, framed by shaded gardens with the Heather Hills standing guard overhead, and the open land stepping smoothly to the Chelmer Valley below.

The Bassett family gave way to the Rawsons around 1390.[100] The last Rawson heiress married John Blake in the early 16th century and a Richard and Mabel Blake lived in Old Bassetts until 1588, when Richard died. His son Giles built New Bassetts. Giles' son, William emigrated in 1630 to Dorchester, Massachusetts. All this time, whilst not rivalling either the Hall or Tofts for size, the owners enjoyed freehold rights as the lords of Bassetts Manor.[101]

It was not until William Blake sold the property that it passed into Toft's possession (under the Penninges). But it regained its independence in 1650 when Sir Moundeford Bramston Master of Chancery, second son of Sir John of Roxwell, made it his principal seat. Incidentally, Moundeford was knighted at the Restoration by Charles II, for supporting the Stuarts throughout the Commonwealth.

Poor William Blake, he gave up this delightful property for better hope in both old and new England, only to see it pass into royalist hands within twenty years!

William Blake's mother was Dorothy, daughter of William Tweedy the trusted Captain of the private militia of the Earl of Sussex at New Hall, Boreham. He may well have been Catholic for his second wife Marjory (Dorothy Blake's step-mother) was a celebrated recusant, outspoken in defence of the Old Faith and out of harmony with her Puritan neighbours at Little Baddow. Her grandfather was Sir Edward Grene of Little Sampford Hall, another outspoken Catholic, with all his family. Marjory and her sisters were frequently presented at the Quarter Sessions for refusing to attend the parish church.

Many of these staunch Catholics were to be dispossessed of their properties following Queen Mary's reign. In retirement, however, Captain Tweedy lived on at Tweedy's Fief, later "Twitty Fee," an old property on the outskirts of Little Baddow, at Danbury, still signposted from The Ridge over the brow of North Hill, but demolished many years ago.

Giles Blake was surely influenced by his wife Dorothy, and together they must have influenced their son William. But he and his wife Agnes were as staunchly Protestant as his parents were Catholic. They are said to have educated their children at Thomas Hooker's school at Cuckoos. One would like to know how it came about that they broke with the family tradition, to the extent of quitting Bassetts for New England. There was no known pressure to emigrate, least of all on a small but prosperous lord of the manor in a strongly entrenched Puritan village like Little Baddow. None of the other Little Baddow landlords did. The suspicion must be that it was for conscience sake.

There was Blake's friendship with William Pynchon of nearby Springfield. Through that he would have contacts with the Roxwell group, and with the Dorchester Puritans, led by the celebrated John White. Perhaps it was also due to the magnetism of Hooker and the captivating charm of the youthful John Eliot down the lane at Cuckoos. Anyway to Dorchester Massachusetts, for whatever reason, the William Blakes sailed with their five children, some of the boys possibly Cuckoos trained, William, James, John, Edward, and Anna.[102]

William Blake was later to be one of the seven who settled Springfield. He went with Pynchon, sailing in Governor Winthrop's boat *The Blessing of the Bay*, to Agawam on the upper reaches of the river Connecticut, and there set up the trading post above the Enfield Falls which became the town. Blake was one of the five (Pynchon, his son-in-law Henry Smith, Jehu Burr, a Mr Michell, and Blake) who signed the Foundation Covenant, "being by God's Providence ingaged together to make a plantation at and over against Agaam, on Conecticot, doe mutually agree certayne articles and orders. It is ordered that William Blake shall have sixteen polle for his home-lott, and of the marsh in bredth abbuttinge at the end of it to the next high land, and three acres more in some other place."[103] Scant recompense for lovely Bassetts, but testimony to William and Agnes Blake's dedication to a reformed theology, in despite of their family history.

Excursions Into Thomas Hooker's Essex, Colchester and its Environs

Colchester, Ancient British Capital.

How to get there.

Colchester, the Fortress of the Colne, is 51 miles from London, 18 from Ipswich, and 21 from the large east coast port of Harwich/Parkstone. You can drive via the A12. There are good car parks and tourist amenities. Or you can travel by train from Liverpool Street Station, London. The railway station is a short bus or taxi drive from the town centre.

This natural stronghold, domain of Old King Cole the legendary father of St Helena (the Helena reputed by the chronicler Geoffrey of Monmouth, 1100–1154, to have married a Roman general, and given birth to Constantine, the first Christian Emperor)[104] sits safely on top of a steep ridge above the river Colne commanding the approaches beneath. The river, like a moat, guards north and east. The smaller Roman River gives natural cover to the south and west. Below it, the land fades into salt-marshes to the North Sea. There is evidence of human settlement from as early as the 5th century B.C.

The town's historical importance dates from the 1st century B.C. Known as Camulodunum[105] (from Camulos, a Celtic warrior-god) it had become the capital of king Cunobelin's loose federation of tribes in southeast Britain. One of Shakespeare's last plays, *Cymbeline*, tells his story.

When the Emperor Claudius directed a Roman invasion of Britain in A.D. 43, Colchester was the prime objective of his commander, Aulus Plautius. Claudius conveniently joined his 50,000 strong army at their

Moulsham (Chelmsford) headquarters.[106] He brought a reinforcement of elephants, a comfortable sort of bodyguard. He arrived in time to preside over the town's capture. He left 16 days later, more of a package holiday than a military campaign, taking his elephants with him for all I know.

It was at Colchester that Claudius received the submission of the seven regional chieftains. Rome controlled southeast Britain from that time on. He rewarded himself with deification. A huge Temple to Claudius and his victory crowned the ridge by A.D. 50. Never was god-head more smoothly gained.

The Norman Castle of c. 1085,[107] to which you should immediately direct your steps, was spread over the ruined Temple. Thus the Keep, which alone remains, is the largest ever built in Europe, because it utilises the Temple foundations. Your best approach is from the High Street, which follows the old Roman road from the West, or Balkerne Gate, now, as the name suggests, cut off from the traffic flow, but part of it still impressively erect. Halfway along the High Street the town hall stands out, with a good tourist information centre on the ground floor. The castle is at the far eastern end, with the attractive Lion Walk shopping precinct on your right, incorporating the library and Museum of Social Life and a lively street market crowding the pavements on Thursdays and Saturdays.

Colchester Castle

A museum now occupies the Norman Keep. In it you will find all the inducement you require to come to terms with Colchester's dramatic history. Here is one of the finest exhibitions of Romano-British antiquities in the country. It was, after all, the very first Colonia in England, set up in A.D. 48 with generous grants of land, villas, and cultural facilities to encourage Rome's veterans to remain in retirement.

There are models of Claudius' Temple, the Balkerne Gate, the Roman Port at the Hythe, and the dire siege of Colchester by Parliamentary troops in 1648. Colchester had declared for Parliament when the Civil War began in 1642 and celebrated the collapse of the Royalist cause after its defeat at the Battle of Naseby. However, King Charles escaped from Carisbrooke Castle in the Isle of Wight in 1647, and the second phase of civil war broke out.[108]

Whilst Cromwell dealt with the Scot's invasion, an insurrection of Kentish Royalists was thwarted by Sir Thomas Fairfax, general-in-chief of the New Model Army. They were driven across the Thames, but raised Royalist sympathisers in Essex as they withdrew towards fortified Colchester. There they heroically resisted Fairfax's encircling army for 74 days, but were pounded and starved into submission. The Royalist commanders, Sir Charles Lucas and Sir George Lisle were barbarously shot after their surrender. An obelisk in the castle bailey commemorates their death.[109]

The grounds outside the Keep delineate the girth of the great castle, and provide splendid views across the Colne valley as well as the relish of their floral displays in what is surely amongst the most enviable of public parks in Britain. In the grounds you will also find Hollytrees, part of the museum, a Georgian house (1718), reminder of Colchester's affluent past, with an enchanting display of childrens' toys, musical instruments, and costumes. The Natural History Museum is housed in the former All Saints Church, across the road outside.

You will find some unusually interesting refreshment places, such as The Red Lion Hotel, with its 15th century exterior and old coachyard, or The George opposite, Roman vaults lurking underneath the 18th century facade, both in the High Street near the Castle; or the Hole-in-the-Wall public house near the Mercury Theatre and Balkerne Gate at the far end of the High Street; and the Siege House at the foot of East Hill outside Hollytrees, which carries bullet holes from the 1648 assault. This is rather a long walk, but there are restaurants on the river bank, and you see parts of the ancient Roman walls as you go.

Far more of the walls is visible from the other end of High Street, where Balkerne Hill road rings the Roman ramparts. They are unique in Britain, dating from the 2nd century A.D., after Boadicea's [Boudicca's] sack of the town. Colchester was among the first targets of her tribesmen when they rose against an oppressive Roman rule in A.D. 60. The town was destroyed, but quickly recovered to become a major centre of trade in eastern England, particularly of the cloth trade by the 16th century. An hour long walk round the oblong circuit of the walls, approximately 3,000 ft by 15,000 ft, has been mapped for hardy walkers in the Museum's *Roman Colchester*, available as a separate pamphlet.

Amongst other places of interest, you may wish to visit St Peter's church on North Hill, again at the west end of the High Street, just beyond the Town Hall.It is mentioned in Domesday Book, though no more remains from Roman and Saxon times than some builders' rubble in the 18th century walls.[110]

St Peter's is the Sarre, Sayer, or Sears church, as several mural brasses inform you when you enter. In the south aisle you will see a plaque to John Sayer, "sometime Alderman of this towne," who died in 1509, and whose descendant Richard emigrated to Massachusetts in 1630, to found the American branch of the Sears family.

The spacious galleries might well have been raised for Thomas Hooker's packed congregations, had he obtained the appointment of Town Lecturer he sought. He would have attached himself to a congenial company of personal friends, with William Ames (then Fellow of Christ's College, Cambridge) lecturer in 1609, William Eyre (Fellow of Emmanuel) in 1610, and Francis Liddal (also a Fellow "of the same college" at the same time as Hooker) 1619. But Liddal was succeeded by Richard Madden (Fellow of Magdalen, Cambridge again contemporary with Hooker) in 1628, and by then it was too late.

The Town Lectures[111] had been given at St Botolph's and St James's churches before St Peter's became the established venue. After the Dissolution of the Augustinian Priory of St Botolph, its great Norman church became the civic church of Colchester, until battered down by Parliamentary siege guns in 1648. You will wish to explore the ruins, part of the glory of Colchester, down Queen Street opposite the Castle and into St Botolph's Street. St John's Abbey Gate, all that remains of a Benedictine Abbey founded by Eudes Dapifer in 1096 (owned by Sir Charles Lucas when he commanded the besieged Royalist forces in 1648) stands further along St Botolph's Street on the south side of the ring road junction, and enhances the walk, and your grasp of the scope and importance of medieval Colchester.

St James's, "the largest of the town's ancient parish churches, the only one built in the grand style of the later Middle Ages," stands hard against the Roman walls, where Minories (outside Hollytrees Museum) joins East Hill. You pass it when walking down to the Siege House. Returning to St Peter's, the interior shows what many Anglican churches looked like in the

16th/17th century days of great preachments, when even the altar could be built over with pews, until Laud began his clearing-up operation. It dates from 1758, to accommodate the large congregations which continued into Victorian times.

One reason for this is that the church has long been influenced by the Simeon Trust, founded by Canon Charles Simeon of Cambridge in the 18th century to ensure the appointment of evangelical clergy to key pulpits, of which St Peter's was one of the first. Simeon did much to restore the credibility of Evangelism in the Church of England after the revulsion brought about by the bigotry of some proselytising Sects during the Commonwealth.

As such, St Peter's is in direct succession to the nonseparating Puritanism of Hooker's persuasion, which had dominated Colchester, and made it a focus of reform. Hooker would have been very happy as Lecturer here, but the political effect of his ministry would have been peripheral in comparison with his opportunities at Chelmsford. Nonetheless, don't miss Colchester. It is unmatched.

The discerning visitor must come to terms with this evidence of the strategic situation, political significance, self-sufficiency, overseas trade and manufacturing power, ease of communication with Protestant Europe and a certain freedom (by distance and distinction from London) from interference with the practise of reform, which made Colchester an equally effective but very different centre of Puritanism from Chelmsford, making its own strong contribution to the moulding of Puritan sentiments, and the rise of revolution in Essex.[112]

Copford Green, Home of John Haynes, First Governor of Connecticut.

Copford Green is about six miles southwest of Colchester. To get there take the A1124 which runs west from Colchester, parallel with the A12 via Lexden, and the B1408 via Stanway and Marks Tey. It is less congested than the A12, and there are some attractive inns along this older route. Just before entering Marks Tey you will see a minor road on your left (south) signposted to Copford. Drive through the village to the Green at the far end. At a staggered crossroads, where the Easthorpe road comes in from your right you will find a signpost to the left marked Copford Church.

If you wish to visit Copford en route to Colchester from Chelmsford, take the Kelvedon exit from the A12 shortly after by-passing Witham. Double back under the A12 on the B1023 towards Inworth, and turn sharp left onto a minor road marked Messing. From Messing, which will be described later on, the same twisting country lane goes to Easthorpe (where you may catch a glimpse of the 500–year old Hall with its distinctive chimney stacks on your left), but turn right at the road junction, at the House

Without A Name, for Copford. You will enter the village at the staggered crossroads noted above, the Rectory on your right hand, the village on your left. Cross over the road, and follow the sign for Copford Church.

Copford Hall and Church of St Mary The Virgin.

John Haynes (1594–1654) third governor of Massachusetts and first of Connecticut, friend and New England next-door neighbour of Thomas Hooker, lived at Copford Hall.[113] That building has long since disappeared, but the present house is a pleasant red brick Georgian structure of seven bays, a porch of four Tuscan columns before a hipped roof, charmingly set in lawns and glades of trees, very different from the first manor house which, from 995 until the deprivation of Edmund Bonner in 1559,[114] had belonged to the bishops of London. There is some suggestion that Bonner, most determined of Queen Mary's persecuting bishops, who died in the Marshalsea prison in London when Elizabeth came to the throne, was buried here. In 1809 a workman is said to have found a coffin bearing his name.

John Haynes owned Copford Hall
prior to his migrating in 1633.

The Hall is a private residence, still owned by descendants of John Haynes, and not open to the public. But it can be seen across the park which encloses the church, "the beau ideal of an English landscape scene" (Pevsner), a plaisance to relish, if from a distance.

John Haynes emigrated with Thomas Hooker. Their ship, the *Griffin*, landed at Boston on 4 September 1633, and they proceeded by prior arrangement to the small settlement at Newtown already dignified by the presence of Thomas Dudley, second Governor of the Bay Colony. In point of fact,

Dudley had designed Newtown as the new State capital before Boston's stronger claims emerged, so that it became "one of the neatest and best compacted Townes in New England having many faire structures with many handsome contrived streets. The inhabitants most of them are very rich, and well stored with cattell of all sorts."[115]

John Haynes was quickly appointed a freeman of Newtown, then an Assistant and third State Governor in succession to Dudley. Bancroft's verdict on his impact on the young colony (in the monumental *History of the United States* by George Bancroft, 10 vols., 1862) was "of a heavenly mind and a spotless life of rare sagacity and accurate unassuming judgment; by nature tolerant, ever a friend of freedom."[116] Some of this rings falsely in the face of Haynes' public censure of John Winthrop, that he "dealt too remissly in point of justice"[117] (a personal attack which helped ease him into the governorship, much to Winthrop's dismay). His banishment of Roger Williams from Massachusetts appears equally harsh. But Williams paid the same tribute. "That heavenly man Mr Hains," he wrote in a letter to Major John Mason, "though he pronounced the sentence of banishment against me at Cambridge, then Newtown."[118]

He was "a gentleman of great estate," as well as of great heart. Both qualities are divulged by his willingness, and by his financial ability, to serve as Governor without remuneration, "partly in respect of their love showed towards him and partly for that he observed how much the people had been pressed lately with public charges, which the poorer sort did much groan under."[119] Yet he was aggressive enough to sustain a significant military career, as colonel of the Massachusetts Regiment in the early days of the Pequot wars, and as one of the Commissioners charged with "all military affairs whatsoever;" and later as a prime originator with Hooker of the New England Confederation of 1643, on which he served as a Commissioner for Connecticut.

The affirmative side of his character is again revealed in his championship of the far reaching Fundamental Orders of Connecticut (1639), which brought him the governorship at the very next General Court, a post he held every alternate year (the alternation was a requirement of the Constitution), until his death.

By his first marriage to Mary Thornton of Nottingham, two sons were born who remained in England, and a daughter, Mary. Robert the elder fought as a Royalist in the English Civil War, his brother, Hezekiah, was Cromwell's Major General for the Eastern Counties.[120] It is Hezekiah's progeny who have continued to own Copford Hall to this day.

John Haynes was married a second time, after Mary's death, to Mabel Harlakenden, by then resident at Newtown, whose family we shall meet at Earls Colne. Five children were born to them, John, Roger, Joseph, Ruth, and Mabel. The Haynes family then joined Hooker at Hartford, building their new home on an adjacent plot. The two men were all but inseparable from Chelmsford days until their deaths. They lie interred as they had lived, side by side, in the old burial ground behind Centre Church, Hartford. It is not unreasonable to see in them kindred characteristics. Without ambition for themselves, with forgiving forbearance to their contemporaries, with an unbending but contagious integrity, and an unvarying vision of a godly commonwealth, each strengthened the other in friendship, and made a political community out of their inner convergence.

Copford Church of St Mary the Virgin.

Twelfth century St Mary's is described by Nikolaus Pevsner as "The most remarkable Norman parish church in the county."[121] The medieval wall-paintings justify this accolade in themselves, a kaleidoscope of incongruous shapes, figures, colours, tossed together in bright confusion some time around 1140–1150. Although the tunnel-vaulted nave was largely destroyed when the south aisle was built, the apse remains with Christ in

Copford Church of St Mary the Virgin

glory, supported by angels and apostles, adorned with zig-zag bands, Greek keys, signs of the Zodiac, mailed figures of the virtues, and the raising of Jairus' daughter for good measure.

I doubt if you will find anything better in England. The tunnel-vaulting is duplicated only in the Chapel of St John in the Tower of London. There are other treasures inside and the verdant setting outside to engage your delight. What must it have meant to John Haynes to quit such a life-style, such artistic riches, for the rigours of early New England!

It is advisable to make certain that the church is open before you time your visit. I am sure that a discreet call to the Rector, or the Rector's Warden, will suffice.

Messing, Home Of The Bush Family.

How to get There.

Follow the directions given for Copford. From Copford Church return to the staggered crossroads and go straight over, taking the minor road signposted Easthorpe and Messing.[122] In Easthorpe turn sharp left at The House Without A Name, into Messing.

Messing has suddenly sprung to prominence from the election of George Bush as President of the United States, and the claim that he is descended from the John Bushe whose baptism is recorded in the Messing Parish register for 20 January 1594. John's son Reynold Bushe emigrated to Massachusetts in 1631. It is thought that he made the passage in the *Lyon*. If so, he journeyed in company with John Eliot. The ship sailed "probably about the middle of August," and made landfall at Natascot (Nantasket) on 2 November. John Winthrop, whose wife was on board, noted in his journal for 3 November 1631, "The wind being contrary, the ship stayed at Long Island ... the next morning, the wind coming fair, she came to anchor before Boston."[123]

A visit to the village will not add to your understanding of Thomas Hooker, who did not come here so far as I know, but it will reinforce certain impressions already received. Drive past the Old Crown inn (a good place for luncheon) to All Saints Church. You can park there, at the bend of the road outside the west end. It stands tall with its prominent brick tower, built in 1840.

Much of the church now dates from an extensive[124] Victorian restoration, but there is also earlier work, and some novel exhibits. Look to your right as you enter by the west door. The American flag flown over the Capitol at Washington, DC in 1989, and afterwards transported and presented to the parish, is displayed on the wall, and other memorabilia.

In front of you, at the far end of what remains of the 14th century nave and its striking roof, is a Chancel "considered one of the finest Jacobean church interiors." Pevsner calls it "rustic," but the effect of the heavy wooden panelling, separated by Corinthian pilasters, with the moulded plaster ceiling above, is admirable. It was designed in 1634 by the lord of the manor Hanameel Chibborne, and Nehemiah Rogers, vicar from 1620–42.

Nehemiah Rogers was one of the Emmanuel College, Cambridge students who "got away."[125] He was a fervent royalist, a friend of William Laud, and on sufficiently good terms with King Charles I for the king to present him to a stall in Ely cathedral. He paid for his loyalty by being sequestered, although reinstated to other parishes in Essex (Little Braxted 1648–50, Doddinghurst 1656–60) after deprivation.

In the Chancel you will find not choir but rare communion stalls.[126] They are a relic of the 17th century restoration of the altar to the centre of the chancel, with seats on either side, which was a feature of reformed worship. Laud did away with it, restored the table to the east end, and fenced it off with altar rails. The Puritans fought hard to retain the practice of gathering round the table in communion, so it is strange to find the practice perpetuated here, in Nehemiah's chancel. It suggests that the hard conclusions that we sometimes draw about 17th century (particularly "Puritan") theology and liturgical practice need to be expressed with some caution.

The east window is very special. It is suggested, in the Church Guide, that it came from New Hall, Boreham, and was placed here by Sir Charles Chibborne (d. 1619). The theme is taken from the Acts of Mercy of St Matthew 24, verses 35–36 ("I was an hungred, and ye gave me meat; I was thirsty, and ye gave me drink; I was a stranger, and ye took me in," etc.). It was made by Abraham Van Linge, one of the celebrated Flemish stained glass painters of that day. The six main scenes are executed in great detail, buildings, furnishings, clothing, and not least the visible expectations of the needy, so that they form a social commentary as well as a work of art. It is worth driving to Messing for this window alone.

It also raises the question of the Puritan's attitude to poverty. This was not simply a subject for stained-glass windows. "There were more and more poor people," writes William Hunt in *The Puritan Moment. The Coming of Revolution to an English County*, quoting, amidst a detailed analysis of increasing destitution in late 16th and early 17th century England, ministers like George Gifford of Maldon ("multitudes—whose wives and children have scarce bread to put in their mouths") and Richard Rogers of Wethersfield ("great beggery").[127]

The causes of increased poverty have been sketchily outlined already. The aftermath of incessant wars, an increasing population, the debasing of coinage, the enclosure of land and increase of landless labourers who could never earn enough to make ends meet, out-of-work craftsmen, the inadequacy of what remained of the manorial system to provide the charity required by these, and all who were handicapped or disabled. The response of popular Calvinism was simple enough. The cause was human sin. The result was an outpouring of justifiable Divine wrath. The resultant human suffering was (a) thoroughly deserved, or (b) good for all sufferers as a learning experience in dependence on God's mercy, and (c) to be countered by penitential fasting and prayer to appease a just God, and fit the soul for whatever he chose to send.

Thus Hooker, in *The Faithful Covenanter*, a sermon preached at Dedham, "Now after he had dealt with them by mercies and judgements, these not prevailing the Lord sends an enemy upon them that sweeps them away as unprofitable dung off the face of the earth. Alas, can you blame the Lord for dealing thus fiercely against a stubborn, rebellious people? What would you have had the Lord done more? He gave them a law, and mercies, and judgments, but they would not serve the Lord."[128] Hooker here speaks of national, not personal calamities, but the message is the same for all cases. There is no sense of social deprivation, only of sin, and no relevant response but penitence, and the banishment of persistent offenders.

Yet Hooker was habitually sensitive and compassionate when dealing with human needs. His limitation was perhaps ours, in that when examining the Puritan scene one tends to step out of the degradation of poverty into the ordered homes of careful merchants, comfortable upright landowners, and earnest beneficed clergy. This was particularly true of the New England they pioneered. As David Cressy says in *Coming Over. Migration and Communication between England and New England in the Seventeenth Century*, it was "a truncated social structure, in which the traditional aristocracy and the poor were missing."[129] The extremes of society were singularly absent from Puritan social plans, neither the idle rich nor the godless artisan included, but only such as might benefit a godfearing and godfavoured community.

The problem of poverty tends therefore to be ignored, whilst that of sin blacks out most other social concerns. But the presence of the godly destitute, in Old and New England, like the beggar named Lazarus who was laid at the rich man's gate, full of sores, who in Christ's parable found his way to heaven whilst the rich man languished in hell (Luke 16, v.19ff.), impressed itself on the Puritans, and, in the case of men like Hooker, increased their drive towards the creation of humane as well as righteously obedient communities, and the dispensation of practical charity to the deserving poor, with whom God might be well pleased. This they did, and generously.[130]

We owe the preservation of the Linge stained-glass to the large 14th century chest which stands to the right of the transept. The window was taken down and stored in the chest, with the church silver, and hidden in the Chibborne vault, when Colchester and other nearby villages like Messing, declared for the king, and were assaulted by the Parliamentary forces.

Tradition links Messing with Queen Boudicca of the Iceni. Where Nazeing was alleged to have been the site of her first easy triumph over the unsuspecting Romans ("Na-sang," no bloodshed), Messing was thought to derive from "messus, much, and sang, blood," betokening the place where Boudicca's army was finally annihilated.[131] There is no linguistic foundation for such fancies, but that does not necessarily affect the strength of a rumour. The fact that children in Essex grew up with such stories of victory for the oppressed, and of the utter destruction of whole communities ringing in their ears, played its part in the Great Migration of 1630, which contrived New England.

Constable Country. Dedham, Flatford Mill, East Bergholt.

How to get there.

From Colchester return to the A12 by driving down East Hill, over the Colne Bridge and past the Old Siege House. Keep to the left at the little roundabout, up the hill on the A1232, to the large roundabout at the Colchester ring-road dual-carriageway. From this major intersection you have a choice of two routes, both less than seven miles distance.

The Fast Route. Continue north over the roundabout on the A1232 signposted Ipswich; rejoin the A12, but take the next exit, marked Dedham.

The Less Congested, More Scenic Route. Turn right (east) at the ring-road roundabout for the A137 to Ardleigh (left-turn at the next roundabout). Ardleigh people will tell you that Constable Country begins there. The crossroads in the village, with St Mary's parish church at the apex, is undeniably photogenic. Turn left at the crossroads, onto the B1029, sign-posted Dedham. The road runs down to the Stour Valley, famed for John Constable's many paintings.

— Supposing that you arrive at Colchester in the morning, and remain for lunch, the place to go for an English Tea is the Essex Rose Tea House in Dedham, across the High Street from the Parish Church in the Centre. I shall expect a picture post-card expressing your thanks for an unforgettable treat!

This prompts me to comment that the Marlborough Head Hotel (c. 1430) in Mill Lane opposite the Essex Rose; The Sun, an old coaching-inn, early 16th century with a Georgian frontage; The Lamb, a thatched inn on the Ardleigh Road; Le Talbooth, at Stratford St Mary, rather further away, a perfectly restored 15th century complex close by "Constable Seat," with views of the Vale he loved to paint—all have especial attractions.

Dedham.

Where will you find anything more comely than Dedham?[132] The wide High Street with its 16th and 17th century houses vying with Georgian facades in variagated appeal; Sherman's Hall (1730), a name to conjure with in American history; the old Grammar School (1732), attended by John Constable; the Countryside and Information Centre down The Drift (which runs beside the old school building); on to Southfields, another shapely Sherman property, 16th century, half-timbered, a wealthy clothier's house built round a courtyard for his trade;—too many to mention, but the

The Parish Church of St Mary, Dedham

information centre will give you fuller details. Everything conspires to corroborate Pevsner's verdict, "easily the most attractive small town in Essex."[133]

Dedham would properly be visited on a peaceful mid-week afternoon, away from the tourist season, when the sun in at the zenith! You will then be able to park your car without difficulty outside the great church of St Mary the Virgin, and catch the radiance of its proportions, in harmony with the High Street outside, its interior invariably decked with floral displays, all glowing in the sunlight.

St Mary the Virgin,[134] its tower rising 130 feet above the Stour Valley, dates from the year Columbus discovered America (1492) and reflects the wealth of the early Essex wool merchants. Look up at the large porch over the north doorway as you enter. Such crowds gathered to hear John "Roaring" Rogers lecture before the weekly markets opened, that at times he had to climb onto the porch to preach from there. Incidentally, the Lectureship from which he profited still functions, though augmented with the living, and generally, I believe, utilised for a course of lectures in Advent or Lent.

Hooker was familiar with St Mary's, and its importance as a focus of Puritan power. In *The Faithful Covenanter*, a sermon preached at the Lecture in Dedham[135] (c. 1629, when John Rogers was under threat of silencing), Hooker had been invited "not merely to expound the principles of federal theology," but to stiffen the congregation's resistance. "Husbands, call upon your wives; and parents, call upon your children, when you see them break the covenant—you begin to be careless of the Sabbath, and cold, and luke-warm, and dull." We become acutely aware of Hooker's personal identification with Puritan congregations all over Essex, and far beyond; and of his authority over them. "Let not the Lord lose; but resolve, whatever becomes of it: 'I will pray constantly and read in my family morning and evening and upon every occasion, and reform my ways. It is not needful that I should be rich; it is that I be sincere, and faithful to the Lord. I will labour for a good conscience and endeavour to walk with God.'"

You will pause in awe on entering so sublime an auditory in so small a town. All truth is relative, even as the experiences of this tour have constantly recalled the relevance of what is small, secret, unexploited and therefore the more unexpected and appreciable. I hope you may slide softly into St Mary's on a tranquil day, with time to imbibe the sublimity of this framework for one of the most effervescent of painful preachers, John Rogers.[136]

The church has been adorned by people the world over, not least from Dedham, Massachusetts. When you have caught your breath after the sudden eruption of height, and light, and grandeur which greets your entry, you will wish to see the Dedham pew, at the end of the nave aisle on the

The Sherman Glass

south side, near the entrance. The carvings include interlaced Ds, the Mayflower, a Settler's house, the Dedham Seal, and other New England emblems. This was part of a post World-War II restoration, which has placed modern carved bench-ends down the length of the nave.

There are New England references in plenty. In the nave roof, heraldic shield No 11 displays the crests of Massachusetts and the Plymouth Fathers; matched by Tudor roses, and the Suffolk county crest in shield No 12. The Sherman Glass is in the window over the Webbe Tomb (they with the Gurdons were principal patrons in the 16th century), on the north aisle wall. The initials E. S. can clearly be seen. They stand for Edmund Sherman,[137] whose house "Shermans" is just across the street. His first cousin, Samuel Sherman, emigrated in 1634, and settled at Contentment near Boston, afterwards known as Dedham. General W. T. Sherman, hero of the American Civil War, claimed descent from Edmund. At least eleven descendents of Edmund's father, Henry Sherman, and their families, are said to have emigrated to New England between 1633–1640. The Revd. John Sherman, 1613–1685, famed mathematician, was among them, sometime minister at Watertown and Wethersfield, early lecturer at Harvard.

You will find John Roger's monument on the north wall of the Chancel, inscribed "John Rogers here expects the Resurrection which he preached, Oct. 18, A.D. 1639, aged 65." His father was probably a cobbler at Moulsham, where John was born in 1574. He may have attended the Edward VIth Grammar School at Chelmsford, went on to Emmanuel, Cambridge, as scholar and fellow, and was appointed Lecturer at Dedham from 1605–1636, a post he barely held onto in an era of exclusions, for 31 years of strenuous Puritan preaching.

His best known publication was *The Doctrine of Faith, Wherein are practically handled twelue principall points, which explaine the Nature and Vse of it*, to the second edition of which, in 1627, Hooker contributed an Introduction of some importance because in it he locates faith in a series of interrelated stages, contrition, vocation, sanctification, glorification—a schema he was to follow throughout his subsequent teaching, known as Preparationist Theology.[138]

At Rogers' funeral so many crowded the church that the west gallery, erected to accommodate the crowds who flocked to his preaching, collapsed. It was regarded as a miracle that no one was injured. The inscription on his tombstone claims

True-hearted worshipper of God
No Boanerges more courageously
Gave forth his thunder, and no Barnabas
The word of consolation sweeter.

He and Hooker were spiritual brothers, exploded off the same granite faith, and we may rejoice that for a few years they were within visiting distance of each other. What a heaven-on-earth they schemed!

Sir Alfred Munnings,[139] the Edwardian equestrian painter, lived at Castle House on the road going east to Ardleigh. This is open to the public at varying times throughout the year. Some of his finest paintings are on view. But you simply must make time to leave Dedham past the Mill, and

Lock, (subject of a Constable painting; you can park and view) via Mill Lane. Then on to the A12 at Stratford St Mary, and up the dual-carriageway still travelling north as if to Ipswich, for East Bergholt, not five miles away. You have to retrace your route at a large roundabout clearly signposted East Bergholt, and return on the other side of the dual-carriageway, where further signposts direct you to the B1070, and the small town, then along a narrow one-way tourist lane, to the car park, and other facilities at Flatford Mill. It is the solitariness of the Stour Valley which necessitates this tortuous, but scenic trail.

The John Rogers
Monument

Diversion to East Bergholt and Flatford Mill.

There is no connection with the Hooker saga, only a wish that you should enjoy the Valley of the Stour to the utmost whilst you are here. You enter East Bergholt from the north on the B1070.

John Constable, born 11 June 1776, grew up at East Bergholt.[140] His father owned Flatford Mill amongst others, and John was first designed to follow his father, but showed such artistic talent that he was allowed to study at the Royal Academy Schools in London. He was a versatile artist, most admired for his landscapes, but his sea-scapes are the more dramatic, and his portraiture can be entrancing (see his *A Suffolk Child*, c. 1835, in the Victoria and Albert Museum, London).

Many of his best-loved pictures are of the Valley of the Stour, and Flatford in particular. *Dedham Vale, The Valley of the Stour, The Mill Stream* (Willy Lotts Cottage), *Boat Building near Flatford Mill, Flatford Mill, Dedham Lock and Mill, The Haywain,* and *A View on the Stour near Dedham,* one of my favourites, now in the Huntington Art Gallery, San Marino, California. These all leap out to embrace you, when you reach Flatford Mill, and wander the tow-path amidst scenes as recognisable now as they were in his day.

At the rear of Flatford Mill the National Trust manages an information and residential training centre, where nature field courses etc. are held. If interested, apply to The Bridge Cottage, Flatford, East Bergholt, Essex, CO7 60L, or call at the National Trust tea-garden and shop when there.

You drive past the parish church of St Mary the Virgin as you go to Flatford. It has a 16th century bell-cage, built at ground level in 1531 to house a ring of bells intended for the tower. But Cardinal Wolsey was financing the building scheme, and funds died with him in 1530. The tower was never completed, and the bells are now rung by hand swinging the wooden headstocks, the ringers standing on a platform a few feet above the ground, the largest handbells in the world! If you were lucky, you might go when the ringers were working their bells, a clamorous but exhilarating event.

The most preceptive tourist would go to Ipswich for the night, and savour that fine county town of East Suffolk next day. But I am in danger of prolonging your stay to the point of bankruptcy. Let the sunset over the Stour in the evening mist at Flatford Mill draw this day to its perfect conclusion.

The Braintree Area.

Braintree and Bocking.

The dividing line between the twin towns of Braintree and Bocking[141] runs along the route of the old Roman Stane Street, now designated the A120. Braintree lies on the south side of the road, Bocking is on the other (north) side. What might today be taken for the centre of Braintree is in fact its northern periphery, hard by the southern edge of Bocking. It will be convenient to explore the two towns together, and important to do so because their joint contribution to the making of New England is of the highest order.

But how can one begin to appreciate what it was like to live in this northeastern part of Puritan Essex? An attempt must be made, if without fanciful embellishment. The result will be entertainingly instructive. It begins in a meeting of land and seaborne wayfarers, hunters, traders, then pilgrims, and refugees skilled in the cloth trade, and the independent, prosperous communities to which they gave birth. It continues in the martyrdom of Protestants: William Pygot, burnt at the stake at Braintree on 28 March 1555; Richard and Thomas Spurge, John Cavel and George Ambrose of Bocking burnt at Smithfield on 24 April 1556; and William Purcas of Bocking, burnt at Colchester on 2 August 1557. Its life was maintained in the spawning of the Braintree Vestry, legislative model for the New England colonies; and of the Braintree Company, with Harvard students and Connecticut Yankees its remote offspring. It continues in a late brood of highly motivated civic benefactors, not least from the international manufactures of Courtaulds' fabrics, and Crittall's metal windows no Asian termites can devour!

Under Roman rule the eastern supply route from Colonia (Colchester) to Verulamium (St Albans) was called Stane Street. It cut a straight line across country to Baldock, where it joined Icknield Way, a prehistoric ridgeway to Dunstable and along the Chilterns to the River Thames at Goring which probably started at The Wash.[142]

Stane Street intersected with Ermine Street at what is now the village of Braughing near Bishop's Stortford, but then "was the first stop on the Ermine Street out of London," an important hub of seven Roman roads effectively linking Colchester to the rest of Roman Britain. Indeed the other Stane Street, from London to Chichester, takes you directly to that important Roman military base and Noviomagnus Regnensium (new market of the Regnenses), now Chichester, on the south coast of Sussex.[143]

Halfway to Braughing from Colchester, Stane Street bisected another Roman road coming up from Chelmsford to Sudbury (A131). Where these two roads crossed the town of Braintree grew up. Bocking was at first a small village en route to Sudbury. They became the twin towns of Braintree and Bocking. Strategically placed for the east coast European trade routes, they also lay athwart an early pilgrim track from the shrine of St Thomas Becket at Canterbury to the shrine of Our Lady of Walsingham in Norfolk and that of St Edmund of Bury St Edmunds in Suffolk.[144]

Walsingham was founded from a vision of the Nazareth home of the Holy Family granted to Richelde de Fervaques in 1061, commanding her to build a replica. It is a place of pilgrimage to this day. St Edmund, king of the East Angles, was murdered by marauding Danes in 870. His body was buried in a great abbey which grew around his shrine. Little now remains, apart from the Gate House in Angel Hill, but so large was it that the extensive Appleby Rose Garden, memorial to the USAAF 94th Bombardment Group who flew from airfields in the vicinity during World War II, covers only a small part of the six-acre site once occupied by monastic buildings. Edmund quickly became a cult figure, and these pilgrimages increased the traffic through Braintree.

Bury St Edmunds deserves a place in this Puritan guide for another reason. Its motto is "Sacrarium Regis Cunabula Legis," meaning "Shrine of a King, Cradle of the Law."[145] It derives from a crucial meeting of the Barons at the Abbey in November 1214, when they swore on the high altar to force King John to sign Magna Carta, and made him do so in June the next year.

Old Inns abound at Braintree, the Boar's Head, the Bull, the Horn, the Horse and Groom, the Six Bells, the Swan, the Wheatsheaf, and the newly renovated White Hart. Sheep and cloth weaving so contributed to the prosperity of the area, that Braintree and Bocking together outshone Chelmsford in the 16th century. The woollen trade predominated into the 18th century.

In 1816 Samuel Courtauld,[146] descendent of Huguenot refugees, brought his silk weaving industry to Bocking, and developed into synthetics. His reformist religious background had fostered a high sense of civic duty. The outcome of this long tradition of manufacture, commerce, and patronage is reflected in the many Courtauld benefactions which range from the Courtauld Institute of Art to the local hospital. You will wish to visit one of these concessions as soon as you can. That is the Braintree Heritage Museum at The Town Hall Centre in the Market Square.

Francis Crittall[147] was the son of a Braintree ironmonger. His mother was injured by a heavy wooden window-sash. He devised a lightweight steel frame and Crittall windows began. He too was a man of social conscience. When he learnt of the problems suffered by people in India, he adapted his frames to withstand tropical heat and ants. He built a model village for his employees and lived there himself in commendable domestic bliss. The lives and works of these two citizens, clearly within the "Puritan" tradition, are attractively exhibited at The Heritage Museum.

There, too, the history of the two towns is displayed from the early lake village to the present day. You will see some of the exquisite illustrations of John Ray (1628–1705) "Father of English Natural History,"[148] and the first complete English botanist with works such as his *Catalogus Plantarum Ang-*

liae (1679), and *Historia Generalis Plantarum* (1704, 3 vols.). He was born the son of the blacksmith at Black Notley, a village outside Braintree. He had a distinguished career at Cambridge as a student and then lecturer in Greek, mathematics, and humanity. He took holy orders, and his college sermons are said to be the basis of his best known book, *The Wisdom of God Manifested in the Works of Creation* (1691). He was forced to resign his university post when unable to subscribe in 1662 to the Act of Uniformity and returned to spend his final years at Black Notley.

You will also find numerous references to the founding of New England, and a model of the *Lyon*, one of the busiest transatlantic passenger ships, which transported "the Braintree Company" to Massachusetts in 1632. The title used by John Winthrop was "Mr Hooker's Party," but it was led by William Goodwin of Bocking (incorrectly described as "of Lyons Hall") in the absence of Hooker in hiding in Holland.[149] A number of influential Braintree/Bocking families also joined in the great migration from 1630 onwards, including John Brainard, John Bridge, Ozias and William Goodwin, Stephen Hart, Nathaniel Kellog, Edward and Joseph Loomis, Nehemiah and Nicholas Olmstead (Bocking and Fairstead), John Talcott, William Wadsworth—names well known amongst historians of New England.

The "Braintree Company" settled first at Mount Wollaston (renamed Braintree) but removed to Newtown, where Hooker joined them next year. Benjamin Trumbull described the reunion in his *A Complete History of Connecticut*. "Finding himself in the midst of a joyful and affectionate people, he was filled with joy himself. He embraced them with open arms, saying 'Now I live if ye stand fast in the Lord.'"[150] They did, and formed the nucleus of pioneers who trekked through the forests with him to establish Connecticut in 1636.

It has been conjectured that Hooker had lived for a time with the Goodwins at Lyons Hall, Bocking, between his eviction from Chelmsford and his flight to Holland, and that he acted as a pastor to a Conventicle organized by William and Ozias. That the relationship was close cannot be questioned. William Goodwin was Hooker's leading Elder in New England, lived alongside him at Hartford, acted as his chief executor when he died, and afterwards married his widow.

However, sadly, there is no evidence either for the Goodwin's residence at Lyons Hall in the 1630s, or of Hooker's at Braintree or Bocking. The document conveying Lyons Hall to a William Goodwin in 1546 is extant, but so is another conveying it to Thomas Fitch of Bocking from a Thomas Goodwin in 1589. There is no record of its returning into Goodwin ownership. It was sold to the Rayneys in 1619, again to the Wentworths in 1627, and to the Hawkins family in 1633. J. J. Goodwin, *Goodwins of Hartford* (1891) loses track of the family from 1589 until a Matthew Goodwin appears in 1608, and a John Goodwin of East Bergholt, clothier, who left £50 in his will for the plantation of New England.[151]

One day, hopefully, evidence will be produced to describe more fully the connection between Hooker, Goodwin, and the Braintree-Bocking members of "Mr Hooker's Party." For the time being it appears that Hooker had no other home than Cuckoos Farmhouse at Little Baddow and that he remained there until he escaped to Holland, whilst his wife and family found temporary shelter at Great Waltham, under the protection of the Earl of Warwick.

Before leaving Braintree you will wish to visit the parish church of St Michael, a short step along High Street from the Town Hall Centre, with the Courtauld Fountain of Youth playing outside. The church is largely 13th century with later additions such as the 14th century shingled spire, but its main interest for us derives from the contribution made by its vicar to Thomas Hooker's career.

Samuel Collins (1576–1667)[152] was instituted in 1610 and remained as vicar until 1657, an indication of his adaptability to the fiercely contradictory situation in which he somehow managed to survive and also to his durability. He was 81 when he retired, and lived to be 91 years of age. T. W. Davids in his *Annals of Evangelical Nonconformity in the County of Essex*, referred to Collins as "one of the Bishop's best friends." This has appeared in the correspondence already quoted, which brought about Hooker's eviction from the Chelmsford Lectureship. But this was, I think, unintentional, and regretted by Collins, whose attitude towards Hooker was friendly if equivocal.

Collins' petition to Laud had been for the quiet removal of Hooker from the vicinity because "His genius . . . haunts all the pulpits in ye county," not for his punishment. Perhaps Collins was amongst the haunted. His career is intriguing. He was 19 when he entered the prestigious Trinity College, Cambridge, an unusually late date. He did not graduate B.A. until he was 24, or M.A. until 27. One is bound to question the recorded date of his birth or the quality of his mind. If he was born in 1576, a decade senior to Thomas Hooker but light-years duller, his admiration might well have been tainted by the subtlest sort of envy. That he went out of his way to warn Hooker whilst at the same time negotiating his dismissal and that he courageously signed the Petition of November 10, 1629 in his favour, reflects his confusion.

Later on Collins was in trouble himself, for playing fast and loose with Laud's ecclesiastical demands. He wrote again, to excuse his failure to discipline his people. "It is no easy matter to reduce a numerous congregation into order that hath been disorderly these fifty years," he pleaded, "and that, for the seven years last past, hath bin encouraged in that way by the refractory ministers in the county, with whom they have had acquaintance in their private meetings and conferences, who have left divers schismatical books among them, and during their continuance here laboured to make my person and ministry contemptible and odious, because I would not hold conversation with them. If I had suddenly and hastily fallen upon the whole parte of uniformity, I had undone myself."[153]

Collins was a survivor and perhaps overready to protect his own interests. On occasions, he lacked the courage of his convictions. We can sympathise with him. On the one hand, there was Braintree's long tradition of independence and Collins' obvious sympathy with it. He had been presented to his parish by Lord Robert Rich, the first Puritan Earl of Warwick. He was clearly overawed by Thomas Hooker, and probably genuinely attracted to him. His long tenure of St Michael's suggests that he was a good parish minister, the fact that he was never sequestered under the Commonwealth, proof of his general acceptability to the reformers.

On the other hand his fear of his bishop, obsequious correspondence with Dr Duck, and preoccupation with his own advantage, weighed too heavily on his weaker will. One wonders if the tablet outside St Michael's commemorating his son, Samuel, who became physician to the Tsar of Russia,[154] reflects the discomforts of a compromising incumbency in a place like Braintree!

From the centre of the twin towns you will wish to make the short journey into Bocking Village, sometimes shown on maps as Bocking Church Street. The old A131 goes north towards Halstead and Sudbury from the White Hart, down Bocking End and Bradford Street, faced by numerous handsome period houses. At the bottom turn left into Church Street, which is the B1053, towards Panfield and Shalford. When the road turns left, bear right down the hill and over the bridge (where the river Pant changes its name to the Blackwater), and so into Church Street and Old Bocking Village. The site was formerly swamped by Courtauld's large weaving sheds, spread all over Parsons Field on the riverfront, where the water mill once stood. Now it is under reconstruction and the village centre is hard to imagine. But the Church lies back proudly from the whisp of village green, and here the cottages first clustered.

The Deanery Church of St Mary, Bocking.

A remarkable church with a remarkable history, half-hidden away behind a triangular green on your left off Church Street. In the year 995 the Saxon noble Aetheric (one who had fought at the Battle of Maldon in 991 and survived), now on his deathbed, in the hope of safeguarding his wife's succession to his other properties, bequeathed Bocking Manor to the Canterbury Cathedral Monastery, and with it the advowson of the priest. He commended his widow to the Archbishop who was also Abbot of the Monastery. It worked. The Archbishop became patron to both parties, and

Deanery Church of St Mary the Virgin, Bocking.

the Rector of Bocking remains a "Dean of the Peculiar" under Canterbury's jurisdiction.[155]

The church has a strong tower (c. 1415), double buttressed, with a matching porch embattled, and a long perpendicular line of nave and chancel which forms an imposing exterior behind the lengthy entrance pathway and spacious churchyard. Inside, there is a 14th century chancel and much of the rest 15th/16th century, including the very fine oak roofs of similar age, richly carved, all carefully restored last century. The roof bosses carry replicas of the arms of Canterbury, the De Veres (Earls of Oxford, see Earls Colne), and the leopard's head of the Fitch family amongst other benefactors.

The Magnificent Window in the south aisle was donated by "James J. Goodwin Esq and the Rev. Francis Goodwin D.D., American Citizens, to the Parish of their Ancestors." The church guide explains "in memory of the Goodwin family of America who originated from Dorewards Hall," but without further substantiation.[156] The two estates of Dorewards Hall and Lyons Hall run side by side, flanking the A131 east of Bocking. This could account for any confusion over the Goodwin's place of residence.

There is a brass memorial to John Doreward (Speaker of the House of Commons) and his wife Isabella Baynard of Messing, dated 1420, on the floor in front of the South Chapel and another in the Choir in memory of Oswald Fitch (d. 1612), "last of the Doreward kin."[157] You will remember that Thomas Fitch purchased Lyons Hall in 1589 from the Goodwins. Oswald was in residence there at the time of his death. Some connection between the families at Dorewards and Lyons Halls must therefore be allowed.

The Deanery Church of St Mary has a further connection with Thomas Hooker. Nathaniel Rogers, second son of Hooker's great friend John Rogers of Dedham, served as curate here. The Dean at that time was Dr Barkham, "so gracious with Bishop Laud," comments Cotton Mather.[158] The two men got on well despite their theological differences, each respecting the other's abilities, until Nathaniel's conscience finally forced him to reject Laud's rigid sartorial regulations, and to discard the surplice. Whereupon Dr Barkham, inspired "with as much disgust against his curate, as his curate had against the surplice itself," terminated the appointment. Nathaniel went as rector to "Puritan" Assington, and then joined John Norton (formerly chaplain to Sir William Masham at High Laver, Essex) at Ipswich, Massachusetts in 1638.

Mather claims that it was Thomas Hooker who intervened, and persuaded Nathaniel Rogers to this act of defiance, communicating from Chelmsford "unto him the grounds of his own dissatisfaction at the ceremonies then imposed."[159] If so, it illustrates Hooker's influence over the younger clergy in Essex. Your sympathies may lie with Dr Barkham for this unwarrantable interference with his curate, but that was the way of the Puritans.

The Deanery Church also has a claim on our attention in Dr John Gauden, to whom the *Eikon Basilike* is attributed. Gauden (1605–1662)[160] was the son of the Vicar of Mayland (in the Dengie Peninsular, Essex). He was appointed Dean of Bocking in 1641 having been chaplain to the Earl of Warwick at Leez Priory. He preached before parliament, one of the peaks of a Puritan's clerical ambitions, was a member of the Westminster Assembly, and "took the solemn league and covenant" with Scottish Presbyterians.[161] However, authorship of the *Eikon Basilike, The Pourtraicture of His Sacred Majestie in his Solitudes and Sufferings*, which appeared in print at the King's death, and was widely assumed to have been written by King Charles because of the intimate nature of the thoughts revealed in it, was claimed by John Gauden in 1660, shortly after his taking up the Bishopric of Exeter.

It is a perplexing sequence of events, but shows Gauden to have been as accommodating in his religious adherence as was his brother minister at Braintree, Samuel Collins. In charity we may assume that he was, together with many other Puritan leaders, sickened by the King's execution. It may have been a coincidence that he publicised his Royalist credentials only just in time for the Restoration of 1660.[162] He was not alone in that. He was translated to the more illustrious see of Worcester two years later, where he died. One of his bequests founded a grammar school at Bocking.

Dorewards Hall, Bocking

Dorewards Hall, Bocking Church Street.

The Hall stands in the middle of a considerable semi-circular segment of land, caused by the straight line of the Roman road (A131) and the loop of Church Street, which runs back from its junction with the B1053 to rejoin the A131 further northeast. This clearly delineated ancient demesne is instantly recognisable by glancing at any large-scale map.

The Hall is reached today from Dorewoods Avenue, opposite the Deanery Church, along a narrow access road signposted to Dorewards Hall Farm Shop. The Durward, or Doreward, family were resident at least from 1216. Later they married into the Thursbys, who owned the Hall until it was sold to a Richard Eden in 1637. I suppose the Goodwins could have rented it, in the 1620s.[163]

What remains of the Hall is a splendid L shaped farm-house of timber, brick and plaster, with a red-tiled roof, warm and welcoming. The Tudor west wing of 16th century red brick, lightened by great windows, decorative string courses, pediments, and chequered buttresses, presents an unexpected grandeur in this secluded place. The whole wing rises to a startling height above a walled garden, and glows in the setting sun. The low-lying central core and eastern wing are older, dating back to c. 1430. Widescale restorations were carried out by Edward Thursby in 1579. It is a most impressive house, open to view from the Farm Shop in the barns which face the Hall across the farmyard.

The hidden away Doreward estate would have offered an ideal location for a prohibited conventicle such as the Goodwins supported at Brain-

Lyons Hall, Bocking

tree-Bocking. It could be that this is where Hooker visited, riding over from Little Baddow, some 12 miles away, and where the Braintree Company and the towns of Braintree and Cambridge, Massachusetts began. It adds a touch of elegant (if unproven) concealment to the Hooker story.

Lyons Hall, Bocking.

Lyons Hall[164] is a mile east of Bocking village and a similar distance from Dorewards. Continue along Church Road eastwards, past the carefully restored post-mill, to the A131. Cross over the main road into Lyons Hall Road and Lyons Hall is down a drive a short distance on your right. It is not open to the public. The late Tudor house, dating from c. 1600, with 18th century additions, is most attractive. Ornamented with barge-boarded gables and carved bressumers, the garden and grounds slope down to the river Blackwater in perfect harmony. I like to think that Hooker found a welcome here.

The Braintree Vestry.

Back in Braintree the impression that you have received from the many gracious old buildings, emphasised by a visit to the Heritage Centre, and the bustling evidences of prosperity on every hand, rightly suggests that the achievements of this small town are exceptional. There is another side which profoundly affected the New England plantations.

A severe recession hit the cloth trade in the 1620s.[165] The first Royal Commission ever to enquire into the causes of unemployment was formed in consequence, in 1622. In April 1629 some 200 weavers from Bocking and

Braintree petitioned the Quarter Sessions at Chelmsford for relief. The Justices who received them included Sir Henry Mildmay and Sir William Masham. They called in the support of the Earl of Warwick, initiated a correspondence with the Privy Council which warned that a violent uprising could be imminent, and that measures to reduce unemployment were fitter than punitive ones.

The truth was that the market had changed, the cottage manufacture of cloth on which Essex' wealth had been founded was no longer viable, and overseas trade was disrupted by constant European wars. The weavers' petition to King Charles I makes sad reading.

"To the King's Most Excellent Majesty The humble petition of the Weavers of Bocking and Braintree in the County of Essex and the neighbouring Towns thereabouts to the number of One Hundred Thousand with them that doe depend upon them. 8th May 1629. Humbly shewing that the trade hath been decaying for this seven years or thereabouts to their utter undoing. Now they have no work at all, by reason whereof they are grown into that extremity, that for themselves and families and are fain to lie in straw—their wives and children are like to perish—they beseech your Majesty to consider that they may not starve in time of plenty. And had it not been that the right honourable the Earl of Warwick, and others, worthy gentlemen, had appeased them many wretched people would have gathered together in Mutiny—they humbly beseech your Majesty graciously to grant for Christ Jesus sake, that they may not perish, but live to do your Majesty's service according to their duties. And continually pray for your Majesty's Long and prosperous Reign."[166]

Little was, or perhaps could be, done to relieve their suffering. In desperation 300 men from Braintree and Bocking marched on Maldon, raided a ship loaded with wheat, ransacked it, and of the handful apprehended, three were hanged by the Chelmsford Court under the presidency of the Earl of Warwick. Agnes Clark of Maldon was hanged with them. She described herself as their captain and had toured the disaffected areas stirring up insurrection. The people of Maldon were "much pleased with the Justices, being before that time much dismayed with the insolence of these people,"[167] but Maldon was a port, not a weaving-town.

Against such a background, the emergence of the Braintree "Company of Twenty-Four" is highly significant. Since every citizen was obliged by law to attend the Church of England it was virtually inevitable that, as the manorial system broke down, the Parish Vestry would gradually displace the Manor Court for most matters of primary justice. By the calling of banns the Vestry could control unsuitable marriages, where homeless and jobless couples might otherwise have burdened the local rates. By administering the poor laws, the Vestry could keep the claims of the indigent within bounds. By upholding conventional morality, it could hope to restrict public disorder, and, a distinct bonus, the number of illegitimate children and petty criminals chargeable to the parish. Puritans were practical people, and looked to secure a comfortable domestic state by their scrupulous observances.

It appears that by the early 17th century this new system had also become moribund. In 1619 the closed vestry of Braintree, known as the Company of Twenty-four, composed of representatives of the rate payers appointed for the dispatch of parochial business (with Samuel Collins a prominent member) "drew up a new set of regulations concerning town government."[168] It was to meet monthly following Sunday worship, to promote religious observance, resist scandalous living, and "make search in such places which we shall suspect for disorderly persons in the manner of a privy watch." Other parishes in Essex followed suit.

The procedure was simplicity itself. The authority behind the Vestry was the godly magistrate. The parson was the front man, liasing between the lord of the manor, local populace, and vestry. The people were effectively controlled by the "chief inhabitants," who constituted the Vestry (largely appointed by cooption), and by the constables they employed. This is precisely the social contract practised in the plantations of New England.

If not actually originating in Braintree, it was there that the closed or select vestry system first received a codified expression. As Sidney and Beatrice Webb, in their *English Local Government* (Part I, "English Poor Law History," 1906) put it, "A more complete example of the government of all the town business by the headboroughs, acting as a municipal council, and not simply through the leet, is that of the four-and-twenty headboroughs of Braintree in Essex."[169] They added, "From first to last we see no trace of corruption, partiality, or jobbery. The members of the Four-and-Twenty, as we have seen, even paid out of their own pockets for their monthly dinners, and were evidently always subscribing money for charitable objects. At no little expense of time and money to themselves, this little company of 'ancients' fulfilled what they doubtless felt as their obligation to give both deliberative and executive service in the administration of their community."

Unintentionally they provided a model which was ready-made for New England by the Braintree Thomas Hooker knew so well. As for the constant dipping into their pockets to pay for public needs, every civic leader would wryly have endorsed the Webbs' comment! Those pioneering Puritans were long accustomed to pay in hard cash (or part with scarce commodities) for their beliefs, a perennial source, we may suppose, of their occasional waspish ill-humours!

Round Trip A. Leez Priory, Felsted, Great Waltham.

    A map of Essex will show that the places listed in this section are within easy distance of Chelmsford, Colchester or Braintree, and may be visited in whatever order suits you best.

Leez Priory, Home Of Richard Rich, First Baron Rochford.

    From Braintree take the A131 as if to Chelmsford. Travel five miles, through Great Leighs, past St Annes Castle (said to be one of the oldest public-houses in England) and Whites Lane on your right. Take the next turning on the right, into Church Lane. Little Leighs Church can be seen on the left of the lane, a half mile from the turning. It is worth stopping to look into the 12th century church of St John, with its rare carved oak figure of a priest dating from the same period. Continue for a mile, then turn left. Turn right at Mattock Farm a further half mile. Continue for two-thirds of a mile along this road. Leez Priory appears on the right hand bend.

    The Priory was a 13th century foundation of the Austin Canons,[170] who followed the rule of St Augustine, and had close associations with the St Bartholomew's and St Thomas's hospitals in London. At the Dissolution, Richard Rich, first Chancellor of the Court of Augmentations, obtained possession. That was in 1536, the year of his appointment, when the act for the Dissolution of Smaller Monasteries was first passed. You notice he wasted no time!

    Richard Rich got hold of approximately one hundred manors in Essex alone. His models had been Cardinal Wolsey and Thomas Cromwell, Earl of Essex, who climbed over other men to positions of power by their own unscrupulous opportunism.

    Rich (1498–1567)[171] was a Londoner born and bred, a lawyer by training at the Middle Temple where he made the acquaintance of Sir Thomas More. He entered Parliament in 1529, and attached himself to Thomas Cromwell[172] who, at More's downfall, as secretary to the king, took over Wolsey's role as Henry's principal parliamentary agent. This made Cromwell's disposal of monastic resources (the dissolution of which he accelerated immediately after More's execution) and other royal revenues, absolute until his dismissal in 1540.

    Richard Rich became Solicitor General, in effect personal secretary to Thomas Cromwell, in 1533. He then played a despicable part in the trial of Thomas More,[173] Wolsey's saintly and reluctant successor as Lord Chancellor. He volunteered the professed contents of a private conversation in the Tower of London, where More was imprisoned for refusing to take the oath of Henry's Supremacy over the Church. He alleged More had treasonably said that no parliament could make a king supreme head of the Church; and was believed.

It is thought that More would have been acquitted but for the gratuitous intervention of Rich's confidential disclosure; and that it was perjury in any case. This probability is increased by Rich's next intervention, at Thomas Cromwell's trial, where again he gave evidence against his master. Yet he had been Cromwell's right hand in disposing of the monasteries, and his mouthpiece as Speaker of the House of Commons.

Rich was now in a situation similar to that which Cromwell had lost; and the king's man at any price. So he was created Baron Rich of Leez; and Lord Chancellor of England (March 1548). As such, under King Edward VI, he actively persecuted Catholics, sharing in the prosecution of Stephen Gardiner, Bishop of Winchester; of Edmund Bonner, the last Bishop of London to die in communion with Rome; and in the harsh confinement of Princess Mary. Both Bishops were stripped of office. Gardiner was imprisoned in the Tower. Both were restored when Mary came to the throne, Gardiner to succeed Rich as Lord Chancellor. But Rich survived.

Lord Rich had too quickly signed the Document of Accession on behalf of Lady Jane Grey, and more hurriedly recanted, asserting he had signed under duress, when popular support for Mary overthrew Lady Jane. Fortunately he could stand by the old faith more easily than by the new when it became appropriate. In fact, his hidden Catholicism reappeared as soon as Mary was enthroned, which enabled him to harry erstwhile Protestant colleagues in his adopted county of Essex without hesitation.

He next served Elizabeth, by suppressing grants of land and money he had diverted to Catholics in her sister's reign. He was a busy man. But by now his health was failing. He did, however, establish a famous school at Felsted, Essex, which you may visit later on. He had incautiously donated revenues to a very Catholic chantry for his own soul at Felsted Church of the Holy Cross, which had to be withdrawn rather quickly under Elizabeth, and a Catholic-style Lenten bequest of fresh herrings to the poor of three neighbouring parishes, which were most conveniently buried in the foundation of a new school. He too lies buried at Felsted in a splendid tomb before which I hope you will meditate on the fragility of human integrity.

On taking up residence, Lord Rich had replaced much of Leez Priory with a more magnificent Tudor palace. Of this only the large gatehouse in red brick patterned with blue remains.[174] It is carefully restored, and stands in spacious gardens visible from the road, a glimpse of past luxury still potent, but not open to the public. The property was bought in 1735 by Guy's Hospital, London, appropriately enough considering the Austin Canons' original involvement with hospital work. But the trustees did not preserve Rich's great house.

The family line continued. Lord Rich's grandson Robert (1560–1619)[175] inherited, and was created first Earl of Warwick. He played a much less conspicuous role in politics, but gained unwanted notoriety from his marriage to Penelope, daughter of Walter Devereux, Earl of Essex, and sister of Queen Elizabeth's favourite. She was a lady of fire and spirit, the reputed lover of Sir Philip Sidney (the Stella of his *Astrophel and Stella*), and assuredly the lover of Charles Blount, Earl of Devonshire, whom she did marry, but only after a disastrous marriage to Robert, and a scandalous divorce.

The tempestuous union of Robert and Penelope produced an heir, Robert, second Earl of Warwick (1587–1658).[176] He had all his mother's engaging brilliance but enough Rich sagacity to profit from a matching piety and the cultivation of popular affection. His was an extraordinary life. From his father he received a solid Puritanism, a personal and domestic morality which ensured the respect of other Puritan leaders in church and politics. He was the outstanding Puritan noble, Lord Lieutenant of Essex, Member of Parliament for Maldon, Leader of the House of Lords, Lord High Admiral of the Fleet, Commissioner for the Government of the Colonies, a man as much responsible for the outbreak and direction of the Civil War as any other.

From his mother he inherited a wilful quality which at times made him no better than a pirate, the leader of highly suspicious naval expeditions, loved by his men but in conflict with more scrupulous trading companies. In some respects he was the epitome of the 16th/17th century English dream of empire, a godly buccaneer blessed of reformed religion and morality, enthusiastically expanding England's Christian culture and commerce.

He was associated with the colonization of Virginia, Bermuda, New Plymouth, Massachusetts, Rhode Island, and, through the Warwick Patent dubiously granted on his own authority, with Saybrook and Connecticut. He had been entered at Emmanuel, Cambridge in 1603, the year before Thomas Hooker, and became both his friend and protector. Thanks to his great-grandfather he had a large number of clergy presentations in his gift. He filled these pulpits with reformist preachers, as his father had done. It is supposed that Essex was partly so Puritan a county from this fact, that if you desired an Essex Parish you had better be reformed upon Calvin's Geneva model mighty quick! Lord Rich, the scheming Royalist who could return to the Catholic faith whenever advisable, would have turned in his grave. Have a look when you reach Felsted. Maybe he did.

Too little of this amazing story appears above ground now, at Leez Priory. But it is thrilling simply to look over the old brick wall, and to ruminate in this pleasant, placid countryside—for instance, on the legacy of despotism the Puritan leaders had stored away in their subconscious minds, ready to reassert itself for emulation when their chance came. Some of it they denounced as damnable, but some, as in the case of men like the 2nd

Earl of Warwick, as laudable, qualifying their concept of the Godly Commonwealth.

Felsted.

Turn left at Leez Priory to the B1417, and right when you reach it, into the centre of Felsted. The original school building founded by Lord Rich in 1564 stands in front of you at what appears to be a T junction, where the B1417 turns at right-angles past the modern school grounds to Bannister Green and Braintree. Ancient tracks crossed here, south of the church, spreading inland from Colchester, along which traders passed with their primitive wares maybe from paleolithic times, long before the Saxons fixed their small settlement strategically between the Roman roads A120 (Stane Street) and the A131 (Braintree to Chelmsford). There is still a Felsted from Saxon days in South Jutland, whence perhaps the founders came.[177]

At the central intersection you will spare a sympathetic thought for the 120 boys crammed into the old schoolroom in the 17th century.[178] They occupied the upper floor of the four small bays which overhang the street. The schoolmaster, who boarded a sizeable proportion of his scholars, lived in the 15th century cottage next door. Its three gables project from the tiled roof bulging with the wraiths of long departed infants. The Boote House, a restaurant of distinction, looks on with winking glass from the other side of the road, its carved inscription running round the eaves, "George Boote made this house 1596." You must book in advance for the pleasure of eating here, but inns abound in the vicinity. The Boote House cottage, carved with rosettes, dragons, a cloven-footed lady of unknown pedigree, is a reminder of Felsted's affluent past. William the Conqueror gave the manor to his brother the Bishop of Bayeux, and then to the Abbey of the Holy Trinity at Caen. The attached settlement prospered with a market charter in the 13th century.

Felsted was later transferred to the Brigittine nunnery at Syon House[179] (St Bridget of Sweden, 1303–1373, friend of St Catherine of Sienna and founder of the Order of Brigittines, spread over Europe, originally a double-order, men and women sharing one campus as in the case of St Gilbert of Sempringham). Henry V founded the nunnery at Syon House, Isleworth, Middlesex, in 1415. Lord Rich's daughter Barbara was a nun there when her father bought back Felsted manor at the Dissolution, and with it further enhanced his considerable domain in Essex.

Syon House, raised upon the walls of the nunnery c. 1550 by the Duke of Somerset, Protector of the realm during the minority of Edward VI, should be a place of Puritan pilgrimage if ever the opportunity arises. Its history is doom-laden, from the savage eviction of Barbara Rich's Catholic companions to the confinement of Queen Catherine Howard before her execution, the ghoulish mauling by dogs of King Henry VIII's corpse as it lay there in state en route to London from Windsor, the beheading of Somerset, then of Lady Jane Grey, her husband, and her father-in-law who succeeded to the property, and the imprisonment of King Charles I's children there by Parliament. This catalogue of woe is only equalled by the magnificence of Robert Adam's (1728–1792) superlative interiors. You will stand astonished in his twelve verde-antique-columned Anteroom (the columns dredged from the Tiber at Rome), breathless in the Red Drawing Room, speechless in the Long Gallery. Syon says it all. The ruthless heritage, the enduring piety, the pursuit of excellence, the proximity to wealth and power, the very structure of English Puritanism.

Felsted's most notable Puritan establishment is its school.[180] Instantly famed as founded by Lord Rich, it sprang to wider prominence under the headships of George Manning (1597–1627) and Martin Holbeach (1627–1649) the great Puritan scholar and teacher.[181] The school grew rapidly to over 100 boys, included Latin, Greek and Hebrew in its curriculum, and numbered amongst its pupils the mathematical genius of two Puritan divines, John Wallis, D.D. (1616–1703), Emmanuel College, Cambridge, professor of Geometry at Oxford, founder member of the Royal Society, notorious for the ease with which he deciphered coded royalist dispatches during the Civil War; and Isaac Barrow D.D. (1630–1677) first professor of mathematics at Cambridge, Isaac Newton's tutor (for whom he vacated his chair, that Newton's even greater genius might adorn it), Master of Trinity College and Vice-Chancellor of the University.

Wallis and Barrow readily acknowledged their debt to the teaching skill of Martin Holbeach. Further renown accrued to the school by the addition of Oliver Cromwell's four sons Robert, Oliver, Richard (Lord Protector after his father), and Henry. Robert lies buried in childhood in the Parish Church. Felsted has long been a major Public School, its influence paramount in the present-day neighbourhood.

From the old school building an archway gives access to the Church of the Holy Cross[182] with its Norman tower of flint and rubble, inset with Roman tiles and stone dressed, with later battlements and 18th century cupola. Enter through the Tudor porch. The south arcade dates from 1180, two great circular piers enclosing one that is octagonal (a 16th century poor-box fixed on it). The nave roof is 14th century, of open-timber construction. The north arcade is of similar date.

You will immediately discover the splendid Rich Chantry Chapel built by the third Lord Rich (first Earl of Warwick) now the south chancel. It contains a 13–foot high monument attributed to Epiphanius Evesham,[183] reputedly the best English sculptor of his day, c. 1619. The first Lord Richard Rich leans on his elbow, resplendent in his Lord Chancellor's robes. Carved panels display scenes from his dubious career. Allegorical figures of virtue and justice, truth and wisdom, hope and charity support the fragile legend. His son Robert kneels in prayer before him. What do you think honest Thomas Hooker made of this, if he ever saw the monument commissioned by his friend the Second Earl of Warwick in memory of his great-grandfather?

At least he could have shared his questions openly with the vicar. Samuel Wharton[184] graduated B.A. from St Johns in the same year as Hooker (1608), and M.A. a year later (1612). He was a solid Essex Puritan, born at Bardfield and cleric at three other Essex churches before his long ministry at Felsted from 1614–1647. His successor, Nathaniel Ranew,[185] was an Emmanuel man from Hooker's period (sizar 1617, B.A. 1620). He remained at Felsted, a confidant of Mary, Countess of Warwick (1625–1678, married to Charles Rich, 4th Earl of Warwick, noted for her piety exhibited in devotional works and diaries now in the British museum, part-published in 1686), until ejected in 1662.

You can return to Braintree (seven miles away) along the B1417, past the imposing school buildings to the A120. Or you may wish to drive south on the A1417, retracing your journey via Hartford End towards Chelmsford, to pick up the A130 into Great Waltham. If so, just beyond Great Waltham, you can join the A131 going back to Braintree, a total distance of 15 miles.

Great Waltham.
It was at Old Park, Great Waltham, "a courteous and private recess,"[186] that, Mather says, the Earl of Warwick sheltered Susannah Hooker and her children whilst Thomas lived in Holland, from the spring of 1631 until July 1633. The whereabouts of Old Park is not certainly known, although there is an Old Park Farm at nearby Ford End, on the A130 going towards Great Dunmow.

Great Waltham derives its name from Wealdam, a settlement in a wood, in this case the great Essex Forest. The road makes an acute bend in the village, around St Mary and St Lawrence, an early Norman church much, and well, restored. There are Roman bricks melded into the walls, 500 years old carved pew-ends, 16th century brasses, alternating tie-beams and hammerbeams in the nave roof enriched with angels, roses, faces lit by a Tudor clerestory, and a peal of eight bells, one cast in 1336.[187]

Additionally there are some eighty other buildings listed as of architectural value by the Royal Commission on Historic Monuments, amongst them the outstanding "Langleys." The Lodge, a miniature version of the great house, you can almost touch from the road. The Hall itself, constructed from 1711–20 over the earlier 1620 Manor house library and dining room, with their exuberant plasterwork, you can only catch in glimpses when passing the park boundaries. These Essex villages are exhilarating simply to drive through.

The stability of many great estates with their hospitable landlords, into which Thomas Hooker was born, and on which he was able to depend throughout his life in England, surely contributed to his confidence in the Kingdom of God on earth. I think that is how it should be, patronage an universal obligation.

Round Trip B. Stisted, Coggeshall, Earls Colne, Castle Hedingham, Wethersfield, And Finchingfield.
From Braintree take the A120 eastwards to Coggeshall, but turn off left (north) into Stisted, a mile out from Braintree.

Stisted, Curacy of Samuel Stone.
Stisted is a picturesque village,[188] little more than one winding street but lined with buildings in pleasing harmony with their environment. Look at those moulded chimney-stacks on the cottages! The Hall is no older than 1823, but All Saints Parish Church has an arcade of c. 1180, the nave pillars elaborately carved, and 16th century Flemish glass in the five lancets of the east window, a reminder of the Lowlands influence on Essex which brought the reforms of Luther and Calvin so deeply into the countryside.

Samuel Stone came as curate to Stisted in 1627 on leaving Cambridge. From his prosperous background at Hertford, and with his new Master's degree, one would surmise that he accepted the lowly appointment of curate in small Stisted for the same reason that John Eliot turned schoolmaster at Little Baddow—to be near Thomas Hooker. He lasted three years before William Laud's prohibitions caught up with his outspoken Puritanism. He withdrew, as we have seen, to Thomas Shepard's hometown of Towcester. I regret no one knows the cottage chimney under which Samuel sat.

Diversion to Cressing Temple.
Due south of Stisted, three miles off, stands a medieval farm complex recently acquired by the Essex County Council which will become a major educational and tourist centre when fully exploited. Should the opportunity occur, you will unquestionably wish to pay a visit, and experience, almost at a glance, a significant segment of the culture which moulded men like Thomas Hooker.

You can quickly drive to the parking and tourist facilities there, either by crossing the A120 (Roman Stane Street) from the left (east) of the two roads out of Stisted, down the lane opposite signposted to Cressing, turning left at the village, and following the signs for Cressing Temple, or via Braintree by the B1018 to Witham, turning left to the Cressing Temple (Templar) site.

The Manor of Cressing was granted to the Knights Templar (originally a military order founded 1118, after the capture of Jerusalem in the First

Crusade, 1069–99; later to become vastly wealthy property owners and bankers, wielding international influence until suppressed by Pope Clement V at the Council of Vienne, 1312) by Queen Matilda in 1137.[189] They administered an estate of "2000 acres which included five mills, two markets and an annual three day fair." The gigantic medieval barns and walled garden, with other estate buildings such as the 16th century Courthall, vividly present the power and size of the organisation (the Templars were amalgamated with the Knights of St John, or Hospitallers, in 1314), and visually excite the most sluggish imagination as today's pilgrims tread the cathedral-like expanses, and enjoy the varied exhibitions or displays mounted by the County Council.

At the expense of a few awed steps into the past, one enters the sanguine world of medieval power-politics which enabled later groups of English mariners to reach out and pluck a New England from the Atlantic ocean.

Coggeshall.

Coggeshall[190] is within five miles of Stisted. Return to the A120, turn right (west), and you will drive into West Street past Paycocke's on your right. This is one of the glories of Essex. It is a stunning timber and plaster house, from about A.D. 1500. The five bays, with intricately carved wood panelling, stretch along the street. A display of Coggeshall lace, and an Old English garden at the rear, complete your visit. The property is administered by the National Trust, and is open 14:00-17:00, Tuesday, Thursday, and Sunday from April to September.

The Paycocks were sheep farmers turned cloth merchants, who precipitated the prosperity of the small town in the 16th century. Flemish weavers seeking refuge from the intermittent persecution of Protestants in the Netherlands, introduced their distinctive, often improved techniques to the material advantage of the whole region. "Coggeshall Whites" became one of the highest quality cloths in England.

The general reputation of Coggeshall was less flattering. The epithet "Coggeshall job" implied something ludicrously inept. The story I recall is of the day when the town clock chimed only eleven strokes at noon. But it was rumoured that the Lexden town clock (at Colchester, not far away) had currently struck twelve at eleven o'clock. So Coggeshall sent a deputation with a pony and trap, to bring back the missing stroke. I think the origin of this "yarn" has to be jealousy!

Proceed along West Street into Market Hill, the Market Charter dating back to 1256. Here you will see the guilty town clock, reconstructed in honour of Queen Victoria's Jubilee in 1887. There is a car park behind it. It is best to walk, otherwise you miss so many interesting buildings, amongst them a number of antique shops for you to explore (the *Town Trail Map* provides a useful guide).

But first go up Church Street, with its many ancient buildings, to the picturesque Woolpack Inn, a late medieval house, and into the Parish Church of St Peter-ad-Vincula, an unusual perpendicular structure, "built to one plan in the 15th century," a parallelogram without chancel or apse, although much of it was rebuilt after being bombed in World War II. There are brass memorials to the Paycocks inside.[191]

The Church and Inn make an attractive stopping place, but our main concern is with Thomas Stoughton, rector at St Peter's from 1600–1606.[192] He was presented to the living by Robert Rich, Puritan first Earl of Warwick, but even Warwick could not shield Stoughton from his inquisitive tongue. He was born, 1557, possibly into the Kent branch of an ancient Surrey family, descendants of a Godwin de Stoctun whose 2,266 acre Manor receives mention in Domesday Book.[193]

Thomas was educated first at Trinity, Cambridge, and Queens', where he obtained a Fellowship exactly 25 years before Hooker followed him. He is said to have been inclined towards the Presbyterianism of the early Tudor period, which owed more to a radical questioning of current ecclesiastical affairs (eg. his *A General Treatise Against Poperie*) than to the authoritarian church management, influenced by John Knox in Scotland, so obnoxious to good Puritans later on.[194]

Thomas Stoughton seems to have questioned everything and everyone, as the Minute Book of the Dedham Classis (of which he was a vociferous member) shows. In 1586 he had received the living at Naughton, Suffolk, not ten miles from Ipswich, some seven miles from Winthrop's Groton, but was deprived within the decade, presumably for his incautious, albeit courageous, nonconformity.

His eldest son Thomas (1588–1661) was baptised at Naughton.[195] Forty-two years later he sailed with his wife (she died almost immediately on arrival) and two children, Thomas and Katherine, from Plymouth (March 20, 1630), in the *Mary and John*, a ship sailing contemporaneously with the Winthrop fleet which made landfall at Nantasket, Massachusetts, on 30 May 1630.

The ship's company settled first at Dorchester, Massachusetts, where Thomas quickly established himself as "a man of position and prominence." This speaks highly of his father's selflessness, for Reverend Thomas died in poverty, his estate exhausted, whereas, whilst himself struggling unavailingly against misfortune, he launched the three sons who claim our attention upon prosperous careers.

Thomas Jr. removed, with other Dorchester families, in 1636, to found Windsor, Connecticut, and to play a leading role in establishing both the new town and the new state.

His younger brother Dr John Stoughton,[196] had been a Fellow of Emmanuel College, Cambridge, and exerted his influence strenuously on behalf of the New England colonies, especially in urging on them the care of the native Indian population, and their need for an Indian College, such as John Eliot strove to secure. He succeeded Ralph Cudworth (father of the Cambridge Platonist of the same name) as Rector of Aller in Somerset, where he married his predecessor's widow. After her death, he married Jane Brown of Dorset, widow of the Rector of Symonsbury, barely 25 miles south. This close Somerset/Dorset link no doubt partly explains the inclusion of his brother Thomas in the predominantly West County ship's company of the *Mary and John*. It was a rare poetic justice, for his father Thomas had been succeeded by Ralph Cudworth, when ousted from Coggeshall.

Dr John died when Rector of St Mary, Aldermanbury, London, in 1639, barely in time to evade prosecution for his outspoken Puritanism. His younger brother, Israel,[197] however, sailed in 1632 to join Thomas Jr at Dorchester, Massachusetts, and there built a lucrative grist mill. He was a wealthy man, having inherited from his mother, and from her second husband William Knight, in whose home Israel grew up, after the death of his father.

In Massachusetts, Israel rose to be Captain of the Dorchester Train Band, saw service in the Pequot War, and then, back in England in 1644, was commissioned Colonel of Horse in the Parliamentary forces, but died of a fever in 1645.

Israel's second son, William,[198] born in England prior to his parent's migration, was educated both at Harvard and at New College, Oxford. He was a Puritan preacher of note, but preferred to practice law, and presided as a Chief Justice over the Salem Witch Trials, for which he was widely criticised. He became Deputy Governor of Massachusetts, and is also re-membered for his gift of Stoughton Hall to Harvard University.

Meanwhile, Thomas Stoughton, Sr. had been silenced at Coggeshall in 1606, and withdrew to Sandwich, Kent, where he was born. He seems to have eeked out an impecunious existence "from my poore lodging in the poore Hospital called St Bartholomewes by Sandwich,"[199] possibly as an underpaid chaplain. As you draw inspiration from the treasures of Cog-geshall, spare a thought for the indomitable spirit of its former Rector, and the achievements of his sons, who had nothing to inherit but his mind and his will.

You will have realized that at Coggeshall you are close to Colchester, and closer still to Messing and Copford. You may prefer to visit them from here rather than the circular tour I have already described. If so, you could very profitably drive via Bridge Street (south of Market Hill) over the Long, or Stephen's Bridge, built by 13th century monks, said to be the oldest brick bridge in the country, onto the B1024 to Kelvedon and the A12.

You should go this way in any case. It brings you immediately to Grange Barn, the oldest surviving timber-framed barn in Europe, c. A. D. 1140, now National Trust property, open from April to the end of October on Tuedays, Thursdays, Sundays, and Bank Holiday Mondays, as Paycocke's is. As a bonus, Grange Hill Farm House stands just beyond, another 16th century timber-frame construction of impressive appearance. Opposite runs Abbey Lane, inviting a long walk to the Cistercian Abbey (1140), with the St Nicholas Chapel (1224), structurally unaltered because used as a cow-byre long enough to thwart improvers; and the Farm House which incorporates the surviving Abbey buildings.

Cross the bridge through the farmyard and there is the Abbey Mill, now restored. The Blackwater river forms a mill-race which opens into a sheet of water for the ancient fish-ponds, a masked corner that whispers of a world long gone, reflective, contemplative, whose affinity with our needs and desires lives on.

Earls Colne.
Follow the B1024 north from Coggeshall. Earls Colne is within four miles. You are now in the Colne Valley (the word colne originally meant river), less than ten miles from Castle Hedingham via Halstead and Sible Hedingham, northwest along the A604; a similar distance from Colchester to the east.

Earls Colne was the heartland of the de Veres, Earls of Oxford.[200] One of their major residences, Colne Place, was here—hence Earls Colne. The de Veres were rated by Lord Macauley (English historian, 1800–1859) as "the longest and most illustrious line of nobles that England has seen."[201] They came with William the Conqueror from Ver, near Bayeux. Their founder, Aubrey de Vere, is named in Domesday book as holding lands all over Essex, Cambridgeshire, and Suffolk.

Henry I created Aubrey's son hereditary Great Chamberlain of England (1133), a title they jealously guarded. This second Aubrey built Hedingham Castle in 1140, one of the best private Keeps in the country, though much reduced now. The Earldom of Oxford was confirmed to his family shortly afterwards.

They created religious houses at Hedingham, Earls Colne, and Hatfield Broad Oak where they were variously interred, strange forerunners of the Puritan strongholds which flourished at each place 500 years later. Godfrey, eldest son of Aubrey de Ver, was responsible for the Benedictine Priory at

Earls Colne in 1100. He was cured of an illness there, and took the habit, to become a monk in his own foundation. He and his wife Beatrice, sister of William the Conqueror, were both buried here.[202]

It is impossible to look in any depth at the story of the Oxfords. Four of them span our period. Edward (1550–1604), "The Spendthrift,"[203] was 17th earl. He held the title for 38 years, and substantially depleted their fortunes.

He was a favourite at Elizabeth's court. "The Queen's Majestie delighteth more in his personage and his daunsing and valientnes than any other," but he squandered talents and inheritance into an embittered, impoverished end. It was from his extravagance that the Harlakendens, whom we soon meet, gained possession of both manors, Earls Colne, and Colne Priory.

Edward de Vere's son Henry (1593–1625) inherited at eleven years of age, leaving his mother the Dowager Countess Elizabeth to retrieve what she could of the forfeited estates. Henry died on campaign at The Hague, fighting in the service of Charles I. His second cousin Robert (d. 1632), became the 19th earl after a dispute over the inheritance; and his son, Aubrey (1626–1703) reaped the reward of their continuous loyalty to the reigning monarchs, after intriguing in the Stuart cause during the Commonwealth.

At the restoration of Charles II, he was given, amongst other honours, command of the Royal Horse Guards known thereafter as "the Oxford Blues." Until then they had been a Cromwellian regiment of horse. They are familiar today as the Blues and Royals, part of the royal Household Cavalry, seen at ceremonial parades, or on duty at London's Horse Guards in Whitehall.

This Royalist, high church heritage of a vast landowning nobility inevitably stamped its mark on the countryside. It helps us to understand the strong bonds of history through which the rising Puritan families had to hack their way, especially in an area like this where the Oxfords regularly resided, and where serfdom was ingrafted upon a dependant populace. A considerable output of spiritual energy was demanded, with its attendant friction, if their pulpits were to be supplied with preaching parsons, who would open to them the new Biblical learning which led to freedom of conscience, and liberty for personal development.

The device of the Puritan Lectureships exactly suited their purpose. These sprang spontaneously to life throughout Essex. To such a Lectureship came Thomas Shepard in 1627.[204]

Thomas Shepard was born at Towcester in Northamptonshire on 5 November 1605, a Gunpowder baby for an explosive life. He went to

High Street, Earls Colne, looking west. House occupied by
William Cosin and Thomas Shepard on the right side

Emmanuel College, Cambridge at about the time Hooker left, came under
his influence, and was one of his most ardent supporters ever after. He
gained his Master's degree in 1627, was ordained deacon by the Bishop of
Peterborough on July 12 that same year, priested next day, and came to Earls
Colne after a brief respite with his friend Thomas Weld at Terling next Little
Baddow, and no doubt with Thomas and Susannah Hooker too.

Shepard's appointment took the familiar pattern, often the only one
open to known Puritans to whom many pulpits were already closed, of
Usher at the Grammar School and Lecturer at the Church outside official
hours. The Schoolmaster was William Cosin, a Cambridge man himself. It
is said that Shepard boarded with him, at Nos 83–85 High Street, formerly
"Matthews Acre," a composite property still standing near the Church, and
looking much as it did in Cosin's day, as I hope you may see for yourself.[205]

One of Cosin's immediate predecessors as schoolmaster had been
Christopher Scott, also Rector of Stisted, who removed to Hawkwell near
Rayleigh, Essex, in 1617. He signed the 1629 Petition to Laud against
Hooker's suppression, as "Parson of Hockeril," a sign of his nonconformity
as well as of his support.[206]

The Parish Church of St Andrew, where Shepard would lecture, is as
noble as its pedigree.[207] Much has changed over the years, not least due to
a large restoration in 1884, but the magnificent tower, emblazoned with the
de Vere arms and five-star emblems capped by a late 17th century copper
corona, and weather vane, will instantly draw your attention. The ground-

Tower of the parish church, Earls Colne.

plan is a square, with the tower and sanctuary projecting. This, and the south aisle, remain from the 7th earl's building (John de Vere, 1313–1360). The nave roof is 14th century too.

You will find a painted monument to Roger Harlakenden and his four wives, dated 1602, in the south chapel. He was steward to the 17th earl of Oxford, and purchased both manors from him. The Dowager Countess Elizabeth tried to repossess the properties after her spendthrift husband's death, objecting to the give-away price, claiming duress, but without success. The Harlakendens were still in residence at The Priory when Thomas Shepard met Roger's grandson Richard, at Emmanuel College (the same Richard who married Alice Mildmay of Great Graces, Little Baddow).[208]

The wealthy Harlakendens became the closest of friends with Thomas Shepard. Richard, his Cambridge contemporary, now lord of the manors, gave him protection too, sheltering him at The Priory when Laud's persuivants were on his trail. He performed the same office for John Hawkesbury, Puritan incumbent from 1612–1640, and for the diarist Ralph Josselin, vicar from 1640–1683. His younger brother Roger emigrated with Shepard, as did his sister Mabell (who then married Governor John Haynes). They settled at Newtown, where Roger purchased Governor Dudley's great house, was commissioned lieutenant-colonel of militia, but tragically died of smallpox when only twenty-seven.

At Earls Colne, Shepard was able to cement his friendship with Hooker, and others of the Cuckoos company. He helped Samuel Stone to a lectureship at his native Towcester, when Laud pressed his censure on them, but could not avoid suspension himself. In 1630 he withdrew into Yorkshire, to become tutor and chaplain to Sir Richard Darley of Buttercrambe, on the river Derwent, northeast of York, and married Margaret Tanteville, Darley's cousin, two years later.

From there the young couple fled even further, to Heddon-on-the-Wall, at Newcastle-upon-Tyne. Shepard would keep preaching, and was in constant danger of arrest. After more than two years in hiding (one wonders if this accounts for the death of their infant son) they escaped to Boston, Massachusetts in the *Defense*. They arrived in time for Shepard to succeed Hooker as Pastor at Newtown when the latter led his one hundred strong party down the Indian trails to Connecticut, but Margaret tragically died that same year. Shepard was happily remarried to Joanna, eldest daughter of Thomas and Susannah Hooker. She bore him three children, of whom one died in infancy.

He was "a poor, weak, pale-complexioned man,"[209] but with the heart of a lion—large enough to send him out with John Eliot and Daniel Gookin (later "chosen to be ruler over the Praying Indians") when Eliot's Indian mission first began. He supported Eliot through all the antagonisms of the Indian work, and contributed largely to the *Eliot Tacts*. He has been called "the most noted evangelist in early New England," and Mather wrote "the character of his daily conversation was a trembling walk with God." His many publications include *The Sincere Convert* (23 editions), *New England's Lamentations for Old England's Present Errors*, and *Subjection to Christ*. Ecclesiastically he stood between the excesses of Laudian persecution and Radical libertarianism, in New England between over authoritarian Puritans and the laxity of some Independents, much as Hooker did. Credit is due to such as these, Winthrop, Winslow, Haynes, Mather, many others, whose balanced statesmanship enabled the new American Congregational churches to emerge from the dangers of sectarianism into full nationhood.

As the pastor of what was now called Cambridge, where the first University was fledged in his time, some credit is also due to Thomas Shepard for Harvard's instant acceptance in parallel with Oxford and Cambridge, whose Faculties quickly recognised Harvard degrees. The Massachusetts Ministers boasted in their ranks some of the English Universities' finest minds, versed in the learning and culture which places like Earls Colne fostered every inch of the pilgrim way.

Castle Hedingham, Wethersfield, and Finchingfield.

If you have time to spare, go on to Castle Hedingham.[210] Continue west from Earls Colne on the A604, through Halstead to Sible Hedingham. There turn right (northeast) onto the B1058 into Castle Hedingham, less than ten miles total. The Castle is open to visitors from April to October inclusive, 10:00–17:00 daily. Light refreshments are available.

You will appreciate that you are now close to Sudbury in Suffolk (another Puritan centre heavily involved in the colonisation of New England) and to Groton, home of the Winthrops, whose Manor House has recently been renovated and is an attractively modernised private home, but not open to view.

Castle Hedingham.

The bridge over the dry moat by which you approach the Castle Keep is Tudor, dating from 1496. The House is Georgian, from 1719. But the Keep is pure Norman and unspoilt. Built by Aubrey de Vere in 1140, the four floors and the roof are still in position. The Great Hall is incomparable. It stands as it was finished by the stone masons, as if waiting for wall drapes, a cheerful fire, and the lord's servants to lay the table before the family moves in; the finest surviving domestic interior of early Norman date in England. If Sir Aubrey appears, and orders off your head for not strewing the floor with clean rushes, you will sense no injustice.

The remainder of the castle buildings have long been demolished, but the Keep, and its situation, repays any effort to get there. A sober, unworldly Puritan like Thomas Shepard would not have dreamed of making the visit, but the castle was in his dreams nonetheless. It symbolised the realistic status of almost everything in Earls Colne and the surrounding countryside.

Wethersfield.

Go back to Sible Hedingham. Turn left (east) onto the A604 as if returning to Earls Colne. Almost immediately turn right onto a minor road running southwest, signposted Wethersfield. Watch out for a left fork shortly afterwards, or you may find yourself at Toppesfield away to the north.

The name Wethersfield is instantly familiar to anyone from Connecticut, for the first 17th century River Plantations were Wethersfield,[211] Windsor and Hartford, with Springfield, Massachusetts, further up the Connecticut river. Until recently Wethersfield, Essex was the long-time Headquarters of the United States Air Force Eastern Command in Britain, with a distinguished record from the days of World War II, commemorated in Chelmsford Cathedral.

Visually just as satisfying as any other Essex village, according to Pevsner, Wethersfield is situated in a pretty countryside of hills gently rising and falling, with some sixty buildings of architectural interest described by the Royal Commission on Historical Monuments, some with overhanging gables enriched by carved bargeboards. The Parish Church of St Mary Magdalene is anchored by a massive early 13th century tower, the nave has 13th century round columns and 14th century octagonal ones. There is a Tudor clerestory and nave roof, and a long history of nonconformity through the pastorates of Richard Rogers, celebrated Puritan preacher and town lecturer from 1572–1618, and of the even more prominent Stephen Marshall from 1618–1625.

Richard Rogers was possibly the grandson of the John Rogers,[212] alias Thomas Matthew, who edited the *Matthew's Bible* (a revision of Tyndale's translation conflated with *Coverdale's Old Testament*, as authorised by Henry VIII for general use in 1537), and became the first Protestant martyr under Queen Mary, burnt at Smithfield, London, on 4 February 1555. He was widely revered throughout the English Protestant community, and when his grandson Richard preached at Wethersfield, it is said, the crowds flocked into the church in such numbers that they overflowed into the two porches, crushed together. This dynamic, 45 year long ministry, held sway over a wide area of Essex and beyond.

Richard's son Ezekial became an Anglican clergyman like his father. He was Chaplain to Sir Francis Barrington of Hatfield Broad Oak, and Rector of Rowley, Yorkshire, a Barrington advowson, before emigrating to Massachusetts in 1638, where he helped to found Rowley, Massachusetts. His cousin, Nathaniel Rogers (son of the famous John Rogers of Dedham, who settled at Ipswich, Massachusetts, in 1636) was one of those for whom Dedham, Massachusetts was named. The Shermans of Wethersfield, Massachusetts, were amongst the others.

We have already met the renowned Shermans at Dedham, England, and have noted that Edmund Sherman emigrated with his two sons, the Rev. John and Samuel. John was called to be Assistant Minister at Watertown, Massachusetts, in 1634. But next year he, with six other members of the Watertown church, was released "with intent to form anew in a church covenant in the River of Connecticut," ie. Wethersfield. His father and brother removed with him, and took up adjoining homesteads on the east side of the High Street.

The *History of Ancient Wethersfield* (Connecticut) suggests that, the name Dedham having already been assigned to the town in Massachusetts, the Shermans commemorated their honoured Rogers connection by naming the new river town Wethersfield. It is also possible that another original settler, John Clarke, may have been the one known to have inherited

Wethersfield Manor in 1629. Mary Chester (neé Neville), wife of Leonard Chester (son of Dorothy Chester, neé Hooker, Thomas Hooker's sister who emigrated with her son to Roxbury, also early Wethersfield settlers) may have descended from the Sir Hugh de Neville, known in England as "Lord of Wetherfield."[213]

Rogers of Wethersfield, Rogers of Dedham, Shermons of Dedham, and Watertown, and Wethersfield in both countries, Hooker of Little Baddow the confidant of Rogers of Dedham, with John Eliot of Roxbury, Pynchon of Springfield in both countries, a founder member of Roxbury, Massachusetts, and Dorothy and Leonard Chester at Roxbury and Wethersfield, and the river towns of Connecticut, Windsor settled from west country Dorsetshire, and Hooker at Hartford with Stone from Hertford, England—the names become interchangeable and the ripples from each individual, inspired by preachers such as Rogers of Wethersfield, or Rogers of Dedham, surge forward in great waves to lap the shores of current history on both sides of the Atlantic. The pebbles they cast into the ocean of time; "Glory to God—Freedom of Worship—Integrity in Practice," a heritage to boast of and maintain!

Finchingfield.

From Wethersfield continue (northwest) on the B1053, for the short drive into Finchingfield. It is part of the Thomas Hooker pilgrim route, one he would have ridden many times, and a pleasure in itself, for Finchingfield is Essex's most photographed village. Deservedly so.[214]

Let us begin with Hooker's connection. Stephen Marshall (1594–1655)[215] lived here. A most celebrated Puritan Divine, born to poor parents at Godmanchester near Huntingdon, one of Hooker's students at Emmanuel and his life-long friend, Stephen Marshall went as Lecturer to Wethersfield (1618), and to St John the Baptist, Finchingfield, as Vicar (1625).

It was as "vicar of Ffinchingfield" that Marshall signed the petition to Laud on Hooker's behalf in 1629. He was one of the most influential members of the Cuckoos Company. Lecturer at St Margaret's Westminster from 1642, a frequent preacher before Parliament (Clarendon complained that his influence over Parliamentarians exceeded that of Laud over the Royalists), a rare Puritan chaplain to King Charles I during his captivity, he had enlisted as a chaplain to the Earl of Essex's regiment in the Civil War, and sustained a reconciliatory ministry as a "moderate and judicious Presbyterian." "No man," it was said, "could rival his power of translating the dominant sentiments of his party into the language of irresistible appeal."[216]

He was a member of the Westminster Assembly (the Synod convened by Parliament in 1643 to reform the English churches), and one of Oliver Cromwell's "Triers" (the body of commissioners appointed "for the approbation of all preachers and lecturers" in 1654). He was buried with much honour in Westminster Abbey, but his body was exhumed and desecrated at the Restoration. That was a risk for principle I think he would have been glad to take. Hooker's disciples had little time for human rewards.

The village is delectable. All roads drop down into a spacious Green, bisected by the little running river Pant, on its way down to Bocking Churchstreet. A hump-backed bridge vaults over the gathered pond-waters in the treeless dell. A cluster of wood and thatch rises from the Green, period cottages to delight in, and a windmill, and the church with its incongruous cupola on top of the sturdy Norman tower, set on the hillocks above. It is a picture-postcard scene.

On the street in front of the church you will find the long low-lying Guildhall of the Holy Trinity. Through a gateway in this building you gain admission to the churchyard. It bursts on you in beauty. Arrange your daughters' weddings here! Stephen Marshall's six daughters were five too many. Only one brought him any comfort. Pepys, the diarist, records that two of them (Beck and Nan) became actresses, and that must have embarrassed their famous Puritan father. Perhaps his marriage to a wealthy heiress, whose fortune he, in conscience, left entirely at her own disposal, exposed the children to too many temptations. It says much for his integrity that the private scandals they brought him scarcely impeded his public ministry. Thomas Hooker must have been fully aware of the situation, and the more determined, for his friend's troubles, to control his own soul's journey without moral compromise.

Inside the church, the spreading Norman tower-arch matches the recessed Norman doorway outside. The chancel arch and the nave arcade are 13th/14th century. The Rood screen is one of the most elaborate in Essex. And Stephen Marshall's impassioned oratory still stirs the silent air. When you can tear yourself away, the B1053 takes you straight back to Braintree.

Villages around Chelmsford

Group One: Writtle, Roxwell, Springfield, Boreham, Terling.

Royal Writtle.

From Chelmsford take the old A414 (the Rainsford and Roxwell roads) going westwards. This route takes you alongside the River Can to its confluence with the Wid just before Writtle begins. Turn sharp left at the junction where the A1060 continues to Roxwell, and cross over the Can into the village centre. On your right you will see the Agricultural College, built on the site of a hunting lodge constructed in 1211 by King John (1167–1216) youngest son of Henry II, best known for signing the Magna Carta. Like most Norman nobles he was an enthusiastic hunter when not occupied with fighting. Part of the moat which surrounded the royal residence, known as

Lordships, is still visible at the pond decked with daffodils in Spring, in the College grounds beside the road.

The old name Writtolaburna means "babbling purling stream,"[217] a reference to the Wid as it came tumbling down from Widford, along the route taken by the main London road round Chelmsford, before the Bishop of London had the Roman bridges rebuilt in 1100. John's hunting lodge was close beside the highway from Westminster, a convenient overnight stop for a hunting monarch.

In the village you enter The Green. You may park your car round the edge if lucky. St John's Green lies further on. Taken together they form as lively and congruous a centerpiece as one could wish. Houses crowd the grassy fringe, Tudor cottages, some with Georgian facades, Aubyns on the south side, an early 16th century half-timbered dwelling, with Mundays beside it, a 17th century plastered house with shell-hood entrance.

The small library and information centre, with the Reformed Chapel alongside the Rose and Crown carvery, and a few shops that have escaped the menace of supermarkets nearer town, spell out the living village community which still survives. The Green slopes down to a pond alive with wildfowl.

Writtle was a Romano-British settlement which became a Royal Manor under the Anglo-Saxons, wrested from Harold after the Battle of Hastings by his Norman conqueror. It was a lordly holding enfolding upwards of a dozen manors within its fief: Lordships; Turges, bought by Nicholas Pynchon (c. 1352), great-grandfather of the founder of Springfield, Massachusetts; Hasets, where his son John Pynchon lived; Fiddlers, where Petres, and then Brownes of Roxwell (and Salem, Massachusetts) lived; Montpelier's, earlier owned by Robert "The Bruce" (1274–1329)[218] until he forfeited his English lands on championing Scottish independence, being crowned king of Scotland on 27 March 1306, an independence secured by his astonishing victory over Edward II at the Battle of Bannockburn, famed in Scottish history; Romans Fee, another Petre property into which one of the Pynchon girls married; and others, some alternating from time-to-time.

Henry III had granted the mega-manor to Philip de Albene in 1216, and it had passed through a number of owners until, by the 16th century, Writtle itself partly passed into the possession of the Pynchon family.

Cross over The Green veering south, and you will glimpse All Saints Church peering over the trees. The stocky tower was rebuilt in 1802 of rough stone held in by narrow brick buttresses, brick battlements atop. The church was built c. 1230, on a pre-Norman site. The nave arcading and clerestory are mostly 13th century, the roof, carried on medieval stone angels with a musical talent, is Tudor.

There are various Weston and Pynchon memorials inside, one the magnificent tomb by Nicholas Stone[219] of Sir Edward Pynchon (deceased 1627) and his wife Dorothy (nee Weston of Skreens, Roxwell). It is an allegory of death, resurrection, and judgement, but it manages to include an air of appropriate respect to its wealthy patrons in the grim theme.

Sir Edward was cousin to William Pynchon of Springfield, Massachusetts. Their fathers were brothers, William of Writtle the major branch, John of Springfield the younger. The generations grew up together, their families resident in neighbouring parishes. The inscription on Edward's tomb runs, in approximate translation from the Latin used, "Sir Edward and Dorothy Weston—formerly one in flesh, now one in dust, await Christ in this tomb. They lived with rare faith to Godward, in undisputed harmony with one another, and in charity to all men. If thou doubt the word of their grief-stricken son, ask those among whom they lived. Meanewhile beware of speaking ill of them, for even the dead have sharp ears."

Roxwell.
Return towards Chelmsford over the river Can, but at the junction of the A414 with the A1060 turn left for a mile, to the Hare and Hounds. Take the narrow road on your left signposted to Roxwell and Skreens Park. The lane twists and turns round the houses to the Parish Church of St Michael and All Angels in The Street. An inviting place to stop awhile.

In Roxwell,[220] the church is much restored, but in the chancel you will find a number of imposing monuments, including one in draped marble on the south side of the sanctuary to the two Sir John Bramstons of Skreens, of whom you will hear shortly. It was also the place of worship of the poet Francis Quarles (1592–1644),[221] a contributor to the Bay Psalter of 1640, America's first printed book, accredited to John Eliot and others of the New England pioneers.

Quarles was an Essex man, born at Romford, educated at Christ's College, Cambridge, at the same time as Thomas Hooker. He became private secretary in Ireland to Archbishop Ussher that so celebrated a Calvinist theologian that Oliver Cromwell ordered a State Funeral in Ussher's honour at Westminster Abbey when he died in 1656.

Ussher[222] lent his considerable authority to every attempt at reconciling Churchmen and Dissenters, without much avail where Quarles was concerned, for Quarles was an ardent royalist, a pamphleteer of great popularity on behalf of Charles I, best remembered for his *Emblems*, printed in 1635, a series of paraphrases on passages of Scripture, with four-line epigrams composed in an ornate metaphorical style, much loved by the King.

Francis and his wife Ursula (Woodgate) had eighteen children, of whom at least four were baptised at Roxwell after their return from Ireland. They resided at the local great house, Skreens Park, Francis presumably in some capacity as a resident chaplain to Sir John Bramston, who had purchased the property from the ennobled Westons of Writtle. They too were committed royalists.

One Weston daughter, Dorothy, married into the Pynchon family, as we have seen. Her brother, Sir Richard Weston, married her sister-in-law Elizabeth Pynchon. This Sir Richard became lord high treasurer under King Charles I, that is to say, one of the most trusted servants of the crown, and rose to be Earl of Portland.[223] He and his immediate descendants remained faithful to the Crown. The Pynchon partners in the Weston alliances were, as you know, first cousins of William Pynchon, arch-Puritan founder of Springfield, Massachusetts. Equally confusing is, as Frances Rose-Troup points out in her *John White, Patriarch of Dorchester and Founder of Massachusetts*, that "there seems to have been a connexion between the Whites and the Westons of Roxwell, Essex."[224]

John White was the moving and sustaining force behind the early Dorchester (1623) and New England (1626) Companies, which matured into the Massachusetts Bay Company (1629). Equally, he was a very celebrated Puritan divine, rector of Dorchester and later of Lambeth, Assessor of the Westminster Assembly which produced the Westminster Confession, and nearly brought England within the Presbyterian Church of Scotland through the Solemn League and Covenant (1643). That he was a family friend, and close associate of William Pynchon in the New England enterprise, occasions no surprise. But that John White's consistently Puritan circle at Dorchester in Dorset was in any way attached across the many dividing miles to Roxwell's Royalist ruling families in Essex, does raise questions about the diversity of contemporary English society, despite the dissuasion from the pursuit of individual belief for which the Tudors and Stuarts worked so energetically. More of this when we come to Pynchon's Springfield.

Skreens has now become the more intriguing! Take the second left-hand exit from St Michael's, towards Shellow Bowells and Willingale (you simply have to be photographed in Shellow Bowells!) Behind you, as you leave Roxwell centre, lies Dukes, a 16th century manorhouse most carefully and well preserved. A short way down the road, on your left, you will find a large notice-board for Skreens Park now a permanent camping-ground for the county Boy Scouts and Girl Guides associations. I suppose you could drive circumspectly down the rough track to photograph the lake. Unless the scouts happen to be encamped, no one will impede a responsible explorer. But only memories whisper among the beds of reeds. The great house was pulled down in 1912.

Skreens[225] was sold by the Westons to Sir John Bramston in 1636, the year following the death of the first Earl of Portland. This terminated the Weston family's residence at Roxwell. His son Jerome, the second Earl, was imprisoned for supporting Charles I, and the line was extinguished with the deaths of Jerome's two sons, Charles and Thomas, both of whom succeeded to the title.

Lord Chief Justice Sir John Bramston (1577–1654),[226] from Maldon in Essex, was also a traditional Royalist. Educated at Cambridge and the Middle Temple, he was Queen's Sergeant and then Justice of the King's Bench, but was impeached by the Commons for giving a legal opinion in favour of the hated "Ship Money" (forced loans by the Crown), and was finally dismissed office for offering his legal advice to King Charles I in prison, after the Civil War. He was one of those who bravely defended John Michaelson, Thomas Hooker's rector at Chelmsford, when the mob turned against him in 1641, and sheltered him and his terrified family "in a small house at Writtle." You will be glad to know that Michaelson was reinstated at the Restoration.

Sir John's son, another John (1611–1700),[227] and a chip off the same royalist block, succeeded his father at Skreens. His *Autobiography*, printed by the Camden Society in 1845, gives many personal insights into the conflicts thrust upon Essex communities by the bitter consequence of civil war. For instance, he records the feud between himself and Colonel Henry Mildmay of Little Baddow.

The Colonel was at that time Governor of Cambridge Castle for Parliament, and contemptuously slighted poor Dr Michaelson when the misused Rector of Chelmsford was taken to the castle on trumped up charges of popery. The younger Sir John Bramston, a lawyer like his father, verbally castigated Sir Henry, who reciprocated with a charge of papistical plotting by Sir John. The case came before the High Court and Colonel Henry was found to have perjured himself. Sir John was exonerated. He became a Member of Parliament for Essex. The case illustrates the tensions between Roundheads and Cavaliers within the closely related families of this small neighbourhood, except that the epithets are too simplistic to carry conviction. The Westons may have been Cavaliers, despite their family alliances with well-known Puritans, but the Bramstons were middle-of-the-road conservatives, loyal to their King and Country, rather than Cavaliers, and many of the Roxwell Puritans were equally loyalist and traditionalist, apart from their determination to cleanse their churches from "unwarrantable" ceremonies, as will next be noted.

Frances Rose-Troup refers to Roxwell as "that Essex village with which, directly or indirectly, a vast number of emigrants were connected, and with which, also, John White was so closely associated."[228] She goes so far as to distinguish "The Roxwell Group," listing amongst its members "The three Brownes, Flyer, Hodson, Pelham, Pyncheon, Vassalls, Waldegrave—to these may be added Eliot, Josselyn and Josias, brother of John White."

The list invites comment. Francis Flyer "of Roxwell" was a London merchant who attended some early meetings of the Massachusetts Bay Company, but Daniel Hodson, a London clothier, was "of Epping" when his second marriage to Agnes Josselyn "of Roxwell" took place. That barely justifies his inclusion, although the Josselyns were well known local Puritans, and some of them emigrated to New England. Herbert Pelham the younger "of Boston, Lincolnshire" first married Jemima Waldegrave of the Waldegraves of Buers, neighbours of the Winthrops in Suffolk, before marrying Elizabeth, widow of Roger Harlakenden, in Massachusetts when his first wife died. The Waldegraves were related to the Gurdons of Assington and bring us to the very heart of the emigration's leading families, but not visibly to Roxwell.

The inclusion of William Pynchon is as hard to justify. His family came from Writtle and Springfield, both larger places which would expect to claim his habitation rather than Roxwell. The two Vassalls, Samuel (an early Associate of the Bay Company) and William (who briefly emigrated in 1628, and again in 1635 before settling in Barbados), London merchants, are said by Rose-Troup to have been "of Eastwood, near Roxwell," but the only Eastwood of consequence in Essex is far away at Prittlewell, Southend-on-Sea. John Eliot was "of Little Baddow," in no way directly linked with Roxwell apart from a vague proximity, and, no doubt, a warm acquaintance with some of the residents.

This leaves the three Brownes and Josias White.[229] Josias, (d February 1623), was Vicar of Hornchurch in Essex from 1611 until his death, and the elder brother of John White of Dorchester. He owned a farm at Roxwell. His son, also Josias (d December 1643) was Rector of Langton Matravers in Dorset. He inherited the Roxwell farm, but bequeathed it to his mother Mistress Anne Drake because "I know not upon what straightes her old age may be cast." From her it passed to his third son William, Dorchester merchant, who moved to London, but there is no evidence that either Josias ever lived at the farm in Roxwell. Nevertheless, the connection was there.

There is, however, a connecting factor which justifies Rose-Troup in bringing together the above as "The Roxwell Group," apart from their tenuous connection with Roxwell itself. So far as can be ascertained, these were moderate Puritans, loyal to the ruling monarch and the established Church. The reason for William Vassall's returns to England was "to petition

Parliament for the liberty of English subjects"[230] under the increasingly restrictive laws of Massachusetts. The Whites, William Pynchon and the Brownes were involved in the same protest. Rose-Troup makes much of this. She concludes that the element of Independency in the Eastern Counties quickly overruled the Puritans' original intention to reform, not replace, the Church of England, and led some of the early settlers to ally themselves with Plymouth Separatism. The Brownes, however, remained aggressively loyal to Church and Crown.

They certainly brought matters to a head at Salem and came close to preventing the progress of the first New England settlements towards Separation. Had they been successful, it could only have been temporary. The forces ranged against the containment of the American colonies inside any English Church or Parliament were irresistible. Nonetheless, these two members of "the Roxwell Group" made the attempt, and it is important that we acknowledge it.

You may know that John Endecott (1589–1665),[231] born into a wealthy Devonshire family but disinherited for his Puritanism and turned soldier of fortune, was engaged by the Massachusetts Bay pioneers to establish a foothold near Cape Ann in 1628, and stockaded himself at Naumkeag (Salem), north of what was to become Boston.

He was appointed governor of the small settlement until John Winthrop and his fleet landed in 1630, and superseded him under the auspices of the newly sealed Massachusetts Bay Company. Two of the Salem settlement's four ministers were Samuel Skelton from Sempringham, Lincolnshire, and Francis Higginson, boyhood companion of Thomas Hooker in Leicester. They organized the Salem Church on the Plymouth Plantation model of Independency, with the approval of the third minister, Ralph Smith, who transferred to the Plymouth Colony.

Francis Bright, fourth of the ministers at Salem, removed to incipient Charlestown "because he was not in sympathy with the tendency to Separatism that was beginning to develope in the colony," and there briefly joined forces with William Blackstone, an anglican clergyman who, as Mather records, "would never join himself to any of our churches, giving his reason for it: "I came from England, because I did not like the lord-bishops; but I can't join with you, because I would not be under the lord-brethren.'"[232] Bright returned to England shortly after.

Endecott sided with Skelton and Higginson. Congregational ordinations took place in defiance of the English episcopal practice and the *Book of Common Prayer* was banned. This was unacceptable to many of the Salem settlers, and the subject of a critical correspondence between Endecott and his governing board in England, pacified by his denial of separation from the Church of England, but only from its corruptions and disorders. The

Brownes led the opposition of the more orthodox Puritans to the unantici-pated schismatic actions of their governor and ministers.

Kellam Browne of Roxwell had signed the Cambridge Agreement of 1629, but did not emigrate. His brothers John (a lawyer) and Samuel (a merchant) sailed to Salem at their own charges in 1629. They were amongst the first gentlemen settlers, had at once been made members of the Gover-nor's Council, and John was sworn as Assistant before his embarkation. They were men of stature unaccustomed to being lightly set aside and they commenced a rival Meeting, at which the Prayer Book was used.

Endecott was an equally colourful character, with a temper to match. Consider his excision of the Cross from the Colony's flag, a sizzling piece of scissor-snipping (what if Laud had caught a shred of it across the ocean!) which called for all Hooker's diplomacy a few years later. Endecott roundly told the Brownes "New England had no place for such as they," and shipped them home (at their own charges!) in the *Talbot* that same year.[233]

They returned to Roxwell, and solicited Pynchon's support when brought before the Bay Company Council.[234] Why not? Pynchon was a Church Warden at Springfield, most probably a Prayer Book man himself. Endecott and his ministers were cautioned and the Brownes received some recompense for their considerable losses. It was a nasty incident which illustrated the speed with which Independency, so dangerous for the settlers who went still under the protection of the English crown, yet so suitable to the requirements of the new colonies, was sweeping aside the original loyalist aspirations of the more moderate Puritan leaders.

This drama unfolded within gunshot of Hooker's Cuckoos Company, a much closer-knit group than anything Roxwell could display. The point to note is that, for all the esteem in which fine old English families like the Westons and the Bramstons were held, and the moderation proclaimed by whole groups of Puritans like that at Roxwell, in the end that moderation led only to revolution. When moderate men build empires, they clarify everything without prejudice, and open the way to radical reform.

Springfield, Home of William Pynchon.

To reach Springfield, return to Chelmsford and exit by Victoria Road going south-east. You then pass in front of Springfield Mill on the River Chelmer (now a restaurant), one reason for Springfield's former prosperity. Turn left (northeast) up Springfield Road (A1113), and turn left again at the second set of traffic lights, into Trump Lane. This brings you to All Saints Church at Springfield Green.[235]

You can park your car outside the church, opposite Springfield Cottage where Oliver Goldsmith wrote his *Deserted Village* c. 1770,—though whether he refers to Springfield (in early English, Springinghefelda, "open country of the dwellers by the spring"), or to some other village, is uncertain. "Sweet Auburn! loveliest village of the plain."

> A time there was, e'er England's griefs began,
> When every rood of ground maintain'd its man;
> For him light labour spread her wholesome store,
> Just gave what life requir'd, but gave no more;
> His best companions, innocence and health;
> And his best riches, ignorance and wealth.
> How happy he who crowns in shades like these,
> A youth of labour with an age of ease.

Essex farm workers might have found it difficult to identify with Oliver Goldsmith's cushy sentiments, but they give a flavour to Springfield Green.

As you enter All Saints you will smile as you read "Prayse God for al the Good Benefactors ano 1586" bricked into the tower, a line which might well have started Goldsmith off, but relates to a renovation scheme of an earlier generation to which the Mildmays largely contributed.

Inside, you will immediately see the Communion Table donated by William Pynchon in 1624, when he was Church Warden, a free-standing table for the comfortable gathering of the reformed congregation round about it, as they supposed the first Christian Disciples had done at their simple meal. And strictly contrary to William Laud's requirements. But it was not until an Archidiaconal Visitation in 1683, forty years after Laud's beheading, that the injunction "the bench under the East Window to be taken down and the communion table to be placed there" was finally complied with,[236] and the fixed altar so important to the 17th century ecclesiastical authorities substituted. Pynchon's Table was placed in the Old Rectory at Trump Lane, removed from the County, forgotten, rediscovered, and miraculously restored to its rightful place, free-standing in the Chancel, in time for the 350th anniversary celebrations of the founding of Springfield Massachusetts, in 1986.

It all seems petty enough to us, but represents one of the few expressions of religious freedom open to church members four hundred years ago. You may even commend the stolid worshippers for their long drawn-out resistance to what seemed to them an unjustifiably imposed conformity, and salute the lovely oak Table affectionately as a symbol of something significant. The Table at New College, Oxford, where William's father worshipped as a student with John White and other young Puritans, was not removed until 1699. Bully for them![237]

I hope the 1624 "Pynchon Board" will be on display with its reference to the Table, and other benefactions. "The belfry enclosed and beautified, and the stairs there altered and amended. Twelve new pews in the bodye of the Church, fowre pewes in the Chancel, a pulpett head, a communion table erected, and the chancel seated round about for the communicants; all of which worke was done by the appointments of John Tansted and William Pynchon, churchwardens."

All Saints may have been a Saxon foundation of 975 on an earlier Roman temple site, but the first Norman overlord, Ralph de Peverel, favoured son of William the Conqueror, built the present Nave and the Font is 13th century. No wonder John and Samuel Brown appealed to William Pynchon for his help when all their trouble came from too great a love of *The Book of Common Prayer*. Would he who treasured this ancient fabric not care for the old ways too?

His great-grandfather Nicholas, clothworker (d. 1552),[238] as we have noted, purchased Sturges, one of the Writtle Manors. He had been Sheriff of London, when the Clothworkers Guild stood in Pynchon Lane, lost long ago. His son John aided the family fortunes by marrying Jayne Empson, daughter and heiress of the loathed Sir Richard Empson, hatchet-man to Henry VII.[239] Sir Richard dispatched his king's enemies with professional speed and was rewarded by Henry VIII, on succeeding his father, by having his own head cut off.

This allowed Jayne to enter into a considerable if ill-begotten fortune, and increased the family holdings at Writtle. There were two sons from this union, William who inherited the major property at Writtle and sired Sir Edward and John, whose son William (1590–1662) inherited the Springfield property, and emigrated to New England in 1630.[240]

William was a founder-patentee of the Massachusetts Bay Company. He signed his name on the original document of 4 March 1629, as "Squire of Springfield." He was made an assistant, sailed in the *Ambrose* in concert with Winthrop's flagship the *Arbella*, as the Company's purveyor of munitions, and was made Treasurer of the Colony. He launched one of the first coastal-trade boats, then negotiated a fur-trade monopoly at Roxbury. There he joined John Eliot as a founder member of the First Church.

He immediately made his mark in the fur-trade. Too much so. He was fined for selling fire-arms to the Indians in order to speed up the supply of furs. He removed to Agawam above the Enfield Falls on the River Connecticut, nicely athwart the Indian fur-trade routes, collared the market, and built up a prosperous trading post, renamed after his native village, Springfield.

A sad story too long for telling here, follows. But having been neighbour to Hooker and Eliot in England, and part of the same dream of a New England, he quarrelled with Hooker over trade restrictions, removed Springfield out of Connecticut, and then fell foul of Massachusetts over his book *The Meritorious Price of our Redemption*, published in London, 1650. The book was judged heretical, publicly burnt in Boston, and Pynchon returned home to resume the life of a leisured gentleman first at Hackney, London, then at Wraysbury in the Thames valley between Staines and Windsor, leaving his son John to expand the prosperity of the Springfield he left behind.

Father and son, frontier magistrates, pioneer merchants, expert Indian negotiators, inventive colonists, forerunners of the Connecticut Yankee who could turn his hand to anything with profit, they were the very stuff of survival. They blazed the trail which led to the emergent United States; and they came from the high-born Writtle manorial class.

No one gave more to the cause. For the sake of his beliefs William gave even livelihood itself. It would have been more profitable by far had he recanted his unorthodox theology of the doctrine of Salvation. But these were more than merchant adventurers. At least in William Pynchon's case it is evident that he went in, and came out, for the Reformed Faith within him first of all.

And his sister married into the principal Catholic family in Essex. Your short stay in the Royal Manor of Writtle cries out aloud the complexities of the route by which the Founding Fathers came to North America.

Pynchon's manor house is not known.[241] Next to All Saints is magnificent, early 18th century Springfield Place, but that was Mildmay property, and the ghost that walks is the ghost of Lady Mildmay. Opposite is Dukes, and that belonged to the Catholic and Royalist Tyrrells.[242] There was a Springfield Hall, a manor house on the site, I believe of Springfield Hall Farm today. It is reached by a narrow track off Lawn Lane which abuts onto All Saints grounds. The original driveway, Springfield Hall Lane, is now blocked up by a new housing estate. Only the attractive gatehouse remains, cut off from its former Hall. The farm fields skirt a new children's playground as they descend to the River Chelmer. It may be that William boated and fished here as a boy. The house can be seen from the new ring-road round the north of Chelmsford, as you turn west from the large roundabout at the end of Lawn Lane (back towards the town centre). It stands proudly, overlooking the open ground on your left, as if with an eye to a takeover bid.

Boreham.

From Springfield Green return to the Springfield Road (A1113) going northeast out of Chelmsford. At the junction up onto the old A12 to Colchester, go underneath the flyover (right) and take the first exit (left) at this large roundabout, onto the B1137 to Boreham.[243] For New Hall, take the next exit (left) at Hart Lane, back over the dual-carriageway below. The entrance gate to New Hall is on your immediate right.

This important house, now a residential Catholic Girls' School, is said to have been first named the new hall of the Canons of Waltham Abbey in the Manor of Walkfares, Boreham (to whom it then belonged), in 1301.[244] It eventually came to Sir Thomas Boleyn, earl of Wiltshire and Ormond (Anne Boleyn's father), and from him to Henry VIII by 1517. He renamed it Beaulieu, "greatly enlarged and beautified" it, and it became a principal residence of the princess Mary during more than twenty years of defiant Catholic usage, until she became the Queen. Elizabeth stayed here during her royal progress of East Anglia in 1561, but permitted Catholic lessees (Sir Thomas Wharton), then granted it in 1573 to Sir Thomas Radcliffe, third Earl of Sussex (1525–1583), "one of the great nobles of the Elizabethan period,"[245] whose tomb you may see at the Parish Church. He was Lord Lieutenant of Ireland, where he campaigned for nearly a decade against the native chieftains vigorously if unsuccessfully on behalf of Queen Mary and Queen Elizabeth; was next Lord President of the North, engaged in suppressing revolts in Northumberland and Westmoreland; and finally, as Lord Chamberlain, was overseer of Elizabeth's Court, and her "progresses" through the country. Few houses in Essex remained nearer the heart of Tudor politics than New Hall, or brought neighbouring villages like Little Baddow closer to the Court. The Earl of Sussex is also commemorated through the bequests of his second wife Frances, daughter of Sir William Sidney, which founded Sidney Sussex College, Cambridge in their joint names.

Incidentally, Sussex' first wife was Elizabeth Wriothesley, daughter of the Earl of Southampton, Chancellor of England before the first Lord Rich.[246] The story was that these two great statesmen entered the torture chamber in the Tower of London to turn the screws of the rack themselves, to torture the young protestant martyr, Anne Askew (1521–1546) in the reign of Henry VIII. An incredible picture of unreformed nobility which, thanks to *Foxe's Book of Martyrs*, penetrated the conscience of every Puritan in the land.

New Hall's next occupant was George Villiers (1592–1628)[247] first Duke of Buckingham, favourite of King James I. He is said to have paid £22,000 for it in 1620, the year he married the Catholic heiress Lady Catherine Manners although himself dissuaded from a profession of Catholicism by William Laud.

Buckingham was assassinated in 1628. His son inherited, but had his estates sequestered in the Civil War. A grateful Parliament voted New Hall to Oliver Cromwell (1650) for the sum of five shillings.[248] He did not take up residence, but his daughter Frances married the grandson of the second Earl of Warwick in 1657, the year when both Cromwell and the Earl died. The young bridegroom died shortly afterwards, else he and his bride might have claimed New Hall, and broken its great Catholic tradition. As we have observed, the Catholic contribution to faith and fortitude in England throughout the upheaval of Tudor times was too valuable to have been so lightly set aside. Hooker would have judged otherwise. The proximity of New Hall would have represented for him further proof of the threat to the Reformed Faith whose servant he was. The dread of "disaster," however scorned, was never far away.

Large alterations, extensions, demolitions, and finally aerial bombardment in 1943, has removed most of the historic buildings above ground, but the Hall remains a noble complex in its modern guise, its spectacular history worthy of your interest even if you cannot visit the site. You will feel a sharp twinge of regret at leaving all this unexplored behind you, as you drive back to the B1137, and turn left (east) again for Boreham village.

You are now on the old Roman Road from London to Colchester up which Claudius' elephants trundled. Can you catch the thunder of Boudicca's avenging chariot-wheels, or is it grumbling tractor-treads from Ford's more prosaic occupation, since 1930, of Boreham House on your right, now the main training centre for Ford International Tractor operations in Europe?

You drive past the shimmering Boreham House, far athwart its ornamental lake. Sir Benjamin Hoare built it after purchasing New Hall from the widow of the famous George Monk, Duke of Albermarle, 1608–69, Parliamentary general at sea as well as on land, and a prime architect of the Restoration, whose deranged widow lingered on in residence at New Hall, and prevented its occupancy by its latest owner. Continue past the Red Lion, and there turn right into Church Road and Boreham Village.

Boreham Old Rectory, home of Benjamin Rush.

As the road makes to turn around the Parish Church, you will see the Old Rectory across the way, a nicely balanced construction of wood-beams and plaster in-fill, the East wing, and the hall in the centre, 15th century, the West wing restored the next century following a fire. The building remains much as John Russhe would remember it.

Was not Benjamin Rush, 1745–1813,[249] physician, humanitarian, patriot, a signatory of the Declaration of Independence in 1776? He was descended from the family of John Russhe who, in 1623, was baptised at Boreham Parish Church, as were his four children, and lived here. One of John's nephews, John Rush from Oxfordshire, Master of Horse in Cromwell's army, and a Quaker, emigrated to Byberry, Pennsylvania, 1683. Benjamin Rush was his grandson.

Born in Philadelphia, he took a part of his medical training at St Thomas's Hospital, London, England, where a friendship with Benjamin Franklin[250] ripened. Returned home, he expanded the Pennsylvania Hospital, and opened its first free dispensary. He was a pioneer of psychiatry, with publications such as his *Medical Enquiries and Observations upon Diseases of the Mind*. He was, at the same time, a firm believer in blood-letting, convinced that the "depletion of spasm" in blood vessels required bleeding (*Medical Enquiries and Observations*). This won him more immediate fame than his *Sermons to Gentlemen upon Temperance and Exercise*, though the latter has a more enduring appeal. He was a man of extraordinary talent, and wide reputation, whose ancestral home rates at least a passing salute.

St Andrew's and the Sussex Tomb.

Opposite the Old Rectory is St Andrew's Church,[251] where John Oakes was Rector when ejected by the 1662 Act of Uniformity. He was housed, you will remember, by the Gobert Barringtons of Tofts, and became the first licensed Nonconformist Pastor of the now separated (from St Mary's, Little Baddow) congregation, whose founding Thomas Hooker had first influenced.

St Andrew's is remarkable for its 15th century porch, said to be the longest in the county; and for the splendid Sussex Tomb inside. All the Radcliffe Earls of Sussex are buried here, twelve coffins dating from the first Earl, Robert, who died in 1542, until that of the fifth, Robert, 1629. They did not move to New Hall, Boreham, until the time of the third Earl, but he removed his father's and grandfather's bodies from St Laurence, Poultney, in London and had them laid to rest in the one tomb.

The alabaster effigies are of these first three earls, Robert , Henry, and Thomas, with the heraldic "man-tiger purpure, feet and head human" of the Radcliffes at their feet, and the Clare family (with whom they were connected) bulls, a ducal crown and chain round the necks, at their heads. The best that the 16th century artist could manage for a "man-tiger" was a baboon! But they sit cheerfully enough. The human figures are 5 feet 9½ inches long, clad in armour, each left leg gartered. The whole tomb is 8 feet 8 inches long, a truly memorable work, though damaged by past neglect.

Lord Thomas' step-sister Frances married Sir Thomas Mildmay (d. 1608). That is how the Mildmays came to inherit one of the Sussex titles—the Barons Fitzwater.[252] How virile the Boreham nonconformists, to impose a Puritan parson (John Oakes, later Pastor at Little Baddow, this *Guide*, page 223) onto so Catholic a patronage.

Terling and Thomas Weld, Bay Company Agent.

Go past St Andrew's, Boreham, to Plantation Road on your left. Follow it back to the A1137. At the T junction turn right (east), towards Hatfield Peverel. Almost immediately take the left-hand exit, via a bridge over the busy A12, into Terling Hall Road. Follow this minor lane, at first alongside the little River Ter, but bear right and then right again at Norells Corner. You cross the Ter by Mill Pool, go up Dairy Hill, and so into Church Green.

The enfolding of agreeable dwellings; the 15th century Manor house with its richly moulded timber, cross-gables and octagonal chimneys; the broad stretch of open greensward; the 18th century red-brick tower of All Saints embracing a 13th century west wall; the brass portraits of William and John Rochester inside, their wives and twenty-two children kneeling round them, dating back to 1490;[253] and Terling Place behind the Church, within its large parkland and riverside vista, now Georgian but formerly a 14th century palace of the bishops of Norwich, from whom Henry VIII took possession, and may have spent his honeymoon here with Jane Seymour:- all command your appreciation.

There is an early Meeting House opposite the Church. The present building dates from 1753, but it retains its 17th century brass candelabra, by the light of which the congregation has sung its praises almost since Thomas Weld came as Parson to the Parish, in 1624. The village repays investigation. Round the corner of Church Green into The Street, you pass the old Congregational Manse, formerly the Manor House of Owl's Hill, or Ockenden Fee, a gracious dwelling sometimes used, as was traditional, for the school-teaching pioneered by many Reformed Ministers before the days of universal education. You can drive back to the A12 at Hatfield Peveril, leaving the superb smock windmill behind you up Owl's Hill, and Norman Hill. It was closed after the tragic death of the miller in 1950, when, 78 years of age, he fell and was crushed to death by the cogs driven from the great spur wheel. It is now a private residence.[254]

Thomas Weld (1595–1661)[255] was not unfamiliar with tragedy. He was born over the Suffolk border at Sudbury, fourth son of a well-to-do Mercer who sent him to Trinity College, Cambridge. There he met Thomas Hooker, graduated MA in 1618, and was ordained by the Bishop of Peterborough, at that time supportive of Puritan clergy in the Church of England.

He was installed first as Vicar of Haverhill in Suffolk, and then at Terling. This was Mildmay territory. Sir Thomas Mildmay, the auditor, had purchased Terling Place in 1563,[256] and made it over to his younger brother John (d. 1580), whose family remained in occupation until the 18th century. As lords of the Manor, the Mildmays would have no difficulty in placing a Puritan Minister in their Parish Church.

Here Thomas Weld served until deposed by the Court of High Commission on 24 November 1631, "for contumacy." He was, after all, a highly qualified graduate of Cambridge's most senior Trinity College, unaccustomed to display subservience to an Oxford man like Laud, and no doubt treated Laud's commissioners with scant respect. He took ship for New England, and landed at Boston on 5 June 1632.

He was immediately appointed pastor of the newly organised First Church of Roxbury (July 1632), and was joined by John Eliot in November as its first teacher. They worked together with remarkable effectiveness, establishing the church and town, and opening the celebrated Roxbury Latin School, at which Weld's elder brother Daniel became teacher in 1650.

They were equally active in colonial affairs, such as the suppression of the antinomian controversy with Anne Hutchinson and her followers, in which Eliot, Weld, and Hooker were all prominent. This was a sad business, but one understands how easily the Colony's security would have been undermined in England had the libertarian, and therefore, as they supposed, anarchic views of the Hutchinsonian party, prevailed.

On 2 June 1641 Weld was commissioned by the General Court of Massachusetts, together with Hugh Peter of Salem, and William Hibbens of Boston,[257] to return to England as its agents, "to congratulate the happy success there" (of the rising Puritan Party in Parliament), and "to make use of any opportunity God should offer for the good of the country here," in other words to attempt to raise funds for the Colony (then in a state of depression) for the new Harvard College, and for the conversion of the Indians. Weld's pamphlet, *New England's First Fruits* (London 1643) was a part of this campaign.

At first they met with success. £2,000 was collected in cash and supplies for the Colony. Then Hibbens returned to Boston, and Peter became heavily involved with the Parliamentary struggle against the King, for which he was beheaded in 1660. In the Civil War, supplies of money dried up. Difficulties mounted. Weld failed to prevent Roger Williams from obtaining a Patent to the Narragansett territory, and he was dismissed, on 1 October 1645. He returned to the English pastoral ministry next year as Rector of Wanlip near Leicester, and from 1650–60, of St Mary's Gateshead near Newcastle-upon-Tyne.

But Weld is to be remembered for his fearless witness at Terling, his consistent support of Hooker in Essex, and of Eliot in the early and often unpopular Massachusetts Indian work. He may have been irascible, he was plainly talented, and he remained indomitable throughout the death of two of his three wives, and the vicissitudes of his pioneer career. Four sons were born to him by his first wife Margaret Deresleye (who died at Roxbury), at least one of whom, Edmund, graduated A.B from Harvard.[258] Judith, whom he married at Roxbury, died at Gateshead, England. Only his third wife, Margaret, outlived him.

Terling conveniently adjoins Little Baddow. Weld was a valued member of the Cuckoos Company, ready to put his name to the Petition of 10 November 1629, risking his own status to save that of his friend Hooker, although in vain.

Group Two: Ingatestone, home of the Lords Petre.

Starting from Chelmsford, travel south-west towards Brentwood and London. At the large intersection of the A1016 with the A12 approaching Margaretting, take the B1002 into Ingatestone, scarcely five miles distant. This leads you into High Street, past the Parish Church where the Petre tombs can be seen, including those of Sir William and his son John, first Lord Petre, to Station Lane on your left. Follow it over the railway crossing, where it becomes Hall Lane. The Hall is on your right, less than a mile from High Street, but is not open to the public, its diminished grandeur only to be admired from afar.[259]

Ingatestone Hall was constructed in 1540 by Sir William Petre (1505–1572) on the site of Abbess Hall, after the estates of Barking Abbey, to which Abbess Hall belonged, had been forfeit to the Crown a few months earlier. Approached by a driveway still in situ, it was planned as a "modern" brick mansion on a traditional courtyard plan, with low ceilinged great hall on entrance, a "fair and stately gallery or walk meet for any man of honour to come into"[260] on the far side, private rooms for family use around, many large windows, and piped water with elaborate drainage works all within a lordly facade of clustered chimney-stacks, crow-stepped gables and ornamental battlements set in well-tended orchards and a formal garden.

Much has been demolished, but the view from the gatehouse is altogether pleasing, and the long gallery mentioned above is still amongst the most attractive rooms in Essex. Sir William's portrait from 1567, his black gown trimmed with fur, his badge as Chancellor of the Order of the Garter hanging pendant from his neck, white wand of office in his hand, a look of careful, reserved interest in his glance both warning and welcoming, presides over the Hall's art collection. If your visit happens to coincide with one of the occasions when the Hall is open to visitors, you will congratulate yourself.

William Petre[261] was a Devonian from Tor Newton in the Parish of Torbryan, twenty miles southwest of Exeter, where his yeomen ancestors had farmed for the past 300 years. His father, a wealthy cattle-farmer-cum-tanner, sent him, aged 14, to Exeter College, Oxford. He was made a fellow of All Souls, and was later admitted a doctor of civil law. At Oxford he became tutor to George Viscount Rochford, Anne Boleyn's brother. Henry VIII's discerning eye may therefore have fallen on him too. He early undertook a "record of continuous service unmatched in mid-Tudor politics,"[262] being appointed seriatim a principal or acting Secretary of State to four monarchs, or five if Lady Jane Grey's short reign is included.

Thomas Cromwell made him his deputy Vicar-General in 1536. This brought him the high-profile if uncongeneal task of personally negotiating the dissolution of the monasteries, but also a touch of their revenues. Many of these gifts, such as an annuity from Barking Abbey presented by the Abbess, Dame Dorothy Barlee,[263] together with the lease of Abbess Hall, no doubt in expectation of favourable treatment, he enjoyed throughout his life; but it should be emphasised that he paid the market rate when he purchased the Hall outright from the Crown, and that he secured a very generous pension for the Abbess, who became godmother to his daughter Dorothy.

This confirms the opinion of Dr F. G. Emmison, in his reconstruction of Sir William's career from an examination of the unique archives which remain from both his public and private life (*Tudor Secretary, Sir William Petre at Court, at Home*) that the "records of his time do not yield a single harsh epithet about him." He was a painstaking and efficient servant of the Crown, but "there is never the slightest hint of brutality or ruthlessness."[264]

Dr Petre became a permanent Secretary of State, was sent as an ambassador to the Emperor Charles V, was knighted, and slowly made himself indispensable. He was appointed a Principal Secretary to Henry VIII, survived, and served Edward VI's protectors in the same capacity. He became the accepted negotiator of all delicate questions, "the only figure always included among the counsellors selected for judicial or admonitory action."[265]

In this capacity Edward dispatched him (regularly accompanied by Lord Rich, or Sir Walter Mildmay—the three families owned adjacent properties at Bartholomew Close and Aldersgate Street in London as well as neighbouring estates in Essex)[266] to discipline the Princess Mary on numerous occasions at one of her mansions, nearby New Hall Boreham among them. This was invariably for her persistently arranging that the Roman Mass should be celebrated in her own home, an unedifying commission. His ability to be acceptable to all parties did not desert him. Mary was so pleased with the manner in which he distributed his censures that she instantly appointed him her principal Secretary of State when she called at Ingatestone en route to London for her enthronement in 1553. By then she was godmother to the Petre's youngest daughter, Catherine (born 1645), and her friendship with Lady Petre, "an uncompromising Catholic," had ripened into frequent visits between Ingatestone and New Hall. At the coronation, Lady Petre rode in attendance on the new Queen as the royal procession flowed from the Tower to Westminster.

The trust displayed by Mary in the Petres is the more remarkable in that it was Sir William, a nominal Catholic at least, who drafted the dubious device for Lady Jane Grey's succession in Princess Mary's place, though at King Edward's command. He even took the oath of allegiance to Lady Jane with the rest of the Council of State before belatedly transferring that allegiance to the rightful Catholic heir. He was a constitutionalist, unswervingly loyal to the acting monarch, and this was, fortunately for him, common knowledge.

Queen Mary in her turn sent Sir William to confront her sister Elizabeth, on suspicion of her complicity in the abortive rebellion of Sir Thomas Wyat in 1554.[267] Wyat had in his youth toured Spain with his poet-statesman father (the Sir Thomas Wyat, 1503–1542, accused of having been Anne Boleyn's lover). He had been embittered by the excesses of the Inquisition, and raised a popular revolt against Mary's pro-Catholic rule. The circumstances were suspicious. Anne Boleyn's daughter Elizabeth was inevitably compromised. But Wyat refused to implicate her, though tortured to that end, and Elizabeth had learnt how to restrain her tongue. Wyat was executed, Jane Grey too.

Despite the drama of this frightening moment, Sir William managed to interrogate the endangered Princess (by then herself detained in the tower) so comfortably, that she too appointed him a principal Secretary of State, though now, in practice, subordinate to Cecil. Petre's was a remarkable gift for survival. With it went a genius for moderate government, an absence of bigotry or cupidity (he paid for the large estates he built up out of his own hard work and able management), and genuine trust in office, with family love at home, generosity to neighbours, and his innovations on behalf of the poor, as his Ingatestone Almshouses and personal pensions schemes witness, not to mention the farsighted reform of his Oxford colleges.[268]

Despite the apparent perfidy of his administration, here for Henry's tyranny, there for Edward's iconoclastic religious reforms, again for Mary's counter-Catholicism with its burnings at the stake ("the remarkable fact remains, however, that his name is never linked with the long persecution in Essex or London"),[269] and the volte face of the Elizabethan Settlement, the practical effect of his more than thirty years in highest office was to provide the State with continuity, probity, and moderation during those Tudor years of crisis and of change.

Petre's lack of unbending principle in office (in contrast to his blameless private life) may compare ill with the selfless devotion to righteousness of a John Winthrop or a Thomas Hooker. That is why God sent them to redeem the times. But, given the quantum leap from medieval despotism towards the free choices of a modern democracy which began to beckon Tudor England, the times, such as they were, were well served by Secretary Petre, and his influence over his Essex properties remains as decisive as it was when William Pynchon, Nathaniel Ward, or more remotely Thomas Hooker lived alongside them.

Sir William's son John was created the first Baron Petre of Writtle, in 1603. He resided at Lordships in Writtle before building Thorndon Hall at

West Horndon, Essex, where the major branch of the family lived for three centuries until fire destroyed it, whereupon they returned to Ingatestone Hall.

The fourth Baron William (1626–1684)[270] married William Pynchon's sister Bridget. It was his second marriage and said to have been a love-match. I hope they had such compensation, for it was an ill-starred union through little fault of their own. Like many Catholics, Lord William had his estates sequestered during the Civil War, and only obtained their restoration after taking the Oath of Abjuration under the 1652 Act of General Pardon and Oblivion, which entailed a renunciation of his faith. Faced with "the choice of remaining steadfast in his religion and risking personal and family ruin, or of compromising with his conscience in order to maintain his status as a great landed magistrate—he chose the latter alternative."[271] It is easy to be judgmental after the events. His dilemma was overwhelming.

Lord William also lacked the gift of contriving good fortune so signally displayed by his great-great-grandfather. He was committed to the Tower when a charlatan named Titus Oates implicated him in a plot to assassinate the king and overthrow the government, which had been shamelessly fabricated.[272] Oates was the son of an Anabaptist preacher of the wild-bunch at Chelmsford who had destroyed poor Michaelson, St Mary's stained-glass, and the good name of true Puritans. Feelings ran high, and Catholics were hunted down in the streets.

Petitions were lodged for Lord William's release, or at least for a trial, without success. He was a member of the most celebrated Catholic family in Essex, and paid the price. He died of gaol-fever in prison, confessing his Catholicism at the end. Bridget lived until 1695. Her portrait hangs in Ingatestone Hall, but not on public view. These events peaked after Thomas Hooker's death, but are indelibly written back into the English scene in which he and his circle developed to maturity.

Stondon Massey.

From the Hall return to Ingatestone High Street. There turn left, drive out of the village and continue on the B1022 across the bridge (over the A12) to Mountnessing. 1.4 miles after joining the B1002 turn right, sign post Doddinghurst and Blackmore. After a further 1.4 miles turn left for Stondon and Ongar. Then follow the signs for Hook End, Stondon and Ongar. Drive through Stondon Massey,[273] passing the Bricklayers Arms on your right, for another 1.4 miles towards Ongar, to the Parish Church.

On the way you will pass, on your left, the Coach House of Stondon Place, a handsome early 18th century building with a central clock tower. Stondon Place lies behind this, though not visible from the road, a large Victorian house built on the site of the mansion which was once the home of William Byrd, the composer.

Further on, also on your left, is Stondon Massey House, formerly the Rectory, standing back from the road amongst trees, built about 1800. Near it, closer to the road, was Nathaniel Ward's Rectory House, seen from an old print to have been a rambling weather-boarded wooden building, with tall chimneys, once the home of the "Simple Cobler of Agawam" when parson of this parish.

The Church of St Peter and St Paul stands on your right a little further along, some distance from where the village now is. The 16th century Stondon Hall[274] lies below the church, on the original manor site, situated from time immemorial in its hollow, the meadows beyond sloping gently to a stream at the bottom of the shallow valley. Here a Saxon settlement was begun which subsequently took its name from the stone, or gravel, hill (dun, or doon) on which the church was erected.

The name Massey derives from the Norman Conquest, when the Marcy family took possession of Marks Hall and its widespread estates, at Margaret Roding less than ten miles to the north. The story of the village is typical of many others, and is told with a wealth of detail in *A History of Stondon Massey in Essex* by a former rector, E. H. L. Reeve (privately printed, 1906). I wish you could read it for its insight into the growth and development of an Essex village.

St Peter and St Paul[275] is a church full of general interest in addition to its affinity with Puritanism in Essex. The main structure of the nave and chancel, their walls three-foot thick, is basically unchanged since their construction, c. 1100, apart from the removal of a rounded apse at the east end. This apse was extended by about 8 feet, probably in the 14th century, and an east window inserted in a squared end, but recent repairs uncovered some corner stones of "random megalithic" pattern, suggesting an earlier Saxon building.[276]

The present Norman structure retains four original windows, narrow slits with round heads and splayed openings inside, more suited to defence than devotion perhaps, but speaking of the dire need of those lonely worshippers for security, in those rough times, as plainly as the Roman tiles coursing with local flintstones in the west exterior wall, and the wooden spire on top, speak of the scarcity of good building stone in Essex.

There are other notable features, such as the shingled spire above a massive timber belfry, whose supporting beams are carried down into the church interior. It holds three bells, one dating from 1400, another from the Armada in 1588. You enter by a south door of rudimentary craftsmanship, but pure early Norman work. Thrust your finger into the bar hole as you go in, first making sure that the blackbirds are not nesting inside. It penetrates six-feet into the solid wall, to ensure your safety when at your prayers.

Once inside, your eye immediately lights on the c. 1480 chancel screen, its cusped ogee arches matching the windows of similar date in the south wall, its delicate tracery a fine setting for the 1630 pulpit where Nathaniel Ward exercised his painful preaching. He is the main reason for our coming here.

Nathaniel, 1578–1652,[277] was born at Haverhill, Suffolk, where his father John Ward was the Puritan minister. He graduated Master of Arts from Emmanuel College, Cambridge in 1603, one year before Hooker's entry, and at first practised Law. He travelled in Europe, and, when ordained, served as Chaplain to the English merchants at Elbing in Prussia, before returning to become the Rector of St James, Piccadilly. From there he was presented to the living at Stondon Massey in September 1626 by Sir Nathaniel Rich, of the celebrated Warwick family. He was by then 48 years of age, and an uncompromising Nonconformist. Laud stepped in, to evict him seven years later.

He was in company with a number of other clergy whose names you will instantly recognise. In *A Memoir of the Rev. Nathaniel Ward, A.M.* (1868) we read "At Keldon, the bishop excommunicated Mr Weld, suspended Mr Rogers, ordered Mr Shepard to leave the diocese, and refused to admit Mr Bridge as lecturer of Colchester, which the people desired. Thence the bishop is said to have gone to Braintree where Mr Wharton, Mr Marshall, Mr Bruer, Mr Car, Mr Ward and others were called before him and received admonition."[278]

Arrived at Ipswich, Massachusetts, Ward served as their minister, but resigned for ill-health four years afterwards. He was employed by the Bay Council on "The Body of Liberties—composed by Mr Nathaniel Ward," Boston's first legal code, approved in 1641. In some directions it could be described as enlightened as it was competent, e.g. Item 80, "Everie married woeman shall be free from bodilie correction or stripes by her husbande, unlesse it be in his owne defence upon her assault."[279]

However, he was opposed to other forms of toleration, as a perusal of his *The Simple Cobler of Aggawam in America Willing to help 'mend' his Native Countrey, etc.* shows. There he wrote "My heart hath naturally detested foure things; The Standing of the Apocrypha in the Bible; Forainers dwelling in my Countrey to crowd our native Subjects into the corners of the Earth; Alchymized coins; Toleration of divers Religions or of one Religion in segregant shapes."[280]

The Simple Cobler, raised quite a stir in England, and went through four editions in 1647, the year of its publication. How could it be otherwise for an author whose pungent versification, however unfair, spoke so closely to popular Parliamentarian opinion!

No King can King it right,
Nor rightly sway his Rod;
Who truly loves not Christ,
And truly fears not God.

He cannot rule a Land,
As Lands should ruled been,
That lets himself be rul'd
By a ruling Romane Queen.

No earthly man can be
True Subject to this State
Who makes the Pope his Christ,
An Heretique his Mate.[281]

Nathaniel Ward's indifferent health (he was 69 years old) forced his return to England shortly afterwards. The General Court of Massachusetts had awarded him some 600 acres of land "as near Pentucket as may conveniently be," and he conveyed this to the infant Harvard College before leaving, thus making a conspicuous contribution to the State's legal and educational systems.

He also left behind him a son, John Ward, and a son-in-law, Giles Firmin. Mather, in the *Magnalia*, wrote glowingly of John as the last of those founding clergy who had been ordained in England before emigrating to America (the First Classis listed at the beginning of his Third Book), as "Bonorum Ultimus, at inter Bonos non Ultimus" ("last of the elite, but by no means last amongst them").[282]

Born, like his father, at Haverhill, Suffolk, he founded Haverhil, Massachusetts, "a new plantation where he could expect none but small circumstances all his days," although "a person of a quick apprehension, a clear understanding, a strong memory, a facetious conversation" (after his father!), "he was an exact grammarian, an expert physician, and, which was the top of all, a thorough divine"[283]—who might well have chosen to minister at some more renowned location, had he not also shared his father's humility.

Giles Firmin (1614–1697), Emmanuel scholar, and medical practitioner at Boston New England from 1632 until he returned to England to be ordained Vicar of Shalford, Essex, also wrote of Nathaniel's self-effacement, despite his fearless polemics. "When Mr Hooker preached those Sermons about the souls preparation for Christ and Humiliation, my Father-in-law, Mr Nathaniel Ward, told him; 'Mr Hooker, you make as good Christians before men are in Christ as ever they are after ... would I were but as good a Christian now, as you make men while they are but preparing for Christ.'"[284]

On his return to England, Parliament honoured Nathaniel Ward with an invitation to preach before its assembly. But Ward was already out of touch with the times. His generation of Puritans were moderate, if unyielding reformers. He had written "We have been reputed a Collunies of wild Opinionists, swarmed into a remote wilderness to find elbow-roome for our phanatick Doctrines and practises—I dare take upon me, to bee the Herauld of New-England so farre, as to proclaim to the world, in the name of our Colony, that all Familists, Antinomians, Anabaptists, and other Enthusiasts shall have free Liberty to keep away from us."[285] But these were the very Levellers who now threatened to take over the English Commonwealth.

He took his text from Ezekial, xix, 14, "And fire is gone out of a rod of her branches, which hath devoured her fruit, so that she hath no strong rod to be a sceptre to rule. This is a lamentation, and shall be for a lamentation." He then spoke of the need for authority in the State, and castigated those whose devotion to religious liberty threatened good order, pleading for moderation. "This sermon," we are told, "gave such dissatisfaction that the House did not order it printed. They did not present him with a piece of plate as usual, nor return him thanks for the great pains he took, according to custom."

"I trust I shall not be grieved with this," he wrote to a friend, "But it grieves me sadly that coming a hard winter voyage over the vast raging seas to doe what service I could to my country in preserving Truth and promoting Peace I am obstructed so far as I am."[286] It grieved many more than the aged preacher. The Puritan dream of an orderly reform of the State and the National Church had already long given way to violent revolution. Ward accepted a call from the parishioners of Shenfield, scarcely five miles from Stondon, to be their Rector, and died there four years later.

It is high time for us to look more closely at Ward's pulpit. You must imagine it as a three-decker, the pulpit set originally above the reading desk and clerk's seat which today lie alongside it. The date "1630" and the text "Christ is all in all," together with simple reproductions of a sheaf of corn and a bunch of grapes, are carved around the desk. The text is thought to have been taken from the title of the first sermon in his brother's *Collection of Such Sermons and Treatises written and published by Samuel Ward, Preacher of Ipswich*, published in 1627.[287] Inside the pulpit is carved "2 TIM 4 1-2" (I charge thee therefore before God . . . Preach the word; be instant in season out of season; reprove, rebuke, exhort with all long suffering and doctrine). How eloquent it all is.

There are other features of interest in the church which may not delay us now: the fine brass memorials, especially the palimpsests, the Victorian Meyer Chapel with an excellent vaulted ceiling, the William Byrd connection. In the Nave, on your right as you enter, you will find a small, modern,

Byrd memorial plaque. In the Vestry there is a framed copy of his Will, with its request that he might be buried near his wife "at Stondon, where my dwelling is." There is no grave to be seen in the churchyard, but the Stondon Singers give a Byrd Memorial Concert in the church, near to the date of his death on July 4th. You will be wise indeed if you arrange your visit to attend it.

William Byrd (1543–1623) came to live at Stondon Place in 1593. He was described in the Cheque Book of the Chapel Royal (a private chapel attached to the English Court) where he and Thomas Tallis shared the post of honorary organists, as "father of musicke." This was the entry marking his death.[288]

The title "Father of English Cathedral music" is generally accorded to Tallis[289] who had been organist at Waltham Abbey (which enjoyed jurisdiction over part of Stondon) before it was dissolved. The British Museum Library has a Waltham manuscript of music with the signature "Thomas Tallys" on the final page, the only specimen known. Soon after the Abbey's closure in 1540, with "20s for wages and 20s for reward" in his pocket, Tallis was made a Gentleman of the Chapel Royal, and for the next forty years laid the foundations of the English school of church music.

Byrd's range was wider if his style was less pure. His output was prolific, and he has claim to be regarded as the greatest composer of his age. The two men together built up an incomparable partnership never to be eclipsed. But Byrd bravely remained Roman Catholic, in defiance of Queen Elizabeth's strictures. And he remained a Gentleman of the Royal Chapel too! He was even commissioned to take part in the Coronation of King James I, yet he had been excommunicated by the then Bishop of London, and was regularly presented by his Protestant Rector at Stondon, to the Archidiaconal Courts, for refusal to attend public worship, throughout his thirty years at Stondon Place.

His last musical publication from The Place was his contribution to Thomas Leighton's *Teares or Lamentations of a Sorrowful Soule* (1614), a possible comment on his own condition. He also there composed his *Medulla Musicke*, both books of *Gradualia*, his *Psalms, Songs, and Sonnets; some solemne, others joyfull, framed to the life of the Words,* and his collection of virginal music with Orlando Gibbons[290] (later organist at the Chapel Royal, and at Westminster Abbey), and with John Bull (another member of the Chapel Royal, organist to James I, long regarded as composer of the National Anthem).[291]

This astonishing eruption of English music plainly owed as much to its Catholic Church origins as to the Elizabethan Renaissance. The influential Catholic families thriving and feuding over Stondon Manor under the Shelleys, and the larger Writtle Manor under the Petres, at least owed this to their Catholic heritage, that they were patrons of church music.

In this respect it is of more than passing interest to note that William Byrd dedicated his tenth Pavan to Sir William Petre, and the second book of the Gradualia to Sir John Petre, son and heir: and that Sir William was a keen musician who saw to it that his children were trained and talented performers. Sir William purchased organs for both his Ingatestone and London houses (one of which might possibly have been played by Thomas Tallis when organist at Waltham Abbey, which, last of all the great monasteries, Petre had been responsible for closing down), innumerable musical instruments, and the professional services of musicians for his family's many social gatherings.[292]

Stondon Place brought Byrd trouble as well as a convenient home in the pleasant uplands of Essex by the old Roman road straight into London. The previous owner, though not resident, had been Sir William Shelley,[293] ancestor of the poet Percy Bysshe Shelley. He was a devout Catholic, who added Stondon to his large estates in Sussex some time in 1521. Trained at the Inner Temple, Sir William became a Judge of Common Pleas, and one of Henry VIII's most trusted advocates. He was the King's man where matters of State were concerned, active in the divorce of Queen Catherine, and the separation from Rome of the Church of England, but staunchly Catholic where his private will prevailed. Thus he and his family presented Catholic priests to Stondon during their tenure of the Manor, in particular John Alford (Stondon 1558–1563),[294] one of the last to be Instituted by ultra-Catholic Bishop Bonner (deprived of his See by Elizabeth when she came to the throne). Alford stomached Elizabeth's new Prayer Book of 1559, but not Archbishop Parker's 39 Articles, with their anti-Catholic clauses, and was deprived of his living. So in 1563 a Stondon Rector was deprived for Catholic tendencies, and within seventy years another Rector suffered the same fate for his firmly held Puritan practices.

Sir William died shortly after Henry VIII, in 1548, and Stondon Hall, with The Place (then a subsidiary farm within the Manor) passed first to his son John (who died two years later), and then to his grandson William, who sublet the property to a Rainold Hollingworth, commemorated by a 1573 brass still to be seen on the wall of the arch leading into the Meyer Chapel (the palimpsest already referred to). From Rainold the Hall passed to his sons, of whom William Hollingworth sublet The Place to William Byrd.

Unlike his grandfather, William Shelley intrigued in the overthrow of his monarch, in favour of Catholic Mary Queen of Scots. He was dispossessed of his estates, but constantly petitioned for their return, as did his widow after him. William Byrd was amongst their objectives. He had benefited by their disgrace, and eventually, in 1610, bought The Place outright; whereas Mrs Shelley maintained her right to repossess it to the end of her life.

The entanglement was endless. Here was Catholic William Byrd wrapped in litigation against the Catholic Shelleys where his new landlords the Protestant Hollingworths had contrived that Catholic John Alford should quit a Parish Church never graced by Byrd although he hoped to be buried there! They had replaced poor Alford with Stondon's first married cleric, the moderate Protestant William Fering (Stondon 1563–1596) whilst the Shelleys continued to contest their manorial rights, and would never have countenanced so Reformed a Rector.

Fering was succeeded by Protestant John Nobbs (Stondon 1596–1626)[295] whose family of ten children forced a complete rebuilding of the former bachelor priests' rectory. Next came Nathaniel Ward, three years after Byrd's death but with the Byrd family still defiant Catholic residents opposite his church, and a new lord of the manor, Sir Nathaniel Rich, as Puritan as his Pastor.

It has to be remembered that this was Petre country. Their estates ran from Barking to Colchester, and bordered Stondon at Mountnessing. Byrd was a frequent visitor at Ingatestone, and indeed only finally secured Stondon Place from the Shelleys by purchasing it in the names of Thomas and John Petre with a reversion to himself.[296] But it was also Rich country (the Earls of Warwick who, with the Earls of Oxford, the D'Arcys, and the Petres were the four largest landowners in the county), and Rich meant Puritan.

We have already met the first Baron Richard Rich, Lord Chancellor of England (c. 1490–1567). He had 15 children by his wife Elizabeth Jenks (Gynkes) of whom the eldest was Robert (1537–1581), who succeeded to the title. To confuse the issue somewhat (and, no doubt, for other reasons) the first Baron also had at least one illegitimate son, named Richard after himself. The eldest son of this Richard was Sir Nathaniel Rich (1585–1636) of Stondon Hall.[297]

He purchased the Manor around 1610, and was in residence at the Hall by c. 1616, ready to bring Nathaniel Ward to the Rectory ten years afterwards. He was a colourful character, trained to the Law, an active Puritan Member of Parliament in turn for Totnes in Devon, East Retford in Notts, and Harwich in Essex. He supported Robert Rich, the second Earl of Warwick, in his expeditions to colonise Bermuda and Providence Island, and was an influential member of the Virginia company. During his residence at the Hall large-scale improvements were undertaken. He presented Puritan Anthony Sawbridge[298] (another Emmanuel graduate) to the Parish in succession to Nathaniel Ward, in 1633, but himself died three years later.

The Hall passed to his nephew, also named Nathaniel Rich (c. 1620-1701),[299] the son of his brother Robert (both the legitimate and the illegitimate lines continued to use the names Richard and Robert sometimes confusingly, and appear to have enjoyed close relationships). It was this Nathaniel who brought Edward Otway to Stondon as a Puritan Lecturer, democratically elected by the congregation.[300] But Oliver Cromwell died that same year (1658), and, at the Restoration of King Charles II, Otway was forced to conform to the Church of England, and did so. Once again the religious tables were turned.

Colonel Nathaniel Rich had fought for Parliament in the Civil War. He rose to the rank of Lieutenant-Colonel, and distinguished himself as a Commissioner for the surrender of Oxford, and by re-conquering Walmer Castle, with Dover and Sandown following suit. He became a Member of Parliament and voted for the beheading of Charles I after some hesitation. But a quarrel with Cromwell led to his temporary dismissal. He was reinstated, and then arrested early in 1661, after King Charles' return.

His Nonconformity was so unremitting that he would not worship in his own squire's pew in his Parish Church. He was presented by his erstwhile Puritan Rector (whom he had himself, as lord of the Manor, presented to the Parish) "for not coming to Divine Service but once this fourteen years and upwards and that when there was a funeral," a change from the run of Stondon Catholics! At his death in 1707, he bequeathed "to Mr Pagit minister of Stondon Meeting the sum of tenne pounds."[301]

Once again the story of Hooker's England presents apparently irreconcilable religious and political conflicts. The truth is that most people managed to live quite comfortably within these religio-social tensions, given the occasional tragic blood-letting. If you were a sufficiently talented composer, your religious stance could be tolerated by concentrating on the music. At the end, however, if you were a Reformed Pastor or Justice of the Peace there was unstable refuge short of the New England colonies.

David Cressy is right to introduce a sense of proportion into the debate. "The thousands who sailed to New England in the 1630s," he notes in his *Coming Over*, "represent less than half of one per cent of the population of England—colonial New England was a sideshow." Again, "the best figures indicate that 69,000 emigrant Britons crossed the Atlantic in the 1630's, of whom only 21,000 went to New England."[302] Even so, these are notable figures in the face of the dangers and deprivation they represent, and cannot be divorced from their outcome, the United States of America. Some sideshow!

Cressy's further contention that "only a handful experienced religious persecution. Only 76 of the 10,000 or more ordained ministers in England joined the migration to New England, and of these only 47 had run into trouble with their episcopal superiors,"[303] also calls for a more sensitive analysis. Civil War erupted within the decade! Add the general harassment of the Puritans, the frustration of their careers, the slighting of their religious ambitions, the threat to their property, and the rapidity with which anxious gossip ran into every corner of the small population of England, so that effects were not experienced only by the individuals who suffered them, but were shared throughout the nationwide kinship networks; and it is difficult to avoid the word persecution. Maybe mostly petty, but insidious, unnerving, nasty, and in the final outcome bloody and lethal.

I have no doubt that Hooker was grateful to have the nimble-witted Nathaniel Ward sandwiched between him and his powerful Catholic neighbours, not to mention William Laud up the road at Westminster. As for Ward, his letter to John Cotton cries his anxiety, and sense of rejection, to all who read it.

> Salutem in Xto nostro.
> Reverend and dear friend,
>
> I was yesterday convented before the bishop, I mean his Court, and am adjourned to the next term. I see such giants turn their backs that I dare not trust my own weak heart. I expect measure hard enough, and must furnish apace with proportionable armour. I lacke a friend help buckle it on. I know none but Christ himself in all our coast fitt to help me, and my acquaintance with him is hardly enough to hope for that assistance my weak spirit will want, and the assaults of tentation [sic] call for. I pray therefore, forget me not, and believe for me also, if there be such a piece of neighbourhood among Christians. And so, blessing God with my whole heart for my knowledge of you and immerited interest in you, and thanking you entirely for that faithful love I have found from you in many expressions of the best nature, I commit you to the unchangeable love of God our Father in his son Jesus Christ, in whom I hope to rest for ever.
>
> Your's in all truth of heart,
> Nath. Ward
> Stondon Mercy, Dec.13, 1631.[304]

Group Three: Danbury, Purleigh, Maldon.

Danbury.

Danbury[305] is next to Little Baddow, on the A414 from Chelmsford to Maldon, and gives its name to the hilltop Common which forms the southern flank of a semi-circle of hills sheltering Little Baddow from the keen East coast winds. This was once a military camp and parade ground, now preserved for the public. It has ample car parks, and offers its visitors spacious views over the Thames Estuary.

Danbury St John the Baptist[306] can be seen for miles around. It occupies the site of a Danish encampment, 365 feet above sea level, as high as anything else in that area. From Chelmsford you come first to the church, secluded from the main A414 by its elongated driveway. Then you reach the Common by turning right at the crossroads at Eves Corner at the top of the hill a little further on.

However, before you get there, as you mount Danbury Hill from Chelmsford, note St Clere's Hall on your left at the foot of the hill, once home of the influential St Clere family, whose unique knightly tombs await you in the church. Then on your right, half-way up the hill, you will see the entrance to Danbury Place, once belonging to Sir Walter Mildmay. It later became the Palace of the Bishops of Rochester (1845–92), and is now a Residential College of Business Studies under the Chelmer Institute.

Most of the old mansion has been replaced by a neo-Tudor construction of 1832, but still magnificent. The setting in what is partly a public park, with tree-lined walks and lakes (attained by driving right round the property from Eves Corner, and entering from the far side) is altogether satisfying.

Inside the 14th century church you will discover the early 13th century St Clere memorials.[307] Three knights lie with crossed legs, a lion at each of their feet, clad in chain mail underneath a tabard, one drawing his sword, the second thrusting his back into its sheath, the third hands folded as if in prayer. They are carved from oak and remain as vividly alive as if but momentarily laid to rest.

If you require details of the embalmed knight, his flesh as firm and white as when first preserved in the aromatic liquids enclosed in his lead-covered coffin, you can buy a descriptive pamphlet in the village. The incident dates from an accidental opening of the tomb in 1779, after five hundred undisturbed years.

There are good inns all round Danbury, one bearing the name of Hooker's transport to New England, The Griffin (late 16th century, timber framed with gabled cross-wings), or The Cricketers on the Common, where you can get good meals. You will have many less enjoyable days on vacations here and there than the one you could spend, the wind in your hair and the sun on your cheeks astride Danbury Common, or around this celebrated Puritan stronghold now commemorated by Danbury, Connecticut. Did Hooker walk here with young Eliot and Shepard, Stone and Weld, debating the adventure which was to bring new life to birth from such ancient soil, Danbury to the south, Lingwood Common running back north along Baddow Ridge to Riffhams Manor with Graces hospitably waiting nearby? If so, the sterner their resolve to leave it all for an even higher view of life.

Purleigh, home of the Lawrence Washingtons.

From Danbury continue south-east along the A414 towards Maldon, but at the first large roundabout take the second exit onto the B1018 to Woodham Mortimer and Purleigh. Once more the village is built on a small hill-top, giving views northwards towards Maldon and the Blackwater estuary, east and south towards the River Crouch valley, across a wide lowland patchwork of hedgerows and fields until they disappear over the horizon or into the North Sea.

The 14th century All Saints Church crowns the hill.[308] The basic construction is of knapped flintstones, interlaced in the chancel and rugged tower with bands of 14th century glazed bricks, small flint crosses adorning the buttresses. Swing open the door within the Tudor porch with reverent care. It hangs on iron strap-hinges which have responded to human pressure for 600 years or more.

Inside you will enjoy the inspired deployment of modern with 14th century stained-glass, and will find references to the Washington connection which brings visitors to this building from all over the world.

From 1632 to 1643 Lawrence Washington of Sulgrave Manor (1602–1652)[309] was the Rector. I hope you know Sulgrave, near Banbury, the manor house built by another Lawrence Washington, c. 1560, beautifully furnished and kept in the Shakespearian style its first owners would have known so well. Residence at Purleigh was not, I fear, as happy for George Washington's great-great-grandfather as his Sulgrave upbringing may have been.

By 1643 the Parliamentarian Sequesters were actively ejecting so-called profane clergy. Lawrence Washington suffered with many others in Essex, "for that he is a common frequenter of Ale-houses, not onely himselfe sitting dayly tippling there, but also incouraging others in that beastly vice, and hath been oft drunk,—and hath published them to be Traitors, that did lend to or assist the Parliament."[310] In other words, Washington was a Royalist.

His reputation was defended by a neighbour Justice of the Peace, one Major Ayloffe, who believed him to be a "very worthy, pious man;—a very modest sober person—a loyal person, and had one of the best benefices in these parts, and this was the only cause of his expulsion, as I verily believe."[311]

He sadly withdrew to Maldon, and died there shortly afterwards. He is said to have been buried in St Peter's churchyard, but the grave is known no longer. Two of his sons emigrated to Virginia, Lawrence, and John from whose son Lawrence of Bridges Creek came Augustine, the father of George Washington, first president of the United States. Incidentally, George Washington's mother was Mary Ball, "The Rose of Epping Forest,"[312] from her childhood home of Epping, Virginia. The Ball homestead stood near to where the Rappahannock River flows into Chesapeake Bay. This suggests a further connection with Essex, supposing that the early settlers named the place from the Epping town in Essex, or from the great Epping Forest which surrounds it.

The unhappy story of the Washingtons of Purleigh illustrates the unhappier state of the countryside around Little Baddow. There were many Puritan clergy who imposed their Calvinistic determinism on a reluctant rural population. There were many more rustic theologians who claimed a Calvinistic faith as their sole means of liberty from a residual feudal bondage, in these remote agricultural estates; and impatiently pressed their reforms on a loyalist, and sometimes reactionary clergy, a recipe for fomenting revolution.

Maldon, ancient port of the Blackwater Estuary.

From Purleigh retrace your journey to the A414 at the large roundabout beyond Woodham Mortimer, and drive into Maldon. There are two car parks off the High Street, well signposted.

Maldon (Saxon Maeldune, "the cross on the hill")[313] is well named. The high ground pitches steeply down to the Blackwater Estuary. Market Hill, on your left at the town centre, descends to the harbour bridge. High Street runs on down to the dockside, with a maze of narrow streets at the top. The 15th century Moot House (now the Town Hall) and other old buildings crowding together amongst the churchyards, early inns scattered generously, the Blue Boar from 1390 once a seafaring home of the Earls of Oxford from Hedingham Castle, make a charming and lively, if congested, shopping area. The smack of salty tar rises from the boatyards on the wind.

Four churches command the harbour heights. To the right, as you go down Market Hill, you will see the United Reformed Church, an impressive facade flanked by what remains of its former Independent School, and an historic graveyard. The first Meeting House was erected in 1696 by Rev. Joseph Billio at his own expense,[314] to accommodate a congregation of 400. This suggests a considerable body of Dissent from earlier times. Billio, by his exuberant and rapidly expanding ministry, gave the English language a new epithet, "like Billyo." The present building dates from 1801, but visibly retains the flavour of Independency at the heart of a town whose affairs it once swayed.

The dominant structure at the town centre is the 13th century Parish Church of All Saints. It had a history of nonconformity from its beloved vicar George Gifford, suspended for his unrepent Puritanism in 1584, to Thomas Horrocks, ejected at the Act of Uniformity in 1662. Gifford, who studied at Christ's College, Cambridge, was celebrated as "a leader of the Puritan party in Essex . . . a great and diligent preacher, and much esteemed by many, and of good rank in the town, and had brought that place to some sobriety and knowledge of true religion,"[315] so much so that the Lord Treasurer Burghley was amongst those who unsuccessfully interceded for his reinstatement.

Thomas Horrocks was a Lancastrian from St John's College, Cambridge.[316] On graduating M.A. in 1638 he taught at Romford Grammar School in Essex, and then (having been ordained by the Bishop of Durham) as a chaplain to Sir John Bramston at Skreens, Roxwell, before his presentation to All Saints, Maldon in 1650. Edmund Calamy (1671–1732) described him in his *Particular Account of the Ministers, Lecturers, Fellows of Colleges etc. who were silenced and ejected by the Act of Uniformity*, as "a diligent and painful preacher for twelve years together, and was instrumental in converting many souls. He was much respected by the Lord Bramston of Roxwell, the Earl of Warwick, Sir Gobert Barrington, Sir Thomas Honeywood, and many others of the nobility and gentry in these parts."[317] There is no History of Maldon Puritans as such, but their influence in the town is easily imagined.

All Saints has also the distinction of the only triangular church tower in England.[318] The external buttresses carry six canopied niches in which you can distinguish carvings of St Mellitus, first bishop of Essex (624); St Cedd, first to establish the church on Essex soil (664); Robert Montell who built Beeleigh Priory (1180) now partially restored but not open to the public; Sir Robert D'Arcy, a powerful medieval family, their major tombs in St Nicholas church, Tolleshunt D'Arcy across the Blackwater; Thomas Plume; and the Saxon Lord Brihtnoth.

Ealdorman Brihtnoth[319] lost his life trying to stem the tide of Danish longships which swarmed up the wide Blackwater estuary in the year 991, when Ethelred the Unready was nominally king of the East Angles, but preferred to buy off the invaders rather than defend the eastern shore. Coins minted at Maldon for this ransom have been found in Scandinavia, after Brihtnoth and his Saxon volunteers were massacred by some 93 Danish ships' crews that bitter day, as recorded in the epic Saxon poem *The Battle of Maldon*.

The interior of All Saints is impressively proportioned. The carved window arcading, and the sculptured arches below, show unusually fine 14th century craftsmanship. There is an American memorial window, showing amongst other scenes the arrival of the Pilgrim Fathers, and the signing of the Declaration of Independence by George Washington. I do not know of any direct contact with Thomas Hooker, but he must have been well aware of everything to do with Maldon. It was his life line to the Protestant Netherlands, and to freedom.

Did not this physical feature contribute to the remarkable absence of apathy in the Puritans' reaction to the petty persecutions they so long endured, which yet did not undermine their theological optimism? Alternative kingdoms beckoned them from a myriad of coastal harbours. They were not trapped by an inescapable despair.

St Peter's, not far from All Saints, retains only its tower, and the unique Plume Library bricked onto it. Dr Thomas Plume (1630–1704) was Archdeacon of Rochester. He founded the chair of Natural Philosophy and Astronomy at Cambridge University, and a Free School at Maldon, as well as bequeathing his library of some 6,000 books, and his collection of paintings, to his native town.[320]

The Library has a copy of Thomas Hooker's *The Soule's implantation into the natural olive*. It also has a copy of the All Saints Register which reads "Burials 1652. Mr Lawrence Washington. 21 Jany."

Underneath the library there is a Museum, with mementos of Edward Bright, born 1721, the heaviest man then known, at 42 stone, with other more serious exhibits. There is also a Tourist Information Centre at the Hythe Quay.

The short journey down the High Street into the Quay (you can take the car) is a pre-requisite of your coming. There you will see the church of St Mary the Virgin, formerly used as a navigational aid by sailors making for the port, which it overlooks below. It boasts a 15th century porch and a Norman nave. But more. Thomas Hooker most probably sailed to Holland from this port. That was when he forfeited bail, and fled Laud's avenging officers leaving Susan and their four children to take refuge at Great Waltham, protected by the Earl of Warwick, one dark Spring day in 1631.

At low tide the mud-flats slop greasily away to Heybridge Yachting Basin on the far side of the Blackwater, the marshes stretching bleakly to the open sea. At high tide it can be an animated picture of brightly coloured sailing boats. But the winds and cross currents of this landlocked arm of the sea can be dangerous for inexperienced sailors. Hooker experienced difficulty in clearing the harbour. Mather records a miraculous change of wind which providentially carried him at the last moment safely from the clutches of his would be captors, riding hard on his fleeing heels.[321]

But nothing can take away the tingle of excitement as you suddenly find yourself at the verge of the North Sea, surrounded by the sounds and smells of a remnant maritime trade once of great importance to this part of Essex.

The canalised Chelmer River runs into Maldon at Wave Bridge, and is still navigable most of the way up to Chelmsford. London's great sailing barges, a common sight in my boyhood plying from the capital to all the small Essex ports, still berth at the Saxon wharf of Hythe Quay. They are chartered for pleasure cruises, or the annual Barge Race up the Thames to London these lesser days, but retain their stolid charms.

For Thomas Hooker the voyage was serious in the extreme. It began for him a loss of homeland and godly hopes almost equal to that of the defeated Brihtnoth and his freedom fighting, Saxon serving men. Even so, a small army of likewise volunteer pioneers poured in ever increasing numbers into the English Channel and across the Atlantic ocean, refusing to accept defeat. And they, at last, were blessed with victory.

John Eliot, Apostle to the Indians, 1604–1690.

A Brief Biography.

His monument at the great timber-framed First Church of Roxbury, which sits like a gigantic white seagull peering down the beautiful Charles River valley, past Harvard University to the Atlantic at Boston, Massachusetts, simply states "Here lie the remains of John Eliot, Apostle to the Indians, Ordained over the First Church, 5 November 1632, died 20 May 1690, aged LXXXVI." It conceals a remarkable story of unexcelled faith and enterprise which signally contributed to the establishment of the New England colonies and the consequent emergence of the United States of America.

John was born at Widford, Hertfordshire, England on 3 August 1604, the son of Bennett and Lettese Eliot.[322] They were prosperous yeomen farmers, who owned land extensively in Herts and Essex. They soon removed to the exciting village of Nazeing, Essex, high on its bluff overlooking royal Waltham Abbey, and the River Lea valley all the way to Bow Bridge at London. John seems to have enjoyed a contented childhood here.

All Saints Parish Church, where the Eliots worshipped, was the centre of a close-knit Puritan community, its ascendant yeomen farmers, Curtises, Camps, Shelleys, Brevitts, Paysons, and Eliots in the Stuart period, "Cromwellian almost to a man," according to J. R. Sutherland's *History of Nazeing*[323] (1950). The presiding clergy also, over a long period, had been predominantly Puritan, as indeed was the whole region, so that it was predictable when a large proportion of the congregation emigrated from Nazeing, with John Eliot as their prospective pastor, to found a new town at Roxbury, Massachusetts in the great migration of 1630–45.

A bright scholar at the local grammar school, John went up to Cambridge when only 14 years of age. At Jesus College,[324] with its reputation for linguistics, he met Thomas Hooker, already a celebrated Puritan tutor at Emmanuel. The course of his later career was set. When he left university he was ordained, joined Hooker at the Cuckoos school at Little Baddow, learnt the fundamentals of educational theory and practice under Hooker's expert tuition, and, now an unflinching advocate of Puritanism, migrated to New England.

In America, Eliot quickly placed himself in the forefront of educational practice. He first proposed a university, five years before John Harvard's

GENEALOGICAL TABLE, NO. 8: THE FAMILY OF JOHN ELIOT, "APOSTLE TO THE INDIANS"

Bennett Eliot
bu. 21 Nov, 1621

m.

Lettese Aggar at Widford, 30 Oct, 1598
bu. 16 Mar, 1620 (both at Nazeing)

Sarah	Philip	John	Jacob	Lydia	Francis	Mary
bapt. 13 Jan 1600	b. 25 Apr 1602	b. 5 Aug 1604	21 Sep 1606	bapt. 1 Jul 1610	10 Apr 1615	11 Apr 1621
Widford	d. 22 Oct 1657	d. 21 May 1690	m. Margery	Nazeing	to Boston	to Roxbury
m. William Curtis	to Roxbury	m. Hannah	to Boston	m. James Penniman		
of Nazeing	Deacon	Mumford	Deacon	m. Thomas Wight		
emigrated to:	First Master	d. 22 Mar 1687		to Roxbury ?		
Roxbury	Latin School	to Roxbury				
		Teacher				
		1st Church				
		'Apostle'				

Hannah	John	Joseph	Samuel	Aaron	Benjamin
bapt.17 Jul 1633	31 Jun 1636	20 Oct 1638	22 Apr 1641	19 Dec 1643	29 Nov 1646
d. 9 Feb 1708	13 Oct 1668	24 May 1694	1 Nov 1664	19 Nov 1655	15 Oct 1687
m. Habakkuk Glover	ordained 1654	ordained 1658	ordained 1660		ord.Asst.
Boston	Newton	Guildford			Roxbury
3 Jun 53	*Ind.54	*Ind.58	*Ind.60		*Ind.

*Ind = Indian (language) ministry, cf. Letter of Jn Eliot to CPPG, 1658,

"I have dedicated my sons to serve the Lord in this work (if he please to accept them) so I do it as they come up; and this year my second son having taken his first degree in the Colledge, I presented him unto our Commissioners and he is accepted for the work" (*Descendants*, p. 230).

Sources, Church Records at Widford & Nazeing, *Descendants of John Eliot* and *John Eliot*, O.E.Winslow, op.cit, relevant refs. I regret that lack of time and means prevent a complete record.

foundation bequest brought Harvard into existence. In a letter recently discovered by Professor Franklin M. Wright of Rhodes College, Memphis (published by Yale,[325] 1954) to Simonds D'Ewes, well known and wealthy Suffolk Member of Parliament, John pleaded for funds sufficient to begin a college. Had Simonds possessed the foresight to advance the money, Harvard might have been "D'Ewes!"

Eliot's appeal failed, but he successfully established the Roxbury Latin School in 1645,[326] America's oldest continuously operative school and high amongst its best private schools today. He assured it should be open to native Indian and to Black children, equally with English settlers. He followed it with at least one other school, at Jamaica Plain, Boston, which specialises still in the service of minority groups. Incredibly, almost beyond belief, he added 14 Indian schools, and trained their teachers, in 14 personally constructed new Indian villages, some of which sent scholars to Harvard (to the first brick-built building erected there, originally known as the Indian College) despite the fact that the Indians did not have even an alphabet, let alone a literature, until he extemporised one for them.[327]

Within a decade of joining his family and friends at Roxbury as their co-pastor with Thomas Weld, Eliot had set about learning the tongue of the surrounding Algonquin tribes. There was nothing to study, apart from the sounds of a spoken language at that time unknown to European linguists. He had the assistance of an English speaking Indian, named Cockenoe, the servant of nearby Dorchester settlers, "a pregnant witted young man who had a clear pronunciation."[328] That was all.

Painstakingly, right up to his death, in spare time from pastoral duties and the settlement of his family in a land of small farmsteads carved from the forests, prey to harsh winters, disease, and hostile tribes, he mastered the language, adapted it to the English alphabet, unravelled and published *The Indian Grammar Begun,* and, chief of all, entered into the soul of the indigenous peoples.

He was one of the first group ever to print a book in America (the *Bay Psalter,* 1640, a consortium). Then he proceeded to translate into his new Algonquin literature books such as bishop Lewis Bailie's *Practice of Piety,* Richard Baxter's *Call to the Unconverted,* and Thomas Shepard's *Sincere Convert.* He attempted to teach illiterate Indians what an educated English child should know! How else could they survive the cultural invasion? His superb confidence was rewarded. At least one of his aboriginal Indians graduated Bachelor of Arts at Harvard, Caleb Cheeshahteamuck.[329]

In addition he translated the Bible into the Algonquian language. How he did it will never be known. The problems were unimaginable. Quill pens and home-made candles! Little of the Indian way of life bore any resemblance to Biblical culture, nor did their concepts of God, individual human worth, or social morality match those of the Jews, or the Graeco-Romano world of the New Testament. Yet so successful was this one-man enterprise that the Algonquian Bible became the text-book of a new "Praying Indian" movement.

Few copies survive. One is in the Old Library at Jesus College, Cambridge, inscribed in Eliot's hand to his Alma Mater. Another was purchased by the Roxbury Latin School on 21 February 1989, when auctioned by Christie's at New York, for $330,000, the highest price ever paid for a book published in North America.

This rare first edition is superbly bound in black morocco, richly tooled in gilt. It is thought to have been the copy presented to Charles II by Robert Boyle,[330] Eliot's friend, and Governor of the Corporation for the Promoting and Propagating of the Gospel of Jesus Christ in New England, largely incorporated to finance Eliot's work.

He had delayed his first evangelistic approach to the tribes round Boston for fifteen years, but by 1646 felt sufficiently fluent to preach and teach in their native tongue. On October 28, he and a few friends (Thomas Shepard, Hooker's son-in-law, amongst them) visited Waban's wigwam at Nonantum, near Watertown Mill on the Charles River, marked today by a stone open air pulpit. There he preached, invited questions, and catechised their children. He thought it unseemly to address the Almighty in his halting Algonquian, so tactfully offered prayer in English.[331]

Waban's people were deeply impressed, as much by the humble demeanour of the English evangelists as by any words spoken. Encouraged, Eliot visited them every two weeks. From the fourth meeting he carried away an urgent plea for schools to train the Indians in the ways of the English. Thus began weekly journeys to all the accessible Indian encampments. As he wrote to Edward Winslow, who piloted the Act "A Corporation for the Promoting and Propagating of the Gospel of Jesus Christ in New England" through the English Parliament in 1649, "I have not been dry night or day from Tuesday to Saturday, but travelled from place to place in that condition, and at night pull off my boots, wring out my stockings, and on with them again, and so continue. But God steps in and helps me."[332]

Under the 1649 Act a public subscription was authorised throughout England. Some £20,000 was raised, encouraged by the so-called *Eliot Tracts*, a stream of pamphlets to which he and others in New England contributed, with titles such as *New England's First Fruits*, and *The Day-Breaking, if not the Sun-Rising of the Gospel with the Indians in New England*, which roused nationwide interest.

Eliot insisted that it was "absolutely necessary to carry on civility with religion."[333] He taught the Indians modern agriculture, building construction, crafts, medicine. He supervised the first Indian town at South Natick, built almost entirely by native labour. He designed a protective stockade, a fort, a meeting house for use as church, school, and store. There were houses for 800 inhabitants, on four streets, with the Charles flowing in between. He showed them how to construct an arched bridge, the very first in North America.

Then he built other towns. By 1670 there were about 3000 Praying Indians in 14 small towns under his protection. He trained over a score of Indian pasters, or catechists and teachers. He restored to the people their dignity and hope. He would have saved Indian culture from virtual extinction in New England, by swinging it into parallel with the first settlers. But King Phillip declared war.[334]

Metacomet, or King Philip, was an educated Pequot chieftain who united the tribes' hostility against the settlers, and led a general uprising which nearly destroyed the colonies, in 1675. It is said that scarcely one family escaped loss or death. All Indians fell under suspicion, and so did Eliot. He, with his followers, was persecuted, and they were dispersed, despite remaining loyal to the English, and incarcerated on Deer Island, a barren rock in Boston Harbour. Few would have survived, despite Eliot's unceasing championship, had not their potential as army scouts been appreciated, almost too late. Some sixty were recruited. It is arguable that New England was delivered only when Eliot's converts put their inside knowledge of the Indians' "skulking way of war"[335] at the disposal of the settlers.

After Metacomet's defeat a small company returned, but to homesteads in ruins. Eliot's work was torn to pieces, towns, schools, even the bibles. "There is a dark cloud upon the work of the gospel among the Indians," he wrote, but his guiding dictum was "Prayer and Pains through Faith in Jesus will do anything."[336] He set about rebuilding his towns and rewriting the Indian Bible, by hand, almost alone. He finished it in 1685. He was 81 years old.

The CPPG resisted the final, heroic act on the ground that too few Indians remained to make it viable. Eliot defied them. He received an unexpected gift of £40 from a well-wisher, authorised his Boston printer to proceed, and charged the outstanding £860 costs to the Society. "Wee are far from Justifying Mr Elliot in his Turbulent and clamorous proceedings," had already come the Corporation's response, "but the best of God's servants have their faylings, and as such soe wee look upon him."[337] The corporation paid in full.

In fact, his character was replete with good humour. Children loved him. So did all who knew him. His title "Apostle" was spontaneously accorded by many, including a French Jesuit priest, Fr. Druilette, who missioned amongst the Canadian Indians, and was his guest one winter.[338]

Such fraternisation with the dreaded papists was almost unheard of in Puritan circles. Said Cotton Mather, "you must write of Charity, or say nothing."[339] An oft recounted story described his Deacon's tying up his monthly stipend in a handkerchief with multiple knots, to prevent his handing any of it over to the first beggar he might meet on his way home. Inevitably he recognised a poor family en route, and tried to extricate a few coins for the mother, but failed. "Here, my dear, take it. I believe the Lord designs it all for you," and he handed over the lot.

His fiancee, Hannah Mumford, possibly one of the Little Baddow Mumfords, sailed out to marry him at Roxbury's first wedding in 1632. She was an equally resolute and generous woman, and needed to be. She managed his precarious estate, brought up their six children , and enjoyed a wide reputation for her "skill in physick and chyrurgery."[340] "He who could prefer the American wilderness to the pleasant fields of Europe, was ready to wander through the wilderness for the sake of doing good. To be active was the delight of his soul; and so he went to the hovels which could not keep out the wind and the rain where he laboured incessantly among the aboriginals of America." And his beloved Hannah made all of it possible.

"There was no man on earth whom I honoured above him,"[341] wrote Richard Baxter, the eminent Puritan Divine, whose *Call to the Unconverted* Eliot had translated into Algonquian. His achievements have been denigrated as paternalistic and short-lived, and for failing to appreciate the worth of Indian civilisation, but what else could any charitable person have done? The Indians lacked the resources to resist the decimation of European techniques and diseases. He more than anyone offered them the life line of equality. And, far from being short-lived, he pioneered a system of universal education for America, free from racial or political interference, at a time when the General Court of Massachusetts strongly favoured control of its schools for religious and political ends.

He was the first considerable Biblical translator in the field of non-classical languages, the forerunner of all contemporary Bible Societies. He cleansed the conscience of the early settlers, whose charter required them to secure the native population within a Western Christian culture. He, more than anyone, made possible the retention of much that is best in the spirit of America, its hospitality, generosity, and practical aid to those in need, irrespective of race, class, or creed.

"I am but a shrub in the wilderness,"[342] he sighed. But the shrub took root. He remains amongst the most honoured of the Founding Fathers. "Welcome Joy"[343] was his last utterance. We should diminish our humanity if we ever forgot him.

Widford, Hertfordshire, Birthplace of John Eliot.

If the reader finds that a diversion into Eliot country necessitates extending the time planned for this "Hooker's England" tour, or a return journey the following year, no apology is required! The recompense from such an adventure will well repay the costs involved, for these are amongst the more secret places of Britain, and provide their own especial reward.

How to get there.

Widford[344] will most easily be reached by car from the northern stretch of the M25 (London Orbital road) Exit 25. Here take the A10 north towards Hoddesdon and Hertford; then turn east at the next exit beyond Hoddesdon, signposted A414; but at the exit immediately following, take the minor road B181 into Stanstead Abbotts. Wind your way through this small town, turning sharp left as you exit, onto the B180, which goes north through Hunsdon to Widford.

It is an isolated village, 25 miles north of the City of London, in the higher rural heartland overlooking the Herts/Essex border, a thriving area enjoying good agricultural land, close to London markets, protected by the early strongholds of Ware and Hertford.

Too much must not be made of this, but John Eliot's confident acceptance of his divinely conceived role as the benefactor of the Massachusetts Indians (not to mention his many other charities, and this despite a natural humility to which his contemporaries all draw attention) suggests a secure infancy. He was not a hungry evangelist greedy for self-assurance, advancement, or adulation. Such an impression will be heightened by a visit to Widford.

The Church of St John the Baptist lies outside the village, on the B1004, announced by its slender tall spire. The location is normally secluded, quiet, breathing its own serene atmosphere of days long gone by. There is the Old Rectory, its gardens merging into the churchyard, and on the nearer side as you approach, Widfordbury Farm, enclosing the former manor house, with a silent graveyard under an archway, opposite. That is all.

St John's dates from AD 1118,[345] as the Norman zig-zag moulding above the south door suggests. To gain admission you go down some steps, said to betoken the Baptist. As a lesser saint than John the Evangelist, it was thought appropriate to go down into his sanctuary, and you may well feel humbled, for you will come at once on the sturdy 14th century font in which John Eliot was baptised. Copies of the Baptismal entry are sometimes available from the church. "John Elliott the sonne of Bennett Elliott was baptized the fyfte daye of Auguste in the yeere of our Lord God, 1604." The officiant was the rector, John Peyton. His initials adorn the foot of the entry. From this it is reasonable to assume that John was born on August 3. Such was the infant mortality in those days that children were invariably baptized on the third day after birth.

His parent's marriage is recorded in the same register. "An° Dom. Bennett Eliot and Lettese Aggar were married xxxth of October an° Sup. Dicto." So are the baptisms of the two eldest children, Sarah and Philip, and the fourth child, Jacob (21 September 1606).

From the font at the west end of the central aisle you look up to the great east window, unveiled by the then American Ambassador, Mr T. F. Bayard, in 1894. The inscription speaks for itself. "To the glory of God, and in Pious remembrance of John Eliot, who was baptised in this Church August 5th, 1604, emigrated to New England A.D. 1631 and died in Roxbury, Massachusetts, May 21st 1690. This window was erected by his descendants A.D. 1894. The righteous shall be in everlasting remembrance."

Ancient murals flank the memorial window. On the north side of the chancel a Last Judgement scene, dated 1299, shows Christ seated on a rainbow, a two-edged sword issuing from his mouth. Also to the left of the window, a knight in the regalia of the Order of the Garter; and on the opposite side of the window, a bishop with his pastoral staff, hand raised in blessing. On the south side there is also a rare Easter Sepulchre (a recess to receive the effigy of Christ), not to be found elsewhere in the county.

Spend a moment wandering around the churchyard if the sun is shining. Peer through the protective trees onto the unspoilt pastures which drift away below. Long may the English countryside escape the spoliation of intensive farming, as it has done in this rough patch of unflattened beauty!

The Old Rectory, alongside the church, is a much later building than the one in Eliot's day, but its splendid Georgian facade provides an attractive reminder of the affluence experienced by many small ecclesiastical and squirarchical landowners in the 17th century. These prosperous families, especially among the wealthier clergy, would need a very strong religious motivation to sell up their possessions, and rebuild their lives in the American "wilderness."

Bennett Eliot had considerable holdings in real estate. He owned land and properties at Widford, Hunsdon, Eastwick, Nazeing (whither the family removed in 1607), and Ware. From such a background John Eliot voluntarily exchanged into the primitive encampments of the North American Indians, and loved every moment of it.

Ware, Hertfordshire, a window on a wider world.

How to get there.

From the Parish Church of St John the Baptist, Widford, return into the village, where sadly there is nothing known of the Bennett Eliot residence to delay you, and take the B1004 westwards into Ware, scarcely five miles away. Bennett owned property in Ware,[346] so it would be well known to John. It was his father's nearest market town, and an important posting stage on the Old North Road (Ermine Street), a mere 24 miles from the metropolis, and strategically set upon the River Lea.

The river marked the boundary between London and Essex. The Lea Valley, running straight north from the Capital, made a natural highway along which the Roman legions marched to their great military base at York. Marauding Danes came later from its confluence with the Thames, and so gained access to the heartlands of Middle England. Widford, and Nazeing occupy the highground to the east of the Lea, and overlook the urgent traffic of this prehistoric route. It was their window on the great world which lay beyond their horizon, a playground for the young Eliots conjuring visions of city splendour and ships to far off lands. A trip to Ware for the boy John would be a rocketing into a many coloured swarm of city merchants trading far and wide, of travelling lords and ladies bound for the court at Westminster, of global gossip in the inns, and gaudy foreign goods in the market place. He had adventured across the oceans in boyish imagination years before he sailed the Atlantic to New England.

Ware was a small but ancient market town,[347] clustered around the river crossing, with a priory to shelter travellers, of the Order of St Francis, founded in 1338 by Thomas Wake Lord of the Manor, now the Council offices.

Fragments of the priory are said to be embedded in the present building, but in Eliot's day it had only just been demolished. The cruciform church of St Mary, its chancel constructed of flint and stone, a gift of Lady Margaret Beaufort, mother of Henry VII, is worth visiting for its elaborate perpendicular font alone. And Inns abound, wherein lay an odd vehicle of Ware's claim to fame, the Great Bed of Ware, 10 feet 8 inches square.

Shakespeare makes reference to this famous furnishing in *Twelfth Night*. When Sir Andrew Aguecheek is persuaded to challenge the lady Viola to mortal combat, Sir Toby Belch incites him to pitch it strong, with "as many lies as will lie in thy sheet of paper, although the sheet were big enough for the bed of Ware in England."[348] It was formerly in the Saracen's Head Inn, but is now at the Victoria and Albert Museum, Kensington. Did John Eliot ever sleep on it with all his friends and relations? It is large enough for half a ship-load of emigrants. If not ever in it, it was nevertheless often full of luckless voyagers, and one of the marvels in his infant mind.

The Bull Inn in Baldock Street, with several adjacent brick and half-timbered houses, together with others in the High Street, date from the 16th/17th centuries. In nearby Bluecoat Yard, the 15th century Manor housed the famous Bluecoat School from 1574–1672, and this too would be

known to the Eliots. They may even have discussed the advisability of
sending young John there before he went up to Cambridge.

And there must have been talk of "The New River,"[349] an unmatched
fresh-water canal, 10–feet wide and 4–feet deep, begun two years before
John's birth by Sir Walter Raleigh's friend, Sir Hugh Myddelton. Its major
source rises at Great Amwell, scarce a mile from Ware and not four miles
from Widford. It flows all the way to London, a revolutionary channel of
clean drinking water, until absorbed into the Metropolitan Water Board's
larger operation in 1904.

The conduit can still be followed to its present termination at Stoke
Newington, but not, alas, the hollowed-out tree trunks, mostly elm, pipes
of up to 10 inch bore, which carried the stream along viaducts, or on wooden
bridges when the land contours could not be followed. However, a specimen remains on display at Chirk Castle, Clwyd, North Wales, now a
National Trust property. The castle came into the possession of the Myddel-
tons when Sir Hugh's elder brother, Sir Thomas Myddelton (Lord Mayor of
London in 1613, the year when the New River was completed) purchased
it in 1595. The wooden water pipe lies in the space at the foot of the Grand
Staircase, an 8–foot long exhibit exhumed at Clerkenwell (near Holborn,
London) in 1895. The project was "partly financed from the profits of his
(Sir Hugh's) lead mines in Wales, reputed to yield £2,000 per month, " but
Sir Hugh was ruined financially, as the total cost was nearer £500,000.[350]

If nine-year old John was not present on Michaelmas Day, 29 September 1613, to hear the populace cry "Flow forth precious stream"[351] when the
Lord Mayor officially opened its terminal reservoir at Islington New River
Head, he, with every schoolboy for miles around, must have known all
about it. Fresh water from 13 springs trickling sedately down a gradient of
2 inches to the mile, over 100 bridges, and forty miles of aqueduct, through
400 miles of tree-trunk pipes, at last to deliver its taintless liquid into the
heart of a city where formerly polluted wells, and festering centuries-old
leather pipes, had spewed their poisoned flood. The taste and sound was
that of a miracle, in an age not unfamiliar with new marvels, nor unwilling
to risk high costs.

The Myddeltons descended from Ririd Flaidd ("the Wolf"—they kept
a live wolf at Chirk Castle), Welsh lord of Penllyn, Pennant, and Bryn in
Meirionydd.[352] They were Parliamentarians rather than Puritans, but rec-
ognisably fashioned from the same mould of adventurous Tudor reformism
met with throughout this journey. City merchants, founders of the East
India Company, investors in the buccaneering, and lucrative, expeditions
of men like Hawkins, Drake, and Raleigh, engineers of a new age. Sir
Thomas (1550–1631) also financed the first popular edition of the Bible in

Welsh, and must have sponsored John Eliot's Indian work had he lived to see the day.[353]

His son, the second Sir Thomas Myddelton (1586–1666), sat in Parliament as a moderate reformer, enlisted with its army in the Civil War, and was appointed General of the Roundhead forces in Wales. But after the beheading of King Charles he, with many other landed Parliamentarians, transferred his sympathies, and in 1659 was forced to surrender Chirk Castle to John Lambert, Major General of Cromwell's New Model Army, only for it to be returned to him at the Restoration, the following year.

One of the keys to an understanding of the rapid rise of Puritanism in 16th and 17th century England lies in this vibrant coexistence of adventurous reformation with a deeper fundamentalism. A confident, often affluent, squirarchy spread through the land, feudal in its gut reaction, and reassured in the recovery of old, well-established Biblical images through the translation of the Bible into the language of the people, and its accessibility for general reading.

The corollary of this, however, was the reawakening of a vision of the Kingdom of God on earth. The Puritans were open to experiment, and above all, to improvement. This profitably matched the age of English Elizabethan renaissance, and generated a radical force sufficient to plant a New England even if, finally, they failed to reform the old.

Their faith remained optimistic. They were interested in improved drinking-water as well as clean consciences. And where freedom of the spirit went hand-in-hand with self-interest, the divine right passed rapidly to commoners from kings.

A short drive westwards from Ware brings the traveller directly into Samuel Stone's Hertford.

Hertford, early English frontier town, cradle of The National Church, home of Samuel Stone, co-founder of Hartford, Connecticut.

How to get there.

The County Town of Hertford[354] (spelt Hart Forde in the Elizabethan Charter of 1589) lies 24 miles north of London, 33 south of Cambridge, and 8 from the stupendous Salisbury Mansion of Hatfield House. Directions for driving by car have already been given.

The town has been split by a busy ring road. Do not be discouraged. There are good central car parks, well signposted. A friendly tourist information centre at the Castle and a small but enterprising, and equally friendly Museum in Bull Plain off Salisbury Square, will provide you with adequate instructions for an enchanting day tour. Both castle and museum are well worth a visit.

If travelling by rail, Hertford East Railway Station (direct connections with London Liverpool Street terminus and with Cambridge) penetrates effortlessly to the heart of the old town. There is a second railway station, Hertford North. This connects with London's Moorgate and Underground systems, but is half-a-mile to the northwest of the old town centre, a short walk or taxi ride down North Road into St Andrew Street and The Wash, opposite the Castle via Mill Bridge.

If you find yourself walking from Hertford East Station down Railway Street do glance at the Friend's Meeting House on your left. It is the oldest in the world still in continuous use. The date is 1669, when it was illegal to attend. The clandestine meetings of the early Quakers are reflected in the laid-back design of this undemonstrative, but significant building. George Fox (1624–1691) and William Penn (1644–1718) worshipped here.[355]

For your passing interest, the oldest house in Hertford is the sumptuous Old Verger's House, c. 1450, now Beckwith's Antique Shop in St Andrew Street. If you arrive at Hertford North Station, you will enter the town this way. Continue now along Railway Street, and you will come to Salisbury Square. Do again glance left, at the oak-timbered White Hart, an Inn familiar to John Stone and his son Samuel. It has been standing there under the same name for over 350 years. The tenant in the Stone's day was Samson Clarke, the rent he paid one penny per year. No wonder the inn has remained solvent for so long.

Turn right out of the Square into Bull Plain, so named for the cattle-market once held nearby. The Museum is next to Beadle House, and Lombard House lies beyond, beside the Folly Bridge. If time permits, cross the bridge and enjoy the houses from the rear, with their unadorned fantasy of mixed-up architectural styles, one generation laid upon another. The countryside at Hertford was intensively cultivated for wheat and malting barley. Large estates hemmed in the borough boundaries. In consequence Hertfordians could not easily increase their buildings outside the town, but built upwards like New Yorkers on Manhattan. Top storeys grew in irregular profusion over the passing years. Nicely tidied up in front but, as exampled in the Lombard House, a neat Georgian facade may conceal an eye-catching medley of medieval gables at the back.

At Folly Bridge you enter the New Cut, made by the Lee Navigation scheme of 1767, which widened the river, and improved its water-borne trade. This ensured that the River Lea (or Lee) remained a major commercial highway to the capital, and Hertford a busy inland port, up to modern times. You may wish to rest a while at the Old Barge Inn by the bridge, now in a quiet backwater, but pregnant with lively memories of maritime cargoes exported round the inhabited globe. What must it have meant to Samuel Stone to grow up, as John Eliot did, at an intersection of trade routes which led into the Port of London, and from it to the farthest bounds of an incipient Commonwealth.

From the 10th century on, Hertford was amongst the most important towns of early England. Three small rivers, the Beane, the Mimram and the Rib converge upon the Lea within its ancient boundaries, conferring on it both protection, and a strategic site. The ford, which at one stage carried the main London traffic across the waterways (where Mill Bridge now traverses the Lea, only a few yards from Bull Plain into The Wash), provided the first reason for the town's prosperity. It was also a frontier town between Saxon England and the Danelaw.

King Edward the Elder,[356] son of king Alfred the Great, first built a palisaded fort on the north bank of the ford at Heorutforda in 911, and a second on the south bank the following year. Hertford immediately became a major fortified township, London's northernmost protection against the dreaded Danish invaders. The Roman Ermine Street ran by Ware but, later, the North Road from London took this route, though alternating at times with its nearby rival. As you know, there was another strategic ford, and then a bridge, over the Lea at Ware. But Hertford had a castle-garrison from Norman days, and politically alert Wardens of the castle generally managed to keep a tight control over Ware bridge, even to draping heavy iron chains across it, so that travellers had to go by Hertford, and the town prospered accordingly.

The Norman invaders ringed London with five protective castles, Hertford and Bishop's Stortford to the north, Rayleigh to the far east guarding the Thames approaches, Windsor to the south, Berkhampstead to the west. At Hertford William erected a motte (mound) and bailey (fortified enclosure) shortly after the Conquest, and garrisoned it with royal troops.[357] Henry II increased the fortification in his struggle against the Barons. The castles were frequently in use as royal residences, and none more so than Hertford.

Henry VIII probably first set eyes on sixteen year old Anne Boleyn when she joined the court in residence at Hertford in 1522.[358] His three children, Mary, Elizabeth, and Edward, spent much of their childhood here. When twelve years of age, Elizabeth compiled a book of prayers for Henry's then Queen, Katherine Parr, comprising her own translations of selected Latin, French, and Italian meditations. She worked the Queen's monogram and initials R. K. P. into the cover in blue and gold thread, with the date "Hertford 20 December 1545." This little treasure is now among the royal collections at the British Museum.

James I allowed the castle to fall into disuse, and Charles I granted it to William Cecil, second Earl of Salisbury, on 29 September 1628. It has remained in the family's possession ever since. In 1911, James Edward

Hubert Gascoyne Cecil, fourth Marquis of Salisbury, leased it to the town for a nóminal rent of 2s 6d per annum, for use as municipal offices and public gardens.[359] Cross over the road at The Wash, where the Lea used frequently to flood, and enter by the ornamental wrought-iron gates. The Norman motte lies to your right on the pretty Lea bank. All that remains of the major castle buildings, the impressive 15th century Gatehouse, lies in front of you, with the lovely grounds spread about, and the commemorative stone to the first conference of English Bishops by the Gatehouse entrance.

On 24 September 673 A.D., Theodore of Tarsus, Archbishop of Canterbury, called a Synod of the five English Bishops, Kent, Wessex, Mercia, East Anglia, and Northumbria.[360] It was the first attempt at reconciliation between the Celtic churches of the north and the later Roman churches founded by St Augustine of Canterbury. By this conference a national church was initiated, the rights and responsibilities of the bishops, clergy and monks regulated, the date of Easter agreed. Hertford may have been selected for this historic meeting because of its centrality to the major highways of that period.

Before disposing of the castle desmene to the Cecils, Charles I commissioned an inventory of his Hertford holdings. John Norden, then the Deputy Surveyor, produced a detailed survey, showing every house and every occupant, in 1621. It is to this survey that we owe precise knowledge of the Stone residence.[361]

The Samuel Stone House in Fore Street.

Speede's early 17th century map of Hartford shows it quite clearly, and John Norden's Survey confirms it. Leave the Castle grounds by the same entrance, turn right into Parliament Square (reminder of the several Parliaments which met at the castle, for instance when London's plagues drove the members outside the capital), pause to admire the War Memorial with its sculpted hart facing the ford at Mill Bridge, bravely defending the town, and there is Fore Street to your left.

As you walk down Fore Street (returning in the direction of Hertford East Station), do take time to admire the 17th century buildings, and their ornamental pargetting. You will pass the Salisbury Arms, with the Shire Hall opposite, both of architectural interest. On the same side of the road as the Salisbury Arms, at Nos 76/78 stands Barclays Bank, with the Stone's home encased behind its facade.[362]

To the left of Barclay's is the Dimsdale Arms. In Norden's 1621 Survey this was the Red Lion Inn "with yard and orchard adjoining," a timber-framed building of about 1600. The home of John Stone was next door, of similar age and construction. Now entirely blocked from view by the Barclay's frontage, the site is marked by a plaque on the wall. Inside, some of the aged oak beams which may have supported the original house have been uncovered, and photographed. I have copies, although the beams are not open to public view.

On the town-centre side of the bank there was another Inn, The Falcon. All together, a group of four adjacent properties, they are clearly visible on Speede's map. Shake off your shoes, this is hallowed ground!

John Stone is credited with two properties in Norden's Survey. One was a "newly erected cottage" on the borough boundary. The other the "ancient messuage" noted above, on the south side of Fore Street. This is within the Parish of All Saints, close to Church Street, through an under-pass beneath Gascoyne Way, the wide ring-road which divides the dominant All Saints from the town centre.

John was evidently a substantial citizen, a "Burgess,"[363] member of the Borough Council, one who could afford to send his son to Cambridge. Samuel was baptised at All Saints on 30 July 1602.[364] He matriculated at Emmanuel College, Cambridge, at Easter 1620, and graduated M.A. four years afterwards. He was ordained by the Bishop of Peterborough, and appointed Curate at Sisted in Essex, 13 June 1627.

He was silenced by Laud three years later and found temporary employment as Lecturer at Towcester, Northants, through the recommendation of Thomas Shepard, a native of that town. It was there that Thomas Hooker found shelter when, after Stones's nomination as his associate, Thomas called on him during a surreptitious visit from exile in Holland, before they sailed for New England in 1633. The two men had, of course, known each other since their days at Emmanuel and we may assume that Stone went into Essex to be near his erstwhile friends in the Cuckoos company.

Mather reveals that Thomas Hooker had asked for John Cotton as his pastoral associate in Massachusetts, but Cotton already had other commitments in the new colony.[365] That Stone's was a wise choice is proved by after events. He and Hooker forged a long-shared and harmonious ministry, first at Newtown, then at Hartford. To survive the dangerous trek to the Connecticut River and all the vicissitudes of founding a new town and a new, fast-growing State, would have taxed the firmest of friendships. Theirs endured.

It was Samuel Stone who negotiated with the Saukiag Indians for land on which to settle in 1636.[366] He gave the name of his home-town to the new venture—Hartford. You will notice the accuracy of the spelling!

In Connecticut he played a vital role in the settlement of the church, and the city. He went to war against the threatening Pequot Indians in 1637, as chaplain to Captain John Mason and his train-band.[367] He succeeded Hooker as principal minister on the latter's death. But not without some conflict. In Cotton Mather's phrase, he was "a Load-Stone and a Flint-Stone." He fell out with William Goodwin, Hooker's chief elder, and executor, who was to marry Susannah after her husband Thomas Hooker's death. It was a complex controversy, "rendered almost as obscure as the Rise of the Connecticut," as Mather put it.[368] It had to do with the endemic problem of reconciling old days with new.

The grandchildren's generation of settlers had not passed through fire and water to found a new world and had no stomach for the self-denying zeal of their forbears. Known as "the Half-Way Covenant," a device was proposed to permit the baptism of their children, even though they were less visibly sanctified than their forefathers.

Samuel Stone wished to practice the humaneness of his mentor, Hooker, and was in favour of relaxing Baptismal regulations, if in his own fashion.[369] He demanded "a speaking Aristocracy in the face of a silent Democracy," that is to say, he reserved to himself a public veto in matters spiritual, requiring an uncomplaining obedience from his members. It could not be sustained.

Thirty-one members of his congregation held to the more rigid codes of an earlier English Calvinism. They were immovably opposed to the compromises demanded by the rising generation of New Englanders. Led by the influential William Goodwin, who withdrew to found a separate town up river at Hadley, they started the opposing South Congregational Church at Hartford, in 1670.[370]

Nevertheless, Samuel Stone earned the tribute paid to him by Samuel Danforth (John Eliot's associate at Roxbury), "the strength and glory of Connecticut." Was it only coincidence that he, who signed the treaty which ceded Hartford, Connecticut, to the English settlers, and established it as the fulcrum of the Connecticut River Towns, came from this pivotal point of the English Church? So much depends on the basic assumptions which unconsciously underlie our expectations and actions. Hertford was an axis of English as well as of Church history, and maybe of America too. Both Hertford and Hartford do well to honour him.

Nazeing, Essex. John Eliot's boyhood home.

How to get there, no more than five miles from Hertford.

If by car from Hertford, south down the A10 to the exit (east) onto the A414, and take the next exit into Stanstead Abbots, and the B181 to Roydon and Broadley Common. Roydon is a pleasant stopping-place, with the stately ruin of Nether Hall, once the home of Jane Colte,[371] wife of Sir Thomas More (1478–1535), Lord Chancellor of England after Cardinal Wolsey, beheaded largely because of his conscientious opposition to Henry VIII's divorce from Catherine of Aragon.

At Broadley Common a minor road runs off to the right (southwest) to Bumble's Green. Do not take the earlier exits to Lower Nazeing (Nazeing-bury, probably marked "Nazeing") as these only land you confusingly in a modern town quite separate from old Nazeing proper, on the hilltop above.

There is a narrow lane (Betts Lane) on your right as you begin to descend the hill to Bumble's Green, immediately after passing The Sun Inn. It is signposted "Nazeing Church," and pursues its circuitous way to All Saints. Only the brave will persevere to the end and be rewarded, for once again you enter a secret Britain, privately in possession of its past. There is ample parking space outside the church, but there are no other facilities.

If from Ware, return south to Stanstead Abbots, and follow the B181 as above.

If from Widford, retrace your route to Stanstead Abbots by the B180, and follow the B181 as above.

Nazeing All Saints.

The Parish[372] is approximately three by two miles in area, bounded by the River Lea to the west, and the parishes of Waltham Abbey and Epping to the south. It encloses a large stretch of common land (Nazeing Common), and was never a compact village but rather a spread of houses with perhaps a small concentration round the Church Green marked on early maps (between the Sun Inn and the Church). Here the Parish Church of All Saints crowns the low lying hills above the river valley, a quiet oasis still, down its narrow lane. John Eliot would quickly feel at home, were he to visit the Church precinct today.

This part of the village, on a bluff standing out above the river plain, provided the name Nazeing ("naze" a nose or promontory, "ing" a meadow or pasture). The Roman Ermine Street ran roughly along the river-bed below. Much of the history of early England coursed up and down this vital route, and Nazeing overlooked it.

The Bennett Eliots removed to Nazeing c. 1607, in time for the baptism of their fifth child, Lydia, three years later. No one knows where they lived, but, again, it must have been a contented home for the manner in which John wrote of it in later years ("a great favour of God unto me"),[373] and the fact of the childrens' emigrating together, and supporting each other in New England.

They worshipped at the striking flint and stone All Saints Church, where Lydia's baptism is recorded with those of two more children (Francis and Mary) and other Eliot entries, in the priceless parchment book of All Saints' marriages, baptisms and burials which goes back to 1598 (with transcriptions of earlier entries from 1559).

As you enter by the 16th century south porch,[374] which screens an ageless doorway hewn from the deep Norman walls, you will see across the Norman nave, in the fine 15th century north aisle, a memorial plaque placed in 1983 by the National Society of the Descendants of John and Elizabeth Hutchins Curtiss. It is dedicated "In memory of all the members of this church who emigrated to America." With them went John Curtiss' nephew, William Curtis of Nazeing, who married the eldest of the Eliot children, Sarah. Her father Bennett Eliot made William his executor (Bennett died 21 November 1621. Lettese predeceased him 16 March 1618: both are recorded in the Nazeing Register).

If the full list had been attached, it must have included the names Adams, Brevitt, Camp, Clarke, Curtis, Eliot, Gore, Graves, Holmes, King, Morris, Payson, Peacock, Pegram, Ruggles, Shelley, and Uffett and many more. W. Winters, *Memorials Of The Pilgrim Fathers, John Eliot And His Friends Of Nazing And Waltham Abbey* (1882) lists 38 names of Massachusetts freemen from Nazeing, recognised between the years 1631–1641, and five times that number from Waltham Abbey.[375]

This is a surprising total, for Nazeing numbered about three hundred residents at that time. It appears that half the village, or more, emigrated. John Eliot had promised to be their minister if they would follow him.[376] No wonder he discovered that, despite the antagonism to his Indian work of the majority of English settlers, who felt threatened by the proximity of his protected Indian towns, he received the courageous support of his Roxbury congregation to his death. They shared his birthrights, his folk law and his convictions.

Nazeing was a "Puritan" village. Sir Francis Swift may have been at Harold's Park, and Sir Richard Lucy at Nazing Park, royalists both, but the Paysons resided at the old manor house of Nazing Bury, and when King Charles I attempted to raise revenue by enforced loans, in 1627, the defaulters included them, and "William Scott, gentleman, Thomas Santrye, gentleman, William Shelley, Edward Adams, and William Brazier," all Nazeing Puritans, all property owners of substance.[377]

A long succession of clergy sympathetic to reform occupied the vicarage. Nicholas Lock, instituted in 1541, was evicted in 1554 when Queen Mary came to the throne, for his Protestantism, and refusing to put away his wife. John Hopkins, 1571, was deprived for nonconformity in 1589. Edward Jude, 1608, ministered to the Puritan congregation for 12 years. Lionel Goodrick, 1631, whose father Lionel Goodrick had been a student at Emmanuel College, Cambridge, went to Caius College in the same university and theological tradition, and was later elsewhere ejected for nonconformity. Jeremy Dyke, 1640, was at Emmanuel as his father had been before him. He came from a line of nonconforming preachers. John Harper, 1648, was also from Emmanuel, and an outspoken Puritan. So were David Leigh, 1648, appointed by the parishioners during Cromwell's Protectorate, and his successor Henry Albury, 1650, who was allowed ten shillings by the Cromwellian sequesters "every Sabbath day" that he preached. He was followed, 1658, by Joseph Browne, ejected in 1662.[378]

What took place at Nazeing followed a pattern repeated throughout the country, even if with greater intensity amongst the freedom-loving people of East Anglia. It was a pattern of voluntary nonconformity alternating with enforced conformity, and it stretched back over more than one hundred years. Puritanism was more of a popular movement than has sometimes been acknowledged.

William and Sarah Curtis seem to have taken responsibility for the family when Lettese and Bennett Eliot died.[379] They paid John's college fees at his father's bequest, and sailed in the *Lyon* with their children Thomas, Mary, John, and Philip in 1632, having sent their eldest son William with his uncle John Eliot in the same vessel the previous year. Altogether four Eliot brothers and three sisters crossed the Atlantic.

Legend has it that John Eliot attended a grammar school at Nazeing along with the other village boys, and returned frequently, possibly to assist in the pastoral work of the parish during and after graduation at Cambridge. This could make sense. The ties between him and the villagers were so intimate that they would never let him go, offer to resign over and again as he did when the pressures of his Indian mission, old age, and infirmity made it impossible to give the attention to his Roxbury congregation he wished.

Nazeing had other lessons to impart, besides the sustaining strength of happy family relationships. Over and above these, his childhood experience had a direct bearing on his espousal of the just causes of the poor, his sensitivity to any exploitation of the weak, so marked a feature of his colonial exploits.

If you walk westwards through All Saints churchyard to the edge of the headland, and look southwards, your sight reaches towards the remains of Epping Forest (once part of a vast royal hunting-ground) and, admittedly by a considerable stretch of the imagination, to the fortified earthworks of Ambresbury Banks, just southwest of Epping, only some four miles away.[380]

There, local legend has it, Boadicea (Boudicca) Queen of the Iceni first rallied the British tribes in A.D. 61, in her revolt against the occupying Roman forces which led to the sack of Colchester, St Albans, and London. Then, cornered by the avenging army of the Roman governor-general Suetonius Paulinus, she made a last stand at Ambresbury Banks, was defeated with fearful loss, and poisoned herself at Cobbins Brook, which runs between the boundaries of Nazeing and Epping.

Never mind whether true or false, the deepest beliefs can be grounded in myths like this. It is impossible to think that children brought up at Nazeing, so close at hand, were unaffected by the memory of this supposed catastrophe.

The fate of the British tribes was in many ways parallelled, 1600 years later, by that of the indigenous Native Americans (always called "Indians" by the European settlers) when the Puritans colonised New England. Can it be merely a coincidence that, almost uniquely amongst the early colonists, John Eliot and his Roxbury neighbours from Nazeing responded positively to the threat of the disintegration of the Massachusetts tribes? Had they not grown up with the threat of tribal extinction a part of their folk-law?

A very different event took place in this same region some time in the year 894. From the western edge of All Saint's grounds you are also looking towards the confluence of the River Lea with the Thames at London, approximately twenty miles away. King Alfred came up that way to trap the Danes somewhere below Nazeing, maybe at Ware, and inflicted on them a decisive defeat.[381] He burnt their warships and drove their forces westwards towards Bridgnorth. It was a dramatic reversal of Boudicca's fate. Alfred lived to see his small kingdom of Wessex delivered from an invader. The experience however, was to be reversed again, in 1066.

The royal Abbey of Waltham nestles in the Lea Valley to the south, and Nazeing was at first under its jurisdiction, its priests appointed by the Abbot and Convent of Waltham, patrons of All Saints up to 1513. It then reverted to the Crown until the mid 17th century, when the Master of Emmanuel appears as patron until the nonconforming congregation at last asserted itself, and , in 1648, chose its own minister, David Leigh.

It could not have been without significance to the gossips of Nazeing when the corpse of King Harold was brought back to Waltham Abbey after his overthrow at the Battle of Hastings in 1066, and reverently laid to rest there.[382] It is impossible that news of the debacle at Hastings, when the undisciplined Saxon house-carls broke ranks and presented a far-from-certain victory to the Normans, which assured the demise of Saxon England, did not filter up from the Abbey to dependant Nazeing.

Was it not also borne into the consciousness of a bright, sensitive boy like John Eliot, and did it not inevitably contribute to his determination to offer the advantages of European culture and education to the illiterate New England Indians, knowing in the depths of his being that they too were in process of elimination, and they too might be saved?

After all, when the Eliot family attended worship at All Saints, they entered by the south door set alongside what came to be known as "the Armada Tower."[383] Stone-built, solid, buttressed, banded and battlemented, the tower rises squarely from the west end of the nave, spreading its message of victory for miles around. It was erected c. 1556, thirty years before the wind of God, as the English claimed, blew away the most oppressive force to menace England since the Norman conquest. The name "Armada" quickly accrued to the tower, and may possibly have contributed further to the growth and development of John Eliot, assured champion of the beleaguered poor.

Think of it. Two warnings of destruction, two instances of deliverance, all four on Nazeing's doorstep! It cannot be fortuitous that the boy brought up with these stories bred into the bone of his community, became the chief advocate of the Indian tribes. He believed in the viability of a divine reversal, he thought they could be saved for his history told him so. He knew the penalty if the hero-figure failed, as Boudicca and Harold did. As he, John Eliot did, and New England's native culture with him and his too few helpers.

He pinned his faith to the power of education.[384] He might even have succeeded in training the Indians to resist the worst effects of the Puritan invasion, the corrosion of its alien culture, techniques, and attendant diseases, had not Metacomet raised insurrection against the colonies, and doomed everyone involved to defeat.

By way of a small compensation, do peep into the front driveway of the Old Vicarage as you leave, only a few steps back along Betts Lane. It is another gorgeous house like that at Widford, much later than Eliot's day, but descending from the privileged position of the clergy whom he knew, whose ranks he joined, whose prosperity he scorned. It was a sacrifice of stern degree to leave Nazeing en masse, and to quarry a holding out of primitive Rocksbury (Roxbury), Massachusetts. But first John Eliot went to Jesus College, a tale already told, then to Little Baddow, before his life's great work unfolded in America.

Waltham Abbey.

How to get there.

From Nazeing it is no more than four miles to Waltham Abbey, and well worth the effort if your schedule can be stretched to include it. The journey can only be made conveniently by car. You return to Bumble's Green, pick up the B194 going south, and positively pierce the ring-road round Waltham Abbey so as to park in the old town centre.[385] Here there are restaurants, the timber frame Welsh Harp Inn first constructed for the medieval pilgrim-trade, and other tourist attractions. Wherever else you may be, Waltham Abbey is close by the northern section of the M25, Exit 25.

The Abbey Church of the Holy Cross and St Laurence[386] provides the main focus of interest. St Laurence (died A. D. 258) was one of the seven deacons of Rome at the time of the Valerian persecution. Valerian, Roman

Emperor A.D. 253–260 initiated a calamitous persecution indiscriminately against all Christians which took place in Italy, Gaul, Spain, Egypt, North Africa, Palestine and Asia Minor, only ceasing when Valerian was captured in battle with the Persians.

St Laurence was reputedly roasted to death on a gridiron by the exasperated Prefect of Rome, who had demanded that he hand over the church's treasures. Instead, Laurence paraded some of Rome's poorest inhabitants, having first distributed the church's wealth amongst them, saying "these are the treasures of the church." I wonder if John Eliot knew the story. He was for ever giving away his possessions to anyone who needed help.

The Holy Cross refers to the Abbey's foundation. A Dane named Tovi,[387] or Tofig, in the days of King Canute (c. 995–1035), held the estates at Waltham. He heard that a black flint figure of the crucified Christ had been unearthed on Mons Acutus, the steep and sacred St Michael's hill which stands above Montacute House, that loveliest of Elizabethan manors near Yeovil in Somerset. It houses many of the National Portrait Gallery's paintings of 16th and 17th century notables, a number of whom feature in this volume.[388]

Tovi, convinced that he had received a divine commission, placed the crucifix on a wagon drawn by twelve red oxen and twelve white cows, pronounced the name of Waltham, and watched with wonder as they set off for his homestead in Essex, nor stopped until the long slow journey across England was completed.

The crucifix was housed in Waltham's church, and pilgrims flocked to touch it when its healing power became apparent. King Harold was cured of a paralysis by its efficacy. He rebuilt Tovi's church on a larger scale, and endowed it for a college of twelve canons under a Dean. The new church was consecrated probably in 1060. After Harold's death at the Battle of Hastings, his college endured for a further one hundred years. Henry II, apparently as part of his penance for the murder of Archbishop Thomas Becket, refounded it (1177) as a priory of Augustinian canons. In 1184 it became an Abbey, and soon a "mitred abbey," giving the status of bishop to its abbot. It was the last to be suppressed under Henry VIII.

Much has been destroyed since those far off days, but seven bays of the Norman nave survive, with some huge cylindrical piers, deeply incised with geometric ornamentation. The 19th century adaptation of the east end is impressive too, with a rose window suspended over three lancets most effectively set under the majestic diamond-patterned painted ceiling, flooded with light atop the massive triforium.

The glass in the east window is by Sir Edward Burne-Jones (1833–1898)[389] of the English pre-Raphaelite school. The lancets hold a "Jesse" window, depicting the descent of Christ from the line of David in the form of a branched tree springing from Jesse, King David's father, while the lights of the rose window depict the several stages of the Creation.

William Morris,[390] central figure of the pre-Raphaelite movement, was born at Elm House in nearby Walthamstow. Water House, where much of his boyhood was spent, on Forest Road in Upper Walthamstow, is now a museum to his memory.

Until the dissolution of the monasteries, Nazeing belonged to Waltham Abbey. The canons were responsible for catechising Nazeing children. Think of that, and the folk-law they left behind for the training of young John Eliot. So much to photograph, so much to share with your less fortunate friends at home!

CHAPTER 6

The Dutch Disillusionment

1631–1633

THE ENGLISH REFORMER BECOMES
THE AMERICAN FOUNDER.

It is arguable that there should be a Seventh Chapter in any assessment of the formative influences in the life of the Founder of Connecticut, namely The New England Experiment.

Thomas Hooker was 47 when he landed at Boston on 4 September 1633, and fifty by the time that Hartford was established. His character was fully developed. But no one could seriously argue that the New England experience was other than determinative for him. The manner in which the emerging townships advanced towards statehood, and with it, the creation of a unique brand of citizen, not previously found on this planet—the Connecticut Yankee—was a process of which he was, to say the least, a part of the beginning.

In that sense, Thomas Hooker's character went on growing to his life's end, even as his career was an unfinished journey, from a secure hamlet in a rapidly changing rural England into the unknown territory of a modern Democracy, as yet unguessed at, held together by the Faith which forged it, and the people who were putting it into practice.

The irreversible situation of most early settlers, only a few of whom could afford, or would dare, to return to England in the first decade; the uncompromising wilderness which impressed its economy on the first colonists; the isolation of the small communities, whose survival depended on self-reliance within a covenantal relationship, requiring each one to serve the whole Commonwealth, or perish—were sufficient in themselves to impose some form of "congregational" government, or group autonomy, on each new Plantation, and therefore on Thomas Hooker.

It is unclear whether Hooker's evolution towards a politico-religious Non-Separating Congregationalism was irrevocable when he left Holland. His last work there, a Preface to William Ames' *A Fresh Suit Against Ceremonies*[1] (Amsterdam, posthumously published in London late 1633) leaves the question open, because it is concerned with the English hierarchy's determination to enforce unpalatable ceremonies on Puritan congregations, rather than with the nature of the Church and the State which Hooker finally upheld.

However, in that Preface, and equally in his answers to John Paget's Twenty Questions,[2] he does reveal his conviction that only a voluntary Association of Believers in hope of Salvation, with a willingness for mutual obedience, whose Ministers are equals because called of God through the Congregation—in contrast to the geographically ordered Parochial system of nominal Christians in the Church of England, led by Bishops appointed under a non-negotiable Monarchical, or State, control—was now acceptable.

John Paget[3] had been Pastor of the English Reformed Church in Amsterdam since its inception in 1607, and remained for thirty years. On 2 July 1631, Hooker was approached by an influential group within Paget's congregation, to become their Associate Pastor, but Paget was apprehensive. He was not looking for change, and feared that Hooker's suspected Separatist, or at best Congregationalist beliefs, would prejudice his own Presbyterian standing.

His congregation was already split into two factions, a Separatist-Reformist group, and an established Presbyterian majority. Paget understandably favoured the latter. They were officially recognized within the local Dutch classis, and this gave them protection under Dutch and English Law. It was not to be lightly imperilled. Paget was also aware that the English authorities, urged on by Laud, had resolved to prevent any English ex-patriots from enjoying unauthorised freedom of worship in Holland, and that Laud's spies had their eyes on Hooker.

Thomas Hooker was involved in another politically damaging relationship. William Ames was Professor of Theology at Franeker, easily within reach. They must have made frequent contact, for Hooker was writing the Preface to the *Fresh Suit*. To come again under the sway of Ames was to espouse Congregationalism.

The reunion must have been joyful. William Ames (1576–1633)[4] had been a Fellow at Christ's when Hooker went up to Cambridge. Their friendship ripened rapidly in the two years before Ames' uncompromising Puritanism led to his removal. Ames went first to Colchester, then to Holland, where he earned universal recognition through his divinity lectures at Franeker University, and his championship of classical Calvinism against the Arminians during the Remonstrative controversies.

Very briefly (since to know is to travel most comfortably) the Remonstrance was a restatement of the teaching of Jacobus Arminius (1560–1609) set out under five headings by his disciples at Gouda.[5] It attacked Calvinist determinist logic, especially in Calvin's dependence on the doctrine of

Predestination as essential to any understanding of God as Sovereign Lord; and in some of his followers' distorted refinements, as, for example, "Supralapsarianism" (that God actually selected individuals for election to sanctity, or for non-election, before Adam was created); and of "Sublapsarianism" (that He chose, or rejected, individuals only after Adam's fall).[6]

The image of God in both is unacceptable. Heavenly quill-pen and parchment in immaterial hand, making eternally long lists before ever we were conceived, to assert His Sovereignty, and to ensure we don't all get saved, and cram heaven uncomfortably full of unworthy residents! Calvin never proposed anything like this. He was content to stand in awe before a Divine Mystery. But others considered it the logical conclusion of his teaching.

Arminius objected. He wished to emphasise the genuine freedom of human will, and might have been better received in his native Holland had he not been identified with the Spanish Party in politics. This damned his followers in the eyes of most Lowlanders. The urgency for us is that into this heated religio-political controversy strode William Ames, soundly on the side of Freedom of Conscience and Faith, but in the name of an Absolutist Deity who willed it for His Elect, which confirmed Traditional Puritans, but permitted Reformist and Imperialist conclusions. And Hooker was his principal ally.

This close association with continental Calvinist-Arminian conflicts, enlarged by his proximity to Ames, must have accelerated Hooker's decision to emigrate to New England (ie. to plant a simplified, purified commonwealth there) as Ames was about to do (and his widow did), when suddenly he died at Rotterdam.

Ames said of Hooker that "though he had been acquainted with many scholars of divers nations, yet he never met with any Mr Hooker's equal, either for preaching or for disputation,"[7] Praise indeed. For Laud's anxious envoys lurking in Hooker's shadow, avid for any hint of indiscretion, the presence of the two men in one Country was threat indeed.

Life was never easy for Hooker in Dutch exile. He suffered recurring ill-health, as we have noted, and a deep disillusionment about the Dutch Reformed churches. To John Cotton he lamented "they content themselves with very forms though much blemished, but the power of godliness, for aught I can see or hear, they know not."[8] If he gained anything from his Dutch disillusionment, it was (a) that there was no remaining place for him and his followers in Protestant North Europe, and (b) that a Congregational doctrine of the Church came nearer to the requirements of Scripture than any other, not least Presbyterianism (an exchange of one authoritarian system for another), or Independency (an unthinkable free-for-all). But he needed the New England experience for proof positive. His growth to maturity did not, in fact, reach its climax until after Hartford was established in Connecticut.

My purpose now, however, is to draw Hooker's English period to a close, and to look on Holland from across the English Channel solely to that end.[9]

At Rotterdam With Hugh Peter.

Thomas Hooker embarked for Holland, probably in June 1631. He first visited Hugh Peter (1598–1660) at Rotterdam.[10] Peter had been Minister of the English Merchant Adventurers' Church there since the Summer of 1629. Born at Fowey in Cornwall, Peter entered Trinity College, Cambridge, in 1613, when Hooker was a Fellow of Emmanuel. After graduation he took a teaching post at Laindon, Essex (now part of Basildon, within acceptable reach of the Cuckoos Company), was ordained, and moved to Rayleigh as Curate.

Rayleigh was as near to Chelmsford, next to Rochford a former home of Richard Rich, first Baron Rochford. The great house exists no longer, but was once one of the homes of Sir Thomas Boleyn, father of the ill-fated Anne, a place of courtly history turned Puritan stronghold when Rich's grandson, Robert, first Earl of Warwick, adopted the Puritan way.

Hugh Peter did not last long. He was suspended in 1627, and emigrated to Rotterdam. He was an early subscriber to the Massachusetts Bay Company, went on to New England, and was called to be Pastor of the Salem Church in 1635. From there he was sent by the General Council of Massachusetts back to England, with Thomas Weld and William Hibbens, to solicit funds for the Colony.

He quickly joined the Parliamentary Army as a chaplain, on the outbreak of hostilities against Charles I, and became one of the English Commonwealth's best-known advocates. He is credited with raising £20,000 during a tour of the Netherlands in 1643 on behalf of Irish Protestants (instead of for the Bay Company, struggling against a wave of economic depression due to the Civil War), and finally was executed at the Restoration, 16 October 1660.

Peter was a rumbustious character, hot-bloodied and impetuous, but he proved a staunch friend to Hooker in Holland, as ill-health and controversies piled up around him. The insecurity of Hooker's situation must have made him the more susceptible to Peter's forthright Separatism. It also displays Hooker's extraordinary patience and humility.

After the July invitation from the English Church at Amsterdam, then meeting at the former Catholic Chapel of the Begijnhof, John Paget insisted on Hooker's answering in writing the Twenty Questions he put to him, before any removal to Amsterdam could be countenanced. Hooker obliged at length, even though "I do apprehend your opinion and affections to be so far settled that you apprehend there cannot be a peaceable concurrence—to deliver you from all fear either of any molestations that might come unto your spirit or division to your congregation."

"These are my poor thoughts for the present touching all the opinions propounded," he had written, "giving wiser and better than myself, loving leave to think and do otherwise, being ever willing to hear better arguments and any converting reason, and to stoop thereunto."[11]

At Delft With John Forbes.

Hooker's forbearance went unrewarded. Instead, he joined the English congregation at the Prinsenhof at Delft, in November 1631, as Assistant to John Forbes. Forbes (1568-1634),[12] a Scottish Presbyterian of noble descent (Lord Forbes of Corse was armour-bearer to King James III of Scotland) had been exiled for life because he had acted as Moderator of the irregular Aberdeen Assembly. He had met Hooker at the home of the Francis Drakes of Esher, where he was a friend of the family; and had received their young son Thomas Drake as an Assistant, at his previous English Church at Middleburg.

It was a much needed welcome for Hooker, but controversy not of his choosing overtook him once more.[13] Forbes decided to enfranchise a group of English craftsmen then working in Delft, by confirming them into Church Membership. The merchants were angered, considering that it lowered their own social status. Forbes was forced to withdraw temporarily to England, and Hooker shared the blame. Nothing ran smoothly for him in Holland.

It was the familiar controversy which was to follow him into Massachusetts. For Hooker, anyone could become a member of the Church (ingrafted into the Body of Christ), and enjoy its franchise, who was prepared to accept sanctification by faith alone. For his Reformed opponents, only those who already possessed a visible sanctity (in this case, as evidenced by the weight of their wealth and social standing). For his Anglican opponents, only those who additionally accepted the dictat of the reigning monarch, and that was another matter altogether.

His first sermon at Delft had been, prophetically enough, "For unto you it is given in the behalf of Christ, not only to believe on him, but also to suffer for his sake" (Phil. 1:29). Hooker's was a suffering of misrepresentation and rejection, of persistent fevers and home-sickness hard to endure.

Preparations For Exile.

By mid-1633 Hooker was back in England, possibly for more than one visit, to be with his family, and to plan the New England passage with companions like John Cotton. Cotton was in hiding, part-time with the beloved Henry Whitefield, at the spacious Ockley Rectory, near Guildford, Surrey. They may well have conferred in the comparative safety of its hospitable walls.

Whitefield[14] was an Oxford graduate, from New Hall, alma mater of John White of Dorchester, John Pynchon, father of William of Springfield, and many another reformer. He emigrated in 1639, taking not only his family but a number of poor families at his own expense. They founded Guildford in Connecticut, and renewed their friendship with Thomas Hooker. When ill-health compelled Whitefield's return to England in 1650, Cotton Mather wrote, "The whole Town accompanied him unto the Waterside, with a Spring Tide of Tears."[15]

The Whitefields were a wealthy couple. They generously entertained other Puritans in distress, such as John Davenport,[16] another Oxford man, the congregationally elected Vicar of St Stephen's, Coleman Street, London. This was an experiment doomed to failure, with Laud in London. There were influential Puritans at St Stephen's, the Vere family amongst them, who contrived to switch certain church funds to the independent upkeep of a Vicar of their own choosing. Laud was horrified. Episcopal control could have been overthrown, and the divine rights of kings openly flouted. If the impropriation of ecclesiastical funds had been generally successful, there would have been no pilgrimage to New England, no Civil War, no Restoration of the monarchy after a peaceably evolved Commonwealth. But Laud ruthlessly put an end to the practice, and Davenport fled to Holland.

He was another founder-subscriber to the Massachusetts Bay Company. For a time he worked in uneasy colleagueship at Amsterdam with John Paget. They are described as slinging pamphlets at each other across the breakfast table, on their conflicting views about baptism and church membership. Davenport was back in England within two years, joined the Theophilus Eaton party which planted New Haven, Connecticut,[17] in 1637, and thus was re-united with Thomas Hooker. Was it not here that the two regicides, Edward Whalley and his son-in-law William Goffe, found sanctuary, after 1660?[18]

A passing note on Theophilus Eaton is illuminating. He was a prosperous London merchant (born at Stony Stratford, Buckinghire, 1590), who for a time acted as advisor, and agent to Charles I in Denmark. An original patentee of the Massachusetts Bay Company, he had known the Davenports since John's childhood, and was a member of St Stephen's, Coleman Street, congregation.

Correctly reading the signs of the times, he transferred his assets to New England, and became founder-governor of New Haven until his death (7 January 1658), with John Davenport as his minister. Together they were responsible for publishing *New Haven's Settling in New England and some Lawes for Government published for the Use of that Colony* (known as the "Connecticut Blue Laws") in 1656. The success of the venture owed much to Eaton's skilful diplomacy with the Dutch at New Amsterdam (New York), who were under increasing threat from the insouciant incursions of the English into their dwindling borders; and something also to his championship of the New England Confederation he helped to bring into being with Winthrop, Hooker and others for the mutual defence of the young colonies.

The fairly rigid development pattern spontaneously adopted in colony after colony, as illustrated by New Haven and the others, bears out their close relationship in Old England. Theirs was "A Family Affair."

These comings and goings amongst the growing company of New England founding figures included Hooker's journey to Towcester, already reported, for a conference with Samuel Stone, his newly elected Associate. The removal to New England for all of them was neither simple nor swift. I think Hooker was reluctant to the end. But there was no more for him to learn, no more for any of them to expect other than persecution, or a narrowing exile in Holland.[19]

Thomas Hooker had exhausted every available means of bringing about a further English Reformation, and had reaped a bitter harvest. Neither satisfaction nor meaningful opportunity had opened for him in northern Europe. His time to leave the Land, the Culture, and the Church he loved so deeply, had come.

The Final Phase.

The Downs is the name given to a Roadstead in the English Channel off Deal,[20] between the North and South Forelands. It is protected on the east by the Goodwin Sands, a dangerous sandbar on which many ships have foundered, but providing calm waters within; and to the north and west by coastal cliffs. Much favoured in the past by sailing vessels on their passage through the Channel, it offered favourable anchorage during heavy weather, yet, being open to the sea, advantageous access to the North European ports, or to the Atlantic and the Americas.

To this exposed haven the families of John Cotton, Thomas Hooker, John Haynes, Samuel Stone, and two hundred more individuals, made their various journeys without capture. Laud's busy pursuivants were scouring the countryside for at least the more celebrated fugitives. The three hundred ton ship, *The Griffin*, hid them aboard, Cotton and Hooker incognito for fear of arrest.

How was it that Thomas Hooker could gather his family from their hiding place at Great Waltham, and move them, baggage, books, servants, furniture, farm implements, food stuffs, afoot through London across the Thames, or by one of the river ferries, into Kent, to the southeastern tip of England for embarkation as a hunted man, under constant surveillance in Holland as well as in England? Did they journey, once again from Maldon port, by coaster down to Deal?

The *Griffin* weighed anchor on 10 July 1633.[21] We see these two courageous princes of the church, John Cotton and Thomas Hooker, hiding below, not daring to show their persons above the hatches until the English Channel was safely cleared. The grey horizons of the ocean stretching before them, when at last they strode the deck, and felt the fresh winds whipping their cheeks with renewed health and hope, must have appeared like pavements of gold reaching out to Heaven.

Come storm and strain, come stench of primitive plantations, come famine and fever, there would be no thought of turning back. They were sailing to Zion, and found it in the humdrum of digging trenches, planting corn, clutching new settlements out of the endless forests, making a way of holiness in the wilderness, as they had done all their lives. Bred to the land, bred to learning, bred in pain and persecution, the Puritan people of the Old Land making it New.

The Vision was flawed, as with all human vision. Their children lacked the heroic disciplines of their mothers and fathers, imposed on the earlier generation by the flowering of Tudor genius and oppression. They could not match the dream of a Divine Commonwealth in their own endeavour. The Founding Mothers and Fathers trusted too much in the perfectability of second-generation saints. A wiser realism had to follow; and it will always be so.

To be fair, Thomas Hooker should be excepted if Mather is correct that "He had sagacious and prophetical apprehensions of the declensions which would attend 'reforming churches' when they came to enjoy a place of liberty—he feared, that they who had been lively Christians in the fire of persecution, would soon become cold in the midst of unversal peace." (*Magnalia* 1:343). But Hooker was exceptional.

The Planting Pilgrims failed also to take that one further step, of accepting the godhead waiting for them in the wilderness. They wanted a God of their own imagination, and a Utopia in America which properly has no basis in Scripture, but belongs rather to pagan, not to Christian dreams.

We forget the lesson at our peril, that the human vision is self-limited, the human achievement never flawless, that allowances must be planned into every settlement of God's Kingdom on earth, which can take care of human follies and weaknesses, that we must so trust in God that no need remains to punish his children for their frailty, only for their anti-social behaviour.

Thomas Hooker understood. Where he went there was compassion, forbearance, mercy tempering justice. "Mr Hooker, being suddenly awakened by an unusual noise, thought he heard a person in his cellar. He immediately arose, dressed himself, and went silently to the foot of the cellar stairs. There he saw a man with a candle in his hand taking pork out of the barrel. When he had taken out the last piece, Mr Hooker, accosting him pleasantly, said, 'Neighbour, you act unfairly; you ought to leave a part for me.' Thunderstruck at being detected, especially at being detected by so aweful a witness, the culprit fell at his feet, condemned himself for his wickedness, and implored his pardon. Mr Hooker cheerfully forgave him, and concealed his crime, but forced him to carry half the pork to his own house."[22]

At his death on 7 July 1647, "a little before sunne-set"—"One that stood weeping by the bed-side said unto him 'Sir, you are going to receive the reward of all your labours,' he replied 'Brother, I am going to receive mercy!'"[23] Do not forget. Take the Hooker Trail.

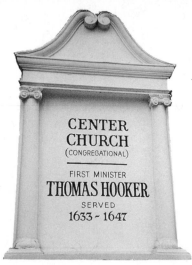

Notes

For list of abbreviations, see pages 23-24. *Guide* indicates this work.

Introduction

1. *Descendants of the Rev. Thomas Hooker, 1586–1908*, Edward Hooker, Comdr. U.S.N., ed Mgt. Huntingdon Hooker, printed Rochester, NY 1909, pp.viiff. NB. Richard Hooker, 1553–1660, alias Vowell, Anglican divine, b. Heavitree, Exeter, Devon, author *Laws of Ecclesiastical Polity*, 8 vols, apologist par excellence of Anglicanism & the Elizabethan Settlement of 1559 (see *Guide* p. 62 and p. 368 n. 51), but no known connection with the Hookers of Leicestershire, cf. *The Rev. Thomas Hooker An Alternative Descent*, J. R. Hutchinson, *New York Genealogical & Biographical Record* 48 (1917), pp. 393–98, quoted NEHGS, pp. 60–65, and all contemporary authorities, eg. *Oxons* 2:741.

2. More disturbing is the disregard for Hooker (and other key New England founders such as John Winthrop, John Cotton, etc) in contemporary English historical studies, orthodox & revisionist, which explore the influence of 16th/17th century Puritans on Britain. One too often looks in vain for meaningful references to the achievements of this fifty year old English notability (Thomas Hooker), whose first opportunity to put into practice his English-bred ideas came only when he reached Connecticut in 1636.

English Puritanism enjoyed two major materialisations, in New England and during the English Commonwealth via the Civil War. For English historians to ignore the New England practitioners of English Puritanism is like a reporter whose evaluation of English cricket is confined to their home tours, and overlooks their experiences in say Australia or New Zealand.

It is inappropriate in this guide to enter in depth into the revisionist debate on Puritanism which has gone on in America and Britain during the last fifty years or so. I have necessarily taken a middle path between traditional and revisionist views, although grateful for the corrective insights which have come from the detailed studies of the local primary sources now available.

3. DNB 9:1189–90 and HTS, p. 2.

4. HTS p.viii.

5. Venn, 2:403.

6. *The Town on the Street*, from the Notebooks of Samuel Ingham, Sturton schoolmaster 1875–1928, ed. J. Ford 1975, Chapter 6, John Robinson *Pilgrim Pastor*, pp. 101–06; cf. *John Robinson Pastor of the Pilgrim Fathers*, Walter H. Burgess, 1920; (Denman Library, Retford, Notts.) DNB 17:18–20; Venn 3:470, "b. 1576. S. of John who d. at Sturston, Notts, 1614. Corpus Christi 1592, Fellow 1598–1604. MA 1599," etc.

Thomas Hooker, A Brief Biography

Available Literature. Magnalia Christi Americana, Cotton Mather, London 1702, new edition: USA, Kenneth D. Murdock, The Belknap Press of Harvard University Press, Cambridge, Mass., 1977; Britain, The Banner of Truth Trust (Silas Andrus ed, 1853) Edinburgh, 1979; *Thomas Hooker: Preacher, Founder, Democrat*, George Leon Walker (Pastor, Centre Church, 60 Gold St, Hartford, Connecticut) New York: 1891; HTS (for Hooker's works see *Establishing the Hooker Canon & A Bibliography*, Bush, pp. 378–425): *Thomas Hooker, 1586–1647*, Frank Shuffleton, Princeton University Press, New Jersey, 1977; *The Writings of Thomas Hooker, Spiritual Adventure in Two Worlds*, Sargent Bush Jr, Wisconsin University Press, 1980: Hooker's published sermons stored in many places, sources such as John Winthrop's *Journal*, ed. J. K. Hosmer, 2 vols, 1908 (rept. 1966), innumerable monographs, articles, some to be found throughout this guide: DAB, 9:199–200: DNB 9:1189–90, *The Pilgrimage of Thomas Hooker (1586–1647) in England, The Netherlands, and New England*, G. H. Williams, Bulletin of the Congregational Library, Boston, Mass., 19 Oct. 1967, Jan. 1968, pp. 5–15, 9–18.

7. The wills of John Hooker of Blaston, 1558; Thomas of Blaston, 1559; admin. of goods of Thomas of Marefield, 1636; Feet of Fines re Thomas of Marefield's Leicestershire properties, and his brother John's (bu. Marefield, bequests to Thomas' sons John & Samuel), etc are all detailed in NEHGS, pp. 34, 60–67, L. Baddow History Centre; cf. G. L., Walker, op.cit. pp. 1–4ff; and Summary Genealogical Table 1, p. 28.

8. NEHGS p. 61; cf. *Guide*, pp.72.

9. NEHGS ibidem.

10. ibidem, p. 62/3.

11. ibidem, p. 63/64; cf. Venn 2:403, "of Birstall, Leics. B. there."

12. NEHGS, p. 63.

13. *Thomas Hooker, 1586–1647*, Shuffleton op.cit. p. 11.

14. *Magnalia*, op.cit. (BOT ed), I, p. 341; cf. HTS pp. 33–35, etc.

15. "a group of Puritans from the general neighbourhood of Chelmsford had gone to the place last named (Mass.) and were known as 'Mr Hooker's company' because they had been his parishioners or listeners in England", DAB 9:199; cf. *Writings of Thomas Hooker*, Bush op.cit. p. 10, etc. NB. *The Goodwins of Hartford, Conn.*, J. J. Goodwin, 1891, chapter *William Goodwin*, G. L. Walker, p. 78, makes it clear that Newtown was developed before Hooker's arrival, by order of the General Council to remove from Mount Wollaston (later Braintree, Mass) where the company had temporarily settled on landing; but see under Braintree, see *Guide*, p. 263.

Edward Johnson, in his highly original *Wonder-Working Providence of Sion's Saviour in New England*, 1654, part I, p. 60 (J. F. Jameson edition, New York, 1910) says the early Winthrop settlers "began to thinke of a place of more safety in the eyes of Man, then the two frontier Towns of Charles Towne, and Boston—and therefore chose a place scituate on Charles River, between Charles Towne and Water-Towne, where they erected a Towne called New-Towne," showing that the feared enemy was not the native Massachusetts tribes, but a sea-borne attack by the English.

16. "At the General Court (of Mass.) in the spring of 1634, those of Newtown complained of straitness for want of land, especially meadow, and desired leave of the court to look out either for enlargement or removal, which was granted; whereupon . . . they would remove." Winthrop, *Journal*, op.cit. 1:124.

17. *Hartford Yesterday & Today*, Robert H. Arnold, 1985, p.4. cf. *The Miracle of Connecticut*, Ellsworth S. Grant, ConnHS, 1992, p. 21.

18. *In and About Hartford*, Marion Hepburn Grant, ConnHS., 1978, p. 30. cf. *Miracle of Conn.*, op.cit. p. 2 ff.

19. Winthrop *Journal*, op.cit. 1:288–290, For Winthrop see *Guide* p. 385 n.14.

20. Winthrop Papers, MassHS 1944, iv, p. 77–78.

21. *The Founding of Harvard College*, S. E. Morison, Harvard, 1935, Appendix B, p. 382; but note *Thomas Hooker the First American Democrat*, Walter S. Logan, 1904, *Thomas Hooker—The Predecessor of Thomas Jefferson In Democracy*, C. S. Thompson, Cheshire Chronicle Press, Conn., 1935; "Hooker was a born democrat," DAB 9:200; cf. "he was the father of the Constitution of the U.S." NEHGS, pp. 14–20.

22. *Sources of our Liberties*, American Bar Foundation, ed Richard L. Parry & John C. Cooper, 1952, IX. *Fundamental Orders of Connecticut*, p. 115. NB. Whilst I concentrate on Hooker's part, it should be remembered that the major work on the Fundamental Orders was probably done by Roger Ludlow, 1590–1664, leading layman of the Dorset Pilgrims who sailed from Plymouth in the *Mary & John* (Mr Ludlow's ship, DAB 11:493), March 1630. Wilts. gentry; Balliol, Oxon; the Inner Temple (London); elected Assistant of the Bay Co., 1630; Deputy Governor of Massachuetts, 1634; a leading founder of Dorchester, Mass. and Windsor, Conn.—he presided over the first Connecticut Court (held at Windsor), drafted the Fundamental Orders (later embodied in the 1662 Charter) following Hooker's sermon, and also *Ludlow's Code*, or *The Code of 1650* which gathered together and codified Conneticut's laws. His enduring reputation has perhaps suffered from his reputedly quick temper, which may have denied him the constancy of high office enjoyed by Governor John Haynes; and by removal to Fairfield, Conn. (1639), & to Britain where he served on Cromwell's Irish Commission, and died at Dublin. But see *Dorset Pilgrims*, Frank Thistlethwaite, Barrie & Jenkins, London 1989 [reprint, Heart of the Lakes Publishing, Interlaken, NY, 1993], for his impact on the early settlement of Connecticut, cf. *Notes on Sources*, Thistlethwaite, op.cit. R. Ludlow, p. 74–5; DAB 11:493–94; cf. J. H. Trumbull letter to D. F. Haynes, dated Nov. 7, 1883, ConnHS Library, Hartford, "the composition of the Constitution of 1638–9, if it was not Hooker's, it was more probably Ludlow's than Haynes.'"

23. *Body of Liberties*, "composed by Mr Nathaniel Ward," Winthrop *Journal* 2:49 (see under Stondon Massey, *Guide* p. 310); cf. S. E. Morison, *Builders of the Bay Colony*, 1930 (Northeastern Ed. 1981), VII. *Nathaniel Ward, Lawmaker and Wit*, pp. 218, 219, 227, etc; cf. DAB 19:433–434.

24. *American Bar Fndt*, op.cit., p. 115.

25. ibidem, p. 120–214: for text, taken down in shorthand by Henry Wolcott Jr now in possession of ConnHS; cf. G. L. Walker, op.cit., p. 125, DAB 9:200, & NEHGS p. 18ff. See my sermon preached at the 350th Anniversary Service of the Fundamental Orders (1639) at Cuckoos Farmyard, Little Baddow, July 1989, Little Baddow History Centre.

26. For *The Half-Way Covenant*; R. G. Pope, Princeton 1969; cf. *Occasional Conformity*, Christopher Hall, in *Reformation, Conformity, and Dissent*, ed. R. Buick Knox, London 1977, pp. 199–220, on easing church membership regulations to accommodate third generation New England settlers; etc.

Preparationist Theology is a title given to Hooker's minute description of the stages of redemption which lead to full union with God. It constitutes the unwavering theme of his sermons. Calvinists were deterministic in their understanding of God's sovereign power at work throughout every part of their lives, but they were not fatalists. Calvin (see *Guide* p. 369, n. 52) had already described the stages through which Saving Grace works in the human soul. Indeed, in the earlier editions of *Christianae Religionis Institutio* (The Institutes) his position had been much closer to that retained by Hooker. "About the election of others we may not ask," he had written, "Towards others we must exercise a judgement of love and regard as elect and members of the Church all who profess the same God and Christ by tongue, by good lives, and by participating in the Sacraments" (cf. *John Calvin*, T. H. L. Parker, Dent, 1975, p. 42ff; ODCC,

p. 695f). The pity was that Calvin moved to a rigidly exclusive position never accepted by Hooker and others in the English tradition like Wm. Perkins & Wm. Ames (see *Guide* p. 361 n. 31) who helped to prepare Hooker's pathway of vocation, justification, sanctification, and glorification, as the steps by which the soul must progress towards the experience of its salvation, to which it must first have been divinely elected. As for the unelected, God demanded obedience to His Laws in any case. It was perhaps unfortunate that Calvin found himself firmly ensconced in established Geneva, whereas Hooker was more fortunately caught up in the dynamic, step-by-step development of a new sub-continent, confirming the need for preparatory (flexible) disciplines which could survive and expand in the new-found settlements. Sargent Bush's description of the preparation for glory offered by Hooker, *Writings of Thomas Hooker*, op.cit. pp. 146–302, is the most helpful that I know. It pointed his people to a new democracy of freely uniting States.

A bibliography of Hooker's known works is printed in HTS pp. 393–425. Even a glance at the titles discloses the direction of his mind. *The Soules Preparation For Christ*, 1632, *The Soules Ingrafting into Christ*, 1637, *The Soules Vocation or Effectual Calling to Christ*, 1637, *The Sinners Salvation*, 1638, *The Unbelievers Preparing For Christ*, 1638, *The Soules Implantation Into The* Naturall Olive, 1640, *The Christians Two Chiefe Lessons, Viz. Selfe-Deniall, And Selfe-Tryall*, 1640, *The Patterne of Perfection*, 1640, *The Covenant Of Grace Opened*, 1649, *The Saints Dignitie, And Dutie, Together With The Danger of Ingnorance and Hardnesse*, 1651, *The Application Of Redemption*, 1656.

27. Desiderius Erasmus, 1466–1536, educated at Delft, entered Augustinian monastery of St Gregory, and was ordained priest. He studied at Paris, came to England, 1499, with his pupil and later patron William Blount, Baron Mountjoy. Alternating between the two countries and Italy, he temporarily settled in Cambridge as Lady Margaret professor of greek and theology, 1509, where he completed his translation of the New Testament. He moved to Brussels, 1516, and Basle, 1521, ever pursuing intellectual freedom, mercilessly exposing superstition and corruption in the Church, thus contributing to the Reformation. But he wished to reform, not overthrow, the Church. His abhorrence of fanaticism, and humanist respect for free will, prevented him from actively espousing Protestantism. But he opened a way in Cambridge for all subsequent Puritan scholars to walk in. cf. Venn 2:105; Oxford Dictionary of the Christian Church, OUP, 1957, p. 459–460.

28. Martin Bucer, 1491–1551, Dominican priest, converted to Luther, married, spent much effort in reconciling both Catholics with Protestants and also internal Protestant divisions. "The dear politicus and Fanaticus of union," Margaret Blaurer, DNB 3:177. Went to Cambridge, 1549, influenced Edward VI, Abp. Cranmer, and Anglican Ordinal of 1550. Buried at Great St Mary's, but exhumed under Mary, 1557, body burnt on Market Hill. cf. DNB 3:172–177; ODCC, p. 204.

29. Theodore Beza, 1519–1605, New Testament scholar whose annotated Latin translation of the Greek New Testament is best known in its 1642 Cambridge University (GB) edition. A French Calvinist theologian, he was professor of Greek at Lausanne & Geneva Switz (where he succeeded Calvin as leader of Swiss Protestants cf. *Jn Calvin*, T. H. L. Parker, etc). His 1565 ed of the Greek NT, pub together with the Vulgate and his Latin trans, and his Codex Bezae (principal representative of the Greek Western Text of the New Testament, presented to the University of Cambridge in 1581, discovered at Lyons 1562), was a landmark in New Testament scholarship. Although playing a leading part in the Colloquy of Poissy, 1561, an attempt to reconcile Catholic and Reformed doctrine, he was rigidly determinist, holding the destruction of free will at The Fall, etc. and defended the burning of Michael Servetus at Geneva. His influence over 16th/17th century Cambridge students was considerable: cf. Mather on Hooker, "he was like Beza," Magnalia op.cit. 1:350. see ODCC pp. 163, 306, 1087, 1244.

30. William Whitaker, 1548–1595, Fellow of Trinity College, CambU, "champion of the teaching of the Church of England, interpreted in the most Calvinistic sense" (DNB 21:21), married Laurence Chaderton's sister-in-law (Venn 1:385), "exercised a wide influence by his devotion to learning and his impartiality," (ODCC p. 1454).

31. William Perkins, 1558–1602, "the first systematic Calvinist theologian in England who also had a clearly defined attitude towards social problems," *Puritanism & Revolution*, Christopher Hill, reprint, Penguin Books, 1990, p. 212. Hill sees Perkins' significance as interpreting the transformation from a medieval economic morality (feudal protectionism, work a curse fallen on mankind, indiscriminate alms-giving to the poor, surpluses consumed not marketed, etc) to a Protestant capitalist work ethic which denounced sturdy rogues, nonproductive monks, and the idle rich (p. 215ff). This led to a coercion of the lower orders of society, who now were visibly not God's elect, and to the reassurance of the middling and gentry classes in their moralising stance, who certainly looked as if they might be the elect, and who tended to become Puritans. There was more to Perkins than this (see *Guide* p. 142) eg. his dialectical pietism inspired by a vision of divine mercy, cf. Th. Fuller, 1608–61, *Worthies of England*, Perkins "humbled the towering speculations of philosophers into practice & morality," DNB 15:894, but it does help to explain the popular appeal of his preaching, & his long-lasting magnetism over Cambridge reformers: ODCC p. 1045–46; DAB 14:6–9; DNB 15:892–95; Venn 3:347; cf. *The Godly Preachers of the Elizabethan Church*, Irvonwy Morgan, 1965, re the concept of Mercy. cf. C. Hill above p. 214 n.5; & Hooker's last words, *Magnalia* 1:350.

Wm. Ames, 1576–1633, a name recurring throughout this guide. His influence over Hooker was incalculable. Old enough to be a mentor, young enough for companionship, he entered Christ's College, CambU, c. 1593, graduating MA 1601, upon which he received a Fellowship. His tutor was William Perkins, his Calvinism similarly uncompromising but progressive, allowing for the exercise of human will within an absolute Divine order. His particular interest (eg. *De Conscientia, eius Jure et Casibus*, 1632, a Protestant examination of casuistry) was to apply general principles to particular ethical cases so that, as a Fellow of Christ's, he refused to wear a surplice in the college Chapel, and openly attacked the "heathenish debauchery" of the students (*EncBrit* 1:850). It was during this period that he and Hooker became firm friends, but he was obliged to withdraw to Colchester (1610), whither Hooker aspired to follow a decade later.

Debarred from a permanent post there, Ames emigrated to Leiden, Holland, and, in 1611, succeeded his father-in-law John Burgess as chaplain to Sir Horace Vere, Baron Tilbury, commander of the English forces in Holland. Later he went on to Franeker University as professor of theology (1622). His wife died "sometime before the Synod of Dort in 1618," at which he had emerged as a European authority on Calvinism (cf. *The Learned Dr Wm. Ames: Dutch Backgrounds to English & American Puritanism*, Keith L. Sprunger, Urbana: University of Illinois Press, 1972, quoted by S. Bush Jr, *Writings of Thomas Hooker*, op.cit. p. 328; see *Guide* p. 348).

He retired to Rotterdam, due to ill health, shortly before his death, even as Hooker, by then also in Holland, prepared to quit for Massachuetts; Ames probably intended to join Hooker there, whither his widow (see below) followed. The two men had been collaborating over Ames' A Fresh Suit Against Ceremonies, to which Hooker was contributing a Preface. Ames' principle works include the *Medulla Theologiae* (1627), a systematic exposition of Calvinism; cf. DBN 1:355–7; Venn 1:27.

NB. i. Dr John Burgess, 1561–1634 "held a unique place in the so-called puritan section of the English clergy" (DNB 3:310–12). At St John's College, CambU, he followed Cartwright's opposition to un-Scriptural ceremonies as not unlawful but inexpedient, and was imprisoned in the Tower for a sermon preached before the King (1604) when James' Council was preparing to enforce new ecclesiastical canons. He emigrated to Leiden on release and took an MD.

Ames joined him there, & succeeded him in his chaplaincy as above. Burgess then returned to London, successfully practised medicine, but reluctantly conformed, and was appointed Preacher at Bishopsgate (1616) despite James' opposition. He moved to Sutton Coldfield, Warwick as rector, was collated to a prebendary stall at Lichfield Cathedral by Bishop Thomas Morton, and in 1631, published *An Answer Rejoyned to that much applauded Pamphlet Of A Nameless Author, bearing the Title, viz. A Reply to Dr Morton's General Defence of three nocent*

Ceremonies, etc. It is just possible that he did not know that Ames was the author of the *Replies* already published against Morton. In any case, the pressures on him to secure his new position were overwhelming.

By this time the daughter who had married Ames was long dead. Ames was stung into issuing *A Fresh Suit Against Ceremonies*. Hooker joined the attack with a demolition of Burgess' arguments in the Preface (see the discussion, and full text in HTS, pp. 299–377). The incident illustrates how deeply disliked were the imposed ceremonies, and how insidious the pressure to support the anti-Puritan measures, when urged upon insecure would-be nonconformists (see *Guide* p. 84; Venn 1:257).

NB. ii. Sir Horace Vere, 1565–1635, of Kirby Hall, nr: Hedingham, Essex, Baron Tilbury, brilliant younger brother of Sir Francis Vere, 1560–1609, "the first soldier of the day" (*EncBrit* 27:1020-21; cf.DNB 20:229–34) who trained many military commanders during his Netherlands campaigns, including his brother Horace & Myles Standish, Captain of Plymouth Plantation. Sir Horace was effectually in charge of English resistance to Franco-Spanish offensives after his brother died, and employed both Burgess & Ames as his chaplains, despite anxious enquiries by the English government. cf. DNB 20:235–9.

NB. iii. Myles Standish, 1584–1656, from a Lancs. Catholic background, became a Protestant soldier under Sir Francis Vere. He was hired in 1620 to defend the Plymouth Plantation. He made himself one of the Pilgrim Fathers, much more than a hired soldier, planning the physical settlement, constructing the fort, nursing the sick during the first calamitous winter, learning the Massachusetts tongue, acting as translator and negotiator, one of the first five Associates of the colony, a leading member to his death. He represents the Christian Warrior tradition so much a part of Puritan New England cf. DNB 18:882–84, DAB 17:500.

NB. iv. William Ames' second wife was Joane Fletcher. She went with their children penniless to Hooker's New Town (Cambridge) Mass., after her husband's death, but took his library intact with her, one of the finest in New England (Mather 1:236). She was the daughter of Giles Fletcher, of Eton & King's colleges, CambU (Venn 2:149). Giles graduated MA and LL.D, was a Fellow of King's, Chancellor of the Diocese of Chichester, MP for Winchester, Envoy to Russia, Treasurer of St Paul's Cathedral. From this background she went into voluntary exile with Ames in Holland, and the Hookers in New England. No doubt human love played its part, but for accuracy one must add "for God and the Faith within her." For Chaderton see *Guide* p. 142.

32. *John Paget's XX Questions (Propositions) and Thomas Hooker's Answers; October 1631*, "Q. 19 whether true repentance or any saving work go before true faith in those that are regenerate? Negatur. A. 19 There is a double repentance . . ." quoted in HTS, p. 290 (full text pp. 277–291). For Paget see *Guide* p. 348.

33. See title page to *The Application of Redemption*—the first eight books—book 3, "The soul must be fitted, etc.," printed in HTS, p. 416f; cf. Shuffleton op.cit. "he required evidence of election prior to admission to the church (but) the overwhelming majority of Hooker's published sermons aimed at leading men to seek Christ." (p. 147)

34. *John Paget's XX Ques*, A. 3, HTS p. 280.

35. *Epistle to the Reader*, anon, printed with *The Danger of Desertion*, Lon. 1641.

36. *The Soules Vocation or Effectual Calling to Christ*, Lon. 1638, 34.

37. American Bar Fndt op.cit. p. 120.

38 *A Survey of the Summe of Church Discipline. Wherein The Way of the Churches of New England is warranted out of the Word, and all Exceptions of weight, which are made against it, answered: Whereby also it will appear to the Judicious Reader, that something more must be said, then yet hath been, before their Principles can be shaken, or they should be unsetled in their practice. By Tho. Hooker, late Pastor of the Church at Hartford upon Connecticott in New England., etc.*, London 1648, cf. Bibliography, HTS p. 413.

Mather's contemporaneous analysis is important. He understood Hooker's work to have fallen into "two great reserves of enquiry for this age—the first, wherein the spiritual rule of our Lord's kingdom does consist, and after what manner it is internally revealed, managed and maintained in the souls of his people?" (ie. the application of redemption, or preparationist theology)—"the second, after what order the government of our Lord's kingdom is to be externally managed and maintained in his churches?" The first he delivered from "pharisaical formality, and familistical enthusiasm" (ie. from Papists and Arminians, from Antinomians and Levellers, etc) by his teaching; the second he secured in the Survey ("by the solicitous importunity of his friends"), agreeing with much of Rutherford, but going on to outline "a church congregational compleatly constituted," including "the consent—the people is to have in the exercise of this discipline." Mather, op.cit. 1:347–350). Here Mather quotes almost verbatim from the *Survey*, printed by A.M. for John Bellamy at the three Golden Lions in Cornhill, near the Royall Exchange, MDCXLVIII, p. ix (my numbering).

39. *EncBrit* 23:940; cf. DNB 17:496–98. The ref. to 'cut off the head of the Papacy, but left the body of it (in Archbishops, Primates, Metropolitans, Archdeacons) yet within his realm,' comes from *Survey*, op.cit. p.vi.

40. Quoted from *Thomas Hooker—Later Years*, David Humphreys, Banner of Truth, 1968, op.cit. p. 35.

41. Cotton's eulogy was bound with the *Survey* (n. 38 above), because the *Survey* was the first postumous publication of Hooker's works: also bound with it were *A Preface of the Authour*, Hopkins' and Goodwin's *To the Reader, especially the Congregation and Church of Jesus Christ in Hartford*, an elegy by Samuel Stone another by Ezekial Rogers and even, occasionally, Cotton's *The Way of the Congregational Churches Cleared*.

42. *Magnalia*, op.cit. I, p. 332, 333.

43. From *The Journal or Diary of a Thankful Christian* (London 1656) by John Fuller, Fellow of Sidney Sussex, Rector of Waltham, Essex, etc., d. 1687, son of Thomas Fuller (1606–1661. NB. Thomas Fuller was a student at Queens' College, CambU in 1622, after Hooker, & curate at Waltham Abbey, next Nazeing, home of John Eliot, & a celebrated contemporary author, eg. *Church History of Britain* 1655, and his much read *Worthies of England*, postumously, 1662). John Fuller represents the younger generation of Anglican sympathisers in England, who kept alive the memory of Hooker's generation's achievements: cf. Venn, 2:184/5; DNB 7: 758.

44. Shuffleton, op.cit. p. 6.

45. *The Danger of Desertion: Or A Farwell Sermon of Mr Thomas Hooker, Sometimes Minister of Gods Word at Chainsford in Essex; but now of New England. Preached immediately before his departure out of Old England*, 1641, printed in HTS, pp. 221–252.

46. I Corinthians, 9, v. 16. Paul S. Seaver, in his *The Puritan Lectureships, the politics of religious dissent 1560–1662*, Stamford University Press 1970, p. 290, seems to me, therefore, to misunderstand Hooker's sermon, "The Danger of Desertion" (above) when he comments "It was Hooker not the Gospel that was departing." Hooker is not an orator, making a point. He is in the grip of an awful prophecy of doom because of his vision of God's departing from England, and that is not to be dismissed by an ironic comment on his subsequent action.

47. *A Comment Upon Christ's last Prayer In the Seventeenth of John. Wherein is opened, The Union Beleevers have with God and Christ, and the glorious Priviledges thereof,'* etc., London 1656.

48 From *The Carnal Hypocrite*, a sermon possibly preached at Chelmsford in 1626, printed in HTS, p. 100: cf. *Foure Learned And Godly Treatises; Viz. The Carnall Hypocrite. The Churches Deliverances. The Deceitfulnesse of Sinne. The Benefit of Afflictions. By T.H*, etc, London 1638, see HTS, pp. 89–123.

49. cf. *The Application of Redemption, By the effectual Work of the Word, and Spirit of Christ, for the bringing home of lost Sinners to God. The first eight Books*: etc, London 1656, pp. 206ff,—"The Plainness of the Ministry appears when the Language and Words are such as those of the meanest Capacity have some acquaintance with, and may be able to conceive; when the Preacher accommodates his Speech to the shallow understanding of the Simplest Hearer, . . . all obscure and unusual Phrases, dark Sentences and Expressions, strange Languages are much

more to be rejected, as opposite even to the end of speaking, much more to plainness of the Preaching of the truth."

Marefield In Leicestershire

1. *History and Antiquities of Leicestershire-Tilton* (East Goscote Hundred: Deanery of Goscote), John Nichols, pp. 462–474. "In 1564, there were 28 families in Tilton; in Halstead 16 families; in South Marfield 6 families," p. 464. NB. John Nichols, 1745–1826, English printer, author of numerous antiquities, ed. *Gentleman's Magazine* 1788–1826, pub. 8 vols. *History and Antiquies of the Town and County of Leicester*, 1795–1815; cf. *Enc. Brit.* 29:657; DNB 14:447–450.

2. The Little Baddow Historical Society was formed for many other reasons, not least the prolonged historical records (see the Parish Chest) and research by local residents (notably Sheila V. Rowley's *Little Baddow, The History of an Essex Village*, 3 vols. 1975–1979), but specifically, in 1985, to organize a 400th anniversary celebration of the birth of Thomas Hooker the following year, which included the unveiling of two civic plaques to him at Chelmsford Cathedral and to him and John Eliot at Cuckoos, the first public memorials to Thomas Hooker in England, see *Guide* pp. 194 and 237; details available from LBHS and Centre Church, 60 Gold St, Hartford, CT 06103–2993.

3. *History of the First Church of Hartford, 1633–1883*, George Leon Walker, 1884, pp. 21, 22ff.

4. See *Vic Hist—Leicestershire*, vol. IV, *Social and Economic History, 1509–1660*, pp. 79–109.

5. *Thomas Hooker, Preacher, Founder, Democrat*, G. L. Walker, op. cit. p. 3–4; cf. *Descendants*, Commander E. Hooker, op. cit. p. viii. NB. NEHGS pp. 62 and 63, n. "bought a house and lands (at Marefield) as early as Easter, 1584, some two years before the commonly accepted date of the Rev. Thomas' birth."

6 For Kenelm Hooker see *Guide*, pp. 28, 56-57, 59, 71-72.

7. *The Founding of Harvard College*, S. E. Morison, op .cit. p. 268.

8. Ibidem The Quest for Revenue 1640–1650, pp.292–328 re Weld, Peter and Hibbens fund-raising mission, p. 303ff (and *Guide* p. 305). See also *Coming Over, Migration and Communication between England and New England in the seventeenth century*, David Cressy, CUP 1987, espc. 8:191ff, eg. Kenelm Digby's correspondence with John Winthrop, p. 209.

9 MassHS collections 8:1792.

10. Rise of the English Yeomen, see *English Social History*, G. M. Trevelyan, Longman, Asa Briggs, editor, 1973, where 3 classes distinguished, ie. peasants, capitalist tenants-at-will, free holders farming own lands, "come to great wealth, insomuch that many of them are able and do buy the lands of unthrifty gentlemen, and often setting their sons to the schools and to the universities and to the inns of court; or otherwise leaving them sufficient lands whereupon they may live without labour, do make them by those means to become gentlemen," p. 26, cf. pp. 109–13, 339–40, 436, 439.

11. For social change under the Tudors, cf. *Henry VIII*, J. J. Scarisbrick, Methuen 1986; cf. *The English Civil War, Conservatism and Revolution, 1603–49*, Robert Ashton, Weidenfeld and Nicolson, 1978 (1989 ed.) pp. 84ff; *The Puritan Moment, The Coming of Revolution in an English County*, William Hunt, Harvard Historical Studies CII, 1983, pp. 4–5, 17–18, *Make-Shift's Inheritance*, p. 23ff; *Essex at Work*, A. F. J. Brown, Essex Record Office, 1969 p. 49ff; etc.

12. Too much has been written about King Charles I, 1600–49, to cover here, but for your interest, cf. *Charles the First*, John Bowle, Weidenfeld and Nicolson, 1975; *King Charles I*, Pauline Dent, 1981; *Charles The Personal Monarch*, Charles Carlton, Routledge and Kegan, 1983;

Charles I and the Road to Personal Rule (how unsuited to his role was his personality), L. J. Reeve, CUP, 1989.

13. William Cecil, 1520–98, son of Richard of Burghley: St John's College, CambU., and Gray's Inn Lon. (cf. Venn 1:313): Eliz's most trusted Secretary of State and Lord High Treasurer, but cf. P. Collinson, *The Elizabethan Puritan Movt*, Cape 1967, especially Part 2, pp. 146–55, shows William as cautiously sympathetic to Puritan objectives (eg. championship of Gifford of Maldon, see *Guide*, p. 321): m. (1) Mary Cheke, sister of Sir John., tutor to Edward VI, (2) Mildred Cooke of Gidea Hall, Romford, Essex (her father Sir Anthony also tutored Edward VI) "most learned lady of her time" (*EncBrit* 5:593) sister of Anne the brilliant wife of Sir Nicholas Bacon and mother of Sir Francis Bacon ("warm adherent to the Reformed or Puritan Church," *Enc. Brit.* 3:135). Such patrons contributed to the rise and influence of Puritanism.

Robert Cecil, 1563–1612, second son of William and Mildred, heir to their gifts and offices; first Earl Salisbury, weakling youth, educated by private tutors and St John's College, CambU (Univ. Chancellor 1600; MA 1605, cf. Venn above, 1 year after Hooker's entry), and Grays Inn: undertook embassies overseas; MP for Westminster 1584–87; Lord High Treas. 1608. Refs. *EncBrit* (15) 3:3–4; DNB 3:1315–21 (William), 1309–13 (Robert); *The Cecils of Hatfield House*, Lord David Cecil, London 1973, Part I, p. 57ff; *Peerage of England* (8 vols), Arthur Collins, 1812, 2:582; *The English Spirit*, A. L. Rouse, Macmillan, 1944, pp. 100–101ff; cf. Rowse's trilogy, *The England of Elizabeth, The Elizabethan Renaissance, The Expansion of Elizabethan England*; and *Great Lord Burghley*, M. A. S. Hume, 1898, etc.

14. ie. Edward Seymour, 1506–52, ultra-Protestant, eldest surviving son of Sir John Seymour (early Tudor supporter who accompanied Henry VIII to Field of the Cloth of Gold etc.) brother of Jane (third wife of Henry VIII, mother of Edward VI), first Earl Hertford, first Duke of Somerset, Protector in the reign of Edward VI, who, as Lieutenant General of the North had led Henry VIII's punitive expedition against the Scots for rejecting his proposed marriage of Edward to Mary Queen of Scots, and pillaged Edinburgh (see n. 80).

As protector he tried to move away from Tudor centralism, repealing treason and heresy laws, resisting land enclosures, permitting social experiment. However, Mary of Guise rejected his plan of pacification for Scotland (her interests lay with a French alliance), and the landed classes resisted his reforms whilst Independents took undue advantage of them. Jn. Guy, *Tudor England*, OUP 1988, p. 210, claims "Somerset mishandled the revolts." He was blamed both for siding with the people and for ordering military reprisals against them, p. 209–10 (eg. Robert Kett's 1549 revolt, see *Guide*, p. 127, and p. 388 n. 33). And he was culpably rapacious in appropriating monastic revenues. Overthrown by the Council of Regency which had appointed him protector, he was placed in the tower and executed. His unwitting contribution to the subsequent history of Puritan expectation and frustration is immediately apparent, cf. *EncBrit* 24:753–55, and 25:386–7; DNB 17:1237–48; Collins *Peerage of England*, etc.

15. *Hatfield House*, Lord David Cecil, St George's Press, Manchester, pp. 12, 14; cf. A. L. Rouse, *The English Spirit*, op. cit., p. 99, and his other Tudor works. NB. *16th century Britain*, CCH, 3:32, attributes the Ermine portrait to William Segar. *The English, A Social History, 1066–1945*, Christopher Hibbert, Grafton, London 1987, attributes the Rainbow Portrait to Zucchero, and regards it as "in a sense the most official; there is the Queen, with an enormous head-dress, the arch of a rainbow in her hand, and with the motto *Non sine sole Iris*" (No rainbow without the Sun, a comment not only on Gloriana herself, but on the self-regard of the English, certainly shared by the Puritan Elect).

Nicholas Hilliard, the first great Elizabethan miniature painter, goldsmith, jeweller, b. Exeter, 1547–1619, Protestant Reformer, protege of Calvinist John Bodley (whose son, Sir Thomas extended and established the Bodleian Library, Oxon) with whom he took refuge at Geneva under the Marian persecution, but returned to paint many Elizabeth notables, incl. the Queen herself, from his Cheapside studio; cf. Victoria and Albert [V&A] Museum, London, brochure for 1947, 400th Anniversary Exhibition (biog, p. 7-11, and of I. Oliver p. 11–12); *Nicholas Hilliard*, Roy Strong, London 1967; *N. Hilliard and I. Oliver*, Graham Reynolds, London

1971, Her Majesty's Stationery Office; DNB 9:880–1. Isaac Oliver, 1565–1617, his more gifted pupil, possibly a Huguenot refugee from Rouen, see above; also *Collecting Miniatures*, Daphne Foskett, 1979, pp. 53–64; Hilliard, p. 51–55); DNB 14:1039–40.

16. *Magnalia*, 1:338.

17. *The Puritan Family, Religion and Domestic Relations in Seventeenth Century New England*, Edmund S. Morgan, Harper, New York, 1944 (1966 ed).

18. Ibidem *Parents and Children* pp. 6—86.

19. See *Vic. Hist.—Leicestershire* 4:76–109.

20. Letter to John Cotton, Apr. 1633, printed HTS, p. 297–298.

21. "New Answering Method", see *Guide* p. 172.

22. *A Survey*, see *Guide* pp. 34-35 and p. 362 n. 38.

23. See *Establishing the Hooker Canon*, Sargent Bush Jr. and *Bibliography, HTS, pp. 378-425.*

24. Magnalia, 1:345 and 346.

25. For Owston and North Marefield, en route to Tilton, see *VicHist—Leicestershire.* 2:270–274. This barely impinges on our story, but the presence of an Augustinian Abbey at Owston from before 1161 (part of an earlier church reform movement) with its history of piety, learning and hospital service, enclosing North Marefield now deserted, but once closest of neighbours to South Marefield, (cf. also *VicHist* op. cit. 2:21), of necessity left its impact on the experience and expectations of South Marefield, where the Hookers resided. For Tilton, see *A Brief History and Guide, The Church of St Peter, Tilton-on-the-Hill*, D. A. Blakesley, 1966, and *The Buildings of England, Leicestershire and Rutland*, Nikolaus Pevsner, 2nd ed. Elizabeth Williamson, p. 411.

26. For the Digby Family see *History and Antiquities of Leicestershire*, J. Nichols, op. cit. p. 462–74, for all succeeding information. NB. Pedigree I, The Digbys of Tilton, p. 473; Pedigree II, The Digbys of Coleshill, Earls of Bristol, p. 474. See also *VicHist—Rutland. 2:222f.*

27. Antiquities op. cit. p. 471, cf. G. L. Walker, *Thomas Hooker* op. cit. p .4. NB. Boyle's Epitaph is at Knossington, Leicestershire, (three miles from Marefield via Owston, see n. 25), where he died, *Antiquities* 2:658.

28. NEHGS pp. 64.

29. Of Sir John Digby, d.1269, Nichols says "was of great account in the time of king Edward the First and Second, serving both those monarchs in their wars, *Antiquities* op. cit. p. 462.

30. Edward the Confessor, 1003–66, son of Saxon Ethelred II and Emma, daughter of Richard Duke of Normandy. Educated in Normandy, he returned to England and was crowned king in 1042, but his interests were religiously Norman (his Archbishop of Canterbury the Norman Robert of Jumieges). He rebuilt Westminster (Thorney) Abbey, adding the great Abbey Church, first English example of Norman Romanesque architecture (*EncBrit* 8:990) part-consecrated, 28 Dec 1065. Politics he largely left to Saxon Earl Godwin, whose daughter Edith he married, 1045. This led at his death to a disputed succession, and the Norman Conquest. He was canonised for his piety, 1161. cf. DNB 6:425–32; ODCC, pp. 439–40.

31. *Antiquities* op. cit. p. 462, quoting John Leland, 4:29. For Leland, see *EncBrit* 16:405–6, DNB 11:892–896.

32. For Everard, d. 1461, see also *VicHist—Rutland 2:223.*

33. Ibidem, pp. 222–223. Their 7 sons were Everard, Simon, John, Lebbaeus, Rowland, Thomas, Benjamin, cf. Nichols, Antiquities op. cit. p. 473.

34, 35. Ibidem, p. 463.

36. Ibidem, p. 464.

37. DNB 5:956–957.

38. *Gunpowder, Treason and Plot*, C. Northcote Parkinson, Weidenfeld and Nicolson, 1979, pp. 61, 62, 76, 77, 82–3, 89-91.

39. *EncBrit* 8:260–261.

40. Antiquities, op. cit. p. 465.

41. Marie de'Medici of Tuscany, 1573–1642, queen consort and regent of France, m:Henry IV of France, mother of Louis XIII of France, Elizabeth (m. Philip IV of Spain), and Henrietta Maria (m. Charles I). Her political power, invariably directed to the Catholic side, and her later intrigues (eg. against Cardinal Richelieu) cast fleeting shadows over English history, cf. DNB 9:429–36.

42 EncBrit 8:261. Sir Kenelm, *Antiquities* op. cit. p. 466f, DNB 5:965–71.

43. DNB 4:961–965.

44. In *England and the Spanish Match*, Thomas Cogswell (pp. 107–130, *Conflict in Early Stuart England, Studies in Religion and Politics 1603–1642* ed. Richard Cust and Ann Hughes, Longman 1989) examines the consternation caused by the proposed match—"we are those on whom the end of the world are fallen" (p. 120); and the unprecedented relief when it failed—335 thanksgiving bonfires from Whitehall to Temple Bar in London (p. 108)—linked with the fear of a Spanish conquest which found expression in *Anti-popery* (previous chapter, by Peter Lake, pp. 72–97), and helped to popularise Puritan policies.

45 cf. *Buckingham, The Life and Political Career of George Villiers, First Duke of Buckingham, 1592-1628*, Roger Lockyer, Longman, 1981; DNB 20:227–237, etc. Buckingham's failures (over-confidence, ambition, vindictiveness, which turned him from a popular into a hated politician—and his effect on the Digbys) is discussed, *Court Politics and Parliamentary Conflict*, Christopher Thompson, pp. 168ff, *Conflict in Early Stuart England* above, cf. "the recall in disgrace, of the Earl of Bristol, England's Ambassador in Spain" (p. 170), see also *Puritanism and Revolution*, Christopher Hill, Penguin edition, p. 376ff, 1990.

46. Enc. Brit. 8:261.

47. *Enc. Brit. 7:576–77;* DNB 5:957–60; cf. *Leaders of the Civil Wars from 1642–48,* G. R. Smith and Margaret Toynbee, re second Earl of Bristol, pp. 18–20.

48. Edward Hyde first Earl Clarendon, 1609–4, Oxon and Middle Temple, Keeper of Rolls of Common Pleas (see Bramston, *Autobiography,* p. 255, *Guide,* p. 294), MP from 1640, constitutionalist, was "deeply stirred by the perversions and violations of the law which marked the twelve years of the king's (Charles I) personal rule—although he did not share the hostility of the puritans to Laud's ecclesiastical policy" (DNB 10:371). Attempted to mediate between Charles I and Parliament, resisted armed conflict, but joined Charles at Oxford, accompanied Prince Charles to Jersey in virtual exile, and to France where he worked ceaselessly for the Restoration of 1660, attained by support of Nonconformist leaders as well as Catholics and Royalists "united at that happy moment by a common loyalty to the throne." Subsequent oppressive measures, the "Clarendon Code" (1661 Corporation Act, which forced members of Corporations to receive Anglican rites; 1662 Act of Uniformity, enforcing use of BCP etc; 1664 Conventicle Act, suppressing Nonconformist worship; Five Mile Act (1665), banning Nonconforming Ministers from residence within five miles of a Borough) were contrary to his wish (eg. he had offered a bishopric to the Puritan divine, Richard Baxter, 1615–1691, author *Reformed Pastor* etc, who had played a prominent part in the recall of Charles II) but received his support once enshrined in law. That he was driven into exile by Charles II's less worthy advisors, not least amongst them Lord George Digby, underlines the tragedy of 17th century England, ie. men of vision and integrity caught in a birth-struggle of dawning liberty and democracy, often destroyed by the libertarianism it unleashed. NB. His influence in New England and Carolina (through the Council for Foreign Plantations) where he was less fettered by vested English interests, upheld their religious freedoms and advanced their material interests. His great literary work was the *True Historical Narrative of the Rebellion and Civil Wars in England,* 4 vols, Oxford, 1702–4: cf. *Enc. Brit.* 6:428–434; DNB 10:370–389. *The Lives of Clarendon,* T. H. Lister, 1838, is perhaps still the best biography; cf. *Clarendon and the Puritan Revolution,* Chaper 6, pp. 197–211, *Puritanism and Revolution,* op. cit.

49. Puritanism as seen by Martyn Lloyd-Jones (former Minister at Westminster Chapel, London, both Minister and Chapel in direct line of succession from the 16th/17th century

English Puritans) can be traced back to William Tyndale (1494–1536), his passion for making the Bible accessible to everyone, and his readiness to make whatever sacrifice was required to effect its translation, cf. *The Puritans, Their Origins and Successors*, BOTT 1987, pp. 237–259, et al). I see it as a wider response to the sociological, economic, and political as well as theological movements of the era, however inextricable they were. There is a plethora of books to argue every point-of-view. *History of the Puritans from 1517–1688*, 5 vols ed. J. Toulmin, 1793–7, is still basic as are Jn. Strype's works, eg. *Annals of the Reformation*, Oxford 1824: cf. *Tudor Puritanism*, M. M. Knappen, Chicago, 1939; *The Worship of the English Puritans*, Horton Davies, 1949; *Society and Puritanism in Pre-Revolutionary England*, Christopher Hill, 1964; *Anglicans and Puritans*, John F. H. New, Stamford, Calif., 1964; *The Elizabethan Puritan Movement*, Patrick Collinson, Berkeley, Calif., 1967; *The Origins of the English Civil War*, C. S .R. Russell, 1973; *The Rise of Puritanism*, W. Haller, New York, 1978; *The Religion of Protestants. The Church in English Society, 1559–1625*, P. E. Collinson, OUP, 1982, are noted in this guide. Contemporary revisionist studies are also covered by the essays in *Conflict in Early Stuart England*, ed. Richard Cust and Ann Hughes, Longman, 1989; *Puritanism and Religion*, op. cit. The particular interest of this guide is also served by eg. *The Puritan Gentry. The Great Puritan Families of Early Stuart England*, J. T. Cliffe, Routledge and Kegan Paul, 1984.

50. Robert Browne, 1550–1633, was a protestant separatist who exercised so considerable an influence over 17th century reformers that his successors eventually gained control of N.E. Puritanism cf. *The Elizabethan Puritan Movt.*, Patrick Collinson, Cape, 1967. Born at Tolethorpe in Rutland not twenty miles from Marefield, related to Lord Burghley at nearby Stamford, he went to Corpus Christi, Cambridge, where he came under the influence of Thomas Cartwright (see *Guide* p. 142 and p. 393 n. 73). He was the first to establish separate congregations from the Church of England, at Norwich and elsewhere. Imprisoned, he removed to Middelburg, Holland, published attacks on the State Church, but then recanted, and was episcopally ordained Rector of Alchurch, Northants. The Brownist movement, however, grew into the Independency and Congregationalism which later took root in England and America: cf. *The Descent of Dissent. A Guide to the Nonconformist Records of Leicestershire Record Office*, ed. Gwenith Jones, 1989, pp. 15–21—"the lines of essential Congregationalism were laid down by Robert Browne;" cf. ODCC pp. 201–222, 329–330, 529; DNB 3:57–61. NB. The Quakers were not organized until 1668, see *Guide* p. 87.

51. The Elizabethan Settlement, initiated in the first year of her reign by the 1559 Act of Uniformity, was designed to re-establish peace and unity in the realm by securing the middle ground between those Catholics (smarting from their loss of power following the death of Queen Mary) and those ultra Protestants (the Puritans, many only recently returned from exile, keen to recapture the power they had sensed under Edward VI's pro-Calvinist reforms) whose interests were on offer under a new regime.

There were four such Acts of Uniformity, all of a similar pattern. The first in 1549, enforced the exclusive use of Edward VI's *Book of Common Prayer*, as a means of national unity through a state church and religious statutes. Disobedience by the clergy could lead to life imprisonment.

The second, in 1552 rectified weaknesses in the last BCP, strengthened its Reformed stance, and threatened penalties against all absenteeism from the new national church, or membership of other denominations.

The fourth, in 1662, as an essential part of the Restoration of the monarchy under Charles II, reimposed the rights of an episcopal Church of England and reintroduced the BCP (both discarded under the Commonwealth), threatened all non-attenders of the state church, and required the renunciation of arms against the throne by all clergy and schoolmasters.

Elizabeth's 1559 settlement, following this same pattern, had repealed much of Mary's pro-Catholic legislation, reimposed Henry VIII's forms of worship (ie. a return to the first tentative steps towards an English reform) and the 1549 compromise BCP, but allowed some adjustment in favour of the Catholics, (not least a more open-ended attitude to church ornaments and usages), and introduced penalties against depracating the BCP, and for absence from public worship in the state church.

Neither of the more extreme Catholic or Protestant wings was satisfied, but the settlement offered a working compromise which lasted throughout Elizabeth's reign. Both disaffected parties were largely free discreetly to pursue their religious convictions within a tolerable degree of harassment, until the advent of the Stuarts shifted the balance of power from Calvinism to an emergent Arminianism which "was aggressively conformist and hierarchical, and in its concern for sacraments, for ceremonial, and for the status of clergy (and thereby the monarchy), was easily seen as a harbinger of a return to popery," cf. *Conflict in Early Stuart England*, op. cit. p. 6, drawing on N. R. N.Tyacke, *Puritanism, Arminianism and Counter-Revolution* in C. S. R. Russell, *The Origins of the English Civil War*, 1973, pp. 119–143: cf. also *Church Politics of the 1630s*, Andrew Foster, *Conflict in Early Stuart England*, above, pp. 193ff. The battle lines were clearly drawn by Arminian leaders like Abp. Laud, with a contradictory assault on the freedom of all nonconformists. Jacob Arminius, 1560–1609, had attacked Calvinism on the ground of respect for God-given human free will, but his followers in the Netherlands were identified with the pro-Spanish party, and this denied him popular support in England until, 100 years later, the Methodist movement under John and Charles Wesley restored Arminianism to its proper perspective, in their insistence on the openness of saving grace to all believers. So-called Laudian Arminianism would therefore be better termed a resurgence of Proto-Anglicanism, a patriotic revulsion against a supposed populist Puritan threat to national unity and sound government under a stable throne which did justice neither to Arminius nor the majority of Puritans.

The alliance of royalists with "Arminians" spelt the end of the Tudor Calvinist-Puritan consensus, as Stuart kings joined Arminian bishops in destroying the working unity achieved under the Elizabethan settlement. Even so, "moderate episcopacy was still to find some staunch defenders among the less extreme Puritans in the debates on religion in the early days of the Long Parliament" (*The English Civil War, Conservatism and Revolution, 1603–1649*, Robert Ashton, Weidenfeld and Nicolson 1978, p. 98), and some of the bishops still managed to protect their nonconforming clergy.

The Elizabethan settlement remains a crucial contributory factor in the making and encouraging of split-loyalists like Thomas Hooker. Whilst it lasted, their ambitions were just about contained. For the reign of Queen Elizabeth in general, commentaries abound. I have enjoyed—*Elizabeth I*, Anne Somerset ("penetrating biography"), Weidenfeld and Nicolson 1991; *Elizabeth*, Christopher Haigh, Longman 1988 (with a useful bibliography, p. 175ff); *The Virgin Queen*, Christopher Hibbert, 1990.

52. John Calvin, 1509–64, born at Noyon, Picardy, France received the tonsure at the age of 12, read theology at Paris, law at Orleans and Bourges, before breaking with the Catholic church in 1553. He withdrew to Basle, began to write the Institutes (a defence of Protestantism "comprising almost the whole of godliness and whatever it is necessary to know on the doctrine of salvation," *J. Calvin*, Parker, op. cit. p. 34), settled at Geneva, and there, not without turbulence, set up a biblio-theocratic state. He sought to influence the reforms of Edward VI, and provided a refuge for English protestants during the reign of Mary Tudor. His ability as a systematic organiser particularly impressed the Puritans, and is mirrored in the New England settlements, as was his austerity, discipline, dedication, logical clarity. His awareness of the divine right and promise will impress people for ever: cf. *John Calvin*, R. N. C. Hunt, 1933; *Calvin and the Reformation*, J. Mackinnon, 1936; *John Calvin*, T. H. L. Parker, Dent 1975; etc.

53. *Magnalia* 1:362.

54. S. E. Morison, *Builders of the Bay Colony*, op. cit. p. 40, 47ff. For John Winthrop see *Guide* p. 385 n. 14. NB. The phrase, para. foll, "The Puritans wanted a democratization of the clergy" is, of course, not to be taken as "a democratic clergy." That never crossed their minds! But their ministers must be chosen and ordained by members of the church locally operating, and all priestly offices must be exercised within a priesthood of believers.

55. *Puritan Spirituality*, Irvonwy Morgan, Epworth Press, London 1973, pp. 41–52; cf. *The Worship of the English Puritans*, Horton Davies, 1948; *Patterns of Reformation*, E. Gordon Rupp, Ep. 1969, pp. 123–30, *Puritan Devotion*, Gordon S. Wakefield, Ep. p. 59, etc.

56. *The Puritan Family*, Edmund S. Morgan, op. cit., II, *Husband and Wife*, pp. 29–64.

57. *The Puritan Movement*, Hunt, op. cit. *The Crisis of Social Polity*, pp. 64–84.

58. *Poverty and Piety in an English Village: Terling, 1525–1700*, Keith Wrightson and David Levine, NY. 1979. Whilst in general agreement with their conclusions, the breadth of popular Puritanism in 16th/17th century England must also be accepted, as shown, eg. in Collinson, *The Elizabethian Puritan Movement*, op. cit. p. 92ff, et al, where instances of nationwide enthusiastic support abound—Abp. Grindal besieged by 60 enraged ladies, "who descended on Grindal in his own house," to protest the exclusion of John Bartlett, minister of St Giles Cripplegate, the 500 Londoners who would "run to the Puritan lectures," the 2–300 women with "exhortations and all kinds of creature comforts," who lined the approaches to London Bridge when Gough and Philpott, Puritan lecturers, were banished, and so on (Collinson, p. 93): see my Windsor, CT lecture *Puritanism in 16th/17th century England, and its effect on the settlement of New England*, 1993, L. B. Papers.

59. See *Borough Of Melton Mowbray*, British Publishing Co., Gloucester 1990, for details.

60. Ibidem pp. 18, 19, 20.

61. Anne of Cleves, 1515–1557, Henry VIII's German protestant wife (4th), a mismatch due to Secretary Thomas Cromwell's ambition for a Continental Protestant alliance (and to Holbein's too flattering portrait; now in the Louvre), which failed from Henry's instant dislike, and a new need for more Catholic alliances which turned his attention to Catherine Howard as wife No. 5. Anne resided principally at Richmond and Bletchingley, Surrey, *EncBrit* 2:69, DNB 1:429–431.

62. *St Mary's Parish Church, Melton Mowbray*, based on Melton Times articles, 1983, ed. Gilbert M. King; cf. Pevsner, *Leicestershire*, p. 315, "St Mary's—The stateliest and most impressive of all churches in Leicestershire" (pp. 315–321).

63. Ibidem p. 18; cf. *The Story of Melton Mowbray*, P. E. Hunt, Appendix II, *Digby and Brokesbury Monuments*, where the reason for demolishing the Digby tomb is given as—"for we find that in 1580, Simon, grandson of the famous Sir John, was attained for the serious crimes of high treason, and dispossessed of all his lands."

NB. "Near this on the floor are three very long and broad flat stones—from which the brasses and inscriptions have now gone." One covers the body of Sir John, on another these words were still legible, "Hic jacet Robertus Digby."

64. For Ab Kettleby cf. Pevsner, *Leicestershire*, p. 71; cf. correspondence, Edward Grindly (Frisby-on-the-Wreake), and B. Jefferies (Eye Kettleby), Little Badlow papers.

65. Marquis of Granby, *EncBrit* 14:715f; for Waltham cf. Pevsner *Leicestershire*, p. 417–8; DNB 12:937–39.

66. Earls of Rutland and Belvoir Castle, *EncBrit* 23:943f; Pevsner *Leicestershire*, p. 95–101; DNB 12:931–42.

67. *The King's England. Leicestershire and Rutland*, ed. Arthur Mee, H&S, 1937, pp. 34–36.

68. Hallaton. *The King's England*, op. cit. p. 79–80; *VicHist—Rutland*, 4:121–132.

69. Blaston is of interest as the earliest known residence of the Leicestershire Hookers. There were 7 households in 1563, only 27 by 1670, a reminder that many New England founders were accustomed to living in tiny, remote hamlets, and made a very good job of it. The Chapel of St Giles, within the parish of St Giles, Medbourne (cf. Pevsner, *Leicestershire*, pp. 313–315, "decidedly lopsided") seems to have been a free organisation, determining its own affairs. This makes sense re Puritan history. It was rebuilt, 1714, again, 1878, in 13th century style (Pevsner p. 104). Nothing of the probable worship centre of the Blaston Hookers remains. It did have a bell-cote (*VicHist—Leicestershire.*, 4:22–27). For Richard Vines, cf. DNB 20:369; Venn 4:305, "B. at Blaston, Leics," M A Magdalene, Camb; schoolmaster Hinckley, Leicster, 1624–42; Master, Pembroke, Cambridge, 1644–50; member Westminster Assembly.

70. *Threnodia Carolina*, Herbert, York royalist, explorer Europe, Persia, Asia; printed in *Collections of Tracts*, C. Goodall, 1702, cf. *EncBrit* 13:340.

71. William Juxon, 1582–1663, another tolerant churchman who, whilst suspended during the commonwealth and only reinstated at the restoration, was happily acceptable to royalist and parliamentarian alike, cf. ODCC, p. 758. Laud "had taken great notice of his parts and temper—but greater of his integrity and polity." Juxon's "gentleness and tolerance" were stretched to breaking point by the extravagance and fickleness of Charles I's behaviour, but his loyalty never wavered, cf. DNB 10:1121–1124; *Leaders of the Civil Wars, 1642–48*, Smith and Toynbee, pp. 106–8.

72. See *Antiquities*, Nichols, op. cit. p. 462ff; Pevsner, op. cit. p. 507–8, "St Andrew. A most lovable church."

73. *VicHist—Rutland* 2:262.

74. For the murals, see Pevsner above; for Edmund king and martyr see *Guide* p. 262.

75. Another aspect of this dichotomy (Preservation and Destruction) is noted by G. M. Trevelyan re Tolerance and Repression. "The toleration of varieties in religion, though not admitted within England herself until 1689, was part of the very liberal practice both of the Stuart kings and of their parliamentary enemies in colonial affairs throughout this period," op. cit. p. 447f; cf. *The English Civil War, Conservation and Revolution, 1603–1649*, Robert Ashton, Weidenfeld and Nicolson, London 1978 (1989 ed); Wrighton and Devine, op. cit. *Tradition and Innovation*, pp. 16–41.

76. Oakham, cf. Pevsner, op. cit. pp. 491–501. He dates the Castle 1340. The Close by the parish Church of All Saints merits a visit; and the school founded by Achdeacon Jonson, 1584. It had a succession of Puritan masters, James Wadeson, John Wallace, Jeremy Whitaker, etc, cf. *Puritan Gentry*, J. T. Cliffe, op. cit. p.80.

77. Lady Anne d. Feb. 17, 1611, cf. *Antiquities*, op. cit. p. 465.

78. *Rockingham Castle*, attractive guidebook, text by Tom Stock, has a brief history of the area as well as of the castle, and the Watson-Wentworth family, resident for over 400 years. See *Vic. Hist.—Northamptonshire* 1:295; DNB 20:958–62.

79. *National Trust Histories, Cambridgeshire and Mid-Anglia*, Christopher Taylor, 1984, pp. 50, 68–69, 73; Pevsner *Northamptonshire*, pp. 176–83. Seventh Earl of Cardigan, DNB 6:136–38; *The Brudenells of Deene*, John Wake, 1953.

80. Mary Stuart, Queen of Scots, 1542–87, daughter of King James V of Scotland and Mary of Loraine (who was daughter of Claude, first Duke of Guise, of that powerful and power-seeking Catholic family of the Dukes of Lorraine, cf. *EncBrit* 12:699–703) was the mother of King James I of England. Her father died shortly after her birth, and she was declared Queen. Henry VIII attempted to make a marriage alliance between her and Edward VI, but through her mother's influence (who acted as Regent during the latter period of the inter-regnum) she was betrothed to the French Dauphin Francis (II), and, at six years of age, was removed to the fatal tutelage of his mother, Catherine de'Medici (1519–89, daughter of Lorenzo II of Florence, niece of Pope Clement VII, implicated in the Massacre of French Protestants on St Bartholomew's Day, 1572, etc; cf. ODCC, p. 250; cf. *The Italian Woman*, Jean Plaidy, 1952), and the corrupt French court. At 15 she married Francis, and reigned with him as Queen of France until his early death in December 1560. She returned to Scotland (1561), her mother having died the previous year.

The tale of conflicting interests, of her demand for Catholic rites against the dominant Presbyterian party, and of her personal duels with John Knox (1505–1572, the much persecuted, oft exiled, inexhaustible leader of the Reformation in Scotland, author of *The First Blast of the Trumpet against the Monstrous Regiment of Women*, 1558, a diatribe against her mother, Mary of Guise, DNB 11:308–28), of her early attempts at conciliation, her personal charm, intelligence and perfidy (A. L. Rouse's comment is revealing; "It pays better to be straightforward, especially when you are the weaker side," *English Spirit*, op. cit. p. 120.) cannot be detailed here. But amidst the Protestant-Catholic/Anglo-Scot political disturbances, the intrusion of her own scandals, especially the murder of her husband Henry Stuart, Lord Darnley, and her rapid marriage to the adventurer James Hepburn, Earl of Bothwell, Darnley's murderer, forced her to seek refuge in England, especially the *Casket Letters*, written to Bothwell by Mary, which linked her with Darnley's murder, DNB 12:1269; cf. Jasper Ridley, *Henry VIII*, 1984, pp. 135–45, calls Mary "cultured, intelligent and brave" but "wilful and obstinate," and comments on Elizabeth and Mary, "Both were sincerely religious, and both betrayed the religion to which they adhered for tactical reasons," a precis of Non-Puritan (ie. Medieval) Tudor attitudes!

In England, Mary's intrigues against Elizabeth , and her continued complicity in French-Catholic designs on both countries, brought about her inevitable downfall. The story of Cecil's attempts at a conditional restoration of the Scottish throne, and of his (and Mildmay's) ultimate trials at Fotheringhay, are well told in Anne Somerset's *Elizabeth I*, op. cit. pp. 38, and 431–7; cf. also DNB12:1258–74; Antonia Fraser *Mary Queen of Scots*, London, 1969; etc. For Fotheringhay Castle and Church, see *VicHist—Northamptonshire*, 2:569–76.

81. Richard III, DNB 16:1044–51, see *Guide* p. 105-6 and p. 379 n. 27.

82. Sir Walter/Sir Anthony Mildmay, DNB XIII, pp. 374ff, and 376. See *Guide*, p. 202. The Cleveland Museum of Art, Ohio, has a portrait of Sir Anthony as ambass. to Henry IV of France by Hilliard, c.1595.

83. Lacock, Wilts, see *The National Trust Guide*, Robin Fedden and Rosemary Joekes, Cape, rep.1980, pp. 270, 285–6, 310.

84. Uppingham, Pevsner, *Leicestershire*, pp. 514–9; Venn 2:480. For Isaac Jonson and Lady Arbella, see *Guide* p. 119-20 and p. 384 n. 13.

85. *By God's Grace, A History of Uppingham School*, Matthews, Whitehead Press, 1984, p.1ff; cf. *Puritan Gentry*, op. cit., *Marriage and Parenthood*, p. 80, re Puritan Schools at Oakham and Uppingham, Leicestershire.; Felstead, Essex; Dorchester and Blandfoot, Dorset; Repton, Derby; Lincoln and Boston, Lincolnshire; Northwich, Cheshire; Beverley, Hull, Doncaster and Sheffield, Yorkshire.

86. Taylor's pulpit remains in situ, *By God's Grace*, op. cit. p. 14; cf.ODCC, p. 132–5; DNB 19:422–9.

87. Bonner, see *Guide* p. 248.

88. *By God's Grace*, op. cit. p. ix.

89. NB. The Hookers were probably resident at Birstall during Thomas' time at Bosworth. I have simply advised that you travel direct from Marefield via Leicester. But it must also be probable that a child would be taken via the safer main roads from Birstall to Market Bosworth through Leicester, rather than cross-country. For Leicester City see *VicHist—Leicestershire, Social and Economic History, 1066–1509*, 4:31–75; *Political and Administrative History, 1509–1660*, pp. 76–109; *Wool Industry and Trade*, pp. 37–41; also *Buildings of England— Leicestershire and Rutland*, N. Pevsner, Penguin, 1984, Intro. pp. 201–7, etc; *Leicester Past and Present*, 2 vols, Jack Simmons, Methuen, 1974.

90. Leicester "until 874 was the seat of a bishopric" (*Enc. Brit.* 16:393). By the time of Remigious, Bishop of Dorchester and Lincoln (d. 1092) it had been transferred to Lincoln as part of a new diocese, then the largest in England (ODCC, p. 810).

91. "In the Civil War the greater part of the county favoured the parliament, though the mayor and some members of the corporation of Leicester sided with the king and in 1642 the citizens of Leicester on a summons from Prince Rupert lent Charles £500. In 1645 Leicestershire. was twice captured by the Royalist forces" (*Enc. Brit.* 23:394; cf. *Leic. Past and Present*, op. cit. vol. i, pp. 86–93).

92. Simmons, ibid. p. 7. NB. Simmons says the King made a further visit, "staying a night at the Countess of Devonshire's house that had displaced the Abbey. On the morning of 19th Aug. he went on to Nottingham where he raised his standard three days later, and the Civil War began" (vol. i, p. 87). For Charles I, see *Guide* p. 364 n. 12, etc.

Henrietta Maria, 1609–66, manoeuvred forcefully against the Puritans. If space permitted, a whole new section would be required of this guide, exposing more completely than I am able to do, the influence of the women whose input history has too often overlooked, or diminished. Indeed, this guide could be rewritten from a feminist point of view with benefit to any conclusions drawn. I regret having embarked too far along the traditional male line to reshape it now.

Henrietta was the daughter of Henry IV of France and Marie de'Medici; her brother, the next king, Louis XIII. She was married to Charles in the year of his accession (1625) on condition that anti-Catholic laws in England were repealed, and was at first estranged from her husband when this did not happen. After Buckingham's assassination, (see *Guide* p. 367 n. 45) the relationship blossomed into one of exceptional love. Her energies seem to have been absorbed by her husband, her children (Charles II, Mary Princess of Orange, James II, Elizabeth, Henry Duke of York, Henrietta Duchess of Orleans), and the gaiety of the Court. She became increasingly enveloped in politics, especially to support Charles' "divine rule," and that of the English Catholics. Her unpopularity intensified. After the Long Parliament was called, in 1640, she found herself under threat of impeachment (*Enc. Brit.* 5:908), and goaded Charles into his rash, fatal raid on Parliament, in an attempt to seize the five members most responsible, Pym, Hampden, Holles, Hesilrige, Strode (Jan. 4, 1642). London stood to arms against the outrage. The Civil War had begun.

Henrietta busied herself throughout the campaign, at first trying to raise support in Europe, then returning at the head of a small band of loyalists, to march to Charles' side at Oxford (1643). She returned to France next year, where she sustained her family in exile, but failed to convert any of them to Catholicism save Henrietta, her youngest. She returned to Somerset House, London, at the Restoration, but her strength was broken. She went back to Colombes, near Paris, to die. Had she but intervened with greater sensitivity for the native independence of her English subjects . . . ! cf. DNB 9:429–36; *Henrietta Maria*, Carola Oman, 1936; *Henrietta Maria*, Elizabeth Hamilton, Hamish Hamilton 1976; or treat yourself to some lighter reading, *Myself Mine Enemy*, Jean Plaidy, 1983.

93. Leicester was the capital of the ancient British Coritani tribe, known to the Romans as Ratae Coritanorum. The Foss Way became Ermine Street beyond Lincoln, and continued to the Humber, thus forming an early frontier boundary line (Latin, limes: cf. Roman Britain, Peter Clayton, Phaidon Press, Oxon, 1980, pp. 22, 178, 182), guarded in this part by Leicester.

94. The Forum (so designated by Kathleen Kenyon after her 1936–39 excavation but now thought to have been on an adjacent site) was more probably a public baths complex, of which the Jewry Wall (prob. Jurats, ie. Aldermen) alone remains above ground: cf. Pevsner, *Leicester-shire*, pp. 207–8, and Simmons op. cit. pp. 1–18. *VicHist—Leicestershire* also has good summaries of Romano-British remains.

95. *King's England, Leicestershire and Rutland*, A. Mee, 1937, p. 120. For Wycliffe see *Guide* p. 87; for Chaucer, See *Guide* p. 374 n. 100. For St Mary de Castro, *VicHist—Leicestershire* 4:369–86, and Pevsner, op. cit. pp. 212–5." Pevsner notes the founder was Robert de Beaumont, first earl of Leicester and the supposed date is c. 1107." He calls the sedilia "the finest piece of Norman decoration in the county," (op. cit. p. 213).

96. Robert de Beaumont (d. 1118) and the first earls of Leicester cf. DNB 2:64ff; G. E. Cokayne Complete Peerage, vol.V., 1893; etc.

97. *VicHist* op. cit., *Castle View*, p. 344, three parts only of the original medieval structure remains, the mound, the hall and some cellars, with gateway and some fragments of enclosure wall all now incorporated with St Mary's in a river-side Castle Park; cf. Pevsner, pp. 217–19.

98. Simon de Montfort, son of Simon of Montfort l'Amaury, Normandy and Alice of Montmorency, DNB 13:731–42. "What the Englishmen of his day saw in him was not so much a reformer of government as a champion of righteousness." (DNB, p. 741). See the remarkable contemporary Song of Lewes, *Political Songs*, ed. T. Wright, Camden Society; *A History of the English Speaking Peoples, The Mother of Parliaments.* W. S. Churchill, Part I, pp. 215–23, etc; *Simon de Montfort*, M. C. Bémont; *The English, A Social History*, C. Hibbert, 1987, Grafton, p. 138ff, etc. NB. re Runnimede (Runnymede), the traditional spot for the signing of the Magna Carta, 1215,

is Charter Island, lying off the meadow on the south bank of the Thames at Runnimede, near Egham (and Windsor), Surrey. The American Bar Association's Magna Carta Memorial (neoclassical temple, 1957), stands on the slope of Cooper's Hill above the River Thames, close by the J. F. Kennedy Memorial, both reached from a riverside car park.

99. Pevsner op. cit. p. 217.

100. John of Gaunt, Duke of Lancaster, see *Guide* p. 108; John Wycliffe, see *Guide* p. 87; Geoffrey Chaucer, English poet. The name derives from Latin calcearius, shoemaker. Chaucer lived in Cordwainer Street, London, the shoemakers' district, from the 13th century, but his father was probably in Thames Street at Geoffrey's birth. His wife, Philippa may have been sister to Sir Hugh de Swynford, whose widow Catherine married John of Gaunt (see Genealogical Table 4, p. 106) from whom both Geoffrey and Philippa received financial support as well as from his royal service under Edward III, Richard II, Henry IV. His significance was that, whilst essentially grounded in French and Italian literature, he first established English as the language of all subsequent English writers, clearing the way for the English Bible, and its effect on the Puritan movement. In addition to his *Canterbury Tales* and numerous other works, he was royal emissary, member of parliament, comptroller of customs, but story-teller par excellence; cf. *Enc. Brit.* 6:13–17, DNB 4:154–67.

101. Richard III, see *Guide* p. 105-9 and p. 379 n. 27.

102. *The Danger of Desertion: or a Farewell Sermon*, see *Guide* p. 214 and my *Growing Towards Greatness*, Hooker Memorial Lecture, Hartford, 1987.

103. The Guildhall, cf. Pevsner, op. cit. p. 221-2.

104. The Augustinian Abbey was founded in 1143. The modern Abbey Park covers 66 acres. Both are detailed by Pevsner, op. cit. p. 249. Cardinal Thomas Wolsey, 1474–1530, came from the middling-sort of family (Ipswich, Suffolk, retail butcher and other trades, property owners, church wardens) who later contributed largely to the Puritan movement. To that extent his success and failure affected Puritan thinking. If he could they could, God willing. His foreign policy when Lord Chancellor was designed to make England the arbiter of Europe, a positive step in the direction of colonising New England. As the first English prelate to accept the jurisdiction of its secular courts he further undermined the authority of the medieval church the Puritans were determined to extinguish; a process accelerated by focusing on himself their antagonism to prelatical tyranny over against the primacy of God's Word, and individual conscience, cf. "had all the qualities necessary for a great minister, and all the vices common to a great favourite," John Foxe, 1516–87, *Book of Martyrs*. p. 130 Book Society edition, London; cf. *The King's Cardinal—The Rise and Fall of Thomas Wolsey*, Peter Gwyn, Barrie and Jenkins, 1990, p. 609ff: Wolsey's death, described p. 813, ironically reveals he stayed at Scrooby, later meeting place of the Pilgrim fathers, see *Guide* p. 17, en route to York, before returning to Leicester to die: cf. DNB 21:769–81.

105. Leicester Cathedral, cf. Pevsner, op.cit. p. 208–9. Robert Herrick, fourth son of Nicholas who practised in London as a goldsmith, entered St John's College, CambU, 1613, but transferred to Trinity three years later, graduated MA from there, 1620, and was ordained by the Bishop of Peterborough, Venn. op. cit. 2:358; cf. DNB 9:704–6. NB. DAB, 8:587 carries a reference to a Henerie Herrick who "was one of the Founders of the First church in Salem in 1629," but I do not know that this was Henry son of Sir William.

106. Quoted from a sermon preached in 1986 at the annual Hooker Memorial Service at Cuckoos farmhouse (generally on the nearest Sunday to his birth and death on July 7th) by Rev. Geoffrey Roper, Minister at Christ Church, Chelmsford, the direct successor to Hooker's 17th century followers at Chelmsford St Mary's, taken from Hooker's *A Comment on Christ's Last Prayer in the 17th of John*, printed Peter Cole, Cornhill, London, 1656, p. 51.

107. St Katherine's Chapel, after Catherine of Alexandria, c. 4th century A.D., symbol of nobility, virginity and learning, who, because of her public protest against the persecutions of the Emperor Maxentius, and her demolition of the arguments of fifty pagan philosophers sent to destroy her faith, was beaten, imprisoned, broken on a spiked wheel, and finally beheaded,

according to a late legend: cf. ODCC, p. 249; *Penguin Dictionary of Saints*, Donald Attwater, 1965, p. 209. NB. Pevsner, "a set of heraldic slates to the Herrick family," op. cit. p. 209.

108. "It was Mr Hooker's manner once a year to visit his native county; and in one of those visits, he had an invitation to preach in the great church of Leicester." Mather 1:337.

109. "By 1632 the Puritans had succeeded in establishing a brotherhood of preachers, working in large measure independently of, though not in direct conflict with, constituted authority. Its members were linked together by ties of youthful association, kindred, friendship, and marriage as well as by conviction and interest. They looked mainly to Cambridge as their seminary and training ground. They had the countenance and support of many of the peers and gentry, merchants and lawyers . . . They did not in most instances go directly from the university to undertake the cure of souls—but perhaps, after an interval as chaplains and tutors in the households of sympathetic patrons, they commonly took up posts as 'Lecturers.' *Liberty and Reformation in the Puritan Revolution,* William Haller, New York., 1955, pp. 11–12. cf. *Puritan Lectureships* Paul S. Seaver, Stamford, 1970 (claims in Puritan strongholds, control of the lectureship gave the laity ecclesiastical power rivalling that of the crown and the bishops. cf. *The Years of Puritan Triumph, 1640–62,* p. 267–88).

110. "One of the chief burgesses in the town much opposed to his preaching there; and when he could not prevail to hinder it, he set certain fiddlers at work to disturb him in the church-porch or church-yard. But such was the vivacity of Mr Hooker, as to proceed in what he was about, without either the damping of his mind, or the drowning of his voice . . . etc.," Mather 1:337–8.

111. St Nicholas, "an unforgettable site, its square and rude forms towering over the Roman foundations and the exposed core of the Jewry Wall," Pevsner *Leicestershire* op. cit. p. 215; cf. *VicHist—Leicestershire* 4:383–87.

112. Francis Higginson, DAB 9:11–12; Venn 2:368 (includes his father John); cf. The Life of Francis Higginson, T. W. Higginson, New York., 1891. The relationships of the Higginsons with Hooker is also told in HTS, pp. 13, 259, 387, etc. For John Jr., cf. DAB, 9:13–14.

113. Mather, 1:347.

114. See HTS, op. cit. *Document X: Preface to Wm. Ames A Fresh Suit* for a comprehensive discussion of the issues involved: pp. 299–319, *Introduction, Background, Authorship* etc; pp. 320–377 full text.

115. DNB 9:833–5—of royal descent, Elizabeth I's "cousin Hildersham," protege of third Earl Huntingdon and William Cecil Lord Burghley, active supporter of Thomas Cartwright, William Bradshaw, etc, suspended, imprisoned, reinstated frequently, but no Separatist ("strong enemy of the Brownists" p. 834) a model Puritan reformer, "he loved all honest men" (Fuller); cf. Venn 2:368, Christ's College, CambU, 1576, MA 1584, Fellow Trinity Hall, Lecturer and Vicar at Ashby 1587–1632; cf. "the famous Arthur Hildersham" p. 119, *The Religion Of The Protestants: The Church in English Society, 1559–1625,* Patrick Collinson, Clarendon Press, 1982.

116. Many Protestant hopes rode with Henry Hastings, third Earl Huntingdon, great-great-grandson of the Baron William Hastings to be met at Kirby Muxloe Castle, see *Guide* p. 93-95. His mother was Catherine Pole (d. 1576) from whose descent from George, Duke of Clarence (1449–78) younger brother of Edward IV (*EncBrit* 6:428) Henry claimed succession to the throne after Elizabeth I. Allied to the Protestant party of John Dudley, Duke of Northumberland, he had been brought up with Edward VI (*EncBrit* 13:951), but escaped Queen Mary's censure through the influence of his uncle Baron Edward Hastings, professed Catholic, and Mary's Lord Chamberlain and Master of Horse. Elizabeth made Henry President of the Council of the North, to contain Mary Queen of Scots' Catholic pretensions. He was her warder for a time when she fled to England. His overlordship of Leicester is described in Simmons, op. cit. pp. 62–69. He "had his own pew in St Martins" (p. 63), and introduced the Wednesday and Friday Puritan Lectures. Dying without issue, the title passed to his brother George. cf. *The Puritan Earl,* Claire Cross, 1966.

117. Mather, 1:337. Mention should also be made of Adam Blackman, b. 1598, of whom Thomas Hooker said "If I might have my choice, I would choose to live and die under Mr Blackman's ministry" (Mather, 1:397). "A useful preacher of the Gospel, first in Leicestershire, then in Derbyshire" (Mather, 1:396), Blackman, a graduate of Christ's College, Oxford University, is claimed in Knapp's *History of Stratford*, Connecticut to have followed Hooker to Massachusetts, settling with his wife Jane and their family first at Wethersfield, and then, in 1639, leading a group of 17 other families, consisting of 65 souls (including "widow Curtis and her sons," ie. Elizabeth Hutchinson, widow of John Curtis of Nazeing, Essex, with her sons John, William and Thomas—their father presumed to have died en route, or shortly beforehand), to open up Connecticut under Hooker (*History of Stratford*, 1989, *Origins*, i, 3ff). They settled at Cupheag, renamed Stratford, presumably after Stratford in Essex whence many of the party originated. Knapp assumes that Blackman met Hooker during the latter's frequent visits to Leicester. If so, this provides a further personal connection between Hooker and his native county, plainly replete with mutual attraction.

118. NEHGS, p. 398 (65) and Genealogical Table, p. 28.

119. Blaby, "Perpendicular west tower of pink granite," Pevsner, op.cit. p. 104.

120. "The middling sort of people," cf. *The Making of the English Middle Class*, Peter Earle, Methuen, 1989, espc. Ch. 1, *The Middle Station*, pp. 3–16. This concept is crucial to any understanding of the rise of the Puritans.

121. "According to the records for 1619 he preached at Blaby where his sister lived, and Earl Shilton, Birstall, and Whetstone," see *Thomas Hooker's Early Life*, David Humphrey, Banner of Truth, 1:34. Pevsner *Leicestershire*, p. 420, portrays Whetstone St Peter's, buttress stone date 1335, 13th century sedilia, ogee headed piscina, 14th century tower, etc.

122. NEHGS, Genealogical Table, p. 1. re: Dorothy m. George Alcock, see Thomas Dudley letter quoted M. C. Rodger correspondence, 30–10–92, Little Badlow Papers.

123. "In 1620 a Leicestershire woman, Constance Wallen, was called to account for her absence from church. She said that she had been "following Mr Hooker" having heard him preach on two occasions, one Sunday at Whetstone and the sabbath following at Birstall," *Thomas Hooker's Early Life*, Humphrey, op. cit., 1:34.

124 For Stoke Golding, see The King's England, Leics, op. cit. p. 196; Pevsner also comments on St Margaret's Parish Church, *Leicestershire*, op. cit. p. 395.

125. Sir Reginald Bray, d. 1503, steward to Sir Henry Stafford (second husband of Margaret, countess of Richmond, mother of Henry VII). After Bosworth he was created Knight of the Bath and of the Garter, constable of Oakham Castle, Chancellor of the Duchy of Lancaster, High Steward of Oxford. Never was the stumbling over a lost crown more richly rewarded! He directed the building of Henry VII's Chapel at Westminster, and St George's Chapel, Windsor, cf. *EncBrit* 4:437–8. How much of this did Thomas Hooker know? He picked up Connecticut!

126. NB. Hinckley and Bosworth official guide, p. 41, "A stone column stands in Fenny Drayton to commemorate one of its famous sons, George Fox." Fox's father was a weaver, he himself an apprentice shoemaker when his quest for an "inner light" began, or an assurance of oneness with God which led to his itinerant mission, and the establishment of the Society of Friends, despite persecution and imprisonment; cf. DNB 7:557–67; ODCC, pp. 516–7.

127. John Wycliffe, early English reformer, born "Spresswel, a good myle from Richmond" (DNB 21:1117–1138): Master of Balliol, Oxford, vicar of Fillingham, Lincolnshire (1361) and Ludgershall, Buckinghamshire (1368; local tradition claims he worked on his translation of the Bible in the parvis, formerly built over the church porch, see Little Badlow papers) before Lutterworth, Leicestershire (1374–84). His attacks on the Pope, the Catholic doctrine of transubstantiation, and his translation of the Bible into English brought about his condemnation, but his Poor Preachers the Lollards (progenitors of Separatism), and particularly John Huss (1369–1415) Bohemian reformer martyred at the stake (ODCC, p. 667–8), spread his challenge against medieval ecclesiastic theocracy to the ends of the English Reformation. cf. G. M.

Trevelyan *The Age of Wycliffe 1898*, K. B. McFarlane *Jn Wycliffe and the Beginning of English Nonconformity* 1952; ODCC, p. 1480.

128. Towcester, see Pevsner, *Northamptonshire*, p. 433 (St. Lawrence), 434 ("Italianate" Town Hall), Lactodorum p. 435–6.

129. See *A Towcester Trail*, a first-rate precis detailing 42 sites, with original illustrations, published by The Towcester Local History Society, also town maps (supplemented by correspondence deposited at the Little Baddow History Centre).

130. See yet another excellent local guide book, *Towcester Parish Church*, James E. Atwell, Vicar, 1984; for Archdeacon Sponne p. 4f and throughout.

131. Samuel Stone, see *Guide* p. 337-39. There is a reference to his Towcester Lectureship in *Album of the Northamptonshire Congregational Churches*, ed. T. Stephens, 1894—"According to the record given in the church book, the church at Towcester dates back to April 6th 1794. But there is evidence from another source, showing that as far back as 1632, Mr Samuel Stone ministered in this town, whose views on church discipline were congregational. Mr Stone is described as a 'pious, learned and judicious divine,' and that his ministry was attended by the powerful demonstration of the truth. But seeing there was no prospect of enjoying liberty in his native country, he was resolved to withdraw from the scenes of persecution and retire to America, where he arrived in 1633." I am indebted to Mr Brian Giggins of the Towcester Historical Society for this extract.

132. *Magnalia*, 1:340.

133. Ibidem, p. 434.

134. Ibidem, p. 435.

135. *Memorials of the Independent Churches in Northamptonshire, with Biographical Notices of their Pastors, and some account of the Puritan ministers who laboured in the county*, Thomas Coleman, London, 1853, 21:357, *Memorials of the Independent Church in Towcester*.

136. Puritan Lectureships, see *Guide* p. 83, cf pp. 36-38.

137. see *Towcester Parish Church*, op. cit.

138. Edward the Elder, d. 924, *EncBrit* 8:989, see also *Guide* p. 336.

139. *Descendants of Thomas Lord*, Kenneth Lord, New York., 1946, p. 3.

140. Ibidem, Preface and pp. 1–6.

Market Bosworth

1. *Kirby Muxloe Castle*, English Heritage, Sir Chas. Peers, 1957, p. 1.

2. *William, First Lord Hastings*, Bernard Elliott, 1989 ed, especially pp. 3–8.

3. DNB 9:148–9 (Sir Hy. Hastings, p. 125); *EncBrit* 13:53. For Simon de Montfort see *Guide* p. 80 and p. 373 n 98.

4. John, King of England, 1167–1216, youngest son of Henry II & Eleanor of Aquitaine, known as Lackland because the royal territories did not stretch far enough to include him, although, as his father's favourite, he was endowed with castles, revenues, the lordship of Ireland. This latter he immediately forfeited by tyrannical mismanagement, a combination which dogged him through life. Involved with his brother Richard Coeur de Lion in conspiracy against his father (1189), he also attempted to seize the throne when Richard was abroad during the Third Crusade (1188–92), and alienated William Longchamp his Chancellor, the Pope, King Louis VIII of France, his wives, the barons, the people, even when submitting to them. Something of the turbulence of English history to which the Puritans were heirs, descended starkly from him. cf. DNB 10:839–54, for Magna Carta cf. *EncBrit* 17:314ff. Of the four copies

authenticated by King John's great seal, I believe two are in the British Museum, one each at Lincoln and Salisbury Cathedrals. Runnimede—see Guide p. 373 n. 98.

5. Hereward the Wake, DNB 9: 691–3; see *Guide* p. 128.

6. *EncBrit* 23:296. For Jane Shore, wife of a London grocer whom St Thomas More, 1478–1535, knew personally see DNB 18:147–8 and 6:616. NB. More was the son of a Sir John More, a student of Christ Church, Oxon (*Oxons*, iii, p. 1025) the devout classicist & jurist author of *Utopia*, 1516, Wolsey's successor as Lord Chancellor, 1529. He was one of the few who put integrity before allegiance to Henry VIII, opposing his divorce, and the Act of Succession entailing the crown on Anne Boleyn's children. He was committed to the Tower and executed, 1535, but canonised by Pope Pius XI, 1935, a model for many Puritans; cf. ODCC, pp. 924-5; DNB 13:876–96; *Thomas More*, Richard Morris, J. M. Dent, 1984. He admired Jane Shore's beauty, and "a proper wit had she and could read well and write, merry in company, ready and quick in answer," *The Life & Times of Edward IV*, ed. Antonia Fraser, Weidenfeld & Nicolson, 1981, p. 200.

For Elizabeth Woodville, Edward IV's Queen, founder of Queens College, Cambridge University (see *Guide* p. 138) and the powerful Earl Rivers, cf. DNB 21:881f, and 6:614–18. For her clamorous, parasitic relations, five brothers, seven unwed sisters, two sons by previous marriage to begin with, see Fraser above, p. 91 (ie. pp. 86–93).

7. Market Bosworth—A New History, Peter Fosse, Sycamore Press, Leicestershire, 1983; cf. Pevsner, op. cit. pp. 302–4, "neat triangular Market Place" etc.

8. See informative *Hinckley and Bosworth Guide*, published by the Borough Council.

9. William Pelsant, cf. Venn 3:338, MA from Clare College, Cambridge University, 1577; Rector Market Bosworth 1588–1634 (succeeded by son John, who married Mary Dixie, d. of the then Sir Wolstan), and Prebendary of Lincon Cathedral, 1589 to his death, 1640. Besides John (Trinity & Peterhouse colleges, Cambridge University), he was father of Henry (St Catherine & Trinity Hall) later Vicar of *Puritan* Wethersfield, 1662–84; Edward (King's College, Cambridge University); and Robert (Pembroke College, Cambridge University)—a notable Puritan family.

10. DNB 5:1027; cf. *Sir Wolstan Dixie*, monograph available from Dixie School, by Penelope, Lady Dixie, 1989; and Fosse above. He died without issue, his brother's grandson succeeding, from whom the family descends to this day.

11. See *Guide* p. 84-85.

12. See Lady Dixie above.

13. Bosworth Hall, cf. Pevsner op. cit. p. 304.

14. Dixie Grammar School Prospectus, 1987, p. 1ff.

15. HTS 18:378–89, and Bibliography, pp. 390–425; re Higginson and the 200 lost mss, ibidem p. 387.

16. "He had a most excellent faculty at the applications of his doctrine; and he would therein so touch the consciences of his auditors, that a judicious person would say of him 'He was the best at an use that ever was heard,'" *Magnalia* 2:335.

17. "Called him back again and again from his refuge (Hartford, Conn.) to face external threats to his community," Shuffleton, op. cit. p. 235.

18. cf. *The Book of Bosworth School, 1320–1950*, Hopewell; *The Bosworth Story* B. Newman, 1967; *School for the Community*, T. Rogers, 1969; and N. T. Parry (former Head of History, Bosworth School) 1984 correspondence, Little Baddow Papers.

19. Sir Wolstan's bequests were for £50 at the foundation of Emmanuel, 1584, and, in his will (1594) for £600 to purchase property to endow his two fellowships and two scholarships, DNB 5:1028. His portrait may still be seen at Emmanuel College.

20. Peterhouse was founded 1284 by Hugh de Balsham, bishop of Ely (see *Guide* p. 130, and p. 389 n. 42) but eg. the library was only built in 1590. For Sir Wolstan's other bequests, cf. DNB 5:1028, eg. £200 for his London Pest House, etc.

21. Bridewell House stood on the west bank of the Fleet River (ditch) at its junction with the north bank of the Thames. It was built in 1525 on the site of a former Norman tower, long

used as an occasional Royal residence, by Henry VIII for the visit of the Emperor Charles V. Afterwards, he and Catherine of Aragon stayed there during their divorce proceedings. It was handed to the city by Edward VI as a penitentiary and was destroyed during the Great Fire of 1666. For the site, see Anthony van den Wyndgaerde's riverfrontage sketches, c. 1543–58, or Samuel and Nathaniel Buck's panorama of Georgian London for the later building (*London*, F. Barker and P. Jackson, Cassells, 1979, pp. 48–55 and 176–183); cf. *EncBrit* 4:528. St Bartholomew's Hospital, Smithfields, is London's oldest, founded in 1123 by Henry I's former jester, Rohere, who turned with others at court to religion following the tragic death of Henry's son in the White Ship (cf. *London*, above, pp. 20, 201). St Thomas's (Thomas Becket, 1118–1170, better known by his contemporaries as Thomas of London, Chancellor and martyred Archbishop of Canterbury) at Southwark, is the other medieval "hospital of any consequence" to survive into modern times. Now rebuilt in Lambeth Palace Road, on the Thames embankment opposite the Houses of Parliament (cf. *London*, above, pp. 201, 370).

22. cf. *The English, A Social History, 1066–1945*, Christopher Hibbert, Grafton, 1987, p. 267, cf. chapter 24, *Schoolboys & Schoolgirls* (17th century) pp. 265–276.

23. Shuffleton, op. cit., p. 8.

24. HTS, p. 354; DNB 2:1090–93, cf. DNB 3:1135; Venn I, p. 202.

25. *Magnalia* 1:333; "Mr Hooker answered 'I can compare with any man living for fears!'" p. 346; but cf. Hooker's conversion under Simeon Ashe, *Guide* p. 146-47.

26. HTS, Document V, Intro, pp. 147–51 and text, pp. 152–86.

27. Richard III, 11th child of Richard, Duke of York & Cecily Neville (see Genealogical Table No 4, *Guide* p. 106), born Fotheringhay Castle, brought up under constant threats to his life, made Duke of Gloucester after his elder brother's victories at Towton and Tewkesbury and ascent of throne as Edward IV. Became Lord Protector at Edward's death and seized throne after mysterious death of princes in the Tower (Edward V and Richard) 1483. Reached Leicester at sunset, 20 Aug. 1485, to oppose Henry Tudor's rebel army; camped outside Market Bosworth 21st; fatally joined battle at Bosworth Field, 22nd: cf. *The Hist. of King Richard III*, Sir Thomas More, ed. R. S. Sylvester, Yale, 1963; *King Richard The Third*, William Shakespeare; *Richard III, A Study in Service*, Rosemary Horrox, CUP, 1989 (CambU studies in medieval life and thought); *Richard III as Duke of Gloucester and King of England*, Caroline A. Halstead, 2 vols, Longman, 1980; DNB 16:1044–51. For Nevilles, cf. DNB 14:243ff, 273.

28. Henry VII, cf. DNB 9:520–27. For his descent & regal claim, see Genealogical Table No 4, p. 106. For John of Gaunt, DNB 10:854–64: Catherine Swynford, DNB 19:243–44; Beauforts, especially Lady Margaret (1443–1509), DNB 2:38ff, 48–9: Owen Tudor, DNB 19:1215: Catherine de Valois (1435–1504) m. Henry V, *EncBrit* 5:331–2.

29. Lord Thomas Stanley, 1435–1504, Earl Derby, whose son Lord Strange was appointed Constable of England by Richard III, cf. DNB 18:962–65. His brother Sir William Stanley (d. 1495) was Justiciar of North Wales with a personal army of 3000 "redcoats." He may have lived at Chirk Castle (see *Guide* pp. 333) & interviewed Henry VII at least twice immediately before the Battle of Bosworth. However, the Stanleys refused to commit their army to either side, and took up a strategic position on Hanging Hill at Bosworth. After intervention for Henry VII, he was made Lord Chamberlain (DNB 18:968–69). The brevity of the battle (about two hours) and the small number of casualties, suggest Richard III had been unable to inspire much enthusiasm or loyalty. NB. see *Guide* p. 392 n. 64.

30. "If this be all they have to say—I shall make them conform themselves, or I will harry them out of the land," DNB 10:606 (for the reign of James I, see pp. 598–618); so *King James I*, David Matthew, 1967; *The Reign of James VI and I*, ed. A. G. R. Smith, 1973; *King James VI of Scotland and I of England*, Antonia Frazer, Weidenfeld & Nicolson, 1974; *James I of England*, Caroline Bingham, Weid. & Nicol 1981; cf. *The Stuarts. A Study in English Kingship*, J. P. Kenyon, 3rd. ed. 1966; etc, etc.

31. The rough but romantic episode of Lady Jane Grey is unavoidable in English 16th century historical literature, but you may enjoy Hester Chapman's (1962), or David Matthew's

(1972) biographies of the same title if you do not know them. Pevsner describes the ruined Great House in his *Buildings of England, Leicestershire & Rutland*, p. 108ff. It was built between 1490–1505 by Thomas Grey, Marquis of Dorset, Jane's father. She was born, and spent most of her short life, there. It is among the earliest examples of lozenge decoration on brick surfaces (bricks interspersed with vitrified headers) typical of later Tudor mansions. When I last visited, red and fallow deer ranged the park in local habitation of the past tragedy.

32. NEHGS op. cit. p. 64–65.

33. Pevsner describes St James the Great (*Leicestershire & Rutland*, p. 102–103). Correspondence with the Birstall and District Local History Society suggests that if Hooker taught at a school here, it must have been in neighbouring Belgrave, now engulfed by Leicester's inner city sprawl.

34. Shuffleton, op. cit. p. 11, "If the people of Birstall wanted a teacher of reading and writing for their children, they would probably have asked the master of some respected grammar school, like Market Bosworth, to recommend a promising scholar." But see above. I think Shuffleton was offering an intelligent guess without the benefit of first visiting Birstall, or coming to know anything about its depressed farm labourers, whose poverty would have prevented a trip to Market Bosworth as surely as it would have stifled any educational ambitions, apart from some other very exceptional farmstead such as may have provided the Hookers with temporary residence.

35. DNB 10:921 (cf. pp. 919–935); cf. Penelope Lady Dixie, 1989 monograph op. cit., p. 3.

36. Thurcaston, Leics, cf. Pevsner *Leicestershire* pp. 40-9. The font "perpendicular unusual circular bowl with a protruding moulding above the octagonal base," p. 407. He thinks the Latimer House, "A mid 15c. cruck-built range," doubtful.

37. Latimer, cf. DNB 11:613–20; Venn 3:49; ODCC, p. 788; *Hugh Latimer*, Harold S. Darby, Epworth, 1953; etc.

38. Thomas Cranmer, 1489–1556, Archbishop of Canterbury, see *Guide* p. 153.

39. "My father was a yeoman and had no lands of his own, only he had a farm of three or four pound by year at the uttermost, and hereupon he tilled so much as kept a dozen men . . .. He kept hospitality for his poor neighbours, and some alms he gave to the poor. And all this he did of the said farm, where he that now hath it payeth sixteen pound by year, or more, and is not able to do anything for his prince, for himself, nor for his children, or give a cup of drink to the poor," quoted from Latimer's *Sermons*, H. S. Darby above, p. 9. Small wonder Henry VIII was displeased at this blunt contrast between his and his father's reigns. For Latimer's burning, cf. Foxe's *Book of Martyrs*, 11:284–93 and 11:303.

40. Nicholas Ridley, 1500–55, bishop of London hailed from Northumberland, but also studied at CambU (Pembroke Hall, becoming Fellow, & Master of Pembroke 1540–53, Venn 3:458), and at the Sorbonne, Paris. Chaplain to Cranmer, 1537, he too was slow to adopt reform. As bishop of Rochester (1547), and, on Bonner's deprivation, of London (1550) he championed the poor. He attempted to woo Princess Mary from Catholicism, campaigned for Lady Jane Grey, and was sent to the Tower when Mary overthrew her rival, despite a humble appeal to her for pardon. He continued to advocate Calvinism from prison, was condemned with Cranmer and Latimer, to "light his candle" with the latter at Oxford, Oct. 16, 1555. DNB 16:1172-5; ODCC, p. 1165; Foxe above.

There are plenty of books about Queen Mary Tudor, 1516–58, eg. *Bloody Mary*, Carolly Erickson, Dent, 1978; *Mary Tudor, A Life*, David Loades, Blackwell, 1989. It is important to remember the impact made on her by the innocent shame and sorrow of her mother Catherine of Aragon, & her own humiliating treatment by Henry VIII, who did not stop at pretending her illegitimacy. I think she never managed to contain her unhappiness and anger; important, too, to recognise the anger and pain of persecuted Catholics in England under the other Tudors, nobles and commoners, and the widespread rejoicing in the temporary relief from often unwanted Protestant Reforms her reign brought to many inarticulate English. For Philip of

Spain, m. Mary 1554 (and his other wives, Maria of Portugal m. 1543; Elizabeth de Valois, 1559; Anna of Austria, 1570), cf. *EncBrit* (15) 9:376–7.

Cambridge

1. Here we take leave of the Welland. It has traced the southern boundary of Hooker's Midlands region from Market Harborough, skirting south of Blaston and Medbourne, past Rockingham where it shortly is joined by the Eye Brook near Stoke Dry, and so to Stamford, Market Deeping, Crowland Abbey, Spalding and The Wash below Boston, hemming in the Marefield area from Northampton's forests, but opening the way to the North European trade routes.

Stamford (cf. *The Town of Stamford. A Survey by the Royal Commission on Historical Monuments*, Her Majesty's Stationery Office 1977, its commentary, maps and illustrations everything that a report should be) boasted 14 churches. Of those remaining, All Saints ("The hub of Stamford." Pevsner, op. cit., *Lincolnshire* pp. 651 and 661–3), referred to in Domesday survey, is in Red Lion Square; St George's, rebuilt in the 15th century, is in St George's Square; St John's, 14th century perpendicular, is in St John's Street; St Martin's, mostly 1430, (where Lord Burghley lies buried, his effigy splendid in armour and garter robes, "Alabaster—a six-poster— recumbent effigy on a half-rolled-up mat," Pevsner, ibid. p. 661), is in High St; St Mary's is in St Mary's Hill,—look at that 13th century tower and later spire!; and St Michael's, now closed, is also in High Street.

The town owed its early prosperity to a fort erected by the Danes on the north bank of the Welland, which enhanced its power as a trading settlement on the great north road: and to an influx of monastic houses, Augustinians (1316), Benedictines (7th c. St Leonard's), Carmelites (1291), Franciscans (also 13th c.), Gilbertines (from 1291), Dominicans (1240). The influence of the monasteries on early England forms a separate study, but every revisionist author needs to be constantly aware that the land of Hooker's (ie. Puritanism's) origins was saturated with religious foundations. The Museum in Broad St runs an excellent Tourist Information Centre.

2. Burghley House (barely over the border, in Cambridgeshire), built between 1552–89, on the manor he had inherited from his father by William Cecil (see *Guide* p. 47: acted as his own architect, cf. *Elizabeth's England*, David Birt, Longmans, 1981, ch.5, *Ministers and Courtiers, Burghley House*, pp. 58–68); cf. *The English Country House and its furnishings*, Michael L. Wilson, Batsford, 1977, pp. 26, 49, 162; Pevsner, op. cit. *Northamptonshire, pp. 48–60*.

3. Hereward the Wake, see *Guide* p. 128. For Bourne, see *VicHist—Lincolnshire* 2:177.

4. Grimsthorpe Castle, seat of the earls of Ancaster, Lord Willoughby de Eresby. Pevsner, Lincolnshire, pp. 71–73 and 554–558, claims the great hall "is unquestionably Vanbrugh's finest room" (p. 557). Constructed on site of a 13th century castle, with Vaudrey Abbey (Vallis Dei, Cistercian, 1147, cf. *VicHist—Lincolnshire* 2:143) formerly on the south side of the dividing lake, the castle was a wedding gift from Henry VIII to the ninth Baron Willoughby when he married Maria de Salinas, lady-in-waiting to Catherine of Aragon. Their sole heir, Catherine, left an orphan at age 5-6, was made a ward of Henry's favourite Charles Brandon, Duke of Suffolk. Brandon later married his ward. On his death she narrowly avoiding being Henry VIIIth last wife, but married a commoner, her trusted estate manager Richard Bertie (cf. *A History of Lincolnshire*, Alan Rogers 1970, pp. 50–55). Devout protestants, they suffered under the Marian persecution and fled as far as Poland. But, a story repeated over and again in this guide, their grandson, Robert Earl Lindsey, commanded the army of Charles I at Edgehill, first battle of the

English Civil War, where he and two of his sons lost their lives, whilst Montague, inheriting as the 2nd Earl Lindsey, lived to attend the king on the scaffold, one of only four peers of the realm at Charles I's burial, cf. *Lincolnshire*, Walter Marsden, Batsford, 1977, pp. 152–4; cf. *Portrait of Lincolnshire*, Michael Lloyd, published by Robert Hale, London, 1983, pp. 22, 23, 32–36; etc. Sir John Vanbrugh, 1664–1726, portrayed almost everything that was abhorrent to Puritans. Born in London, he continued his studies in France, and also saw military service there, where he was imprisoned in the Bastille on a charge of espionage. He used the time to write *The Provok't Wife*, one of the many libertine comedies to pour from his pen. But his greater fame derived from his flamboyant genius in Palladian architecture (the neo-classical style of the 16th century Italian, Palladio). Charles Howard, third Earl of Carlisle, commissioned him to build Castle Howard (1714). Kneller Hall, Hounslow, London, followed, and Blenheim Palace, Greenwich Hospital, Eastbury in Dorset, Seaton-Delaval in Northumberland, King's Weston at Bristol, Claremont, Grimsthorpe and many more. His was the unrestrained exuberance of the post-pilgrim period, a casting to the winds of the moral restraints which distinguished the Puritans. Typically, Vanbrugh's designs took little account of comfort or convenience, sacrificing everything for artistic effect. At least the sober Puritans would have kept the kitchens nearer to the dining rooms! cf. DNB 20:86–94; *EncBrit* 27:880; *EncBrit*(15) 12:260. For Capability Brown see *Guide* p. 133 and p. 391 n. 51.

    5. cf. *Excavations on the Site of Sempringham Priory*, Rose Graham and H. S. Braun, Journal, British Archaeological Association, 3rd series, V, 1940; St *Gilbert of Sempringham and the Gilbertines*, R. Graham; DNB 7:1194–96; *St Gilbert of Sempringham His Life and Achievement*, Raymonde Foreville; also, useful summaries in the church guide, *Sempringham*, C. F. Ward, & *VicHist— Lincolnshire* 2:179–186.

    6 HTS p. 17; cf. DAB 20:287. The meetings are described in Sempringham & St Gilbert & the Gilbertines, Eric W. Iredale, Pointon, Lincolnshire, 1992, pp. 32–34.

    7. John Cotton, "Patriarch of New England" (DAB 4:460–2), born at Derby, Dec. 4, 1584, into the pious family of an affluent lawyer (Roland Cotton), was sent to Trinity, CambU in his 13th year, gained his MA at 21, and, that same year (1606) a Fellowship at Emmanuel in recognition of his excellence at Hebrew, and Old Testament studies. There he received a spiritual awakening after the Puritan pattern, took holy orders (priested at Lincoln Cathedral, July 13, 1610), and, at 27, was inducted into the important living of St Botolph's, Boston by his bishop, and it is said, by popular vote inasmuch as the mayor twice accidentally gave his casting vote in favour of Cotton (*Magnalia* 1:257)! His ministry continued in persuasive controversy. He introduced Puritan practices into the liturgy to the annoyance of some, but the enthusiastic approval of the many who followed him even to New England. He travelled to Southampton to preach the farewell sermon before Winthrop's company sailed in 1630, but not until 1632 was he arraigned before the Court of High Commission. He fled to London (see *Guide* p. 352), sent a letter of resignation to his bishop (7 May 1632), whose support had been unfailing, and emigrated with his second wife, Sarah (Hawkbridge) Story, and with Hooker, in the *Griffin* (July, 1633), reaching Mass. Sept. 4 that same year. Their first son, Seaborn, was born during the voyage. Within a month Cotton, already a firm friend of John Winthrop, was appointed teacher at Boston, and began to exercise a dominant ministry. "Whatever he pronounced in the pulpit became either the law of the land or the practice of the church" (DAB 4:461). But he had his failures. His *Abstract of the Lawes of New England*, based too strictly on Mosaic law, was rejected by the Massachuetts General Court, 1636. His championship of Anne Hutchinson (see *Guide* p. 125 and p. 387 n. 27) and subsequent volte face, not only led to a loss of face, "from that time he became more narrow and bitter in his views" (DAB 4:461). However, in Mass., his will generally prevailed, as, eg. over that of his proposed colleague, Roger Williams, both in Williams' assault on Boston's ties with the Church of England, and on the shared authority of Magistrates with Clergy which Williams abhorred where Cotton's stance was altogether more reconciliatory.

Cotton was an indefatigable preacher, an assiduous writer eg. *The Keyes of the Kingdom of Heaven* (1644), *The Way of the Churches of Christ in New England* (1645), *Milk For Babes*, his famous Catechism (1646), *The Way of the Congregational Churches Cleared* (1648), etc., an able advocate, invited to advise the Westminster Assembly in 1643, as was Hooker, though both wisely refused to make the Atlantic crossing, his brilliance and charm, added to his spirituality and over-whelming belief, led Mather fulsomely to apply a Latin quotation to him, which may be translated—"He is perfect, in whom the flame of religion and devotion is not stifled by the smoke which is generated from the lights of science. But who is he, that we may worship him? Answer: Behold him here!" ("Hic Est!," *Magnalia* 1:252): cf. *Magnalia* 1:252–286; Venn1: 403.

8. R. Williams, cf. DAB 20:286–289; DNB 21:445-450; Venn 4:417; Mather, "Little Foxes; or, the spirit of rigid separation in one remarkable zealot," *Magnalia* 2:495–507. Son of a wealthy freeman of London, of the Merchant Taylors Guild, he attended Charterhouse School and Pembroke College, CambU. Ordained 1629, his whirlwind romance with the Masham's niece, and subsequent marriage to their lady-in-waiting Mary Bernard, is told at *Guide* pp. 227-28, all within the same year, cf. Mather's "rapid motion of a windmill" below! But his sensitivity to the needy, his championship of the underprivileged, his work amongst the Massachusetts Indians, and his founding of Rhode Island, bespeak the quality of his mind equally with his warmth of temperament.

9. Sir William Masham, d. 1705, cf. Venn 3:155; well known Essex Puritan family, see *Guide* pp. 227; cf. *Essex Heyday* , William Addison, J. M. Dent, 1949 pp. 29, 37, 323; DNB 11:1295–98 re the pious and celebrated Ladies Damaris (1658–1708) and Abigail (d. 1734).

10. HTS, p. 18, n. 44.

11. DAB 20:287. Williams had sailed to Boston, Mass., in the *Lyon*, 1 Dec 1630, welcomed as "a godly minister" (Winthrop Journal, op. cit. I, 57) but was angered "because they would not make a publick and solemn declaration of repentance for their communicating with the church of England" (*Magnalia* 2:496): "there was a whole country in America like to be set on fire by the rapid motion of a windmill, in the head of one particular man. Know, then, that about the year 1630, arrived here one Mr Roger Williams:"Mather 2: 495. For John Haynes, see *Guide* p. 248. For John Wilson see *Guide* p. 155.

12. John Norton, 1606–63, cf. *Norton Honoratus, the Life of Mr John Norton, Magnalia* 1:286–302; DAB 13:572-4; Venn 3:268. Born at Bishop's Stortford, Hertfordshire; to Peterhouse, CambU at 14 years; he returned to Stortford as curate, and usher at the grammar school before going to Otes as a Masham chaplain, emigrating to New England with Thomas Shepard (see *Guide* pp. 283-86) 1634. Teacher, then Pastor in succession to Nathaniel Ward (see *Guide* pp. 311-12) at Ipswich, Mass., he succeeded Cotton at Boston after controversial disagreement between the two churches. A harsh unyielding Calvinist, he was charged to dispose of William Pynchon's (see *Guide* pp. 297-300) *The Meritorious Price of our Redemption* by the Massachuetts clergy, in his *That Great Point in Divinity, The Sufferings of Christ*. He insisted on a death penalty for Quakers, but was respected for his *The Orthodox Evangelist* (1654), *Abel Being Dead Yet Speaketh, or, the Life and Death of John Cotton* (1658), etc.

13. Sempringham came into the possession of Edward Fiennes Clinton, 1512–85, ninth Lord Clinton of Saye, first Earl of Lincoln, at the Dissolution of Smaller Monasteries (Act of 1536, cf. ODCC p. 407) in 1538. NB. only four out of the 26 Gilbertine houses enjoyed revenues anywhere near £200 p.a. (Rose Graham, *VicHist—Lincolnshire* 2:179–86). Sir William Petre (see *Guide* pp. 306-9) attended in person at Sempringham, to enforce their surrender from Robert Holgate, 1481–1555, then Master of the Order.

This was concluded amicably, Holgate receiving the rectorial income of Fordam, Cambridgeshire and a pension of £30 per annum, even though he had already accepted the See of Llandaff (1537) and was to become Archbishop of York (1545). A two-story chapel (now known as the Lady Chapel) still stands independently against the north side of the Church of St Peter at Fordham, near Ely. It is assumed to have been part of the Gilbertian Priory founded there by Sir Robert de Fordham in 1227 (E. W. Iredale op. cit. pp. 136–7, 148–9), see Canon Arnold

Nicholas correspondence, Little Badlow papers, including leaflet *Fordham, The Church of St Peter*; cf. ODCC p. 645. Holgate's marriage and promotion of the protestant reforms of Edward VI, suggest that he was able to make the best of both worlds, monastic and reformed. He was understandably deprived under Mary Tudor, but it must not be assumed that the dissolution of the monasteries necessarily injured the residents, cf. *Master of Sempringham—Robert Holgate*, E. W. Iredale (a mine of detailed information) op.cit. pp. 28–29.

Edward Clinton successfully served four Tudor monarchs, Henry VIII, Edward, Mary and Elizabeth, rising to be Lord High Admiral, created Earl of Lincoln by Elizabeth (cf. DNB 4:547–55), founding a family which holds the title to this day, though merged since 1768 (when Henry Clinton, ninth Earl, succeeded his uncle Thomas Pelham (see *Guide* p. 166) with the Dukes of Newcastle (*EncBrit* 16:702–3).

Theophilus, fourth Earl, a devout Calvinist, took his place in the forefront of Puritan reformers, though succeeding to the title young, his influence extended via his vibrant family circle (cf. HTS, p. 17, but note the Lincoln property at Sempringham was the manor house, not a "castle" as there stated. There never was a Sempringham Castle, see *Sempringham Seat of the Clintons*, Lincolnshire Archive Office correspondence GTYH/MC, Little Badlow papers, and E. W. Iredale, op. cit. pp. 32ff.). This included his sisters: (1) Arbella, married to Rev. Isaac Jonson (grandson of Archdeacon Jonson of Leicester, see *Guide* pp. 77-78), who, with his brothers Ezekial and Samuel, went to Emmanuel, CambU, was ordained Deacon at Peterborough Cathedral, 1621 (Venn 2:477), and died during the first winter of the 1630 settlement of Mass., his wife predeceasing him on landing. The presence of this illustrious couple amidst the hardships of the ocean passage and the primitive settlement, coupled with their tragic death, made its impression on the whole enterprise.

(2) Lady Susannah, who married John Humfry, gentleman, of Chaldon near Dorchester, wealthy London merchant, friend of the pilgrim patriarch John White (see *Guide* p. 293 and p. 428 n. 224). Treasurer of the New England Company (predecessor of the Mass. Bay Co., of which he became Deputy Governor), the man perhaps most responsible for combining the power of leading London Puritans with the earlier colonising exploits of the Dorset adventurers who had settled Salem, Mass. and who sent out Endecott as Governor in 1628, thus making possible the success of the Winthrop plantation in 1630. Humfry emigrated to Salem in 1634, but returned, c. 1642, to serve as a colonel in the parliamentary army, and to bear the sword of state before the President at the trial of Charles I. He died, 1651. cf. *Dorset Pilgrims*, op.cit., p. 19ff & 102, etc; Venn 2:430.

(3) Lady Frances, who married John Gorges son and heir of Sir Ferdinando Gorges (d. 1647). Ferdinando, imperious naval and military Commander, governor of Plymouth (England) but also "father of English colonisation in America," (DNB 8:241) was constantly in rivalry with puritan leaders like the Earls of Warwick, and Lincoln. He obtained patents over vast tracts of the eastern territories of North America, and established Maine, but he and his son John proved incapable of retaining their interests. However, theirs was a name to conjure with apprehensively, amongst aristocratic Puritan circles of the day.

Of the others involved in the Sempringham meeting, see n. 14 following for John Winthrop. Thomas Dudley, 1576–1653, recurrent Deputy Gov. and Gov. of Mass., was the son of a Capt. Roger Dudley of Northampton. He joined the entourage of the Earl of Northampton as a page and, after military service with the rank of captain in France, transferred to the young Earl of Lincoln as Steward of his large estates. His skill in management brought him to prominence with the Bay Company founders, of whom he was one. He sailed on the *Arbella* in 1630, to Newtown (Hooker followed in 1633) where his ambitious mansion and scheme to make it the State capital, and his robust leadership, led to an estrangement from Winthrop. He removed to Ipswich, and finally settled at Roxbury, where he supported John Eliot in founding the independent Latin School (see *Guide* p. 326), and his Indian work. NB. Eliot was one of Dudley's executors and received a bequest of £5, to "Worthy & beloved friends, John Elliott, teacher of the church at Roxbury." cf. *Descendants of John Eliot* 1905, p. 224. A pious, uncompromising Calvinist, "in him New England Puritanism took on some of its harshest and least pleasing aspects" (DAB 5:485), but "his integrity was unimpeachable." Mather 1:73 and 132–5; DAB 5:484–5.

The effect of this godly yet glittering circle on Hooker could only confirm his belief in the viability of a Puritan Commonwealth in a free land overseas, if not immediately in England, and add spice to the adventure.

14. John Winthrop, 1588–1649, first Governor of Mass., features throughout this guide. He was the son of Adam, squire of Groton manor, Suffolk, whose sister had married into the Mildmay family (see *Guide* pp. 198-201 and 221-22). A pensioner at Trinity, CambU, John's legal status derived from his attendance at Grays Inn and the Inner Temple. He practised as Attorney of the Court of Wards and Liveries, but inherited Groton, and employed all his assets in superintending the recruitment and equipment of "the Winthrop fleet" which transported "over 700 people across the Atlantic" (Thistlethwaite, op. cit. p. 21) to settle Mass. He acted as Governor or Deputy Governor until his death, and kept a voluminous diary, published as the *History of New England*, the colonies' major primary source of information. Massachusetts owed its survival and distinctive qualities as much to his introverted, religious, oligarchic yet disinterestedly public-spirited, incorruptible and magnanimous character, as to any other. cf. *Magnalia* 1:118–131; *The Life and Letters of John Winthrop*, 2 vols, R. C. Winthrop, 1864; DAB 20:408–11; DNB 21:697–702; Venn 4:441; *EncBrit* (15) 12:709; *Builders of the Bay Colony*, S. E. Morison, ch. III; etc., etc.

Emmanuel Downing, 1569–1660, son of George (so Venn 2:62, but St John Mildmay, *A Brief Memoir*, p. 29, see *Guide* p. 223-24 and p. 412 n. 62, names him Emmanuel—a signatory with Sir Walter Mildmay of the Emmanuel College Statutes, 1585; MA Corpus Christi, CambU; master of Ipswich Grammar School, Suffolk; d. 1610) was b. Ipswich 1569, d. Edinburgh 1660. Entered Trinity Hall, Cambridge 1602, & Inner Temple, London where he practised law, also Dublin, Ireland. Played influential part in the Massachusetts Bay Co, with John Winthrop whose youngest sister Lucy he married. Spent most of 1638-64 at Salem, Massachusetts, whence his son George (Bart) attended Harvard, cf. DAB 5:419; DNB 5:1304–06;

15. Samuel Skelton, 1592–1634, is a key, if only a minor figure in the development of Massachusetts from the Reformed Anglicanism of John White and the Dorchester group to the full-throated Independency which rapidly overtook the Nonseparating Congregationalism of Cotton and Hooker (see *Guide* pp. 61-63 and 296). He was at Clare, Cambridge, when the latter two were at Emmanuel (entered 1608); Vicar of Sempringham, in remote succession to St Gilbert and his experimental religious community, by 1615 (where he married Susanna Travis, 27 April 1619. Venn 4:83); Chaplain to the Earl of Lincoln by 1622; but was silenced for nonconformity and joined Endecott's party at Salem, Mass, with Francis Higginson as its two foundation ministers. Endecott had sailed with a small advance party in the Abigail, in June 1628, Skelton and Higginson followed in the *Talbot* on 25 April 1629 (DAB 6:155–6). They immediately set about the creation of an Independent church, to the extent that the Brownes (see *Guide* p. 295ff) and others in the Anglican tradition could neither tolerate nor be tolerated, and Massachuetts began to swing into the Plymouth Plantation Separatist tradition originally unacceptable to the Bay Company planners. Mather (*Magnalia* 1:68) wrote of him as "eminent for learning and virtue," but in him the dream of a New England was already beginning to move towards the awakening of an independent United States of America. I wonder how clearly Hooker's deductive, logical intellect foresaw the outcome of his championship of the Congregational way. Probably more than he is known to have admitted. He was, after all, Francis Higginson's confidante.

16. Simon and Anne Bradstreet receive special treatment in S. E. Morison's delightful *Builders of the Bay Colony*, 1930, ch. XI. Anne was Thomas Dudley's daughter, born 1612 at Tattershall Castle (a seat of the Earl of Lincoln; the great keep, 15th century brick, rising through four storeys over 100 feet high, on the A153 from Sleaford to Horncastle, Lincolnshire, now National Trust property, open to the public, cf. *National Trust Guide*, 1980 ed, p. 318) and married

Simon Bradstreet at 16, in 1628, they sailing together to Massachuetts in the *Arbella*, two years later. Simon Bradstreet, 1603–97 (son of the Simon d. 1621, who was one of the first Emmanuel students, cf. Venn 1:203, nonconforming vicar of Horbling, Lincolnshire) was, according to Mather (*Magnalia* 1:138) taken under Thomas Dudley's wing in the Earl of Lincoln's household. He attended Emmanuel, gaining his MA in 1624, and later took over his father-in-law's duties as Lincoln Steward, after marrying Anne. Appointed Assistant of the Bay Colony in 1629, he accompanied Dudley to New England, and remained in public employment for over 60 years, as State Secretary, and Governor from 1679–86, and 1689–92. His second marriage was to Anne (Downing) Gardner, sister of Sir George Downing (see *Guide* p. 224), niece of John Winthrop. At the very heart of the colony, he exercised a moderating influence, particularly towards England and the Church, so much so that he was accused as "an enemy of his country" (DAB 2:580).

His first wife, Anne Dudley, gained a reputation as the first English poetess in America. She was influenced by Francis Quarles (see *Guide* p. 292), but more by her better masters the Elizabethan poets Edmund Spencer (1552–1599, author of the *Faery Queen*) and Sir Philip Sidney (1554–86, *Arcadia*, etc), which in no way damaged her reputation in Mass., evidenced by the acceptability of her work (of which the *Contemplations* is most highly rated). Mather enthuses "whose poems, divers times printed, have afforded a grateful entertainment unto the ingenious, and a monument for her memory beyond the stateliest marbles" (*Magnalia* 1:135). She and Simon lived at Ipswich, under the protection of the wry rhymester Nathaniel Ward (see *Guide* pp. 311–13), and, for a time, of her own father. To understand New England Puritanism is to accommodate Simon and Anne Bradstreet for they were amongst its most influential founders. cf. *Mather* 1:138–40; DAB 2:579–80; Venn 1:203.

17. *Sempringham* Church Guide, C. F. Ward, p. 7. " 1633. The Rev. John Cotton, Vicar of St Botolph's, Boston, felt it wise to leave his parish and spend some time at Sempringham while awaiting the opportunity to join those who had previously sailed to America," E. W. Iredale, op. cit. p. 34.

18. The story of St Gilbert is told in C. F. Ward's *Sempringham*, op. cit.; by Rose Graham in *VicHist—Lincolnshire* 2:179–186; *EncBrit* 12:256–7; most fully by E. W. Iredale, *Sempringham & St Gilbert & the Gilbertians* , op. cit. wh. includes Capgrave's *Life of St Gilbert*, pp. 55–114, & *The Constitutions* pp. 115–34.

19. HTS, p. 17 "on the same day in the house in London of the deputy governor of the company, Thomas Goffe, the principal stockholders (called the general court) convened. At this London meeting Governor Matthew Cradock proposed that the government of the projected colony be transferred to the inhabitants thereof," etc.

20. Matthew Cradock, a wealthy Puritan merchant-adventurer, and M.P. for London, active in promoting citizen rights eg. in opposing Charles I's attempt to fortify the Tower against Londoners. Died 1641. DNB 4:1361–2.

21. The current *Boston Official Guide*, pub. E. J. Burrow, London SW2 4TR, provides widescale information; cf. *Portrait of Lincolnshire*, Michael Lloyd, pub. Robert Hale, London 1983, pp. 86–88; *Lincolnshire.*, Walter Marsden, Batsford, 1977; etc.

Bristol's development as an international port also reaches back to the Middle Ages, the city incorporated 1155, the harbour opened 1247 principally for export of woollen cloth, but "late mediaeval Bristol was no Venice or Bruges" (*The City and County of Bristol*, Bryan Little, 1967, p. 76), 130 ships plying from the port mid-1400s, "the largest was the *Mary and John* which cost the sum of £2,660" (ibid. p. 77). But the Society of Merchant Adventurers was not incorporated until 1532. Sturmy's Voyage in the *Cog Anne* to Joppa (160 passengers, many for Jerusalem pilgrimage) to trade with Venetian satelite ports, 1446, seems to have been the first major venture (ibid. pp. 78f): further prosperity, sadly, came with the slave trade, late 16th/17th century, for which a misguided popular Calvinism (ie. backward/poor = unelected/abandoned by God) philosophy must accept some responsibility. However, the plus side was the volume of vital exports to New England, eg. shipping lists of supplies ordered by Eliot for his Indian work, held at South Natick Museum, Massachuetts. Cf. also *Bristol and its Adjoining Counties*, ed. C. M. MacInnes & W. F. Whittard, 1955, especially chapter 11 *Bristol in the Middle Ages*, pp. 73ff; *EncBrit* (15), 2:524,. etc.

22. William Brewster, 1567–1644, Elder of the Pilgrim Church at Scrooby, Leiden, and Plymouth, Mass., lived at Scrooby (Notts) manor house as a child, went to Peterhouse, CambU in 1580, saw minor diplomatic service at Elizabeth's court but returned to Scrooby manor in 1589, and succeeded his father as bailiff and regional post-master (a lucrative appointment due to the Ermine Street traffic). His leadership of the Scrooby Separatist Meeting forced him to take his congregation into the larger religious freedom of Holland, where he printed Puritan books to ship back to England. At Leiden he acted as chief envoy to the Mayflower venture, securing royal consents, but withdrew into England because of opposition to his unorthodox publications. He emerged again in Plymouth Plantation as presiding Elder, "of a cheerful Spirite, and sociable and pleasant amongst his friends" (DAB 3:29–30; *Magnalia* 1:63; Venn 1:213, DNB 2:1212–13.

23. William Bradford, 1590–1657, Governor of Plymouth Plantation, Mass., was born at Austerfield, Yorkshire into a family of substantial yeomen such as the Hookers, bred to independence. He joined the Scrooby congregation under Brewster, and sailed with them to Holland, like them much influenced by John Robinson (see *Guide* p. 18). A liberal attitude remained with him, eg. Father Druillette the Jesuit Indian missionary who conferred the title "Apostle" on John Eliot ('Dec. 28–9, 1650 during a visit, cf. *The Genealogy of the Descendents of John Eliot*, 1598–1905, ed. Wilimena Emerson, Ellsworth & George Edwin Eliot, 1905, p. 223. cf. DAB 5:462) also stayed overnight with Bradford in the same year. Nonetheless, Bradford took part in every aspect of the new colony (following John Carver as governor), the terrible hardship, shortage of essential commodities, physical weakness etc., and not only guided it to permanence, but compiled a *History of Plimmoth Plantation* between 1630–51. cf. DAB 2:559–63; DNB 2:1069–72.

24. A comprehensive guidebook, *Boston Parish Church*, by Mark Spurrell, third ed. 1987 supplies most details. For St Botolph (Botulph), d. c. 680, said to have founded a monastery at Icanhoh (Boston, Botulph's Stone) with his brother St Adulf, see *Saints*, p. 73; ODCC p.189.

25. eg. "The personal rivalry between Hooker and Cotton was much more of a factor in his removal than I had naively supposed," The New England Mind, Perry Miller, New York, 1936, p. 17; cf. Alan Heimert (Cabot Professor, Harvard), "Hooker had harboured, probably unconsciously, an animosity towards Cotton—or at least an envy of him—ever since their days at Emmanuel," (*The Cambridge Review*, pp. 177–182 , Nov. 1985). But this is going too far. Heimert's reasons do not bear examination, eg. "Hooker had preceded Cotton to Emmanuel, and yet Cotton was appointed Fellow first." In fact, Cotton preceded Hooker to CambU (Trinity) by six years, and gained his fellowship on graduating MA in 1606 when Hooker was only in his second year, whereas Hooker got his fellowship only two years later, on graduating BA; and "Cotton's pulpit at Old Boston gave him a voice to be heard throughout old England; Hooker darting from place to place, never did better, by way of settlement, than a modest lectureship at Chelmsford," when the "darting about" was ten years of privileged enjoyment of an Emmanuel fellowship, and at Chelmsford he was a threat to the government at Westminster, not wasting in a Lincolnshire backwater! Heimert's misunderstanding is shown also in his use of the phrase "probably unconsciously." That Hooker never was!

26. eg. "All these in Hooker's spirit did remain,
　　　A son of Thunder and a show'r of rain;
　　　A pourer forth of lively oracles,
　　　In saving souls, the sum of miracles . . .," etc. *Magnalia* 1:351.

27. Anne Hutchinson, 1591–1643, born at Alford, Lincolnshire, into the home of Rev Francis Marbury, d. 1611, a Christ's, CambU student in regular conflict over his nonconformity, imprisoned, but later vicar of St Pancras, London, and St Margaret's New Fish Street. cf. Venn 3:139. She married, gave birth to 14 children, and attended Cotton's Boston church, scarce 25

miles away. Bred to theological debate, intelligent, well read, articulate, she and her family followed Cotton to Massachuetts in 1634, her eldest son having emigrated in his company the previous year. There she held private meetings in her home for female friends, but, being an acceptable midwife, attractive, and exceptionally kind, the numbers swelled into the 80s, and from neighbouring towns. She expounded a covenant of grace which denigrated the moralis-ing of the clergy, and smacked of anti-nomianism (disregard for moral law). Her open criticism posed a threat to the young theocracy, aggravated by her group's political challenge to Winthrop's governorship, and to John Wilson, senior minister at Boston. Charged with heresy, she was excommunicated, and banished to Rhode Island. There her husband died. She removed to Long Island where she and members of her family were massacred by hostile Indians.

It was a sad story from which no one escaped unscathed. At first Cotton stood by his church member, but his support dwindled as the case grew more critical. Hooker was already in Connecticut, but his position was also under threat, ie. that moral behaviour was an outcome of indwelling grace, and therefore an indication of it; and that preparation for salvation, however passively received (and thereby for citizenship with its essential property rights) necessitated good conduct. He returned to act as moderator, with Peter Bulkeley of Concord (cf. *Magnalia* 1:399–404), of a Synod to examine charges against Anne. John Eliot, Thomas Weld, Thomas Shepard (see below) and most of the clergy were equally antagonistic. Anne Hutchin-son became a figure of persecution and pity. Given rather more charity by those in authority, and less intolerance on her part, Massachuetts might have been spared that decline into censorious morality which became a feature of later New England Puritanism. But it was not to be. cf. Shuffleton's able summary, *Thomas Hooker* op.cit. pp. 238–52; DAB 9:436–7; DNB 10:33–/8.

Anne Hutchinson has been much written about, eg. *Unafraid: A Life of Anne Hutchinson*, Winifred K. Rugg, 1930; *A Woman Misunderstood: Anne Hutchinson, Wife of William Hutchinson*, R. P. Bolton, 1931.

28. Details of Essex Puritan clergy will in general be found in the next chapter. For Shepard, see *Guide* pp. 283–87; Weld, see *Guide* pp. 304–5; The Rogers, see *Guide* pp. 257–59 and 267; Eliot, see *Guide* pp. 324–30, etc.

29. Peterborough Cathedral, cf. *The Cathedrals of England*, H. Batsford & C. Fry, Batsford 1936 ed. pp. 71–75; *EncBrit* (15) 9:334.

30. King's Lynn. Pevsner, North West & South Norfolk, pp. 220–37, quotes Daniel Defoe, 1659–1731, author *A Tour through the whole Island of Great Britain*, "more gentry & gaity;" St Margaret pp. 221–6, St Nicholas pp. 226–28, Red Mount Chapel p. 229, Saturday Market p. 232, Tuesday Market p. 234, etc.

31. Norwich, Pevsner *North East Norfolk & Norwich*, pp. 204–87. "Norwich has every-thing" (p. 204), demonstrated by full accounts of the Cathedral, Castle, etc; cf. *Portrait of Norfolk*, David Yaxly, London: 1977, ch I; *The City of Norwich*; *Norwich—a Fine City. An Historical Miscellany*, Norwich City Council, second ed. 1991, etc.

32. Walter Tyler, d. 1381, of indistinct origin, Essex/Kent, a soldier (fought in "the French War," *Enc Brit* 27:495) led rebels in south-east England against excessive poverty resulting from the Black Death, a devastating Oriental plague pandemic throughout 14th century Europe (named for its dark splotches on the skin, *Oxford English Dictionary*, concise ed, 1979, vol. I, pp. 656, 73. cf. *A History of the English Speaking Peoples*, W. S. Churchill, Part I pp. 278–92). They sacked Rochester and Canterbury, marched on London, but were thwarted by the bravery of boy-king Richard II (see *Guide* p. 136). Tyler was decapitated, the peasant-rights promised by the king revoked. cf. DNB 19:1347–8.

33. Robert Kett, d. 1549, raised 16,000 rioters against the excesses of land-owners made newly rich by the Dissolution of the Monasteries. The revolt was touched off by his landlord's despoliation of the abbey church at Wymondham (Norfolk), purchased for parish use. One thing led to another. Norwich was invested, demands issued for the protection of common

lands. To no avail. John Dudley, earl of Warwick, raised an army and overthrew the rebels. Kett was executed, 3000 peasants slain, 300 executed, DNB 11:76–77, cf. *Portrait of Norfolk*, op. cit. p. 2.

34. Admiral Nelson, 1758–1805, hero of Trafalgar. For Burnham see *Horatio Nelson*, Tom Pocock, Bodley Head, 1987, pp.2–3,5–7, etc.; also Robert Southey, *Life*, 2 vols, 1813, now suspect but cf. *Nelson*, David Walder, Hamish Hamilton, 1978, a good biography purged of mythology, with a useful bibliography; cf. DNB 14:189–207. For Burnham Thorpe see *Horatio Nelson*, Pocock, above.

35. Holkham Hall, Norfolk, "one of the greatest memorials to the Palladian age" (*Great Houses of Britain*, N. Nicolson, Weidenfeld & Nicolson, 1965, p. 230; cf. Pevsner *North West & South Norfolk*, pp.199–215), with stately interiors, Ruben's Return from Egypt, Roman sculptures, etc, cf. *Portrait of Norfolk*, op. cit. p. 45–46, built 1610 by Ld. Chief Justice Sir Edward Coke, centre of agricultural improvement espc. under William C. Coke (*Coke of Norfolk*) from 1776.

36. Blicking, Norfolk, 17th century red brick, by Lord Chief Justice Sir Henry Hobart (cf. *Puritan Gentry* op. cit. p. 9), fine furniture, pictures, tapestry (Pevsner *North-East Norfolk & Norwich*, pp. 96–99. cf. *National Trust Guide*, 1980, pp. 65–8), "one of the last of the great Elizabeth prodigy houses" (*Portrait of Norfolk*, pp. 109–10ff). A copy of Eliot's Indian Bible is in the muniment room. For Walsingham, cf. *VicHist—Lincolnshire* 2:394–402; see also p. 154.

37. Hereward, "that noble native of Lincolnshire who must surely be partly responsible for the proud and defiant character of all true Fenmen," Edward Storey, Spirit of the Fens, London: Robert Hale, 1985, ch. 21 *Out of the Mists*, p. 162. If a legendary figure, Hereward was at least tenant of lands conveniently held from Peterborough Abbey around Bourne, Lincolnshire—at Witham-on-the-Hill, four miles southwest of Bourne, Lincolnshire; at Barholme, a further five miles south (within five miles of Market Deeping, and ten of Crowland Abbey); and at Rippingale 4½ miles north of Bourne, three miles across the fields from Sempringham Priory. He held other lands under Crowland much further to the north at Stow, not far from Sturton-le-Steeple (see *Guide* p. 16) and possibly in Warwickshire and Worcestershire as well: indeed, *Hereward Country—Information for the Visitor 1990*, informative booklet issued by the Tourist Board, claims the whole region from Cambridge in the south and Peterborough in the west to The Wash in the north and the East Coast, as the effective area of natural independence up to modern times; cf. DNB 9:691–3; EncBrit 13:363; and eg. *The Changing Fenland*, A. C. Danby, CUP 1983 chs. 1, *The Medieval Fenland*, 2, *The Fen Project: 1600–63*, etc.

38. EncBrit 13:363.

39. Boudicca, cf. DNB 2:741–2, but see *Guide* pp. 246, 342.

40. Robin Hood, see *Guide* p. 132, and p. 391 n. 47.

41. Ely, Cambs. A useful *Official Guide* is obtainable from the City Council, with a short history, including Hereward. *The Story of Ely Cathedral* is beautifully illustrated by Rena Gardiner's 1973 1300th anniversary booklet and detailed in the Pitkin *Pride of Britain History*, C. P. Hankey, 1962.

42. Hugh de Balsham, d. 1286 (probably born at Balsham village, ten miles west of Cambridge, just north of the A1307–A604 on the old Roman road), a sub-prior chosen in defiance of The Crown by the monks as their Bishop, a benefactor who consolidated Ely's political independence; the "father of the collegiate system of Cambridge" University, cf. DNB 1:1012–17. For Bishop Alcock, see *Guide* p. 152.

43. St Etheldreda, c. 630–679, "most revered of Anglo-Saxon women saints" (*Saints*, op. cit. p. 119), for her reputed intercessionary powers. Her second marriage was to Egfrid, son of Oswy, Christian King of Northumbria, who released her—an interesting sidelight on marital (ie. human) relations which belongs, however remotely, to Cambridge's student heritage, cf. ODCC p. 465.

44. St Wilfrid (634–709) changed the course of English Church History by unifying the hitherto independent Celtic Church of the North under the Roman Church founded by St Augustine of Canterbury (597) in the South. Born in Northumbria, educated at Lindisfarne

(Holy Isle, St Aidan's early centre of Celtic learning & missionary enterprise, see *Guide* p. 207), contemporary with St Oswy (605–642, cf. ODCC, p. 997) and the brothers St Cedd (d. 664, Bishop of the East Saxons, see *Guide* pp. 207-8), and St Chad (d. 672, cf. ODCC, p. 259), he broke with the Celtic tradition, and, at the Synod of Whitby in 664 established a unified Roman rule (ODCC p. 1454). In an oblique sense the Elizabethan English antipathy to Rome, and the Puritan demand for a Church to their own liking, sprang from the seeds of discontent sown by Wilfrid's imposition of Roman authority, as a fresh flowering of native English independency.

His life was wracked by controversy, his courage equal to it. King Oswy, impatient at Wilfrid's long absence in France (where he sought consecration to the See of York at the hands of Roman bishops, rejecting the authority of his Celtic brothers in England) introduced Chad to the See. Wilfrid appealed to the Pope, and was reinstated, Chad graciously removing to Lichfield. He was next in conflict with Canterbury over its exercise of authority over York. Again he appealed to Rome, and, on his return, was imprisoned by King Egfrid. But he exercised the role of evangelist wherever he went. His powerful preaching regarded as the inspiration of the successful missions to pagan Sussex, to Friesland and the Germanic people of Europe. cf. ODCC, p. 1459; *Saints*, op. cit. p. 340–1; DNB 21:238–42.

45. Oliver Cromwell's contribution to an English Commonwealth built upon Puritan beliefs was unequalled, defying summarisation in a passing Footnote. His achievements also belong to the period immediately following the story of Thomas Hooker in England. Although elected MP for Huntingdon in 1628, it was not until his membership of Parliament for CambU in 1640 that his hour struck. Even so his image is discernible throughout this Guide.

Born in 1599, 13 years younger than Hooker, he went to the University in 1616 whilst Hooker was at the height of his academic career. Bred to the Fenlands of East Anglia, he looked to the men of the Eastern Association for the New Model Army which turned the tide against the Royalist forces at Marston Moor and Naseby. He was related to the Barringtons later of Little Baddow (see Guide pp. 225-26), corresponded with Hooker in Connecticut (see *Guide* p. 230), and at one stage considered emigration himself (*EncBrit* 7:487). New Hall, Boreham, next Little Baddow, was one of his final homes (see *Guide* p. 301). He was a late developer as was Hooker, a man who had to wait until middle-life for his destiny.

We can recognise many of the same characteristics in both men, shared with many Puritans. There was the rustic origin, the coming-of-age of the solid yeoman stock, the contrasting mysticism, the spiritual intensity, a tremendous zest for life bound within a love of law and order, the ruthlessness of convictions forged in the fire of persecution, an inner willingness for the pains of power together with scorn for the outward trappings of empire be it secular or religious. Either man, and many more, would sacrifice a king or a kingdom for principle, yet kept a redeeming tolerance of opponents. Both failed to find the balance by which belief might become practical politics. They exchanged the lighter touch of Elizabethan creativity for the awful burden of the Kingdom of God, and knew no solution but to soldier on, to experiment with reforms of the law and of the church, of education and of manners, to assume responsibilities they knew properly belonged to God, and never flinched. The unwilling Lord protector, the Pastor who longed to retreat into the wilderness and discover truth in simplicity, they complement each other, and in them we see the strength and weakness of everyReform movement.

For Cromwell this meant all out war against his compatriots the Scots and the Irish, suppression of the Parliamentary rule he wanted, the Independents with whom he had so much in common, accommodation of the centralised system of Presbyterianism which he held in suspicion, Continental wars to supplant the Catholic with Protestant powers and to claim a reformed Christendom which totally eluded him, a last resting place in the pomp of Westminster Abbey, a body disinterred and hung in derision at Tyburn at the restoration of the monarchy he had swept away.

Carlyle wrote of him (W. C. Abbot edition, 4 vols, 1904), so did John Morley (1900), John Buchan and Hilaire Belloc in lighter vein (1934); E. Barker, *Oliver Cromwell & the English People* (1937); C. V. Wedgewood *Oliver Cromwell*, Duckworth, 1973; Roger Howell *Cromwell*, Hutchinson, 1977; C. Hill *God's Englishman: Oliver Cromwell & the English Revolution*, London 1970 (cf. C. Hill *Century of Revolution*, 1964), and William Halle *The Rise of Puritanism*, 1938, represent a contemporary viewpoint; but S. R. Gardiner *Oliver Cromwell*, 1909, reprinted 1976, Epworth Press Pub. Co., is probably still standard; also *Cromwell, A Profile*, ed. Ivan Roots, Macmillan 1973 with a comprehensive introductory biography; cf. Venn 1:423; DNB 12:135–86; ODCC p. 356 for potted histories.

46. John Bunyan, 1628–88, belongs to the post-restoration period, his autobiographical *Grace Abounding to the Chief of Sinners*, and *Pilgrims Progress* written after 1666, coming out of his prison experiences from 1660–72. But he represents the Puritan mind in its pious aspirations, now forced into Indepednency by the renewed Anglican-Royalist repression of nonconformity.

47. Robin Hood, legendary English hero, cf. *EncBrit* 23:421; DNB 9:1152–7, "mythical forest elf," cf. *Legendary Britain*, Stewart & Matthews, Blandford Press, 1989, ch. 7, p. 93 *Robin Hood & the Green Man*.

48. William Langland, 1332–c.1400 (C. Hibbert *The English, A Social History, 1066–1945*, 1987, Grafton, p. 764). Details of his life come from *Piers the Plowman* since he is not mentioned in contemporary documents. Thought to be an early follower of John Wycliffe from the West Midlands (Shropshire, Worcestershire) he claims to have lived mostly in London (Cornhill). He was a keen, sensitive observer of people, especially the poor; a part of that early prophetic protest (cf. K. S. Latourette *History of the Expansion of Christianit'*, 1938, Eyre & Spottiswoode, vol. ii, p. 384) which led to Puritanism; cf. DNB 9:545–9; *EncBrit* 16:174–6.

49. Quotations from *EncBrit* 18:420 and 421.

50. St Ivo, patron saint of St Ives, whose remains, including a bishop's insignia, were discovered near Ramsey Abbey (Hunts, now Cambridgeshire, Ram-Eye, or Isle, rising ground surrounded by impenetrable marsh), Benedictine, founded Ailwin "Earl of the East Angles" (*EncBrit* 22:880) 969. Only the 13th century Lady Chapel remains, incorporated into Ramsey School: cf. *Saints*, op. cit. p. 181–2. Cromwell may not have been over impressed, but the long-assumed Providential protection of even the smallest settlements was imbedded in every Puritan's folk-memory.

51. Lancelot Brown, 1715–83, b. in Northumberland, a gifted kitchen-gardener whose genius was to become "founder of the English style of landscape gardening" in contradistinction to the French geometric style of Versaille. cf. DNB 3:22.

52. Cambridge. The large Official Guide contains most of the information likely to be needed by visitors, including the surrounding district. *The Cityscape 1990–91* panoramic street map is amongst the best produced. Two hour guided walks leave the tourist office daily. The *Victoria County Histories* series on Cambridge is outstanding. Vol. 3:1–100 contains a History of Cambridge, with *Early Stuarts and Civil War* detailed pp. 191–210; the Colleges, pp. 334–498. Vol. 7 has Roman Cambridge (p. 1ff), showing evidence of the Eastern Counties' struggle for independence from earliest English times (pp. 4, 5ff). Every college has its own "History." Endless "Guides" etc are also available.

53. Grantchester, from Granta-Setan, "settlers beside the Granta," *VicHist—Cambridgeshire* 5:198. Built on the Roman Akerman Street, which ran west of the modern highway; the church is St Mary & St Andrew (p. 211). For R. Brooke, see ibidem p. 200; also *Cambridge Official Guide*, p. 37.

54. Tobias, or Thomas Hobson, cf. *Cambridge Official Guide*, pp. 6, 7, 11; DNB 9:946.

55. Stourbridge. There is a file in the local history section on the 3rd floor of the Central Library in Lion Yard, with articles on the Fair by T. D. Atkinson (*Cambridge Described & Illustrated*, pp. 203–213); C. Caraccioli, *An Historical Account of Sbdge Fair*; P. H. Ditchfield, W. Hove, & Bron Surrey (all *Sbdge Fair*); J. Nichols, *The History & Antiquit. of Barnwell Abbey & Sbdge*

Fair; J. Heywood and T. Wright, *Cambridge University transactions during the Puritan controversies of the 16th & 17th Centuries*, 1854, pp. 414–20 & 438; C. Walford *Fairs Past & Present*, p. 403; I. Ward, *A Step to Stir-Bitch Fair, 1977*; etc, which offers a fascinating day's reading if still available.

56. cf. VicHist—Cambridgeshire, 2 *The Religious Houses*, pp. 197–318.

57. Wat Tyler, see *Guide* p. 127.

58. John Ray, see *Guide* p. 262-63.

59. Humphrey Tyndall, DD, 1549–1614, graduated BA from Christ's at 18, MA three yrs later, was President of Queens at thirty, Vice-Chancellor of the Univeersity by 36. He was also Dean of Ely Cathedral, and at the height of his remarkable powers, but within ten years of death when Hooker went up. Venn 4:284, cf. Shuffleton op. cit. pp. 11–13.

60. Margaret of Anjou, 1430–82, was reputedly strong-minded, aggressive, accustomed to intrigue, ever favouring her native France, never conversant with English ways (DNB 12:1023–33). In contrast her successor, Elizabeth Woodville, 1437–92, was English born and disliked for her equally strong-willed nepotism on behalf of the Woodvilles (DNB 4: 614–18). Mother of the murdered princes in the tower, her daughter Elizabeth of York married Henry VII, bringing reconciliation after the Wars of the Roses. Despite conflicting interests, Elizabeth had been a Lady of the Bedchamber to Margaret, &, seriatim, they established Queens'. cf. *Cambridge University Official Guide*, p. 13.

61. Erasmus, see *Guide* p. 33 and p. 360 n. 27.

62. John Fisher, 1469–1535, student at Michaelhouse, CambU, later Master, (cf. *Vic Hist—Cambridgeshire* 3:472), was President of Queens' 1505–08, then Chancellor of the University 1504–35. Chaplain to Lady Margaret Beaufort, he used her patronage to raise university standards, & was first Lady Margaret Professor of Divinity. Bishop of Rochester, 1504, he was confessor to Catherine of Aragon, and protested against Henry VIII's plan of divorce, and design to be head of the English Church. He was sent to the Tower and executed. But the Pope made him a cardinal (1535), and Pius XI canonised him, 1936. A great scholar and pastor, he helped CambU become a creative centre of 17th century Reform, cf. DNB 19:58–63; Venn 2:143; ODCC pp. 506–7; E. E.Reynolds *St John Fisher*, 1955.

63. For Latimer & Ridley see *Guide* pp. 112-13 and p. 380 n. 40.

64. Lady Margaret Beaufort, 1441–1509, Countess of Richmond, a remarkable lady, m. Edmund Tudor (d. 1456) & gave birth to Henry VII (see *Guide* p. 108). Her second husband was Sir Henry Stafford, her third Lord Thomas Stanley, first Earl Derby. Thus at the Battle of Bosworth, 1485, she was mother of the rival claimant to the throne, Henry Tudor, and married into the Stanley family whose uncommitted troops held the power of overthrowing Richard III's hope of victory, and did so (see *Guide* p. 108f). It is quite extraordinary that Richard should have expected otherwise. Did the acquisition of positions of power really carry with them such expectations of overriding acquiescence? If so, what appears to us as irrational behaviour on the part of so many whose lives we have touched on in this Guide, not least amongst the, at times aggressively authoritarian middling Puritan leaders, magistrates, ministers, becomes more understandable. NB. Lady Margaret also had a hand in her son's reconciling m. to Elizabeth of York, bringing to an end the Wars of the Roses. John Fisher, see *Guide* n. 62 above, her spiritual director in later life, encouraged her to a life of prayer and the founding of the Lady Margaret professorships at OxfordU and CambU, and the CambU colleges of St John's and Christ's, cf. DNB 2:48–49, & 18:964; ODCC pp. 855–6.

65. Thomas Cartwright, see *Guide* p. 142 and p. 393 n. 73.

66. Roger Ascham, 1515–68, English scholar, from Kirby Wiske on the A167 north of Ripon, Yorks, entered St John's, 1630, where he came under the influence of Sir John Cheke (1514–57, zealous Reformer, gifted classical scholar, Fellow by 1529, Regius Professor in 1540, tutor to Edward VI, MP, Secretary of State to Lady Jane Grey, banished by Queen Mary, later imprisoned in Tower, forced to become Roman Catholic, died partly of remorse—an example of a Tudor Protestant martyr, cf. Venn 1:328; DNB 4:178–83). In 1548 Ascham became tutor to Princess Elizabeth, and Latin Secretary to Queen Mary. On accession, Elizabeth appointed him

a canon of York Minster, where he added *The Schoolmaster* to his other celebrated work *Toxophilus* (in support of Henry VIII's compulsory Archery Act, cf. *EncBrit* 2:720–22. cf. DNB 1:622–31; Venn1:43; *Elizabeth I*, Anne Somerset op. cit. p. 20–21.

    67. William Cecil, Lord Burghley, see *Guide* p. 47.

    68. William Wilberforce, 1759–1833, English Evangelical philanthropist, typical post-Puritan off-shoot, who brought about the abolition of the slave trade, from Wilberfoss Manor, on the A1079 east of York, born at Hull, of delicate health but MP (Hull 1780) where he renewed friendship with William Pitt (1759–1806, parliamentarian and Prime Minister) whom he had met when Pitt was at Pembroke College, CambU cf. ODCC, p. 1458; DNB 21:208–17; cf. *Life* by his sons Robert & Samuel, 5 vols, 1833.

    William Wordsworth, 1770–1850, English Poet Laureate (tho' not until 1843), his early sympathies were radical if not revolutionary. Much of his work sprang from the spiritual meaning he perceived in commonplace events. This every Puritan shared, but his starting point was Natural not Biblical, as suggested by his growing appreciation of Anglicanism, and the Oxford Movement which aimed at restoring the 17th century High Anglican ideals of William Laud & Co. cf. *The Religion of Wordsworth*, A. D. Martin, 1936; ODCC, pp. 1476–7; DNB 21:927–42.

    69. Robert Herrick, see *Guide* p. 81.

    70. Emmanuel, "that happy Seminary both of Piety & Learning," "Mr Hooker one of the choicest Tutors in the University," Cliffe *The Puritan Gentry* op. cit. pp. 92–93; cf. ch. 5, *The Puritan Undergraduate*, pp. 83–103. Among available publications I recommend *Emmanuel College, An Historical Guide*, 1983, &, also by Dr Frank Stubbings, former Librarian, *Forty-Nine Lives: an anthology of portraits of Emmanuel Men* (1983). This includes Mildmay, Chaderton, Preston, Cotton, Ralph Cudworth, Harvard, but not (an interesting comment on his almost total neglect in Britain) Thomas Hooker.

    71. Sir Walter Mildmay, 1520–89, Emmanuel's founder, occurs throughout this guide, eg. see Guide pp. 198-204; but cf. Stubbings, *Forty-Nine Lives*,op.cit. Chapter 1; Venn 3:188, etc.

    72. Laurence Chaderton, c. 1536–1640, but cf. Stubbings, op.cit. Chapter 3, says born c. 1527, making him 113 at death? A convinced protestant, he aimed, when Fellow of Christ's, to make it "a Puritan seminary in all but name." But he upheld Church of England practices as by law established, thus avoiding suppression. His intellect was above petty controversy. cf. *Laurence Chaderton and the Cambridge Moderate Puritan Tradition, 1570–1604*, Peter Lake, PhD Thesis, 1978, quoted by Patrick Collinson, *The Religion of Protestants* 1982 op.cit. p. 5. He raised Emmanuel to be the foremost college of his day. He was ordained, 1568, and held the Lectureship at St Clement's, CambU for fifty years (Venn 1:313). The Mastership of Emmanuel he held with outstanding success from 1584–1622, when he resigned only to accommodate the election of John Preston. DNB 3:1339–43.

    73. Thomas Cartwright, 1553–1603, from Royston, Hertfordshire, uncompromising Puritan but no Separatist, he entered St John's, 1550, but had to withdraw throughout Mary's reign (1553–58). Elected to a Fellowship at Trinity, he pressed for organisational and ceremonial reform. He became Lady Margaret Professor (1569) but was deprived three years later, and visited Geneva. He espoused Presbyterianism. To avoid arrest he travelled between Antwerp, Middelburg, and the Channel Islands, but spent time in prison too. Gifted, learned, a shaper of Puritanism to come. At James I's accession he wrote the Millenary Petition on behalf of "1000 ministers," (NB. Collinson, *Eliabethian Puritan Movement* op. cit. p. 464 claims "not more than ninety benefited clergy preferred deprivation to subscription & conformity"!) pleading relief from imposed Anglican ceremonies, which brought about the Hampton Court Conference, but died. DNB 9:226–30; ODCC, p. 242; Venn 1:303.

    74. Irvonwy Morgan Puritan Spirituality—Illustrated from the life and times of the Rev. Dr John Preston, etc., Epworth, 1973, p. 24; re Perkins, see *Guide* p. 33 and p. 361 n. 31.

    75. John Preston, 1587–1628, b. Northamptonshire, graduated MA from Queens', 1611; BD, 1620; DD 1623. Ordained Peterborough, honours quickly came—Fellow and Dean of Queens' (the college chapel could not contain the crowds who mustered to his preaching);

Professor at Dublin; Master of Emmanuel; Prebendary of Lincoln; Chaplain to Prince Charles (on the advice of the Duke of Buckingham, who hoped to use him to ingratiate the government with the ruling Puritan cause, cf. I. Morgan above, p. 9 etc); Preacher at Lincoln's Inn; Town Preacher of Cambridge (a post he valued above the bishopric Buckingham offered). His influence declined as Laud's increased and Puritan political power waned. Sickness overtook him. He died at 41. Venn 3:393; DNB 16:308–12; cf. *Life of Preston*, Thomas Ball (pupil), 1628; Neal, *History of the Puritans*, 1822, ii, 124ff; cf. Fuller's *Worthies*, 1662 (Northamptonshire) p. 291; and Heywood & Wright, *Cambridge University Transactions*, 1854, ii, p. 312.

76. Dr Richard Bancroft, 1544–1610, was determined to promote the authority of the state church, and of bishops as its chief agents under the Crown. Puritans and Presbyterians were prime targets, and robustly handled (cf. Bancroft's sermon at St Paul's Cross, 9 February 1589, *A Warning Against Puritans*, quoted in *The English Sermon*, Martin Seymour Smith, vol. i, 1550–1650, p. 123–7 —"Spew out the poison of their slanders—they stick at all things which are enjoined, they require the reason of everything, they suspect amiss of every precept, and will never willingly hold themselves contented but when they hear that, which peradventure doth please them") cf. *Elizabethian Puritan Movement*, Collinson, op. cit. p. 391. He made sure that the Hampton Court Conference failed. Venn 1:78; ODCC, p. 123.

77. Thomas Plume, 1630–1704, b. Maldon, Essex, at Christ's, CambU (1645) whence he received a doctorate (1673). Vicar of Greenwich, Archdeacon of Rochester, he endowed a school at Maldon (where his library in now housed), and also the Plumian Chair of Astronomy at CambU. Venn 3:372; Essex Heyday op. cit. pp. 202, 327.

78. Shuffleton, op. cit. p. 26. NB. re King James, see *James I*, David Matthew, op. cit., which has a good bibliography.

79. *Emmanuel College, An Historical Guide*, Stubbings, p. 7.

80. *Emmanuel College Chapel*, Stubbings, 1986.

81. *The Emmanuel College Gardens*, George Sealy, 1979.

82. *An Historical Guide*, Stubbings op. cit. p. 32.

83. cf. *Historical Guide*, ibidem, p. 3.

84. cf. *Magnalia* 1:333 ff.

85. *Oxford English Dictionary*, compact ed. 1979, 2:2843 (123).

86. Simeon Ashe, cf. DNB 1:640; Calamy op. cit., 1:85. From CambU he was ordained (Peterborough, 1619) and "early ejected from living in Staffs" (Venn 1:143), so that he depended on a patron for a living, see n. 88 below. For Arthur Hildersham, see *Guide* p. 85.

87. cf. *Magnalia* 1:333 & 351.

88. "When Simeon Ashe was deprived of his Staffordshire living in the reign of Charles I, Sir John Burgoyne gave him sanctuary at Wroxall where he probably acted as assistant to Ephraim Huett", or Huitt (*Puritan Gentry*, op. cit. p. 183). Both Burgoyne and Huett had been his contemporaries at college. Huett was a sizar at St Johns (1611), then curate at Knowle, Warwickshire, lecturer at Shotwick in the same county, and chaplain to Burgoyne. But Laud had him silenced. He emigrated to Massachuetts (1639), to be teacher at Windsor until his death, 1644 (*Magnalia* 1:236; Venn 2:361).

Sir John Burgoyne, 1592–1657, went to Emmanuel in 1607, graduating BA in 1611, the year Hooker gained his MA. Sir John entered the Middle Temple, became Sheriff of Bedforshire, and MP for Warwick, 1649 (Wroxall is five miles north-west of Warwick), always a stout Parliamentarian (Venn 1:258). He was evidently pleased to provide shelter for his college friends.

Next Ashe moved to the service of Robert Greville, 1607–43, a younger man but well able to offer patronage. He was the adopted son and heir of Fulke Greville, 1554–1628, first Baron Brooke, of Jesus College, CambU, poet, favourite of Queen Elizabeth, boon companion of Sir Philip Sidney who entered Shrewsbury School on the same day to form a lasting friendship. In late life Fulke Greville became Chancellor of the Exchequer & possessed of Warwick Castle. He was stabbed to death by a disgruntled servant (cf. Venn 2:265; DNB 8:603) & was succeeded by Robert Greville as second Baron Brooke. He too had graduated from CambU (MA 1629), became Speaker of the Lords, a moderate in politics, but credited with bringing the Midlands Counties to the Parliamentary side in the Civil War (cf. *Conflict in Early Stuart England*, R. Cust & A. Hughes, Longman 1989, ch. 8:245ff). He fought with the Earl of Essex, and was killed at Lichfield, 1643. He lent his name, with William Fiennes, 1582–1662, first Viscount Say & Sele ("the oracle of those who were called Puritans in the worst sense" Clarendon, *EncBri.* 24: 277) to the Saybrook colony which later joined itself to Connecticut, cf. Venn 2:265, DNB 8:607–08. Simeon Ashe moved in high company.

During the Civil War, Ashe served as chaplain to Edward Montague, second Earl of Manchester. He too came from a powerful family, claiming descent from the Norman conquest. His great-grandfather, Sir Edward Montague (d. 1557) was Chief Justice of the King's bench under Henry VIII, one of the King's executors, a governor of the young Edward VI. Similarly his father Sir Henry, first Earl (1563–1642, although at "puritan" Christ's, CambU) was Chief Justice under James I (he ordered Sir Walter Raleigh's execution), and rose to be Lord High Treasurer, Lord Privy Seal, one of Charles I's most trusted advisers, supporting him in his undemocratic taxation policy (see *Guide* p. 218), resolutely on the side of monarchy v. parliament. He was created Earl of Manchester in 1626. cf. Venn 3:201; DNB 8:696–8.

In almost total reversal, Edward, second Earl (1602–71: popularly known as Lord Mandeville before succeeding his father, a Sidney Sussex man like Oliver Cromwell, and also MP for Huntingdonshire), became a leading Parliamentarian. When his first wife, related to the Duke of Buckingham (Charles I's confidant, cf. see *Guide* p. 59) died, he married Anne, daughter of the second Earl of Warwick (see *Guide* p. 274), joined forces with his father-in-law (then High Admiral of the navy), was made major general of the eastern counties, with Cromwell as his second-in-command. His moderation opposed all-out conflict. Cromwell forced his resignation. He continued to urge restraint, opposed the King's trial, negotiated the return of Charles II, and was reappointed general, with other honours, at the Restoration. cf. Venn 3:201; DNB 13:674–9.

89. cf. *EncBrit* 5: 913. Charles was living at Breda when his declaration of amnesty was issued. NB. Venn 1:43 says Ashe was "Lecturer at Cornhill Rector of St Austin's," a highly significant post; cf. Edmund Calamy DD, 1671–1732, *The Non-conformist's Memorial* (ed. Samuel Palmer, 1775, cf. DNB 3:683–7) p. 85.

90. Ramus, French humanist b. into the home of a Picardy charcoal-burner, worked his way thro the College of Navarre, found the courage to defy theological conservatism with his *Dialectical Partitiones* (1543) attack on scholasticism (educational tradition of the medieval schools, cf. ODCC, p. 1225), was silenced in 1544 by Francis I, King of France (1494–1547, cf. *EncBrit* 10:934–5), but reinstated by King Henry II (1519–59, cf. *EncBrit* 13:291), astonishingly, because Henry (m. to Catherine de 'Medici, daughter of Lorenzo II de 'Medici of Florence, a merciless anti-Protestant intriguer, cf. *Enc. Brit.* 3:528f), "showed to the Protestants even less mercy than his father" (*EncBrit* 13:291). cf. ODCC p. 1137; *EncBrit.*22:881.

91. ODCC, p. 222, cf. The Cambridge Platonists, F. J. Powicke, 1926.

92. Whichcote, DNB 21:1–3; Venn 4:382; ODCC p. 1453; *49 Lives*, Stubbings, op. cit. 12.

93. Cudworth, DNB 5:271–2; Venn 1:431; ODCC p. 360; *49 Lives* above, 14.

94. Culverwell, DNB 5:288–9; Venn 1:432, Fellow Emmanuel, 1642–51.

95. Cumberland, *EncBrit* 7:622.

96. Glanville, *EncBrit* 12:77.

97. Norris, *EncBrit* 19: 756.

98. Henry More, ODCC, p. 924. Re Hobbes, cf *'Puritanism & Revolution*, ch. 9, *Thomas Hobbes and the Revolution in Political Thought*, C. Hill, op. cit. pp. 267–88; *The World Turned Upside Down, Radical Ideas During the English Revolution*, Appendix, *Thomas Hobbes*, C. Hill, Penguin, 1975; DNB 9:931–9, etc.

99. Plato, 427–347 BC, of Athens, pupil of Socrates the extension of whose philosophy occupies Plato's early dialogues. He set up his own school at Athens in the grove of Academus,

hence The Academy. A summary of his teaching can be found in *The Cambridge History of Later Greek and Early Medieval Philosophy'*, ed. A. M. Armstrong, CUP, 1967 (eg. *Aspects of the theory of ideas in Plato's dialogues, the One & the Good*, pp. 19–23; *Plato's cosmogeny & psychology*, pp. 23–29, etc); cf. *An Examination of Plato's Doctrines*, I. Crombie, 2 vols, Routledge & Kegan Paul, 1962; *Plato*, J. C. B. Gosling, R. & K. P., 1973, etc.

100. John Hooker Jr, see *Guide* p. 195 and p. 407 n.6.

101. Second Earl of Warwick, see *Guide* p. 274.

102. Stephen Marshall, see *Guide* pp. 289–90.

103. *Emmanuel, Historical Guide*, op. cit. p. 9.

104. John Eliot, see *Guide* p. 324-29.

105. Lady Margaret Beaufort, see *Guide* p. 140 and p. 392 n. 64. For Christ's College, cf. *VicHist—Cambridgeshire* 3:429–36.

106 Sidney Sussex, EncBrit 5:93, and 26:163-5; *VicHist—Cambridgeshire*. 3:481–87.

107 Elizabeth m. Cromwell on 20 August 1620. She was a year his senior, the daughter of Sir Jn. Bouchier, a prosperous city merchant who had bought an "estate at Felsted in Essex" altho' "no kin to the noble Bouchiers of that shire" (Oliver Cromwell, John Buchan, 1934, p. 64; cf. "a model of female perfection after the Peridean standard"—a woman least spoken of amongst men—*Oliver Cromwell*, S. R. Gardiner, rep. 1976, p. 4; *Cromwell*, Roger Howell, Hutchinson, 1977, p. 10–11). Pilloried by the royalist opposition for her frugality, dowdiness and dullness as the first lady of the land, she displayed every virtue which might endear her to her husband and the Puritans. Buchan calls her "homely and dignified"; Howell, "she provided the quiet stability and love that Cromwell needed at all points of his career" (p. 11–12). With her proudly walked so many of the Pilgrim wives, whose simple, practical, self-effacing devotion brought New England to lasting life.

108 cf. S. Bush Jr, Sp. *Adventure in Two Worlds*, p. 96ff.

109. See *Guide* pp. 324-29. For Jesus College, cf. *VicHist—Cambridgeshire* 3:421–28; or the official college History.

110. John Alcock, 1430–1500, of Beverley, Yorks, educated at CambU, had a varied career. Rector of St Margaret's, Fish Street (London), Dean of St Stephen's, Westminster, Prebendary of St Paul's and Salisbury, Privy Councillor, Master of the Rolls, Bishop of Rochester (1472), Lord Chancellor, Bishop of Worcester (1476) & Ely (1486). Founder of Jesus College (1491), he also built or restored churches, the Bishop's Chapel and Palace at Ely, Great St Mary's, Cambridge, etc, and improved the standards of the clergy. "No one in England had a greater reputation for sanctity," DNB 1:236, cf. Venn 1:12.

111. St Radegund, cf.ODCC p. 1136; *Saints* p. 95. For V. Fortunatus, cf. ODCC p. 1411.

112. Cranmer, Fellow of Jesus, University Preacher (1526), roving plenipotentiary for Henry VIII, Arcbishop of Canterbury 1533, supported accession of Lady Jane Grey, dispossessed, tried for heresy at Oxford, 1555, burnt there Mar. 21, 1556. cf. Martyrs pp. 303–29; DNB 5:19ff; Venn 1:413; *Cranmer and the English Reformation*, A. F. Pollard 1904; etc. NB. Thomas Erastus Luber, German-Swiss theologian, 1524–83, cf. ODCC p. 460. "Erastian" implies the supremacy of the State in ecclesiastical matters. Andreas Osiander, 1498–1552 was a controversial Reform professor at Konigsberg, author *De Justificatione*. cf. ODCC p. 996.

113. Thomas Thirlby, the sole Bishop of Westminster, also bishop of Norwich and Ely; b. Cambridge, trained Trinity Hall, Fellow & Dr. Civil Law (1528); Dean, Chapel Royal, Privy Council, scourge of Anabaptists ("re-baptizers," requiring believers' baptism, generally hostile to all other authority, a threat to the English Puritan Party because they tended to provide a refuge for outlandish Independents). He presided over the trials of Marian martyrs John Hooper, Bishop of Gloucester and Wocester, disciple of Continental Reform, burnt at stake 1555; ODCC, p. 654 (cf. *Martyrs*, pp. 369–83), John Rogers, first Marian martyr, editor of Matthews Bible (first complete translation in English) burnt at Smithfield, London, 4 February 1555 (cf. *Martyrs*, pp. 313–327; Venn 3:479), and others; deposed on Elizabeth's accession, imprisoned in the Tower, and at Lambeth Palace until he died, cf. DNB 19:615–18; Venn 4:220.

114. Thomas Ithell, d. 1579, was indeed "a safe man" *(VicHist—Cambridgeshire* 3:424): b. Billesdon, Leicestershire., student of Magdalene, CambU, where he proceeded LL.D, 1563, he was Chancellor of Ely as well as Fellow & Master of Jesus (1563–79); cf. Venn 2:452.

115. Lancelot Andrewes, b. at Barking, Essex, educated at the Merchant Taylors school & Pembroke, Cambridge, where he was both Fellow & Master (1589–1605), was chaplain to the Queen, Bishop of Chichester (1605) and Ely (1609): best known as Bishop of Winchester, and for his devotional writings; Venn 1:30; DNB 1:401–5.

Roger Andrewes, his brother, was also at Pembroke, Ordained at Lincoln (1602) he served churches in Essex and Sussex before being made Chancellor & Archdeacon of Chichester Cathedral (Sussex) and Master of Jesus College, 1618–32. He resigned, 1635. Venn 1:31.

NB. F. Washington Jarvis claims "Not until long after Eliot's time—did the college lose its tolerant tranquility, eschewing Puritanism & siding with King Charles," unpublished manuscript of *History Roxbury Latin School,* Jarvis, chapter 1, p. 7, & n. 7 (publication due 1995).

116 Richard Hooker, see *Guide* p. 15 and p. 357 n. 1.

117. See *Jesus College, VicHist—Cambridgeshire* p. 424 and 425.

118. cf. *John Eliot Apostle to the Indians*, Ola Elizabeth Winslow, Boston, 1968, pp.15–20, and Venn 2:94. But Winslow is wrong in claiming Eliot was only 13 on entering Cambridge, cf. unpub. mss. *History Roxbury Latin School*, op. cit. chapter 1, p. 7f, & n. 7, n. 10. Eliot Matriculated 20 March 1618 Old Calender, ie. 1619.

119. Magnalia 1:530; cf. Venn 2:94 "Probably in Holy Orders," cf. my article *The Founders' Formative Years*, Roxbury Latin Newsletter vols. 65, no.3 and 66, no. 1 (April and Oct. 1992).

120. *Magnalia* 1:235.

121. Tyack, 1951 unpublished doctoral manuscript, vol. ii, p. xxvii. cf. Winthrop's *History of New England* op. cit. Boston, 1853, vol. i, p. 76 "He adjoined to the church at Boston, and there exercised in the absens of Mr Wilson who had gone back to England;" Eliot's *Church Record (Report of the Boston Record Commissioners*, Document 114, 1880. Margaret (Tyndal) Winthrop, third wife, John Winthrop. In a booklet published by Essex County Council for the U.S. Armed Forces in the U.K. (chiefly Airforce, based at Wethersfield, Essex), 1967, William Finch wrote, "without doubt the finest & greatest lady in the early story of your country" (p. 12f); "of singular prudence, modesty, & virtue, & especially beloved & honoured of all the country", DNB 21:700.

122. John Wilson, 1591–1667, entered King's, CambU as a scholar from Eton at 14 years (1605), and remained to enjoy a Fellowship (1608–10) before being deprived for nonconformity. He entered the Inns of Court but in 1620 accepted the Lectureship of Sudbury (Suffolk) near to the Winthrops at Groton, tho' "frequently suspended," Venn 4:429. He sailed with Winthrop in 1630 and shared in founding Boston, Mass., as Teacher, then Pastor of the First Church until he died. He was implicated in the Hutchinson case, being a main object of Anne's criticisms. Mather (*Memoria Wilsonia, Magnalia* 1:302–21) speaks of his humility, DAB 20:336–7 of his "hospitality," "great zeal with great love" (*Magnalia* 1:312). His son John married the Thomas Hookers' daughter Sarah.

123. *EncBrit* 21:694f. NB. Jarvis (*History Roxbury Latin School*, op. cit. chapter 1, p. 11 & n. 15) has uncovered the Jesus College Register entries for Eliot's MA and the testimonial for his ordination, both 1625, thus confirming my speculations.

124. Genealogy of the Descendants of John Eliot, op. cit., p. 259.

125. *Magnalia* 1:562.

Esher and Amersham

1. See *The Story of Esher*, Ian D. Stevens, 1966; *VicHist—Surrey* 3:447–9; cf. Philpott File, compiled Hilda Philpott, 1991, (hereafter Philpott File) on behalf of Esher Historical Society in answer to my questions re Hooker and Esher, Little Baddow Papers.

2. Redundant Churches Fund, St Andrew-by-the-Wardrobe, Queen Victoria Street, London EC4V 5DE.

3. There is no biography of Sir Richard Drake, but information about the Drakes of Esher can be gleaned from *The Family and Heirs of Sir Francis Drake*, Lady E. F. Eliott-Drake, 2 vols., Smith, Elder & Co., 1911, arising particularly from Don Pedro de Valdes' captivity at Esher Place, cf. pp. 95–96, etc; cf. also *Sir Francis Drake*, John Sugden, Barrie & Jenkins, 1990; and the brief histories of the Richard Drakes and Thomas Hooker, in St George's Esher Church Guide, John Floyer, Rector, 1908–34, pp. 8–15.

4. Christ Church, cf. *St George's Church, Esher*, R. R. Langham-Carter, 1968, p. 11; Floyer op. cit., p. 4; *VicHist—Surrey* 3:450; Philpott File.

5. Biographies of Queen Victoria, 1819–1901, are too numerous to list, but cf. EncBrit (15) 12:349–50 and 29:505–10 with good bibliography; and for your pleasure, try *The Life & Times of Victoria*, Dorothy Marshall, Weidenfeld & Nicolson, 1972; *Queen Victoria, Her Life and Times*, Cecil Woodham-Smith, Hamish Hamilton, 1972; *The Young Victoria*, Alison Plowden, Weidenfeld and Nicolson, 1981; *Victoria, Portrait of a Queen*, Richard Muller and Jas. Munsen, 1987, BBC Books; *Letters of Queen Victoria*, 3 vols., ed. A. C. Benson, London, 1911; *Further Letters* ed. H. Bolitho, London, 1938, etc. have numerous and revealing refs. to Esher: eg. *Letters* 1:10, 11, 13, 18, 19—Claremont; 14—outbreak of dysentery at Esher; 32–42—Leopold of Belgium.

6. Leopold, King of the Belgians, see *Guide* p. 400 n. 21. The monument is in the West Vestry at Christ Church, Esher.

7. Leopold George Duncan Albert, 1853–88, 4th and youngest son of Queen Victoria, b. Buckingham Palace, a delicate, studious, artistic child, attended Christ Church Oxford U, and lived at Claremont from 1879. He married Princess Helena Frederick Augusta of Waldeck-Pyrmont in 1882 (see *Further Letters*, p. 252, "that poor, loving young wife," p. 255), and died suddenly at the Villa Nevada, Cannes (ibid. "I am profoundly shattered and crushed," p. 254–5). He was buried at St George's Chapel, Windsor. cf. DNB, 11: 944–5.

8. Charles Howard, 1536–1624, Lord High Admiral of Armada fame, first Earl of Nottingham, "a great public servant, and of absolute integrity" (A. L. Rowse, *The English Spirit*, Macmillan, 1944, p. 104); "unlike many of the Howards, was a staunch Protestant" (*EncBrit* 19:826). This scion of England's premier family, who traced their ancestry back to the Norman Conquest and owned vast estates from Vanbrugh's stupendous Castle Howard near York to Arundel Castle in Sussex, seat of the present Howards Dukes of Norfolk, was immediately descended from Thomas Howard, second Duke of Norfolk, his grandfather. His father, William Howard (1510–73) was the first Lord Howard of Effingham (a small village in Surrey not ten miles from Esher, cf. *VicHist—Surrey* 3:323) a title bestowed after his defence of London against Sir Thomas Wyat's anti-catholic rebels in 1554 (see *Guide* p. 308). He too had been lord high admiral of the fleet, under Henry VIII.

The sister of this Lord William, Elizabeth Howard, married Sir Thomas Boleyn and was the mother of Queen Anne Boleyn (mother of Queen Elizabeth). Thus close to the monarchy, the Howards of Effingham drew closer under Lord Charles of Esher Place, for Elizabeth seems to have solicited her younger kinsman's counsel, even to the extent of allowing him to over-persuade her to sign Mary Queen of Scots' death warrant. His was an iron hand, if velvet gloved.

He possessed great charm but steady statesmanship. "A striking, almost heroic figure" (*EncBrit* 19:826), he exercised great responsibilities under successive monarchs, and only retired as high admiral in 1618, over 80 years of age, having held the office since 1585, well before the Armada. See further *Guide* p. 168: cf. DNB, 10:1–6.

9. Eliott-Drake, op. cit. pp. 62, 63.

10. DNB 5:1338. cf. Eliott-Drake op. cit. p. 176.

11. For the early history of the Drake families see Eliott-Drake, Pt. 1, Ch. 1, pp. 3–32 (Genealogical Tree p. 11) and J. Sugden op. cit. pp.1–6; DNB 5:1329 re Sir Bernard of Ashe; DNB 5:1330ff re Sir Francis and Drakes of Tavistock; cf. *EncBrit* 8:473–4; and biographies, eg. *Sir Francis Drake*, George Malcolm Thomas, 1972.

12. Crownedale lies one mile from Tavistock on the west bank of the river Tavy. Francis Russell, 1527–85, second Earl of Bedford, was descended from wealthy reformist Weymouth, Dorset, merchants who rose to power under the Tudors. He was an active Puritan, implicated in Wyat's revolt (see above), and lived for a time in exile in Calvin's Geneva. His father, John, had entered Henry VIII's service, as soldier, envoy, knight-marshall of the royal household, Lord Privy Seal, and executor of Henry's will. At Edward VI's crowning he was made Lord High Steward, and First Earl of Bedford (1550). Altho Protestant, Mary reappointed him Lord Privy Seal. He died, 1555, vastly rich, not least from the dissolution of monasteries, among them Tavistock, Thorney Abbey, Cambridgeshire, and Woburn Abbey, Bedfordshire which became the chief seat of the family. His son Francis was appointed, under Elizabeth, Lord Lieutenant of the Northern Counties, where he was caught up in border unrest, but his interest in Sir Francis Drake was invaluable, another instance of newly-enriched merchants advancing others with reformed beliefs, and thereby, the Puritan cause. cf. Sugden, op. cit. pp. 2 and 171; *EncBrit* 23:862; DNB 17:431–3; CCH., ed. Boris Ford, vol. IV, *17th Century Britain*, CUP, pp. 34–35 etc. wide reforming influence of the Bedfords, religious, agricultural, architectural.

13. The Western Rising of 1549 was "the closest thing Tudor England saw to a class war," according to John Guy, Tudor England, OUP, 1988, pp. 208–9, 213. "No single cause was responsible, agrarian, fiscal, religious, and social grievances fused. It was a hot summer, the crops failed, prices rose and the Protector compounded the problem by fixing maximum prices at terrifyingly high metropolitan levels. The Devon rebels—misunderstood the Prayer Book— both Devonians and Cornishmen disliked the service in English; they claimed to prefer Latin or Cornish," etc. The Act of Uniformity, 1549, imposed the use of Edward VI's Prayer Book. Devonians, with others, failed to grasp the muted Calvinism underlying it, or wanted more. So Protestant subject fell out with Protestant ruler and Puritanism's failure as a political system was born.

14. cf. Eliott-Drake, Pt. IV, *Sir Francis Drake, Second Baronet*, pp. 249–419; re m. to Dorothea Pym, see ibidem p. 276; cf. *EncBrit* 22: 680–82; DNB 5:1346. John Pym 1584–1643 (DNB 16:518–26) was from an ancient west country family (Brymore, Somerset), a lawyer of the Middle Temple, he was receiver-general of royal revenues for Wiltshire, and Member of Parliament for Calne. He represented the anti-catholic, pro-Parliamentarian party, defended their privileges, incurred James I's displeasure, and was confined to house-arrest.

Francis Russell, fourth Earl of Bedford supported his return, as Member of Parliament for Tavistock, 1624. He continued to work for political discrimination against Catholics, in opposition to the royal policy, moved for Buckingham's impeachment, and, later, that of William Laud, pushed for the Petition of Rights, and, from the Short Parliament of 13 April 1640, emerged as leader of the anti-royalist group, provoking the Grand Remonstrance of 1643, and Charles I's fatal attempt to arrest him first among the "Five Members," leading to civil war. It is pertinent for us to note (i) that all this furore seethed up from the west country, inseparably linked with the efforts of eg. the Dorset Pilgrims to establish a Protestant New England in North America (see *Guide* p. 293), and (ii) the nodal involvement of men of stature like the west country

Pyms and Drakes, known to Hooker nationally, as well as from his Esher residence, built confidence into his positive hopes for statutory reform.

15. Sugden, op. cit. p. 158, and E. Drake op. cit. p. 100; cf. also re young Francis of Esher's visit, 1593, and terms of Sir Francis Drake's will, E. Drake, pp. 118–20; and Sugden p. 306 re the £1500 ransom money.

16. See Sugden, op. cit. ch. 13, *Sir Bernard Drake*, p. 158ff, and DNB 5:1338.

17. John Aubrey, 1626–97, wealthy antiquary, b. near Malmesbury, Wiltshire, educated at Malmesbury Grammar School (where he met Thomas Hobbes, see Guide p. 149, a former pupil) and Trinity, OxfordU. A non-political socialite, he loved celebrities. A member of the Royal Society, he casually collected information for his *Minutes of Lives*, and *Miscellanies*, resulting in a *Perambulation of Surrey*, incorporated in Rawlinson's *Natural History and Antiquities of Surrey*, 1719. cf. DNB 1:716–7; *EncBrit* 2:891; re the Santa Domingo bell, cf. Floyer op. cit. p. 9; *Story of Esher*, op. cit. p. 22; and Philpott File—Answer No. 3.

18. The Don Pedro de Valdes incident is detailed in Sugden, op. cit. p. 241ff: He "remained over four years with Richard Drake at Esher, " see ibidem p. 100).

19. Sugden op. cit. throughout: cf. "In his prime he spent several hours a day in worship. The earliest evidence, from the 1560s shows that Drake's religious convictions were not only deep but extreme and uncompromising. In time he would find himself a spiritual home among the Eliz. Puritans," (ibidem p. 7). He even unsuccessfully attempted with Sir Walter Mildmay to pilot a strict Sabbath Observance Bill through Parliament, but Elizabeth vetoed it (ibidem p. 172).

20. The history, architecture and furnishings of St George's are described in Floyer, Langham-Carter, I. D. Stevens, and the Philpott File. cf. also *VicHist—Surrey*, 3:451; Pevsner—*Surrey*, pp. 220–21.

21. The Princess Charlotte tomb receives special treatment in Philpott File; her story is outlined in DNB 4:120–22 and *EncBrit* 2:744f. Leopold I of Belgium, 1790–1865, was born a younger son into the house of Saxe-Coburg-Saalfeld, at Coburg, in what is now Germany, 100 miles west of Frankfurt-am-Main. He fought as a general of cavalry in the armies of Alexander, Emperor of Russia, against Napoleon, visited England, and married Princess Charlotte (DNB 4:121) being thereupon created Duke of Kendal. After his wife's tragic death he continued to reside at Claremont, but, in 1831, was elected King of Belgium, a country but recently separated from Holland. His leadership helped establish Belgium as a viable independent kingdom (cf. *EncBrit* 16:460–61). His platonic affection for his niece, the young Princess Victoria, whom he addresses as "My Dear Little Heart," or "My Dear (or Dearest) Love," see *Letters*, op. cit. pp. 31–55, and his instruction for a budding Queen (he dares to call it "preaching" at times cf. ibidem p. 41) endears him also to other readers. I do not think the Puritans would altogether have disapproved (see Edmund S. Morgan, *The Puritan Family*, Harper 1944).

22. Francis John Williamson, see *Victorian Sculpture*, Benedict Reed, Yale, 1982, pp. 14, 69; cf. Philpott File, Enclosure No. 4.

23. George IV, 1762–1830, eldest son of George III (cf. DNB 7:1071–83), handsome, talented, artistic, but humanly flawed, "either the most polished gentleman or the most accomplished blackguard in Europe—possibly both" (so his tutor, Richard Hurd, 1720–1806, bishop of Worcester, Emmanuel, Cambridge scholar and fellow, like Hooker also of farming stock, and, strong coincidence, Rector of Thurcaston 1756–76, pop. known as "the beauty of holiness"' cf. Venn 2:436; *EncBrit* 13:958) entered into a private illegal marriage contract with Mrs Fitzherbert, a Roman Catholic, in 1785, but was publicly married to his cousin Princess Caroline of Brunswick ten years later. George's rejection of his wife and enforced separation of their daughter Charlotte from her mother brought Caroline popular support, cf. DNB 3:1059–63; Lewis Melville, *The First Gentleman of Europe*, 1900; and *George IV, Regent and King*, Christopher Hibbert, Lane 1973. This is a long way from Thomas Hooker, but to interpret the present one needs to look forward as well as back in time. Esher was such a community as could sustain the widest contrasts. Geneva wasn't. So Hooker differed from Calvin.

24. The Pelhams, a later generation of Esher residents, show how the two main properties evolved. Thomas Pelham Holles was the elder brother, 1693–1768, Duke of Newcastle, and Prime Minister in succession to his brother. He was born into a family which, like the Barringtons of Little Baddow, claimed independent Saxon descent from before the Conquest, at Laughton, Sussex (after defunct Pelham in Hertfordshire, the family's main seat), six miles east of Lewis, not far from Glyndebourne Opera House. Reputedly honest, devout, he amassed wealth and titles from his father Thomas, mother Grace Holles, and wife Henrietta Godolphin granddaughter of Churchill, Duke of Marlborough. He used his position to advance Whig policy (roughly, following the Civil War, the party favouring parlimentary power over the crown and some toleration for dissent, versus the Tories who, roughly, upheld the sovereign's rights and, pro-Catholic, opposed dissent) in Lords and Commons, as Secretary of State for thirty years, 1724–54. DNB 15:702–6.

Henry Pelham, 1695–1754, Oxford student, soldier, traveller, entered Parliament for Sleaford, Sussex (1717) as treasury lord, paymaster the armed forces, and Prime Minister (1743). He had difficulty emerging from his brother's shadow, but secured peace at home and abroad. He purchased Esher Place in 1729 (employing William Kent to improve its grounds, see *Guide* p. 112), thus preserving a line from the Puritan Drakes to Whig "dissent" at Esher. DNB 15:689–92. For Vanbrugh, see *Guide* p. 383 n. 4 and p. 403 n. 56.

25. Sir Thomas Lynch, d. 1684, DNB 12:337–8; Langham-Carter op. cit. p. 9; cf. *VicHist—Surrey*, 3:448 re Esher Episcopi (Place) "Sir T. Lynch held it in 1680." re Sir Henry Morgan, 1635–88, DNB 8:914. "The principal and peculiar industry of Jamaica at that time was the support of the buccaneers," ie. privateers commissioned by the English crown, see DNB 7 above.

26. John Flaxman of York, 1755–1826, sculptor, draughtsman, cf. *Dictionary of British Sculptors 1660–1851*, Rupert Gunnis, Oldhams, pp. 147–51; DNB 7:254–60.

27. Sir Thomas Masterman Hardy, 1769–1839, scarce impinges on our narrative, save as a noble part of the long line of Dorset mariners (born Portisham, six miles west of Weymouth and Dorchester, Dorset) who pioneered the northeast plantations. Serving before the mast at twelve years, he rose to be Nelson's Captain of the Victory at Trafalgar, Vice-Admiral, First Sea Lord; DNB 8:1243–5.

Charles Rose Ellis, 1771–1845, first Baron Seaford, second son of George Ellis, Chief Justice of Jamaica, and grandson of Colonel John Ellis whose family had settled there during Sir T. Lynch's time. Charles returned to invest his colonial fortune in a political career. Member of Parliament from 1793–1826, he purchased Claremont 1798; DNB 6:692–3. Both he, and William Pitt, the great parliamentarian and Prime Minister (DNB 15:1253–72), lie outside the scope of this guide.

28. Bishop William Wayneflete, 1395–1486, of Wainfleet, Lincolnshire, educated OxfordU, Headmaster Winchester, Provost and possibly first headmaster of Eton, Lord Chancellor to Henry VI, 1457 (no wonder his effigy in Magdalene College Chapel, OxfordU, is garbed as a merchant not a bishop, *EncBrit* 28:433) etc, cf. DNB pp. 996–100.

29. *EncBrit* 21:826; see *Guide* p. 398 n. 8.

30. HTS, p. 4; BOT, op. cit. 1, pp. 35–36; but NB. David Cressy, *Coming Over, Migration and Communication Between England and New England in the 17th Century*, OUP, 1987, p. 118, "Beneficed clergy received stipends ranging from £10 to £100 a year." The median salary for a vicar in the West Midlands in 1650 was £42.2–8.

31. *The Firebrand Taken out of the Fire. Or, the Wonderful History, Case, and Cure of Mis Drake*, London 1654, 6; cf. Eliott-Drake refs, p. 193. For the Tothills, and the saga of *Mrs Drake Revived*, see ff. pages, and under Amersham.

32. Ibidem, 8, 9–10.

33. Eliott Drake, op. cit. pp. 176–7. For a detailed review of the damaging litigation between Francis of Esher and Joseph Bodenham v. Thomas Drake, see ibidem pp. 174–93, and Sugden, op. cit. pp. 288–9, 313, etc.

34. Hartwell, op. cit. 10–14.

35. John Dod, 1549–1645, cf. Venn 1:50; DNB 5:1050–1. He had been University Preacher at Cambridge, and according to *Puritan Gentry* op. cit. p. 152, preached before Sir Francis Barrington when the latter was imprisoned by Charles I in the Marshalsea for opposing forced loans (see ibidem p. 147). His text was "Behold the devil shall cast some of you into prison that you may be tried" (Rev. 2:10). Charles was not amused.

36. Hartwell op. cit. 120; cf. HTS 28:4ff.

37. John Drake was born in late 1619, or early 1620, the pathetic inscription on his tomb at Amersham reading "dyeing ye 2 of Aprill in the 4 yere of his age 1623," see *Guide* p. 183. The Hookers married two years before John's death, on April 3, 1621. Their first child Joan was born the next year. Their love was mutual and abiding. They provided a serene oasis within the disturbed Esher household. To have had this daily before her eyes yet beyond her reach, their child thriving whilst the baby on whom she doted declined, could only have increased Mrs Drake's vexation.

38. Shuffleton, op. cit. p. 31. Re Chaderton and Preston, see *Guide* p. 142ff: John Rogers, *Guide* p. 257-58.

39. John Forbes, 1568–1634, see *Guide* p. 351.

40. James Usher (Ussher), 1581–1656, Dublin born, early student at Trinity College Dublin (founded 1591), Dublin's first professor of divinity (1607), Bishop of Meath, 1621, Archbishop Armagh, 1625, he preserved the independence of the Irish Church; eminent scholar, hugely humane, Calvinist yet friend of Laud, lived in England following the Irish Rebellion of 1641, and endeavoured to reconcile church and dissent; granted a state funeral at Westminster Abbey by Cromwell. DNB 20:64-72; ODCC p. 1400.

41. G. L. Walker, *Thomas Hooker, Preacher, Founder, Democrat*, op. cit. p. 38. Francis Drake's will is dated 13 March 1634, cf. also HTS 28:5, n. 14.

42. The *Poor Doubting Christian* is printed in full in HTS, pp. 152–86 with an Introductory Essay, pp. 147–51. The extracts are from pp. 152, 157, 155, 162, 176.

43. *Magnalia* 1:334.

44. Langham-Carter op. cit. prints the St George's Clergy List from 1280, with Thomas Hooker 1620–26, p. 12.

45. *Magnalia* 1: 334.

46. S. Bush, op. cit. p. 4; cf. A. E. Van Dusen, State Historian, *Connecticut*, ERO 13404349, 1961, p. 12, "Hooker's first charge was a humble one—the rectorship of a small village," could scarcely be more misleading!

47. Emmanuel College Charter, see *Guide* p. 145.

48. Humphreys, BOTT op. cit. 1, p. 34.

49. For the Freakes (Frekes) of Purleigh, Essex and Washington DC, see *Guide* p. 175. The list of Freake livings is too long for total inclusion here, but Edmund (1516–91) also received the rectory of Fowlmere, Cambridge from Queen Elizabeth (who then appointed him to Purleigh, he having been one of her chaplains) which he held in plurality until handing it, too, to his son John. He became Bishop of Norwich, 1575–84, on leaving Rochester, and of Worcester (1584–91). He was a noted persecutor of the Puritans in East Anglia. The Freakes may have had as little conscience over their attitude to the ordained ministry as many of their contemporaries, but they knew what the Puritans thought of them! cf. Venn 2:176; DNB 7:670–1; *The Elizabethan Puritan Movement*, Collinson, pp. 187/8, 192, 201–5, etc.

50. *The Church's Deliverance*, printed in *FOVRE/LEARNED/AND GODLY/TREATISES: VIZ./The Carnall Hypocrite./The Churches Deliverances./The Deceitfulnesse of Sinne./The Benefit of Afflictions./By T.H./Printed at London by Tho. Cotes,/for Andrew Crooke, etc, 1638*; Introductory Essay HTS op. cit. pp. 53–59, Text, pp. 60–88; extracts, pp. 67–8.

51. eg. Sir Everard "Gunpowder" Digby, *Guide* p. 58f.

52. Cardinal Wolsey, see *Guide* p. 81 and p. 374 n. 104.

53. "It was for this reason that Francis Drake, an outspoken critic of Arminianism, managed to recruit Thomas Hooker for his donative cure of Esher in Surrey," *Puritan Gentry*, op. cit. p. 170; cf. Floyer op. cit. p. 10.

54. Floyer op. cit. p. 12–13; cf. Langham-Carter p. 12.

55. "Originally part of the manor of Esher Episcopi, now bought by Sir John Vanbrugh," also re Lord Clive's purchase, 1768; Leopold's and Charlotte's occupancy, 1816; and that of Louis Philippe I of France, 1848, *VicHist—Surrey*, 3:447. NB. Louis' daughter Louise returned to Claremont after his death as second wife of Leopold I of Belgium, eg. his letter to the Princess Victoria, 31 August 1832, "You told me you wished to have a description of your new aunt—she is extremely gentle and amiable, her actions are always guided by principles," etc, *Letters of Queen Victoria*, op. cit. p. 34; cf. *EncBrit* 17:51–52: cf. *National Trust Guide*, 1980, op. cit. pp. 239–41; *Claremont Landscape Garden, Surrey—The History 1708–1722*, National Trust, 1984, pp. 6–12.

56. Vanbrugh's fortunes were at a low ebb. The unpaid costs of Blenheim Palace, and fierce disputes with the Duchess, Sarah, "the wicked woman of Marlborough," a source of endless embarrassment, *EncBrit* 27:881. NB. John Churchill, 1650–1722, First Duke of Marlborough, was the son of Winston Churchill of Dorset and Elizabeth (daughter of the Sir John Drake of Ashe who died 1636), *EncBrit* 12:737, cf. DNB 4:342. A page in the household of the Duke of York (afterwards James II) at 17 years, he was commissioned into the Guards, and second in command of the royal army at the Duke of Monmouth's revolt, 1685. Monmouth was an acknowledged illegitimate son of Charles II by his mistress Lucy Walters, and the obvious if unworthy Protestant rival to the throne when James declared himself a Catholic. On the death of Charles II, Monmouth raised an abortive insurrection, and was defeated at Sedgemoor, Somerset. cf. *Monmouth's Rebels, The Road to Sedgemoor 1685*, Peter Earle, Weidenfeld and Nicolson, 1977. *James, Duke of Monmouth*, Bryan Bevan, Robert Hale, London 1973. Churchill helped save the day for an inept royal army by his personal leadership. When William III ousted James II, Churchill was made Earl of Marlborough; but fell under suspicion as a favourite of the last two Stuart kings. He emerged as the greatest general in Europe under Queen Anne, with victories at Blenheim, 1704; Ramillies, 1706; Oudenarde, 1708; Malplaquet, 1709, cf. *Marlborough*, Corelli Barnett, Eire Methuen, London 1974; *Life of Malborough*, Garnet Wolsey, 1894, etc. This has no bearing on the Hooker cycle, except as illustrating the illustrious history surrounding Claremont, Esher, to which Hooker also dramatically contributed.

57. Clive of India, 1725–74, cf. *EncBrit* 3:532–6; DNB 4:564–76.

58. *EncBrit* 28: 28–37: cf. Victoria biographies (previous note 5) for Leopold.

59. Charles Bridgeman, d. 1738, cf. *Claremont Landscape Garden*, op. cit. pp. 7–12; cf. *The English Garden*, L. Fleming and A. Gore, 1979, p. 241–2. re William Kent, 1684–1748, painter, sculptor, landscape gardener, see *Claremont* above, pp. 13–21, cf. DNB 11:23–25; re Capability Brown, see ibidem pp. 21–23, see also *Guide* p. 133.

60. See *Hampton Court*, R. J. Minney, Cassell 1972 (for Huguenot Jean Tijou, pp. 179, 181, 187; and *Hampton Court Palace*, June Osborne, Kaye and Ward 1984 (Tijou pp. 138–9, 149), amongst many other publications. The impact of Hampton Court on Esher can hardly be exaggerated, except that in the intimate social networks of Tudor England, with its tiny population closely interdependent, many people lived much closer to royalty and the nobles than has been possible ever since.

Details of Hampton Court's artists are not relevant to this guide, except, again, to note the opulence which beckoned Hooker from many sections of his Cambridge, London, and Essex days. This may not have conditioned his ambitions to any degree, but had its echoing effect in New England, where Dudley attempted a great mansion at Hooker's Newtown, where a consortium of peers essayed noble estates at Saybrook, and remembered glories resurfaced as New England grew to prosperity. The Puritans could not altogether avoid becoming what they had fled from.

Puritans were also not without native-bred artists, see CCH 4, *17th Century Britain*, op. cit. ch. 8, *Painting*, pp. 235–67. Despite their problems with images, every Puritan would have his/her portrait painted! CCH suggests, to uphold law and order by aggrandizement of the ruling-class image, hence the preponderence of portraits: cf. *Music*, ch. 6, *Paradise and Paradox*, CCH pp. 179–221; *Sculpture*, ch. 9, pp. 267–75; cf. book-illustrators, silversmiths, etc, etc. Puritanism cannot be separated from artistry.

Sir Christopher Wren, 1632–1723, made his major architectural impact after the Great Fire of London (1666), but has work to be seen eg. at Emmanuel and Queens (the College Chapels) which has interest for followers of Hooker, cf. DNB 21: 995–1009.

Grinling Gibbons, 1648–1721, master-carver to George I, again belongs to the post-pilgrim period. A wood-carver of sublime genius, he worked with Wren, and is best known for his ornamental carving at Windsor Chapel, in the choir at St Paul's, at Burghley, Chatsworth, etc. cf. *EncBrit* 2:936; DNB 7:1138–40.

Sanzio Raphael, 1483–1520, of Urbino, bordering Tuscany and Umbria, Italy, where his father Santi painted before him, belongs to the Renaissance and to Italy not to the Reformation and New England, even if his lifespan covers that of Martin Luther (1483–1546). But if Cromwell could purchase the Mantegna Cartoons, contemporary Christians in the reformed tradition could delight in Raphael! ODCC, p. 1138; *EncBrit* (15) 9:941–3.

Andrea Mantegna, 1431–1506, was adopted by Francesco Squarcione of Padua, Italy, and trained in his art school. He settled at Mantua where he painted the *Triumph of Caesar*, and there died. My guess is that, if Oliver Cromwell did indeed influence its purchase, it was in part because he could identify with Caesar's conquests, a facet of the Puritan mind (triumphalism) symmetrically noted in this guide with its perfectionism and mystical humility. cf. ODCC p. 850; *EncBrit* (15) 8:794–6.

61. For Amersham cf. *VicHist—Buckinghamshire* 3: 141–154; *The History and Antiquities of the County of Buckinghamshire*, George Lipscomb, vol. 3, 1847; Pevsner, op. cit. *Bucks*, 1960, pp. 46–51, 233 (Shardeloes Manor); *Amersham An English Country Town*, Nicholas Salmon, 1991; *Buckinghamshire*, Town and County Books, London 1984; *Yesterday's Town: Amersham*, Nicholas Salmon and Clive Birch, Barracuda Books, Buckinghamshire, 1991.

62. John, King of England, 1167–1216, see *Guide* p. 94. For the 1682 Market Hall, gift of William Drake, nephew of Sir William (the son of Francis and Joane Drake of Esher), cf. Pevsner op. cit. *Bucks*, p.48–9. This first Sir William Drake of Shardeloes was born and brought up at Esher Place. He died, 1669, not surprisingly unmarried after so hectic a family background. The estate passed to his nephew, son of his younger brother Francis (cf. Salmon, op. cit. p. 56). There is no definitive history of the Drakes of Amersham. Information is available from Nicholas Salmon above, who makes use of *The Shardeloes Papers of the 17th and 18th Centuries*, ed. G. Bland, OUP, 1947, and *Records of Buckinghamshire*, G. Bland, vol. XIV. cf. also sources quoted in Salmon Correspondence, Little Baddow Papers; and Drake Family sources quoted under Esher, and incorporated into this Amersham section.

63. Parish Church of St Mary, cf. Pevsner, above, p. 46, *VicHist—Buckinghamshire* 3:152–4 and church guide leaflet.

64. The history of Amersham Lollardy, originally followers of John Wycliffe (see Guide p. 87; ODCC p. 819), has been researched by local historian Nicholas Salmon (see Little Baddow Amersham papers) whose publications are available from The Amersham Museum, 49 High Street, Amersham Old Town, Buckhamshire. cf. *The Lollards of the Chiltern Hills*, W. H. Summers, 1906; *The Lollards or some account of the witnesses for the truth*, Religious Tract Society, 1825; *The Book of Amersham*, L. E. Pike and C. Birch; etc. Salmon traces the high proportion of Amersham residents who espoused Wycliffe's reforms back to 1414, when 20,000 Lollards marched on London "from the Chilterns, Bristol, Essex and the Midlands," and four Amersham Lollards were executed. Further arrests took place in 1462–4, but the cause of reform increased (eg. Thomas Man, burned at Smithfield, 1518, held unauthorized meetings and "turned seven hundred people to his religion," Foxe *Acts and Monuments*, 4:213). Tylsworth, another prominent preacher, was burnt in 1511, to be followed by others at Ruckles Field, Amersham, in 1521–22. Eleven names are listed on the 15 foot high Martyrs Memorial erected in 1931. Salmon

considers that not all were burnt to death, but the number of local dissenters was phenomenally high.

65. Sir William and Lady Catherine Tothill, see Salmon op. cit. pp. 49ff, also Hartwell, see p. 95ff. re their daughter, Joane Drake. Salmon is surely correct in crediting them (op. cit. p. 50) with only three daughters, in place of the 33 unnamed children quoted in other Amersham publications! But Salmon assumes that Joane's cure took place at Shardeloes, where "her husband Francis—himself a puritan—entertained numerous religious men who he hoped would effect a cure." This cannot be the whole story, since Joane's parents were still in residence, as were the Drakes at Esher. Thomas Hooker was certainly brought to Esher, not Amersham, to exercise his share in Joane's cure.

66. The reason given by Salmon (op. cit. p. 55) for Sir William Drake's inheritance of Shardeloes is that his aunt, Miss Catherine Tothill, "having bin from hir infancy taken with a palsy, and beeing thereby very weake and inferne of body, unfitt to be troubled with the managing of an estate," was persuaded to relinquish her inheritance to her nephew. After Christ Church, OxfordU (1624, cf. *Oxons*, vol. 1), and the Middle Temple where he worked with Sir Simmons D'Ewes (see *Guide* p. 326), Sir William purchased Amersham Manor, entered Parliament, and started the long association of the Drakes with parliamentary representation of the borough. However, despite his youthful tuition by Thomas Hooker, he did not espouse the Puritan cause, but discreetly withdrew to Italy "during much of the 1640s" (Salmon, p. 54).

67. The Drake Chapel is described by Pevsner, op. cit. p. 46–48, cf. *VicHist—Buckinghamshire* 3:153–4; but far better to visit it yourself.

68. See under Esher, see *Guide* pp. 160-63. The William Drake who built the present Shardeloes in 1766 died in 1796, and the estate passed to his younger son Thomas, who had by then assumed the surname and arms of Sir John Tyrwhitt of Stainford, Lincolnshire, whose properties he had inherited. Thus the family became the Tyrwhitt Drakes; cf. Salmon op. cit. pp. 60–6; *Oxons*, 1:386 has a large number of Tyrwhitt-Drakes of Shardeloes, all at Brasenose College.

69. Salmon, op. cit. pp. 52–53 and 55 notes that Joane Drake was not the only member of her family to suffer mental disorder. Her maternal uncle, John Denham (1615–69), whose young wife, Margaret, was seduced by James II when Duke of York, became so disturbed that he called on King Charles II, "and told him quite seriously that he was the reincarnation of the Holy Ghost." He was suspected later on of murdering the wayward lady "with a cup of hot chocolate."

70. Cf. *Buckinghamshire Parish Registers Marriages* 1908, 4:13.

71. See NEHGS, p. 1.

72. Ibidem, *Children of Rev. Thomas Hooker and Susan Garbrand*, p.4 ; see *Guide* p. 195-98, and p. 407 n. 6.

73. Susannah, c. 1593–1676. For her dates see NEHGS, pp. 42–3; and *The Goodwins of Hartford, Connecticut*, James Junius Goodwin, 1891, section *The Goodwin Family* by G. L. Walker, "Susannah—died in Farmington about three years later (ie. than her second husband, William Goodwin), May 17, 1676;" see *Guide* p. 418 n. 149. For Dr. John Herks Garbrand, 1542–89, DNB 7:845–6; and John (son of Tobias Herks Garbrand, MD) d. 1695, political writer, DNB 7:846: cf. also *Oxons* 2:546, see below.

74. Bishop John Jewel or Jewell, 1522–71, of Merton College, OxfordU, Fellow, Vicar of Sunningwell, Oxfordshire until deprived under Queen Mary, when he fled to Frankfurt (1555), to return under Elizabeth as Bishop of Salisbury, 1560, he published his support of the Elizabethan Settlement, aiming at an Anglican compromise, see DNB 10:815–19, *Oxons* 2:813, and further here, on *Guide* p. 188. "The great interest attaching to Jewel's writings is the insight which they give into the process by which the anglican system was established on a logical basis" (DNB, p. 817). For this volte face the Puritan party found it difficult to excuse him.

75. *Oxons* above records Garbrand Herks "Dutch bookseller in Oxford," his sons Thomas, b. 1539, chorister Magdalen College, fellow 1557-70; Dr John alias Herks, 1542–89,

fellow New College 1560–67, DD 1582, canon Salisbury and Wells, rector North Crawley, Buckinghamshire 1566–89; William, b. 1549, Magdalen, fellow 1570: his grandsons John, 1583/4–1618, son of Dr John above, also of New College; Tobias, 1579–1638, Magdalen, fellow 1605–19; Nicholas, b. 1600, Magdalen, fellow 1619–39, canon of Chichester; his great-grandson Dr Tobias, 1611–89, MD; and his great great grandsons John b. 1647, New Inn Hall, and Inner Temple, and John of Christ Church; a formidable list for a family of refugees.

76. *Magnalia* 1:338.

77. Ibidem, p. 336.

78. See *The Making of the English Middle Class, Business, Society and Family Life in London 1660–1730*, Peter Earle, Methuen, 1989, ch. iii, *The Independent Businesswoman* (a misleading term) pp. 166–174; cf. "Some of London's business continued to be run independently by women" etc.

79. NEHGS, p. 43, "In 1618, in the will of her brother John Garbrand, she is mentioned as not having received her part of her parents' estate."

80. See *History and Antiquties—Buckinghamshire* 3:159 re the "six Almes' houses "built by Sir William Drake "for the relief of six Poor Widows" in 1617; and "The Free-School" endowed by Robert Challoner. It opened at "A Tenement called 'the Church-House,'. . . Another Tenement given at the same time, by Charles Croke, for the Dwelling of the Schoolmaster," in 1624, with a curriculum of Latin, Greek, Religious Education and Hebrew. But there may well have been a less ambitious school in the care of the rectory before that. See also *VicHist—Buckinghamshire* 2:213, *Amersham Grammar School*, which, besides details of the Challoner School, gives the date of his death as "1 May 1621," a month after Susannah's marriage.

81. "The Master is usually the Curate of the parish" (*History and Antiquties—Buckinghamshire* 3:159). A Mr Edward Rayner appears to have been the first Master, "Mr Angel, probably the next master" (*VicHist—Buckinghamshire* 2:213).

82. *A Comment Upon Christ's last Prayer* is one of the last known sermons of Thomas Hooker, printed in London by Peter Cole at the sign of the Printing Press in Cornhill, 1656, 187.

83. *The Soules Humiliation*, printed for Andrew Crooke at the signe of the Beare in Paul's Church-yard, 2nd ed. 1638, 73–74.

84. *The Application of Redemption By the Effectual Work of the Word, and Spirit of Christ, for the bringing home of lost Sinners to God.* The Ninth and Tenth Books, printed by Peter Cole, near the Royal Exchange, London 1659, 137.

Chelmsford And The County Of Essex

1. For Chelmsford see *The Sleepers and the Shadows—Chelmsford: A Town, Its People and Its Past*, Hilda Grieve, Vol. 1, *The Medieval and Tudor Story*, ERO 1988. Unfortunately Volume 2 has not been published at the time of writing, but will undoubtedly prove as carefully researched, balanced and indispensable as Volume 1: cf. *VicHist—Essex*; esp. vol. III, *Roman Essex*, p. 1ff re fortified settlement west of the River Cam, ie. Moulsham; and *Chelmsford*, pp. 63–72. See also *Chelmsford with its Surroundings, Ordnance Map and Plan*, H. G. Daniels (the key John Walker map, 1591, is beautifully reproduced in *The Walkers of Hanningfield Surveyors and Mapmakers Extraordinary*, A. C. Edwards, K. C. Newton, 1984, Plate V); *A History of Essex*, A. C. Edwards, Unwin 1978; *The Place Names of Essex*, P. H. Reaney, 1935; *Chelmsford Hundred*, p. 23—282 (25 different spellings, from Celmeresforde, 1086, to Chelemanford, 1285, and The Ford of Ceolmaer, Assize Rolls, cf. p. 245); *Chelmsford Through The Ages*, Gilbert Terry, 1977; general works such as *The History and Antiquities of Essex*, P. Morant, 2 vol. 1768, rep. 1816; and numerous ERO

monographs, Nos 34 *Elizabethian Essex*; 36 *Medieval Essex*; 44 *Stuart Essex*, etc. NB. in Domesday two towns only are listed, Colchester and Maldon. The 438 other settlements were small rural communities, cf. *History from the Sources* (reissue of Domesday Book), No 32, Essex, ed. John Morris, 1983, "3. Land of the Bishop of London—(Hundred of Chelmsford) 12. Bishop William held Chelmsford before 1066—value £8," "6. Land of St Peter's Westminster," 15a, "14. St Peter's has always held Moulsham—Value—£12," etc.

2. *EncBrit 6:24*, but cf. *The English*, C. Hibbert, op. cit. p. 67, shows that whilst a fowl might then cost 1d, a sheep 1/5, ox 13/-, a palfrey could cost up to £15, so £30 was maybe a considerable rent; cf. H. Grieve, op. cit. p. 8ff. re the bridges, Grieve p. 5, cf. sketch map showing all three bridges in relation to medieval town and market, p. 16.

3. Known as "Shoprow," Grieve, op. cit. pp. 53–54, 60. Grieve traces the Mildmays from their first market stall in Shoprow, leased by Anne, widow of Guy Harling's son-in-law John Cornish (Mildmay too was related to Harling) in 1506, to Thomas Mildmay's purchase of the Guy Harlings house in 1533, pp. 89, 90,ff.

4. "Mr Hooker, preacher at Chelmsford, 1625," HTS 28:6, n. 19. However, the quotation is misleading in that the only reference to Hooker in John Marshall's will (deposited ERO, reference D/ABW 47/103) does not state his residence at Chelmsford, eg. "Item I give unto Mr Hooker by whose paines in the preachinge of the gospell I have received much spirituall comfort the somme of 40s to be payed upon the day of my funerall whome also I desire to preach at my funeral." If the inference is "at Chelmsford," then the Hookers could have been in residence prior to October 1625, not early in 1626. I incline to this conclusion, but for convenience retain the generally accepted dates 1626–1629.

5. Genealogical details of the Hooker family are to be found in Tables 1 and 6 (see *Guide* pp. 28 and 197). Sources include Hooker's *Genealogy*; NEHGS especially *Children of Reverend Thomas Hooker and Susan* p.44ff; Essex Record Office, Parish Registers, especially for Ann's baptism, ERO D/P 65/1/1 (Great Baddow St Mary) and burial, ERO D/P 94/1/2 (Chelmsford St Mary): for Sarah's baptism and burial, ERO D/P 92/1/2 (Chelmsford St Mary); for Reverend John, Buckinghamshire Record Office re Marsworth and Leckhampstead Parish Registers, marriage, births, etc, and Hugh Hanley, County Archivist, correspondence, including extracts from *History of the County of Buckinghamshire*, George Lipscomb, 1847, Little Baddow Papers; also Venn 2:403, John Hooker, from Essex, pens. Emmanuel 1649, matric 1650, no other details; for third son, unnamed, d. 1634, J. Winthrop papers, MHS, Boston, 1943, 177: cf. also major biographies, G. L. Walker, etc.

NB. DAB 17: 75–6, claims Joanna (Joan) Hooker was married in 1637, "who bore him four children, one of whom died at birth and another in infancy," but that Samuel and John (2) survived. DNB 18:51 repeats the marriage date. But this would make her no more than 15 years of age at marriage. I have preferred the date given in NEHGS, op. cit. p. 44, "m. 1640 Reverend Thomas Shepard, as his second wife," and also, "They had three children: Samuel, John and John 2d," as per my genealogical tables, see also *Guide*, pp. 286.

6. Reverend John Hooker MA. Commander Hooker's account (*Genealogy* op. cit. pp. 8–9) is largely speculative. No birthdate is known save that, according to Thomas Hooker's will, John was not 21 when his father died in 1647, and that Thomas was possibly apprehensive that John would remain in England (where he is assumed to have been at University, though neither *Alumni Oxonienses* nor *Cantabrigienses* make specific reference to his attendance), and might "Marry and Tarry" there (in which case he would forfeit his full inheritance; for Hooker's Will and Inventory of Estate, cf. NEHGS, pp. 21–22). Commander Hooker assumes John did not marry, and describes him as a "very dissipated" curate, collated reluctantly by the bishop, as Vicar of Mazeworth in Buckinghamshire, with "a suicidal ending, and a secret burial to avoid the severe inflictions which the penal laws of England at that time prescribed for the bodies of suicides" (*Genealogy*, op. cit. p. 9).

As no place named Mazeworth is listed in Buckinghamshire, I wrote on the off chance to the Rector of All Saints, Marsworth, Buckinghamshire, and to the Buckinghamshire County

Archivist, and found that John Hooker had been collated Vicar there, 12 February 1660 (Bishops' Transcripts, Buckinghamshire Record Office, D.A.T. 132; which also show that John signed as Vicar from 1659–82, there being no entries for 1683–85; cf. Lipscomb, *History of Buckinghamshire* op. cit. 3:412); that he was also presented to the rectorship of Leckhampstead, Buckinghamshire (some twenty miles from Marsworth) in 1669, where "John Hooker, clerk and Miss Mary Lovell were Married April 23, 1659" (Leckhpstd Parish Register, PR 127/1/1); and that "Elizabeth daughter of Mr John Hooker Rector of this parish and Mary his wife was baptised 24 August and was buried 24th" (NB. number obscure) in 1660.

That John was already rector of Leckhampstead in 1660 may be doubted. A second hand has added the words "Rector of this parish," with "the Revd" over "Mr," to the above parish register entry. There is no doubt, however, that John held the two livings in plurality, that he was married, and that he and his wife had at least two children, a second being recorded in the Bishops' Transcripts for Marsworth, "the baptism of a Mary Hooker on 24 Jan. 1662" (NB, Marsworth Parish Registers only go back to 1720). Lipscomb further adds "He died suddenly, in his bed, on a Sunday morning, 1684, and was buried obscurely" (*History* op. cit. p. 412). He also refers to John as MA, which may tie in with Venn's indecisive entry re a John Hooker "of Essex," pensioner at Emmanuel, 4 February 1649 (2:403), when John might have been 22–23 years of age, altho it is generally assumed he went to Oxford ("became a student at Oxford," Hooker's *Genealogy* op. cit. p. 9: but cf. Shuffleton, op. cit. p. 278, "John was preparing for Cambridge University," having already written, "John—went to England—to continue his education at Oxford," p. 273, but presumably not both at the same time). The enigma remains, but perhaps John Hooker's character was more stable than has hitherto been allowed. For Roger Newton, first pastor, Farmington, 1652, who completed his theological training in the Hooker home, see NEHGS, op. cit. p. 44, and *Magnalia* 1:237. For John Wilson Jr, son of Boston's, (Mass.) first Minister (DAB 20:336–7), colleague of Richard Mather at Dorchester, Massachusetts, see NEHGS p. 44; DAB 12:394–5. For Samuel Hooker and Mary Willett, see NEHGS pp. 44–58; *Magnalia* 1:88 and 2:30.

7. *Banner of Truth*, op. cit. 2:33, "When Thomas and Susan Hooker moved to Essex they established their home in the village of Great Baddow, about three miles outside Chelmsford. It was in Great Baddow that their daughter Ann was born and baptised." H. C. Wooley, *Hooker Bibliography*, Centre Church, Hartford, Monographs No. I, 1932, suggests that the Hookers lived next door to John Haynes (later Governor of Connecticut), in Great Baddow, but I know of no evidence for this.

8. *The Friendly Inn, Essex Heyday*, op.cit. pp. 146–62; cf. Sir Thomas Mildmay's control of Chelmsford Inns at political elections, etc., ibidem p. 26ff.

9. The Mildmays appear at every stage of this guide. Information is readily available, eg. *Sir Walter Mildmay and Tudor Government*, Stanford E. Lehmberg, University of Texas Press, Austin, 1964, first full biography of Sir Walter, presented as "a towering parliamentary figure, leading the House of Commons from 1576–1589—a skilled negotiator—a shrewd analyst of foreign affairs—a dutiful member of the Privy Council" (p. vii): cf. also works listed under n. 1, especially Grieve op. cit. pp. 99–120; DNB 13:372–76; *A Brief Memoir of the Mildmay Family*, Lt. Col. H. A. St John Mildmay, Bodley, 1913, to whom I am indebted for many details in Genealogical Table 7, *Guide*, page 200-201; *The Mildmays and their Chelmsford Estates*, J. H. Round, Essex Archaeological Society, TEAS xv, 1921, pp. 1–16, NB. "these nine several families of Mildmays," detailed p. 8, cf. The *Account Books of Benjamin Mildmay, Earl Fitzwalter*, A. C. Edwards, Regency Press, "nine branches of the family in Essex alone," p. vi; *Sir Humphrey Mildmay: Royalist Gentleman Glimpses of the England Scene 1633–1692*, Philip Lee Ralph, Rutgers University Press, draws on the Diary of Sir Humphrey of Danbury; *Guy Harlings, New Street, Chelmsford*, F. Chancellor, ERO xxv, 151; etc. Sir Thomas and Lady Avice's fine cathedral monument, with its "fifteen pledges of their prosperous love," erected 1571 (described Pevsner, *Essex*, p. 115), stands beneath brasses commemorating some forty Mildmays buried in the vaults

or within the cathedral precinct. Hard by is the ornate memorial to Benjamin, Earl Fitzwalter, d. 1756.

10. Grieve op. cit. p. 102.

11. Ibidem, p. 129; cf. *In Search of Essex*, S. M. Jarvis and C. T. Harrison, pub. Essex Countryside (undated, c. 1960s), p. 17.

12. Grieve above, especially. pp. 91ff; DNB 13:374-76; Venn 2:188; and *Sir Walter Mildmay*, Lehmberg, op. cit. "b. in Chelmsford, Essex, son of Thomas Mildmay, a mercer" (p. 3ff), "acquired the manor of Seynclers and Herons in Danbury—there is no indication that he resided on any of these estates" (p. 24f; cf.*Guide*, p. 319). NB. but St John Mildmay *A Brief Memoir*, op. cit. claims "Danbury, Essex, was purchased by Sir Walter from the Earl of Northamptonshire in the reign of Edward VI, and he is said to have built the house in which his younger son lived" (p. 4); founded Emmanuel (Lehmberg p. 222ff); etc, cf. *Guide* pp. 76f and 141-43.

13. Cy Pres, as near as possible to the testator's intentions; cf. Grieve op. cit. p. 100–101, "Sir Walter and his colleague Robert Keilway found five parishes with chantry objects worthy of support. At Harwich—the upkeep of the sea walls, at Witham provision for the poor, at Romford a travelling preacher, and at Rayleigh a grammar school." At Chelmsford they agreed to continue "the revenues of the late chantry of Our Lady otherwise Mownteneye chantry—the schoolmaster there has had for his yearly wages £9.12s, which school is very meet and necessary to continue." For Sir John Mounteneye, see Grieve p. 31.

14. Sir Henry of Wanstead, DNB 13:372-74; Morant, *History*, op. cit. 30, ii, 29; Bramston, *Autobiography*, op. cit. p. 29. NB. Cecile Rodger, re the royal treasure, says the guilt was to have "yielded the King's treasure to the 'unlawful' Commonwealth authorities," LBHS Newsletter, April 1990, p. 8.

15. DNB, 13:373.

16. Mather 2:30, "Gulielmus Mildmay, Mr" graduated AB, 1647 (but does not allow him the double asterisk which stands for AB and AM as per Morison, cf. *Founding of Harvard College*, op. cit. p. 349, 375; cf. St John Mildmay op. cit. p. 32; Venn 3:188. For Dunster, Lyon, and the whole incident, see *Life of Mr Henry Dunster*, Mather 1:405–8; Morison, *Builders of the Bay Colony* op. cit. ch.VI *Henry Dunster, President of Harvard*, pp. 183–213; Venn 2:76, notes Dunster was admitted at Magdalen, Cambridge University, 1627; was curate and teacher at Bury, Lancashire; emigrated to Cambridge, Mass. 1640; President of Harvard 1640–54.

17. For Essex see works listed at n. 1. For Havering-atte-Bower, *VicHist—Essex* 7:1–5; *King's England*, op. cit. p.188–190; for Romford (Roman Durolitum) *VicHist—Essex* 7:56-63.

18. General Richard Deane, 1610–53, regicide, *EncBrit* 7:898; *Essex Heyday* p. 277.

19. John Norden, 1548–1625, notable English topographer. His first finished essay into a *Speculum Britanniae* (1593) was Middlesex. The original has annotations in Burghley's handwriting. Five other counties (including Essex—the "English Goshen" quotation is taken from *Essex Heyday*, op. cit. p. 308) were completed by his death, with much besides. His London maps are the best known for Tudor times. *EncBrit* 19:740; DNB 14:550-53.

20. Barking, cf. A. C. Edwards A History op. cit. p. 29; Discovering Essex in London, Kenneth Neale, Essex Countryside, 1969, pp. 22, 26, 38, 59, etc. It is surely significant that, in Domesday, "not a single market appears in Essex" (*VicHist—Essex* 1:1903). There were chartered markets over the Suffolk border, at Sudbury, Clare, Haverhill, and no more until London was reached, ringed by street markets as is still the case today, the termini to which Essex traders brought their goods for sale.

21. See *English Nonconformity*, Henry W. Clark, London 1911, 1:254–5; *The Reformation*, Owen Chadwick, *Pelican History of the Church* 3:225–32, ff; etc.

22. William Laud, 1573–1645, held a number of livings before Dean of Glostershire, ie. Stamford, North Kilworth (Leicestershire), West Tilbury (Essex), Cuxton (Kent); but he was not aiming at the "painful" ministry of the word within a congregation beloved of Puritans, pointing rather at a managerial office which could only militate against a Pastoral (Shepherd) Episcopacy. Charles Carlton, Archbishop William Laud, Routledge and Kegan, 1987, says his

father was a clothier (owned looms) not a tailor, but comments "His humble origins produced a drive to succeed that influenced his career, his death, a martyrdom that he embraced heroically, has exaggerated the importance of his life" (p. 1ff). Christopher Hill, *Economic Problems of the Church* 1971, summarises Laud as an insecure academic obsessed with detail, a petty bureaucrat promoted beyond his capabilities (p. 229): cf. *Archbishop Laud*, H. Trevor-Roper, 1940; DNB 11:626; *EncBrit* 16:276–8; *Oxons* 3:885, Venn 3:50; *The Laudians*, Chadwick *The Reformation*, op. cit. pp. 225–30, etc.

Andrew Foster, *Conflict in Early Stuart England* op. cit. ch. 7, *Church Policies of the 1630s*, p. 193–223 notes "after years of being regarded as an unsuccessful and unlikeable little martinet, Laud is suddenly the object of sympathy" (p. 194, ref. Sharpe, *The Personal Rule of Charles I*, in *Before the English Civil War*, ed. H. Tomlinson, 1983, pp. 53–78) and that some revisionist works portray Laud as "essentially a mild-mannered, misunderstood bureaucrat in Bancroft's mould, with no novel theological ideas" (p. 196), but rejects this view. "Laud was 'indeed the greatest calamity ever visited upon the Church of England.'" (p. 194).

23. cf. *The Diary of John Evelyn*, 1620–-706, wealthy dilettante (DNB, "virtuoso"), consistent royalist and Protestant who avoided embarrassment by travelling abroad during the civil war, offended by laxity of Charles II's court and antipathy to Church of England; patron of arts and Oxford University: Secretary Royal Society; prolific diarist, DNB 6:943–47, "then was the University exceedingly regular, under the exact discipline of William Laud, Archbishop of Canterbury, then Chancellor" Everyman ed. 1966, p. 10.

24. cf. *Early Essex Town Meetings*, F. G .Emmison, 1970, p. xii etc; Hunt *Puritan Moment* op. cit. pp. 10, 47, 69, 78, 79; Grieve op. cit. *The Poor* pp. 143–48, innumerable instances of acute poverty. re. Roman Winchester, *EncBrit* 28:805ff.

25. VicHist—Essex 3:52ff describes the Ythancaestir of Bede (the *Venerable* scholar and English historian, c. 673–735, cf. ODCC p. 148. His *Historia Ecclesiastica Gentis Anglorum* was completed, 731). See also St Cedd, ODCC p. 254, and Chelmsford Cathedral guide books. Sts Aidan, Chad, Cedd, Columba of Iona, Cuthbert, Egbert, Oswald, Wilfrid each contributed to the establishment of Christianity in Britain. Their stories of independent, inaugural evangelism, are outlined severally in ODCC, *Dictionary of Saints*, Essex guide books etc: to whom Puritan belief owed credal succession.

26. Bradwell-Juxta-Mare: Pevsner, *Essex*, p. 99; *St Thomas's Church* guide, K. and K. Bruce 1986. For the Sherman family, see also *Guide* p. 258. Contentment, Massachuetts was renamed Dedham.

27. For the Dengie Peninsular, see *In Search of Essex*, Jarvis and Harrison op. cit. pp. 50, 55–58; *Essex*, Crouch, op. cit. pp. 71–78; etc. Burnham-on-Crouch is well described by Pevsner, *Essex*, pp. 107–9.

28. *A History of the Diocese of Chelmsford*, Gordon Hewitt, 1984 is available from the cathedral, with cathedral guidebooks: see also Pevsner *Essex* p. 114ff; and *A Short History of the Cathedral Church*, Wykeham Chancellor, 1938.

29. *Banner of Truth*, op. cit. 2:33, "Two lectures were delivered each week, one on the Sabbath afternoon and the other on the market day at which Hooker preached, whilst upon the Lord's Day he helped Mr Michaelson in the worship." "Drew ... away from the ale-houses," *Essex Heyday*, op. cit. p. 217.

30. John Michaelson, BD, Venn 3:183, cf. Mather, "Mr Mitchel, the incumbent of the place," 1:335; cf. T. W. Davids, "seldom coming to church until prayers was ended," *Annals of Evangelical Nonconformity in the County of Essex from the time of Wycliffe to the Restoration, with Memorials of the Essex Ministers who were ejected or silenced in 1660–1662*, London 1863, p. 171.

31. *Essex Heyday* op. cit. p. 218; NB. Michaelson is accredited by Venn 3:183 with BD, not DD. "Doctor" is therefore a courtesy title. cf. W. Chancellor, *Short History* op. cit. p. 21; re the offending escutcheons in the east window, cf. Grieve op. cit p. 72; re Michaelson's retreat to Writtle, see *Essex Heyday* p. 324.

32. HTS, p. 11, from Plume Ms, No 25, cf. *Dr Plume's Pocket-Book*, Andrew Clark, *Essex Review* 19 (1905): 67.

33. *Magnalia* 1:345.

34. Hooker's known sermons are detailed in the authoritative bibliography in HTS, pp. 390–425, following Sargent Bush Jr's Essay 4, *Establishing the Hooker Canon*, pp. 378–89. Some sermons are printed, including the 5 here, *Spiritual Munitions, Church's Deliverances, Carnal Hypocrite, Faithful Covenanter, Danger of Desertion*. Copies can also be found in a number of New England libraries, the Williams library, Bloomsbury, London, even small libraries such as the Plume at Maldon, Essex.

35. HTS above, pp. 232, 245; cf. my fuller treatment in *Growing Towards Greatness*, 1987, 14th Thomas Hooker Lecture, Centre Church., Hartford, Conn..

36. *Magnalia* 1:337.

37. *Banner of Truth*, op. cit. "we have a record of his being actively engaged in the Gospel in and around London for a period before being called to Chelmsford," 1:35–36.

38. "A judicious person would say of him, 'He was the best at an use (ie. personal application of the point under discussion) that ever he heard,'" *Magnalia* 1:335.

39. Quoted from Hunt, *Puritan Moment*, op. cit. p. 257, cf. n. 75, from Shepard's *A Memoir of His Own Life*, in *Chronicles of the First Plantation of the Colony of Massachusetts Bay*, ed. Alex Young, Boston, 1846, pp. 236–7.

40. *Annals,* T. W. Davids, op. cit. p. 150–1, ironically re Samuel Collins, "one of the bishop's best friends," cf. Venn 1:374 (Trinity College 1595, MA 1603, ordained Norwich 1601, Curate of Ash Bocking, Suffolk, Vicar of Braintree 1611–61, d. 1667).

41. Collins was an active member of the Braintree Vestry (see *Guide* p. 269) but was evidently so agitated by the insecurity of his situation that he failed in his normal secretarial duties, "which probably explains why no minutes were recorded" for that May, suggests Emmison, *Early Essex Town Meetings*, 1970, p.60.

42. Sir Arthur Duck, DNB 6:87. Richard Hooker, see *Guide* p. 15 and p. 357 n. 1.

43. Davids, op. cit. p. 151–2.

44. *Magnalia* 1:338.

45. Davids op. cit. pp. 152–55; so *Magnalia* 1:345, and Shuffleton, op. cit. p. 128–9. For Raweth, and Rayleigh see *In Search of Essex*, op. cit. pp. 72–73; for Wickford and Elizabeth Reid, p. 84; for Ashingdon and Canute, p. 74.

46. Davids, op. cit. p. 152–3.

47. *Essex Heyday*, op. cit. p. 179–94; cf *The Story of the King's Highway*, Sidney and Beatrice Webb, Vol. V, *English Local Government*. 1913, eg. Chapter 5, *New Uses of the Roads in the 17th and 18th Century*, pp. 62–76.

48. Davids op. cit. p.150 re tonnage and poundage; cf. *EncBrit* 27:11. For the wider issues cf. *EncBrit* 5:906–12, and all histories, eg. *The Outbreak of the English Civil War*, Anthony Fletcher, published Arnold, 1981, especially pp. 71–72, 169, 241 ("pressed 'with great violence'"); *Charles I, The Personal Monarch*, Pauline Gregg, Dent, 1981, pp. 40–41, 129–34, 138, 183–6; *The Life and Times of Charles I*, D. R. Watson, Weidenfeld and Nicolson, 1972, p. 53, 60–66.

49. *The Diary of Ralph Josselin, 1616–1683*, ed. Alan Macfarlane, OUP, 1976, p. 648.

50. The Little Baddow Historical Society is fortunate to have a three volumed *History of an Essex Village* carefully and widely researched by a former resident, Sheila V. Rowley, covering almost every aspect of the life of the village, together with numerous other historical papers (hereafter as Rowley). Cambridge Historian Dr R. Buick Knox has written the *History of Little Baddow United Reformed Church*. Pevsner has written of St Mary's Parish Church, *Essex*, p. 271, as has *VicHist—Essex* 3:22, 46. re John Newton, then Vicar, cf. Rowley 2:19; Cecile Rodger LBHS Newsletter, Apr. 1990, p. 4; Venn 3:252, who notes Newton possibly baptised St Mary Abchurch, London, 1596, and entered St Johns Cambridge where he graduated MA at 24 yrs, 1620. His student days were thus entirely spent under the shadow of Thomas Hooker, which may be significant.

51. Susan Cook, cf. Buick Knox *History*, p. 5, and Rowley 2:19.

52. "A hypocaust is said to have been found here and there are many Roman tiles in the church," VicHist—Essex 3:46.

53. Danbury and Little Baddow, Peter Came, European Library, published Zaltbornmel, Netherlands, 1987, Intro. p. 1. The Sketch Map of Little Baddow in the Middle Ages, Rowley 2:48, accurately conveys the contained-scatteredness of the village.

54. Information about the Little Baddow Mildmays comes from sources detailed in *Guide* p. 408 n. 9. St John Mildmay, op. cit. pp. 27–35 has a chapter on Sir Henry of Great Graces; Rowley op. cit. 1:6ff, and *Some Aspects of the History of Little Baddow* (1970), with LBHS Newsletters Aug. 1988, Ap. 1990, contain studies of local (16–17 century) families: cf. *The Mildmays and their Essex Estates*, J. H. Round, TEAS XV, 1921, 1–16. Round suggests the name Mildmay comes from the Little Baddow Manor of Mildemet (p. 5, cf. *Guide* p. 224). For Great Graces, cf. Pevsner, *Essex*, p. 141.

55. Pevsner, *Essex*, op. cit. p. 271.

56. Rowley 1:6. For the Gurdons of Assington, Suffolk, cf. DNB 8:795–6, and Venn 2:275. Brampton's (d. 1649) sons John (1595–1675), Ipswich MP and High Court of Justice for Trial of Charles I (refused to attend), Robert and Brampton, entered Emmanuel, Cambridge respectively in 1611, 1614, 1614. Of John's sons, five followed, of whom Nathaniel D.D. was Rector of Chelmsford (1681–96).

57. Re J. Rogers' *Doctrine of Faith*, and Hooker's Preface, see *Guide* p. 258: also HTS pp. 133, 140–42, 144–46 (text of the Preface), 393. "The way which the author of this treatise hath followed in making a saving contrition to go before faith will be found to be beyond exception," Hooker wrote (p. 144), revealing his "concern with the contrite state . . . without contrition there can be no saving faith" (p. 133), which underlay his preparationist theology.

58. Came op. cit. 53; cf. St John Mildmay op. cit. p. 31: cf. Lady Alicia's "ghost of Graces," Rodger, LBHS Newsletter, April 1990, p. 8.

59. Pevsner, *Essex*, p. 156.

60. St John Mildmay, op. cit. p. 35.

61. Rowley op. cit. I, p. 22.

62. St John Mildmay, op. cit. pp. 28–30, cf. DNB 5:1304–6.

63. *EncBrit* 8:459. cf. DAB 5:419.

64. C. Rodger, LBHS Newsletter, Apr. 1990, p. 8; cf. S. E. Morison, *Harvard College* op. cit. p. 197, and Venn 2:307.

65. The Hall, Pevsner, *Essex*, op. cit. p. 271: the Manors, Rowley op. cit. 1:1–11.

66. *VicHist—Essex*, 1:334, cf. Rowley, op. cit. I, p. 2. NB. For Domesday Little Baddow, see *History from the Sources* op. cit. book No 32.

67. LBHS Newsletter, Aug. 1988, devoted to Sir John Smythe, articles by M. and P. Herniman and C. Rodger, cf. Rowley, op. cit. 1:3.

68. Rowley, op. cit. 1:49.

69. Barrington family, "whose ancestors I can aver to be knights before English was in England," quoting first Earl of Warwick *Puritan Moment*, op. cit. p. 167. cf. Rodger, LBHS Newsletter Apr. 1990, p. 9–10, with ref. to the family accounts kept by steward John Kendall from 1622; Buick Knox, *Little Baddow URC A History*, pp. 6–8 ff; Rowley op. cit. p. 4–5, etc; DNB 1:1209, and extensive refs. in many historical works, eg. *The Puritan Gentry*, pp. 11, 21, 25, 26, 38, 44, 57, etc. For Hatfield Forest, cf. *VicHist—Essex* 1:166; *National Trust Guide*, 1980, p. 483–4.

70. Hatfield Broad Oak, one of the largest ancient parishes of Essex, cf. *VicHist* 8:158ff, "its assessed valuation of £85 ranked 6th," at Domesday, (p. 159), the manor held by King Harold, later to Geoffrey de Mandeville, Earl of Essex, and to Baron Rich at the dissolution (1547), sold by him to Sir Francis Barrington (p. 165): cf. *St Mary's Church Guide; Hatfield Broad Oak Village Trail*, produced by St Mary's Primary School; various Guide Books.

71. *St Mary's Church, Hatfield Broad Oak*, Church Guide.

72. Sir Francis Barrington, 1550–1628, see n. 69 above; cf. DNB 1:1209; DAB 17:75f; *EncBrit* 3:436–8; *Essex Heyday*, op. cit. p. 312.

73. *EncBrit* 17:773.

74. The general effect of Barrington's and Masham's opposition to the forced loans is discussed in *Conflict in Early Stuart England, Studies in Religion and Politics, 1603–42*, ed. Richard Cust and Anne Hughes, 1989, pp. 155, 157, 161, etc., see especially Essay 5, *Politics and the Electorate in the 1620s*, Re Sir William Masham of Otes Manor, High Laver cf. *Essex Heyday*, op. cit. p.323; *VicHist—Essex* 4:87–97 (Otes held by Barringtons from 14th century purchased by Masham 1614, p. 91).

75. Roger Williams, see *Guide* p. 383 n. 8 and n. 11. For the mischievous correspondence with Lady Barrington, cf. *Essex Heyday*, pp. 72–76, cf. DNB 21:445–50.

76. Edward Whalley, 1615–75 and William Goffe, cf. DNB 21:1305–07, DNB 8:71–73, and DAB 20:25; *EncBrit* 28:574; *Leaders of the Civil War, from 1642–48*, G. R. Smith and Margaret Toynbee, pp. 210–13.

77. DAB 20:287–89. The marriage took place on 15 Dec. 1629 (ibidem p. 287).

78. Sir Thomas Barrington, d. 1644, Member of Parliament for the last Parliament under James I and first under Charles I, cf. A. C. Edwards, *A History of Essex*, 1978, p. 106; Buick Knox *History* op. cit. pp. 5–9. NB. "Sir Thomas Barrington of Hatfield Broad Oak became one of the leading members of the Providence Company, whose aim was to settle a Puritan Colony in Providence Island in the Caribbean Sea," *A History of Braintree and Bocking*, W. F. Quin, Laverham Press, 1981, p. 106.

79. Act of Uniformity, ODCC pp. 1389–90: National Covenant, ibidem p.939.

80. For Thomas Gilson and John Oakes, cf. Buick Knox *Little Baddow History* op. cit. pp. 6, 7, 23.

81. March 15, 1672, ODCC p. 381, the third Indulgence under Charles II, in accord with the 1660 Declaration of Breda, which promised liberty of conscience should the king be restored, but the first two made little difference because Charles ignored them.

82. Buick Knox *History* op. cit. pp. 7, 18. St Antholin's Church, a noted Puritan centre, was in Watling Street, between Cheapside and Cannon Street, in the City.

83. *Butler's Charity*, J. Berridge, E. R. liv, 11; cf. Rowley, op. cit. 3:25–40 for the story of education in the village, and Buick Knox *History*, op. cit. for the independent congregation's charitable trusts.

84. Quoted from *A Discourse on Early Nonconformity in Maldon*, Robert Burls, 1840 (former pastor) p. 20. Act of Uniformity, ODCC p. 1389–90; Conventicle Act, ODCC p. 338; Five Mile Act, ODCC p. 507; Toleration Act, ODCC p. 1365.

85. DNB 1:1209–11.

86. Ibidem p. 1210, similarly quotations below. John Locke's life, 1632–1704, covers the early New England period, through the English Civil War, Commonwealth, Restoration, and Glorious Revolution of 1688, yet it is scarcely relevant to the Hooker saga, which had fulfilled its destiny before Locke's influence could be felt. Nonetheless he represents an important element of the era, the growth of individualism, rationalism, free enquiry, intellectual toleration, all sustained within a Christian framework developed from but strikingly different to the Puritan experience. It is significant that a leader of contemporary congregationalism like Shute Barrington could live emotionally so close beside Locke. By coincidence, Locke lived for his last 14 years as guest of Sir Francis and Lady Damaris (daughter of the Cambridge Platonist Ralph Cudworth, see *Guide* p. 148, long standing friends of Locke) Masham, at Otes Manor, High Laver, not far from Little Baddow, where Roger Williams and John Norton had been chaplains to the celebrated Essex Puritan leader, Sir William Masham, d. 1705, see *Guide* p. 119. Locke's works include *Letters concerning Toleration* (1689, 1690, 1692), *Two Treatises of Government* (1688), *Essay Concerning Human Understanding* (1690), *Reasonableness of Christianity as Delivered in the Scriptures* (1695), *A Discourse on Miracles* (posthumously, 1716): cf. DNB 12:27–36; *EncBrit* (15) 23:221–25.

87. Buick Knox, *History,* op. cit. p. 8.

88. Ibidem, p. 9; cf. Rowley op. cit. III, p. 54.

89. Buick Knox, above, pp. 10–14 and 17. Joseph and David Marven, ibidem pp. 16, 17–19.

90. Ibidem p. 10, from *Night Thoughts* Edward Young, 1683–1765, DNB 21:1283–88, poet, priest (son of Edward, Dean of Salisbury) chaplain to William and Mary. *Night Thoughts* was partly autobiographical, and had wide appeal to Church going people.

91. Cf. *John Eliot, Apostle to the Indians,* O. E. Winslow, Boston 1968, p. 101.

92. Cuckoos Farmhouse and its occupants, cf. Rowley op. cit. 1:44–45, and Roy Warsop (L. B. historian), Porter Family Memo, Little Baddow Papers. NB. *Dorset Pilgrims,* Thistlethwaite, op. cit., gives throughout detailed information re John Porter Jr. of Felsted and his brother-in-law Joseph Loomis of Braintree, and families, who sailed to Windsor, Connecticut, 1638, with the Ephraim Huett (Huitt) Party, see *Guide* p. 241.

Huitt, see Venn 3:88, emigrated to Windsor as replacement teacher for Windsor Pastor John Warham's first teacher John Maverick, who died (see Thistlethwaite above, pp. 142–44, etc.). Grants of adjacent land were made to Porter and Loomis in Plymouth Meadow, Plimmoth Plantation having been the first to attempt to settle the area, but perforce gave way to the more numerous Windsor settlers from Dorchester, Massachusetts. Porter, a wealthy trader who retained his London connections, became the second constable at Windsor.

The settlement of Dorchester, Massachusetts, and later of Windsor, Connecticut, was carried out predominantly by the west country company who sailed in the *Mary and John,* first ship to reach Massachusetts in 1630 in advance of, though under the aegis of the Massachusetts Bay Co., led by Warham, Ludlow (see *Guide* pp. 31-32 and p. 359 n. 22) and others, was both a separate development under John White of Dorchester's earlier *Dorset Adventurers* (see *Guide* p. 293 and p. 428 n. 224), and also closely associated with Thomas Hooker and the settlement of Hartford, Connecticut, as the presence of East Anglia families like the Porters/Loomis' shows—further illustrating the trans-England Puritan kinship networks. A Mary and John Clearing House, c/o Burton W. Spear, 5602 305th Street, Toledo, Ohio 43611, has been established. Its many publications deal in detail with the *Mary and John* story.

93. *Magnalia,* 1:336.

94. Ibidem, 1:335.

95. DAB 20:393–4 re Edward Winslow's defense of Plymouth Plantation v. changes brought about by Lydford and John Oldham.

96. *Magnalia* 1:336.

97. Davids *Annals,* op. cit. p. 151 f, cf. Banner of Truth, op. cit. 2:38. The following list of members of *The Cuckoos Company* is also from Davids, who prints the names of Hooker's petitioners in full, pp. 153–61.

98. See Note 92 above and Thistlethwaite op. cit. pp. 138, 157, 161, etc.

99. Tofts manor, cf.Rowley op. cit. 1:3, 4, 24–32, etc; and C. Rodger, Little Baddow Newsletter, Aug. 1988, Apr. 1990, for all details quoted here.

100. Bassetts Manor, cf. Rowley op. cit. 1:5, 9, 19–23, etc.

101. For the Blakes of Bassetts, see *William Pynchon (1590–1662) Founder of Springfield, Massachusetts, and Thomas Hooker,* D. C. Collingwood, *The Connecticut Nutmegger,* Journal of the Connecticut Society of Genealogists, vol. 23, Nos 3 (Dec. 1990) and 4 (March 1991), pp. 389, 395, and footnotes, 6, 42, 43. pp. 628, 632.

For the Pennings, cf. C. Rodger, op. cit. Little Baddow Newsletter, Apr. 1990, p. 9; and also for Sir Moundeford Bramston ibidem p. 11–13; Venn 1:204, Queens' 1632, LL.D. Trinity Hall, Chief Justice of the King's Bench, d. 1679; and DNB 2:1115 (see also *Guide* p. 243).

For the Tweedys and local recusants, see Rodger ibidem, p. 3–4; Rowley op. cit. 2:18.

102. *Migration from East Anglia,* Tyack, op. cit. 2:xxi; but Tyack is over-dependent on Colonel Charles Edward Banks, whose books, eg. *The Planters of the Commonwealth,* and *The Winthrop Fleet of 1630* (both 1930) contributed much to contemporary genealogical studies, but

are not without error. Tyack must therefore be treated with reservation, eg. he confuses the Blakes of Little Baddow with a family of the same name who migrated from Pitminster, Somerset, with the Dorset pilgrims, and therefore mistakenly supposes the Little Baddow family to have sailed in the *Mary and John*. In fact, the west country Blakes ventured in the *Hopewell*, 1635, cf. Burton Spear correspondence, Mary and John Clearing House, Feb. 1993, Little Baddow Papers.

103. *The First Century of the History of Springfield. The Official Record from 1636–1736*, Henry M. Burt, 1898, 1:40–46.

104. Old King Cole, cf. *Folklore Myths and Legends of Britain*, Readers Digest Assoc. 1973, p. 234: St Helena, 255–330, ODCC p. 619: Geoffrey of Monmouth, Bishop of St Asaph, Wales, chronicler *Historia Britonum* ODCC p. 548.

105. Colonia Camulodunum, cf. *VicHist—Essex* 3:2ff (NB. a new section on the history of Colchester is currently being written); *History and Antiquities of the Borough of Colchester*, Philip Morant, 1748; Pevsner *Essex* pp. 129–48; *Essex County Standard Guide*, Geoff H. Martin, 3rd edition 1967, p. 5ff; *Colchester Official Guide*, G. H. Martin, 5th edition 1982, p. 12ff; and all Essex Guidebooks. There is an imaginative illustrated *Colchester Town Trail* available from the information centre.

106. *A History of Essex*, A. C. Edwards, 1978, 4th impress. pp. 15–17.

107. *The History and Antiquities of Colchester Castle*, J. H. Round, 1882; *Colchester Castle*, Duncan W. Clark, 1948; *Colchester Castle: A History, Descrition and Guide*, D. T–D. Clarke, 3rd ed. 1974; Pevsner *Essex*, pp. 138–9, on the Balkerne Gate, "one of the largest and most impressive town gates in Roman Britain, 107 feet long, it projects 30 feet in front of the wall. There were four arched entrances, two of them 17 feet wide for wheeled traffic."

108. *The English Social History*, Christopher Hibert, Grafton 1987, pp. 252–64; *EncBri.* 5:910ff, 6:660–1; *The Outbreak of the English Civil War*, Anthony Fletcher, 1981; *The King's War 1641–46*, C. V. Wedgewood, Penguin 1983; *The Causes of the English Civil War*, Conrad Russell, Clarendon Press, 1990; etc. For local impact of the royalist march to Colchester, cf. *Boreham, History, Tales and Memories of an Essex Village*, Burgess and Rance, 1988, account of a council of war at New Hall, June 9, 1648, p. 12; cf. *The Impact of the English Civil War*, ed. John Morrill, 1991, *Siege of Colchester*, p. 15; etc.

109. *Colchester Castle*, D. T-D. Clarke, op. cit. p. 17, *Official Guide*, 1982 edition, p. 15; cf. *The Siege of Colchester*, D. T-D. Clarke; *History Essex*, A. C. Edwards op. cit. pp. 5–60; *The Civil Wars of England*, John Kenyon, Weidenfeld and Nicolson 1988, , pp. 176–99, *Siege of Colchester* pp. 184–6, NB. claims Lucas and Lisle were shot as "mere soldiers of fortune," p. 192, surely sophistry.

If irrational action inevitably follows armed conflict, it must be said that Thomas Fairfax, 1612–71, was generally "Chivalrous and punctilious in his dealings with his own men and the enemy. Honour and conscientiousness were equally the characteristics of his private and public character" (EncBrit 10:132). Son and heir of the Second Baron Cameron of Denton, nr. Otley, Yorks; educated St Johns, CambU; his military training begun in Holland under Sir Horace Vere (see *Guide* p. 362 n. 31); he joined his father in the service of Charles I, who knighted him, 1640. Both, however, opposed the king's arbitrary prerogative. When civil war erupted, Lord Fairfax was made Parliament general of the north, Thomas his cavalry lieutenant-general. They exercised their commands through the campaign which won the north of England for Parliament at the battle of Marston Moor, 1644. Thomas became Commander-in-chief, with Cromwell his second in command. His gifts were military not political, but under the Commonwealth his steadying influence over the army, especially its anarchically independent officers, remained. In him we see again the 'non-separating' Puritan so representative of New England's founders. DNB 6:1005–13.

"The execution of Lucas and Lisle was a solitary instance of severity, and by no means an indefensible one" (ibid. p. 1012), "for the trouble, damage and mischief they have brought upon the town and kingdom" (ibid. p. 1009). They were responsible for prolonging the Civil

War into a second phase, and forcing revolt on Colchester, which was by choice a Parliament town.

110. The Roman Walls are described by *VicHist*—*Essex* 3:92–96; and by Pevsner, *Essex* p. 230. For St Peter's Church see ibidem p. 135, and *Church History*, R.M.Wilson, 1982.

111. Town Lectures, cf. Morant Antiquities of Colchester, op. cit. p. 96. The lecturers listed by Morant can be traced in Venn (1:27; 2:114; 3:125); cf. also ERO correspondence, Little Baddow Papers, and *Official Guide*, p. 39 (St Botolph's), p. 47 (St James's) for the Lecture Churches. For St John's Abbey, cf. p. 46. For C. Simeon, 1759–1836, ODCC p. 1257, cf. *St Peter's Church History*, op. cit. p. 15.

112. See, for instance, the witness of the Colchester Protestant martyrs, as told in Foxe's *Martyrs*, Book Society of London edition, p. 329ff.

113. Copford, cf. *Treasures of Britain*, op. cit. p. 148; H. C. Edwards *History of Essex*, op. cit. p. 27; *King's England, Essex*, op. cit. pp. 99–102. John Haynes, DAB 8:459–60; DNB 9:301–2. Copford Hall, Pevsner, *Essex*, op. cit. p. 150.

114. Edmund Bonner, 1500–69, Wolsey's loyal chaplain, Bishop of Hereford, and of London (1539) but temporarily deprived for opposition to Edward VIth's Protestant reforms, he was restored by Mary Tudor and presided over the martyrdom of some 200 Protestants, including Latimer, Ridley, and Cranmer. He refused the oath to Elizabeth I in her 1559 Act of Supremacy, and was committed to the Marshalsea. ODCC p. 186, *EncBrit* 4:210–12; DNB 2:818–22.

115. *New England's Prospect*, William Wood, Prince Society, Boston, 1865, No 3, 4—44, quoted from Shuffleton, op. cit. p. 164 (cf. p. 161–5).

116. *History of the United States*, George Bancroft, 1862, 1:364.

117. Winthrop, *History of New England*, Boston 1853, 1:188.

118. DNB 9:302. NB. John Mason, c. 1600–72, professional soldier in the Low Countries prior to emigration to Massachusetts, 1633; captain of militia at Dorchester and Windsor, Connecticut; later deputy, magistrate, deputy governor, and military officer to Connecticut Colony—was promoted major after his victory in the Pequot War, 1636-37. He is titled major here but captain on *Guide*, p. 338, because it has not been possible to maintain a strict chronological sequence in this work. *Guide*, p. 338 relates to his earlier period. cf. DAB 12:367; *Fowles History of Windsor, Connecticut*, Uricchio, op. cit. pp. 30–32.

119. Winthrop, *History*, op. cit. 1:150.

120. DAB 8:459–60; cf. *Stuart Essex*, ERO No 44, 1974, Sect. 20.

121. Copford Church, cf. Pevsner *Essex*, op. cit. pp. 149–50; *The Parish Church of Copford in Essex*: re Chapel of St John, cf *Tower of London*, C. Hibbert, 1971, p. 2.

122. Messing, cf. *King's England, Essex*, p. 258. For the Bush connection cf. *Essex Chronicle*, editions Nov.11, 1988, May 26, 1989, and attractive Church Guide, Martin Clarke, 1990.

123. cf. *Descendants of John Eliot 1598–1905*, op. cit. p. 215.

124. Pevsner *Essex*, op. cit. p. 298.

125. Venn 3:479. Nehemiah Rogers entered Emmanuel, Cambridge in 1613, remaining to take his MA five years later, so he was contemporary with Thomas Hooker throughout his student period, but, rarely, resisted Hooker's persuasion.

126. Illustrated in ERO *Stuart Essex*, op. cit. Sect. 12.

127. Hunt, op. cit. pp. 41, 42,ff: cf. *William Perkins and the Poor*, in *Puritanism and Revolution*, Christopher Hill, Penguin reprint 1990, pp. 212–33, eg. *A Treatise of the Vocations or Callings of Men*, preached after the 1597 Poor Law statute, "Art thou a poore man and wouldst thou have sufficient foode and raiment for thy temporall life? Then first set thy heart to seeke God's kingdom, follow the word, and labour therein for regeneration and new obedience; and doubt not, but if thou be upright and diligent in thy lawful calling, thou shalt find sufficient for this life." As for "so many beggars," Perkins says "They are (for the most part) an accursed generation. They join not themselves to any settled congregation for the obtaining of God's kingdom, and so the promise belongs not to them," p. 223.

128. HTS p. 191ff. The sermon is printed in full, pp. 190–220.

129. *Coming Over*, David Cressy, op. cit. p. 293; cf. Ch.2, *A Mixed Multitude Furnished With Means* pp. 37–53.

130. For Hooker's generosity to the poor, cf. Magnalia 1:346. His quarrel with Pynchon over the price of corn during the Pequot wars derived from his policy of reducing costs in times of scarcity to enable all to purchase essential supplies, as was the practice advocated by Lord Burghley's "remarkable order—some time between 1586 and 1597," described by the Webbs in *English Local Government.* (see below), and carefully followed in Puritan towns like Dorchester, where grain was purchased in bulk for sale to the poor at prices below cost, as then required by the Privy Council, cf. *Fire From Heaven: 17th Century Dorset*, David Underdown, New Haven, CT: Yale University Press, 1992, p. 118ff— whereas Pynchon followed market prices, always inflated under shortages, cf. *Growing Towards Greatness*, Collingwood, 14th Hooker Lecture, op. cit. p. 4, n. 28; cf. *Pynchon and Hooker*, Collingwood, Connecticut Society Genealogists, *Nutmegger* 23, No 3, p. 391 and No 4, p. 631 n. 21. NB. *English Local Government: English Poor Law History*, Sidney & Beatrice Webb, Part I, vol. 7, Longmans 1927, re Burghley's "remarkable order in Council, c. 1586, for bulk purchases and distribution below costs to keep down prices," pp. 66–7 and 22–30.

131. *Memorials of the Pilgrim Fathers*, W. Winters, 1882, p. 13.

132. Every Essex Guide Book eulogises Dedham, and the Dedham Vale Countryside Centre will provide a selection for your choice, cf. *A History of Dedham*, C. A. Jones, 1907; *Dedham in the 17th Century*, G. H. Randall, *Essex Review* 39:75, 128, 188.

133. Pevsner, *Essex*, pp. 157–60.

134. *The Parish Church of St Mary Dedham*, A. R. Johnston, 1971.

135. HTS, Document VI, *The Faithful Covenanter*, pp. 187–9, text pp. 190–220, following quotations pp. 210, 213, 217 and conclusion, p. 220.

136. John Rogers, 1572–1636, "The most popular preacher of the seventeenth century in Essex" (*Essex Heyday*, op. cit. p. 224), son of a Moulsham shoemaker, educated at Chelmsford's new grammar school, entered Emmanuel, Cambridge, Feb. 4, 1588, ordained at Peterborough, April 16, 1595, vicar of Haverhill, Suffolk, 1603, vicar and lecturer at Dedham 1605–36. His son Nathaniel (1598–1655) was well known in New England, educated at Dedham grammar school and Emmanuel, ordained at Peterborough, Curate at Bocking and Rector of Assington before emigrating to Ipswich, Massachusetts where "he was wondrous careful to omit nothing from his daily duties," *Magnalia* 1:415, 423–8 for John; 415–23 for Nathaniel; cf. Venn 3:479 and DNB 17:129–30 for John and 17:135–36 Nathaniel.

137. DNB 17:82. For General William Tecumseh Shermon (1820–91) cf. DAB 17:93–97; for John of Watertown (1613–85), DAB 17:83–4, *Magnalia* 1: 511–18: but there is, so far as I know, no history of the family.

138. cf. HTS Document 4:140–46.

139. Sir Alfred Munnings, 1878–1959. cf. *Dictionary of British Artists, 1880–1940*, 1976, p. 368; b. Mendham, Suffolk, studied Norwich School of Art and Paris, best known for his sporting scenes, eg. *Epsom Downs, City and Suburban Day*.

140. John Constable, 1776–1837, cf. DNB 4:962–7; *John Constable*, John Lloyd Fraser Hutchinson, London 1976; *John Constable* Peter D. Smith, Bonfini Press, 1981; *Constable's England*, Graham Reynolds, Metropolitan Museum of Art, NY, in conjunction with their Exhibition 1983; *The Discovery of Constable*, Ian Flemming-Williams and Leslie Parris, 1984; and *Constable, Paintings, Drawings and Watercolours*, Basil Taylor, Phaidon, 1973, cf. Plate 80 *View on the Stour near Dedham*, as exhibited 1822, "better than any I have done yet," n. 33, p. 204, now at Huntington Library and Art Gallery, San Marino, California.

141. *A History of Braintree and Bocking*, W. F. Quin, op. cit.: cf. Pevsner *Essex*, pp. 9—93 and Braintree *Guide*; Urban District Council Official Guide.

142. *Essex*, M. Crouch, op. cit. p. 154: cf. *The Old Roads of England*, Sir William Addison, 1980, p. 33, etc.; *Roads and Tracks of Britain*, Christopher Taylor, Dent 1979, p. 191, etc. Icknield

Way, cf. *Roman Roads in Britain*, David E. Johnson, 1979, p. 183, "begins on the north coast of Norfolk, near Wells-next-the-Sea. It runs via Swaffham, Royston, Luton to Goring, Oxfordshire where it crosses the River Thames and becomes the Ridgeway:" cf. *Roman Britain*, Peter Clayton, Phaidon Press, Oxford, pp. 129–32; *VicHist—Essex*, 3:24–31 (Roman roads), p. 26 (Stane St), p. 28 (Icknield Way).

143. David E. Johnson, op. cit. p. 62; cf. *Illustrated Guide to Britain*, Drive Publications 1972, op cit. p. 223: cf. Addison, op cit. p. 43; P. Clayton, op cit. pp. 174–192.

144. Pilgrim Ways, cf. *Old Roads of England*, Addison above, pp. 57–63. Great and Little Walsingham, *VicHist—Norfolk* 2:394–401; cf. *The Shrine of our Lady of Walsingham* (ie. Little Walsingham) J. C. Dickinson, 1956; cf. Pevsner *North East Norfolk* p. 185–9; ODCC p. 1437. St Edmund, king and martyr, said to have been used, after capture, as a living target by invading Danish archers for refusing to renounce Christianity by making alliance with their leader, Inguar: *Saints*, p. 109–10; ODCC p. 439.

145. *Treasures of Britain*, op. cit. p. 108; for political manoeuvres preparatory to signing Magna Carta, cf. *EncBrit* 17:314ff.

146. *In Search of Essex*, op. cit. p. 139; Crouch *Essex*, op. cit. pp. 144, 17—8, etc. Pevsner *Essex* pp. 91–93, rates the Courtauld Town Hall "a successful building"—high praise!

147. *In Search of Essex*, above, p. 140; Crouch above, p. 153, etc.

148. John Ray, 1628–1705, *EncBrit* 22:91–2; cf. DNB 16: 782–87; Venn 3:427 (entered Trinity, Cambridge 1644; Fellow '49; Tutor '53–60; Sub-Dean; ordained, Lincoln, 1660).

149. That William Goodwin was "of Lyons Hall" seems to be an English (specifically Braintree) fiction. There is no such reference in *The Goodwins of Hartford, Connecticut, Descendants of William and Ozias Goodwin*, compiled by James Junius Goodwin, Hartford, Connecticut, 1891; nor elsewhere in American Sources that I have noted. Indeed, Augustus Jessopp (J. J. Goodwin above, pp. 5–30) claims "As early as the end of the fifteenth century there was at Bocking a family of gentry who bore the name Goodwin. They resided in a mansion of some pretentions in the parish, called Goodwin Place" (ibidem, p. 24). It is, eg. *Emigration to New England on The Lyon in 1632, The Braintree Company*, John Corley, Braintree and Bocking Heritage Trust, 1984, p. 3, which makes the specific claim of Goodwin's residence at Lyons Hall (only one of a number of inaccuracies).

William Goodwin 1595–1673 (see Braintree Historical Society correspondence, March 31, 1993, Little Baddow Papers, and *William Goodwin*, by G. L. Walker in J. J. Goodwin above, pp. 76–94), is said to have graduated, OxfordU, 1621, but I find no confirmation in *Oxons* 2:586, none of the five Williams fitting his curriculum vitae; m. (1) Elizabeth White of Braintree, Essex, (2) Susannah Hooker; as presiding elder held the early "Braintree" immigrants together in voyaging in the *Lyon*, 1632; establishing Newtown (Cambridge) Massachusetts and its congregation in readiness for Hooker's arrival (1633); led preliminary expedition (1635) to Connecticut; obtained a treaty with the Native Americans (signed with Samuel Stone); prepared Hooker's arrival (1636); was a founder of Hadley, Massachusetts after quarrel with Stone over the "Half-Way" covenant (see *Guide* p. 339); and early resident with Susannah at Farmington, Massachusetts (Samuel Hooker Pastor); where he died Mar. 11, 1673, followed by Susannah May 17, 1676. NB. Hooker's power over his followers.

150. *A Complete History of Connecticut, 1630–74*, Benjamin Trumbull, 1797, rep. 1918, p. 26. Trumbull, 1735–1802, Congregational minister and historian, descended from John Trumble, who joined Eliot's Church of Roxbury, Massachusetts, 1639. From Yale he was licensed to preach, 1760, and called to New Haven, Connecticut where he served the next sixty years, save about six months chaplain to General Wadsworth at the Revolution, 1776. Criticised for some inaccuracies, he nevertheless spent twenty years preparing his first volume, and I find his early comment illuming, cf. DAB 19:7–8. However, Braintree (Quincy) was not established by Hooker's Party, but rather by single families as became convenient. "About a month before William Goodwin and the party with him arrived, the Court (ie. Massachusetts) had ordered the "Braintree Company, which had begun to sit down at Mount Wollaston—afterwards

Braintree, Massachusetts—to remove to Newtown" (Winthrop's Journal, Savage, 1853, 1:104, 105, cf. J. J. Goodwin, op. cit. p. 78; cf. *Braintree Massachusetts Its History*, H. Hobart Holly, Braintree Historical Society 1985, pp. 26–28; cf. *History of Old Braintree and Quincy*, William S. Pattee, 1878; and Braintree Historical Society correspondence, Mar. 31, 1993, Little Baddow papers.

151. The Conveyances were at Lyons Hall when I inspected them in 1989, cf. Roger Thompson, University East Anglia, correspondence July 29, '89; also J. J. Goodwin op. cit. pp. 22 and 56. This book shows how widespread was the unsuccessful search for a Goodwin genealogy and home (cf. *Report on English Investigations*, Henry F. Waters, ibidem pp. 32–74): but see re Dorewards Hall, Bocking, *Guide* pp. 268, as a possible venue for Goodwin Place, *Guide* p. 418 n. 149.

152. Saint Michael the Archangel, cf. *VicHist—Essex* 3:55; Pevsner *Essex*, p. 99 ("a disappointing church", superbly situated near the town centre, alas mostly locked against vandals, so arrange your visit in advance. For Collins, see *Guide* p. 215ff; Davids op. cit. pp. 150f,168; Venn 1:374.

153. Davids above, pp. 168–9. In Collins' favour, he boarded John and Oliver Barrington (sons of Sir Francis and Lady Joan?) for their schooling, and earned their praise. "Precious among saints" was their verdict, according to *Puritan Gentry*, op. cit. p. 78: cf. also Will of Robert Woodward of Braintree, father of Mary (m. Ozias Goodwin), "Item I giue and bequeath unto Mr Collins my faithfull paster Twenty shillings," quoted J. J. Goodwin, op. cit. p. 35.

154. *Kings England, Essex*, op. cit. p. 52. The inscription is to be found on the east end outer wall, viewed from the churchyard. It could represent Sam Jr's personal enterprise, or need to get as far away as possible!

155. cf. *The Deanery Church of St Mary Bocking—A Short Guide*, p. 1; cf. Pevsner *Essex* , p. 91.

156. *A Short Guide*, op. cit. above, p. 2.

157. Ibidem; cf. *VicHist—Essex* 5:183 makes reference to John Doreward's licence, May 14, 1440, to found a "Maison Dieu" for seven poor men on two acres of his land. Correspondence with the present dean, the Very Reverend Alistair M. Haig shows that a Thomas and James Fitch emigrated to New England in the 1630s. Mather lists a James Fitch as magistrate in Massachusetts, 1681 (*Magnalia* 1:163).

158. *Magnalia* 1:415–6. For Rogers and Norton together at Ipswich, Massachusetts, cf. *Magnalia* 1:419; and 286–302, *Norton Honoratus, The Life of—*.

159. Ibidem 1:416.

160. Dr John Gauden, cf. DNB 7:948–51; ODCC p. 542; Venn 2:200; A.C. Edwards *A History of Essex* op. cit. p. 110.

161. DNB 7:948. The Solemn League and Covenant was an agreement between the General Assembly of the Church of Scotland, the Westminster Assembly and Parliament (Sept. 25, 1643) aiming at uniformity between churches in Britain along Presbyterian Reformed lines, upholding the liberties of parliaments whilst also defending the King's just rights, cf. ODCC p. 1268.

162. Gauden's *Cromwell's Bloody Slaughterhouse, or his damnable Designs in contriving the Murther of his sacred Majesty King Charles I discovered*, claimed by Gauden to have been written at the time, only saw the light of day in 1660 (DNB 7:949–51). A happy coincidence! He used his publications to advance his request for the See of Worcester, more lucrative than Exeter.

163. Photocopied extracts from unspecified History of Essex *Dorewards Hall*, deeds, estate map, etc. in possession of Braintree Heritage Trust, Little Baddow papers; cf. Pevsner *Essex*, p. 92. Is this the *Goodwin Place* cf. J. J. Goodwin, op. cit. p. 24 (see n. 149)?

164. cf. Pevsner *Essex*, p. 93: he dates it "c. 1600." Some of the replacement bargeboards were carved by the previous occupant, Mr Dixon-Smith, who also showed me the collected Deeds, cf. *Guide* p. 419 n. 151.

165. Depressions in the cloth trade, "still no authoritative and comprehensive history of this vital aspect of Essex history," wrote F. G. Emmison, *Early Essex Town Meetings, Braintree, 1619–36: Finchingfield, 1626–1634*, p. vii, as he went on to describe waves of recession from 1622–29, "unsold cloths were piling up in the sheds of clothiers, especially at Coggeshall, Braintree and Bocking; but cf. *English Local Government*, S. and B. Webb, op. cit. vol. 7 throughout, especially pp. 60ff; *The Church, the State, and the Poor*, W. E. Chadwick, London 1914; *Essex At Work, 1700–1815*, A. F. J. Brown, ERO 1969, especially ch. I, *The Cloth Trade in Decline*, pp. 1ff.

166. Quoted from *Essex Heyday*, p. 136.

167. Ibidem p. 137.

168. Hunt, *Puritan Moment* op. cit. pp. 82–83,142–3; F. G. Emmison *Early Essex Town Meetings*, op. cit. "conceivable that they originated in the manorial homage" p. vi.

169. *English Local Government*, Webbs op. cit., 1:221–7, 234, and 192–3: for later developments, cf. Webbs ibidem, Part Two, vol. 3, 1908, *From the Revolution to the Municipal Corporations Act: The Manor and the Borough*, etc. PS. In examining the transcripts of the Braintree/Finchingfield Vestry Meetings Emmison (see above) found that the following families were engaged in emigration from Braintree to New England, 1631–38—"James Wall carpenter, John Talcott, William Wadsworth, John White, Edward Elmer, Henry Adams, Samuel Adams, Edward Loomis, John Wall, William Skinner, John March, Joseph Loomis, Nathaniel Sparhawk" (pp. xiv–xv), although he placed a ? after some, to "indicate that definite identification as Braintree inhabitants awaits further research" (p. xv).

170. Pevsner *Essex*, op. cit. p. 265. For St John the Evangelist see Pevsner, p. 255.

171. Richard Rich, 1498–1567, first Baron of Leez Priory, see *Guide* p. 272ff; cf. DNB 16:1009–12 (which gives date of birth as "c. 1496,") which quotes Sargeaunt's *History of Felsted School*, as containing the best *Life* of Lord Rich; cf. Venn 3:449 (date of birth "c. 1497," death "1567"), probably CambridgeU," but no college named; barrister, Middle Temple; Member of Parliament for Colchester 1529, Speaker '36; Lord Chancellor '48, etc.

172. Thomas Cromwell, c. 1485–1540, Earl of Essex, and son of a notoriously turbulent Putney brewer-cum-fuller (Walter, arraigned for "sanguinary assualt"), seems to have enjoyed early life as a European mercenary (fighting for the French in Italy) and roving consultant in commercial and legal affairs. On return he extended his legal transactions, which brought him into favour with Wolsey. Member of Parliament from 1523, accepted into Gray's Inn the following year, he assisted Wolsey in everything, especially the suppression of minor monasteries. He was at Esher Place with Wolsey after the latter's fall (1529), but rode to Westminster, offered his services to the crown, and by 1534 was chief Secretary of State. Unscrupulous, he lacked neither courage nor devotion to the twin Protestant doctrines of the supremacy of the sovereign in government and of the scriptures in belief. As Vicar General he advised Henry on ecclesiastical affairs. He was responsible for introducing a public copy of the Bible into every church, for reforming the clergy, and for the registration of births, marriages and deaths. He advanced England's alignment with German Protestant powers, not least by the marriage of Henry VIII to Anne of Cleves. She was utterly repugnant to Henry. Easier relations developed between England and France. Henry had no further need of a German alliance, political or marital. Cromwell was sentenced for treason, and beheaded. Renouncing a Protestantism for which he had given his life, he died professing the Catholic faith. DNB 5:192–202; ODCC p. 357; *EncBrit* 7:499–501.

173. Sir Thomas More, 1478–1535, son of Judge Sir John More (1453–1530, cf. DNB 13:871–2), b. Cheapside, London; entered service of Archbishop Canterbury J. Morton; further educated Christ Church OxfordU (1492–4) and Lincoln's Inn; brilliant career as barrister; Member of Parliament 1504, Speaker, '23; Lord Chancellor after Wolsey; author *Utopia* (1516); ascetic, deeply religious, absolutely honest, he opposed Henry VIII's divorce; refused oath at Act of Succession, 1534; was committed to the Tower, and beheaded for high treason, 6 July 1535; canonized by Pope Pius XI, 1935: cf. DNB 13:876–96; *Thomas More, A Biography*, Richard Marius, Dent 1984, especially examination of Rich's false evidence, p. 505ff, cf. *Henry VIII*, Jasper

Ridley, Constable 1984, pp. 231–2. The earliest biography was *The Life Arraignement and death of that Mirrour of all true Honour and Vertue, Syr Thomas More*, by his son-in-law William Roper, Paris 1626, which also deals at length, and censoriously, with Rich's intervention. See *Guide* p. 340.

174. Pevsner, *Essex*, p. 266; cf. M. Crouch, *Essex*, op. cit. p. 134; etc.

175. Robert Rich, first Earl of Warwick (1560–1619), DNB 16:1007–8. His political career may not have equalled that of his grandfather, but NB Thistlethwaite's comment, *Dorset Pilgrims*, op. cit. p. 9, "It was the heyday of the privateer. During the last years of Elizabeth's reign Lord Rich had built up one of the largest privateering fleets in England," ready for Robert the second Earl, and obliquely for the Puritan invasion of New England. For Penelope Lady Rich. (1562–1607) cf. DNB 16:1006–9.

Philip Sidney, 1554–86 (son of Sir Henry, lord deputy of Ireland, lord president of Wales, his godfathers Philip II of Spain and ultra-Puritan John Russell, first Earl of Bedford), must also be accepted into the Puritan movement, however uncomfortably for some 20th century critics. "A paragon of the Elizabethan courtier" (CCH p. 145), brilliantly compelling admiration from all he met, equally admired at Elizabeth's Court, or the European embassies on which she sent him, radiant, lovable, in poetic Arcadian fantasy or paraphrasing the psalms, in armour, on horseback, he belongs to the gravely courteous but steely, fervent Protestant core of a rising generation which swept the seas of Spaniards for God and Gloriana, and spilled its faith back into the ruling families and rural squirarchy of 16th–17th century England, building international alliances against the Catholic powers, cementing a militant holiness into the nation. He died of a bullet wound in battle, gallantly forfeiting the cup of water he craved in favour of a dying soldier at his side, leaving a posthumous translation (from French into English) of Mornay's *Worke Concerning the Trewnesse of the Christian Religion*, and a quest for purity: cf. *EncBrit* 25: 42–45; DNB 18: 219–36.

176. Robert Rich, second Earl of Warwick (1587–1658), DNB 16:1014–19; cf. *Leaders of the Civil Wars, 1642–48* G. R. Smith and Margaret Toynbee, 1977, p. 208–10; Venn 3:449 (Emmanuel 1603 when he matriculated, but only received his MA by courtesy in 1624); and especially *Dorset Pilgrims*, op. cit. pp. 6–25, Thistlethwaite's sensitive appreciation and detailed account of *The Earl of Warwick and the Colonising of America 1600–35*. NB. "The Rich family group of livings was smaller that it had been in Elizabethan days, but the Earl of Warwick was still patron in nearly twenty parishes, and he kept a chaplain at Leez Priory," ERO, *Stuart England*, No 44, op. cit. Intro.

177. Cf. Church of the Holy Cross, Felsted, 1969, Historical Outline, p. 3, M. R. Craze (former Senior English Master and Historian of Felsted School); NB. the name Felsted probably denotes "the place on the hill" (Nicholas S. Hinde, Archivist, Felsted School, correspondence, 15 January 1992, Little Baddow Papers). Whilst Essex is mostly flat country, "Felsted is on an eminence between two and three hundred feet above the valley of the Stebbing Brook which becomes the Chelmer—and all roads approaching the village rise more or less steeply," an obvious site for an early settlement.

178. Felsted School, "there were over 100 boys at the school" by 1630, cf. *A History of Felsted School*, M. R. Craze, Cowell, Ipswich, 1955, p. 51; cf. Pevsner *Essex* p. 163.

179. Craze, *Church of the Holy Cross*, op. cit. p. 4. For St Bridget, cf. ODCC p. 198/9 (Catherine of Sienna, 1347–80, Dominican tertiary famed for sanctity, charitable works, moral instruction, and fervent political involvement on behalf of *Avignon* Popes Gregory XI and Urban VI, somewhat in the mode of later Puritan Independents, cf. ODCC, p. 250; *Saints*, pp. 211–12). For Syon House, cf. *Great Houses of Britain*, Nigel Nicolson, 1965, pp. 239–245; *Treasures of Britain*, op. cit. p. 453.

180. Craze, *History Felsted School*, op. cit. cf. *Lord Rich and his Chantry*, p. 13–26, a more sympathetic appraisal of Baron Rich than is usual, "his decrees were just, his dispatches quick, his judgement speedy, his sentences irrevocable" is quoted with approval, the conveyance of his Catholic chantry revenues to the School commended, "nor was it a pirate's attempt to salve

his conscience by disgorging loot" (ibidem p. 24): and *The Foundation of the School, 1564–67*, pp. 27–33. NB. The Lenten herring doles ("as you pass thro the archway from the old school buildings to the church, on the left hand side may be seen hatches which may well have been those through which the herring dole, one of Lord Rich's charities, was distributed," N. S. Hinde correspondence, op. cit.) may have been embarrassingly different from the more secularly Protestant-dictated Elizabethan poor laws, but a kindly benefaction nonetheless, cf. Herring *Dole for the well-behaved*, M. Craze, C. L. 117:926.

181. Craze *History Felsted School*, op. cit. *The First Three Headmasters, 1564–97*, pp. 34–40; *George Manning 1597–1627*, pp. 41–49, "rising standards" (p. 41); *Martin Holbeach, 1627–49*, pp. 50–64. Holbeach was at Queens', Cambridge, then master at Halstead (Essex) and Braintree, a born teacher, he attracted the sons of royalist families (Craze, *Essex Review*, vol. 60, 1951, *Five Seventeenth-Century Vicars of Felsted*, p. 156) as well as Oliver Cromwell's four sons, and the young Colonel Henry Mildmay of Great Graces (but note Sir John Bramston, 1611–1700, *Autobiography*, pub. Camden Soc, 1845, "pestilent sectary—that scarce bred anyone loyal to his prince" p. 63); cf. Venn 2:387 ("Queens' 1617; ordained, London, 1624; Felsted 1628–49; Vicar High Easter, Essex, ejected 1662 etc").

For Dr John Wallis, DNB 20:598–602, *EncBrit* 28:284; Venn 4:322. cf. his tribute to Holbeach as "a very good School-Master—At this school, though in a Country Village, he had at that time an hundred or six score Scholars; most of them strangers, and sent thither from other places upon reputation of the School; from whence many good Scholars were sent yearly to the University" (Craze, *History Felsted School*, op. cit. p. 51. For Dr Isaac Barrow, cf. DNB 1:1219–25, *EncBrit* 3:440; Venn 1:98; ODCC p. 134.

182. *Church of the Holy Cross*, Craze, op. cit.; cf. Pevsner *Essex* p. 162–3.

183. Epiphaneus Evesham, cf. Index of Sculptors, *Treasures of Britain*, op. cit. p. 527; *European Sculpture*, H. D. Molesworth, 1965 p. 224 (passing ref only).

184. Samuel Wharton, Venn 4:378; cf. Craze, *Essex Review*, 60, 1951, op. cit. p. 154 which shews that his wife occasionally filled in the Parish Register for her husband—"martha wharton writ this"—a surprising comment on the role of at least one 16th century housewife.

185. Nathaniel Ranew, 1602–78, DNB 16:731, "generally esteemed and valued" (Calamy), subscribed to *Testimony of Essex Ministers*, and *Essex Watchman's Watchword* (see *Guide* p. 442 n. 378), ejected 1662; cf. Venn 3:420 (Emmanuel with Hooker, 1617–24; Felsted 1648–62) cf. Essex Review above. For his patroness Mary, Countess of Warwick, sister of Robert Boyle principal founder the Royal Society, cf. *EncBrit* 4:354–6; DNB 2:1026–31; *Essex Heyday* p. 59–63, etc. For Boyle see *Guide* p. 436 n. 330.

186. *Magnalia* 1:338, cf. Pevsner *Essex*, pp. 210–13. The Puritan Everard family of Langleys, Great Waltham, intermarried with the Mashams of High Laver (see *Guide* pp. 119, 227). In November 1629 Sir Richard Everard wrote his mother-in-law, Lady Joan Barrington, that "Thomas Hooker's case would go hard with him as the Bishop was extremely hostile," cf. *Essex Heyday*, 317.

187. *In Search of Essex*, op. cit. pp. 33–4; cf. *King's England*, p. 171.

188. Pevsner *Essex*, op. cit. pp. 372–3; *Braintree and Stisted*, J. H. Round, EAT, n.s. xix, 51. For Samuel Stone, see *Guide* pp. 88ff, 337-39. NB. One of only two passing references to Martin Luther, 1483–1546 (*EncBrit*(15) 23:305–13), founder of the German Reformation, occurs here. This neglect may appear to be quite astonishing. But for all Luther's prominence in the Protestant Reformation, he was currently, in 17th century England left in the back alleys of Puritan thinking by the immediacy of Calvin's modifications to reform, via Geneva. I defer to Luther's greatness, but find no pressing event to include him further in Hooker's story. However, you would enjoy *Martin Luther, An Illustrated Biography*, Peter Mann, and *Luther*, John M. Todd, both published 1982.

189. *Cressing Temple*, Essex County Council, 1990. Knights Templar, ODCC p. 1327–8. Queen Matilda, 1102–64, daughter of Henry I of England (1068–1135), wife of Geoffery Plantagenet, count of Anjou. Although her father's nominated successor, the English and

Norman Councils preferred Henry's nephew Stephen. He ascended the throne in 1135. Matilda waged intermittent war, and ruled England from 1141–48, but Stephan regained power. Matilda retired to Normandy where her husband now ruled, leaving the eventual succession of both countries to her son, Henry II, first of the Plantagenet kings (1133–89), and spent her energies on religious and charitable works, cf. *EncBrit* 17:888, DNB 13:54–58.

190. Coggeshall, *A History of Coggeshall in Essex*, G. F. A. Beaumont, 1890; cf. Pevsner *Essex*, p. 199; and all guide books, eg. *National Trust Guide*; op. cit. p. 348.

191. St Peter-ad-Vincula, cf. Pevsner above; *King's England* p. 83–85; etc.

192. cf. *The English Ancestry of Thomas Stoughton, 1588–1661, and His Son Thomas Stoughton, 1624–84 of Windsor, Connecticut, His Brother Israel Stoughton, 1603–1645, and His Nephew William Stoughton, 1631–1701 of Dorchester, Massachusetts*; and *The Stoughton Families of Dorchester, Massachusetts, and Windsor, Connecticut*, Ralph M. Stoughton, published by The American Genealogist, 116, vol. 29, No 4, Oct. 1953, pp. 193–204 (both mss available in photocopy, Little Baddow papers).

193. cf. *English Ancestry*, op. cit. p. 2 ff; Venn 4:172.

194. cf. *The Presbyterian Movement of the Reign of Queen Elizabeth.*, Camden Soc, 3rd series, vol. viii; cf. *English Ancestry* above, pp. 69, 70; re the Dedham Classis, p. 73; cf. *The Elizabethan Puritan Movement* Collinson, op. cit. Part Three: *The First Presbyterians*, pp. 101–55; ODCC, p. 1101–02; etc.

195. 1588 is the date given by *English Ancestry* op. cit. but *The American Genealogist*, op. cit. 29:193, prints the Naughton Church Register entry "1593 January: Thomas Stoughton ye sonne of Thomas and Katherine his wife was bapt. on ye 23rd of this month." This different date is also given in Venn (4:171) for Dr John Stoughton, "undoubtedly the eldest surviving son" (*English Ancestry* op. cit. p. 193). Not being competent to judge, I have simply followed the order accepted in *English Ancestry*.

196. Dr John Stoughton, 1593(?)–1639; cf. DAB 18:13; Venn 4:171; *American Genealogist*, p. 195ff; *Magnalia* 2:554. For Ralph Cudworth, see *Guide*, p. 148

197. Israel Stoughton, baptized Coggeshall, Feb. 18, 1603 (*American Genealogist*, p. 194, cf. also p. 198ff). The influence of the Stoughton family, not least for a more democratic management of the New England townships, is disclosed throughout Frank Shuffleton's *Dorset Pilgrims*, op. cit.

198. William Stoughton, (1631–1701) *American Genealogist*, op. cit. p. 202; *Magnalia* 1:141, 2:11, 30, 489, 584; *Oxons* 4:1432; DAB 18:113–4.

199. *English Ancestry*, p. 71, cf. pp. 69–72.

200. *Earls Colne*, Local History, R. Hunt and Co, 1946, p. 23ff; cf. *Herein I Dwell—A History of Earls Colne Houses from 1375*, pub. by Earls Colne W. E. A. History Group, 1983; also *VicHist—Essex* 1:102; Pevsner, Essex, p. 165. NB. The best source of information about 17th century Earls Colne is *The Diary of Ralph Josselin A Seventeenth Century Clergyman* (Vicar 1641–83), edited Alan Macfarlane, OUP, 1976, to which I am indebted. Josselin's cousin Abraham emigrated to New England, cf. *The Family Life of Ralph Josselin*, CUP, 1970.

201. Quoted from *EncBrit*, *Vere Family*, 28:1019 cf. foll. pages, and vol. XX, *Earls of Oxford*, p. 402,ff; DNB 20:219ff. NB, John Evelyn's description of his visit to DeVere, 1614, *Diary*, Everyman edition 1973, p. 118.

202. Pevsner *Essex* p.163; *VicHist* p. 103; DAB 17:75.

203. *Earls Colne*, R. Hunt, op. cit. p. 48–9. The 17th Earl m (1) Anne Cecil, daughter of Lord Burghley, (2) Elizabeth Trentham, the Dowager Duchess, *EncBrit* 20:402–3.

204. Thomas Shepard, DNB, 13:330–31; DAB, 17:75; Davids *Annals*, p. 164ff; "Pastor Evangelicus", *Magnalia* 1:380–394; Venn 4:60, etc.

205. *Wherein I Dwell*, op. cit. p. 42; cf. *Earls Colne Grammar School, A History* A. D. Merson, pub. School Governors, 1975, ch. 4, p. 33, ch. 5, p. 34f.

206. Christopher Scott, Vicar of Hawkwell, near Rayleigh, Essex, 1617–32 (Venn 4:30), his funeral oration was delivered by the Puritan Vicar of Castle Hedingham, Edmund Brewer,

(despite royalist Oxford patronage) cf. Venn 1:212, cf. *E. C. Grammar School History*, above, p. 30, 39; Davids, op. cit. p. 155;

207. *A Short History and Guide to St Andrew's*, S. M. Hammock; cf. *Earls Colne*, R. Hunt, op. cit. p. 23–44, cf. F.Chancellor, *Earls Colne Church*, E.A.T. n.s. xii 65, *Earls Colne Priory*, ibid 63.

208. Harlakendens, cf. DNB 8:459f; Venn 2:307; *Harvard College*, S. E. Morison, p. 197ff; and Kinship Diagram, *Diary Ralph Josselin*, Macfarlane op. cit. Appendix I, p. 666, details Rich. m Alice Mildmay etc; for local events see also *History of Essex*, A. C. Edwards, op. cit. p. 14; *Magnalia* 1:382; etc.

209. DNB 18:31 and DAB 8:75 (re John Eliot's Indian work); *Harvard College*, S. E. Morison, op. cit. p. 400; cf. *Magnalia* 1:380-94, "trembling walk with God" p. 390. NB. In addition to Joanna's sons Samuel and John, his third wife Margaret (Boradel) bore him Jeremiah (DAB p. 75).

210. *Hedingham Castle*, English Life published 1986; Pevsner *Essex* pp. 110–4; *Norman Castles in Britain*, Derek Renn, 1973 ed. TL787359.

211. Wethersfield, Pevsner, ibid. p. 421-2; cf. *History of Ancient Wethersfield*, "the most Auncient Town for the River is determined by the Court to bee Wethersfield", p.23 (ie. The General Court of Connecticut, 1650 declaration), photocopy extracts per courtesy The Griswold Family Association of America, Little Baddow papers.

212. The difficulty with the Rogers family is that there were at least four branches with some Essex roots—John the Marian Martyr, alias Thomas Matthew (pseudonym under which, for safety, he published the Matthew's Bible), father of eleven children; John of Moulsham, father of "Roaring" Rogers of Dedham, England (grandfather of Nathaniel of Ipswich, Massachusetts); Richard, a Steward of the Earls of Warwick, father of Richard of Wethersfield, England (grandfather of Ezekial of Rowley, Massachusetts); and Vincent of Stratford-at-Bow, father of Nehemiah of Messing.

Lineage from John Rogers Martyr has been claimed by American descendants of all these families, claims researched by Joseph Lemuel Chester (genealogist, descendant of Nathaniel of Ipswich, DNB 17:135) in *John Rogers: The Compiler of the first Authorised English Bible, the Pioneer of the English Reformation; and Its First Martyr*, London 1861, who concluded that John of Dedham, "supposed to have been a grandson of the Martyr—a nephew of Richard Rogers of Wethersfield" (p. 248) was "no other than a relative or kinsman" (p. 249); that Richard of Wethersfield (cf. pp. 238–45) was "possibly a relative but certainly not a son of the Martyr" (p. 245); and that Vincent Rogers, "Minister of Stratford Bow, Middlesex" (p. 252), said to be "grandson of the Martyr," he "presumed to be the case" (p. 254).

DNB 16:126–32, says "according to a persistent tradition, Richard Rogers of Wethersfield was a grandson of the martyr Rogers", and that Vincent "may have been the martyr's grandson" (p. 129). The problem lies with the names of the Martyr's eleven children, none suitable to the above statements. However, taking into consideration the mass of information in Venn (III, pp. 478–80), where some 21–22 Rogers relevant to our period are named, the following Summary Genealogical Table No 9, *Guide* p. 426-27, indicates the possible relationships of those who figure in the Thomas Hooker saga. The significance of having the proto-martyr in their families cannot, of course, be exaggerated.

NB. Rowley, Yorks no longer appears on English Ordnance Survey maps. For Ezekial Rogers, cf. *Magnalia* 1:408–14; for Nathaniel, ibid, pp. 414-2, ff.

213. For the naming of Wethersfield, cf. *History Ancient Wethersfield*, op. cit. pp. 52-5.

214. Finchingfield, Pevsner, *Essex*, p. 180–1; and all guide books.

215. Stephen Marshall, 1594–1655, DNB 12:1128–31: m Susanna Castell, heiress of Woodham Walter, next Little Baddow en route to Maldon, so would know Hooker's Little Baddow intimately. His appointment as Chaplain to Charles I was entirely political. It is said the king never attended his chaplaincy sermons (DNB above). A justifier of Charles' trial, he did not sign the king's death warrant. He d of consumption, November 19, 1655, was buried in the South Aisle of Westminster Abbey, but exhumed, June 19, 1661, by royal requisition at the

Restoration, his corpse thrown into a pit at the back door of the Prebend's lodgings (DNB p. 1130). NB. Emmison, *Essex Town Meetings*, op. cit. pp. 107–36, shows Marshall as chairman of the Finchingfield Select Vestry: cf. *History of the Rebellion*, Clarendon, 1707, 1:204, 302, 2:81; *History of the Puritans*, Neale 1822, 3:204, 211, 218; Davids, op. cit. p. 154ff—all affirm his influence.

216. DNB XII, p.1131. Re the *Triers* cf.ODCC p. 1375. The trials occasioned by Marshall's too-lively daughters is enlarged in *Essex Heyday*, op. cit. pp. 76–80, etc: but DNB 12:1128ff questions any attack on their reputation.

217. Writtolaburna. There are reference files in the small Library on The Green which, at least when I last visited, could be examined on application (NB. ERO at Chelmsford is a superb resource centre, but information locally discovered has a flavour all its own). Much of what follows comes from the library files; but cf. *William Pynchon and Thomas Hooker*, Collingwood, ConnSG *Nutmegger* 23, Nos 3, 4, 1990, op. cit. pp. 392–394 and Notes, pp. 626, 631–2; Pevsner *Essex* op. cit. pp. 401–2. For King John see *Guide* p. 94 and p. 377 n. 4.

218. Robert. *The Bruce, 1274-1329*, DNB 3:117–28 (Bannock Burn, p. 122). For the Writtle Manors see Library File, and Morant, below, ii, pp. 65, 66. For *The Church of All Saints*, D. C. George, 1963, and Pevsner, above.

219. Nicholas Stone, 1586–1647, b Woodbury near Exeter, Devon, quarryman's son, trained under Peter de Keyser, Holland whose daughter he married, *A Dictionary of British Sculptors*, M. H. Grant, London 1953, pp. 231–3; *European Sculpture*, H. D. Molesworth, p. 224, cf. Plate 230 (J. Donne); cf. *Church of All Saints*, D. C. George, 1963.

The large Pynchon memorial stands against the north chancel wall, blazing white stone chased with gold, a symbolic corn-shovel bearing the family arms below, flowing water, rock and corn, the sun above with gilded rays, an angel reaper towering over all, originally with sickle in hand, the theme is repeated almost exactly for a Lady Clerke, 1633, in Southwark Cathedral, London NB. Stone's monument in St Paul's Cathedral of its metaphysical (the vision which goes beyond observable natural law) poet-Dean, John Donne (1573–1631, DNB 5:1128–39, ODCC p. 415–6; *Life of John Donne*, Izaac Walton, 1640, etc). Stone shared Donne's perception, and made him pose in the Dean's study, naked inside a winding-sheet as you will understand if you see the monument. Donne is said to have kept the carving in his bedroom to remind him of his mortality. Crowds surged to hear Donne preach. Does this not highlight 16th century piety, vividly alert to Life in Death, in which all Puritans participated?

220. *Roxwell Revealed, An Anthology of Village History* published by the Roxwell Revealed Group, via Pat Smith, The Mill, Roxwell, 1993, a well documented and illustrated local history; cf. also *Roxwell, A Pictorial Record*, Revealed Group; *Roxwell, An Excursion into History*, Pat Smith 1987; cf. *The Histories and Antiquities of the County of Essex, From Domesday-Book, Inquisitiones Post Mortem and other most valuable Records and Mss., etc.*, Philip Morant, 1768, vol 2, pp. 69–71; Pevsner, *Essex*, p. 329.

221. Francis Quarles, 1592–1644. DNB 16:535–39, says "a sturdy royalist," but CCH *17th Century Britain*, p. 154, says "restrained Anglican puritan," both correct as we have seen; cf. *Roxwell Revealed*, 1993, op. cit. pp. 40–43. His works include *The Loyall Convert, The Profest Royalist in his Quarrel with the Time*; cf. *EncBrit* 22:711; ODCC p. 1131; Venn 3:411; *A History of Essex*, A. C. Edwards, op. cit. p. 119, etc.

222. James Ussher, 1581–1656, see *Guide* p. 402 n. 40.

223. Westons of Skreens, Earls Portland, DNB 20:1275–8; *EncBrit* 22:118. Sir Richard Weston, 1577–1635, son and heir of Sir Jerome, 1550–1603; Member of Parliament under James I and Charles I; succeeded Buckingham as personal counsellor to Charles; lord high treasurer, 1628; Earl of Portland, 1633; died in office 13 March 1635. He features as a tight-fisted financier in *Myself My Enemy*, Jean Plaidy's historical novel about Henrietta Maria (pub. Robert Hale, 1983, pp. 149, 151, etc.), who, "in his final moments he sent for a Catholic priest to administer the last rites" (p. 167), as indeed he did. C. Hill, *The Century of Revolution 1603-1714* Nelson 1980, p. 9, also comments, "Weston effected numerous economies and a variety of financial expedi-

GENEALOGICAL TABLE, NO. 9: DESCENDANTS OF JOHN ROGERS MARTYR

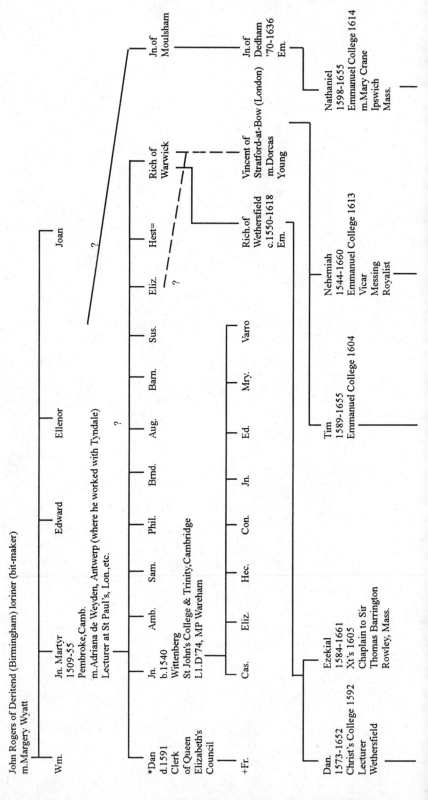

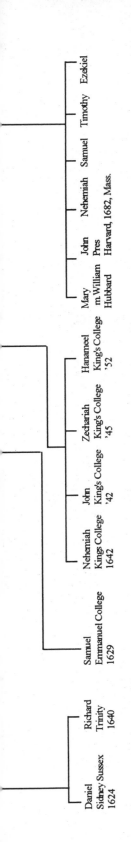

* full names:- Daniel, John, Ambrose, Samuel, Philip, Bernard, Augustine, Barnaby, Susan, Elizabeth, Hester: - no ref. to Richard of Warwick or John of Moulsham?

+ full names:- Francis, Cassandra, Elizabeth, Heckuba, Constantine, John, Edward, Mary, Varro:- no ref. to Richard or Vincent?

NB. These Puritan Rogers were solidly Cambridge-trained.

ents was adopted which alienated all sections of the population." He sounds a worthy member of the gifted and proficient Pynchon family!

224. *John White The Patriarch of Dorchester (Dorset) and the Founder of Massachusetts 1575–1648, with an Account of the Early Settlements in Massachusetts 1620–1630,* is Frances Rose-Troup's major biography (New York: G. P. Putnam's sons, 1930, quote from p. 156). See also *The Massachusetts Bay Co and Its Predecessors,* Rose-Troup, Grafton, NY, 1930; DNB 21: 59–61; *Oxons* 4:1614; S.E. Morison *Builders of the Bay Colony* op.cit. 2:27ff; *Fire From Heaven,* op. cit. extensive refs. NB. White was educated at Winchester; fellow of New College OxfordU, 1595 where WilliamPynchon's father John attended (1577, at 19 yrs, *Oxons* 4:1614). His brother Josias White (New College, OxfordU, 1593) became Vicar of Hornchurch, Essex, near Roxwell, and owned property there inherited by his son Josias (New Inn Hall, OxfordU, 1627, at 13 yrs, *Oxons* 4:1615; see *Guide* p. 295). Sir Edward Pynchon was also at OxfordU (at 14 yrs, with his brothers Henry 13 yrs, and William 11 yrs, all entered Hart Hall, 1596). Dorchester did indeed spread into Essex!

225. Skreens, described and illustrated, *A Pictorial Record,* op. cit. p. 4–5; cf. Skreens Park, *A Short History,* C. Treacher, 1983; Morant op. cit. pp. 70, 71, "several Manors but they are all within the Manor of Writtle."

226. Sir John Bramston, 1577–1654, Chief Justice of the King's Bench, cf. DNB 2:1115–18; Venn 1:204 (son of Roger of Boreham, Essex; Jesus College, Cambridge, 1593. NB. High Church;) *Roxwell Revealed* 1993 op. cit. pp. 23–26. For his championship of John Michaelson, cf. *Essex Heyday* op. cit. p.218.

227. Sir John Bramston Jr, 1611–1700, autobiographer, barrister, Member of Parliament, cf. DNB 2:1118–19; brother of Sir Moundeford of Little Baddow, Master of Chancery, cf. Venn 1:204 (Queens' Cambridge LLD Trinity), see *Guide,* p. 243, and of Francis, baron of Exchequer, cf. Venn, ibid (Queens' Cambridge), cf. DNB 2:1114. For his quarrel with Colonel Henry Mildmay see *Essex Heyday* op. cit. pp. 219–20.

228. *John White Patriarch,* op. cit. p. 145. For "The Roxwell Group," see *Massachusetts Bay Predecessors,* op. cit. p. 162, and re its members, Vassals (pp. 60–63), Flyer (p. 141), Hodson, Josselyn (p. 145), Josselyn (p. 146), Pelham (p. 150), Waldegrave (pp. 150–1, 157). Re William Pynchon, the link, in addition to his living at Springfield next Roxwell, may be his family connection with John White of Dorchester (see my 1993 Windsor, Connecticut Lecture "Puritanism in 16–17 Century England and its effect on New England," L. Baddow papers), and "landed first at Dorchester," Massachusetts; and his wife Anna (Andrew) having died, m (2) widow Frances Sanford, also from Dorchester, DAB 15:292. NB. Tyack, op. cit. II, Appendix I, includes also amongst Roxwell New England immigrants Jehu Burr, Matthew and Anne Irons, Joseph and Anne Mygatt, Robert Sharp (cf. *John White Patriarch,* p. 298), but is not altogether trustworthy. However, for so small a village, it is an incisive number.

229. The Brownes of Roxwell, cf. *Massachusetts Bay Predecessors,* op. cit. pp. 145–58; *Coming Over,* Cressy, op. cit. pp. 11, 21, 22; S. E. Morison, *Builders of the Bay Colony* op. cit. pp. 37ff. They held Fidlers Manor, cf. Pat Smith, Roxwell historian, Little Baddow papers. The Cambridge Agreement referred to six paragraphs further on, was a meeting ("ad-hoc caucusus" Rose-Troup, *John White Patriarch,* op. cit. p. 180) of some twelve early patentees of the Massachusetts Bay Co., Kellam Browne and William Pynchon among them. They signed a declaration of intent to emigrate, wh. included financial penalties should they withdraw, but only two failed to go. For Josias White, father and son, cf. *John White Patriarch,* op. cit. p. 391; *Oxons* 4:1615. NB. Pat Smith, above, says Josias Sr owned the farm named Fetches (today Thatchers) and that the White family were in possession up to 1705 (quoted from Essex court rolls and wills of White family, ERO, Little Baddow papers), cf. *Roxwell Revealed,* 1993, op. cit. pp. 93–7, ch.XIII *The Roxwell Group who helped to found Massachusetts.*

230. *Massachusetts Bay Predecessors,* op. cit. p. 156.

231. Capt. John Endecott, 1589–1665, Governor of the Dorchester Company Settlement at Salem (1628–29) and of Massachusetts, was a professional soldier who fought with the Protestant armies in the Low Countries, and supported Skelton's rigid separatist noncon-

formity (see *Guide* p. 120 and p. 385 n. 15). He married Anne Gower, cousin of Matthew Craddock (Governor of the Bay Company before Winthrop's appointment), and was early involved in the Bay Company's affairs. Labelled "bloodthirsty and brutal" (DAB 6:156), he not only banished John and Samuel Browne for their Church of England sentiments but excised the cross from the colony flag, (an incident which called for Hooker's peace-making gifts, described by F. Shuffleton, op. cit. pp. 187–91, cf. Hooker's *Touching Ye Crosse in Ye Banners*, Proceedings of the Massachusetts Historical Society, XLII, series three, 2:272–280), and mishandled Indian affairs to the point of being accused of inciting the first Pequot wars (Thistlethwaite, op. cit. p. 127). "Forceful," "domineering" (Thistlethwaite, pp. 41, 42), "hamfisted and headstrong" (ibidem, p. 127), he was nonetheless steadfast to his vision of an Independent New England, honest, ready to suffer for it, and served Winthrop loyally when himself summarily displaced in 1630 as governor, and the Colony when reappointed in later life, with integrity. cf. *Magnalia* 1:67, 137; DAB 6:155–6, cf. *John Endecott A Biography*, L. S. Mayo, Boston, Mass.: Harvard, 1936; *Massachusetts Bay Predecessors*, op. cit. 3:16–31; *Builders of the Bay Colony*, op. cit. p. 29ff espc. re Roger Conant, who withdrew from Plymouth Plantation for its "narrowness" and held the Cape Ann/Salem ground (*Magnalia* 1:67, claims Hebrew equivalent to Naumkeag = Comfort Haven) until displaced by Endecott's party. For Winthrop see *Guide* p. 120 and p. 385 n. 14, Higginson pp. 61, 84, 375 n. 112.

232. *Magnalia* 1:243. The events leading both Bright and Blackstone to resist the Salem move towards Separatism are related by Rose-Troup, *Massachusetts Bay Predecessors*, op. cit. ch. IV, who continues, "West Country men who began the settlement of the North Shore were Puritans not Separatists, while those who came over in 1630, mostly from the East Coast" (of England) "had been much affected by the Separatist opinions so widely held in that district— Skelton had apparently advanced much further on the road to Separation, and Endecott . . . ," pp. 32–34,ff, cf. *John White, Patriarch*, op. cit. pp. 143, 144,ff. The Brownes of Roxwell incident follows, pp. 145ff, 179, cf. *Magnalia* 1:67, etc.

233. Winthrop *Journal*, op. cit. 1:137; cf. HTS XXVIII, *Touchinge ye Crosse in ye Banners*, 1634, p. 422; cf. Mayo op. cit. pp. 84–90; Shuffleton, op. cit. p. 191 (NB. ibidem n. 65 "It seems likely that Cotton sided with Endicott and against Hooker on this issue").

234. Cressy, op. cit. p. 197; *John White Patriarch*, op. cit. p. 154,ff; etc.

235. cf. *A Brief History of All Saints Church, Springfield, Essex*, Church Guide; *Springfield Church*, F. Chancellor, E.A.T., n. 5, xix, 57; *Essex Churches—All Saints, Springfield*, E. R. iii, 113; *A History of Springfield*, Ian Clark, Chelmsford, 1985; Pevsner *Essex*, pp. 362–3; *In Search of Essex*, op. cit. p. 20, etc.

236. *A Brief History*, op. cit. p. 3.

237. So Smith's *Ecclesiastical History of Essex*, op. cit. p. 72: the connection between Writtle/Roxwell and New College OxfordU (refs. Writtle Library File already noted) is of interest. William de Wykeham, 1324–1404, Bishop of Winchester, Edward III's Chancellor, clerk of the royal works, founder of New College and Winchester College (cf. ODCC, 1464; EncBrit 28:677–81, and 703–4, Winchester; 20:410, New College), secured a part of his possessions, including Writtle and Hornchurch (cf. *Discovering Essex in London*, K. Neale, 1969, p. 126 and Writtle File) for the upkeep of New College—a connection extended by a bequest (1572) from Sir William Petre of Ingatestone and Writtle to New College of "two tenements in Writtle formerly belonging to Carpenter's Chantry there. The rents of 13s 4d a year" (Emmison, *Tudor Secretary*, op. cit. p. 284) to support Writtle and Roxwell boys at the college, eg. John, father of William Pynchon of Springfield, Massachusetts, attended New College (*Oxons* 3:165).

238. A Nicholas Pinchon from Wales, clothworker, Sherrif of London, purchased Sturges in 1532, *History and Antiquities of Essex*, P. Morant, 1768, op. cit. 2:65, 66, cf. 1:305; see also Writtle Library File and *A Short History of the Clothworkers' Company*, No I of series of Livery Company leaflets, Clothworkers' Hall, Mincing Mane, London, 1985, etc.

239. Sir Richard Empson, son of Peter Empson of Towcester, Member of Parliament Northamptonshire, Speaker of Commons, High Steward of Cambridge University, crime of "Constructive Treason," beheaded 1510, *EncBrit* 9:361; DNB 6:782–3.

240. William Pynchon, 1590–1662. *The First Century of the History of Springfield (Massachusetts) The Official Records from 1636–1736,* Henry M. Burt, 2 vols, Springfield 1898; *William Pynchon, Frontier Magistrate and Fur Trader,* Chapter 12, *Builders Bay Colony,* op. cit. pp. 337ff; *Pynchon John—Account Books 1651–c.1694,* 6 vols., Connecticut Valley Historical Society, Springfield, Massachusetts; *Colonial Justice in Western Massachusetts (1630–1702), The Pynchon Court Record* Joseph H. Smith, Harvard 1961; "William Pynchon," E. G. Byington, *Connecticut Valley Historical Society Proceedings,* 1904, 2:20–40; *William Pynchon, Merchant and Colonizer,* Ruth A. McIntyre, Connecticut Valley Museum, 1961; *Pynchon Letters, Proceedings,* Massachusetts Historical Society 48:35, 36; *The Secession of Springfield from Connecticut,* Simeon E. Baldwin, Colonial Society of Massachusetts 21:55–82; *A Glimpse of Sion's Glory, Puritan Radicalism in New England,* Philip F. Gura, Wesleyan University Press, Middletown, Connecticut 1989, ch. 11, *William Pynchon* pp. 304–22; *William Pynchon and Thomas Hooker, Neighbours and Friends in Essex, England,* Collingwood, ConnSG, op. cit. vol. 23, No. 3–4, 1990–91; and Pynchon's own publications, *The Meritorious Price of our Redemption, Justification, etc.—Clearing it from some Common Errors etc.* by *William Pinchin, Gentleman in New England,* pub. London 1650 (answered by John Norton, *A Discussion of that great point of Divinity THE SUFFERINGS OF CHRIST: and the Questions about his Active and Passive Righteousness, and the Imputation thereof,* discussed in *Magnalia* 1:.291f); together with *Jews Synagogue,* 1652; *How the Sabbath was ordained,* 1654; *Covenant of nature made with Adam,* 1662; cf. DNB 16:528; DAB 15:292–3; Morant op. cit. 2:65–66.

241. Pynchon signed the Patentee Agreement of the newly-forming Massachusetts Bay Co., March 4, 1629 "Squire of Springfield in Essex," cf. *A General History of New England from the Discovery to MDCLXXX,* W. Hubbard, Boston 1878, p. 308, "Mr Pynchon who had his mansion house at a town of that name, near Chelmsford in Essex before he removed to New England."

242. Sir John Tyrrell, "pot-fellow" of Sir Humphrey Mildmay of Danbury (b. 1592, grandson of Sir Walter, and a surprising Royalist), inherited anti-Puritan sentiments from his mother's family, the Capels of Rayne Hall, Essex (eg. Baron Arthur, 1610–19, Royalist General), strengthened by his marriage into the family of Sir John Crofts of Little Saxham, Suffolk "whose fifteen children were known for their gaity," cf. *Essex Heyday* op. cit. pp. 300, 314, and 298–300, cf. DNB 19:1364, etc.

243. *Boreham, History, Tales and Memories of an Essex Village,* editors Eleanor Burgess, Mary Rance, art editor Ken Keeble, architectural drawings and information by Mark Rowland, 1988, proves to be all that a local history should be; see also Pevsner, *Essex,* op. cit. pp. 93–94, and all guide books.

244. New Hall, cf. *Boreham* op. cit., pp. 118–125, 126–136; cf. Pevsner op. cit. p. 94.

245. *EncBrit* 26:165; cf. DNB 16:579–86 (the third Earl; for the Sussex Earls, cf. pp. 577–87). For Lady Frances (Sidney) Sussex, d. 1589. cf. ibid p. 586; *EncBrit* 5:93–4.

246. Thomas Wriothesley, 1505–1550, DNB 21:1063–7, State Secretary under Thomas Cromwell (see *Guide* p. 301), Lord High Chancellor (1544) when the notorious torture and subsequent burning of Anne Askew took place (*EncBrit* 25:490, cf. ODCC p. 95; DNB 1:662). He was succeeded by his son, Henry, one of the Catholics who conspired on behalf of Mary Queen of Scots.

247. Villiers, Duke of Buckingham, cf. *Boreham,* op. cit. p. 121–22, 132 (see *Guide* p. 59).

248. Ibidem, p. 122f: re Frances Cromwell, cf. *Essex Heyday,* op. cit. p. 331. For George Monk (DNB 13:594–609, cf. *Leaders of the Civil Wars,* op. cit. pp. 1–3), and Benjamin Hoare, cf. *Boreham* op. cit. p. 123; for Boreham House, pp. 113–4; cf. Pevsner *Essex* p. 83.

249. Boreham Old Rectory is described and illustrated, ibidem p. 158. For Benjamin Rush, cf. DAB 16:227; *EncBrit* 23:857.

250. Benjamin Franklin, 1706–90, b. Boston, Massachusetts, printer, author, diplomat (DAB 6:585–98).

251. *Boreham*, op. cit. pp. 138–48; *Essex Churches, III, St Andrew's, Boreham*, F. Chancellor, E. R. i, 212; cf. Pevsner *Essex* pp. 95–96. Re John Oakes, see *Guide* p. 228. Re *The Sussex Tomb*, Boreham Histories, No. 3, W. J. T. Smith, 1973, and *Boreham* above, p. 144.

252. Sir Thomas Mildmay of Moulsham (d. 1608), son of Thomas the Master Auditor, cf. Grieve *Sleepers and Shadows* op. cit. 1:111.

253. *A Guide to Terling Church*, Richard Seymour, 1987, p. 13, Pevsner *Essex* p. 378 (Terling Place p. 379).

254. *Terling Guide*, above, p. 4.

255. Thomas Weld, *Magnalia* 1:236; cf. DAB 19:627–8; Venn 4:360. His exploits in America are also covered in, eg. *Builders of the Bay Colony* (Chapter 10) and, especially *Founding Harvard College*, op. cit. both S. E. Morison.

256. *Terling Guide*, op. cit. p. 5.

257. Weld, DAB 19:627–8; Hugh Peter, see *Guide* p. 350: William Hibbens, DAB 9:2 (he fell into financial difficulties, and his wife, soured, was hanged at Boston for witchcraft, the sentence passed by Governor Endecott, but J. Norton wrote, "executed because she had more wit than her neighbours." There were no witch trials in Thomas Hooker's Connecticut).

258. Mather, Catalogue of BA graduates, 1650, "Edmundus Weld," 1:30.

259. Ingatestone, Pevsner, *Essex*, pp. 250–52. The Hall's history and architecture is also detailed in *Tudor Secretary, Sir William Petre at Court, at Home*, F. G. Emmison (County Archivist) ERO, 1961, ch. 3, pp. 22ff.

260. *Tudor Secretary*, op. cit. p. 32.

261. We are fortunate to have Emmison's scholarly and detailed *Tudor Secretary*, above, an eminent book in every way: cf. DNB 15:979–81; *EncBrit* 21:315; NB. ERO has printed *Petre Family Portraits, A Catalogue*, David Piper, No. 26, 1930, including that of Bridget Pynchon, m. William, Fourth Baron (DNB15:983).

262. *Tudor Secretary*, op. cit. p. xv.

263. Ibidem p. 23, cf. p. 24.

264. Ibidem p. 296.

265. Ibidem p. 122.

266. Ibidem p. 84.

267. Wyat's Rebellion, cf. DNB 21:1098–1102 (Thomas Poet), 1102–4 (Thomas Rebel). cf. Venn 4:480.

268. *Tudor Secretary*, op. cit. pp. 276–78, 291; and pp. 270–85—he re-established Exeter College, OxfordU, with grants equalling £111 p. a.

269. *Tudor Secretary*, op. cit. cf. Epilogue p. 293ff, "records of his time do not yield a single harsh epithet about him—There is never the slightest hint of brutality or ruthlessness" (ibidem p. 296).

270. cf. *The Misfortunes of William, Fourth Baron Petre*, 1627–83, *Recusant History*, Christopher Clay, No. 2, 2:87 "estates inherited—in 1637 were large enough to place him in the ranks of the great landed magnates—about 11,000 acres, ie. "about 11,000 acres of freehold land and the lordship of several manors, and those produced some £5,500 per annum" in addition to his Devon holdings (Axminster, Dartmoor) and London properties, although this compares ill with the 45,000 acres Sir William was said to have amassed in his life-time (*Tudor Secretary* ch. xiv, *Man of Fortune and Charity*, pp. 266–76); cf. *EncBrit* 21:315; DNB 15:979-81 (Sir William), pp. 982–3 (William Fourth Baron). Elizabeth Savage, d. 1665, his first wife, descended from Thomas D'Arcy, Viscount Colchester, who succeeded the Woodville Earls Rivers (Elizabeth Woodville, Edward IV's queen), but was named by Pepys (Diary, April 1664) impudent, lewd, a drunken jade, DNB 15:983, cf. 17:831–34. Bridget Pynchon bestowed no renown on the Petre name, but one trusts she brought comfort, and sober Puritan good sense.

271. *Misfortunes of Fourth Baron*, op. cit. "On the 4th of May 1652 he went before the Lord Mayor of London and took the notorious oath," but he "remained a Catholic at heart," and so described himself in a death-bed letter to Charles II from the Tower of London (p. 106).

272. Titus Oates, 1649–1705, son of an Essex Anabaptist Minister (cf. *Essex Heyday* p. 218–9. Anabaptists were rebaptizers whose demand for individual Believers' Baptism on Scriptural grounds under radical leaders like Thomas Munzer, 1490–1525, led to open violence and the German Peasant's Revolt of 1524–6 in which Munzer was captured and executed: a deadly threat to Luther's—and all Puritan-Reformation. Titus went to St John's, Cambridge, contentiously held a variety of ecclesiastical posts, Catholic and Protestant, and embroiled King and country in his fraudulent revelations of a Popish plot against both. Public unrest surged for several years around 1678, many Catholics suffered, but Oates was finally discredited and imprisoned; cf. *EncBrit* 19:938–9; DNB 14:741–8; Venn 3:273 (NB. Venn knows of no Essex connection, DNB says Titus was b Oakham and that his father's ministry was exercised in Norfolk and Hastings, Sussex).

273. *A History of Stondon Massey in Essex*, E. H. L. Reeve (Rector) MCMVI, gives detailed accounts of history, people, buildings, a local historian's treasure trove; cf. *VicHist—Essex*, op. cit. 4:240–49; Pevsner *Essex* p. 373–4; and Dr. F. McGown Notes, Little Baddow papers, on all of which the following text is based.

274. Stondon Hall, *VicHist—Essex* 4:242, cf. p. 240-42 and Reeve *Hist.*, op. cit. pp. 3–6, etc.

275. *Essex Churches—St Peter's and St Paul's* F. Chancellor, E. R. vii, 139; cf. *St. Peter's and St. Paul's Church Guide*; *VicHist—Essex* 4:245–7, etc. above.

276. *Church Guide*, op. cit. p. 4.

277. Nathaniel Ward, *Magnalia*, op. cit. 1:236, 521f; cf. DAB 19:433–4; DNB 20:785. Venn 4:333; *Builders of the Bay Colony*, op. cit. Ch. VII, *Nathaniel Ward, Lawmaker and Wit*, p. 218ff; Reeve *Hist*, op. cit. pp. 71–74, etc. NB. Elbing is now known as Elblag, Poland, inland from the Gulf of Danzig (Gdansk).

278. *A Memoir of the Reverend Nathaniel Ward A.M., Author of the Simple Cobler of Agawam in America with Notices of his Family*, by John Ward Dean, Albany, NY: J. Munsell, 1868, p. 37.

279. Quoted from DAB 19:434. "The first code of laws to be established in New England," cf. Winthrop *Journal*, J. K. Hosmer, 1908, 2:49.

280. *The Simple Cobler*, published by James Munroe and Co, Boston, 1843, edited by David Pulsifer from 1647–1713 editions, p. 5.

281. Ibid. p. 85–86: re Harvard bequest, see Reeve *Hist*, op. cit. p. 73.

282. *Magnalia* 1:524, cf. pp. 236, 521–4.

283. Ibidem, pp. 522–3.

284. Giles Firmin, 1614–97, *The Real Christian*, London 1670 p. 19; cf. DNB 7: 45–46; *Magnalia* 1:427, 588; Venn 2:140; *Essex Heyday*, pp. 77, 317. Davids lists 17 of Firmin's publications, including *Separatism Examined*, 1651; *Stablishing against Shaking* (Quakers), 1656; *The Question between the Conformist and the Nonconformists*, 1681.

285. *Simple Cobler*, op. cit. p. 3: for sermon before Parliament, cf. Reeve, op. cit. p. 143.

286. Ibidem p. 73.

287. Reverend Samuel Ward, cf. Venn 4:334, DNB 20:790, cf. Reeve *Hist*, op. cit. p. 74: Pevsner *Essex* p. 373 on the pulpit, "good work with strap decoration and bands of diamonds," cf. *Church Guide* op cit., p. 3.

288. W. Byrd, 1543–1623, CCH IV, op. cit pp. 10, 181–2, etc; cf. DNB 3:575–78; ODCC, p. 212. Two disastrous fires, 1866 and 1877, gutted the old Place, apart from the surviving stables. The present Place dates from c. 1879, Reeve *Hist*, op. cit. p. 51–52; cf. Pevsner p. 341.

289. Thomas Tallis, 1515–85, *EncBrit* 26:377–8; cf. DNB 19:348–51; ODCC 1320.

290. Orlando Gibbons, 1583–1625, b Cambridge into musical family of William Gibbons. His brothers, Edward, Bachelor of Music and organist Bristol and Exeter Cathedrals, DNB 7:1138, *Oxons* 2:560: Ellis, second son, organist Salisbury Cathedral, DNB 7:1138: Orlando, youngest, Doctor of Music. *Oxons* 2:560, Venn 2:209, most gifted of all, my favourite church musician, his too few compositions a mastery of controlled polyphony. The family were Royalists, Orlando dying from smallpox contracted when travelling to Canterbury to compose

music for Charles I's wedding to Henrietta Maria; cf. *EncBrit* 11:937; DNB 7:1140–3; *17th century Britain,* CCH 4:11, 182–88, etc.

291. John Bull, 1562–1628, a West Country man (b Somerset), organist at Hereford Cathedral and Chapel Royal, Bachelor of Music, OxfordU, Doctor of Music, CambU (Venn 1:251), Music Professor Gresham College, London (see *Guide* p. 436 n. 330, cf. DNB 3:239–42; CCH 4: 8, 11). He travelled abroad for health, and died at Antwerp, organist at Notre Dame Cathedral. These royal musicians orbited away from Puritan conventicles, but were not unknown, or unappreciated. Ask Milton's ghost!

292. cf. *Tudor Secretary,* op. cit. pp. 210–214.

293. Shelley family, cf. Reeve *Hist,* op. cit. pp. 27–32; cf. *VicHist—Essex* 4:243; cf. DNB 18:41–2.

294. John Alford, cf. Reeve op. cit. pp. 66ff; Venn 1:15.

295. Fering had been Rector of Broomfield (Reeve *Hist.,* op. cit., p. 67), a moderate as was John Nobbs, from Corpus Christi, Cambridge (Venn 3:259).

296. Reeve *Hist.,* op. cit. p. 42.

297. The Stondon Branch of the Rich Family, and Sir Nathaniel Rich, 1585–1636: DNB 16:1005–6; *EncBrit* 23:293; Reeve *Hist.,* op. cit. p. 37; cf. *VicHist —Essex,* op. cit. p. 244, "John Shelley sold the manor of Stondon in c. 1610 to Sir Nathaniel Rich." NB. Richard first Baron Rich may have been Catholic at heart, but his offspring consistently espoused Puritanism.

298. Anthony Sawbridge entered Emmanuel 1597, and took his MA in 1604, the year of Hooker's entry. However, he remained for a further nine years as a fellow, so was for five of them co-fellow with Hooker. He moved on to Hadleigh, Essex, 14 miles from Little Baddow, 1613–33 before going to Stondon, one more practising Puritan in and around Thomas Hooker, cf. Venn 4:23.

299. Colonel Nathaniel Rich, 1620–1701, DNB 16:1005–6; cf. Reeve *Hist* op. cit. pp. 38–39, 144–5.

300. Edward Otway, b. St Neots, Cambridge, sizar at Christ's, Cambridge 1636, Puritan Lecturer at Stondon Massey, 1658, Rector 1660–91 (d), Venn 3:287.

301. Both quotations from Reeve *Hist,* op. cit. pp. 145 and 39.

302. *Coming Over,* op. cit. p. vii and p. 68.

303. Ibidem, p. 87.

304. Quoted from Reeve, *Hist,* op. cit. p .72.

305. In 1547 Sir Walter "acquired the manors of Seynclers and Herons in Danbury and built Danbury Place, but handed it to his second son, Humphrey" (S. E. Lehmberg, *Mildmay and Tudor Government,* op. cit. pp. 24–25); cf. Pevsner, *Essex,* pp. 154–7; *In Search of Essex,* op. cit. pp. 24–26; *Danbury Place-Park-Palace in the 18th and 19th Centuries,* M. Hopkirk, *Essex Review* lviii, 8; Danbury Society Handbook, 1980.

306. *Essex Churches, IV, St John the Baptist,* F. Chancellor, E. R. ii. 17; *A Short History of Danbury Parish Church,* J. M. Bull, 1939.

307. Described in *King's England, Essex,* op. cit. p. 110–111, and *In Search of Essex,* op. cit. p. 25.

308. Purleigh. Pevsner *Essex,* p. 316–7; *Essex churches, V, All Sts Purleigh,* F. Chancellor, *Essex Review* ii, 82.

309. Lawrence Washington, cf. *EncBrit* 28:344–8; cf. Pevsner *Essex* p. 317; F. H. Laws, *Maldon's Links With America,* Maldon, Essex, 1977, pp. 16–17. For Sulgrave see *Great Houses of Britain,* Nigel Nicolson, London 1971, pp. 70–75 etc.

310. Quoted from *A First Century of Scandalous Malignant Priests,* Thomas White, 1643, photocopy, Little Baddow papers "9. The Benefice of Lawrence Washington, Rector of Purleigh in the County of Essex, is sequestered, for that he is a common frequenter of Ale-houses, etc."

311. *Essex Heyday,* op. cit. p. 216.

312. *EncBrit* 28:344–5. NB. Mary Ball (1708–89) was Augustine's second wife, DAB 19:509. re. George Washington, cf. DAB 19:509–27; *EncAmericana* 8:590–92; *EncBrit*(15), 29, p. 212 and Biographies.

313. Maldon, Maeldune, cf. Reaney, *Place Names*, op. cit. p. 218; Pevsner *Essex* op. cit. pp. 290–94, cf. F. H. Laws *Maldon's Links with America*, 1977.

314. *A Discourse on Early Nonconformity in Maldon*, R. Burls, 1840, photocopy 1926 reprint, Little Baddow papers; *The Church on Market Hill*, M. G. L. Earnshaw, 1988. Joseph Billio, Venn 1:151 (Sidney Sussex, Cambridge 1675, son of Reverend Robert of Hatfield Peveral, Felsted school), cf. Earnshaw above p. 3–5.

315. George Gifford, Venn 2:213; cf. Davids *Annals*, op. cit. p. 117–118, and Burls *Early Nonconformity*, op. cit. pp. 6–11, "a great and diligent preacher" etc. NB. Maldon petitioned Parliament "that nearly all their learned and useful ministers were forbidden to preach, or deprived of their livings" (Burls, p. 10) evidence of the strong Puritan settlements of the town before civil war broke out.

316. Venn 2:409; Burls op. cit. p. 18–19. The reference is to Sir John Bramston the Elder (d. 1654), see *Guide* p. 294.

317. Edmund Calamy, 1671–1735, chronicler of Nonconformity, known especially for his *account of 1662 ejected ministers* (originally the ninth chapter of his Abridgement of Richard Baxter's 2 vol. *History*, cf. ODCC pp. 143, 217) came from a well known family of Essex nonconformist divines. His father, Edmund the Younger (1635–85) was rector of Moreton (five miles northwest of "Nathaniel Ward's" Stondon Massey, on the old Roman road to Great Dunmow, next village to "the Mashams'" High Laver), presented by the Earl of Manchester, son-in-law of the second Earl of Warwick, DNB 3:682–3. His grandfather Edmund the Elder (1600–66) was Puritan Lecturer at Rochford, also under the second Earl's patronage, and succeeded Dr John Stoughton at London's St Mary Aldermanbury (DNB 3:679–82; Venn 1:281, DNB 3:679–82, cf. Davids *Annals* op. cit. p. 424; DNB 3:68—7.

NB. Sir Thomas Honeywood, 1586–1666, of Marks Hall, Coggeshall, came from another celebrated Essex Puritan family. He commanded an Essex regiment in the Civil War, one of three, the other two commanded by the second Earl Warwick and Sir Thomas Barrington (d. 1644) who married Frances Gobert, foundress of the Little Baddow line (*Essex Heyday*, op cit., p. 312). He commanded Colchester after its siege, dismantling the fortifications (*Essex Heyday*, op cit. p. 320).

318. All Saints commemorates St Mellitus, d. 624. He came with the second group of missionaries to join St Augustine at Canterbury (601), and was consecrated by Augustine bishop to the East Saxons, with London his headquarters. King Sabart was converted, but not his sons, who drove Mellitus into exile in Gaul on their father's death. He returned to become Archbishop of Canterbury (619), his missionary work in Essex to be completed by St Cedd, ODCC pp. 254, 884; *Saints*, op. cit. pp. 83, 242; see *Guide* pp. 207-8.

319. Brihtnoth (Bryhtnoth), Earl of Essex, benefactor of the Church, his remains were interred in Ely Cathedral, cf. *Maldon A Thousand Years Ago*, F. H. Laws, 1952, pp. 1–5, including a translation of *The Song of Malden*.

320. Thomas Plume, A. C. Edwards *A History* op. cit. p. 119; cf. *Essex Heyday* op. cit. pp. 202, 327.

321. *Magnalia* 1:338.

322. Sources—*Magnalia* 1:526–583, *The Triumphs of the Reformed Religion in America: or, The Life of the Renowned John Eliot; A Person justly famous in the Church of God; not only as an eminent Christian, and an excellent Minister among the English; but also as a memorable Evangelist among the Indians of New-England. With some account concerning the late and strange success of the Gospel in those parts of the world, which for many ages have lain buried in Pagan ignorance. Essayed by Cotton Mather*, based, we remember, on personal acquaintance with Apostle. The lengthy life concludes with a letter from Richard Baxter, August 3, 1691, "I am now dying, I hope, as he did. It pleased me to read from him my case, 'my understanding faileth, my memory faileth, my

tongue faileth, and my hand and pen fail but my charity faileth not,'" ibid. p. 583: cf. *Descendants of John Eliot, Apostle to the Indians, 1598-1905*, new ed. 1905, W. H. Emerson, E. Eliot, G. E. Eliot Jr, including a Life, memorials of the Apostle, etc.; S. E. Morison, *Builders of the Bay Colony*, op. cit. chapter 10, *John Eliot*, cf. pp. 290–320; *John Eliot, Apostle to the Indians*, Ola Elizabeth Winslow, Boston, 1968, with a useful Bibliography, pp. 213–18; *The History of New England from 1630–1649*, Boston, 1825, John Winthrop; articles, eg. *The Life of John Eliot*, Nehemiah Adams, Boston, 1847, ditto Convers Francis, 1896; E. H. Byington, *John Eliot the Puritan Missionary to the Indians*, American Society of Church History 8:1897, pp. 109–45; *Notices of the Pilgrim Fathers, John Eliot and his Friends of Nazeing*, William Winters, Royal Historical Society *Transaction* 10:267–311, London 1882; *The Founder's Formative Years*, the story of John Eliot in England, 1604–31, a convenient summary of what appears here, closely followed in this text, D. C. Collingwood, The Newsletter, Roxbury Latin School, vol. 65, No. 3, 66, No. 1 (April 1992–October 1992), p. 11–15, 10–16 (illustrated); DAB 6:79—80; DNB 6:607–12; Venn 2:94. For Widford, Nazeing, etc. see followling pages.

NB. If my references to North American Indians, instead of the more acceptable title of Native Americans, causes any offence, I apologise, but the best the English could do in the 17th century was the general title Indians, and I have not found it feasible to get round their misunderstanding. What most pleased the Native Americans, it was said, was John Eliot's humility in his bearing towards them, a humility shared by all his personal assistants, me too.

323. *History of Nazeing*, J .R. Sutherland, 1950, pp. 13–15.

324. Jesus College, "an excellent reputation for scholarship, especially in the classics," DAB 6:79-80. re Ordination, see *Guide* p. 154f and p. 397 n. 118, 123; cf. Jarvis op. cit. ch. 1, p. 8, n. 10.

325. *A College First Proposed, 1633, Unpublished Letters of Apostle Eliot and William Hammond to Sir Simond D'Ewes*, Franklin Wright, offprint, Yale Library Bulletin vol. III, No. 3, Autumn 1954. Yale University, third oldest in USA, was developed too late for this guide, but may not be overlooked. Higher education was the life-blood of New England. Land was set aside for a college by the New Haven founders as early as 1647, and Hopkins Grammar School was opened c. 1668. Yale was not formally established until 1701. It was a community venture, students being at first accommodated in other centres of New Haven and Saybrook. It was deliberately orientated towards a stricter Calvinism than then prevailed at Harvard. The curriculum broadened with the passage of time, as did its Puritan heritage, carrying, as it did, seeds within it of intellectual expansion and adventure from its inception, cf. *EncAmericana*, op. cit. 29: 639–41, 1986 ed; *EncBrit* 18:899–901. For Elihu Yale, 1649–1721, b Boston, Massachusetts, East India Company, Madras governor, large donor to Saybrook college, his name incorporated in the 1745 Charter, see DAB, 20:590–91: *EncBrit* (15) 12:807–08.

Sir Simonds D'Ewes, 1602–50, son of Paul of Stowlangtoft Hall, Suffolk, one of the six wealthy Chancery Clerks (Joane Drake's father Sir William Tothill of Shardeloes, Amersham, was another). His grandfather Gerrard was a London printer, but he spent much of his childhood with his maternal grandfather, Richard Simonds in Dorset, whose fortune he inherited. He entered St John's, Cambridge 1618, and the Middle Temple, became a barrister and Member of Parliament for Sudbury, 1640–48. DNB calls him an "antiquarian writer." The author of *Journals of all the Parliaments During the Reign of Queen Elizabeth*, he seems never to have made the higher grades of politics. Deeply pious, richly pedantic, influential for his prolific writings rather than actions. He m Anne Clopton heiress of most desirable Kentwell Hall, Long Melford, Suffolk (go if ever you can) but lived and was buried at Stowlangtoft; cf. DNB 5:900–903; Venn 2:38.

326. The Roxbury Latin School: "A grammar-school he (ie. John Eliot) would always have upon the place, whatever it cost him; and he importuned all other places to have the like ... God so blessed his endeavours, that Roxbury could not live quietly without a free school in the town; and the issue of it has been one thing, which has made me almost put the title of Schola Illustris upon that little nursery; that is, that Roxbury has afforded more scholars—first

for the colledge, and then for the publick—than any town of its bigness, or, if I mistake not, of twice its bigness in all New-England," *Magnalia* 1:551; cf. *Tercentenary History of the Roxbury Latin School, 1645–1945*, Richard Walden Hale, 1946; *Forty Years On*, Francis Russell, 1970; and *The Catalogue for the Three Hundred and Forty-Eighth Year, 1992–3*. Look out for important Eliot biography in new *History of Roxbury Latin School*, A. W. Jarvis, publication due 1995.

327. Eight years after Eliot's death, statistics of the New England Co. revealed "some 30 congregations of praying Indians, which were served by 37 full-time native preachers, teachers, and catechists and only seven or eight native-speaking English ministers, usually on a part-time basis." By the outbreak of the American Revolution a century later, "there had been at various times in New England 22 Indian churches, 91 praying towns or reservations, 72 white missionaries, and 133 native preachers and teachers." Jarvis, op. cit. 1:68.

Mather includes in the Harvard Graduate (AB) Class of 1665, "Caleb Cheeschaumuk Indus," *Magnalia* 2:31. Eliot's 1689 gift of 75 acres "for the support of a school and schoolmaster at that end of Roxbury, commonly called Jamaica or Pond Plain" (*Descendants of John Eliot*, op. cit. p. 249), "for the teaching of Indians and negroes in Roxbury," DNB 6: 610, cf. *Magnalia* 1: 576.

328. DNB 6:608; cf. *Magnalia* 1:561–2; *John Eliot's First Indian Teacher and Interpreter, Cockenoe-de-Long Island*, William Wallace Tooker, New York, 1896, p. 12ff.

329. *The Bay Psalm Book* 1640, Richard Mather, John Cotton, Thomas Welde, Francis Quarles (see *Guide* p. 292-93, credited with contributing psalms 6, 16, 25, 57, 88, 137), and John Eliot: cf. Winslow op. cit. ch.V, *A Share in New England's First Public Book*, pp. 65–70; Zoltan Haraszti *The Enigma of the Bay Psalm Book*, Chicago, 1956. Eliot's many other publications, including the Eliot Tracts (see following paragraphs), are listed in *Descendants*, op. cit. pp. 257–63. Caleb Cheeschaumuk see *Guide* n. 327 above.

330. See Jarvis op. cit. 1:60 re Eliot Bible First Edition. Robert Boyle, 1627–91, "father of chemistry" no less (ODCC, p. 190) was governor from 1661–89, of the "Corporation for the Promoting and Propagating the Gospel of Jesus Christ in New England" (CPPG, enacted by Parliment 27 July 1649, later known as *The New England Company*, Winslow, op. cit. pp. 116, 117). The 14th child of Richard, Earl of Cork, b at Lismore Castle, Munster (Ireland), he was educated at Eton, and in Europe, especially Geneva, and Florence shortly before the astronomer Galileo (1564–1642) died there. His inheritance of privilege and wealth enabled him to devote his life to scientific research, particularly the enunciation of "Boyle's Law" (that the volume of a gas varies inversely as the pressure, EncBrit 4:355). He helped draw together a group of natural philosophers, Isaac Newton, Edmund Halley Astronomer Royal, Isaac Barrow, Christopher Wren, John Aubrey, Samuel Pepys, John Evelyn, most of whom appear in this guide. They met frequently at Gresham College (ie. Sir Thomas Gresham, London merchant, 1519–79, had built the London Royal Exchange and bequeathed a series of lectures which at first were held there as an independent academy, London's first seat of higher learning; cf. CCH *17th century Britain*, op. cit. 4:7–9, etc.) and expanded into the Royal Society of London for Improving Natural Knowledge, incorporated by Charles II, 1662. Boyle was offered the Presidency in 1680, but declined. His underlying concern seems always to have been for the reconciling of religion and science. To this end he gave of his energy and money, not least to promote the spread of Christianity. He was an outstanding governor of the CPPG, a sympathetic supporter of John Eliot, the epitome of the new age pragmatic evangelical Protestant so familiar to us in men like Thomas Hooker, whom Boyle may not have met, but who belonged to his era. DNB 2:1026–31; CCH ibidem 4:32ff; EncBrit (15) 2:447; The Works of the Honorable Robert Boyle to which is Prefixed the Life of the Author, 5 vols, 1744 (rep. 1965–66), with Letters from John Eliot, 1:ccv-ccxiv, and CPPG Charter, Appendix pp. cliv-clviii.

331. "Upon October 28, 1646, four of us (having sought God) went unto the Indians inhabiting within our bounds, with desire to make known the things of theire peace to them." "Upon November 11, 1646, we came the second time unto the same Wigwam of Waawbon," quoted in *Descendants*, op. cit. pp. 220, 221. The four were probably Eliot, Shepard, Elder Heath

of Roxbury, and Daniel Gookin ibidem p. 271. "Mr Eliot's way of Opening the Mysteries of the Gospel to our Indians" is described by Mather, *Magnalia* 1:563ff; Winslow *John Eliot*, op. cit. p. 96–110, etc. Daniel Goodkin, 1612–87, "colonist, soldier, magistrate" (DAB 7:417) is another multi-coloured character thrown up by the New England adventure. Third son of Daniel of Carrigaline, Ireland, his mother was Mary Boyd, daughter of Richard, Canon of Canterbury Cathedral. Daniel worked on his father's plantation in Virginia, then, a Puritan, removed to Roxbury, Massachusetts 1644, where he met Eliot. "One of the founders of the free grammar school" (Roxbury Latin) the following year (DNB 7:417), he then moved to Cambridge, Massachusetts, where he served as Captain of the train-band, Deputy, and Assistant. He accompanied Shepard (Pastor of Cambridge) and Eliot in the early mission to the Indians, and was "chosen to be ruler over the praying Indians," ie. Eliot's successor; cf. DAB 7:417–8. Mather lists him among the "Magistrates of the Massachusett-Colony" (*Magnalia* 1:141), and one of the eight "Major-Generals of the Military Forces in the Colony," with Thomas Dudley, John Endecott, Edward Gibbons, Robert Sedgwick, Humfry Atherton, Daniel Denison and John Leveret (ibidem p. 142), and adds "The Indian church at Natick (which was the first Indian church in America) is, since blessed Eliot's death, much diminished and dwindl'd away. But Mr Daniel Gookin hath bestow'd his pious cares upon it" (2:439).

332. *Magnalia* 1:563–4;

333. DNB 6:608. re Eliot's "civility" projects, cf. *Magnalia* 1:564f; *History of South Natick*, Little Baddow papers, p. 3, "a foot-bridge of timber in the form of an arch and resting upon abutments of stone;" narrated by Winslow, *John Eliot*, op. cit. ch. X, *Natick, First of the Praying Towns*, "it spanned an 80–ft riverbed, was arched 9–ft high and had stone abutments on either bank." pp. 122–36: cf. Eliot, "I set them therefore to fall and square timbers, for an house, and when it was ready, I went, and many of them with me, and on their shoulders carried all the timber together, etc. These things they chearfully do; I pay them wages carefully for all such works I set them about, which is a good encouragement to labour," ibid. p. 126: cf. Eliot Tract No. 6, *The Light appearing more and more towards the perfect Day*, London 1651, p. 138; cf. Tracts 3, *The Day-Breaking, if not the Sun-Rising of the Gospell with the Indians in New England*, London 1647; 5, *The Glorious Progress of the Gospell, Amongst the Indians in New England*, London 1649; 7, *Strength out of Weaknesse*, London 1652, etc: cf. *History of the Town of Natick, Massachusetts*, William Biglow, Boston, 1850.

Edward Winslow's part in Eliot's singular achievement should be acknowledged. Winslow, 1595–1655, was b at Droitwich (Worcester), a "gentleman of the best family of any of the Plymouth planters" (DNB 21:672). He travelled to Leyden (possibly to the University) and there came under John Robinson's sway. He allied himself to that reforming congregation, sailed, 1620, in the Speedwell (with his wife and two servants), crossed the Atlantic in the Mayflower and served as one of the five first assistants of the infant Plymouth colony. He rose to be g overnor (1633, 36, 44). His most considerable contribution lay in representing the colony as its envoy in England, defending it from criticism, negotiating the liquidation of its crippling debts. Thus he was in London at the time of presenting the Bill to Parliament for "A Corporation for the Promoting and Propagating the Gospel of Jesus Christ in New England" which financed Eliot's work, enacted largely through his skilful diplomacy; cf. DAB 20:393–4; DNB 21:672–4.

334. For Eliot's comments on King Philip's War, 1675, and his Praying Indians' imprisonment on Deer Island, Boston Harbor, cf. *Descendants*, op. cit. pp. 239–42; Flintlock and Tomahawk, NY: D. E. Leach, 1958; etc.

335. Letter to Robert Boyle (see *Guide* p. 436 n. 330), 23 October 1677, "In our first war with the Indians, God pleased to show us the vanity of our military skill, in managing our arms, after the European mode. Now we are glad to learn the skulking way of war," quoted *Descendants*, op. cit. p. 242.

336. *Magnalia* 1:577 and 562. DAB 6:80, only four of Eliot's 14 Praying Indian Villages survived Metacomet's War.

337. Letter to Eliot, signed William Steele, First Governor CPPG, 18 February 1653, quoted *Descendants*, op. cit. p. 225.

338. Fr. Druillete(s), Dec. 28–9 1650, Winslow, op. cit. p. 185, cf. *Descendants* op. cit. p. 223: but ibid. p. 213, "Mr Eliot is for the first time 'stiled the Indian Apostle' by Thomas Thorowgood" (*Jewes in America or Probabilities that the Americans are Jewes*, 1660, a thesis much favoured by Eliot and other New England leaders, cf. *Magnalia* 1:560f). cf. DNB 7:607.

339. *Magnalia* 1:540; cf. "The papooses always found small gifts in his deep pockets," DNB 6:608. The story of the knotted kerchief is variously told, eg. Winslow, op. cit. p. 120, "Sister, I think the Lord meant it all for you.": cf. Jarvis op. cit. ch. 1, n. 46, authentic quote from Letter, James May Collection, MassHS, X (1809), 186–87.

340. *Magnalia* 1:529, 541, cf. p. 547, and for her management of the family estate, cf. p. 538, "Once when there stood several kine of his own before his door, his wife, to try him, asked him 'Whose they were?' and she found that he knew nothing of them."

341. Richard Baxter, 3 August 1691, "I knew much of Mr Eliot's opinions, by many letters which I had from him. There was no man on earth whom I honoured above him. It is his evangelical work that is the apostolical succession that I plead for," quoted by Mather, *Magnalia* 1:583. NB. Baxter's *Call* was translated by Eliot into Algonquian, 1664. "Before the end of August, a thousand copies—had been printed and distributed to the Indians," *Descendants*, p. 233.

342. Letter to Robert Boyle, August 26, 1664, quoted in Winslow, op. cit. p. 188, see n. 330.

343. "His last breath smelt strong of heaven, and was articled into none but very gracious notes; one of the last whereof was, 'Welcome Joy!' and at last it went away, calling upon the standers by to 'Pray, pray, pray!' which was the thing in which so vast a portion of it had been before employed," Mather 1:578.

344. Widford, cf. *VicHist—Hertfordshire* 3:402–7; cf. Pevsner *Hertfordshire* p. 406.

345. *St John the Baptist, Widford, Herfordshire*, Roddy Hill-Smith; and Hill-Smith correspondence, Little Baddow papers.

346. Bennett Eliot's Will, November 5, 1621, "And first I give and bequeath all the rents and profitts of all my coppy and customary lands and Tenements wth theire appertenncs lyeinge and beinge in the sevall p'shes of Ware, Widford, Hunsdon and Estweeke in the County of Hartford unto my Trusty and welbeloved friends William Curtis my sonne in lawe, Nicolas Camp the younger and John Keyes all of the sayde parishe of Nasinge for the space of eight yeares from the time of my decease quarterly to pay unto my sonne John Eliott the some of eight pounds a yeare of lawfull money of England for and towards the maintenance in the univ'sity of Cambridge where he is a Scholler," quoted in *Descendants*, op. cit. p. 269–70.

NB. Hunsdon House temporarily brought the court to secluded Widford because it was "a favourite with Henry VIII,' who lavished improvements on it (*VicHist—Hertfordshire* 3:323–32). Edward VI and Mary (perforce) spent long periods there, but Elizabeth conferred the estate on Sir Henry Carey, with Eastwick Manor. Carey, first Baron Hunsdon, chamberlain of Elizabeth's household, was high in her affections (DNB 3:977). Bennett Eliot bought into a regal enclave.

347. Ware, *VicHist—Hertfordshire*, 3:380–97. Originally, Ware took precedence over present county capital, which, in 14th century was known as"'Hertford-by-Ware" (ibidem p. 383); cf. Pevsner *Hertfordshire*, pp. 376–82, "Its character has been eroded by the destruction of several of its most distinguished buildings" (ibidem p. 378), nevertheless Pevsner's *Preambulation* still excites curiosity. The Parish Church of St Mary is described ibid. pp. 376–78, and in *VicHist—Hertfordshire* 3:392–4. For Lady Margaret Beaufort-Tudor see *Guide* p. 140 and p. 392 n. 64. Her interest was secured by the restoration, 1513, of two local manors formerly in her family's possession (*VicHist—Hertfordshire* 3:381). The Church the Puritans sought to reform may have been corrupt, but had bitter memories of benefits yielded only by threats and bribery!

348. *Twelfth Night*, William Shakespeare, Act III, Scene II, line 52. The Great Bed of Ware is 10–ft 8–ins square, of finely carved oak with inlay and painted decoration, cf. *VicHist—Hertfordshire* 3:382; *Dictionary of English Furniture* 3 vols, 1, p. 41–42, Illustrated, Fig. 14.

349. The New River, *EncBrit* 28:323, and 19:111; cf. *London*, Barker and Jackson, op. cit. p. 112; *London Metropolitan Water Board*, *EncBrit*, 16:946–7; Great Amwell, *VicHist—Hertfordshire* 3:414. NB. "a ferment of technological invention was rising out of the soil of proto-capitalism," CCH *17th century Britain* 4:9.

Sir Hugh Myddelton, 1560–1631, sixth son of Sir Richard, Governor of Denbigh Castle, North Wales (a constituency Sir Hugh represented in Parliament) was a wealthy London goldsmith in addition to his family's Welsh silver and lead mines. He advanced his fortune by venturing on the Spanish Main with Sir Walter Raleigh. It was his brother William, "Welsh poet and seaman" (DNB 13:1340) who commanded the "pinnace, like a fluttered bird, came flying from far away: Spanish ships of war at sea! We have sighted fifty-three!" ("The Revenge," Tennyson, i: The *Revenge* was Drake's ship against the Armada, 1588). By this daring act William Myddelton saved Lord Howard's fleet of 16 vessels, sent against the Spanish treasure ships, 1591—but not Sir Richard Grenville in the *Revenge*, who died as his rearguard action heroically engaged the Spaniards single-handed. Every Eliot in Massachusetts knew the story by heart! Sir Hugh received a Baronetcy in recognition of his work as first Governor of the New River Company, cf. *EncBrit* 19:110–11; DNB 13:1333–36.

NB. Grenville, 1541–91 (son of Sir Roger Greynvile commander Henry VIII's flagship, Mary Rose, who died on board when she capsised, 1545, recently recovered), Privateer; Member of Parliament and Sheriff Cornwall; commanded support fleet for his cousin Walter Raleigh's Virginia Colony, 1585 and '88; vice-admiral, 1591, under Thomas Howard (first Earl Suffolk, second son of Thomas fourth Duke Norfolk, DNB 10:71—NB. Lord Howard of Effingham was first son of Thomas second Duke Norfolk); Commissioner of Works, Dover Harbour; Commander Western Defences, England—there was no end to these devout-Christian-respected-fighting-magistrate-models for Puritans in need of human as well as divine inspiration in New England settlements! DNB 13:565–67.

350. *Chirk Castle, Clwyd*, Naional Trust, 1990, p. 15; *The Wooden Water-Pipe* p. 14–5; cf. Pevsner, *Denbighshire*, pp. 121–8 (Chirk Village, pp. 128–31).

351. *London*, Barker and Jackson, op. cit. p. 112.

352. The Myddeltons of Chirk, *Chirk Castle*, National Trust, op. cit. pp. 51–57; cf. DNB 13:1333–41.

353. Sir Thomas Myddelton, 1550–1631, and the Welsh Bible, *EncBrit* 19:111; cf. DNB 13:1337–38. His son, General Sir Thomas, 1586–1666, ibid. pp. 1338–40.

354. Hertford is well served by its Museum, Information Centre, and local publications, eg. *Hertford County Town Guide*, current edition *Discovering Hertfor*d, four illustrated walks, detailed in house-to-house historical, architectural notes (2nd edition, 1987); *The Chronicles of Hertford Castle*, H. C. Andrews, 1947; an attractive mini-guide for the day-tourist; occasional papers, eg. *The Standard of Honour*, "within a chaplet of roses Gules a stag's head caboshed" (facing front), thrice repeated, with "Argent, a hart lodged in water; *A Brief History of Hertford Castle*, etc; cf. *VicHist—Hertfordshire* 3:490–511; Pevsner *Hertfordshire* pp. 185–92—on all of which I have gratefully drawn. cf. also Hertford Correspondence, A. G. Davies, former Museum Curator, 1987; R. R. Dunkley, Manager Barclays Bank (home of Samuel Stone) 1989; Ann Kirby, Town Clerk, 1990, Little Baddow papers.

355. George Fox, see *Guide* p. 87 and p. 376 n. 126: William Penn of Pennsylvania, 1644–1718, son of Admiral Sir William (1621–70) whose erratic career may be represented in the individualism of his son. Sir William was a Parliament naval captain in the Civil War, an able naval tactician who switched loyalties when Charles I was beheaded, yet commanded Cromwell's 1654 West Indies expedition which captured Jamaica, then supported the Restoration as "great captain commander" under James II (then Duke York), cf. *EncBrit* 21:99; DNB 15:753–6).

His son, William Penn, Essex bred at "Puritan" Wanstead, and Chigwell's high-church Harsnett Grammar School (Samuel Harsnett, 1561–1631, another Essex man, b Colchester, educated Pembroke, Cambridge, D.D. 1609 and University Vice-Chancellor, censured for "Romish tendencies," chaplain to Archbishop Bancroft, see *Guide*, p.143ff; Vicar of Chigwell in later succession to J. Rogers (First Marian martyr, see *Guide* p. 288)—what a topsyturvy world it was! Archdeacon Essex; Bishop Chichester; Archbishop York; unloved of Puritans, he left a legacy of High Churchmanship which produced many a reactive Reformer, cf. *Essex*, Crouch, op. cit. p. 99–101; *EncBrit* 13:30; Venn 2:319). Penn was sent down from Christs, OxfordU, 1661, for nonconformity. He joined the Quakers, and wrote prolifically in their defence. He was briefly imprisoned in the tower (as his father had been tho' not for any religious reason), where he wrote *No Cross, No Crown* (1669); and founded Pennsylvania (1682). He returned to England two years later, nor visited the colony again until 1699; but continued to write (eg. *Primitive Christianity*, 1696) and preach, upholding the Quaker way by his personal example. He is buried at Jordans, Chalfont St Giles, close by Amersham (*EncBrit* 21:99–104; DNB 15: 756–65; DAB 14:433–7; ODCC p. 1042–3.

356. Edward the Elder, d. 924 (second son of Alfred the Great, see *Guide* p. 89) was constantly occupied, with his sister Aethelflaed the Lady of Mercia, in consolidating their father's gains over the Danes by a policy of strategically placed forts, and burghs (fortified towns); and in pushing back the Danish frontiers, until Britain was virtually reunified under his rule, cf. *EncBrit* 8:990–1; DNB 6:419–23, "the 'Unconquered King,'" p. 423.

357. *Town Guide*, op. cit. p. 18; cf. *Chronicles of Hertford Castle*, op. cit. *The Norman Period, 1066–1272*, pp. 6–16; *VicHist—Hertfordshire* 3: 501–6; Pevsner *Hertfordshire* p. 187, "flint curtain wall, which may belong to the work recorded for 1171–4."

358. *Chronicles of Castle* op. cit. Part V, *The Tudor Period* (pp. 60–75), p. 63. For Elizabeth's 1535 *Prayer Book, Town Guide*, op. cit. p. 19; Hertford occasional papers, op. cit. *Brief History of Hertford Castle*, G. Moodey; etc.

359. *Chronicles of Castle*, op. cit. p. 84.

360. The Synod Stone, cf. *Town Guide*, p. 17. For Council of Hertford, 673 AD, cf. ODCC p. 632.

361. *Chronicles of Castle*, pp. 76–79. For John Norden, see *Guide*, p. 204 and p. 409 n. 19.

362. Samuel Stone's House, cf. *Discovering Hertford*, p. 31; A. G. Davies correspondence, *The Birthplace of Samuel Stone*, Little Baddow papers. John Speede's Map is reproduced in miniature in *Discovering Hertford*, p. 9, but you need to traverse the short perambulations, book in hand, to reap full benefit. The Map is also in *Chronicles of Castle*, p. 72. A larger reproduction is available at the Museum. John Speed, 1552–1629, historian, cartographer, was born into a Cheshire taylor's home, and became a member of the Merchant Taylor's Company (cf. DNB 18: 726–28). At first he made maps in his leisure hours, but the patronage of Fulke Greville (see *Guide* p. 394 n. 88) enabled him to follow full-time his interest in cartography and the Society of Antiquaries, eg. his *The History of Great Britaine under the Conquests of ye Romans, Saxons, Danes and Normans*, also his *Genealogies Recorded in Sacred Scripture* which ran through 33 editions, many bound with copies of the Bible. High Church, he shared the Puritans' fascination with religion and life, reflected in his dwellings-directed maps (eg. also, *A Cloud of Witnesses*, dedicated to John Whitgift, 1530–1604, Elizabeth's Puritan-repressing Archbishop of Canterbury, cf. *Elizabethan Puritan Movement* Collinson, op. cit. pp. 123 through p. 455ff; ODCC p. 1456), successor to Grindal, 1519–83, Puritan sympathiser to Elizabeth's chagrin, cf. ODCC pp. 591, 1456.

363. John Stone, Hertford Councillor (Burgess) 1605, cf. A. G. Davies, *Birthplace of Samuel Stone*, op. cit. Little Baddow papers.

364. Samuel Stone, 1602–63, was baptized at All Saints (Alhallowes) close behind his father's Fore Street house. The Norden Survey (1621) shows it to have been outside the town boundary. Indeed it had belonged to Waltham Abbey before the Dissolution, and thereby linked with John Eliot's Nazeing (*Discovering Hertford*, op. cit. p. 33). The church burnt down

(*VicHist—Hertfordshire* 3:508) the present structure a reconstruction, dating from 1891. Adjacent, north-east, lies Hale's Grammar School, 1617, where Samuel may have been amongst the earliest scholars as he did not enter Emmanuel, Cambridge, until 1620. At Emmanuel he graduated MA in 1627 (Venn 4:168), but also spent some time studying under the celebrated Puritan teacher, Richard Blackerby (cf. Mather 1:434; Venn 1:160), at Ashen, north Essex, on the River Stour border with Suffolk, at "the enchanting village of Stoke-by-Clare" (*Essex*, Marcus Crouch, op. cit. p. 197). Ashen's tall flint church-tower is c. 1400, the brick stair-turret 1520, the nave Norman. Samuel had no interest in tourism, and would only have invited your visit to argue theology under Blackerby (Mather dubbed Stone "Doctor Irrefragabilis," "whom none could confound"); nor would he have approved the old churching stool (for the purification of women after childbirth) the back of which Crouch saw against the church wall in 1969, inscribed "This hath bin the churching the mearring stool and so it shall be still," but I have not been so lucky! NB. Mearring = Marrying stool (?) on which one sat for Banns to be called, cf. Oxford English Dictionary, compact edition vol P-Z, p. 1018, Stool (i) "Any kind of seat for one person"—1626, Minute Book, Archdeaconry of Colchester, "A couple that came to be married, which, by custome, should have sitten in the stoole aforesayd." From Ashen, Samuel went to Stisted, Towcester, and with Hooker to Massachusetts (see *Guide* pp. 88, 278), cf. DAB 18:83–4; DNB 18:1302; Mather 1:434–8, where his Epitaph stands, "Crowned by the clouds through which he passed."

365. *Magnalia* 1:434, cf. DAB 9:199.

366. *Magnalia* ibid, also re "both a Load-Stone and a Flint-Stone," and the immediately following complementary sentence "He had a certain pleasancy in conversation, which was the effect and symptom of his most ready wit."

367. DAB 18:83. For Major John Mason, see *Guide* p. 416 n. 118.

368. *Magnalia* 1:436; cf. *The Half-Way Covenant*, R. G. Pope, Princeton, 1969; *Reformation, Conformity and Dissent*, ed. R. Buick-Knox, London 1977, essay by Christopher Hall, *Occasional Conformity* (in Britain), pp. 199–220; etc.

369. *Magnalia* 1:437, with the added comment "He was an extraordinary person at an argument; and as clear and smart a disputant as most that ever lived in the world."

370. DAB, 18:84; cf. *In And About Hartford*, Marion Hepburn Grant, Connecticut Historical Society, 1978, p. 108–9, *South Congregational Church, 277 Main Street*, outlines the dispute between Stone, Goodwin, and the 31 members.

371. Roydon, cf. *In Search of Essex*, op. cit. p. 130; Pevsner *Essex*, pp. 329–30. Sir Thomas More m. Jane Croft, 1505. "The battered gatehouse of Nether Hall—once towered in the grand Essex manner—of red brick patterned with blue" (*Essex*, Couch, op. cit. p. 234) was replaced by a house in Chelsea, London which became a "centre of intellectual life" (ODCC, p. 924), frequented by Erasmus and John Colet (1466–1519, Dean of St Paul's, ODCC 310) who together shared an abhorrence of the extravagant worldliness of the higher clergy which fostered succeeding Puritans (ODCC p. 924). See *Guide*, p. 272.

372. Nazeing. *VicHist—Essex* 5:140–50; Pevsner *Essex*, p. 304–5; and all guide books. *Memorials of the Pilgrim Fathers, John Eliot and his friends of Nazeing and Waltham Abbey*, W. Winters, 1882, especially re Nazeing Village, pp. 10–15, eg. p. 13, "Nazeing is situated on the north-west corner of the half-hundred of Waltham; part of it being on an elevation—From east to west it is four miles, and nearly the same from north to south—pleasant and healthy," etc; All Saints, pp. 15–21; Eliot family, pp. 26–30, etc; *The Ecclesiastical History of Essex under the Long Parliament and Commonwealth*, Colchester, H. Smith; c. 1931, *History of Nazeing*, J. R. Sutherland, 1950; *History of All Saints, Nazeing Parish Church*, David Read. There is an active Waltham Abbey HistoricalSociety, Essex; and the John and Elizabeth Curtis/Curtiss Society of Connecticut, formerly National Society of the Descendants of John and Elizabeth Curtiss (kin to John Eliot), both valued sources of information, cf. Dr K. N. Bascombe (Waltham), and Nelson G. Curtis (Southbury, Connecticut) correspondence, Little Baddow papers (including copy John Chapman and Peter Andre's map of Nazeing Parish, 1777).

373. "I do see that it was a great favour of God unto me, to season my first times with the fear of God, the word, and prayer," *Magnalia* 1:529.

374. Nazeing All Saints, "as fine a position as any in the county. The tall tower looks across a valley gleaming with water and glass to the hills of Hertfordshire", Crouch, Essex, op. cit. pp. 236–7; cf. History, D. Read above; Pevsner *Essex*, op. cit. p. 304; *VicHist—Essex* 5:149.

375. Winters, op. cit. pp. 10; *The Curtis Family*, 42ff; *The Ruggles Family*, 50f; *The Graves Family*, 52f, etc; cf. Nazeing and Waltham settlers' lists, pp. 68–69, etc.

376. "Mr Eliot had engaged unto a select number of his pious and Christian friends in England that, if they should come into these parts before he should be in the pastoral care of any other people, he would give himself to them, and be for their service. It happened that these friends transported themselves hither the year after him, and chose their habitation at the town which they called Roxbury," *Magnalia* 1:531.

377. Winters, op. cit. *Notes on the Nonconformists of Nazeing*, p. 7–78; cf. Bascombe correspondence, Little Baddow papers. NB. Nazeing had been a royal manor, attached by King Harold to his college at Waltham for revenue, and so remained up to the Dissolution, when it reverted to the Crown.

378. Clergy references. cf. Winters op. cit. *Vicars of Nazeing*, pp. 22–25. Nicholas Lock, cf. Winters, p. 22, Sutherland, op. cit. p. 12, cf. Bascombe correspondence; J. Hopkins, cf. Winters, "deprived," p. 22–23; E. Jude, cf. Venn 2:491 (Emmanuel, 1596), cf. Winters p. 23; L.Goodrick, cf. Venn 2:237; J. Dyke, cf. Venn 2:79; J. Harper, cf. Venn 2:309, cf. Winters p. 23, "signed the "Essex Testimony" ('A Testimony of the Ministers in the Province of Essex to the Truth of Jesus Christ and the Solemn League and Covenant, as also against the Errors, Heresies and Blasphemies of these times and the Toleration of them," 1648, cf. "The Essex Watchman" of 1649, a further manifesto in favour of Presbyterianism, and an alliance with the Scots against the Royalists in the Civil War, put forward in sympathy with similar statements by London Ministers, cf. *Ecclesiastical History of Essex*, Smith, op. cit. pp. 102ff) cf. *VicHist—Essex* 5:148; D. Leigh, cf. Winters, p. 23; Henry Allbury, cf. Winters, p. 23; J. Browne, cf. Venn 1:235, cf. Winters, pp. 23–4.

379. *The Curtis Family*, Winters, op. cit. pp. 42–49; cf. Winslow, *John Eliot*, op. cit. pp. 18, 28; Curtis correspondence, Little Baddow papers. The children of Bennett and Lettice Eliot who emigrated to Massachusetts with their families were Sarah, baptized Widford, January 13, 1600, m. William Curtis, Nazeing, August 16, 1618; Philip, baptized April 14, 1602, first Master of Roxbury Latin School; Reverend John, baptized August 5, 1604; Jacob, baptized September 21, 1606, m. Margery, Boston Freeman, March 6, 1632, ordained deacon, May 17, 1640; Lydia, baptized Nazeing, July 1, 1610; Francis, bapized April 10, 1615; Mary, baptized March 11, 1621, Widford and Nazeing Parish Registers: cf. Winters op. cit. pp. 26–30, but NB, he muddles the order, p. 27; cf. Genealogical Table 8, *Guide* p. 325.

380. *VicHist—Essex* 5:151 re Ambresbury "an Iron-Age Hill Fort" cf. p. 155: re Boudicca, see p. 145; cf. DNB 2: 741–2; *EncBrit* 4:94; *Essex In London*, op. cit. p. 18. Winters' description of Boudicca's campaign is impaired by his supposition that Nazeing derives from "Na-sang," a bloodless victory presumed to have been won by Boudicca at this site (Winters, p. 13–14).

381. *Essex In London*, op. cit. p. 23. Alfred (Aelfred) The Great, c. 848–901, was born at Wantage, Berks, fourth son of Aethelwulf. He was confirmed by Pope Leo IV at Rome in 853, when only five yrs of age, and crowned King of Wessex after a co-regency with his brother Aethelred from 866. They began Britain's successful resistance to the Danes. 870 was Alfred's "Year of Battles," nine engagements, some won, some lost, leading at last to the Peace of Wedmore, 878, although London, East Anglia and Midlands remained in Danish hands. Fresh Danish invasions were partially thwarted, but Alfred's final push northwards from the Thames, of which his victory near Nazeing was a part, confined the Danes largely to East Anglia (leaving Essex under their rule), and Northumbria. It was left to Alfred's son, Edward the Elder, to free Essex, until, under Aethelred the Unready, the Danes once more gained ascendancy, and

Canute (995–1035) became King of Denmark and of England, cf. *EncBrit* 1:582–84; DNB 1:152–61.

382. *In Search of Essex*, op. cit. p. 128. King Harold II, c. 1022–66, was second son of Earl Godwine (d. 1053, kingmaker of Hardicanute, Edward the Confessor to a lesser extent, of Harold, the most powerful Saxon nationalist of his day, opposed to the Normanization of Edward's court, DNB 8:50–55). Harold succeeded to the Saxon interest when his father died. He crushed the Welsh under King Gruffyd (1063, DNB 8:748–50), mediated his brother Tostig's banishment from Northumbria, and, having succeeded Edward, defeated Tostig at Stamford, Sept. 25, 1066. Meantime William of Normandy claimed the English crown, protesting his kinsman Edward had bequeathed it to him, and that Harold had broken his sworn allegiance. Harold's army, weakened by its forced march from Stamford, was defeated at Senlac Hill, Battle, near Hastings, Oct.14, leaving Harold and his brothers Gyrth and Leofwine slain; *EncBrit* 8:11; DNB 8:1302–10.

383. D. Read *History*, op. cit.: *VicHist—Essex* 5:149, says "early 16th century."

384. "Lord, for schools every where among us! That our schools may flourish! That every member of this assembly may go home, and procure a good school to be encouraged in the town where he lives! That before we die, we may be so happy as to see a good school encouraged in every plantation of the country," *Magnalia* 1:551.

385. Waltham Abbey, *VicHist—Essex*, 5:151–80 (population 320 houses in 1662, p. 151; photo Market Square, p. 164); Pevsner *Essex*, p. 400–06.

386. Holy Cross and St Laurence, *VicHist—Essex* 5:171f, "richest monastery in Essex" (ibidem 5:151) when refounded by Henry II; cf. King's England *Essex*, op. cit. pp. 357–66, etc. For St Laurence, ODCC, p. 790; *Saints*, p. 214; for Valerian, *The Expansion of Christianity*, K. S. Latourette, Eyre and Spottiswoode, 1938, vol. 1, *The First Five Centuries*, p. 149–50, "the last surviving deacon of the Roman Church, Lawrence, perished," p. 151–2.

387. Tofig *The Proud*, d.1042 (*VicHist—Essex* 5:151, 155), *The Staller* (ie. Master-of-Horse, see Bascombe correspondence, op. cit. Little Baddow papers), cf. Pevsner *Essex*, p. 401.

388. Montacute, mons acutus, *National Trust Guide*, 1980, pp. 145–7—"The heraldic stained-glass in the great parlour and great hall is as good as or better than any surviving from the Elizabethan period, and forty-seven coats of arms celebrate the Phelips family, their connections, and West Country neighbours. The depth of the spirited plaster friezes in some of the rooms is also distinctive—the great hall with its 16th century panelling—one of the most engaging halls of the period—the elaborate screen is in stone with rusticated arches and flamboyant strapwork cresting" (p. 146), the Elizabethan Age encapsulated!

389. See *The Abbey Church*, Pevsner *Essex*, pp. 400–403. Burne-Jones, 1833–98, *Encyclopaedia of Painting*, edited B. S. Myers, 1956, p. 62; *Dictionary of Victorian Painters*, Chris Wood, rep. 1985, p. 74.

390. William Morris, 1834–96, *Encyclopedia of Painting*, op. cit. pp. 350–51; *Nineteenth Century Decoration: The Art of the Interior*, Charlotte Gere, Weidenfeld and Nicolson, 1989, pp. 11, 12 "late-comer to the Pre-Raphaelite Circle, William Morris, was to achieve the transformation of taste dreamt of by Holman Hunt and Rosetti."

*

The Dutch Disillusionment.

1. NB. Keith L. Sprunger, New England Quarterly, XLVI, March 1973, p. 17, claims "when he left the Netherlands for America, Hooker's Congregationalism was publicly and firmly established." Hooker's Preface to *A Fresh Suit Against Ceremonies*, Ames (posthumous), Amsterdam, 1633, is printed in HTS, XXVIII, op. cit. pp. 320–77, with Introduction, pp. 299–320.

444   *Notes*

2. Paget's XX Questions (Propositions), and Hooker's Answers are printed ibid. pp. 277–91, with introduction, pp. 271–76. Sprunger above (p. 22) "boils down" the XX Questions to three issues, (i) Brownists "no sin to hear them occasionally:" (ii) Baptism of non-members' children, Hooker side-steps the Questions: (iii) Congregations had full authority without recourse to the Classis.

3. John Paget, d. 1640, ibid. pp. 22 (n. 52), 25–27; cf. Venn 3:295 (Trinity, Cambridge 1592; Rector of Nantwich, dispossessed for nonconformity, to Holland 1604, Amsterdam 1607–37).

4. William Ames, see *Guide* p. 361 n. 31; cf. DNB 1:355–7; Venn 1:27.

5. Arminius and The Remonstrance, 1610, cf. ODCC, pp. 87 and 1152. Arminius (Jakob Hermandszoon), son of a Dutch cutler of Oudewater, was educated at Utrecht and Marburg, but returned to Holland when many of his Protestant family were massacred by their Spanish overlords. It was ironic that, later, his followers should lose Dutch support for their supposed pro-Spanish sympathies. The fact was that he taught submission to Christian rulers. His studies continued at Leyden (where he became Professor, 1603) and Geneva, Basle, Padua, Rome, but he again returned to become Pastor of the Reformed Church at Amsterdam. He opposed the rigidity of Calvin's predestination, and upheld the reality of human choice. He avoided charges of Pelagianism (Pelagius, a late fourth century British monk who advocated a personal responsibility towards the moral law which contradicted Augustine's doctrine of the Fall, see below, and brought Pelagius excommunication), and, amidst controversy and condemnation, enabled a more liberal Protestantism for posterity, cf. *Arminianism*, A. W. Harrison, Epworth Press, 1937; etc. The narrow line between Christian morality and secularism still perplexes observers of busybody Puritans. But they resolutely lived by both truths, Grace and Casuistry.

A passing glance at St Augustine, 354–430, Bishop of Hippo, North Africa, one of the four "Doctors of the Church" (with St Ambrose, 339–97, Statesman Bishop of Milan, who influenced Augustine's conversion; St Jerome, 342–420, supreme Biblical scholar; St Gregory, 540–604, "The Great," father of medieval Papacy) may appear impertinent and insulting, but is not so intended. Lack of space and skill alone determine. But some acknowledgement must be made to (a) the forging by Augustine of his faith in the burning heat of self-examination and public controversy (eg. his *Confessions*, his combating Pelagius, his "City of God," published after the sack of Rome in 410 by Alaric the Goth) so reminiscent of Puritans' experiences of inward and outward distress, so descriptive of their aims; (b) the sense of sinful humanity's absolute dependance on a Creator whose will was essentially good, as appears in Thomas Hooker's preaching, and many others (cf. Bush *Writings of Thomas Hooker*, op. cit. pp. 225f, 241f, 246f, etc.—where Hooker's dependance on Augustine is carefully exposed); (c) Calvin's response to much of Augustine's teaching, which informed the whole Puritan movement, and firmed up its acceptance of predestination alongside the promissory demands of holiness, unity, and obedience. The literature is too vast to hint at, but I found Peter Brown's *Augustine of Hippo, A Biography*, Faber 1967, very readable, and *St Augustine Pastoral Theology*, Trevor Rowe, Epworth 1974, would win Hooker's approval. The article in *EncBrit* (15) 14:397–401 by John Burnaby is most comprehensive (cf. his *Amor Dei, A Study of the Religion of St Augustine*, rep. 1960). NB. "'The true philosopher is the lover of God'—In those words from the *De Civitate Dei*, Augustine has left at once the best portrait of himself, and the fullest justification of his life's work", *EncBrit* above, p. 400.

6. Sub and Supralapsarianism, ODCC pp. 1300, 1306.

7. *Magnalia* 1:339.

8. Letter to John Cotton from Rotterdam, April 1633, HTS, p. 297.

9. It is not my purpose to research Hooker's *Dutch Disillusionment* in detail, but the literature available should be noted, eg—*The Dutch Career of Thomas Hooker*, Keith L. Sprunger, New England Quarterly, XLVI (Mar.1973), pp. 17–44; *Early English Dissenters*, Champlin Burrage, Cambridge 1912, pp. 274ff; *The English Reformed Church in Amsterdam in the 17th Century* (which draws on the Register of the Begijnhof English Church, 3, 1626–1700), A. C. Carter,

Amsterdam, 1964; *Congregationalism in the Dutch Netherlands: The Rise and Fall of the English Congregational Classis, 1621–35*, R. P. Stearns, Chicago, 1940; etc.

10. Hugh Peter, 1598–1660, cf. DNB 15:955–63; DAB 14:496–8; Venn 3:351; *The Strenuous Puritan: Hugh Peter 1598–1660*, R. P. Stearns, Urbana, 1954; etc.

11. HTS, p. 291; see my *Growing Towards Greatness*, op. cit. p. 5; *After the Dutch said No to Thomas Hooker*, Joseph A. Bassett, Bulletin of the Congregational Library, Boston, MA, vol. 35, No. 2, 1984.

12. John Forbes, DNB 7: 402–4. NB. *The Walloon Congregation and Church at Delft*, church guide, Little Baddow papers, "1621–1635. During this time, the church was leased to a group of English merchants, the Court of Merchant Adventurers."

13. *Thomas Hooker*, Shuffleton, op. cit. ch. 4, *The Netherlands Experiment*, especially pp. 150–55.

14. Henry Whitefield, "one who abounded in liberality and hospitality; and his house was always much resorted unto," *Magnalia* 1:593 (see pp. 592–4); cf. *Oxons* 4:1620.

15. *Magnalia* 1:592.

16. John Davenport, 1597–1670, profoundly independent, utterly opposed to union of New Haven with Connecticut (bemoaned as "Christ's interest miserably lost," DAB 5:85–87). re the influential Veres, related Earls Oxford, cf. *EncBrit* 27:1019–21, HTS pp. 304, 375 n. 189.

17. Theophilus Eaton, 1590–1658, *EncBrit* 8:838–9; DAB 5:612–3. He encountered large financial losses in return for spiritual freedom.

18. Whalley and Goffe, regicides, see *Guide* p. 227. Welcomed with open arms by Davenport and Eaton.

19. For William Laud's *Regulation of the English Factories in Holland*, and continuing persecution of Puritan exiles, see *History of the Puritans*, Daniel Neal, i, pp. 265f, 337f; *Ecclesiastical History* Colyer, p. 752; etc.

20. The Downs, roadstead off Deal, *VicHist—Kent* 2:244, "the Downs were not only a refuge for merchantmen but formed a strategic centre from which, under favourable circumstances, war fleets could command the North Sea and English Channel"; cf. *Kent*, Weidenfeld and Nicolson, 1988, p. 30, "the favourite anchorage between the shore and the Goodwin Sands."

21. HTS, pp. 34–35. *The Griffin* reached Boston on September 4, cf. Winthrop Journal, i, p. 137. The Hooker and Stone families "went presently to Newtown, where they were to be entertained" by Deputy Governor Thomas Dudley (Winthrop, Journal, i, pp. 105–7). The Meeting House, its bell transported all the way from England, was waiting the commencement of their ministry, *History of Cambridge, Massachusetts*, Lucius R. Paige. Boston 1877, p. 247.

22. *Travels in New England and New York*, Timothy Dwight, 1752–1817, edited B. M. Soloman, Harvard 1969, 4 vols, i, pp. 172–3, quoted by Shuffleton, op. cit. p. 306. Dwight (descended from John Dwight of Dedham, England who emigrated to Dedham, Massachusetts 1635) was a Congregational Minister/author who became President of Yale, 1795–1817, cf. DAB 5:573–77.

23. *Magnalia* 1:350.

Bibliography

The method of research adopted for this guide to Thomas Hooker's England was to visit every place known to have had some personal association with him in England and America, to open communications with the local historical societies, county record offices and libraries, and to read whatever books or documents might be discovered from these sources, in order to assess what facts were most likely to have contributed to Hooker's character and career in the general history of England and of New England, and in the social events connected with each place. This, of course, applies to following as well as to preceding and current events. What happens after residence in a place may well reflect what happened in an earlier generation, and throw light on that period as well as its own.

The following is a list of the books which most influenced the author in reaching his conclusions. It is not a bibliography of 16th/17th century English history, nor of the New England story, so fully documented in countless other books about this vivid period of world history. The choice of the books, pamphlets, articles and documents quoted here was determined by their relevance to Thomas Hooker. The briefer documents will mostly be found in the Footnotes. They are readily accessible from the appropriate county record office or library. The major works are listed below.

1. General Background Literature to the Social History of Hooker's England

Magnalia Christi Americana; or, The Ecclesiastical History of New-England; from its first planting, in the year 1620, unto the year of Our Lord 1698. In Seven Books, Cotton Mather, first published London, 1702, is basic to any study of the founders of New England, but, so far as I am aware, no one has researched the reason for Mather's copious classical allusions, quotations from ancient history, and world literature. They may simply be an explosion of effusive scholarship, or Mather's claim for recognition by European scholars, but at least, and rightly, they place the planting of the New England colonies within a world view.

I have used two recent editions, one edited by Kenneth D. Murdock, Belknap Press, Harvard University, 1977, the other a reprint of Silas Andrus & Son's edition, Hartford, Ct, 1853, published The Banner of Truth Trust, Edinburgh, 1979.

Encyclopaedia Britannica. I have also relied on two editions, the eleventh (1910/11, for its full, if dated, biographies of early European and English celebrities), and the 15th, 1992.

The Oxford History of England, edited Sir George Clark, 15 vols (especially vol. 7, "The Early Tudors," J. D. Mackie, 1952; vol. 8, "The Reign of Elizabeth, 1558–1603," J.

B. Black, 2nd edition, 1959; vol. 9, "The Early Stuarts, 1603–1660," Godfrey Davis, 2nd edition, 1959), Clarendon Press, Oxford.

The New Cambridge Modern History, 12 vols (especially vol. 3, "The Counter Reformation and Price Revolution, 1559–1610, edited R. B. Wernham, 1963), CUP, 1958.

The Cambridge Cultural History, edited Boris Ford, 9 volumes, see especially 2: *Medieval Britain*, 3: *Sixteenth-Century Britain*, 4: *Seventeenth Century Britain*, CUP 1992.

Dictionary of National Biography, Smith & Elder, London, 1908.

The Cambridge Biographical Encyclopedia, David Crystal, CUP 1994 (sadly repeats earlier Hooker errors, ie., born Markfield for Marefield, escaped to Holland 1630 instead of 1631).

A History of the Expansion of Christianity, 7 vols, K. S. Latourette, Eyre & Spottiswoode, 1938–47.

The Oxford Dictionary of the Christian Church, edited F. L. Cross, London, 1957.

The Pelican History of the Church, edited Owen Chadwick, 6 vols, 1960–70, Penguin Books.

Alumni Cantabrigienses, J. & J. A. Venn, Part I, vols. 1–4, CUP, 1922–27.

Alumni Oxoniensis 1500–1714, James Foster, 4 vols, London, 1887–91.

The Penguin Dictionary of Saints, Donald Attwater, Penguin Books, 1965.

History from the Sources, reissue of *Domesday Book*, 1086, edited John Morris, OUP 1980 (especially No. 32 "Essex").

English Social History, G. M. Trevelyan, edited Asa Briggs, 1973.

A Social History of England, Asa Briggs, London, 1983.

The English, A Social History 1066–1945, Christopher Hibbert, London, 1987.

A History of the English Speaking Peoples, W. S. Churchill, 4 vols, Cassell, 1957, (especially 2: "The New World," 3: "The Age of Revolution").

The Canterbury Tales, Geoffrey Chaucer, edited Neville Coghill, Penguin 1951 (rep. 1970).

Treasures of Britain, Drive Publications, 1968.

Folklore, Myths and Legends of Britain, Readers Digest Association, 1973.

"Anglo-Saxon England, c. 550–1087," Sir Frank Stenton, vol. 1, *The Oxford History of England*, 3rd edition, 1971.

2. Thomas Hooker's England

The Life of Thomas Hooker

Piscator Evangelicus, or The Life of Mr. Thomas Hooker, Cotton Mather, Boston 1695, later incorporated into *The Light of the Western Churches, or, The Life of Mr. Thomas Hooker*, Cotton Mather, *Magnalia*, op cit, 1:332–52, BOTT edition.

Thomas Hooker: Preacher, Founder, Democrat, George Leon Walker, NY, 1891.

Thomas Hooker the First American Democrat, Walter S. Logan, 1904.

Descendants of the Rev. Thomas Hooker, 1586–1908, Edward Hooker, NY, 1909.

Thomas Hooker—The Predecessor of Thomas Jefferson In Democracy, C. S. Thompson, Cheshire Chronicle Press, CT, 1935.

Thomas Hooker and the Puritan Contribution to Democracy, Roland H. Bainton, Bulletin of the Congregational Library, Boston, vol. 10, no. 1, October 1958.

Thomas Hooker Writings in England and Holland, 1626–1633, Harvard Theological Studies XXVIII, by George H. Williams, Norman Pettit, Winfried Herget and Sargent Bush Jr., Harvard, 1975.

Thomas Hooker, 1586–1647, Frank Shuffleton, Princeton University, NJ, 1977.

The Writings of Thomas Hooker, Spiritual Adventure in Two Worlds, Sargent Bush, Jr., WI, 1980.

The Pilgrimage of Thomas Hooker (1586–1647) in England, The Netherlands, and New England, G. H. Williams, Bulletin of the Congregational Library, Boston, October 1967, January 1968.

Called By Thy Name, Leave Us Not: The Case of Mrs. Joan Drake. A Formative Episode in the Pastoral Career of Thomas Hooker in England, G. H. Williams, Harvard Library Bulletin XVI, April & July, 1968.

Hooker Genealogical material compiled by the New England Historic Genealogical Society, Little Baddow Historical Society 400th celebratory publication, NEHGS, Boston, 1986.

Hartford Centre Church Monographs, from No 1, *Thomas Hooker Bibliography, together with a Brief Sketch of His Life*, H. Clark Wooley, 1932, to No 14, *Growing Towards Greatness*, D. C. Collingwood, 1987.

Thomas Hooker's Publications referred to in the *Guide*, listed in the order adopted in HTS, *Bibliography*, pp. 393–425.

"To the Reader," *The Doctrine of Faith*, John Rogers, London, 1627.

The Poor Doubting Christian Drawne Unto Christ, London, 1629.

The Soules Preparation For Christ, London, 1632.

"The Preface," *A Fresh Suit Against Human Ceremonies*, William Ames, Rotterdam, 1633.

The Soules Humiliation, 1637.

The Soules Ingrafting into Christ, London, 1637.

The Soules Vocation Or Effectual Calling to Christ, London, 1637.

The Soules Implantation, 1637.

The Soules Implantation Into The Naturall Olive, 1640.

Four Learned And Godley Treatises; Viz. The Carnall Hypocrite. The Churches Deliverances. The Deceitfulnesse of Sinne. The Benefit of Afflictions, London, 1637.

The Sinners Salvation, London, 1638.

Spiritual Munition, London, 1640.

The Unbeleevers Preparing For Christ, London, 1638.

The Christians Two Chief Lessons, London, 1640.

The Patterne Of Perfection, London, 1640.

The Danger of Desertion, London, 1641.

The Faithful Covenanter, London, 1644.

A Survey of the Summe of Church-Discipline, London, 1648.

The Covenant Of Grace Opened, London, 1649.

The Saints Dignitie, and Duty, London, 1651.

The Application Of Redemption, London, 1656.

A Comment Upon Christ's Last Prayer, London, 1656.

"Touchinge ye Crosse in ye Banners," *Proceedings*, Massachusetts Historical Society, XLII, April 1909.

Reigns Affecting The Life of Thomas Hooker

John

King John, Ralph V. Turner, Longman, 1994.
Magna Carta, Geoffrey Hindley, Constable, 1990.
Simon de Montfort, Earl of Leicester, Charles Bemont, London, 1930.
Simon de Montfort, Margaret Wade Labarge, Eyre & Spottiswoode, 1972.

Edward I

The Life and Times of Edward I, John Chancellor, Weidenfeld and Nicolson, 1981.
Edward I, Michael Prestwich, Methuen, 1988.

Edward IV

The Life and Times of Edward IV, edited Antonia Fraser, Weidenfeld & Nicolson, 1981.

Richard III

King Richard The Third, William Shakespeare, 1592–93.
The History of King Richard III, Sir Thomas More, edited R. S. Sylvester, Yale, 1963.
Richard III as Duke of Gloucester and King of England, Caroline A. Halstead, 2 vols, Longman, 1980.
Richard III, Charles Ross, Methuen, 1981.
Richard III, A study in service: Cambridge University studies in medieval life and thought, Rosemary Horrox, CUP, 1989.
Bosworth Field and the Wars of the Roses, A. L. Rowse, 1966.
The Battle of Bosworth, Michael Bennett, New York, 1985.

Hastings

William, First Lord Hastings, Bernard Elliott, Leicester Research Department of Chamberlain Music and Books, 1989.

Henry VII

The Reign of Henry VII, R. L. Storey, Blandford Press, 1968.
Henry VII, S. B. Chrimes, Methuen, 1972.
Lives of the Tudor Age 1485–1603, Ann Hoffman, Osprey, 1977.
The Tudor Age, Jasper Ridley, Constable, 1988.
Tudor England, John Guy, OUP, 1988.

Henry VIII

Henry VIII, J. J. Scarisbrick, Methuen, 1986.
Henry VIII, Jasper Ridley, Constable, 1984.

Wolsey

The King's Cardinal-The Rise and Fall of Thomas Wolsey, Peter Gwyn, Barrie & Jenkins, 1990.

More

Utopia, Sir Thomas More, 1516, Everyman's Library, Dent, 1970.
Thomas More, Richard Marius, Dent, 1984.

Fisher
St. John Fisher, E. E. Reynolds, 1955.

Mary Tudor
Bloody Mary, Carolly Erickson, Dent, 1978.
Mary Tudor, A Life, David Loades, Blackwell, 1989.

Cranmer
Cranmer and the English Reformation, A. F. Pollard, 1904.
Cranmer and the English Reformation, F. E. Hutchinson, 1951.

Latimer
Hugh Latimer, Harold S. Darby, Epworth, 1953.

Foxe
Foxe's Book of Martyr (Acts and Monuments of matters happening in the Church, 1554), Book Society Edition, London.

Elizabeth
Elizabeth, Christopher Haigh, Longman, 1988.
The Virgin Queen, Christopher Hibbert, 1990.
Queen Elizabeth I, J. E. Neale, Penguin Books, rep. 1990.
Elizabeth I, Anne Somerset, Weidenfeld & Nicholson, 1991.
Elizabeth's England, David Birt, Longman, 1981.
The English Spirit, A. L. Rowse, Macmillan, 1944.
The England of Elizabeth, A. L. Rowse, Macmillan, 1950.
The Expansion of Elizabethan England, A. L. Rowse, Macmillan, 1955.
The Elizabethan Renaissance, A. L. Rowse, Macmillan, 1971, 1972.

Burghley
Burghley, Tudor Statesman, 1520–1598, B. W. Beckingsale, 1967.
The Cecils of Hatfield House, Lord David Cecil, London, 1973.
Great Lord Burghley, M. A. S. Hume, London, 1989.

Bacon
Francis Bacon, Anthony Quinter, OUP, 1980.
Francis Bacon, B.H.G. Wormald, CUP, 1993.

Mildmay
Sir Walter Mildmay and Tudor Government Stanford E. Lehmberg, Texas University, Austin, 1964.
A Brief Memoir of the Mildmay Family, St. John Mildmay, Bodley, 1913.
The Sleepers and the Shadows, 2 vols, Hilda Grieve, Essex Record Office, 1988 & 1994.
The Mildmays and Their Chelmsford Estates, J. H. Round, Transcripts of the Essex Archaeological Society, 15:1921.

Lord Petre

Tudor Secretary: Sir William Petre at Court at Home, F. G. Emmison, Essex Record Office, 1961.
Recusant History, Christopher Clay, 2:11, *The Misfortunes of William, Fourth Baron Petre*.

Drake

The Family and Heirs of Sir Francis Drake, E. F. Eliott-Drake, 2 vols, Smith, Elder & Co, 1911.
Sir Francis Drake, G. M. Thomas, Seckar & Warburg, 1972.
Sir Francis Drake, John Sugden, Barrie & Jenkins, 1990.
The Elizabethan Deliverance, Arthur Bryant, Collins, 1980.
The Spanish Armadas, Winston Graham, Collins, 1987.
Armada, Duff Hart-Davis, Bantam Press, 1988.

Hilliard

Nicholas Hilliard, Victoria & Albert Museum, London, 400th Exhibition brochure, 1947.
Nicholas Hilliard, Roy Strong, London, 1967.
Nicholas Hilliard and Isaac Oliver, Graham Reynolds, H. M. Stationery Office, London, 1971.
Collecting Miniatures, Daphne Foskett, London, 1979.

Mary Queen of Scots

Mary Queen of Scots, Antonia Fraser, London, 1969.

James I

King James I, David Mathew, 1967.
The Reign of James VI and I, edited A. G. R. Smith, 1973.
King James VI of Scotland and I of England, Antonia Fraser, Weidenfeld & Nicholson, 1974.
The Wisest Fool In Christendom, William McElwee, Faber, 1988.
The Stewarts, A Study in English Kingship, J. P. Kenyon, 1966.
Gunpowder, Treason and Plot, C. Northcote Parkinson, Weidenfeld & Nicolson, 1979.

Charles I

The Life and Times of Charles I, D. R. Watson, Weidenfeld & Nicolson, 1972.
Charles the First, John Bowle, Weidenfeld & Nicolson, 1974.
Charles I, The Personal Monarch, Pauline Gregg, Dent, 1981.
Charles The Personal Monarch, C. Carlton, Routledge & Kegan, 1983.
Charles I And The Road To Personal Rule, L. J. Reeve, CUP, 1989
The Personal Rule of Charles I, Kevin Sharpe, Yale, 1992.

Henrietta

Henrietta Maria, Carola Oman, 1936.
Henrietta Maria, Elizabeth Hamilton, Hamish Hamilton, 1976.
Myself Mine Enemy, Jean Plaidy, Robert Hale, London, 1983.

Villiers

Buckingham, The Life and Political Career of George Villiers, First Duke of Buckingham, 1592–1628, Roger Lockyer, Longman, 1981.

Clarendon

True Historical Narrative of the Rebellion and Civil Wars in England, Edward Hyde, 1st Earl Clarendon, 4 vols, Oxford, 1702–04.
The Lives of Clarendon, T. H. Lister, 1838.

Laud

Archbishop Laud, H. R. Trevor-Roper, Oxford, 1940.
Archbishop William Laud, Charles Carlton, Routledge & Kegan, 1987.

Cromwell

Oliver Cromwell, S. R. Gardiner, 1909, rep. E. P. Publishing, 1976.
Oliver Cromwell, John Buchan, Hodder & Stoughton, 1934.
Oliver Cromwell and the English Revolution, edited John Morrill, Longman, 1990.
Oliver Cromwell, C. V. Wedgewood, Duckworth, 1973.
Cromwell, Roger Howell, Hutchinson, 1977.
God's Englishman: Oliver Cromwell and the English Revolution, Christopher Hill, 1970.

Josselin

The Diary of Ralph Josselin, 1616–1683, edited Alan MacFarlane, OUP, 1976.

Evelyn

John Evelyn and His World, John Bowle, Routledge & Kegan Paul, 1981.
The Diary of John Evelyn, selected, edited John Bowle, OUP, 1983.

Aubrey

The Natural History and Antiquities of Surrey, (posthumously) 1719.
John Aubrey A life, David Tylden-Wright, Harper Collins, 1991.

Pepys

The Diary of Samuel Pepys, (1633–1703), 11 vols, edited Robert Latham & William Matthews, G. Bell & Sons, London, 1970–83.

Bramston

Autobiography, Sir John, of Roxwell, The Camden Society, 1845.

Other Significant Events

Augustine and the Reformation

City of God, new translation, John O'Meara, Penguin Books, 1984.
De Civitate Dei Contra Paganos, W. C. Greene, 7 vols, Harvard, 1960.
The Confessions of St. Augustine, E. M. Blaiklock, Hodder & Stoughton, a new translation, 1983.
Amor Dei, A Study of the Religion of St. Augustine, J. Burnaby, rep. 1960.
Augustine of Hippo, A Biography, Peter Brown, Faber, 1968.
St. Augustine Pastoral Theologian, Trevor Rowe, Epworth, 1974.

The Dawn of the Reformation, H. B. Workman, 2 vols, Epworth, 1933.
The English Reformation, A. G. Dickens, Batsford, 1968.
The Reformation, Owen Chadwick, Pelican History of the Church, No. 3, Penguin Books, rep. 1973.

Wycliffe
The Age of Wycliffe, G. M. Trevelyan, 1898.
John Wycliffe and the Beginnings of English Nonconformity, K. B. McFarlane, 1952.
The Later Lollards 1414–1520, J. A. F. Thomson, OUP, 1965.

Luther
Luther's Works, edited J. Pelikan & H. T. Lehmann, 54 vols, New York, 1955–76.
Luther, A Biography, H. G. Haile, Sheldon Press, London, 1980.
Martin Luther, An Illustrated Biography, Peter Mann, 1982.
Luther, Heiko A. Oberman, Yale, 1989.

Calvin
Christianae Religionis Institutio, final vol. 1559, J. Calvin, (English translation, *The Institutes*, H. Beveridge, 2 vols, 1949).
Calvin and the Reformation, J. Mackinnon, 1936.
John Calvin, T. H. L. Parker, Dent, 1975.
Calvin, Geneva and the Reformation, Ronald S. Wallace, Scottish Academic Press, Edinburgh, 1988.
A Life of John Calvin, Alister E. McGrath, Blackwell, 19990.

The Church of England and The Puritans
A History of the English Church and People, Bede, 731, translated R. E. Latham, Penguin Books, 1968.
The Book of Common Prayer, Elizabethan, 1559; revised James I., 1604; confirmed, *Act of Uniformity*, Charles II, 1662.
Treatise on the Laws of Ecclesiastical Polity, Richard Hooker, 8 volumes, 1594–1662 (vols 6–8 posthumously).
A Short History of the Church in Great Britain, W. C. Hutton, 1900.
The Church in England, 597–1688, S. C. Carpenter, Murray, 1954.
The Early Tudor Church and Society 1485–1529, J. A. F. Thomson, Longman, 1993.
The Religion of the Protestants, The Church in English Society 1559–1625, Patrick Collinson, Clarendon, OUP, 1982.
Grace Abounding to the Chief of Sinners, John Bunyan, 1666.
Pilgrim's Progress, John Bunyan, 1684.
Of Plymouth Plantation 1620–1647 by William Bradford sometime governor thereof, edited S. E. Morison, NY, 1952.
Worthies of England, Thomas Fuller, posthumously 1662.
The History of the Puritans, Daniel Neal, 4 vols, London, 1732.
Annals of Evangelical Nonconformity in the County of Essex, T. W. Davids, London, 1863.
History of English Nonconformity, Henry W. Clark, 2 vols, London 1911–13.
The Rise of Puritanism: Or the Way to the New Jerusalem, William Haller, New York, 1938.

The Worship of the English Puritans, Horton Davies, 1949.

Cambridge University Transactions During the Puritan Controversies of the 16th and 17th Centuries, J. Heywood & T. Wright, CUP, 1954.

Society and Puritanism in Pre-Revolutionary England, C. Hill, 1964.

Anglicans and Puritans, John F. H. New, Stamford, CA, 1964.

The Godly Preachers of the Elizabethan Church, Irvonwy Morgan, Epworth, 1965.

The Elizabethan Puritan Movement, Patrick Collinson, Cape, 1967.

Patterns of Reformation, Gordon Rupp, Epworth, 1969.

The Puritan Lectureships, the politics of religious dissent, 1560–1662, Paul S. Seaver, Stanford University, 1970.

Puritan Spirituality, Illustrated from the Life and Times of the Rev. Dr. John Preston, Master of Emmanuel, Irvonwy Morgan, Epworth, 1973.

The Puritan Gentry, The Great Puritan Families of Early Stuart England, J. T. Cliffe, Routledge & Kegan Paul, 1984.

The Making of the English Middle Class, Peter Earle, Methuen, 1989.

The English Civil War

True Historical Narrative of the Rebellion and Civil Wars in England, Edward Hyde 1st Earl Clarendon, 4 vols, Oxford, 1702–04.

The World Turned Upside Down. Radical Ideas During the English Civil War, Christopher Hill, Penguin Books, 1978.

The English Civil War, Conservatism and Revolution, 1603–1649, Robert Ashton, Weidenfeld & Nicolson, 1978.

The Outbreak of the English Civil War, Anthony Fletcher, Arnold, 1981.

The Puritan Moment, The Coming of Revolution in an English County, William Hunt, Harvard Historical Studies CII, Harvard, 1983.

The King's War 1641–46, C. V. Wedgewood. Penguin Books, 1983.

The Civil Wars of England, John Kenyon, Weidenfield & Nicolson, 1988.

Conflict in Early Stuart England, Studies in Religion and Politics, 1603–1642, edited Richard Cust & Ann Hughes, Longman, 1989.

The Causes of the English Civil War, Conrad Russell, Clarendon, 1990.

Puritanism and Revolution, Christopher Hill, Penguin Books, rep. 1990.

The Impact of the English Civil War, John Morrill, Longman, 1991.

The Nature of the English Revolution, John Morrill, Longman, 1993.

Thomas Hooker's English Resorts

Every large town in Britain has its Tourist Information Centre and, with the Public Libraries, provides information about Guide Books and places of local historical interest. The following, however, were of particular value.

The Victoria History of the Counties of England, OUP, London, contained in many and large volumes in Central Libraries where they are displayed for reference. This magnificent series is under constant review.

The Buildings of England, Sir Nikolaus Pevsner, 2nd edition, Penguin Books, an architectural survey of England (drawing on The Royal Commission on Historical Monuments publications) printed in separate county editions for study in Central Libraries but also small enough for personal use.

Earlier materials included *A Tour Through the whole Island of Great Britain*, Daniel Defoe, 1724–26, edited P. N. Furbank & W. R. Owens, Yale, 1991, and *Rural Rides*, William Cobbett, 1830 (by no means unrepresentative of an earlier rural England), edited E. W. Martin, MacDonald, 1975. Mention should also be made of *The National Trust Guide. A Complete Introduction to the Buildings, Gardens, Coast and Country owned by the National Trust*, Robin Fedden & Rosemary Joekes, Cape, 1980; *AA Illustrated Guide to Britain*, Drive Publications, 1972, *AA Illustrated Guide to Country Towns and Villages of Britain*, Drive Publications, 1985, etc. etc.

Other Guide Books are listed in the Footnotes.

1. Marefield, Leicestershire

Marefield
Victoria History Leicestershire.
History and Antiquities of the Town and County of Leicester, John Nichols, 8 vols, 1795–1815, (2: Tilton-East Goscote Hundred).

Leicester
The King's England. Leicester and Rutland, county series edited Arthur Mee, Hodder & Stoughton, 1937, outstanding in its time for local history and human interest, now out of print.

Higginson
The Life of Francis Higginson, T. W. Higginson, NY, 1891.
The Puritan Earl. Henry Hastings, 3rd Earl Huntingdon, Clair Cross, 1966.
Leicester Past and Present, Jack Simmonds, 2 vols, Methuen, 1974.
The Descent of Dissent. A Guide to the Nonconformist Records of Leicestershire Record Office, edited Gwenith Jones, L. R. O., 1989.

Towcester
Northamptonshire, Pevsner.
Memorials of the Independant Churches in Northamptonshire, with Biographical Notices of their Pastors, and some account of the Puritan ministers who laboured in the county, Thomas Coleman, London, 1853.
Album of the Northamptonshire Congregational Churches, edited T. Stephans, 1894.
Descendants of Thomas Lord, Kenneth Lord, New York, 1946.

2. Market Bosworth, Leicestershire

Market Bosworth-A New History, Peter Fosse, Sycamore Press, Leicester, 1983.
The Book of Bosworth Schook, 1320–1950, Hopewell.
The Bosworth Story, B. Newman, 1967.
School for the Community, T. Rogers, 1969.

3. Cambridge And Related Places

Burghley House
Victoria History, Lincolnshire.

The Town of Stamford. A Survey by the Royal Commission on Historical Buildings, H. M. Stationery Office, 1977.

The English Country House and its furnishings, Michael L. Wilson, Batsford, 1977.

Elizabeth's England, David Birt, 5: "Ministers and Courtiers, Burghley House," Longman, 1981.

Lincolnshire, Pevsner.

Lincolnshire, Walter Marsden, Batsford, 1977.

Portrait of Lincolnshire, Michael Lloyd, Robert Hale, 1983.

Sempringham
St. Gilbert and the Gilbertines, Rose Graham, 1901.

"Excavations on the site of Sempringham Priory," R. Graham & H. Braun, *Journal, British Archaeological Association*, vol. 5, 1940.

Sempringham and St. Gilbert and the Gilbertines, Eric W. Iredale, Pointon, 1992.

Boston and Bristol
A History of Lincolnshire, Alan Rogers, 1970.

Trade, Plunder and Settlement: Maritime Enterprise and the Genesis of the British Empire 1480–1630, K. R. Andrews, CUP, 1984.

The City and County of Bristol, Bryan Little, Bristol, 1967.

Bristol and its adjoining counties, edited C. M. MacInnes & W. F. Whittard, Chapter eleven "Bristol in the MIddle Ages," Bristol, 1955.

Cotton
Ten New England Leaders, Williston Walker, Boston, MA, 1901.

The Career of John Cotton: Puritanism and the American Experience, Larzer Ziff, Princeton, 1962.

King's Lynn
Victoria History, Norfolk.

North West & South Norfolk, Pevsner.

Fenland Freemen
Fen, fire and flood: scenes from Fenland history, Edward Storey, Cambridgeshire Libraries publications.

Life of Nelson, Robert Southey, 2 vols, 1813.

Nelson, David Walder, Hamish Hamilton, 1978.

Horatio Nelson, Tom Pocock, Bodley Head, 1987.

Norwich
North East Norfolk and Norwich, Pevsner.

Norwich—A Fine City. An historical miscellany, Norwich City Council, 1991.

Robert Kett
Portrait of Norfolk, David Yaxley, London, 1977.

Hereward The Wake
The Cambridgeshire Fens, BBC Radio Cambridge, 1989.
Spirit of the Fens, Edward Storey, Robert Hale, 1985.
The Changing Fenland, A. C. Danby, CUP, 1983.
Hereward The Wake, Charles Kingley, 1866.

Ely
The Cathedrals of England, H. Batsford & C. Fry, Batsford, 1936.
Pride of Britain—Ely Cathedral, series, C. P. Hankey, 1962.
The Story of Ely Cathedral, Rena Gardiner, 1973.

Oliver Cromwell
See under Reigns—Charles I.

Robin Hood
Robin Hood, J. C. Holt, London, 1982.
Legendary Britain, Stewart & Matthews, Blandford Press, 1989.

Langland
The Vision of William Concerning Piers the Plowman, edited W. W. Skeet, 1886.
Social Life in the Days of Piers Plowman, 1922.
Piers The Plowman, translated J. F. Goodridge, Penguin Books.

Cambridge
Victoria History, Cambridgeshire.
Cambridge, Pevsner.
Cambridge. Official Guide, Tourist Information Centre.
The History and Antiquities of Barnwell Abbey and Stourbridge Fair, J. Nichols.
Emmanuel College, An Historical Guide, Frank Stubbings, CUP, 1983.
Forty-Nine Lives an anthology of portraits of Emmanuel Men, Frank Stubbings, CUP, 1983.

Platonists
The Cambridge Platonists, F. J. Powicke, 1926.
An Examination of Plato's Doctrines, I. Crombie, 2 vols, Routledge & Kegan Paul, 1962.
The Cambridge History of Later Greek and Early Medieval Philosophy, edited A. M. Armstrong, CUP, 1967.

Plato
Plato, J. C. B. Gosling, Routledge & Kegan Paul, 1973.

Hobbes
Thomas Hobbes, Arnold A. Rogow, W. W. Norton, New York, 1986.
Hobbes, Tom Sorell, Routledge & Kegan Paul, 1986.

4. Esher, Surrey and Amersham, Buckinghamshire

Esher

The Story of Esher, Ian D. Stevens, 1966.
Natural History and Antiquities of Surrey, Richard Rawlinson, 1719.
Victoria History, Surrey.
Surrey, Pevsner.
St. George's Esher Church Guide, John Floyer, Rector, 1908–34.
St. George's Church, Esher, R. R. Langham-Carter, 1968.

Victoria

The Life and Times of Victoria, Dorothy Marshall, Weidenfeld & Nicolson, 1972.
Queen Victoria, Her Life and Times, Cecil Woodham-Smith, Hamish Hamilton, 1972.
The Young Victoria, Alison Plowden, Weidenfeld & Nicolson, 1981.
Victoria, Portrait of a Queen, Richard Muller & James Munsen, BBC Books, 1987.
Claremont Landscape Garden, Surrey, National Trust Guide, 1980.
The English Garden, L. Fleming & A. Gore, London, 1979.

Vanbrugh

Life of Marlborough, Garnet Wolsey, 1894.
Marlborough, Coreli Barnett, Methuen, 1974.
Hampton Court, R. J. Minney, Cassell, 1972.
Hampton Court Palace, June Osborne, Kaye & Ward, 1984.

Amersham

History and Antiquities of the County of Buckinghamshire, George Lipscomb, London, 1847.
Victoria History, Buckinghamshire.
Buckinghamshire, Pevsner.
Buckinghamshire, Town and Country Books, London, 1984.
The Book of Amersham, L. Elgar & C. Birch, Barracuda, 1991.
Yesterday's town: Amersham, N. Salmon & Clive Birch, Barracuda, 1991.
The Lollards of the Chiltern Hills, W. H. Summers, London, 1906.
The Shardeloes Papers of the 17th and 18th Centuries, OUP, 1947.

5. Chelmsford, Essex

Chelmsford

Victoria History Essex
Essex, Pevsner.
The Sleepers and The Shadows-Chelmsford: A town, its people and its past, Hilda Grieve, 2 vols, Essex Record Office, 1988, 1994.
A Short History of the Cathedral Church, Wykeham Chancellor, 1938.
A History of the Diocese of Chelmsford, Gordon Hewitt, 1984.
To Frame The Heart-Thirty Godly Preachers in Essex under Elizabeth I and the Early Stuarts, Gordon Hewitt, Chelmsford Cathedral, 1985.

The History and Antiquities of Essex, Philip Morant, 2 vols, 1768.
The Walkers of Hanningfield Surveyors and Mapmakers Extraordinary, A. C. Edwards & K. C. Newton, 1984.

Essex

Speculum Britanniae pars Essex, John Norden, posthumous edition, Sir Henry Ellis, Camden Society, 1840.
The Place Names of Essex, P. H. Reaney, CUP, 1935.
The King's England, Essex, Arthur Mee, Hodder & Stoughton, 1943.
Essex Heyday, William Addison, Dent, 1948.
In Search of Essex, S. M. Jarvis & C. T. Harrison, Essex Countryside.
Discovering Essex in London, Kenneth Neale, Essex Countryside, 1969.
A History of Essex, A. C. Edwards, Unwin, 1978.

Little Baddow

The History of an Essex Village, Sheila Rowney, 3 vols, 1975–79, Little Baddow Historical Society.
A Country Teacher Looks Back, C. L. Turner, Essex Library, 1980.
Little Baddow United Reformed Church. A History, R. Buick Knox, 1976.

Colchester

History and Antiquities of the Borough of Colchester, Philip Morant, 1748.
Colchester Official Guide, 5th edition, 1982.
History and Antiquities of Colchester Castle, J. H. Round, 1882.
Colchester Castle, Duncan W. Clark, 1948.
Colchester Castle. A history, description and guide, D. T-D. Clarke, 3rd edition, 1974.

Rome

"Roman Britain and the English Settlement," R. G. Collingwood & J. N L. Myres, *Oxford History of England*, 2nd edition, 1937.
Roman Britain, John Wacher, Dent, 1978.
Roman Britain, Keith Branigan, Readers Digest Association, 1980.
Roman Britain, Peter Clayton, Phaidon Press, Oxford, 1980.
Map of Roman Britain. Ordinance Survey, 4th edition, 1978.
Roman Roads in Britain, David E. Johnson, 1979.
Roads and Tracks of Britain, Christopher Taylor, Dent, 1979.
The Old Roads of England, William Addison, 1980.
The Story of the King's Highway, vol. 5, Sidney & Beatrice Webb, *English Local Government*, 7 vols, Longman, 1913–27.

London

Victoria History, London.
London. The Biography of a City, Christopher Hibbert, Longman, 1969.
London, F. Barker & P. Jackson, Cassells, 1979.
Tower of London, Christopher Hibbert, Newsweek, New York, 1971.

Dedham

A History of Dedham, C. A. Jones, 1907.

The Parish Church of St. Mary Dedham, A. R. Johnston, 1971.

John Constable, John Lloyd Fraser, Hutchinson, 1976.

John Constable, Peter D. Smith, Bonfini Press, 1981.

Constable's England, Graham Reynolds, Metropolitan Museum of Art, 1983.

The Discovery of Constable, I. Fleming-Williams & L. Parris, 1984.

Constable, Paintings, Drawings and Watercolours, Basil Taylor, Phaidon Press, 1973.

Braintree and Bocking

A History of Braintree and Bocking, W. F. Quin, Lavenham Press, 1981.

The Story of the Lyon, Winifred Ashwell, Braintree Heritage Centre, 1981.

Goodwin

The Goodwins of Hartford, Connecticut Descendants of William and Ozias Goodwin, James Junius Goodwin, Hartford, CT, 1891.

History of Old Braintree and Quincy, William S. Pattee, 1878.

Braintree Massachusetts, Its History, H. Hobart Holly, Braintree Historical Society, 1985.

Select Vestry

Early Essex Town Meetings, Braintree, 1619–1636: Finchingfield, 1626–1634, F. G. Emmison, Essex Record Office, 1970.

English Local Government, Sidney & Beatrice Webb, vol. 7, *The Old Poor Law,* Longman, 1927.

The Church, the State, and the Poor, W. E. Chadwick, London, 1914.

Essex At Work, 1700–1815, A. F. J. Brown, Essex Record Office, 1969.

Felsted and Lord Rich

Church of the Holy Cross, Felsted, M. R. Craze, 1969.

Coggeshall

A History of Coggeshall in Essex, G. F. A. Beaumont, 1890.

The English Ancestry of Thomas Stoughton, 1588–1661, and his son Thomas Stoughton, 1624–1684 of Windsor, Conn., His Brother Israel Stoughton, 1604–1645, and His Nephew William Stoughton, 1631–1701 of Dorchester, Mass.

"The Stoughton Families of Dorchester, Mass., and Windsor, Conn.," Ralph M. Stoughton, *The American Genealogist,* October, 1953.

The Presbyterian Movement of the Reign of Queen Elizabeth, Camden Society, 3rd series, vol. 8.

Earls Colne

Earls Colne, a history, R. Hunt & Co., Earls Colne, 1946.

The Family Life of Ralph Josselin, Alan Macfarlane, CUP, 1970.

The Diary of Ralph Josselin, 1616–1683, edited Alan Macfarlane, OUP, 1976.

Earls Colne Grammar School, A History, A.D. Merson, published by the School Governors, 1976.

Wherein I Dwell—a history of Earls Colne Houses from 1375, published by Earls Colne History Group, 1983.

A Short History and Guide to St. Andrew's Earls Colne, S. J. Hammock.

Shepard

The Clear Sun-Shine of the Gospel breaking forth upon the Indians of New England, London 1648, Eliot Tracts, Joseph Sabin reprints, New York, 1865.

"The Autobiography of Thomas Shepard" in _Chronicles of the First Planters of the Colony of Massachusetts Bay_, Alexander Young, Boston, 1846.

Wethersfield

The History of Ancient Wethersfield Connecticut, edited Henry R. Stiles, 2 vols, Grafton Press, New York, 1904.

John Rogers Martyr

John Rogers: The Compiler of the first Authorized English Bible, the Pioneer of the English Reformation; and its first Martyr, Joseph Lemuel Chester, London, 1861.

Writtle

The Church of All Saints, D. C. George, 1963.

N. Stone

A Dictionary of British Sculptors, M. H. Grant, London, 1953.

Life of John Donne, Isaac Walton, 1640.

John Donne: A Life, Robert C. Bald, edited W. Milgate, 1970.

Roxwell

Roxwell Revealed, An Anthology of Village History, Roxwell Revealed Group, 1993.

Roxwell, An Excursion into History, Pat Smith, Roxwell, 1987.

The Massachusetts Bay Company And Its Predecessors, Frances Rose-Troup, Grafton Press, New York, 1930.

White

John White, The Patriarch of Dorchester (Dorset) and the Founder of Massachusetts 1575–1648, with an Account of the Early Settlements in Mass. 1620–1630, Rose-Troup, Putnam's, New York, 1930.

Fire From Heaven, Life in an English Town in the Seventeenth Century, (Dorset) David Underdown, Yale, 1992.

Springfield

A History of Springfield, Ian Clerk, Chelmsford, 1985.

"Springfield Church," F. Chancellor, Essex Archaeological Society, _Transactions_, T, n. 5, xix, 57.

Springfield, 1636–1886, Mason A. Green, Nichols & Co., Springfield, Massachusetts.

The First Century of the History of Springfield (Mass.), The Official Records from 1636–1736, Henry M. Burt, 2 vols, Springfield, 1898.

Pynchon

The Meritorious Price of our Redemption, Justification, etc.—Clearing it from some common errors etc. by Wm. Pinchin, Gent. in New England, London, 1650.

The Jewes Synagogue, William Pynchon, London 1652.

The Time When the First Sabbath Was Ordained, William Pynchon, London 1654.

The Covenant of Nature Made with Adam, William Pynchon, London, 1662.

"William Pynchon," Ezra Hoyt Byington, *Proceedings*, Connecticut Valley Historical Society, 2:20–40, 1904.

Builders of the Bay Colony, Samuel Eliot Morison, 1930 (Northeastern edition, 1981).

Colonial Justice in Western Massachusetts 1636–1702): The Pynchon Court Record, Joseph H. Smith, Harvard, 1961.

William Pynchon, Merchant and Colonizer, Ruth A. McIntyre, Connecticut Valley Museum, 1961.

A Glimpse of Sion's Glory, Puritan Radicalism in Seventeenth-Century New England, Philip F. Gura, Wesleyan University Press, Middletown, CT., 1989.

"William Pynchon and Thomas Hooker, Neighbours and Friends in Essex, England," D. C. Collingwood, *The Connecticut Nutmegger*, Connecticut Society of Genealogists, No. 23: 3 & 4, 1990 & 1991.

Boreham

Boreham, History, Tales and Memories of an Essex Village, Burgess & Rance, 2 vols, 1988 & 1995.

Terling

Poverty and Piety in an English Village: Terling, 1525–1700, Keith Wrightson & David Levine, New York, 1979.

Weld

A Guide to Terling Church, Richard Weymour, 1987.

Stondon Massey

A History of Stondon Massey in Essex, E. H. L. Reeve, 1906, privately printed.

Essex Churches—St. Peter's and St. Pauls," F. Chancellor, *Essex Review*, 7:139.

Ward

The Simple Cobler of Agawam in America, Nathaniel Ward, London, 1647, published by James Munroe & Co., Boston, edited by David Pulsifer from 1647 & 1713 editions, 1843.

A Memoir of the Rev. Nathaniel Ward A.M., Author of the Simple Cobler of Agawam in America with Notices of his Family, John Ward Dean, Albany, 1868.

The Real Christian, Giles Firmin, London, 1670.

Maldon

A Discourse on Early Nonconformity in Maldon, R. Burls, Maldon, 1840.

The Church on Market Hill, M. G. L. Earnshaw, rep. Maldon, 1988.

Maldon A Thousand Years Ago, Fred H. Laws, Maldon, 1952.

Maldon's Links With America, Fred H. Laws, Maldon, 1953, rep. 1977.

John Eliot, Apostle to the Indians

"The Triumphs of the Reformed Religion in America: or, The Life of the Renowned John Eliot," *Magnalia*, Cotton Mather, BOTT edition, 1:526–83, 1979.

The Life of John Eliot, Nehemiah Adams, Boston, 1847.

The Life of John Eliot, Convers Francis, Boston, 1896.

Descendants of John Eliot "Apostle to the Indians" 1598–1905, edited Wilimena H. (Eliot) Emerson, Ellsworth Eliot, George Edwin Eliot Jr., 1905.

Builders of the Bay Colony, S. E. Morison, Chapter 10, "John Eliot," 1930.

The Enigma of the Bay Psalm Book, Zoltan Haraszti, Chicago, 1956.

The Roxbury Latin School

Tercentenary History of the Roxbury Latin School, 1645–45, Richard Walden Hale, 1946.

Forty Years On, Francis Russell, 1970.

350th Anniversary History, F. Washington Jarvis, due publication, 1995.

The Founder's Formative Years," D. C. Collingwood, *The Newsletter*, Roxbury Latin School, vols. 65 & 66, Nos. 3 & 1, 1992.

Harvard

A College First Proposed, Franklin Wright, Yale Library Bulletin, vol. 3, no. 3, 1954.

The Founding of Harvard College, S. E. Morison, Harvard, 1935.

Yale

Sketch of the History of Yale University, Dexter, Franklin, Bowditch, New York, 1887.

Glimpses of Saybrook In Colonial Days, Harriet Chapman Chesebrough, Saybrook, CT, 1985.

Indian Bible

"John Eliot, the Puritan Missionary to the Indians," E. H. Byington, *American Society of Church History* 8, 1897.

John Eliot's First Indian Teacher and Interpreter, Cockenoe-de-Long Island, William Wallace Tooker, New York, 1896.

John Eliot, Apostle to the Indians, Ola Elizabeth Winslow, Boston, 1968.

Flintlock and Tomahaw,, D. E. Leach, New York, 1958.

Boyle

The Works of the Honourable Robert Boyle to which is Prefixed the Life of the Author, 5 vols. (Eliot letters vol. 1), 1744.

Widford, Hertfordshire

Victoria History, Hertfordshire, vol. 3.

St. John the Baptist, Widford, Herts, Roddy Hill-Smith, Widford, Ware, Hertfordshire.

Hertfordshire, Pevsner.

Dictionary of English Furniture, edited Ralph Edwards, 3 vols., The Antique Collectors Club, 1983.

Chirk Castle, Clwyd, National Trust Publications, 1990.

Denbighshire, Pevsner.

Hertford, Hertfordshire

Hertford County Town Guide, Hertford.

Discovering Hertford, Hertford Civic Society, 1987.

The Chronicles of Hertford Castle, H. C. Andrews, Hertford, 1947.

Stone

"Doctor Irrefragabilis: The Life of Mr. Samuel Stone," *Magnalia*, BOTT Edition, 1:434–438, 1979.

Hartford, Connecticut

In And About Hartford, Marion Hepburn Grant, Connecticut Historical Society, 1978.
Hartford Yesterday and Today, Robert H. Arnold, Farmcliff Press, Glastonbury, CT, 1985.
The Miracle of Connecticut, Ellsworth S. Grant, Connecticut Historical Society, 1992.
The Connecticut River, Edmund Delaney, Globe Pequot Press, 1983.
The Half-Way Covenant, R. G. Pope, Princeton University, 1969.
Reformation, Conformity and Dissent, edited by R. Buick Knox, London, 1977.

Nazeing, Essex

Victoria History Essex.
Essex, Pevsner.
Memorials of the Pilgrim Fathers, John Eliot and his friends of Nazeing and Waltham Abbey, W. Winters, Waltham Abbey, 1882.
History of Nazeing, J. R. Sutherland, 1950.
History of All Saints, Nazeing Parish Church, David Read.

6. The Netherlands

Congregationalism in the Dutch Netherlands: The Rise and Fall of the English Congregational Classis, 1621–1635, R. P. Stearns, Chicago, 1940.
The English Reformed Church in Amsterdam in the 17th Century, Alice C. Carter, Amsterdam, 1964.
"The Dutch Career of Thomas Hooker," Keith L. Sprunger, *The New England Quarterly*, XLVI, 1973.
After the Dutch Said "No" to Thomas Hooker, Joseph A. Bassett, Bulletin of the Congregational Library, Boston, vol. 35, No. 2, 1984.

Arminius

Arminianism, A. W. Harrison, Epworth, 1937.

Robinson

John Robinson, Pastor of the Pilgrim Fathers, Walter H. Burgess, Retford, Nottinghamshire, 1920.
The Town on the Street, edited by J. Ford, Retford, Notts., 1975.
John Robinson and the English Separatist Tradition, Timothy George, 1982.

Rotterdam

The Strenuous Puritan: Hugh Peter 1598–1660, R. P. Stearns, Urbana, 1954.

The Downs, England

Kent, Weidenfeld & Nicolson, 1968.

7. New England

In order to judge the English roots from their American flowering, it has been essential to follow Hooker's trail into Massachusetts and Connecticut. The following is a selection of books which have enriched that further journey, as well as others already listed, to all of whose authors I express my appreciation and thanks.

Dictionary of American Biography, Hibber & Jarvis, OUP, 1928.

The Encyclopedia Americana, 30 vols, 1829, Grolier Incorporated edition, 1986.

A Journal of the Transactions and Occurrences in the Settlement of Massachusetts and Other New England Colonies from the Year 1630 to 1644, John Winthrop, Hartford, 1790, J. K. Hosmer edition, *Winthrop's Journal, History of New England, 1630–1649*, 2 vols, New York, 1908.

Winthrop Papers (1498–1649), edited Allyn B. Forbes, 5 vols, Boston, 1929–47.

The Life and Letters of John Winthrop, 2 vols, R. C. Winthrop, Boston, 1864.

The Puritan Dilemma: The Story of John Winthrop, Edmund S. Morgan, Boston, 1958.

The Winthrop Woman, Anya Seton, Hodder & Stoughton, 1958.

Wonder-Working Providence of Sions Savior in New England, Edward Johnson, 1654, edited William F. Poole, Andover, MA, 1867.

A Complete History of Connecticut, 1630–1674, Benjamin Trumbull, 1797 (rep. 1918).

History of the Discovery of America, Henry Trumbull, New York, 1802.

The Founding of New England, James Truslow Adams, 1921 (rep. Boston 1972).

History of the United States from the Discovery of the American Continent, George Bancroft, 10 vols., 1834–74.

Sources of Our Liberties, American Bar Foundation, edited Richard L. Parry & John C. Cooper, 1952 (Chapter 9, "Fundamental Orders of Connecticut").

Unafraid: A Life of Anne Hutchinson, Winifred K. Rugg, 1930.

A Woman Misunderstood: Anne Hutchinson, Wife of William Hutchinson, R. P. Bolton, 1931.

Saints and Sectaries: Anne Hutchinson and the Antinomian Controversy, Emery Battis, 1962.

The New England Mind: The Seventeenth Century, Perry Miller, New York, 1939.

From Colony to Province, Perry Miller, Harvard, 1953.

Errand Into the Wilderness, Perry Miller, Harvard, 1956.

"Migration from East Anglia to New England," W. C. P. Tyack, unpublished thesis, Essex Record Office.

The Winthrop Fleet of 1630, Charles Edward Banks, 1930 (rep. Baltimore, 1972).

The Planters of the Commonwealth, C. E. Banks, 1930 (rep. Baltimore, 1975).

Search for the Passengers of the Mary & John 1630 Books, Burton W. Spear, The Mary & John Clearing House, Toledo, OH.

Dorset Pilgrims, The Story of West Country Pilgrims Who Went to New England in the 17th Century, Frank Thistlethwaite, Barrie & Jenkins, 1989,(rep. Heart of the Lakes Publishing, Interlaken, NY, 1993).

The Fowles History of Windsor, Connecticut, William Joseph Uricchio, The Loomis Institute, Windsor, 1976.

Henrietta Maria de, 58, 214, 218
Medoca, Don Vascoe de, 163
Medway Ports, Kent, 161
Mellitus, St., 322, 434 n.318
Melton Mowbray, Leics., 41, 55, 63-66, 98, 97
Merton, Walter de, 136
Messing, Essex, 248, 252-54, 281
Metacomet (King Philip), 328, 344
Michaelson, John, 213, 217, 240, 294, 309
Middleburg, Holland, 351
Middlemead, 224
Mildemet, 224, 242
Mildmay, —, 48, 74, 195, 198-204, 211, 213,
    215, 221-24, 241, 298, 300, 303,
    304
  Abraham, 77
  Anthony of Apethorpe, 76, 200-2
    m. Grace (Sharington), 76
  Avice, 199
  Elizabeth, 77
  Henry of Little Baddow, 200-1, 203
    221, 223-225, 236
  Henry of Wanstead, 200-1, 203, 270, 409
    n.14
    m. (1) Alicia (Harris), 184, 200-1, 221,
    223, 285
    m. (2) Amy (Gurdon), 200-1, 221-22
  Henry, Colonel, 198, 200-1, 221, 294
  Humphrey, 202
  John, 199
  Thomas, the Auditor, 198, 199-201,
    223, 303-304
  Walter, Chancellor, 76-77, 103, 141, 145,
    175, 199-203, 222, 307, 219, 400
    n. 19, 409 n.12, 409 n.13
  William, 199
Minehead, Somerset, 216
Monk, George, 302
Monmouth, Duke of, 403 n.56
Montacute, Somerset, 345, 443 n.388
Montague, Edward, 147, 154, 394 n.88
Montaigne, Bishop of London, 214
Montfort, Simon de, 80-81, 90, 94, 222, 373
  n.98
Montpelier's, 291
More, Henry, 149
  Thomas, 272, 339, 378 n.6, 420 n.173
    m. Jane (Colte), 339
Morell, Stephen, 233
Morgan, Edmund S, 48
  Henry, 166
  Thomas, 233
Morison, Samuel Eliot, 31, 45
Morris, William, 346, 443 n.390
Moulsham, 245, 258
Mount Wollaston, MA, 263
Munnings, Alfred, 259
Myddelton, —, 333-34

Hugh, 333, 439 n.34

–N–

Nantasket, MA, 280
Naseby, Battle of, Nthants., 90, 246
Nash, Yeoman, 48, 216
Nassington, 76
Naughton, Suffolk, 280
Nazeing, Essex, 63, 254, 324, 339-44, 346, 441
  n.372, 442 n.374
Nazeing Company, 324, 341-343
Nazeing Puritan Clergy, 324, 341
Nelson, Horatio, 127, 167
Neville, Hugh de, 289
  Thomas, 139
Newbold Vernon, 96
Newcastle-upon-Tyne, 305
Newfoundland, Canada, 162
New Hall, 151, 243, 300-2, 352
New Haven, CT, 31, 352-53
Newmarket, Suffolk, 129
Newton, John of Little Baddow, 220, 240,
  411 n.50
  Isaac, 138-39, 436 n.330
  Roger, 28, 185, 197, 195
    m. Mary (Hooker), 28, 185, 195, 197,
    276
Newtown, MA, see Cambridge, MA
New York, 353
Nichols, John, 51
Nobbs, John, 316
Nonantum, MA, 327
Norden, John, 204, 337, 409 n.19
Norfolk, 127
Norris, John, 148
Northampton, Nthants., 20, 87, 90
Northamptonshire, 73, 76, 202
North Hill, 223, 242-43
North Luffenham, 71
Northumbria, 207
Norton, John, 119, 241, 267
Norwich, Norfolk, 19, 127-28, 176, 304
Nottingham, Notts., 18, 79,97
Nottinghamshire, 124

–O–

Oakes, John, 223, 228, 303
Oakham, Leics., 73, 77, 371 n.76
Oaklands Park, 213
Oates, Titus, 309, 432 n.272
Okay, —, 224
Oldham, 142
Old King Cole, 244
Oliver, Isaac, 48, 365 n.15
Olmstead, Nehemiah, 263
  Nicholas, 263
Ongar, 309
Orange Tree Hill, 204

Osiander, Andreas, 153, 396 n.112
Oswald, St., 207
Othona, 207
Otterton, Devon, 161
Owston, Leics., 50, 366 n.25
Oxford, Oxon., 112, 136, 138, 184-87, 205-
206, 226, 266, 352
All Souls, 306
Exeter, 306
Magdalene, 186, 288
Merton, 136
New College, 184, 186, 281, 298, 352
St. John's, 70

–P–

Paget, John, 317, 348, 350, 352
Paley, Robert, 240
Panfield, 265
Paris, France, 148, 200-201
Parish Vestry, 270
Parker, Matthew, 315
Parkstone, 244
Parry, William, 233-34
Paycocks of Coggeshall, 279-80
Payson, —, 324
Pelagius, 444 n.5
Pelham, Henry, 166, 401 n.24
Herbert, 295
Thomas, 166, 178, 401 n.24
Pelsant, William, 96, 103, 378 n.9
Penn, Sir William, 439 n.355
William, 335, 439 n.355
Penninges of Tofts, 242
Pepys, Samuel, 132, 190, 224, 290
Pequot Tribe, 163, 250, 281, 328, 338
Perkins, William, 33, 142, 361 n.31, 416 n.127
Peter, Hugh, 29, 241, 305, 350
Peterborough, Cambs., 75-76, 115, 126, 128,
202
Petre, —, 48, 291, 306-8, 314-16
John, 315
William, the Founder, 300, 306-7, 315, 431
n.269
William, 309, 431 n.270
m. (1) Elizabeth (Savage), 431 n.270
m. (2) Bridget (Pynchon), 300, 309
Pevsner, Nikolaus, 251-52, 258, 288
Peyton, John, 330
Philadelphia, PA, 302
Philip II of Spain, 45, 328
m. (1) Mary of Portugal, 56
m. (2) Mary Tudor, 56, also see
Mary Tudor
m. (3) Elizabeth de Valois, 56
m. (4) Anne, 56
Philip III of Spain, 56, 59
Picot, Roger, 136
m. Hugoline, 136

Pilgrim Fathers, 16, 123, 239-40, 257-58, 322
Pitt, William, 167
Platius, Aulus, 245
Plato, 149, 395 n.99
Pledger, Elias, 229
Plume, Thomas, 143, 322, 323, 394 n.77
Plymouth, Devon, 162, 280
Plymouth, MA, 19, 30-31, 185, 258, 273, 296
Portland, 293
Porter, —, 236, 414 n.92
John, 236, 241, 414 n.92
m. Sible (Vessey), 241
Possevino, Antonia, 43
Presbyterians, 35, 152, 228, 231-32, 267, 280,
289, 293, 351
Preston, John, 143, 172, 393 n.75
Providence Island, 316
Purcas, William, 261
Puritans, 19, 30, 45-49, 61-63, 68, 70, 74, 78,
80, 82-85, 87-88, 103-4, 109, 120-
21, 132, 138, 140-148, 150, 153-
54, 163, 170-71, 177, 189, 198,
203-4, 206-207, 215, 248, 253-54,
257-58, 261-62, 271, 276, 293-94,
295-96, 298, 301, 309, 313, 315-
17, 321-24, 328, 341-42, 367 n.49,
399 n.13, 403 n.60, 433 n.291
Puritan Lectureships, 83, 89, 143, 205, 257-
58, 264, 283, 288-89
Purleigh, Essex, 175-76, 320-21
Pygot, William, 261
Pym, John, 162, 399 n.14
Pynchon, —, 291-92, 295
Edward of Writtle, 292, 299
m. Dorothy (Weston), 292-93
Elizabeth, 293
John of Springfield, Mass., 299, 352
John of Writtle, 291-92, 299
m. Jayne (Empson), 299, 430
n.239
Nicholaus, 291, 299, 429 n.238
William of Springfield, 21, 222, 241, 243,
292-93, 295-98, 300, 308, 430
n.240
m. (1) Anna (Andrew), 428 n.228
m. (2) Frances (Sanford), 428 n.228
Pynchon Lane, 299

–Q–

Quakers, 61, 87, 335
Quarles, Francis, 292-93, 425 n.221, 436 n.329
m. Ursula (Woodgate), 293
Queens College, 17, 138 (See also
Cambridge)
Quorn, 64

Paget, John,   delete 317

Paris, France,   add 76, 202,   delete 200-201

Pepys, Samuel   150   not 190

Pelham, Herbert   295,   remove from between Henry & Thomas

  add m. Jemima (Waldegrave) 295   (no relation)

Petre, -   306-9   not =8

        John,   add 308-9

        William the Founder, delete 300,   306-9 not 306-7

Pevsner, Nikolaus,   257   not 258

Philip II of Spain,   56   not 45   delete 328

Philip III,   57   not56

Plautius, (not Platius), Aulus, 244   not 245

Plymouth, MA.   17   not 19   274   not 273

Possevino, Antonio (not Antonia) 44   not 43

Pynchon, -

        Elizabeth 293,   delete (see under m. R.Weston)

    add John of Springfield, 292, 299, 352

        John of Springfield MA, 300   delete 299, 352

    add William of Writtle, 292, 299

THOMAS HOOKER - Index errata - may be pasted opposite page 480

Radcliffe Earls of Sussex
      Thomas, 3rd Earl
         m. Elizabeth Wriothesley,   301 not 151
Rainbold,   -233   delete
Raphael, Sanzio,   404 n. 60 not 403
Rayney, -,   263   not 264
Retford, East,   16   not 18

Rich, -,   delete 47
      Mary,   277   rewrite Charles, Fourth Earl, 277
                                      m. Mary (Boyle) 277
      Richard   delete 285
      Robert, 2nd Earl,   delete 280
Robinson, John,   16, 17   not 18, 19
Rochester, Kent,   138   not 128   add 207
Rockingham, Nthants.,   18   not 20
Rogers Families,   add to all names 426-7 (Genealogical Table No 9)
      Nehemiah of Messing 252-3   not 252
      Richard of Wethersfield,   add 288-9
Rotterdam, Holland, delete 340
Roxbury, MA,   add 325
Roxbury Latin School,   19   not 21
Roxwell Group,   294-97   not -95
Russhe, John,   302   delete
Rutherford,   delete 138

St. Ives, Cambs.,   133   not 131
Salisbury, Wilts.,   delete 334
Sayer, John,   247,   delete   (see Sears below)
Scrooby, Notts.,   17   not 19
Sears, -   247
    add John (Sayer), 247

social reformer, 199, 205, 213-19, 229,
240-41, 351, 353
m. Susannah (Garbrand), 28, 29,
116, 173, 183-89, 195, 197, 198,
220, 235, 239-40, 277, 284, 339,
418 n.149
university (Cambs), 29, 96, 126, 137-
50, 168
Hooper, John, 396 n.113
Hopkins, Edward, 35
John, 341
Hornchurch, Essex, 295
Horrocks, Thomas, 321-22
Horsfield, William, 241
Howard of Effingham, 160, 168, 176, 398 n.8
Hudson, Michael, 117
Huguenots, 233, 262
Huitt, Ephraim, 241, 394 n.88
Humfry, John, 120, 383 n.13
m. Lady Susan (Clinton), 120, 383
n.13
Hunsdon, Herts., 330-31, 438 n.346
Hunt, Rex, 100
William, 62, 253
Huntingdon, Cambs., 85, 96, 131-33, 226
Hutchinson, Anne, 125, 305, 387 n.27
Hyde, Edward, 58, 203, 289, 367 n.48
Hythe Quay, 246, 323

–I–

Icanhoe, 124
Ieiden, 124
India, 262
Ingatestone, Essex, 306-309, 315-16
Innocent X, Pope, 60
Iona, Hebrides, 207
Ipswich, Suffolk, 126, 222, 244, 255, 260, 280
Ipswich, MA, 240-41, 267, 288, 311
Ireland, 77, 207, 231, 292-93, 301
Ithancester, 207
Ithell, Thomas, 153, 397 n.114
Ivo, St., 133, 391 n.50

–J–

Jacob, Robert, 29
Jamaica, West Indies, 166
James I, 19, 56, 58-59, 67, 74, 110, 140, 142,
144, 170, 203, 205-6, 201, 314,
336, 379
m. Anne of Denmark, 56
James II, 230, 402
James III, 351
Jersey, Channel Island, 104
Jerusalem, 278
Jewel, John, 185, 188, 405
Jewry Wall, 93
John I, 80, 94, 180, 262, 290, 377
John of Gaunt, 80, 106, 108

m. (1) Blanche of Lancs., 106
m. (2) Constance of Castile, 106
m. (3) Catherine (Swynford), 106,
108
Johnson, Ben, 59
Samuel, 111
Joiner, Isaac, 240
Jones, Evan, 223
Jonson, Ben, 59
Robert, 77
Isaac, 77, 119, 399
m. Lady Arbella (Clinton), 119
Josselin, Ralph, 218, 285
Jude, Edward, 341
Juxton, William, 70, 371

–K–

Kellogg, Nathaniel, 263
Kelvedon, Essex, 248, 282
Kenilworth, Warwcks., 93
Kennedy, Joseph P, 124
Kensington, 332
Kent, 136, 280
Kent, William, 178
Kett, Robert, 127, 388
Kettering, Nthants., 135
King's Lynn, Norfolk, 126-27
Kirby Muxloe, Leics., 67, 93-96, 109
Knight, William, 281
Knightsbridge, —, 211
Knights Templar, 134, 278
Knox, John, 280

–L–

Lacock, Wilts. 76-77
Laindon, Essex, 350
Lambert, John, 334
Lambeth, 293
Lancashire, 142
Langland, William, 132, 394
Langton Matravers, Dorset, 295
La Rochelle, France, 218
Latchington, Essex, 209
Latimer, Hugh, 112, 138
Laud, William, 18, 29, 48, 60, 70, 77, 83, 119,
154-55, 166, 205-206, 211, 215,
217-20, 238, 240, 248, 252, 267,
278, 284, 285, 286, 289, 298, 301,
304, 311, 318, 338, 348, 352-53,
409
Lawrence, St., 345, 443
Lees Hall, 142
Leez Priory, Essex, 267, 272-75
Leicester, Leics., 19, 29, 41, 48-49, 55, 64, 77-
85, 87, 90, 93, 95, 96, 110, 112,
135, 138, 168, 216, 305, 373 n.93,
373 n.97

478   Inde:

Leicestershire, see Chapters 1 and 2,
    especially 17, 27, 41, 43, 49, 67,
    74, 90, 138, 154, 216
Leiden, Holland, 19, 124
Leigh, David, 342
Leighton, Thomas, 104, 314
Leland, John, 54
    Arabella, 54, 119
Leofric, 64
Leopold I of Belgium, 160, 165-66, 178
    m. (1) Princess Charlotte, 165-66,
    178
    m. (2) Princess Louise, 403
Lewis (Battle) Sussex, 80
Liddal, Francis, 247
Lincoln, Lincs., 74, 77-79, 85, 120, 122
Lincolnshire, 54, 102, 115, 125-26
Lindisfarne, North., 207
Ling, William, 229
Lingwood, 221
Little Baddow, Essex, 20-21, 29, 33, 42, 86,
    88, 151-52, 154, 175, 186, 198-99,
    209, 217, 222, 224-243, 264, 268-
    69, 278, 297, 205, 318, 321, 324,
    344
Little Braxted, Essex, 253
Little Leighs, Essex, 252
Little Sampford Hall, Essex, 243
Little Walsingham, Norfolk, 128, 266
Lisle, George, 246
Lock, Nicholas, 341
Locke, John, 235, 413
Lollards (Wycliffites), 87, 181
Lombard House, 335
London, City of, 48, 55, 70, 81, 86, 88, 95, 97-
    98, 121, 123, 135, 141, 143, 148,
    155, 169, 174, 193-95, 202, 204-
    206, 216, 229, 242, 244, 249, 295,
    299, 300, 314, 323, 332-36, 342-
    43, 352, 278 n.21
    See Also Westminster
    Southwark, 29, 74
Loomis, —, 241, 263
Lord, —, 89
Lougborough, 110
Louis XIII of France, 56, 59, 218
    m. Anne of Austria, 56, 59
Lucas, Charles, 246, 247
Lucy, Richard, 341
Ludlow, Roger, 32, 359 n.22
Luther, Martin, 153, 278, 422 n.188
Lutterworth, Leics., 87
Lyford, John, 239
Lynch, Thomas, 166
    m. Vere (Herbert), 166
Lyon, Richard, 203
Lyons Hall, 263, 266-67, 269

–M–

Macauley, Lord, 282
Madrid, Spain, 59
Madden, Richard, 247
Maldon, Essex, 143, 202, 209, 224, 235, 242,
    253, 265, 270, 274, 294, 318-24,
    249
Maldon, Jacob, 225
Manchester, Earl of, 147, 154
Mandeville, Geoffrey de, 181
Manners, Dukes of Rutland, 58-59, 67, 73
Manning, George, 276
Mantegna, Andrea, 179, 403 n.60
Mararet Rodin, 310
Marblehead, MA, 98
Marcy, —, 310
Marefield, Leics., 17-18, 27, 41-46, 48-51, 75,
    85, 90, 111, 115, 127, 364 n.1
Market Bosworth, Leics., 29, 41, 49, 78, 86-
    87, 93, 95-112
Market Deeping, 126
Markfield, Leics., 17, 19-20, 27, 42
Marks Hall, 310
Marshall, John, 195, 407 n.4
    Stephen, 131, 151, 241, 288-90, 313, 424
    n.215
Marsworth, Bucks., 407 n.6
Marven, —, 233, 241Massachusetts, 31, 34,
    55, 77-78, 84, 98, 102, 125, 128,
    155, 174-75, 206 222-23, 249-50,
    263, 273, 280, 296, 312, 350-51
Mayland, 267
Mary Queen of Scots, 56, 74, 168, 308, 315,
    371 n.80
Mary Tudor, 56, 62, 112, 139, 142, 153, 199,
    202, 243, 249, 273, 288, 301, 307,
    336, 380 n.40
    m. Philip II of Spain, 56
Masham, William, 119, 227, 267, 270, 383,
    n.9, 413 n.86
    m. Elizabeth (Barrington), 227
Mason, John, 250, 338
Massachuestts Bay Co., 77, 119-21, 124, 222,
    274, 293-97, 299, 311, 327, 350,
    352
Mather, Cotton, 36, 61, 83, 85, 88, 104, 146,
    154, 175, 186, 214, 235, 267, 277,
    286, 312, 323, 329, 338, 352, 357
    n.6
    Richard, 36, 195
Matilda, Queen, 278, 422 n.189
Matthew, —, 233
Maurice, Bishop of London, 194
McLean, J. Allen, 42
Medbourne, Leics., 68, 70
Medici, Catherine de, 56, 371 n.80
    Marie de, 56, 59, 214, 367 n.41

Leicestershire,   delete 154   68 not 67,   78 not 74
Leiden, Holland,   17   not 19
Leland, John,   54
  delete Arabella , 54, 119
Leofric,   64
  add m. Lady Godiva   64
Leopold I,   add 400 n. 21
  m. (2) Princess Louise   403 n. 55   add n. 55
Little Baddow,   delete 268   18, 19   not 20-21,   305 not 205
Little leighs, Essex,   272   not 252
Little Walsingham, Norfolk,   261   not 266
Locke, John,   230   not 235   413 n. 86   add n. 86
London,   58   not 48   378 n. 21   not 278
Louis XIII of France,   57   not 56
  m. Anne of Austria,   57   not 56

Maldon, Essex   354   not 249
Manchester, Earl of,   add 395 n. 88
Margaret Roding, Essex   not Margaret Rodin
Marefield, Leics.,   15-16   not 17-18
Markfield, Leics.,   delete   19-20   add 18
Marshall, Stephen,   132   not 131   311   not 313
Marven,   -233, 241   remove Massachusetts refs. to alphabetical place
Mary Queen of Scots,   add 75   delete 308
Mary Tudor,   delete 199   113   not 112   add 308
Mather, Cotton,   358 n. 6   not 357
Matilda, Queen,   279   not 278
  delete   Matthew, -, 233
Medici, Catherine de
          Marie de,   57, 58   not 56, 59

	Henrietta Maria		see m. Charles I
Melton Mowbray, Leics.,			delete 98
Mildmay, -		

      Abraham, 77   delete

      Avis, 199   delete (see Thomas Auditor below)

      Elizabeth, 77   delete   and rearrange as follows:-

      Henry of Little Baddow,   200 delete -1,   221-25 i.e. add 222

        m. (1) Alicia (Harris),   184 delete,   285 delete

        m. (2) Amy (Gurdon),   200 delete - 1

      Henry Colonel,   delete 198, 224,   201 not 200-1 add 223, add

        m. (2) Mary (Mildmay),   200

      Henry of Wanstead   200 delete - 1

      Humphrey,   add 200

      John of Terling,   add 200 add 304

  add Thomas, the Mercer,   199, 200

      m. Agnes Read,   199, 200

      Thomas, the Auditor,   199-201, 222 , 304   delete 198, 223, 303-

  add m. Avice Gunson,   199, 200

      Thomas of Springfield Barnes   200, 223

      m. Alice (Winthrop),   200, 223

      Thomas Fitzwalter,   199, 200, 303

      m. Frances Radcliffe,   200, 303

      Walter the Chancellor   add 142,   319 not 219

      m. Mary (Walsingham),   200

      William of Springfield Barnes   add 200, 223

      m. Agnes (Winthrop)   200, 223

Morell, Stephen   233,   restore brother, slipped 3 lines down

      Thomas,   233

Moulsham   add 193 - 194, 198, 199

Myddleton, -

      Hugh,   439 n. 349   not n. 34

New Hall, Boreham,   253   not 352

Newton,

      Isaac   add 276

      Roger,   delete 28

      m. Mary (Hooker),   add 184,   delete 276

Northampton   delete 20

North Luffenham   77   not 71

Norwich, Norfolk,   17   not 19

Nottingham,   16   not 18   delete 97

Okey,   not Okay   add John not -

Oldham,   add Lancs.,

THOMAS HOOKER - Index errata - may be pasted opposite page 479

Gifford, George, 253, 321, 434 n.315
Gilbert, St., of Sempringham, 118, 120-21, 275
Gilson, Thomas, 228
Glanville, Joseph, 148
Glaston, 77, 115
Glenfield, 110
Gloucester, 95, 206
Godiva, Lady, 64
Godmanchester, Cambs., 132-33, 151, 289
Goffe, Thomas, 121
    William, 227, 352, 445 n.18
Goldsmith, Oliver, 297-98
Gonville, Edward, 130
Goodrick, Lionel, 341
Goodwin, John, 264
    Matthew, 264
    Ozias, 263, 266, 268
    William, 30, 35, 241, 263, 266-68, 339, 418 n.149, 418 n.150
    m. (1) Elizabeth (White), 418 n.149
    m. (2) Susannah (Hooker), 418 n.149
Gookin, Daniel, 286, 437 n.331
Gorges, Ferdinando, 120, 383 n.13
    John, 120, 383 n.13
    m. Lady Frances (Clinton), 120, 383 n.13
Goring, Oxon., 180, 261
Green, Samuel, 203
Grantchester, Cambs., 133-4, 391 n.53
Great Amwell, Herts., 333
Great Baddow, Essex, 198, 202, 220
Great Bentley, Essex, 241
Great Graces, 221-25, 242
Great Leighs, Essex, 272
Great Waltham, Essex, 29, 48, 186, 199, 217, 240, 277, 354
Greenwich, Kent, 162
Grene, Edward, 243
Grenville, Richard, 439 n.349
Greville, Fulke, 394 n.88, 440 n.362
    Robert, 146, 394 n.88
Grey, Lady Jane, 110, 112, 273, 275, 306, 308, 379 n.30
Grimsthorpe, Lincs., 117, 381 n.4
Grindal, Edmund, 147, 155, 440 n.362
Groton, Suffolk, 280
Guildford, Surrey, 352
Guildford, CT, 352
Gunson, Avice, 199
Gurdon, —, 221-22, 241, 295
    Adam, 222
    Amy, 221
    Brampton, 222, 241, 258

–H–

Hackney, London, 200
Hadley, MA, 227, 339

Hallaton, Leics., 68, 70
Halstead, Essex, 265, 287
Halstead, Leics., 50
Halton, 222
Hammond, John 141
    Robert, 86
Hampton Court, Midsex., 86, 110, 160, 163, 179, 227
Hardy, Thomas Masterman, 167, 401 n.27
    m. Anne (Berkeley), 167
Harlakenden, —, 285, 295
    Richard, 200-1, 226, 285
    m. Alice (Mildmay), 200-1, 226, 285
    Roger Sr, 285
    m. Elizabeth, 285, 295
    Roger Jr, 226, 285, 295
Harling, Guy, 199
Harold, King, 291, 343-45, 443 n.382
Harper, John, 341
Harsnett, Samuel, 439 n.355
Hart, Stephen, 263
Hartford, CT, 21, 30, 42, 70, 84, 102, 213, 224, 233, 241, 251, 287, 289, 338, 347, 350
Hartwell, Jasper, 169, 173
Harvard, John, 144, 324
Harvard, MA, 44, 60, 144, 203, 224, 241, 261, 281, 286, 305, 312, 324, 326
Harwich, Essex, 244, 316
Hastings (Battle) Sussex, 95, 343
Hastings, George, 95
    Henry, 94
    John, 94
    William, 85, 375 n.116
    William, Baron, 67, 93-96
Hatfield Broad Oak, Essex, 151, 226, 282, 412 n.70
Hatfield Heath, Essex, 226
Hatfield House, Herts., 47-48, 115, 334
Hatfield Peveril, 303-304
Haverhill, MA, 312
Haverhill, Suffolk, 304, 311-12
Havering-atte-Bower, Essex, 204
Hawkesbury, John, 285
Hawkins, John, 161, 263
Hawkwell, Essex, 284
Haynes, —, 248-49
    Dorothy (Bird), 90
    John, 25, 90, 119, 224, 227, 241, 249-50, 286, 353
    m. (1) Mary (Thornton), 250
    m. (2) Mabel Harlakenden, 251, 286
Heavitree, Devon, 216
Hedingham Castle, Essex, 282, 287, 321
Helena, St., 244
Hendon, John 188
Henrietta Maria, Queen, 79
Henry I, 282

Henry II, 108, 290, 345
Henry III, 80, 94, 130, 136, 222, 291, 340
Henry IV, 106, 108
    m. Mary (Bohun), 106
Henry V, 106, 108, 275
    m. Catherine de Valois, 106, 108
Henry VI, 106, 108, 134, 138, 218
    m. Margaret of Anjou, 106, 108, 138,
        392 n.60
Henry VII, 47, 51, 77, 87, 106, 108, 134, 140,
        299
    m. Elizabeth of York, 106, 108
Henry VIII, 35, 47, 56, 61, 64-65, 67, 76, 106,
        112, 139, 145, 153, 163, 167, 179,
        199, 272, 275, 288, 299, 301, 304,
        306, 307, 315, 336, 345
    m. (1) Catherine of Aragon, 56, 153,
        315, 339
    m. (2) Anne (Boleyn), 153, 308, 336
    m. (3) Jane (Seymour), 225, 242, 304
    m. (4) Anne of Cleves, 64, 153, 370
        n.61
    m. (5) Catherine (Howard), 275
    m. (6) Catherine (Parr), 336
Herbert, Thomas 70
Hereward The Wake, 18, 94, 116, 128, 131,
        389 n.37
Herrick, Robert, 82, 83, 140, 374 n.105
    William, 81, 83
Herrys, Arthur, 225
Hertford, Herts., 20, 30, 278, 289, 334-37
Herts., 324
Heybridge, Essex, 249, 323
Hibbens, William, 305, 350, 431 n.257
Hieron, 155
Higginson, Anna (Herbert), 84
    Elizabeth, 84
    Francis, 61, 84-85, 98, 120, 296, 375 n.112
    John, 84, 102
High Laver, Essex, 249, 323
Hildersham, Arthur, 84-85, 96, 146, 375 n.115
Hilliard, Nicholas, 48, 145, 365 n.15
Hinchingbrooke, Cambs., 132, 226
Hinckley, Leics., 96
Hitchin, Herts., 180
Hoare, Benjamin, 302
Hobbes, Thomas, 149, 395 n.98
Hobson, Tobias, 17
Hodson, Daniel, 295
    m. Agnes (Josselyn), 295
Holbeach, Martin, 276, 422 n.181
Holbein, Hans, 67
Holgate, Robert, 383 n.13
Holkham, Norfolk, 127, 389 n.35
Holland, 18-19, 29, 81, 84, 124, 175, 186, 189,
        224, 263, 348-51, 352
Hollingworth, —, 315, 316
Holwell, Leics., 65

Honeywood, Thomas, 322, 434 n.317
Honiton, Devon, 161
Hood, Robin, 128, 132-33, 222, 391 n.47
Hook End, 309
Hooker, —, 17, 27-28, 41-51, 68, 72, 78, 111,
        128, 195, 198, 221-36, 407 n.6
    Edward, 17
    John of Blaston, 27, 28
Hooker (cont.)
    John of Marsworth (son of Thomas), 27,
        28, 106, 150, 185, 195, 407 n.6
        m. Mary (Lovell), 28, 106
    Kenelm, 72
    Richard, 17, 154, 216, 357 n.1
    Samuel (son of Thomas), 28, 106, 185, 195
        m. Mary (Willet), 28, 106, 185
    Thomas
        birth (Marefield), 27, 29
        boyhood, 41-50, 60, 75, 78-81, 95-96
        church membership, 31-32, 34, 174,
            339, 351
        Company, Mr Hooker's, 29, 214,
            236-37, 239-40, 262-63, 357 n.15
        conciliator, 49, 146, 239, 297
        conversion, 104, 108-10, 145-50
        death, 35, 355
        democracy, 31-32, 79-81, 90, 194
        exile (Holland), 88, 217, 277, 322,
            323, 347
        experimental theologian (Preparat-
            ionist), 30-32, 149, 173-74, 257,
            259, 313
        federalism, 51, 250, 352
        flight to New England, 119-21, 185-
            86, 249-50, 263-64, 352-55
        Fundamental Orders of Connecticut,
            31-32, 34, 90, 104, 250
        ill-health, 49, 101-102, 188, 349
        late-developer, 40, 101-102, 146
        lecturer (Chelmsford), 210-11, 213-20,
            247-48, 257, 263-64
        non-separating congregationalism,
            33, 34-35, 49, 61-62, 150, 228 29,
            230-32, 238-39, 248, 268, 282 ˙˙ ,
            296, 312-13, 247-48, 368 n.51
        pastoral counsellor, 150, 160-61,
            167-74, 176-77
        persecution, 83, 88, 215-19, 317,
            323, 348, 353
        preacher, 35-37, 79-80, 82-86, 102,
            163, 165, 173-75, 189, 205, 214-
            15, 225, 253-54, 257-58, 363 n.4
        rector (Esher), 160, 163-165, 174
        school (Market Bosworth), 29, 96-1
            110-12
        schoolmaster (Little Baddow), 229,
            233, 234-39

Henry II,   delete 108,   add 336
Henry III   delete 340
Hereward the Wake.   delete 18
Hertford, Herts.,   delete 20   334-38   not -37
Heybridge,   240   not 249
Higginsons,   rewrite as follows
Higginson, Francis,   61, 84-85, 98, 120, 296, 375, n. 112
    m. Anna (Herbert)   84
    John,   84
Higginson (contd)
    m. Elizabeth   84
    John Jr.,   84, 102
High Laver,   119, 227, 241   not 249, 323
Hobson,   134   not 17
Holland,   delete 18-19
Holwell, Leics.,   65-66   add -66
Hooker, -   15 not 17, 68-70 not 68,   add 197, 220-21, not 221-36
Edward,   15   not 17
Hooker (contd)   delete
    John of Marsworth, delete 27, delete 106,   add 197
    m. Mary (Lovell),   delete 28, 106   add 197, 407 n. 6
    Kenelm,   add 28
Hooker, Richard   15   not 17   NB. no relation: separate entry
    Samuel,   delete 106   add 197
    Thomas
    church membership, 32-34   not 31-32, 34
    Company, Mr. Hooker's, 30, not 29   add 213,
                            delete 236-7, add 238
                            239-41 not 239-40,   263-64, not 262-63
    conversion,   109-110 not 108
    death,   36,   not 35
    exile,   218   not 217,   delete 322,
                            323-24 not 323   347-55   add -55
    experimental theologian   32-34 not 30-32,
                            258   not 257, 259   312   not 313
    federalism,   30   not 51,   251   not 250,   353   not 352
    flight to N.E.   118-21   not 119, 183   not 185-86
    ill health,   102   not 101
    late developer,   49   not 40
    non-separating,   347   not 247-48
    pastoral counsellor,   176-78   not 77
    preacher,   36-38   not 35-37,   228-29 not 225
    rector (Esher)   add 159, 163-67   not '65, 174-78 add -78

social reformer, 163 not 199
    m. Susannah, add 42 delete 116
    university 29, 97 not 96, 125 not 126
Hudson, Michael, 177 not 117
Humfry, John 384 n. 13 (2) not 383 n. 13
    m. Lady Susan 384 n. 13 (2)
Hythe Quay delete
Ieiden, delete (misspelling of Leiden)

James I, 17 not 19, 143 not 142, 301 not 201, 379 n. 30 add 30
James II 403 n. 56 not 402
James III of Scotland, 351
Jewel, John, 405 n. 74 add 74
John I 377 n. 4 add n. 4
Johnson, Ben, delete (see Jonson, Ben, 59 below NB. no relation to Isaac)
Jonson, Isaac, 77, 119, 384 n. 13 (1) not 399
    m. Lady Arabella (Clinton), 119. 384 n. 13 (1)
       Robert 77
Jones Evan, add 234
Juxon, William, 70, 371 n. 71 add n. 71
Kent, add 281
Kett, Robert, 388 n. 33 add n. 33

Langland, William 391 n. 48 not 394
Laud, William, delete 18, 409 n. 22 add n. 22
Laurence, St., not Lawrence 345, 443, n 386 add n. 386
Leicester, add 17-18 78-85 not 77

Edward, the Confessor, 54, 204, 226, 366 n.30
Edward, the Elder, 89, 336, 440 n.356
Edmund, King & Martyr, 72, 262, 266, 418
    n.144
Edward I, 74, 80, 222
Edward II, 291
Edward III, 80, 86, 106
    m. Philippa of Hainaut, 86,106
Edward IV, 54, 93-95, 106, 108, 138
    m. Elizabeth (Woodville), 95, 106,
      138, 392 n.60
Edward V, 95, 106, 108
Edward VI, 47, 61, 112, 145, 161, 165, 202,
    259, 273, 307, 336
Effingham, Surrey, 160, 176
Egbert, St., 207
Elbing, Prussia, 311
Eliot, —, 324, 332, 339-40, 342, 442 n.379
    Bennett, 154, 324-25, 331-32, 340, 342
    m. Lettese (Agar), 324-25, 331, 342
    John, The Apostle, 18, 21, 86, 101,
      130, 151-52, 154-55, 186, 203,
      225, 229, 235-37, 240-41, 252,
      278, 281, 289, 295, 299, 305, 324,
      326-28, 330, 331, 333, 339-42, 344
    m. Hannah (Mumford), 325, 329
    Philip, 331, 315
Eliott-Drake, Lady, 161, 169-70
Elizabeth I, 48, 62, 76, 78, 81, 101, 103, 110,
    143-45, 161-62, 168, 170, 181,
    188, 202, 225, 273, 301, 308, 314,
    315, 334, 336, 368 n.51
Ellis, Charles, 167
Ely, Cambs., 18, 20, 94, 128, 129-30, 151-54,
    252
Emmison, F. G, 307, 420 n.165, 420 n.169
Empson, Richard, 299, 430 n.239
Endecott, John, 296, 297, 429 n.231
Enderby, 96
Epping, Essex, 321, 340, 342
Epping Forest, Essex, 320, 342
Erasmus, Desiderius, 33, 138, 360 n.27
Erastus, Thomas, 153, 396 n.112
Erle, Randolf, 133
Esher, Surrey, 29, 159-89, 351
Essex, see Chapter 5, especially 20, 30, 123,
    127, 141, 174-75, 181, 193-94,
    202, 204-11, 213, 221, 223, 225-
    31, 244-48, 260-70, 292-95, 310,
    321-24, 332
Etheldreda, St., 130-31, 389 n.43
Ethelred II, the Unready, 226, 322
Evelyn, John, 410 n.23
Evesham (Battle) Worcs., 93-94, 222
Evesham, Epiphanius, 276
Exeter, Devon, 79, 154, 216, 267, 306
Eye-Kettelby, Leics., 55, 64, 66
Eyre, William, 247

–F–

Fairfax, Thomas, 246, 415 n.109
Falstaff, John, 128
Farmington, CT, 185, 195
Fawkes, Guy, 58
Felstead, Essex, 151, 241, 273, 275-77, 421
    n.177
Fen Drayton, Cambs., 133
Fen Stanton, Cambs., 133
Fenlands, 87, 116, 124, 127-28, 131-34
Fenny Drayton, Leics., 87
Fering, William, 316
Fervaques, Richelde de, 262
Fiddlers, 291
Fiennes, Wm., 394 n.88
Finch, John, 219
Finchingfield, Essex, 241, 289
Firebrace, Henry, 86
Firmin, Giles, 312, 432 n.284
Fisher, John, 138, 392 n.62
Fitch, —, 263, 266, 419 n.157
Flatford Mill, 255
Flaxman, John, 167
Floyer, J., 177
Flyer, Francis, 295
Forbes, John, 173, 351
Fordham, Cambs., 128, 383 n.13
Fortunatus, Venantius, 152
Fotheringhay, Nthants., 74, 95
Fowey, Cornwall, 350
Fox, George, 87, 335, 376 n.126
Foxe, John, 301
France, 60, 67, 76, 105, 135, 207, 218
Francis of Assissi, 83
Franeker, Holland, 84, 348
Franklin, Benjamin, 302, 430 n.250
Freake, Edmund, 175, 402 n.49
    John, 175
Fuller, John, 36, 357 n.4

–G–

Gainsborough, Lincs., 19
Garbrand, —, 183, 185-88, 405 n.75
    Dr. John, 185-88
Gardiner, Stephen, 273
Gateshead, Tyne., 305
Gayhurst, Bucks., 52, 58, 71
Geneva, Switzerland, 61, 104, 177, 205
Gauden, John, 267, 419 n.162
Geoffrey of Monmouth, 244, 415 n.104
George I, 235-36
George II, 179
George IV, 165, 400 n.23
    m. Caroline of Brunswick, 165
Gerard, John, S. J, 58
Gibbons, Grindling, 179, 403 n.60
    Orlando, 314, 432 n.290

Index

Dapifer, Eudes, 247
Darby Fort, MA, 98
Darley, Richard, 286
Davenport, John, 35, 352, 445 n.16
Davids, T. W., 264
Dean Prior, Devon, 83
Deane, Richard, 204
Deanery Church of St. Mary, 265
Dedham, 126, 172
Dedham, Essex, 205, 209, 241, 254-59, 267,
    280, 288, 289
Dedham, MA, 257-58, 288
Deene Park, 74
Defoe, Daniel, 135
Delft, Holland, 29, 84, 351
Dengie Peninsular, Essex, 209, 224, 267
Denham, John, 181
Denmark, 217
De Peverel, Ralph, 299
Deptford, Kent, 162
Derbyshire, 76
Deresleye, Margaret, 305
Desford, 96, 110
De Vere, Earls of Oxford, 226, 266, 282-83,
    316, 321
    Aubrey the Founder, 282-83, 287
    Edward the Spendthrift, 283
      m. (1) Anne (Cecil), 423 n.202
      m. (2) Elizabeth (Trentham), 283,
      285
Devereux, Walter, 54, 274
    m. Jaquetta (Ellis), 54, 72
    Penelope, 274
Devine, —, 62
Devon, 154, 160-61, 182
D'Ewes, Simonds, 326, 435 n.325
Dickens, Charles, 59, 88
Digby, Lincs., 54
Digby, —, 27, 44, 50-66, 71-73, 79, 366 n.29
    Everard (Gunpowder Plot), 51, 55, 58, 64,
      65, 71, 72
      m. Mary (Mulsho), 55, 58
    George, 59-60
    John, 52, 55-56, 59,64
    Kateryn, 55
    Kenelm, 44, 52, 58-60, 71
      m. Venetia (Stanley), 59
    Richard, 72
    Simon, 55, 65
      m. Agnes (Clarke), 71
Dillingham, Gilbert, 240
Dixie, —, 96-105, 111-12, 146
    Alexander, 98
    Anna, 98
    Lady Penelope, 100
    William, 98
    Willoughby, 99
    Wolstan, 96-102, 112, 134, 146, 378 n.10

    m. Agnes (Draper), 97
Docket, Andrew, 138
Dod, John, 171-72, 401 n.35
Doddinghurst, Essex, 253, 309
Donne, John 425 n.219
Dorchester, Dorset, 243, 293, 352
Dorchester, MA, 195, 242-43, 280-81, 293, 326
Dorchester Company, 293-4
Doreward, John, 266, 268
    m. Isabella (Baynard), 266
Dorewards Hall, 266-69
Downing, Emmanuel, 120, 223, 385 n.14
    m. Lucy (Winthrop), 223
    George, 223
Downs, The, Kent, 353
Drake, —, 160-63, 167-70, 177, 181-82, 295
    Bernard of Ashe, 162
    Edmund, 161
    Lady Eliott-, 161, 169-70
    Sir Francis, 145, 160-63, 167, 169, 170
    Francis, 162
      m. Dorothea (Pym), 162
    Francis of Esher, 160-61, 168-70, 173, 177,
      180-83, 188, 351, 402 n.53
      m. Joane (Tothill), 163, 167-72, 173,
      180-83, 185, 188
    John, 161, 183
    Margery, 161
    Richard of Esher, 160, 161-63, 167, 168-70
    Thomas, 170, 351
    Tyrwhitt, 182
    William of Amersham, 181, 404 n.62, 405
      n.66
    William, of Shardloes, 182
Draper, Charles, 97
Druillettes, S. J, 328, 387 n.23
Dryden, —, 138
Dry Drayton, Cambs., 133
Dry Stoke, Leics., 55, 58, 68, 71-72
Duck, Arthur, 215-16, 240, 265
Dudley, Thomas, 30, 120, 155, 224, 249, 286,
    383 n.13
Dukes, 293
Dunstable, Beds., 180, 261
Dunster, Henry, 203, 409 n.16
Dutch, 30, 218, 347-49
Dyke, Jeremy, 341

–E–

Earls Colne, Essex, 218, 224, 241, 250, 282,
    287
East Anglia, 72, 136, 206
East Bergholt, Suffolk, 255, 259, 264
Easthorpe, Essex, 248, 252
Eastwick, Herts., 331
Eaton, Theophilus, 352, 445 n.17
Edgehill (Battle) Warwcks., 90
Edmund, Ironside, 217

Edward III,		add 108		
Edward V		107	not 106	
Edward VI,	delete 259			
Eliot, -,				
John, the Apostle,		18,19	not 21	
Philip,		325	not 315	331
Ely, Cambs.,	delete 20	151, 152, 153, 154,	not 151-54	
Endecott, John,		428 n. 231	not 429	
Epping Forest, Essex,		add 321		
Essex		18	not 20	
Evesham (Battle) Worcs.,		94-95	not 93-94	
Felsted,	not Felstead			
Fiennes, Wm.,	restore title		Viscount Saye & Sele	
Fitch, Thomas	not -			
Fotheringay,	add 75			
Fuller, John		363 n. 43	not 357 n. 4	

Gainsborough, Lincs.,		17	not 19
George I,		230	not 235 - 36
Gibbons, Grinling	not Grindling		

Goodwin,   add
        James Junius,   263, 266
Gorges, Fernando   384 n. 13 not 383   ditto John & Lady Frances
Grey, Lady Jane,   276   not 275   379 n. 31 not 30
Grindal,   delete 147

Hackney, London   300   not 200
Hampton Court,   add 159
Harlakenden -
        Richard   224   not 226
        Roger Jr.   224   not 226
Harling, Guy,   add 215
Hartford, CT,   19   not 21
Hastings (Battle), Sussex,   add 345   (for Lords Hastings rewrite as   Hastings, George, 1st Earl
Huntington   96   not 95   follows)
        Sir Henry,   94
        Henry, 3rd Earl Huntington,   85, 96, 375 n. 116
        John,   94
        William, Baron,   67, 93 -96
        delete William,   85, 375 n. 116
Hatfield House, Herts.,   116   not 115
Hawkins, John,   delete 263
Haynes, -
        delete Dorothy (Bird)
        John   29   not 25   249-51   not 249-50
Henden, John,   188   not Hendon
Henrietta Maria, Queen,   79   delete (see Charles I)